OXFORD TELEVISION STUDIES

General Editors **Charlotte Brunsdon**
John Caughie

Feminist Television Criticism

A Reader

Feminist
Television Criticism
A Reader

Edited by
Charlotte Brunsdon,
Julie D'Acci, and **Lynn Spigel**

Clarendon Press · Oxford

1997

Oxford University Press, Great Clarendon Street, Oxford OX2 6DP

Oxford New York
Athens Auckland Bangkok Bogota Bombay
Buenos Aires Calcutta Cape Town Dar es Salaam
Delhi Florence Hong Kong Istanbul Karachi
Kuala Lumpur Madras Madrid Melbourne
Mexico City Nairobi Paris Singapore
Taipei Tokyo Toronto
and associated companies in
Berlin Ibadan

Oxford is a trade mark of Oxford University Press

Published in the United States
by Oxford University Press Inc., New York

British Library Cataloguing in Publication Data
Data available

Library of Congress Cataloging in Publication Data
Data available

ISBN 0–19–871152–2
ISBN 0–19–871153–0(Pbk)

10 9 8 7 6 5 4 3 2 1

Typeset by Hope Services (Abingdon) Ltd.
Printed in Great Britain
on acid-free paper by
Biddles Ltd.,
Guildford & King's Lynn

Acknowledgements

WE WISH TO THANK the Department of Film and Television Studies, University of Warwick, the Department of Communication Arts, University of Wisconsin-Madison, and the Department of Critical Studies, University of Southern California; Fran Breit, John Caughie, Andrew Lockett, David Morley, Lisa Parks, Niki Strange; and Matthew Murray for the lion's share of work on the bibliography.

Contents

List of Contributors

IEN ANG is the author of *Watching Dallas* (1985), *Desparately Seeking the Audience* (1991), and *Living Room Wars* (1996). She is currently Professor of Cultural Studies at the University of Western Sydney, Nepean, Australia.

JULIE D'ACCI is an Associate Professor in the Department of Communication Arts at the University of Wisconsin-Madison, and a co-editor of the journal *Camera Obscura*. She is the author of *Defining Women: Television and the Case of* Cagney and Lacey (University of North Carolina Press, 1994) and a range of articles on television. She is currently writing a book on television and gender.

JACQUELINE BOBO is Associate Professor in the Women's Studies Program/Film Department at the University of California, Santa Barbara. She is the author of *Black Women as Cultural Readers* (Columbia University Press 1995), and the editor of the forthcoming book *Black Women Film and Video Artists*, to be published by Indiana University Press.

CHARLOTTE BRUNSDON teaches in the Department of Film and Telelvision Studies at the University of Warwick, England. She is author of *Screen Tastes* (Routledge, 1997), editor of *Films for Women* (BFI, 1986).

ANITA DIGHE is Senior Fellow at the National Institute of Adult Education in New Delhi and co-author of *Affirmation and Denial: Construction of Femininity on Indian Television* (Sage New Delhi, 1990).

ANNE GRAY teaches Cultural Studies at the University of Birmingham. She is the author of *Video Playtime: The Gendering of a Leisure Technology* and is currently writing a book on ethnographic research methods in Cultural Studies.

PRABHA KRISHNAN is co-author, with Anita Dighe, of *Affirmation and Denial: Construction of Femininity on Indian Television* (Sage New Delhi, 1990).

HILARY HINDS is a lecturer in English Studies at Cheltenham and Gloucester College of Higher Education. Her other publications include *Her Own Life: Autobiographical Writings by Seventeenth-Century English-women* (Routledge, 1989), co-editor with Elspeth Graham, Elaine Hobby, and Helen Wilcox; and *God's Englishwomen: Seventeenth-Century Sectarian Writing and Feminist Criticism* (Manchester University Press 1996).

KATE KANE is Assistant Professor of Communication at DePaul University in Chicago. Her research interests centre around the representation of the body in mediated culture, and she is active in the Union for Democratic Communications.

ROSANNE KENNEDY teaches Women's Studies and English at the Australian National University. She is currently working on a study of rep-resentations of history and trauma in contemporary film and literature.

ANNETTE KUHN's books include *Family Secrets: Acts of Memory and*

Imagination (Verso, 1995) and as editor *Queen of the Bs: Ida Lupino Behind the Camera* (Flicks Books 1995). She is an editor of *Screen* and Reader in Film and Television Studies, University of Glasgow.

PURNIMA MANKEKAR is the Assistant Professor of Anthropology at Stanford University. She is currently completing a manuscript that analyses the place of Indian television in the construction of women's subjectivities. Other articles include 'National Texts and Gendered Lives: An Ethnography of Television Viewers in the North Indian city', *American Ethnologist*, 20 (3): 543–63 (1993), and 'Reflections on Diasporic Identities: A Prolegomenon to an Analysis of Political Bifocality', *Diaspora*, 3 (3): 349–71 (1994). Her areas of specialization include feminist ethnography, cultural studies, and critical theory.

MICHELE MATTELART was born in France. She lived many years in Chile and participated actively in the debate about media during the revolutionary period of Salvador Allende's popular regime. Presently, she lives and works as a researcher in Paris. She has written extensively on Politics, Mass Culture, and Feminism. Her books are translated in many languages. Among them, *Women, Media, Crises: Femininity and Disorder, Rethinking Media Theory, International Image Market*. In 1995, she has published with Armand Mattelart *Historie des Theories de la Communication*.

JUDITH MAYNE is Professor of French & Women's Studies at Ohio State University. She is author of several books, including *The Women at the Keyhole* (1990), *Cinema and Spectatorship* (1993) and *Directed by Dorothy Arzner* (1994).

PATRICIA MELLENCAMP is a Professor of Art History and Visual Culture at the University of Wisconsin–Milwaukee. She is the author of *High Anxiety: Catastrophe, Scandal, Age and Comedy* (Indiana University Press, 1992) and the editor of *Logics of Television: Essays in Cultural Criticism* (Indiana University Press, 1990). Her recent book on cinema is *A Fine Romance: Five Ages of Film Feminism* (Temple University Press, 1996). She also wrote *Indiscretions: Avant Garde Film, Video, and Feminism* (Indiana University Press 1990). Her current project is a book about women, money, and age.

TANIA MODLESKI teaches film, literature, and popular culture at the University of Southern California. She is author of *Feminism Without Women: Culture and Criticism in a 'Postfeminist' Age* and *The Women Who Knew Too Much: Hitchcock and Feminist Theory*. She is finishing a book about women who are popular genres, such as minstrelsy, Westerns, romance, and melodrama.

SUVENDRINI PERERA completed her BA at the University of Sri Lanka, Kelaniya, and her Ph.D. at Columbia University, New York. She teaches in the School of English at La Trobe University, Australia. She is author of *Reaches of Empire* (Columbia, UP, 1991) and editor of *Asian and Pacific Inscriptions: Identities/Ethnicities/Nationalities* (Meridian, 1995). Her forthcoming book, written with Joseph Pugliese, is titled *Erased Bodies: The Making and Unmaking of Ethnicity in Australia*.

ELSPETH PROBYN is Head of Gender Studies at the University of Sydney.

Her publications include *Outside Belongings* (Routledge, 1996), *Sexing the Self: Gendered Positions in Cultural Studies* (Routledge, 1993), and *Sexy Bodies. The Strange Carnalities of Feminism* (co-editor, Routledge, 1995).

TRICIA ROSE is an assistant professor of History and Africana Studies at New York University. She is author of *Black Noise: Rap Music and Black Culture in Contemporary America* (Wesleyan Press, 1994) and co-editor with Andrew Ross of *Microphone Fiend Youth Music and Youth Culture* (Routledge, 1994).

KATHLEEN ROWE KARLYN is the author of *The Unruly Women: Gender and the Genres of Laughter*. Her work has appeared in *The Quarterly Review of Film and Video, The Journal of Film and Video, Jump Cut* and numerous anthologies. She is currently working on a book about film and television for and about teenage girls and their rites of passage.

ELLEN SEITER is Professor of Communication at the University of California at San Diego where she teaches courses in media studies and women's studies. She is the editor of *Remote Control: Television, Audiences, and Cultural Power* (Routledge, 1989) and the author of *Sold Separately: Children and Parents in Consumer Cultures* (Rutgers UP, 1983).

LYN SPIGEL teaches film and television in the school of Cinema-Television at the University of Southern California. She is author of *Make Room for TV: Television and the Family Ideal in Postwar America* (University of Chicago Press, 1992), as well as numerous essays and anthologies.

CORRINE SQUIRE teaches at the University of East London. She is the author of *Significant Differences, Feminism in Psychology* (Routledge, 1989), and, with Ellen Friedman, of *Morality USA: Representative of Morality in Contemporary Culture* (Minnesota University Press, 1997). She is also the editor of *Women and AIDS: Psychological Perspectives*, and is currently researching notions of identity and community as they appear in the narratives of people affected by HIV.

LYN THOMAS teaches contemporary French popular culture, cinema and women's writing at the University of North London. Her research on *Inspector Morse* and its audience is to be published as part of a book on the relationship between feminism and readings of 'quality' media texts in contemporary Britain. She is also writing a book on Annie Ernaux for Berg.

REBECCA WALKOWITZ is a graduate student in English and American literature at Harvard University, where she is writing about the twentieth-century novel, the media, and metropolitan culture. She is editor of *Media Spectacles* (Routledge, 1993), *Secret Agents: The Rosenberg Case, McCarthyism, and Fifties America* (Routledge 1995), and *Field Work: Sites in Literary and Cultural Studies* (Routledge, 1996).

Introduction

Charlotte Brunsdon, Julie D'Acci, and Lynn Spigel

FEMINIST TELEVISION CRITICISM: A READER is a collection of essays on television by critics who repeatedly engage, in different ways, with the problems of feminism and femininity—what these terms mean, how they relate to each other, what they constitute and exclude.

Since the 1970s, feminists have become increasingly interested in television as something more than a bad object, something that offers a series of lures and pleasures, however limited its repertoire of female roles. For its part, over the last twenty-five years, television too has engaged with the themes and tropes of feminism. Indeed, while some feminists have defended women-targeted genres such as soap opera and situation comedy, and embraced programmes like *The Women of Brewster Place* and *Oranges Are Not the Only Fruit*, television has responded in its own way. For example, US TV has featured its own brand of feminism in 'New Women' sitcoms like *Kate and Allie* and *Murphy Brown*, while the Indian state channel has shown daytime serials aimed at the 'modern' woman. Even genres that were once widely male identified have been touched by feminist sentiments. Crime shows such as the US-produced *Cagney and Lacey* and Britain's *Prime Suspect* feature action heroines in detective roles (and these genres are also widely available on the export market). Indeed, much of the current entertainment output of television features strong women, single mothers, and female friends and lovers—that is, female types who are integral to feminist critique and culture.

The essays in this book are collected together to trace some of the contradictions and reciprocities of the relationships between feminism and television that have emerged over the last twenty years, with a concentration on the anglophone US/UK axis. Although the time space of twenty years is short, the collection is historical, mapping the emergence and formation of an area of study which has both a political and an academic address. During the years in which these essays were written, feminism and television have each found uneasy and marginal niches in the academy. Still, even in the margins, power hierarchies have their way of producing certain kinds of knowledge and excluding others. In this sense, the production of knowledge that we now recognize as 'feminist television criticism' has emerged against the traditional disciplines, but also within a field of unequal power relations among feminist critics in both national and international contexts. These essays and their selection, then, are symptomatic of a certain set of social and institutional hierarchies among feminist intellectuals, and for this reason they beg critical reassessment from a new wave of scholars. It is with an eye towards critical review and the stimulation of future research—rather than canonization—that we have gathered them together.

This anthology largely focuses on feminist television studies in the USA and Britain, which seems to us to reflect deep structurings of the field at more than one level. In other words, feminist television scholarship, and the conferences and publishing companies that have promoted it, have traditionally located their points of commerce in the English-speaking academy, particularly the USA and Britain. At the same time, US television is both national and, in its continuing prominence in the cultural imagination of the global markets, supra-national in a way that is true of no other national television system. Thus, Ien Ang's article, written in the Netherlands, is about responses to two US exports, *Dallas* and *Cagney and Lacey*; Elspeth Probyn writes in Canada about another US programme, *thirtysomething*; and Rosanne Kennedy's article, from Australia, is about a third, *L.A. Law*. US shows such as *Roseanne* and *Oprah*, discussed in Parts 1 and 3, have wide national and international circulations, whereas, for example, British programmes such as *Portrait of a Marriage* are much more clearly national products (although definitely part of Britain's most exportable 'quality' period drama).[1] Purnima Mankekar, writing in the USA, discusses the reception of *The Mahabharata* in Delhi on Doordarshan, the Indian government monopoly channel (colloquially, in India, 'Doordarshan' is often used to mean television in general). As Marie Gillespie has traced, the screening of this sacred serial attracted audiences of about 650 million in India, with diasporic viewings elsewhere on cable, satellite, and video, and broadcast in Britain. We would suggest, however, that, despite these huge international audiences, US entertainment hegemony naturalizes the idea that *The Mahabharata* is an instance of 'national television' that expresses some specific formation of 'Indianness' whereas US television is just 'television'.[2] In other words, through regulations and practices such as international copyright law, trade and quota agreements, syndication, diplomatic negotiations in organizations such as Unesco, and by the naturalization of its representational conventions, US television has historically wielded power on the international entertainment market. It has in effect secured world 'consent' to the idea that its technology, its institutional practices, and its media products are 'standard' forms against which all other television systems are then compared for their difference or expected to mimic. This anthology attempts both to recognize, and to some extent disrupt, these hegemonic notions and practices.

Most of the articles included in the volume deal with genres and topics that have been the dominant subjects of feminist television analysis—soaps, telenovelas, serials, sitcoms, housewives, 'new women', heterosexual and lesbian romances, female audiences, and domesticity. The focus of our selection is the feminist engagement with femininity and what are seen as feminine genres. To a much lesser degree, we have also included articles dealing with issues and genres more traditionally associated with the public sphere. While we agree with scholars such as Christine Geraghty, Liesbet van Zoonen, and Philip Schlesinger *et al.*, that feminist criticism should focus on all areas of television representation—news, political coverage, documentary, as well as fiction—in Geraghty's words, on 'blue' as well as 'pink' topics, we would suggest that our emphasis accurately reproduces the founding

---

1 See Mandy Merck's essay, 'Portrait of a Marriage?', in Mandy Merck (ed.), *Perversions: Deviant Readings* (New York: Routledge, 1993), 101–17.

2 Marie Gillespie, *Television, Ethnicity and Cultural Change* (London: Routledge, 1995), 87–95. See also Jeremy Tunstall, *The Media are American* (London: Constable, 1977).

contours of the field.[3] Indeed, in some quarters, feminist work is identified with an emphasis on the feminine. For example, Meaghan Morris, a critic who repeatedly addresses the wider sphere of political economy, has discussed the curious and vexing ways in which her work on the economy—as with some feminist historical work—has generally not been received as 'feminist'. That is, it is almost as if research has to be on a stereotypically girly topic—which violence, the news, and political–economic structures are not—before it can be considered feminist.[4]

The history of the development and visibility of the field 'feminist television criticism' is particularly problematic when it is recognized that 'femininity' has generally meant white femininity. To be able to address issues of gender alone would be a luxury for those critics ethnicized by dominant culture, as white feminists have been repeatedly reminded by writers and cultural workers such as Karen Alexander, Lola Young, Michele Wallace, bell hooks, and Pratibha Parmar.[5] However, as the work of these and other scholars reminds us, it has also been a luxury, one often reflecting greater security within the academic and critical establishments, to be able to address one medium alone. The work of black female scholars in Britain and the US has in general been characterized by its cross-media address and the fluency with which it traces the imbrication of ethnicity, race, and gender across a range of

3 Philip Schlesinger, R. Emerson Dobash, Russell P. Dobash, and C. Kay Weaver, *Women Viewing Violence* (London: BFI, 1992); Christine Geraghty, 'Feminism and Media Consumption', in James Curran, David Morley, and Valerie Walkerdine (eds.), *Cultural Studies and Communications* (London: Arnold, 1996), 306–22; Liesbet van Zoonen, *Feminist Media Studies* (London: Sage, 1994).

4 Many feminist media scholars have, of course, discussed public sphere issues. Meaghan Morris, open discussion at Console-ing Passions, Television, Video, and Feminism Conference, Tucson, 1994; Liesbet van Zoonen, 'Rethinking Feminist Media Politics', *Socialist Review*, 23/2 (1993), 35–56; 'A Tyranny of Intimacy? Women, Femininity and Television News', in Peter Dahlgren and Colin Sparks (eds.), *Communication and Citizenship: Journalism and the Public Sphere in the New Media Age* (London: Routledge, 1991), 217–35; *Feminist Media Studies*. Susan Honeyford, 'Women and Television', *Screen*, 21/2 (1980), 49–52. Association of Cinematograph and Television Technicians (ACTT), *Patterns of Discrimination Against Women in the Film and Television Industries* (London: ACTT, 1975). Jeanne Allen, 'The Social Matrix of Television: Invention in the United States', in E. Ann Kaplan (ed.), *Regarding Television* (Frederick, Md.: University Publications of America, 1983), 109–19; Pat Auferhide, 'Latin American Grassroots Video: Beyond Television', *Public Culture*, 5/3 (1993), 579–92; Alexandra Juhasz, *AIDS TV: Identity, Community, and Alternative Videos* (Durham, NC: Duke Univ. Press, 1995); Laura Marks, 'Tie a Yellow Ribbon Around Me: Masochism, Militarism, and the Gulf War on TV', *Camera Obscura*, 27 (1991), 55–75; Patricia Mellencamp, *High Anxiety: Catastrophe, Scandal, Age and Comedy* (Bloomington: Indiana Univ. Press, 1992); Eileen Meehan, 'Heads of Household and Ladies of the House: Gender, Genre, and Broadcast Ratings, 1929–1990', in William S. Solomon and Robert W. McChesney (eds.), *Ruthless Criticism: New Perspectives in U.S. Communication History* (Minneapolis: Univ. of Minnesota Press, 1993), 204–21, 'Why We Don't Count: The Commodity Audience', in Patricia Mellencamp (ed.), *Logics of Television: Essays in Television Criticism* (Bloomington: Indiana Univ. Press, 1990), 117–37; Kathryn Montgomery, *Target Prime Time: Advocacy Groups and the Struggle Over Entertainment Television* (New York: Oxford Univ. Press, 1989); Margaret Morse, 'Talk, Talk, Talk—The Space of Discourse in Television', *Screen*, 26 (1985), 2–15; Mimi White, *Tele-Advising: Therapeutic Discourse in American Television* (Chapel Hill: Univ. of North Carolina Press, 1992); Barbie Zelizer, 'CNN, the Gulf War, and Journalist Practice', *Journal of Communication*, 42/1 (1992), 66–81; Lana F. Rakow and Kimberlie Kranich, 'Woman as Sign in Television News', *Journal of Communication*, 41 (1991), 8–23; Heather Hendershot, 'Media Reform in the Age of Toasters: *Strawberry Shortcake*, the Continuum of Gender Construction, and the Deregulation of Children's Television', *Wide Angle*, 16/4 (1994), 58–82.

5 Karen Alexander in 'Karen Alexander: Video Worker, Interviewed by Mica Nava', *Feminist Review*, 18 (1984), 29–34; 'Mothers, Lovers, and Others', *Monthly Film Bulletin*, 56/669 (1989), 314–16; Lola Young, *Fear of the Dark: 'Race', Gender and Sexuality in the Cinema* (London: Routledge, 1996); June Givanni (ed.), *Remote Control: Dilemmas of Black Intervention in British Film and TV* (London: BFI, 1995); Michele Wallace, *Invisibility Blues: From Pop to Theory* (London: Verso, 1990); bell hooks, *Black Looks: Race and Representation* (Boston: South End Press, 1992); Pratibha Parmar, 'Hateful Contraries: Media Images of Asian Women', *Ten. 8*, No. 16 (1984).

textual sites. For example, Michele Wallace discusses, among other topics, literature, cinema, and television in her collection of essays *Invisibility Blues: From Pop to Theory*. Similarly, June Givanni's recent collection, *Remote Control*, specifically addresses black interventions in film and television in Britain, and bell hooks's *Black Looks: Race and Representation* analyses films, novels, poetry, magazines, autobiographies, documentaries, and music videos.[6] Indeed, it is only in the last year, 1995, that the first two single-author academic books dealing with race and film have been published in English. In Britain, Lola Young's *Fear of the Dark: 'Race', Gender and Sexuality in the Cinema* traces the representation of race and black people in British cinema since World War II. In the USA, Jacqueline Bobo's *Black Women as Cultural Readers* investigates the reception of *The Color Purple* and *Daughters of the Dust* by African American female audiences. Bobo uses some of the theoretical paradigms that have been developed in television and cultural studies to approach the audience (see Part 2 below) and it is thus also virtually unique in its investigation of a social audience for cinema.[7]

Whereas the regulated absence of blacks on television has historically rendered feminist African American criticism directed solely at television a fairly futile pursuit, recent industry developments have opened onto new critical possibilities. Music videos and talk shows, among other forms, have increasingly addressed black audiences and provided more representations of black women and greater spaces for black women's agency. The work of Robin Roberts and Tricia Rose on music video and Corinne Squire on *Oprah* offer prime examples of these newer critical interventions. Of course, African American feminist scholarship such as that of Jane Rhodes on *L.A. Law* testifies to the fact that the industry's limitations and constraints have never totally determined or shaped the critical impulse.[8]

Feminist television criticism was formed initially through two quite different agendas, one directed at the medium itself and the other at the existing traditions of critical scholarship about television.

In the first case, as with other 1960s political movements, feminists took the media to task for their demeaning and stereotypical images of women.[9]

---

6 See above, n. 5.

7 The other notable exception here is Jackie Stacey's *Star Gazing* (London: Routledge, 1993). Jacqueline Bobo, *Black Women as Cultural Readers* (New York: Columbia Univ. Press, 1995). See above, n. 5.

8 Robin Roberts, '"Ladies First": Queen Latifah's Afrocentric Music Video', *African American Review*, 28/2 (1994), 245–57, 'Music Videos, Performance and Resistance: Feminist Rappers', *Journal of Popular Culture*, 25/2 (1991), 141–52, '"Sex as a Weapon": Feminist Rock Music Videos', *National Women's Studies Association Journal*, 2/1 (1990), 1–15; Tricia Rose, 'Never Trust a Big Butt and a Smile', *Camera Obscura*, 23 (1990), 108–31 (Ch. 20 in this volume); Corinne Squire, 'Empowering Women? The *Oprah Winfrey Show*', *Feminism and Psychology*, 4/1 (1994), 63–79 (Ch. 7 in this volume); Jane Rhodes, 'Television's Realist Portrayal of African-American Women and the Case of *L.A. Law*', *Women and Language*, 14/1 (1991), 29–34.

9 For information and sources on feminist responses to television in the 1970s see the pioneering work: Gaye Tuchman, Arlene Kaplan Daniels, and James Benet (eds.), *Hearth and Home: Images of Women in the Mass Media* (New York: Oxford Univ. Press, 1978); esp. Helen Franzwa, 'The Image of Women in Television: An Annotated Bibliography' (US Commission on Civil Rights, 1976), 273–99; and Josephine King and Mary Stott, *Is This Your Life? Images of Women in the Media* (London: Virago, 1977); Matilda Butler and William Paisley, *Women and the Mass Media: A Sourcebook for Research and Action* (New York: Human Sciences Press, 1980); and Margaret Gallagher, *Unequal Opportunities: The Case of Women and the Media* (Paris: Unesco, 1981). See also US Commission on

Many of the initial feminist dealings with television were, in fact, calls to action growing out of a deep conviction that women's oppression was very much related to mass media representations and that change was not only urgent, but possible. The famous iconic moments of this are the protests against the 1968 Miss America contest in the US and the 1970 Miss World pageant in London.

In the second case, feminists took issue (often implicitly) with the existing critical work on television that disregarded femininity, gender, and sexuality in discussions of the 'political'. Here, the political was interpreted in very narrow terms of the market and public policy (arenas that were mostly populated by male executives, producers, and policy-makers). As in other disciplines, feminist critics broadened the meaning of the term 'political' to include a general interest in everyday life, especially the female-associated spheres of domesticity and consumerism.

Given this, it is no surprise that one of the first subjects feminist television critics turned to was daytime programming and soap opera in particular. As the articles included in this volume suggest, perhaps more than in any genre, the interest in soap opera (both daytime and prime time) has been international in scope, from the work of Michèle Mattelart and Ana Lopez on the telenovela to the early British work on *Coronation Street* by Richard Dyer, Christine Geraghty, Marion Jordan, Terry Lovell, Richard Paterson, and John Stewart, to work on US serials by Carole Lopate, Ellen Seiter, Tania Modleski, Jane Feuer, and Mimi White, to work on *Dallas* by Ien Ang and Tamar Liebes and Elihu Katz, to that on Indian serials by Prabha Krishnan and Anita Dighe, and on to Robert Allen's recent anthology on global soaps and Charlotte Brunsdon's recent work on feminist critics who study soaps.[10]

Civil Rights, *Window Dressing on the Set: Women and Minorities in Television* (Washington, DC: US Government Printing Office, 1977).

10 Michèle Mattelart, 'Women and the Cultural Industries', *Media, Culture and Society*, 4/2 (1982), 133–51; Ana Lopez, 'Our Welcomed Guests: Telenovelas in Latin America', in Allen (ed.), *To Be Continued . . . Soap Operas Around the World* (New York: Routledge, 1995), 256–75; Richard Dyer, Terry Lovell, Jean McCrindle, 'Women and Soap Opera', repr. in Ann Gray and Jim McGuigan, *Studying Culture* (London: Edward Arnold, 1993), 35–41; Richard Dyer, Christine Geraghty, Marion Jordan, Terry Lovell, Richard Paterson, and John Stewart, *Coronation Street* (London: BFI, 1980); Carol Lopate, 'Daytime Television: You'll Never Want to Leave Home', *Radical America*, 11/1 (1977), 32–49; Tania Modleski, 'The Search for Tomorrow in Today's Soap Operas: Notes on Feminine Narrative Form', *Film Quarterly*, 33/1 (1979), 12–21 (and Ch. 2 in this volume), 'The Rhythms of Reception: Daytime Television and Women's Work', in E. Ann Kaplan (ed.), *Regarding Television* (Frederick, Md.: University Publications of America, 1983), 67–75; Ellen Seiter, 'The Role of the Woman Reader: Eco's Narrative Theory and Soap Operas', *Tabloid*, 6 (1981), 36–43, 'Promise and Contradiction: The Daytime Television Serials', *Screen*, 23 (1982), 150–63; Jane Feuer, 'Melodrama, Serial Form and Television Today', *Screen*, 25/1 (1984), 4–16; Mimi White, 'Women, Memory and Serial Melodrama: Anecdotes in Television Soap Opera', *Screen*, 35/4 (1994), 336–53; Ien Ang, *Watching* Dallas: *Soap Opera and the Melodramatic Imagination* (London: Methuen, 1985); Tamar Liebes and Elihu Katz, *The Export of Meaning: Cross-Cultural Readings of Dallas* (Oxford: University Press, 1990); Prabha Krishnan and Anita Dighe, *Affirmation and Denial: Construction of Femininity on Indian Television* (New Delhi: Sage, 1990); Robert Allen (ed.), *To Be Continued . . . Soap Operas Around the World* (New York: Routledge, 1995); Charlotte Brunsdon, 'The Role of Soap Opera in the Development of Feminist Television Scholarship', in Allen (ed.), *To Be Continued . . . Soap Operas Around the World*, 49–63, 'Identity in Feminist Television Criticism', *Media, Culture and Society*, 15/2 (1993), 309–20 (and Ch. 8 in this volume); Dorothy Hobson, Crossroads: *The Drama of a Soap Opera* (London: Methuen, 1982); Muriel G. Cantor and Suzanne Pingree, *The Soap Opera* (Beverly Hills: Sage, 1983); Robert C. Allen, *Speaking of Soap Operas* (Chapel Hill: Univ. of North Carolina Press, 1985); Louise Spence, 'Life's Little Problems . . . and Pleasures: An Investigation into the Narrative Structures of *The Young and the Restless*', *Quarterly Review of Film Studies*, 9 (1984), 301–8; Sandy Flitterman-Lewis, 'The *Real* Soap Operas: TV Commercials', in Kaplan (ed.), *Regarding Television*, 84–96, 'All's Well That Doesn't End: Soap Opera and the Marriage Motif', *Camera Obscura*, 16 (1988), 118–27;

Critics often explore these programmes with ambivalence, at once challenging their romantic glorification of women's isolation at home, but also embracing soaps for their strong female characters and other narrative conventions (e.g. multiple point of view, cliffhanger closure) that many think speak to female concerns and pleasures in ways classical novels and films do not. In fact, for some—most notably Beverle Houston and, by extension, the work of Sandy Flitterman-Lewis—television as a medium is organized around female desire and thus essentially different from the classical Hollywood cinema that many early critics saw as male-centred, soliciting visual pleasures that objectified female characters and encouraged ways of seeing based on voyeurism and fetishism.[11]

In the inaugural work on soap opera, the desire for the institutional legitimation of the feminist television critic within the academy was often central and explicit. In this regard, it was also very much an attempt—like the early women's movement itself—to render visible the invisible (and often culturally disregarded), everyday conditions of women's lives in the home. This is very clear, for example, in the work of Dorothy Hobson, whose 1970s research in Birmingham (from which she developed the *Crossroads* project) was about the ways young mothers at home with their children used both television and radio in their daily routines.[12]

In this early feminist attention to soap opera, we find traces of what developed into a number of methodological pursuits (sometimes related, sometimes not). First, there has been a large body of work that employs textual analysis (or the close reading of programmes for their narrative structures, iconography, symbolic codes, themes, and their solicitation of pleasure, identification, and subjectivity). Evidently, the preoccupation with textual analysis stems from its more general methodological prominence in critical writing in the humanities. Moreover, particularly since the widespread availability of the video recorder, there are also economic and institutional reasons why feminist work should cluster in this cheapest of research fields. Textual analysis, ultimately, can be conducted at home by an individual working alone. No need to apply for research funding—and perhaps even more pertinently, no need for grant awarders to be sympathetic to feminist projects. Certainly, the pattern of paper submissions to both the US Consoling Passions conference and the Screen conference in Scotland would suggest that the textual analysis of individual programmes, series, personae (Roseanne, Oprah), and events (such as the Hill/Thomas hearings) provides

Christine Geraghty, *Women and Soap Opera* (Oxford: Polity Press, 1991); Mark Finch, 'Sex and Address in *Dynasty*', *Screen*, 27/6 (1986), 24–42; Martha Nochimson, *No End To Her: Soap Opera and the Female Subject* (Berkeley: Univ. of California Press, 1992); Mary Ellen Brown, 'The Politics of Soaps: Pleasure and Feminine Empowerment', *Australian Journal of Cultural Studies*, 4/2 (1987), 1–25, *Soap Opera and Women's Talk: The Pleasure of Resistance* (Thousand Oaks: Sage, 1994); Laura Stempel Mumford, *Love and Ideology in the Afternoon* (Bloomington: Indiana Univ. Press, 1995); Gloria Abernathy-Lear, *African American Viewers and Daytime Serials* (Philadelphia: Univ. of Pennsylvania Press, forthcoming).

11 Beverle Houston, 'Viewing Television: The Metapsychology of Endless Consumption', *Quarterly Review of Film Studies*, 9 (1984), 183–95; Sandy Flitterman-Lewis, 'Psychoanalysis, Film, and Television', in Robert C. Allen (ed.), *Channels of Discourse, Reassambled* (Chapel Hill, NC, 1992), 203–46.

12 See citations for Dorothy Hobson, as well as Carole Lopate, Michèle Mattelart, Tania Modleski, Ellen Seiter, and Charlotte Brunsdon in n. 10 above.

what is now seen as a replicable model of feminist engagement with television.[13]

While still often engaged in textual analysis, a second area of research seeks mainly to relate programmes to their discursive, social, and institutional contexts, as well as their social and institutional histories. This work, for example, focuses on such subjects as the symbolic placement of television in the home, the larger socio-discursive history of sexuality that informs the production and interpretation of television texts, the extra-textual promotional materials through which television producers direct audience interests and interpretations of female characters, and the institutional imperatives and constraints which shape these characters. Such work is often historical in nature. Typically based on archival research methods, it treats popular sources such as women's fashion magazines, books on interior décor, or fanzines as primary historical documents that shed light on women's culture rather than treating them (as does much traditional history) as mere anecdotes. Moreover, it (either implicitly or explicitly) argues that these 'feminized' sources are just as useful as the more 'masculinized' and so-called 'official' sources such as network files and policy reports that were usually recorded by men in male-dominated institutions. It may, on the other hand, analyse these official, institutional sources through feminist interpretative strategies. In other words, as with feminist history in general, these kinds of feminist television histories are interested in finding women's voices, or the conditions under which femininity is produced, and this means either looking in places that are not conventionally regarded as 'legitimate' or revisiting and re-visioning traditional sites and sources.[14]

This issue of context is manifested in a somewhat different way in a third area of research which investigates the gendered audience and the sexual politics of family viewing.[15] Qualitative and usually critical in nature, much of

13 See Wahneema Lubiano, 'Black Ladies, Welfare Queens, and State Minstrels: Ideological War by Narrative Means', in Toni Morrison (ed.), *Race-ing Justice, En-Gendering Power: Essays on Anita Hill, Clarence Thomas, and the Construction of Social Reality* (New York: Pantheon Books, 1992), 323–63.

14 e.g. in this volume, Lynn Spigel's research on television's relationship to the reception context of the suburban home; and Elspeth Probyn's and Rebecca Walkowitz's analyses of current TV fictions in relation to the discourses of post-feminism and family values use these types of 'feminized' source materials to flesh out the contexts in which television programmes were produced and interpreted by their audiences. See also Mary Beth Haralovich, 'Sitcoms and Suburbs: Positioning the 1950s Homemaker', *Quarterly Review of Film and Video*, 11/1 (1989), 61–83, 'Suburban Family Sitcoms and Consumer Product Design: Addressing the Social Subjectivity of Homemakers in the 50s', in Phillip Drummond and Richard Paterson (eds.), *Television and its Audience* (London: BFI, 1988), 38–60; Lauren Rabinovitz, 'Sitcoms and Single Moms: Representations of Feminism on American TV', *Cinema Journal*, 29/1 (1989), 3–19; Tara McPherson, 'Disregarding Romance and Refashioning Femininity: Getting Down and Dirty with *Designing Women*', *Camera Obscura*, 32 (1993–4), 103–23; Edith Thornton, 'On the Landing: High Art, Low Art, and *Upstairs, Downstairs*', *Camera Obscura*, 31 (1993), 27–46; Julie D'Acci, *Defining Women: Television and the Case of* Cagney and Lacey (Chapel Hill: Univ. of North Carolina Press, 1994), 'Nobody's Woman? *Honey West* and the New Sexuality', in Lynn Spigel and Michael Curtin (eds.), *The Revolution Wasn't Televised* (New York: Routledge, forthcoming); Moya Luckett, 'Patty Duke and Girl Culture', *The Revolution Wasn't Televised*; Jeffrey Sconce, 'Families at the "Outer Limits" of Oblivion', *The Revolution Wasn't Televised*; Anna McCarthy, 'Reach Out and Touch Someone: Technology and Sexuality in Broadcast Ads for Phone Sex', *Velvet Light Trap*, 32 (1993), 50–7.

15 In this volume see articles by Ann Gray, Prabha Krishnan and Anita Dighe. See also Dorothy Hobson, *Crossroads: The Drama of a Soap Opera*; David Morley, *Family Television: Cultural Power and Domestic Leisure* (London: Comedia, 1986), *Television, Audiences and Cultural Studies* (London: Routledge, 1992); James Lull, *Inside Family Viewing: Ethnographic Research on Television's Audiences* (New York: Routledge, 1990), also (ed.), *World Families Watch Television* (Newbury Park, Calif.: Sage, 1988); Minu Lee and Chong Heup Cho, 'Women Watching Together: An Ethnographic Study of

this work is a hybrid of sociological, anthropological, and in some cases, historical method, and it is generally concerned with the way women view television, how they interpret it, and/or how the context of domesticity relates to these modes of reception. In contrast to textual analysis, this work is potentially very expensive in terms of research time and funds as it typically necessitates assistants and/or extensive data-gathering. This certainly does not make it a priori more rigorous or qualitatively better than textual analysis, but it does make it more logistically difficult to do.

As various articles in this volume will demonstrate, while we want to separate these critical approaches for discussion here, they have become increasingly intertwined in television criticism. For example, in this reader, authors such as Lyn Thomas and Jacqueline Bobo and Ellen Seiter perform close readings of *Inspector Morse* and *The Women of Brewster Place* respectively, but they are also concerned with audience research methods. In this regard, one of the main contributions of feminist television criticism now is its insistence on a wider interdisciplinary approach to method. As in much feminist work, the reasons for this are not simply whimsical, but rather determined by a rejection of the ideology of scientism that so many television historians, audience researchers, and policy analysts had employed when media studies was dominated by the male-centred concerns and empiricist/positivist methods of the 1930s–1960s (the time when industry- and government-funded 'administrative' social scientific research first flourished in the States and when paternalistic notions of public service and policy formation reigned in Britain). Even while feminist scholars are interested in the social world and often have a historical and empirical dimension to their work, much feminist scholarship implicitly rejects the idea that empirical facts can be marshalled to make universal truth claims that speak for an imaginary *everyone*. The idea of difference—sexual, racial, ethnic, and otherwise—so central to feminism, mitigates against universal truth and the methods that aspire to find it.

That said, it should be clear why the problem of legitimation was so central for early feminists working in these non-scientific interpretative paradigms on what was widely perceived as trivial subjects like soaps and housewives. But if the early work on soap opera was explicit in its attempts to authenticate female pleasures and low-status genres aimed at women, the rhetoric of legitimation and polemical calls to arms were rarely heard by the mid-1980s. In addition, as in feminist criticism more generally, the idea of an essential form of 'feminine' pleasure and desire was increasingly contested over the course of the 1980s. For feminist television critics this has meant a more self-conscious move away from reflection theories that posit a fit between representation and 'real' women or even 'real' women's pleasure, and towards a

Korean Soap Opera Fans in the United States', *Cultural Studies*, 4/1 (1990), 30–44; Valerie Walkerdine, 'Video Replay: Families, Films and Fantasy', in Victor Burgin, James Donald, and Cora Kaplan (eds.), *Formations of Fantasy* (London: Methuen, 1986), repr. in *The Media Reader*, ed. Manuel Alvarado and John O. Thompson (London: BFI, 1990), 339–57, and in Valerie Walkerdine, *Schoolgirl Fictions* (London: Verso, 1990); Henry Jenkins, '"Going Bonkers!": Children, Play and Pee-Wee', *Camera Obscura*, 17 (1988), 168–93; Ondina Fachel Leal, 'Popular Taste and Erudite Repertoire: The Place and Space of Television in Brazil', *Cultural Studies*, 4/1 (1990), 19–29; Aniko Bodroghkozy, '"Is This What You Mean By Color TV?": Race, Gender, and Contested Meanings in NBC's *Julia*', in Lynn Spigel and Denise Mann (eds.), *Private Screenings* (Minneapolis: Univ. of Minnesota Press, 1992), 143–68; Ellen Seiter *et al.* (eds.), *Remote Control: Television, Audiences, and Cultural Power* (New York: Routledge, 1989). See citations for Ien Ang and Gloria Abernathy-Lear in n. 10 above.

critique of television's constructions of all social categories, including gender, sexual identity, race, nation, and everyday life itself. Now, in a more post-structuralist move, none of these categories is seen as self-given or self-evident.

This shift toward the idea of social construction was accompanied by a new set of problems. Some scholars concentrated on the social construction of domestic space and the gendered relations of leisure that define television viewing in the home. Some of this work, such as Lynn Spigel's study of the introduction of television, was in explicit dialogue with feminist history and theory, while other work, such as David Morley's ethnographic research on TV viewers or Ann Gray's study of the use of the video recorder, provides empirical investigations of individual families watching TV. So too, Andrea L. Press interviews women about their experiences watching television, although her study is less concerned with viewing context than with how women identify with television characters; and Evelyn Cauleta Reid questions young black women in London to ascertain the *differences* in their attitudes toward television rather than a homogeneous 'black perspective'. More recently, Gloria Abernathy-Lear's study of African American female soap opera fans is explicitly interested in detailing the viewing strategies and pleasures of a group of African American women engaged with a predominantly white-dominated genre.[16]

Over the course of the 1980s, feminist criticism also began to take a broader range of genres as objects of study, especially sitcoms and detective programmes. Still interested in issues of representation and interpretation, and still often employing some degree of textual analysis, critics focused on how these genres construct female types. So, for example, Mary Beth Haralovich examined how classic US sitcoms like *Leave It to Beaver* and *Father Knows Best* address post-war women as arbiters of suburban consumer culture. Helen Baehr, Serafina Bathrick, Cathy Schwichtenberg, Judith Mayne, Jackie Byars, Lauren Rabinovitz, Bonnie Dow, Caren Deming and Mercilee Jenkins, Julie D'Acci, Danae Clark, Lorraine Gamman, Beverley Alcock, Jocelyn Robson, and Shari Zeck look at US and British representations of 'feminist' heroines during the 1970s and 1980s in shows such as *Charlie's Angels, Kate and Allie, Mary Tyler Moore, L.A. Law, Cagney and Lacey, Murphy Brown,* and *Cheers.*[17]

Whether in its more specifically textual or historical inflections, this focus on 'constructed' femininities poses particular questions for feminist reinvestigation. First, as we noted above, the original problem of legitimation is not made explicit in this later work. That is, the feminist critic no longer feels it necessary to make television a 'visible' and worthy concern in the academy.

16 Lynn Spigel, *Make Room for TV: Television and the Family Ideal in Postwar America* (Chicago: Univ. of Chicago Press, 1992), 'Installing the Television Set: Popular Discourses on Television and Domestic Space, 1948–1955', *Camera Obscura*, 16 (1988), 10–47; David Morley, *Family Television: Cultural Power and Domestic Leisure* (see above, n. 15); Ann Gray, 'Behind Closed Doors: Video Recorders in the Home', in Helen Baehr and Gillian Dyer (eds.), *Boxed-In: Women and Television* (London: Pandora, 1987), 38–54 (and Ch. 16 in this volume), *Video Playtime: The Gendering of a Leisure Technology* (London: Routledge, 1992); Andrea Press, *Women Watching Television: Gender, Class, and Generation in the American Television Experience* (Philadelphia: Univ. of Pennsylvania Press, 1991); Evelyn Cauleta Reid, 'Viewdata', *Screen*, 30/1–2 (1989), 114–21; Gloria Abernathy-Lear (see above, n. 10); see also citations for Ondina Fachel-Leal, James Lull, and Valerie Walkerdine in n. 15.

17 Please refer to the bibliography for full citations from these authors.

This is obviously related to the increasing visibility of feminist media studies in the curriculum as well as to the more general rise of Cultural Studies. But even while it had gained a measure of institutional legitimacy, this second wave of television criticism still had a certain 'inferiority' complex, especially with regard to the more 'rigorous' and established fields of feminist literary and film studies. For this reason, at the implicit level, this work was still striving for a way to legitimate itself. This struggle for legitimation is written into its attempts to find models outside of psychoanalytic feminist literary and film studies. While still within the psychoanalytic discourses of early feminist film theory, Patricia Mellencamp, for example, turns to Freud's work on humour rather than the body of work on voyeurism and masochism traditionally used in cinema studies. In the more historical and audience-based research, a move towards Antonio Gramsci's model of hegemony (as inflected by British Cultural Studies) differentiates television studies from early film theory's fascination with notions of ideology based on the writings of Louis Althusser.[18] This interest in hegemony has meant a focus on how television incorporates feminist dissent and turns it into consensual and non-threatening notions of women's liberation that are ultimately good for consumerism (for example, *The Mary Tyler Moore Show* drew on the feminist movement in such a way as to make it appealing to the girl next door, and it became a favourite of advertisers interested in targeting working women with buying power).[19] But the use of the concept of hegemony has also meant a growing interest in the possibility of women's 'agency' and the power to be critical of television, over the Althusserian notion of 'interpellation' that gave the television text more power to manipulate the spectator. For this reason, the Gramscian model has often generated ethnographic, audience-based studies or else textual studies that foreground the possibility of 'resisting' the text's dominant meanings. For example, a large body of work on *Star Trek* and soap opera fandom has shown how the fans often rework the programme to the point of actually producing their own 'slash' texts that recombine features of the original show to make new narratives (for example, in separate studies, Constance Penley, Camille Bacon-Smith, and Henry Jenkins have all shown how (mostly female) *Star Trek* fans create homoerotic texts by reworking scripts or re-editing video clips to produce, among other things, sexually charged exchanges between Captain Kirk and Mr Spock).[20]

Also during the 1980s and 1990s, a focus on intertextuality, production

---

18 See Patricia Mellencamp's article in this volume and also her *High Anxiety: Catastrophe, Scandal, Age and Comedy*.

19 See Serafina Bathrick, '*The Mary Tyler Moore Show*: Women at Home and at Work', in Jane Feuer, Paul Kerr, and Tise Vahimagi (eds.), *MTM: 'Quality Television'* (London: BFI, 1984), 99–131; Helen Baehr, 'The "Liberated Woman" in Television Drama', *Women's Studies International Quarterly*, 3/1 (1980), 29–39; Lauren Rabinovitz, 'Sitcoms and Single Moms: Representations of Feminism on American TV'; Robert Deming, '*Kate and Allie*: "New Women" and the Audience's Television Archive', *Camera Obscura*, 16 (1988), 154–67; Bonnie Dow, 'Hegemony, Feminist Criticism, and *The Mary Tyler Moore Show*', *Critical Studies in Mass Communication*, 7 (1990), 261–74, 'Femininity and Feminism in *Murphy Brown*', *Southern Communication Journal*, 57/2 (1992), 143–55.

20 Constance Penley, 'Brownian Motion: Women, Tactics, and Technology', in Constance Penley and Andrew Ross (eds.), *Technoculture* (Minneapolis: Univ. of Minnesota Press, 1991), 135–61; Henry Jenkins, '*Star Trek*: Rerun, Reread, Rewritten: Fan Writings as Textual Poaching', *Critical Studies in Mass Communication*, 5/2 (1988), 85–107; Camille Bacon-Smith, *Enterprising Women: Television, Fandom and the Creation of Popular Myth* (Philadelphia: Univ. of Pennsylvania Press, 1992); Cathy Schwichtenberg (ed.), *The Madonna Connection: Representational Politics, Subcultural Identities, and Cultural Theory* (Boulder, Colo.: Westview Press, 1993).

conditions, and the social history of texts—rather than close textual readings of individual programmes—became important to scholars looking at the social construction of woman.[21] In these studies, it is assumed, for example, that *Cagney and Lacey* needs to be understood within the more general framework of media portrayals of feminism and the networks' institutionalization of it; or that the black sitcom *Julia* needs to be understood within the broader field of debates about black single mothers and the politics of civil rights in the 1960s.[22] In a powerful demonstration of intertextuality, Wahneema Lubiano makes clear how one of the most significant television events of the early 1990s—the Anita Hill/Clarence Thomas Congressional hearings—had to be analysed on a multiplicity of sites. She shows how the event circulated a complex repertoire of images and narratives about 'blackness' not simply on television but in numerous other media including newspapers and magazines.[23] In taking this intertextual approach, critics not only demonstrate how television produces meanings that coincide with or else contradict broader areas of women's culture, but they also show how audiences are positioned to interpret television programmes within the context of previous encounters with other media forms and aspects of material culture.

A consideration of television as a contemporary mode of popular festival and ritual likewise gained prominence over the course of the 1980s, and this mode of inquiry also worked to differentiate TV studies from film theory. Drawing especially on the work of Mikhail Bakhtin, Natalie Zemon Davis, and Victor Turner (all of whom focus on pre-industrial European popular culture), these models foreground television's relationship to cultural belief systems and draw analogies between pre-industrial popular culture and the media culture of late capitalism. For example, Mary Ellen Brown draws analogies between soap opera fan gossip and pre-industrial oral culture, while Gloria Abernathy-Lear investigates how African American oral traditions are taken up by soap opera fans. In this volume, Kathleen Rowe uses *Roseanne* as a case study to show how tropes of femininity in pre-industrial carnivals carried over into the genre of television comedy.[24]

A focus on postmodern theory, most fully developed in the work of

21 See Mary Beth Haralovich, 'Sitcoms and Suburbs: Positioning the 1950s Homemaker'; Lauren Rabinovitz, 'Sitcoms and Single Moms: Representations of Feminism on American TV'; Danae Clark, '*Cagney and Lacey*: Feminist Strategies of Detection', in Mary Ellen Brown (ed.), *Television and Women's Culture* (London: Sage, 1990); Julie D'Acci, *Defining Women: Television and the Case of Cagney and Lacey*; Aniko Bodroghkozy, ' "Is This What You Mean By Color TV?" ': Race, Gender, and Contested Meanings in NBC's *Julia*'; Denise Mann, 'The Spectacularization of Everyday Life: Recycling Hollywood Stars and Fans in Early Television Variety Shows', in Lynn Spigel and Denise Mann (eds.), *Private Screenings*, 41–70; Nina Leibman, 'Leave Mother Out: The Fifties Family in American Film and Television', *Wide Angle*, 10 (1988), 24–41; Jackie Byars and Eileen Meehan, 'Once in a Lifetime: Constructing the "Working Woman" through Cable Narrowcasting', *Camera Obscura*, 33–4 (1994–5), 13–41; Eithne Johnson, 'Lifetime's Feminine Psychographic Space and the "Mystery Loves Company" Series', ibid. 43–74; Pamela Wilson, 'Upscale Feminine Angst: *Molly Dodd*, the Lifetime Cable Network and Gender Marketing', ibid. 103–30; Jane Feuer, 'Feminism on Lifetime: Yuppie TV for the Nineties', ibid. 133–45; Sasha Torres, 'War and Remembrance: Televisual Narrative, National Memory, and *China Beach*', ibid. 147–64.

22 Aniko Bodroghkozy, ' "Is This What You Mean By Color TV?" ': Race, Gender, and Contested Meanings in NBC's *Julia*'.

23 Wahneema Lubiano, 'Black Ladies, Welfare Queens, and State Minstrels: Ideological War by Narrative Means', 323–63.

24 Mary Ellen Brown, *Soap Opera and Women's Talk: The Pleasure of Resistance*; Gloria Abernathy-Lear, *African American Viewers and Daytime Serials*; Kathleen Rowe, 'Roseanne: Unruly Woman as Domestic Goddess', Ch. 5 in this volume.

Patricia Mellencamp, Lynne Joyrich, E. Ann Kaplan, and Margaret Morse, also implicitly separates television studies from other objects of analysis— especially film.[25] Though not always about women *per se*, the work on post-modernism often dovetails with specifically feminist concerns because it centrally foregrounds issues of high and low culture that feminist media studies had initially investigated by embracing the traditionally 'low' forms such as soap opera. This work also explores new forms of subjectivity that might trouble the modes of identification more typically offered by realist and modernist art forms in western patriarchies. The interest in postmodern subjectivity moved many feminist critics away from the search for a female subject in film and literary analysis towards a notion of distracted, frag-mented, schizophrenic identities engendered (in part) by television.[26] This work also engages Jean Baudrillard's notion of 'simulation' and the waning of historical consciousness that postmodern critics have more generally developed. For television critics this has meant a move away from psychoan-alytic film theory's obsession with the imaginary and symbolic (terms based on the writings of psychoanalyst Jacques Lacan) which it developed in rela-tion to questions of the unconscious and identification. Instead, television critics moved toward Lacan's concept of the 'real' and the phenomenology of perceptual experience. Here, for example, critics such as Mary Ann Doane, Patricia Mellencamp, and Margaret Morse, respectively, explored how real-ity formats from catastrophe coverage to exercise tapes altered perceptions of time and space as well as the sensory relation of the body to each.[27] These ideas of the special connection between television and postmodernism also gave feminist critics ways to speak about television as an area of study linked to, but also different from, feminist film studies.

Another central problem for feminist television criticism is the relation between the feminist critic and 'women' in general. Within ethnographic projects, the intersubjective relation of 'self–other' has become most explicit. Ethnographic and interview-based studies such as Tricia Rose's study of female rap artists and Lyn Thomas's essay on *Inspector Morse* fans (included in this volume) as well as Constance Penley's study of female *Star Trek* fans, question the degree to which 'feminism' is an operative term for the fans and producers themselves. So too, in the spirit of self-reflexive ethnographic method, these authors often question their own stake in the fandom.[28] This has been especially important in terms of critiques of racism. In the essay

25 Patricia Mellencamp, 'Situation and Simulation: An Introduction to *I love Lucy*', *Screen*, 26/2 (1985), 30–40, *High Anxiety: Catastrophe, Scandal, Age and Comedy*; Lynne Joyrich, 'All That Television Allows: TV Melodrama, Postmodernism and Consumer Culture', *Camera Obscura*, 16 (1988), 129–54, 'Going Through the E/Motions: Gender, Postmodernism, and Affect in Television Studies', *Discourse*, 14/1 (1991), 23–40; E. Ann Kaplan, *Rocking Around the Clock: Music Television, Postmodernism, and Consumer Culture* (London: Methuen, 1987); Margaret Morse, 'Artemis Aging: Exercise and the Female Body on Video', *Discourse*, 10/1 (1987–8), 20–53, 'Talk, Talk, Talk—The Space of Discourse in Television'; Susan White, '*Veronica Clare* and the New *Film Noir* Heroine', *Camera Obscura*, 33–4 (1994–5), 77–100.

26 See above, n. 25.

27 Mary Ann Doane, 'Information, Crisis, Catastrophe', in Patricia Mellencamp (ed.), *Logics of Television*, 222–39; Patricia Mellencamp, *High Anxiety: Catastrophe, Scandal, Age and Comedy*; Margaret Morse, 'Artemis Aging: Exercise and the Female Body on Video'.

28 Tricia Rose, 'Never Trust a Big Butt and a Smile', *Camera Obscura*, 23 (1990), 108–31 (Ch. 20 in this volume); Lyn Thomas, 'In Love with Inspector Morse: Feminist Subculture and Quality Television', Ch. 13 in this volume. For Penley see n. 20 above.

included in this volume, Jacqueline Bobo and Ellen Seiter (1991) demonstrate the institutional and methodological bias of ethnographic research, which, they suggest, has typically excluded the voices of women of colour. In addition, they argue, the whole field of feminist television criticism has been preoccupied with notions of 'woman' that are decidedly white and middle class, and has marginalized issues of civil rights and public life that centrally touch the lives of women of colour.

Bobo and Seiter's important reflections on the political stakes of method and research design make us consider specifically the project and political future of feminist television criticism that this collection implicitly imagines. If we are indeed embarking on a future for feminist television criticism, new directions will involve further critique of what is and has been meant by terms such as 'woman' and 'feminist'. For certainly, within the Anglo-American context, particular conceptions of what a woman is and what feminism is have helped to regulate the kinds of knowledge feminists are interested in generating and the objects that they want to explore.[29]

Sometimes, we hear our colleagues and students describe their work as 'not really feminist', a phrase that marks the confusion and ambivalence about this category. What does it mean to be 'not really feminist'? Does it mean there are real feminists and borderline feminists? Perhaps the phrase 'not really feminist' has at least something to do with the fact that feminist television criticism has not adequately conceptualized its own meanings for feminism, but instead has mirrored the 'common sense' meanings of feminism that circulate in both popular and academic cultures, meanings which, among other things, were fashioned around the place and concerns of white, middle-class, heterosexual, western women. As stated at the outset, this mode of feminist inquiry belies power dynamics within the academy and tells us more about the social construction of feminist knowledge in Anglo-American contexts than it does about television as a world or even national practice. It is in this sense, again, that we would stress the double-edged nature of our project in this anthology. To say that a field developed in a certain way is not necessarily to endorse it—but it is perhaps to suggest certain historical specificities of the figure 'feminist' and the critical engagement with television she inaugurated.

This book has three parts, which are organized partly historically, partly thematically, and partly in relation to the arguments we have already made about the main contours of feminist work on television. Each part is fully introduced later in the book, but let us here explain the principles of our organization.

The first part, 'Housewives, Heroines, Feminists', groups together early feminist work on television *for* women with analyses of different representations *of* women. The section as a whole thus displays what has been a significant method for feminist television criticism, textual analysis, while at

---

29 Several African American feminist scholars whose work centres on cultural forms other than television—most notably Michele Wallace, bell hooks, and Wahneema Lubiano—point to a number of directions for future television scholarship. See Michele Wallace, *Invisibility Blues: From Pop to Theory*, esp. 241–55; bell hooks, *Black Looks: Race and Representation*; Wahneema Lubiano, 'Black Ladies, Welfare Queens, and State Minstrels: Ideological War by Narrative Means'.

the same time showing the very different ways in which the 'text' has historically been conceptualized. The earliest work in this section, that of Michèle Mattelart and Tania Modleski, has been chosen to represent the feminist engagement with soap opera. As with other contemporaneous research, such as that of Carole Lopate and Dorothy Hobson, the main concern was with the rhythm and flow of serial melodrama in relation to domestic labour and the career 'housewife'. The text here is 'soap opera/telenovela' as it is watched in everyday life. This contrasts with the extract from Prabha Krishnan and Anita Dighe's analysis of the general representation of women on Indian state television (Doordarshan) in 1990 where the text (such as that which emerges in the tradition of mass communications content analysis) is the whole output of the channel for the period in which the researchers studied it. The other articles in Part 1 all focus on the 'text' most familiar to arts and humanities traditions of textual analysis, the individual programme. However, various essays use different theoretical frameworks and methods to focus their analyses. All are to some extent concerned with how ideas of 'feminism' and 'femininity' are made meaningful in relation to each other and to categories like 'women'. Patricia Mellencamp tries in part to claim sitcom stars Lucille Ball and Gracie Allen for feminism while Judith Mayne queries what she calls 'prime-time feminism' in the case of *L.A. Law*. Corinne Squire, whose work emerges from the discipline of psychology, examines the way Oprah Winfrey articulates particular versions of 'blackness' and 'femininity/feminism', while Kathleen Rowe analyses the particular challenges to conventional femininity offered by what she characterizes as the 'disorderly body' of 'Roseanne'. Charlotte Brunsdon's article takes feminist television criticism itself as the text, and traces the ambivalence of feminist critics towards the pleasures and viewers of programmes such as television soap opera. Her article echoes the changing attitudes of feminist critics towards programming which clearly engages with female audiences. Finally in this part, Elspeth Probyn uses a discussion of *thirtysomething* to raise broader questions about 'post-feminism' and the renewed emphases in current debates about the importance of home and family for women, returning us to questions about everyday life, but posing them in a context where she is also trying to address the issue of 'generations' in feminist thought.

The second part of the book shifts concerns from textual analysis to audiences and reception contexts. We have already argued that one of the distinctive contributions of feminist television studies is its concern with the female viewer. In this part, we try to show the historical evolution of what is now a complex methodological debate without using a chronological 'and then' 'and then' structure. We have chosen articles that exemplify different approaches and generate knowledges about different audiences within what is now a significant tradition of feminist reception research. Approaches in Part 2 range from Ien Ang's analysis of *why* melodramatic identifications might be particularly pleasurable to women to the empirical investigation of female viewers and the conditions of watching that we find in the work of Ann Gray and Lyn Thomas. Each of these empirical projects, however, is also very different, with Ann Gray tracing the use of the video recorder in Britain in 1987 and Lyn Thomas working with fans of the British quality crime programme *Inspector Morse*. Annette Kuhn's 1984 article, 'Women's Genres', which opens the section, offers an early overview of the different theoretical which disciplinary origins from which much of this research on female spectators has been generated. Jacqueline Bobo and Ellen Seiter, writing in 1991, combine a textual analysis of *The Women of Brewster Place* with a critique of the ethnocentricity of much extant feminist reception analysis. And Hilary Hinds makes strikingly plain the relationship of text to context in analysing the unpredictably positive reception of *Oranges Are Not the Only Fruit*—a British programme about a young lesbian's fundamentalist Christian upbringing. We would suggest that the juxtaposition of these various pieces of research allows us to trace an increasingly differentiated understanding of the figure of the female viewer. However, as these pieces also show, feminist analysis of reception contexts has also been concerned with the ways in which spaces like the living-room or the suburbs are made meaningful through the social categories of class, ethnicity, and gender. Here Lynn Spigel's essay offers one example of the historical reception of television itself in 1950s US suburbia.

The essays that comprise the final part of the book for the most part combine textual, reception, and contextual analyses to grapple with the public/private divide that has shaped so much feminist scholarship. The articles in this heterogeneous section illustrate some of the myriad ways that 'private' women's bodies are mobilized to represent public issues and crises—are made to figure social meanings other than themselves. Squarely confronting cultural myths about the female body, Kate Kane explicates feminine hygiene commercials on US television, showing how a woman's body—in the most 'private' and 'personal' of its zones—is made to appear unclean so that it can be publicly regulated and tied into overall commodity culture. The female body—in its ever contested dimension of reproduction—is also at the centre of Julie D'Acci's study of US television documentaries on abortion. D'Acci brings together textual, contextual, and institutional analyses to illustrate how control of female sexuality and reproduction became one of the battlegrounds on which the racist, classist, sexist, *and* feminist struggles of a nation got played out during the late 1960s and early 1970s.

Other articles in Part 3 zero in on individual programmes and specific incarnations of femininity. Purnima Mankekar, Rebecca Walkowitz, and Suvendrini Perera perform textual and reception analyses on eminently different objects of study, but each makes abundantly clear the ways televised femininity is made to bespeak and stand in for wider public struggles. In her research on the televised version of the Hindu 'sacred serial' *The Mahabharata,* Mankekar interviews New Delhi families and discovers how the depiction of a publicly humiliated Hindu woman comes to symbolize 'Indian femininity' as a whole and also a particular version of Indian nationalism. Walkowitz focuses on the public reception of US sitcom *Murphy Brown* and the uproar over an episode in which the white, heterosexual, middle-class, main character has a baby 'out of wedlock'. She demonstrates how this particular embodiment of femininity, sexuality, and reproduction comes to figure the death of 'family values' in the US and triggers a phenomenon in which television-femininity and 'real' public life implodes. Suvendrini Perera analyses an Australian television programme's depiction of a stereotyped Asian 'temptress' who seduces the entire Australian diplomatic corps and ultimately represents not simply a caricatured 'Oriental' femininity but *cultural difference*—particularly cultural difference between Australia and Malaysia in a post-colonial world. Perera insists, however, that such depictions, in order to be fully mined—in order, that is, to yield both progressive and regressive dimensions—need to be analysed from the place of the 'ethnic' spectator, and she uses herself—a Sri Lankan woman viewer—as an example of such reception.

Rosanne Kennedy and Tricia Rose, writing in different countries with variegated aims and approaches, each make clear the complex character of popular portrayals of women—portrayals that on the one hand marshal the tropes of femininity to signify things other than 'the feminine' and so ensure repression, and on the other hand speak forcefully of female agency. In her analysis of *L.A. Law*'s bisexual female character, Kennedy illustrates how a lesbian body and its sexuality is severely constricted by the text and shoulders the weight of traditional constraints on female sexuality; but she also shows how 'queer' readings and a general 'queering' of the text can work to emancipate it. Rose's 'Never Trust a Big Butt and a Smile' illustrates how music and music videos are sites in which a number of African American women have used their bodies and the stereotyped ways their bodies have been evaluated and caricatured to take control of their own sexuality and gain both a place and prestige in the worlds of rap and popular culture. Through interviews with black women rap artists, Rose adds a production dimension to her textual analyses and shows how women's bodies and their representations can be used by female cultural producers for liberating and power-producing ends.

All of the articles in these three parts are more fully discussed in the introductions that follow. We offer this outline of the logic behind our selections as a rough map to guide the reading of our volume.

1

Housewives, Heroines, Feminists

1

Introduction to Part 1

As **A MEDIUM THAT OFFERS** the fantasy of seeing the outside world while sitting in the interior space of the family home, television has largely reproduced the ideology of separate spheres which sees the home as a space of femininity and leisure and the public world as a place of masculinity and work. For feminists, who have been deeply concerned with issues of women's labour both at home (where it goes mostly unrecognized) and in public (where it is often underpaid and undervalued), television's relationship to this ideology of separate spheres has been an ongoing concern. In addition, particularly because the study of television as a social form has been so biased towards the male/public arenas of work (the industry and policy makers), feminist critics have intervened in these debates by demonstrating how women's culture, and especially the domestic economies of everyday life, impacts on the entire institution of television, its narrative features, and its ultimate response from viewers.

As we discuss in the general introduction, the issue of separate spheres served as an impetus for early work on soaps. This early scholarship considered the ways television addresses women as housewives engaged in daily chores, and (less often) how it also relates to women's work outside the home. Much of this writing opened up an interest in television's relationship to women's everyday lives, an interest also taken up by articles in Part 2 that deal with gendered viewers and domestic space. In addition, this kind of work is concerned with the degree to which television contributes to the 'symbolic annihilation of women', or else on the more positive side, how it offers women some relief from, consciousness of, and even resistance to the various forms of disempowerment they encounter in their everyday lives.[1]

Two examples of inaugural thought on these subjects are included in this part. Michèle Mattelart writes about Chile, where she lived until the coup that brought down Allende's government in 1973. More explicitly than any

---

[1] Gaye Tuchman, 'The Symbolic Annihilation of Women by the Mass Media', in G. Tuchman *et al.* (eds.), *Hearth and Home: Images of Women in the Mass Media* (New York: Oxford Univ. Press, 1978), 3–45. The phrase 'symbolic annihilation' is originally George Gerbner's in 'Violence in Television Drama: Trends and Symbolic Functions', in G. A. Comstock and E. A. Rubenstein (eds.), *Media Content and Control* (Washington, DC: US Government Printing Office, 1972), 44.

other of the authors in this part, she writes from a Marxist tradition, but one also strongly informed by French feminism, and particularly some of Julia Kristeva's early work.[2] Mattelart too discusses women's consumption of telenovelas (melodramatic drama serials) in terms of routine, everyday life and time. Her perspective is more international than many of the other writers in this section, and she tries to move between granting significance to women's unseen household labour and understanding how this labour is linked to international movements of capital and global patterns of development and underdevelopment.[3]

Tania Modleski's 1979 article 'The Search for Tomorrow in Today's Soap Operas' also examines the relationship of a woman-orientated television genre and women's everyday lives by arguing that the soap opera offers forms of pleasure and identification different from those encouraged by the Hollywood cinema (which, of course, at this point in feminist film theory, was largely seen as privileging masculine desire). She maintains, for example, that soaps even provide female revenge fantasies with their well-loved villainesses who manipulate femininity in ways that defy male power and privilege. Writing in dialogue with feminist critics and artists concerned with the formation of a feminist avant-garde cinema that challenged Hollywood's male bias, Modleski concludes that the television soap's narrative form might serve as a model for a feminist cinema capable of appealing to large numbers of women.

Written eleven years later about Indian television, Prabha Krishnan and Anita Dighe's essay is also concerned with television's place in the gendered division of public and private spheres. For these authors, who are interested in the social contradictions that Indian women face under modernization, television plays a key role in a process they refer to as 'affirmation and denial'. Excerpted from their book of that title, the section included here examines Indian television commercials and news programmes, focusing on how women and their concerns are handled by the medium. Krishnan and Dighe argue that Indian television (or what is colloquially known as Doordarshan, the name of the government public service station) affirms a limited definition of womanhood as embodied by the housebound woman, while at the same time denying viewers insight into women's ongoing social and political struggles. They further suggest that the demarcation of public and private social spaces characteristic of Doordarshan programming reinforces state and masculine hegemony by locating affirmed aspects of womanhood in the home and denied aspects within public, male-dominated domains.

A second set of essays in this part considers how television has represented female heroines and performers. Many of these essays are part of a more general feminist concern with the way television negotiates traditional ideals of bourgeois domesticity and womanhood with the newer role models offered by feminism. Much of this work has argued against the idea that television simply reflects 'progress', and it questions the very meaning of progress for

2 Julia Kristeva, 'Le Temps des Femmes', *Revue du Département de Sciences des Textes* (Université de Paris VII, Paris, 1979), 34/44.

3 See also Ana M. Lopez, 'Our Welcomed Guests: Telenovelas in Latin America', and Jesus Martin-Barbero, 'Memory and Form in the Latin American Soap Opera,' in Robert C. Allen (ed.), *To Be Continued . . . : Soap Operas Around the World* (New York: Routledge, 1995), 256–75; 276–84.

feminism itself. (Progress for whom, and at the expense of what groups?, etc.) An implicit critique of 'enlightenment' history, then, is evident in much of the criticism here.

Patricia Mellencamp's 1986 'Situation Comedy, Feminism and Freud: Discourses of Gracie and Lucy' grapples with the rebellious female comedy of the early 1950s before, according to Mellencamp, television spawned a bevy of contented, understanding homebodies. She reads the performances of Gracie Allen and Lucille Ball through Freud's work on jokes, humour, and the comic, concluding that we are left with a double bind of enormously complicated proportions, a bind that critical models are hard-pressed to resolve. Given the social repressions of the 1950s, the humour of these virtuoso comediennes could be seen as a woman's weapon—a tactic offering release from domesticity and ensuring survival, sanity, and self (although with racist implications in the more 'acceptable' challenge to the Cuban Ricky Ricardo's patriarchy). The vexing conundrum, however, is that the comedy replaces anger and rage (no matter how tacit or buried) with pleasure. As Mellencamp so succinctly summarizes, '[w]hether heroic or not, this pleasure/provoking cover-up/acknowledgement is not a laughing but a complex matter, posing the difficult problem of women's simulated liberation through comic containment'.

Taking us into the 1990s, Kathleen Rowe's 'Roseanne: Unruly Woman as Domestic Goddess' is also concerned with the way comedy encourages critical perspectives on women's roles in society and the family in particular. Using theoretical frameworks from Mikhail Bakhtin and Natalie Zemon Davis, Rowe argues that *Roseanne* harks back to the trope of the 'unruly woman' used in pre-modern European literature, a trope that inverted the dominant power hierarchies by literally turning social relations among men and women, Kings and subjects, topsy-turvy. Rowe suggests that Roseanne's star persona and her television sitcom replace the 'perfect wife and mother' with a 'domestic goddess' whose sensibilities and physique challenge the norms of femininity. As a blue-collar 'woman-on-top' Roseanne is a modern-day unruly woman who provides audiences with a pleasurable release from normative power hierarchies between men and women as well as classes.

In '*L.A. Law* and Prime-Time Feminism', Judith Mayne confronts the representation of feminism on US prime time and specifically analyses the relationship between feminism and narrative. It is feminism, according to Mayne, that both stimulates *L.A. Law*'s stories and grounds its multiple-plot structure. *L.A. Law* emerges as a text that is supremely ambivalent about the law, sexual politics, and feminism, projecting its contradictions onto the bodies of women and producing the woman lawyer as the very emblem of ambiguity. For Mayne, the narratives are constructed around two 'swinging doors', one opening onto the equality of men and women under the law (feminism) and the other, onto their difference (femininity). The narratives operate by producing an 'echo effect' in which the multiple plots reflect off each other—in one, the female narration bespeaks the equivalence of men and women, while in another, the stereotypically feminine returns to undermine feminist challenges to male power. The episodes incessantly work to open up and close down the gap between feminism and femininity, but most conclude with a shot of 'heterosexual utopia' signalling that the challenge to patriarchy does not extend to sexual preference or desire (a theme also taken up by Rosanne Kennedy in Part 3 of this volume).

Writing in 1994 from Britain about the widely successful and internationally syndicated *Oprah,* Corinne Squire turns the focus from prime-time fiction's heroines and stars back to daytime genres. However, in the 1980s and 1990s, with the advent of the talk show—and one produced and hosted by an African American woman—daytime has changed considerably. Squire argues that *Oprah* is often better able to recognize the shifting and interrelated agendas of class, gender, and race than is much feminist theory. She trains a critical eye on the show and its star's handling of these issues, citing *Oprah*'s most valuable contributions as a feminism rooted in African American women's history and writing, and a 'super-realism'—an emotional and empirical excess—that puts common assumptions about gender, race, and class in doubt. She also sees the psychology produced by the show as infused with a particular type of black feminism—one rooted in community, a belief in personal and spiritual power, and hope.

The next article in Part 1 continues to raise general questions about the representation of, and address to, women on television. As with all the other articles in this section, the starting-point is textual analysis, but here the text is taken to be the sum of the journal articles through which feminist television criticism has constituted itself. Charlotte Brunsdon argues that this critical literature also has produced meanings of 'woman', and she suggests that the identity 'feminist intellectual' was partly established through the constitution of the 'ordinary woman'—the woman who is not a feminist. Brunsdon argues that there have been historical shifts in the relation between the two terms 'feminist' and 'woman' in second-wave feminism and offers a typology for approaching this history.

The questions of generation posed by Brunsdon recur in Elspeth Probyn's article which concludes the section. As one of her starting-points, Probyn uses the popular US 'yuppie' series, *thirtysomething.* Writing in the late 1980s, Probyn examines the renewed emphasis in contemporary North America on the importance of the family and home for women. She suggests that this 'new traditionalism' can be found together with views of feminism as outmoded and *passé* in shows like *thirtysomething.* Probyn uses the idea of the 'choice-oisie' to approach what she sees as a new generation of female-centred shows, suggesting that in these we are typically presented with a television world where every woman can make a choice between having a successful career or a family. Choosing 'home' just seems natural.

Probyn's essay, like many of the others in Part 1, raises questions about the relationship between television texts and the larger social and cultural milieu. Theorizing this fit between representations and social 'reality' is one of the most complex and difficult tasks for media theory generally, and the way different feminists approach it here will no doubt spur debates among readers of this volume. The next part on audiences and contexts engages with similar problems in relation to interpretation.

1

Everyday Life (Excerpt)

Michèle Mattelart

1. From Soap to Serial: The Media and Women's Reality

AN EPISODE FROM the 1920s—in other words, right at the beginning of that important technological medium that radio was to become—provides a good illustration of the close link between symbolic mass-production and the production of material goods in the nascent industrial society of the United States. At the same time, it shows us how women were straightaway singled out, from this commercial point of view, to become the favourite target for mass media messages, an essential factor in the planning of programmes.

Glen Sample worked at the time for a small advertising agency (later to become in the 1960s Dancer, Fitzgerald and Sample). He was the first person to adapt for radio a serial that had appeared in a newspaper—'The married life of Helen and Warren'. On the air this became 'Betty and Bob' and was sponsored by the well-known flour brand Gold Medal, at the time manufactured by the firm Washburn Grosby and Co., later to become General Mills.

Shortly afterwards, Mr Sample turned his attention to Oxydol washing powder. The manufacturers, Procter and Gamble, were then on the point of going to the wall under the attack of the English company Unilever, which had successfully launched the brand Rinso. Massively plugged by Mr Sample's radio serials and the advertising that interrupted them, Oxydol triumphed over Rinso. The serial, called 'Ma Perkins', whose career on the air went on and on for almost thirty years, gave Oxydol the decisive impetus.[1] 'Soap opera', the radio (and subsequently television) version of the 'lonely hearts' press, was born.

The name given to the new genre is as interesting as it is unusual. Isn't it unprecedented for a cultural product to indicate so crudely its material origin (here linked to the sale of soap and detergent) and its conscription in the battle between different commercial brands? At the same time, a whole *household* definition of a broadcast literature reveals itself plainly, making unambiguously clear a twofold function: to promote the sale of household products, and to subsume the housewife in her role by offering her romantic gratification.

Only much later did the feminine factor come to be important in the programming of European radio stations, notably in France. In fact, French

© Michèle Mattelart, 1986.

Excerpt from 'Everyday life' in Michèle Mattelart, *Women, Media and Crisis: Femininity and Disorder* (London: Comedia, 1986), 5–18.

1 Miles David and Kenneth Costa, 'Since 1895, radio finds its niche in the media world', *Advertising Age*, 19 Apr. 1976.

radio did not start as a public service. There were state stations before the war, but they coexisted with private ones. Advertising certainly existed, but not (as in the same period in the United States) as the norm around which programming was structured.[2] It usually came in only as a subsidy for cultural programmes (often concerts), which were also supported by groups of listeners. We can therefore observe a certain continuity between the classic forms of cultural life (concerts, plays, shows put on by local associations, etc.) and the programming of these radio stations. The history of television was likewise marked by the same preponderance of classic culture—plays, films, and concerts—rather than a specifically televisual genre.

These radio programmes included, in the morning, 'Women's Hour' (the day's menu, recipes, etc.), but overall the programming, whose high spot was undoubtedly the news, was made up essentially of rebroadcast concerts, cultural and scientific broadcasts, radio plays, and entertainment programmes like quiz games—all types of programme which do not immediately segregate their audience by sex.

After World War II, when so-called 'peripheral' radio stations made their appearance, escaping the previous state monopoly on broadcasting, the commercial model became dominant. And this model was progressively to acknowledge the tremendous importance of the mass female public.

Radio Luxembourg came into existence in 1933 with the lofty aim of 'acquainting listeners in different countries with the artistic and cultural masterpieces of the whole world'. In 1935 it introduced 'L'heure des dames et des demoiselles' (Women's Hour), which became a feminine byword and continued right through to 1966. In 1935 the introduction of radio serials coincided with the beginnings of a wider development of programming: as with all private radio stations, entertainment began to nibble away the airtime hitherto reserved for classical music. Regularly, radio games, weekly radio plays, and the 'hurly-burly of the music hall' (sponsored by Cadoricin Lotion) made their appearance. From 1955 Europe-1 and Radio Luxembourg (now RTL—Radio Television Luxembourg) competed vigorously through radio serials. To Europe's serial, RTL responded with 'Nicole et l'amour' (Nicole and Love). It was also in competition with RTL that Europe-1 introduced Ménie Grégorie's well-known programmes of advice on sexuality and family psychology.[3]

RTL rapidly multiplied its claims to be the leading commercial radio station. The first multinational radio station in Europe, it was also the first to broadcast throughout the day. In 1977 this same station calmly admitted that advertising could account for 20 per cent of its air-time, that most of its public was female, and that these considerations laid down certain lines of programming. 'Women's attitude towards radio is significant: what they fundamentally want is somebody there . . . RTL will therefore fill this space

---

2 The advertising revenue of commercial radio stations in the United States was soon to become very high and sponsors used to take over part of a programme and organize it as they saw fit. The volume of advertising revenue made it possible to launch some very ambitious programmes. Certain sections of the public soon expressed concern at the increasing impact of advertising on radio broadcasting; and a motion for reducing this impact was tabled in the senate as early as 1936. Information assembled in Pierre Miquel's *Histoire de la radio et de la télévision* (Paris, Éditions Richelieu, 1972).

3 Information assembled in René Duval's *Histoire de la radio en France* (Paris, Éditions Alain Moreau, 1979).

and accompany our listener with its voice, in her home, *in her everyday life*' (author's italics).

Everyday life. Day-to-day life. These phrases represent a specific idea of time within which women's social and economic role is carried out. It is in the everyday time of domestic life that the fundamental discrimination of sex roles is expressed, the separation between public and private, production and reproduction. The sphere of public interests and production is assigned to man, that of private life and reproduction to woman. The hierarchy of values finds expression through the positive value attached to masculine time (defined by action, change, and history) and the negative value attached to feminine time which, for all its potential richness, is implicitly discriminated against in our society, internalized and experienced as the time of banal everyday life, repetition and monotony.

■ **Invisible Work**   For a few years now, the international feminist movement, with the aid of analytical work by specialists in social science (male and female), has been vigorously denouncing the negative value attached to women's household work. This becomes transparently obvious when we think that it has always been assumed that this work should be unpaid. Now, 'as a rule, once manual work is paid, it takes on economic value, so that any unpaid work (such as women's housework) becomes economically, and thus also socially and culturally, devalued'.[4]

The part played by this *invisible work* in the functioning of economies has been amply demonstrated. Everywhere, in developed and developing countries alike, women form the mainstay of the *support economy* which makes it possible for all the other activities to be carried on. A woman at home performs a fundamental role in any economy: she services the labour force each day. This economic activity, carried on by most layers of the female population, is of great importance; but the indicators by which the socio-economic position of each country is defined, and its development measured, conceal the economic value of household work.

The arrival of capitalism, which introduced the factory and institutionalized the sale of labour power, undoubtedly represented a decisive moment in the segregation of sex roles in the productive process, mainly by depriving the family of its old function as a productive unit. But we should beware of a nostalgic attitude, and of the tendency to idealize the situation that traditional society gave women in productive activities. It has been shown (with reference to Africa, for example), that this often went hand in hand with forms of slavery. Capitalism merely continued and deepened a hierarchical division of labour which had come into being long before, reserving for males the most prestigious and best-rewarded work and restricting women

4 Rodolfo Stavenhagen, 'Invisible Women', *Unesco Courier*, July 1980. Many women and many women's associations have studied this problem. Cf. Rosalyn Baxandall, Elizabeth Ewen, and Linda Gordon, 'The working class has two sexes', in *Monthly Review*, 28/3 (July–Aug. 1976). See also the articles in the 'Special Issue on the Continuing Subordination of Women in the Development Process', *IDS Bulletin*, 10/3 (Apr. 1979) (Univ. of Sussex). Reference may also be made to Harry Braverman, *Labour and Monopoly Capitalism* (New York: Monthly Review Press, 1974), and above all to the study which must be considered as the classic monograph on the subject, namely Mariarosa Dalla Costa, 'Donne e sowversione sociale', trans. into English as 'Women and the Subversion of the Community', in *The Power of Women and the Subversion of the Community* (Bristol: Falling Wall Press, 1972).

to the lowest kind. This sex role discrimination is fundamental to the maintenance of the capitalist economy, and it has been shown that

> but for this vast female underpinning—the women who provide food and clothing for the proletariat in a world where the necessary facilities for a collective restoration of labour energy simply do not exist—the hours of surplus value extorted from the worker by capital would be fewer. We can even say that women's work in the home is expressed through men's work outside by the creation of surplus value.[5]

Gradually isolated from the world of production through the long process of consolidation of the monogamous family and its close links with the system of private property, women, by virtue of the kind of tasks they carry out at home and their dependence on men, become the cement of class society. This division of labour finds expression in a definition of masculine and feminine qualities transmitted, reinforced, and rearticulated by the different institutions of society (the Church, schools, the media). Girls will be docile, submissive, clean, chaste, prudish; they will play quiet games and enjoy indoor activities. Conversely, boys will be sexually aggressive, prone to show off their physical strength, encouraged to develop their 'innate' sense of leadership, and so forth.

The invisibility of women's work and the concealment of the productive value of their household tasks are of decisive importance in determining the image of women projected by the media and the media's relationship with them. The media have made a point of following the traditional household timetable. Radio and television programming is particularly revealing in this respect: it punctuates the day with moments that make women's condition 'all worth while', and helps to compensate for being shut up at home all day. It makes women's work legitimate, not as work, but as a duty (sometimes pleasurable) that *forms part of their natural function.*

The genre of these women's broadcasts may differ (afternoon magazines, television serials, radio serials); the values around which their themes are structured can correspond to different points in women's relation to capital, and to the more or less modern and free-thinking character of the sections of the bourgeoisie that produce them. But they still have in common the purpose of integrating women into their everyday life.

■ The Exception Confirms the Rule— Adventure Consecrates Routine

In this process of integration, the melodramatic serial, whether on radio or television, has traditionally played a crucial part. The serial can take several different forms and has several different tendencies, which it is not our job to analyse here. Suffice to say that most serials take as their target the family audience. But the melodramatic serial, which carries on in radio and television where 'lonely hearts' columns leave off, addresses primarily the working-class female public. Because of the immense impact of this genre in Latin America and other Catholic countries, there is a tendency to think of it as a

---

5 Isabel Larguia and John Dumoulin, 'Toward a Science of Women's Liberation', New York, North American Congress on Latin America (NACLA), *Latin America and Empire Report*, No. 6.

Latin genre. Yet we can see that it exists, with variations, on the screens and the air-waves of every country in the world—at least the capitalist part.

It is all too well known that the more a channel declares itself to be fulfilling a cultural function and/or that of a public service, the fewer serials it will broadcast; and this is even more true of melodramatic serials. On the other hand, they are ubiquitous on commercial channels. The profile of their audience, and their inherent regularity, make them excellent terrain for advertisers. In one hour of these serials in Venezuela, for example, there are twenty minutes of advertising. It has also been noted that there is a close link between the kind of products advertised and the subject of the day's episode.

In Latin America, undoubtedly the major territory for this genre (known there as *Telenovela*), the state channels—insignificant compared with the commercial ones, attracting only 10 per cent of the audience—have tried to win over viewers by making the serials more 'up-market'. Major authors of contemporary Latin American literature (Salvador Garmendia in Venezuela, Gabriel García Marquez in Colombia, Jorge Amado in Brazil) have been invited to contribute to this strategy, opposing to the commercial model of the dominant channels the alternative of 'cultural television'. There is no doubt that the results of this collaboration offer female audiences (and others) the chance to encounter cultural products with a much richer and more complex approach to human experience and emotion. But are we still talking about melodramatic serials or 'telenovelas'?

The production systems currently prevalent in commercial Latin American broadcasting companies encourage directors to keep costs down and profits up by sticking to the rules of serialization. Shooting time is minimal: the script for the following day's episode is improvised from one day to the next within the basic formulae of these mass-produced artefacts. This 'on-the-spot' shooting makes it possible to take into account some social and even political issues, as well as the reactions of the public and comments by critics; but the stereotyped structure of these products, channelling the serial through a set of hackneyed recipes, reduces the effective possibilities for openness. The rules of commercialism, whose first principle is to mine the same vein to exhaustion, mean that these stories go on and on interminably. The Venezuelan government had to limit the number of episodes by law.

There is no denying, however, that the interplay in a particular country between cultural channels (even in a minority) and commercial ones, can lead the latter to modify their programming, especially when they realize that the new 'cultural serials' attract large audiences. Even so, in the current circumstances, these serials, like the 'lonely hearts' press, remain dominated by a principle of segregation of audiences. That is the key to the matter. This genre conforms to the principle of market division that governs the culture industry. In the press, to refer to socially distinct targets (from the standpoint of both purchasing and cultural power), publishers speak of 'upmarket' and 'downmarket'. In the field of television, the melodramatic serial indisputably belongs in the second category. And this duality of the female market increasingly pervades the whole mass cultural apparatus (a process of market democratization and segregation at the same time).

This segregation of female audiences is so marked that the international distribution of photo-novels (for example) is carried out by firms which can certainly be described as transnational, although their position none the less remains marginal compared to the largest multinational publishers. This market is dominated by Italian and Spanish companies and, to a lesser extent, French companies with Italian connections,[6] along with companies based in Miami, but actually the inheritors of exiled businesses that were already flourishing in Batista's Cuba. One example is the De Armas group, at the head of a real 'lonely hearts' empire, which at the same time transmits transnational power in Latin America and acts as the Latin American distributor there for the Spanish versions of magazines such as *Good Housekeeping* and *Cosmopolitan*. It also publishes an international women's magazine for the Latin American market, *Vanidades*.[7] (It is worth noting that Cuba was among the pioneers of the radio serial, right from the 1930s, and exported it to other Latin American countries.)

Only in June 1978, under the titles *Kiss* and *Darling*, did the so-called 'photo-novel magazines' make their appearance in the United States, in supermarkets and drugstores. As *Advertising Age* announced: '*Kiss* and *Darling* mark the first American attempt at photo-novels, a form exceedingly popular in Europe. Photo-novel magazines are similar to comic books, except that, instead of drawings, the panels contain photos of people with dialogue balloons inserted above their heads.' Establishing continuity between this genre and 'Mills and Boon'-style literature, these magazines are aimed at the women who read the 'Harlequin' collection—Harlequin is a large multinational publisher of sentimental literature, whose parent company is based in Canada. Its French offshoot, which has operated from Paris since 1978, sold in 1980 between seventeen million and twenty-five million copies of this collection, 'which carries you off into a wonderful world whose one and only dazzling heroine will be *YOU*'. It publishes eighteen titles per month, 140 per year.[8] These figures certainly carry us off into a fabulous dream-world.

Today, the international distribution of television serials is the province of independent Latin American firms, who are greatly helped by the existence of a large Spanish-speaking market in the United States. This international distribution is sometimes reflected in international production, or at least script-writing. Spanish-speaking inhabitants of Miami are thus persuaded to lend a hand. This expansion has up to now taken place primarily in the United States, Central and South America, and the Caribbean. It has now got as far as the Arab countries (notably Saudi Arabia) and, via Brazil, those

---

6 This confirms the Latinity of the genre. With regard to this Latinity, it would be interesting to study the particular moment at which, in individual countries, this type of serial was introduced into pro-gramme schedules, and to try to determine whether it is descended from earlier forms of expression (literature, the press, cinema), in order thereby to assess to what extent it corresponds to particular trends in specific socio-cultural environments. It is here that one feels the absence of historical studies which might show how one genre is descended from another, and trace the gradual development of certain forms of traditional culture towards forms of mass culture.

7 Mexico, a vital link in transnational publishing in Latin America, also has a large national output of photo-novels and romance magazines. The same is true of Argentina and Brazil. In all these countries production is professional and industrial, whereas in Colombia it is still very artisanal.

8 In 1979 Harlequin Enterprises, leader of the 'romance' novel publishers, declared its intention to set up a publishing empire in the United States. It began by acquiring the Laufer company, which publishes *Tiger Beat*, several magazines for adolescents and, above all, the Rona Barret gossip magazines. Cf. Benjamin M. Compaine (ed.), *Who owns the media?* (New York: Harmony Books, 1979).

African countries which were once Portuguese possessions. European countries, such as Spain and Portugal, are also fertile territory. In 1979, according to figures from Televisa (the monopoly Mexican commercial television station), Mexico exported 24,000 programme-hours per year of programmes and serials to the United States, Central and South America, the Caribbean, and now Arab countries as well.

It is easier to grasp the size of this figure if we bear in mind that (according to a classic Unesco study of 1972) neither French nor British television exported more than 20,000 programme-hours in that year.[9] North American television in the same period was exporting anything from 100,000 to 200,000 programme-hours and, at the time, Mexico exported only 6,000 hours at the most. Its expansion is now in full flight. The infiltration of the United States by Mexican television has caused friction between the two countries. The firm Univision, controlled by Televisa, had made it possible, thanks to the satellite Westar, to receive Televisa programmes directly in New York and Los Angeles, whence they are channelled to the rest of the United States. This meant that by the end of 1976 more than thirteen million households watched Televisa in the United States. While nowhere near so large as the Mexican industry, Venezuela is also launching an attack on the international market. Between 1975 and 1977, twenty-three 'oil serials', as they are known, were exported to North and South America, Spain, Portugal, and Saudi Arabia.

It remains true that the melodramatic serial on radio or television is the fictional genre most clearly addressed to a mass female public. These productions usually have a woman's name as their title—*Natacha, Simplemente Maria, Rafaela,* or whatever—a strategy which has proved successful: those serials whose titles included men's names had less of an impact. In Latin American countries, these productions continue to exist side by side with imported series (generally North American), or more up-to-date programmes which deal with the industrialized world and reflect the relative emancipation of women participating in professional life on an equal footing with men. But the traditional productions still enjoy more success. It is through these serials that the principal audience battle between the different stations is fought out.

There have been enough content analyses and ideological readings of melodramatic serials and linked genres (such as photo-novels) for us to feel able to give a highly condensed summary here.[10] The plot generally revolves round the ups and downs of a love affair which brings together people separated by social class (or age, or previous ties, or a combination of all three). The family context tends to be riddled haphazardly with social pathology and individual problems—unhappy homes, incurable diseases, illegitimate children, alcoholism, incestuous or quasi-incestuous cohabitation. The variations run the whole gamut from romantic adventures to social dramas. In Latin America, the serials are very much marked by sex and violence, obses-

9 See A. and M. Mattelart, X. Delcourt, *International Image Markets* (London: Comedia, 1984).

10 Cf. Michèle Mattelart, *La cultura de la opresión feminina* (Mexico: Editorial Era, 1977); Anne-Marie Dardigna, *La Presse féminine* (Paris: Maspero, 1978); Cornelia Butler Flora and Jan L. Flora, 'The *Fotonovela* as a Tool for Class and Cultural Domination', in *Latin American Perspectives*, special issue entitled 'Culture in the age of mass media', issue 16, vol. 5, No. 1 (Winter, 1978).

sively present (though always shrouded in implication and innuendo) in the form of blackmail or rape. The unrolling of the story through all kinds of ambiguities, avowals, mistaken identities, and interventions by a *deus ex machina* reveals a highly normative message: the good and the virtuous are rewarded. Love sanctioned by the legitimate union of marriage is better than passion, which is always punished by fate. The female characters ennoble the values of purity and virginity for girls, and often become heroic martyrs to men who in fact get away with abusing their masculine authority and class power; but, after putting her through great suffering and temptation, they confirm the happiness of the girl from a modest background by offering her a ring and married life. The sacrifice, courage, and self-denial of wives and mothers are other attitudes reinforced by these messages, crowned as they are by the return of the husband, the renewed gratitude of the son, or the simple satisfaction that comes from doing one's duty.

Monotony is countered by exceptions. The serial makes possible a symbolic revenge on the triviality of everyday life, whose monotonous repetition is countered by the day-by-day episodes of the heroine's unusual adventures. Household work, experienced as unproductive and of low socio-economic standing, is countered by programmes which give value to the area of private life and a female world dominated by 'love' and 'emotion'.

Even before 1917 Alexandra Kollontai, writing about the social basis of the female question, observed how very far from innocent love stories were, and how the realm of private life had been sedulously infiltrated by bourgeois standards: 'Even that bourgeoisie that proclaimed love to be a "private matter" knew how to use its moral guidelines to channel love in the direction that best suited its class interests'.[11]

The greatest of the repressions carried out by what we have elsewhere called 'the order of the heart'—the order that governs the organization of this kind of melodramatic discourse—is that it invalidates any form of struggle against social inequalities (the existence of which is admitted) by means of this diffuse explanation: only love can cross class barriers. Not only is the solution individual—never collective—it is also linked to the miracle of love. Love comes to be a universal explanation which can resolve social contradictions through denying them, for the order of society, like love, is founded on Fate. The repressive order of the heart has two helpmates: Nature and Fate.

But we can notice that from the 'content' point of view a tendency to increase the realism of these discourses brings them closer to the real situations of working and poor people. These new serials, at any rate in Venezuela and much more in Brazil, show an increasing concern to stick to real life. Let us look at one such example, and observe the manner in which it continues to smooth over points of conflict. The Venezuelan serial 'Dõna Juana' explicitly refers to a problem that affects all social strata, but principally working people, and implacably brings out the sexist character of society— that of irresponsible paternity, of illegitimate children brought up by their mother alone and not recognized by the father, who abandons the mother after making her pregnant. 'Dõna Juana' portrays these women, and their brave struggle against male hostility and fecklessness. But Dõna Juana, of

---

11 Alexandra Kollontai, *Marxisme et Révolution sexuelle* (Paris, Petite Collection Maspero, 1977).

humble background, does not learn to define herself as an independent individual, even though her struggle shows the strength and energy she can display as head of the family. The dénouement still follows a conservative and conventional pattern: thanks to an almost miraculous stroke of luck, the father finds his daughter and recognizes her. He thereby satisfies simultaneously the mother's dream and that of the daughter—that the child can bear its father's name and thus escape the stigma of illegitimacy.

It is no secret that the ideological function of these narrative discourses rests primarily in the fact that they are given as representations of reality, and therefore cling to certain features of the reality of social and class conflict, which they implicitly explain (through the mechanisms of the story) from a certain point of view, itself likewise linked to the objective reality of class struggle. The serial's twin task—of representing reality and explaining it—defines its role of reproducing the conditions of production of the social system, predisposing women to accept the 'natural' explanation of their domination.

2. Women as Consumers

One recent important strand in the theory of media studies has been a rejection of the inevitably passive way in which people react to the messages addressed at them. What is questioned is the act of consumption itself, the process by which a subject receives and appropriates. This means that the monolithic nature of the ideological effect of domination is likewise questioned. For that is the key problem. The media transmit a set of values corresponding to the interests of a particular power system. Can we infer that the recipients, reacting to the signals like Pavlov's dogs, internalize these structures of domination once and for all?

The spotlight is turned, in other words, on the act of looking and consuming: what is the relationship between the message and the subject that receives it within a personal history, or the history of a group or class? Oddly enough, there are a great many studies of media power structures, national and international, and a great many, too, of the content of media messages, but very few on the manner in which the 'dominated' groups and individuals read and respond to them, or resist them (if need be through a diversion of the original intention, implicit or explicit) in the name of some ideas of their own.

Our study of the Popular Unity regime in Chile led us to try to ascertain if that historical moment, characterized by intensified social confrontations and a mobilization of popular consciousness, led to a critical attitude towards such messages as the melodramatic serials which continued to appear on television, just as in the past. In the most active strata of working-class women, we discovered that these messages were not necessarily read as their senders intended, and that the way in which they were received denied their internal logic, leading to a roundabout process of consumption. These demystifications, particularly of the illusory social mobility often presented in the serials, emerged in comments such as the following:

> The lovers in these serials are always from a wealthy family, or a well-heeled profession, never workmen. The working class always appear as

servants, or else in the character of a girl who, thanks to some miraculous encounter, becomes a great lady overnight.

Perhaps episodes can occur in real life like those depicted in these serials, but at what cost? In real life one cannot become rich without exploiting somebody else, and the serials show that the road to riches is an easy one. At whose expense do these young men and women make their wealth? It all goes to give the working class false hopes.[12]

What is disturbing, however, is the fact that these stories still provide *pleasure* for women viewers who are critically aware of how alienating they are and who have located the mechanisms through which their work is carried on. We cannot simply ignore the appeal and the pleasure (however bitter-sweet it may be when it goes hand in hand with a social and political awareness) produced by these fictional products of the cultural industry. There *is* a problem here, and one hitherto scarcely tackled. As an initial approach to it, we shall merely put forward some hypotheses about women's expectations and exhilaration.

We shall refer later to the 'temporality' of women (see Part Two, *The myth of modernity*).[13] We should recognize that the mythical hostility between the notion of women and that of change goes back to the association between the image of femininity, and of permanence and the concept of fertility. The image of woman is linked with the idea of continuation, perpetuation, duration. To the timescale of disruption and crisis can be contrasted the female timescale—a fluid perception of time, inhabited by eternal functions.

This specific inflection given by femininity to time can be defined as simultaneously *repetition* and *eternity*: the return of the same, eternal recurrence, the return of the cycle that links it into cosmic time, the occasion for unparalleled ecstasy in unison with the rhythm of nature, and along with that the infinite, womb-like dimension, the myth of permanence and duration.

It was this notion of a specifically female idea of time that led us to formulate the hypothesis that, above and beyond their themes and images forever retracing the dominant ideology, these lengthy stories, unfolding over protracted periods in regular daily consignments, might have much in common with this experience of repetition and eternity. These tales could well correspond to the psychic structures of women not caught up in a forward-looking idea of time, a time of change. These vast stories, delivered in daily instalments and repeated daily, would then serve, through their stereotyped rhythms, to satisfy the expectations of female subjective time. By cultivating the enjoyment of this non-forward-looking sense of time, these stories would tend to hinder women's access to the time of history, the time of project.

---

12 M. Mattelart, 'Chile: Political Formation and the Critical Reading of Television', in *Communication & Class Struggle* (New York: International General Editions, 1983). Countries with a socialist orientation know how difficult it is to do away with serialized TV melodramas, which have a broad public appeal. In Chile, under Allende, Channel 9 decided to use the serial entitled *Simplemente María* to entice viewers into watching the news programme which followed. The government of Nicaragua, faced with popular discontent over the disappearance of TV 'novels', decided to reintroduce them. In Mozambique, a similar problem has arisen over Indian melodramas.

13 In Part 2 of her book Mattelart uses Julia Kristeva's notion of women's time to discuss the temporality of women. See Kristeva, 'Le Temps des femmes', *Revue du Département de Sciences des Textes* (Univ. de Paris VII, Paris, 1979), 34/44; trans. into English as 'Women's Time' by Alice Jardine and Harry Blake and repr. in Toril Moi (ed.), *The Kristeva Reader* (Oxford: Blackwell, 1986), 188–213.

We shall need to check this hypothesis in the light of recent scientific researches in the field of subjectivity and the unconscious structures of personality. But what is certain is that hitherto we have been too satisfied with looking for the alienating quality of the products of the culture industry merely in the arrangement of image and word. For what continues to pose a problem, as we said earlier, is the fascination these products still exercise over spectators (of either sex) who are perfectly capable of giving an acute analysis of the serials' alienating characteristics. What collective masochism, what suicidal group-attitude can explain this fascination?

One theory is that the power of the culture industry is also to be found outside the subjects with which it deals, the anecdotes it transmits, which are but foreshadows of its real message. What is not said would then count for more than what is said. Does the culture industry not restore the psychic patterns of the mass of people, patterns which are elements of nature as well as of culture? Could its ideological function not also be fulfilled in this constant restimulation of the deep structures of a collective unconscious? The crucial importance of the question in terms of formal or informal strategies for resistance should be plain. One complement to the basic development of self-awareness should surely be the need to sound out the 'group unconscious'.

We cannot leave the problem here. We have to see what these questions can contribute to the construction of an alternative, and how we can give a *non-alienated* answer to these deep unconscious structures. African film makers such as the Ethiopian Haile Gerima, director of *Harvest: 3,000 Years*,[14] have clearly understood the importance of adopting these structures of perception. They have modelled their narratives on a psychic demand which can perfectly well be satisfied in a completely different manner from the old Indian melodramas which enjoy such great popularity in Africa.[15]

14 The critic Robert Grelier described the film in the following terms in *La Revue du Cinéma* (No. 320–1, Oct. 1977): 'A film with three central pivots—the exploiting landlord, the "madman" and the peasants—*The 3,000-year Harvest* draws its inspiration from a song which has given the film its title and is heard three times. The words of the song are as follows: "Our bride, our new bride, your bridal gown has never been torn in all its 3,000 years". It inspires the dream of the young peasant helping his father with the plough and is repeated as a theme song throughout the film. This poor land, still with its feudal structures, is depicted without condescension or compassion, but with much nobility of spirit. The sweat and the fatigue appear on the peasants' faces like stigmata of the exploitation they are suffering. The spoken word does not pervade the whole film but lets the image follow its own course. People speak only when necessary. Sounds, i.e. noises, are given the place they deserve, the place they enjoy in everyday life. Oral traditions, dreams, allegories and symbols are used by the director as active elements linked to this documentary vision but never as pretexts for aestheticism or for embellishing the form of the work, whose principal quality resides in the sobriety of the images. Time and technology, like the cloud of dust in which a convoy of lorries is just visible, pass through this landscape but never stop. Omnipresent traditions preserve the privileges which may be in the process of changing; but it seems that a price will have to be paid, and that the class relationships which govern this society will have to be tackled sooner or later. These relationships are merely hinted at in the lines spoken by "madman" but are not evident to most of the protagonists.'

15 The melodrama is the principal genre in the commercial cinema in India. In India today, the cinema is a major means of mass communication. The country ranks as first in the world for the production of films: the 714 films produced in 1980 (72 per cent of them in colour) were seen by three billion people. Television, on the other hand, is still in its infancy: its sixteen channels, in black and white, only cover 12 per cent of the country and its programmes are viewed by less than 8 per cent of the population (about 600,000 households own a television set). (Source: *Le Monde Diplomatique*, Mar. 1981.)

Many of these commercial films (which contain a mixture of songs, mythology, violence, humour, dancing, and tears and suffering, and feature popular stars idolized by the masses) are exported to Africa, both black Africa and the Maghreb. A country such as Mozambique has still to come to terms with the fascination exercised on its urban population by Indian melodramas. The proportion of Indian films imported into Mozambique is still very large, large enough indeed to maintain the

Shot very slowly, these old films, whose rhythm is linked to a specific measure of time, have clearly motivated the demands that Tanzanian peasants
have made on film makers who want to get them to participate in the production of their own image.[16] But the misguided identification of technological with human progress has often led to the error of colonizing the
production of a national image through the stereotyped techniques of the
modern image industry. This blocks the contribution to culture that could
be made by groups which have remained deeply connected with the rhythm
of country life, close to the cycle of nature, and still uncontaminated by a
system of production which (on the symbolic level at least) is increasingly
dominated by sensationalism and ellipsis. At a time when the ideas of development and growth are being called into question by the very countries
which do not want to repeat the mistakes of others, is it not also necessary to
take account of the contribution these countries can make to the relation
between images and filmic time?

The question of women brings us face to face with the same problem. The
notion that women, as a dominated group, have of time can be viewed in two
ways: on the one hand as alienated, on the other as a positive alternative to the
dominant idea of time as geared to linear industrial productivity. There is no
doubt that greater value will be attached to the temporality of women as
development models are questioned and the limitations of a society governed by the rule of the highest possible GNP become plain. Increasingly
influential social movements and social theories tell us that work and career
are not everything. This new consciousness gives a heightened value to
women's work and the patterns of their everyday life. The division of labour
which has resulted in the definition of specifically feminine and masculine
qualities has reduced the emotional and intellectual capacity of women as
much as that of men. And it is now plain that, however urgent it is to increase
awareness of the productive value of household tasks, it is also vital to restore
value to areas that are not directly productive.

When, in *Jeanne Dielman,* the Belgian director Chantal Akerman films the
everyday banalities of a woman's existence at full length, she does two things
at once: she attempts to endow with its own language her subjective experience as a woman, silenced by culture up to now, and at the same time she

dominating position which such films have enjoyed in the past (a domination of the market which
they share with karate films from Hong Kong, another major film production and distribution centre
for Africa). Of the 714 films imported in 1976, 223—approximately a third of the total—came from
India, 122 from the United States, ninety-eight from Italy, sixty-four from France and forty-nine from
the Soviet Union and other countries. (It is clear, therefore, that these Indian films are much more
popular than North American westerns and comedies.) Today, Mozambique is pursuing a policy of
diversification with regard to imports of films. Out of 162 new films imported in 1980 from twenty-
three different countries, there were still thirteen from India, but half of these had been made by progressive film directors who have set themselves apart from the mainstream of commercial films in
India. There are, in fact, increasing signs of the emergence in India of a local and realistic school of
cinema, of a high standard, which is modifying in a progressive direction the basic premisses of the
melodrama. Egypt is another major production centre for romantic films, which are mostly exported
to Middle Eastern countries.

16 Cf. the mimeographed study entitled *Understanding and Use of Educational Films in Villages in
Tanzania,* by M. Leveri, P. Magongo, S. Mbungira and J. Siceloff, presented to the Audio-Visual
Institute, Dar es Salaam, in February 1978. The villagers expressed their preference for a linear montage of the shots taken, and for a pace of shooting which would make it possible to illustrate in every
detail, and with all its natural slowness, the process of manufacturing objects or performing certain
tasks. Also, they clearly wanted the theme of work to be related to the themes of everyday family and
community life.

gives us a creative shock which makes it possible to understand (by contrast) what the customary norm of film time is.

This feminine time is, along with increased awareness of the body, at the heart of the effort being made by women today to give cultural expression to what they as women feel. Beyond the supposedly equal status they may have acquired in the world of production, women are trying to get across what makes them unique and different on the level of subjective experience and symbolic representation. This is leading them to delve into their age-old memory linked to the space and time of reproduction, and in which today part of their specific sensitivity is still shaped. And this is a specific, and unalterably different, sensitivity because it is linked with psychological, biological, and sexual differences which have traditionally been used to subordinate them, but which today need to be expressed as an alternative world of symbols and meaning.

It is stimulating to observe that this research seems to be paralleled by the exploration of the time-sense of dominated and marginal races and continents being carried out in, for example, Latin American narrative fiction. This allows us to think that it will really be possible to give a non-alienated answer to the female internalizing of the twofold dimension of time—repetition and eternity. Novels such as Gabriel García Marquez's *One Hundred Years of Solitude,* or José Donoso's *The Dark Bird of Night,* are vast epics based on cyclic progress and monumental stretches of time, majestic replies to unconscious demands which provide democratic and liberating outlets, rather than the feeble and imitative products that merely conform to the commercial precepts of market democracy.

2

The Search for Tomorrow in Today's Soap Operas

Notes on a Feminine Narrative Form

Tania Modleski

IN SOAP OPERAS, the hermeneutic code predominates. 'Will Bill find out that his wife's sister's baby is really his by artificial insemination? Will his wife submit to her sister's blackmail attempts, or will she finally let Bill know the truth? If he discovers the truth, will this lead to another nervous breakdown, causing him to go back to Springfield General where his ex-wife and his illegitimate daughter are both doctors and sworn enemies?' Tune in tomorrow, not in order to find out the answers, but to see what further complications will defer the resolutions and introduce new questions. Thus the narrative, by placing ever more complex obstacles between desire and its fulfilment, makes anticipation of an end an end in itself. Soap operas invest exquisite pleasure in the central condition of a woman's life: waiting— whether for her phone to ring, for the baby to take its nap, or for the family to be reunited shortly after the day's final soap opera has left *its* family still struggling against dissolution.

According to Roland Barthes, the hermeneutic code functions by making 'expectation . . . the basic condition for truth: truth, these narratives tell us, is what is *at the end* of expectation. This design implies a return to order, for expectation is a disorder.'[1] But, as several critics have observed, soap operas do not end. Consequently, truth for women is seen to lie not 'at the end of expectation', but *in* expectation, not in the 'return to order', but in (familial) disorder.

As one critic of soap opera remarks, 'If . . . as Aristotle so reasonably claimed, drama is the imitation of a human action that has a beginning, a middle, and an end, soap opera belongs to a separate genus that is entirely composed of an indefinitely expandable middle.'[2] The importance of this difference between classical drama and soaps cannot be stressed enough. It is not only that successful soap operas do not end, it is also that they cannot end. In *The Complete Soap Opera Book*, an interesting and lively work on the subject, the authors show how a radio serial forced off the air by television

Originally published in *Film Quarterly*, 33/1 (1979), 12–21.

1 Roland Barthes, *S/Z*, trans. Richard Miller (New York: Hill and Wang, 1974), 76.

2 Dennis Porter, 'Soap Time: Thoughts on a Commodity Art Form', *College English* (Apr. 1977), 783.

tried to wrap up its story.[3] It was an impossible task. Most of the story-line had to be discarded, and only one element could be followed through to its end—an important example of a situation in which what Barthes calls the 'discourse's instinct for preservation'[4] has virtually triumphed over authorial control. Furthermore, it is not simply that the story's completion would have taken too long for the amount of time allotted by the producers. More importantly, I believe it would have been impossible to resolve the contradiction between the imperatives of melodrama—i.e. the good must be rewarded and the wicked punished—and the latent message of soaps—i.e. everyone cannot be happy at the same time. No matter how deserving they are. The claims of any two people, especially in love matters, are often simply mutually exclusive.

John Cawelti defines melodrama as having

> at its center the moral fantasy of showing forth the essential 'rightness' of the world order. . . . Because of this, melodramas are usually rather complicated in plot and character; instead of identifying with a single protagonist through his line of action, the melodrama typically makes us intersect imaginatively with many lives. Subplots multiply, and the point of view continually shifts in order to involve us in a complex of destinies. Through this complex of characters and plots we see not so much the working of individual fates but the underlying moral process of the world.[5]

It is scarcely an accident that this essentially nineteenth-century form continues to appeal strongly to women, whereas the classic (male) narrative film is, as Laura Mulvey points out, structured 'around a main controlling figure with whom the spectator can identify'.[6] Soaps continually insist on the insignificance of the individual life. A viewer might at one moment be asked to identify with a woman finally reunited with her lover, only to have that identification broken in a moment of intensity and attention focused on the sufferings of the woman's rival.

If, as Mulvey claims, the identification of the spectator with 'a main male protagonist' results in the spectator becoming 'the representative of power',[7] the multiple identification which occurs in soap opera results in the spectator being divested of power. For the spectator is never permitted to identify with a character completing an entire action. Instead of giving us one 'powerful ideal ego . . . who can make things happen and control events better than the subject/spectator can',[8] soaps present us with numerous limited egos, each in conflict with one another and continually thwarted in its attempts to 'control events' because of inadequate knowledge of other peoples' plans,

---

3 Madeleine Edmondson and David Rounds, *From Mary Noble to Mary Hartman: The Complete Soap Opera Book* (New York: Stein and Day, 1976), 104–10.

4 Barthes, *S/Z*, 135.

5 John Cawelti, *Adventure, Mystery, and Romance* (Chicago: Univ. of Chicago Press, 1976), 45–6.

6 Laura Mulvey, 'Visual Pleasure and Narrative Cinema', in Karyn Kay and Gerald Peary (eds.), *Women and the Cinema* (New York: E. P. Dutton, 1977), 420.

7 Ibid. 420.

8 Ibid.

The Soap Formula

Currently, twelve soap operas are shown daily, each half an hour or an hour long. The first goes on the air at about 10 a.m., and they run almost continuously until approximately 3.30 p.m. With the exception of *Ryan's Hope*, which takes place in a big city, the soaps are set in small towns and involve two or three families intimately connected with one another. Families are often composed of several generations, and the proliferation of generations is accelerated by the propensity of soap characters to mature at an incredibly rapid rate; thus, the matriarch on *Days of Our Lives*, who looks to be about 65, has managed over the years to become a great-great-grandmother. Occasionally, one of the families will be fairly well to do, and another will be somewhat lower on the social scale though still, as a rule, identifiably middle class. In any case, since there is so much intermingling and intermarrying, class distinctions quickly become hopelessly blurred. Children figure largely in many of the plots, but they don't appear on the screen all that often; nor do the very old. Blacks and other minorities are almost completely excluded.

Women as well as men frequently work outside the home, usually in professions such as law and medicine, and women are generally on a professional par with men. But most of *everyone's* time is spent experiencing and discussing personal and domestic crises. Kathryn Weibel (see n. 11) lists 'some of the most frequent themes':

the evil woman
the great sacrifice
the winning back of an estranged lover/spouse
marrying her for her money, respectability, etc.
the unwed mother
deceptions about the paternity of children
career vs. housewife
the alcoholic woman (and occasionally man)
(Weibel, p. 56).

Controversial social problems are introduced from time to time: rape was recently an issue on several soap operas and was, for the most part, handled in a sensitive manner. In spite of the fact that soaps contain more references to social problems than do most other forms of mass entertainment, critics tend to fault them heavily for their lack of social realism (on this point, see Edmondson and Rounds (n. 3), pp. 228–47). As for the fans, most insist on soap opera's extreme lifelikeness and claim that the characters have to cope with problems very like their own.

motivations, and schemes. Sometimes, indeed, the spectator, frustrated by the sense of powerlessness induced by soaps, will, like an interfering mother, try to control events directly:

Thousands and thousands of letters [from soap fans to actors] give advice, warn the heroine of impending doom, caution the innocent to beware of the nasties ('Can't you see that your brother-in-law is up to no good?'), inform one character of another's doings, or reprimand a character for unseemly behavior.[9]

Presumably this intervention is ineffectual, and feminine powerlessness is reinforced on yet another level.

The subject/spectator of soaps, it could be said, is constituted as a sort of ideal mother: a person who possesses greater wisdom than all her children, whose sympathy is large enough to encompass the conflicting claims of her family (she identifies with them all), and who has no demands or claims of her own (she identifies with no one character exclusively). The connection between melodrama and mothers is an old one. Harriet Beecher Stowe, of course, made it explicit in *Uncle Tom's Cabin*, believing that if her book could bring its female readers to see the world as one extended family, the world would be vastly improved. But in Stowe's novel, the frequent shifting of perspective identifies the reader with a variety of characters in order ultimately to ally her with the mother/author and with God who, in their higher wisdom and understanding, can make all the hurts of the world go away, thus insuring the 'essential "rightness" of the world order'. Soap opera, however, denies the 'mother' this extremely flattering illusion of her power. On the one hand, it plays upon the spectator's expectations of the melodramatic form, continually stimulating (by means of the hermeneutic code) the desire for a just conclusion to the story, and, on the other hand, it constantly presents the desire as unrealizable, by showing that conclusions only lead to further tension and suffering. Thus soaps convince women that their highest goal is to see their families united and happy, while consoling them for their inability to bring about familial harmony.

This is reinforced by the image of the good mother on soap operas. In contrast to the manipulating mother who tries to interfere with her children's lives, the good mother must sit helplessly by as her children's lives disintegrate; her advice, which she gives only when asked, is temporarily soothing, but usually ineffectual. Her primary function is to be sympathetic, to tolerate the foibles and errors of others.

It is important to recognize that soap operas serve to affirm the primacy of the family not by presenting an ideal family, but by portraying a family in constant turmoil and appealing to the spectator to be understanding and tolerant of the many evils which go on within that family. The spectator/mother, identifying with each character in turn, is made to see 'the larger picture' and extend her sympathy to both the sinner and the victim. She is thus in a position to forgive most of the crimes against the family: to know all is to forgive all. As a rule, only those issues which can be tolerated and ultimately pardoned are introduced on soaps. The list includes careers for women, abortions, premarital and extramarital sex, alcoholism, divorce, mental and even physical cruelty. An issue like homosexuality which, perhaps, threatens to explode the family structure rather than temporarily disrupt it, is simply ignored. Soaps, contrary to many people's conception of them, are not conservative but liberal, and the mother is the liberal *par excellence*. By constantly presenting her with the many-sidedness of any question, by never reaching a

---

9 Edmondson and Rounds, *From Mary Noble to Mary Hartman*, 193.

permanent conclusion, soaps undermine her capacity to form unambiguous judgements.

These remarks must be qualified. If soaps refuse to allow us to condemn most characters and actions until all the evidence is in (and of course it never is), there is one character whom we are allowed to hate unreservedly: the villainess,[10] the negative image of the spectator's ideal self. Although much of the suffering on soap operas is presented as unavoidable, the surplus suffering is often the fault of the villainess who tries to 'make things happen and control events better than the subject/spectator can'. The villainess might very possibly be a mother, trying to manipulate her children's lives or ruin their marriages. Or perhaps she is avenging herself on her husband's family because it has never fully accepted her.

This character cannot be dismissed as easily as many critics seem to think.[11] The extreme delight viewers apparently take in despising the villainess[12] testifies to the enormous amount of energy involved in the spectator's repression and to her (albeit unconscious) resentment at being constituted as an egoless receptacle for the suffering of others. This aspect of melodrama can be traced back to the middle of the nineteenth century when *Lady Audley's Secret,* a drama about a governess turned bigamist and murderess, became one of the most popular stage melodramas of all time.[13] Discussing the novel upon which the stage drama was based, Elaine Showalter shows how the author, while paying lip-service to conventional notions about the feminine role, managed to appeal to 'thwarted female energy':

> The brilliance of *Lady Audley's Secret* is that Braddon makes her would-be murderess the fragile blond angel of domestic realism. . . . The dangerous woman is not the rebel or the blue-stocking, but the 'pretty little girl' whose indoctrination in the female role has taught her secrecy and deceitfulness, almost as secondary sex characteristics.[14]

Thus the villainess is able to transform traditional feminine weaknesses into the sources of her strength.

Similarly, on soap operas, the villainess seizes those aspects of a woman's life which normally render her most helpless and tries to turn them into weapons for manipulating other characters. She is, for instance, especially good at manipulating pregnancy, unlike most women, who, as Mary Ellmann wittily points out, tend to feel manipulated by it:

---

10 There are still villains in soap operas, but their numbers have declined considerably since radio days— to the point where they are no longer indispensable to the formula. *The Young and the Restless*, for example, does without them.

11 See e.g. Kathryn Weibel, *Mirror Mirror: Images of Women Reflected in Popular Culture* (New York: Anchor Books, 1977), 62. According to Weibel, we quite simply 'deplore' the victimizers and totally identify with the victims.

12 'A soap opera without a bitch is a soap opera that doesn't get watched. The more hateful the bitch the better. Erica of "All My Children" is a classic. If you want to hear some hairy rap, just listen to a bunch of women discussing Erica. "Girl, that Erica needs her tail whipped." "I wish she'd try to steal my man and plant some marijuana in my purse. I'd be mopping up the street with her new hairdo."' Bebe Moore Campbell, 'Hooked on Soaps', *Essence* (Nov. 1978), 103.

13 'The author, Mary Elizabeth Braddon, belonged to the class of writers called by Charles Reade "obstacles to domestic industry".' Frank Rahill, *The World of Melodrama* (University Park: Pennsylvania Univ. Press, 1967), 204.

14 Elaine Showalter, *A Literature of Their Own* (Princeton: Princeton Univ. Press, 1977), 165.

At the same time, women cannot help observing that conception (their highest virtue, by all reports) simply happens or doesn't. It lacks the style of enterprise. It can be prevented by foresight and device (though success here, as abortion rates show, is exaggerated), but it is accomplished by luck (good or bad). Purpose often seems, if anything, a deterrent. A devious business benefitting by indirection, by pretending not to care, as though the self must trick the body. In the regrettable conception, the body instead tricks the self—much as it does in illness or death.[15]

In contrast to the numerous women on soap operas who are either trying unsuccessfully to become pregnant or have become pregnant as a consequence of a single unguarded moment in their lives, the villainess manages, for a time at least, to make pregnancy work for her. She gives it 'the style of enterprise'. If she decides she wants to marry a man, she will take advantage of him one night when he is feeling especially vulnerable and seduce him. And if she doesn't achieve the hoped-for pregnancy, undaunted, she simply lies about being pregnant. The villainess thus reverses male/female roles: anxiety about conception is transferred to the male. He is the one who had better watch his step and curb any promiscuous desires or he will find himself saddled with an unwanted child.

Moreover, the villainess, far from allowing her children to rule her life, often uses them in order to further her own selfish ambitions. One of her typical ploys is to threaten the father or the woman possessing custody of the child with the deprivation of that child. She is the opposite of the woman at home, who at first is forced to have her children constantly with her, and later is forced to let them go—for a time on a daily recurring basis and then permanently. The villainess enacts for the spectator a kind of reverse *fort-da* game,[16] in which the mother is the one who attempts to send the child away and bring it back at will, striving to overcome feminine passivity in the process of the child's appearance and loss. Into the bargain, she also tries to manipulate the man's disappearance and return by keeping the fate of his child always hanging in the balance. And again, male and female roles tend to get reversed: the male suffers the typically feminine anxiety over the threatened absence of his children.

The villainess thus continually works to make the most out of events which render other characters totally helpless. Literal paralysis turns out, for one villainess, to be an active blessing, since it prevents her husband from carrying out his plans to leave her; when she gets back the use of her legs, therefore, she doesn't tell anyone. And even death doesn't stop another villainess from wreaking havoc; she returns to haunt her husband and convince him to try to kill his new wife.

15 Mary Ellmann, *Thinking About Women* (New York: Harvest Books, 1968), 181.

16 The game, observed by Freud, in which the child plays 'disappearance and return' with a wooden reel tied to a string. 'What he did was to hold the reel by the string and very skilfully throw it over the edge of his curtained cot, so that it disappeared into it, at the same time uttering his expressive "o-o-o-o." [Freud speculates that this represents the German word "*fort*" or "gone".] He then pulled the reel out of the cot again by the string and hailed its reappearing with a joyful "*da*" ["there"].' According to Freud, 'Throwing away the object so that it was "gone" might satisfy an impulse of the child's, which was suppressed in his actual life, to revenge himself on his mother for going away from him. In that case it would have a defiant meaning: "All right, then go away! I don't need you. I'm sending you away myself." ' Sigmund Freud, *Beyond the Pleasure Principle*, trans. James Strachey (New York: W. W. Norton, 1961), 10–11.

The popularity of the villainess would seem to be explained in part by the theory of repetition compulsion, which Freud saw as resulting from the individual's attempt to become an active manipulator of her/his own powerlessness.[17] The spectator, it might be thought, continually tunes in to soap operas to watch the villainess as she tries to gain control over her feminine passivity, thereby acting out the spectator's fantasies of power. Of course, most formula stories (like the Western) appeal to the spectator/reader's compulsion to repeat: the spectator constantly returns to the same story in order to identify with the main character and achieve, temporarily, the illusion of mastery denied him in real life. But soap operas refuse the spectator even this temporary illusion of mastery. The villainess's painstaking attempts to turn her powerlessness to her own advantage are always thwarted just when victory seems most assured, and she must begin her machinations all over again. Moreover, the spectator does not comfortably identify with the villainess. Since the spectator despises the villainess as the negative image of her ideal self, she not only watches the villainess act out her own hidden wishes, but simultaneously sides with the forces conspiring against fulfilment of those wishes. As a result of this 'internal contestation', the spectator comes to enjoy repetition for its own sake and takes her adequate pleasure in the building up and tearing down of the plot. In this way, perhaps, soaps help reconcile her to the meaningless, repetitive nature of much of her life and work within the home.

Soap operas, then, while constituting the spectator as a 'good mother' provide in the person of the villainess an outlet for feminine anger: in particular, as we have seen, the spectator has the satisfaction of seeing men suffer the same anxieties and guilt that women usually experience and seeing them receive similar kinds of punishment for their transgressions. But that anger is neutralized at every moment in that it is the special object of the spectator's hatred. The spectator, encouraged to sympathize with almost everyone, can vent her frustration on the one character who refuses to accept her own powerlessness, who is unashamedly self-seeking. Woman's anger is directed at woman's anger, and an eternal cycle is created.

And yet . . . if the villainess never succeeds, if, in accordance with the spectator's conflicting desires, she is doomed to eternal repetition, then she obviously never permanently fails either. When, as occasionally happens, a villainess reforms, a new one immediately supplants her. Generally, however, a popular villainess will remain true to her character for most or all of the soap opera's duration. And if the villainess constantly suffers because she is always foiled, we should remember that she suffers no more than the good characters, who don't even try to interfere with their fates. Again, this may be contrasted to the usual imperatives of melodrama, which demands an ending to justify the suffering of the good and punish the wicked. While soap operas thrive, they present a continual reminder that woman's anger is alive, if not exactly well.

---

17 Speaking of the child's *fort-da* game, Freud notes, 'At the outset he was in a *passive* situation—he was overpowered by experience; but by repeating it, unpleasurable though it was, as a game, he took on an *active* part. These efforts might be put down to an instinct for mastery that was acting independently of whether the memory was in itself pleasurable or not.' *Beyond the Pleasure Principle*, 10.

We must therefore view with ambivalence the fact that soap operas never come to a full conclusion. One critic, Dennis Porter, who is interested in narrative structures and ideology, completely condemns soap operas for their failure to resolve all problems:

> Unlike all traditionally end-oriented fiction and drama, soap opera offers process without progression, not a climax and a resolution, but mini-climaxes and provisional denouements that must never be presented in such a way as to eclipse the suspense experienced for associated plot lines. Thus soap opera is the drama of perepetia without anagnorisis. It deals forever in reversals but never portrays the irreversible change which traditionally marks the passage out of ignorance into true knowledge. For actors and audience alike, no action ever stands revealed in the terrible light of its consequences.[18]

These are strange words indeed, coming from one who purports to be analysing the ideology of narrative form! They are a perfect illustration of how a high-art bias, an eagerness to demonstrate the utter worthlessness of 'low' art, can lead us to make claims for high art which we would ordinarily be wary of professing. Terms like 'progression', 'climax', 'resolution', 'irreversible change', 'true knowledge', and 'consequences' are certainly tied to an ideology; they are 'linked to classical metaphysics', as Barthes observes. 'The hermeneutic narrative, in which truth predicates an incomplete subject, based on expectation and desire for its imminent closure, is . . . linked to the kerygmatic civilization of meaning and truth, appeal and fulfillment.'[19] To criticize classical narrative because, for example, it is based on a suspect notion of progress and then criticize soap opera because it *isn't* will never get us anywhere—certainly not 'out of ignorance into true knowledge'. A different approach is needed.

This approach might also help us to formulate strategies for developing a feminist art. Claire Johnston has suggested that such a strategy should embrace 'both the notion of films as a political tool and film as entertainment':

> For too long these have been regarded as two opposing poles with little common ground. In order to counter our objectification in the cinema, our collective fantasies must be released: women's cinema must embody the working through of desire: such an objective demands the use of the entertainment film. Ideas derived from the entertainment film, then, should inform the political film, and political ideas should inform the entertainment cinema: a two-way process.[20]

Clearly, women find soap operas eminently entertaining, and an analysis of the pleasure that soaps afford can provide clues not only about how feminists can challenge this pleasure, but also how they can incorporate it. For, outrageous as this assertion may at first appear, I would suggest that soap operas are not altogether at odds with a possible feminist aesthetics.

---

18 Porter, 'Soap Time', 783–4.

19 Barthes, *S/Z*, 76.

20 Claire Johnston, 'Women's Cinema as Counter-Cinema', in Bill Nichols (ed.), *Movies and Methods* (Berkeley: Univ. of California Press, 1976), 217.

'Deep in the very nature of soaps is the implied promise that they will last forever.'[21] This being the case, a great deal of interest necessarily becomes focused upon those events which retard or impede the flow of the narrative. The importance of interruptions on soap operas cannot be overemphasized. A single five-minute sequence on a soap opera will contain numerous interruptions both from within and without the diegesis. To give an example from a recent soap opera: a woman tries to reach her lover by telephone one last time before she elopes with someone else. The call is intercepted by the man's current wife. Meanwhile, he prepares to leave the house to prevent the elopement, but his ex-wife chooses that moment to say she has something crucial to tell him about their son. Immediately there is a cut to another couple embroiled in an entirely different set of problems. The man speaks in an ominous tone: 'Don't you think it's time you told me what's going on?' Cut to a commercial. When we return, the woman responds to the man's question in an evasive manner. And so it goes.

If, on the one hand, these constant interruptions and deflections provide consolation for the housewife's sense of missed opportunities, by illustrating for her the enormous difficulty of getting from desire to fulfilment, on the other hand, the notion of what Porter contemptuously calls 'process without progression' is one endorsed by many innovative women artists. In praising Nathalie Sarraute, for example, Mary Ellmann observes that she is not

> interested in the explicit speed of which the novel is capable, only in the nuances which must tend to delay it. In her own discussions of the novel, Nathalie Sarraute is entirely antiprogressive. In criticizing ordinary dialogue, she dislikes its haste: there not being 'time' for the person to consider a remark's ramifications, his having to speak and to listen frugally, his having to rush ahead toward his object—which is of course 'to order his own conduct'.[22]

Soap opera is similarly antiprogressive. Just as Sarraute's work is opposed to the traditional novel form, soap opera is opposed to the classic (male) film narrative, which, with maximum action and minimum, always pertinent dialogue, speeds its way to the restoration of order.

In soaps, the important thing is that there always be time for a person to consider a remark's ramifications, time for people to speak and listen lavishly. Actions and climaxes are only of secondary importance. I may be accused of wilfully misrepresenting soaps. Certainly they appear to contain a ludicrous number of climaxes and actions: people are always getting blackmailed, having major operations, dying, conducting extramarital affairs, being kidnapped, going mad, and losing their memories. The list goes on and on. But just as in real life (one constantly hears it said) it takes a wedding or a funeral to reunite scattered families, so soap opera catastrophes provide convenient occasions for people to come together, confront one another, and explore intense emotions. Thus in direct contrast to the male narrative film, in which the climax functions to resolve difficulties, the 'mini-climaxes' of

---

21 Edmondson and Rounds, *From Mary Noble to Mary Hartman*, 112.

22 Ellmann, *Thinking About Women*, 222–3.

soap opera function to introduce difficulties and to complicate rather than simplify characters' lives.[23]

Furthermore, as with much women's narrative (such as the fiction of Ivy Compton-Burnett, who strongly influenced Sarraute), dialogue in soap operas is an enormously tricky business. Again, I must take issue with Porter, who says, 'Language here is of a kind that takes itself for granted and assumes it is always possible to mean no more and no less than what one intends.'[24] More accurately, in soaps the gap between what is intended and what is actually spoken is often very wide. Secrets better left buried may be blurted out in moments of intensity, or they are withheld just when a character most desires to tell all. This is very different from night-time television programmes and classic Hollywood films with their particularly naïve belief in the beneficence of communication. The full revelation of a secret on these shows usually begins or proclaims the restoration of order. Marcus Welby can then get his patient to agree to treatment; Perry Mason can exonerate the innocent and punish the guilty. The necessity of confession, the means through which, according to Michel Foucault, we gladly submit to power,[25] is wholeheartedly endorsed. In soap operas, on the other hand, the effects of confession are often ambiguous, providing relief for some of the characters and dreadful complications for others. Moreover, it is remarkable how seldom in soaps a character can talk another into changing his/her ways. Ordinarily, it takes a major disaster to bring about self-awareness—whereas all Marcus Welby has to do is give his stop-feeling-sorry-for-yourself speech and the character undergoes a drastic personality change. Perhaps more than men, women in our society are aware of the pleasures of language—though less sanguine about its potential as an instrument of power.

An analysis of soap operas reveals that 'narrative pleasure' can mean very different things to men and women. This is an important point. Too often feminist criticism implies that there is only one kind of pleasure to be derived from narrative and that it is essentially a masculine one. Hence, it is further implied, feminist artists must first of all challenge this pleasure and then out of nothing begin to construct a feminist aesthetics and a feminist form. This is a mistaken position, in my view, for it keeps us constantly in an adversary role, always on the defensive, always, as it were, complaining about the

---

23 In a provocative review of *Scenes from a Marriage*, Marsha Kinder points out the parallels between Bergman's work and soap operas. She speculates that the 'open-ended, slow paced, multi-climaxed structure' of soap operas is 'in tune with patterns of female sexuality' and thus perhaps lends itself more readily than other forms to the portrayal of feminine growth and developing self-awareness (*Film Quarterly* (Winter 1974–5), 51). It would be interesting to consider Kinder's observation in the light of other works utilizing the soap opera format. Many segments of *Upstairs Downstairs*, for instance, were written by extremely creative and interesting women (Fay Weldon, for one). The only disagreement I have with Kinder is over her contention that 'The primary distinction between *Scenes from a Marriage* and soap opera is the way it affects us emotionally. . . . Instead of leading us to forget about our own lives and to get caught up vicariously in the intrigues of others, it throws us back on our own experience' (p. 53). But soap opera viewers constantly claim that their favourite shows lead them to reflect upon their own problems and relationships. Psychologists, recognizing the tendency of viewers to make comparisons between screen life and real life, have begun to use soap operas in therapy sessions (see Dan Wakefield, *All Her Children* (Garden City, New York: Doubleday & Company, 1976), 140–3). We may not like what soap operas have to teach us about our lives, but that they *do* teach and encourage self-reflection appears indisputable.

24 Porter, 'Soap Time', 788.

25 Michel Foucault, *La Volonté de Savoir* (Paris: Éditions Gallimard, 1976), esp. pp. 78–84.

family but never leaving home. Feminist artists *don't* have to start from nothing; rather, they can look for ways to rechannel and make explicit the criticisms of masculine power and masculine pleasure implied in the narrative form of soap operas.

One further point: feminists must also seek ways, as Johnston puts it, of releasing 'our collective fantasies'. To the dismay of many feminist critics, the most powerful fantasy embodied in soap operas appears to be the fantasy of a fully self-sufficient family. Carol Lopate complains:

> Daytime television . . . promises that the family can be everything, if only one is willing to stay inside it. For the woman confined to her house, day-time television fills out the empty spaces of the long day when she is home alone, channels her fantasies toward love and family dramas, and promises her that the life she is in can fulfill her needs. But it does not call to her attention her aloneness and isolation, and it does not suggest to her that it is precisely in her solitude that she has a possibility for gaining a self.[26]

This statement merits close consideration. It implies that the family in soap operas is a mirror-image of the viewer's own family. But for most viewers, this is definitely not the case. What the spectator is looking at and perhaps longing for is a kind of *extended* family, the direct opposite of her own isolated nuclear family. Most soap operas follow the lives of several generations of a large family, all living in the same town and all intimately involved in one another's lives. The fantasy here is truly a 'collective fantasy'—a fantasy of community, but put in terms with which the viewer can be comfortable. Lopate is wrong, I believe, to end her peroration with a call for feminine solitude. For too long women have had too much solitude and, quite rightly, they resent it. In a thought-provoking essay on the family, Barbara Easton persuasively argues the insufficiency of feminist attacks on the family:

> With the geographical mobility and breakdown of communities of the twentieth century, women's support networks outside the family have weakened, and they are likely to turn to their husbands for intimacy that earlier generations would have found elsewhere.[27]

If women are abandoned to solitude by feminists eager to undermine this last support network, they are apt to turn to the right. People like Anita Bryant and Mirabel Morgan, says Easton, 'feed on fears of social isolation that have a basis in reality'.[28] So do soap operas.

For it is crucial to recognize that soap opera allays *real* anxieties, satisfies *real* needs and desires, even while it may distort them.[29] The fantasy of community is not only a real desire (as opposed to the 'false' ones mass culture is

---

26 Carol Lopate, 'Daytime Television: You'll Never Want to Leave Home', *Radical America* (Jan.–Feb. 1977), 51.

27 Barbara Easton, 'Feminism and the Contemporary Family', *Socialist Review* (May–June 1978), 30.

28 Ibid. 34.

29 A point Hans Magnus Enzensberger makes about mass consumption in general. See *The Consciousness Industry* (New York: Continuum Books, 1974), 110.

always accused of trumping up), it is a salutary one. As feminists, we have a responsibility to devise ways of meeting these needs that are more creative, honest, and interesting than the ones mass culture has come up with. Otherwise, the search for tomorrow threatens to go on, endlessly.

3

Affirmation and Denial

Construction of Femininity on Indian Television
(Excerpts)

Prabha Krishnan and Anita Dighe

Introduction

THIS STUDY WAS designed to examine the kind of consciousness—feminine, female, feminist—that was constructed on Indian television. We hypothesize that the hegemonial process within Indian society serves to entrench patriarchy, and that the media as an organization within the 'civil society' resonates with patriarchal ideology. In order to consolidate a national–popular collective will, the ruling class takes note of women's struggles for empowerment. Mechanisms for containment now exist at the level of the state within 'civil society' in the form of organizations and as segments of mainstream media. We see feminist scholarship in the field of media as an attempt to decode and decipher 'myths' and promote critical analysis of media content so as to disrupt the hegemonial process.

■ Objectives of the Study

The broad objective of the study was to examine the content of television programmes in relation to women. The specific objectives were:

1. To understand what were considered women's concerns on television;
2. To examine how women and their concerns were reflected in sectoral and general programmes;
3. To investigate the manner in which sectoral programmes for women reflected or did not reflect issues of national and international concern; and
4. To ascertain the patterns of women's representation in TV programmes in terms of the functions they performed and the roles they played.

Analysis of TV Programmes—An Eclectic Approach As noted in our discussion of theoretical considerations, the traditional approach of content analysis does not produce a complete picture of television programming. It was necessary, therefore, to supplement it with elements of structural analysis.

© UNICEF, 1990/New Delhi Sage.

Prabha Krishnan and Anita Dighe, *Affirmation and Denial: Construction of Femininity on Indian Television* (New Delhi: Sage, 1990), selection is excerpted from pp. 23–5, 70–86.

This combination of approaches became particularly necessary since we decided to include all TV programmes, irrespective of their format, content, and duration, in the sample. This led to our using semiologic analysis in order to understand how meaning was generated and conveyed through the various television programmes.

As analytical tools, we used content analysis, semiology, structuralism, and the like, with all their potentials and shortcomings. We have attempted not only immanent criticism but, wherever possible, transcendent criticism of various media texts.

While content analysis was sparingly used and that, too, mainly for the analysis of TV news, its aim was twofold. First, it was used to establish a quantitative base for more qualitative analysis of the message. Second, it helped us to categorize TV programmes according to content in a way not based on any prior assumptions or empirical categories previously applied to the depiction of women in mass media. Three researchers watched TV programmes consistently for one month in order to ascertain the patterns of programme structure. Constant interaction and discussion enabled them to evolve a common perspective. This exercise also enabled them to categorize programmes and to evolve analysis sheets in order to study them. Seven different analysis sheets were designed to analyse seven different categories of TV programmes. These analysis sheets were piloted over a one-week period of TV viewing, then modified and finalized. Thereafter, one master sheet for each programme was constructed on the basis of the sheets filled in by the three individual researchers. Each analysis sheet was discussed and debated until a consensus was reached.

Sample Size   The total sample consisted of every alternate day of Delhi Doordarshan programmes over a one-month period (July 1986). The researchers watched TV programmes that

1. Start at 6 p.m. on weekdays and continue up to 11–11.15 p.m. every night;
2. Begin at 1.45 p.m. on Saturday and continue up to 4 p.m. and later continue from 6 p.m. to 11–11.15 p.m.; and
3. Begin at 9.30 a.m. on Sunday and continue all through the day, evening, and late evening.

Every single programme (inclusive of commercials) over a total of 15 days became part of the sample. However, the daytime educational broadcasts aimed at school and college students and the one- or two-minute 'fillers' and continuity programmes were not included in the sample.

Discussion   There is a continuity of perspective that informs the total output of Doordarshan with regard to male and female roles. Two main trends were visible in the treatment of women and their concerns on this medium—that of affirmation and of denial.

There was affirmation of a limited definition of womanhood as embodied by the physically and mentally housebound woman, engrossed in the minutiae of home-making, deriving meaning for her existence and achievements from her husband and children. Together with the affirmation and entrenchment of passive, subordinate roles for women, Doordarshan programmes tended to deny viewers an insight into ongoing struggles of women to achieve personhood. Women in several parts of the country are engaged in isolated struggles for economic autonomy, political and legal rights, for a meaningful identity within marriage, and for relevant education. We got, if at all, token glimpses of such struggles, and even these were treated in a superficial manner.

The demarcation of public and private social spaces is a way of congealing the ongoing processes of affirmation and denial. The affirmed aspects of womanhood are situated and contained within the home, the most private of social spaces. The denied aspects of womanhood are largely located in public spaces which, as we shall see, are the domain of the male.

In effect, the construction of these two spaces results in the construction of femininity and masculinity, of gender. To retain the integrity of the public realm as male space, several exclusionary mechanisms are brought into force with the complicity of the inhabitants of the private realm. Our findings help to explicate the role of television in this hegemonic process, which is the maintenance of the integrity of the public and private realms.

■ The Public Realm

In a commercial for a soap, we see a young man working in his office. Later, through a crush of people in the elevator and on the road he goes to his club where he plays a hard game of tennis. When he returns home, he scrubs himself with the soap. Then, purified and sanitized after his interaction with the world outside, he goes to meet his wife. She is waiting in the garden, tea-table prettily set with lace and silver. She herself is young, soft, fresh, unhurried, quite untouched by the cares of the world, cushioned and contained within the home. She is enclosed, on one side by the walls of the house, on two sides by the garden, and in the front by the camera. There appears to be only one way to gain access to the garden where she sits, that used by the man. He is her protector and he alone has access to her. The active energetic male goes to the passive, waiting, and accepting woman.

In a commercial for a toothbrush, we are urged to enter a happy home contest. The house featured in the visual has large eyes, long eyelashes, and a large, painted mouth. The house is woman personified.

There can be no rigid, material distinction between the private and the public realms. In terms of activities we note that women often perform in public what are extensions of their private roles—that is, they work as child-minders, nurses, maids, and housekeepers in hotels and hostels. In terms of the locus of decision-making, we note that both in our culture and in the media it is men who make the comparatively more important decisions within the home and wield greater economic autonomy. The distinction that we sense intuitively and emotionally will have to be crystallized in ideological terms.

O'Brien (1982) notes that the Marxists offer a partial explanation about why certain men had access to the public realm by defining that realm as the social space within which the ruling class is free to perpetuate the praxis of its own survival *qua* the ruling class. She goes on to add that for feminists, focusing on production processes as the basis for the establishment of ruling class hegemony is unsatisfactory and proposes that we concentrate instead on the reproduction process. Applying the dialectical model of the evolution of human consciousness to the analysis of human reproduction, she points out that for men, physiology is fate. They do not experience birth and therefore are alienated from integration with the actual continuity of species. In Marxist terms, it is women who, through their labour, create a value, that is the child. Men's reaction to their alienation from the product is to appropriate the child, that is bestow on it paternity, which is not a natural event, but an ideology. For men, therefore, potency and virility are essentially political and ideological attributes and stem from their need to cancel out the alienation built into the reproductive process. Together with the appropriation of the child comes the need to control the sexuality of the women. These twin needs result in the differentiation of the private realm from the public realm, with men effectively in control of both.

In describing the 'dualist' man, Arendt (1958) notes that the nature of man is said to be *dual*, composed of both animality and humanity, while a woman's nature is thought of as being *single*, composed of animality alone. This philosophy, cast in concrete terms, results in the separation of public and private realms.

The private realm is the realm of man's animality; it is where woman lives, and where she is governed by necessity. The public realm, on the other hand, is where man lives as a human being. This realm is created in freedom, and represents the space where man can overcome his animal nature. The private or the domestic realm is seen by men as a work-free place, a refuge from the competing world of the market place and politics. In truth, however, it is women's unpaid labour within the home which enables men to work outside it.

The distinction between these two social spaces and their respective inhabitants has also resulted in these inhabitants being marked in psychic and social ways, which differentiates them into two genders. The social construction of gender takes place through the working of ideology, which is a system of beliefs and assumptions—unconscious, unexamined, invisible—that represents 'the imaginary relationships of individuals to their real conditions of existence' (Green and Kahn, 1985).

Ideology is also a system of practices that informs every aspect of our daily lives, and though it originates in particular cultural conditions, it authorizes its beliefs and practices as 'universal' and 'natural'. In the context of gender it presents 'woman' as eternally and everywhere the same. Further, ideology as a universalizing mechanism offers partial truths in the interests of false coherence; it obscures the actual conditions of peoples' existence, and can often make them act contrary to their own existence (Green and Kahn, 1985). In the last section of this discussion, when we consider the support structures for male hegemony, we will enlarge on two major Indian epics, the *Mahabharata*, and the *Ramayana*, as universalizing ideological mechanisms that even today are implicated in the construction of femininity.

Cross-culturally, gender is found to be a learned quality, an assigned status, with quantities that vary independently of biology and an ideology that attributes these qualities to nature (Mackinnon, 1982). Further, when *woman* as a social construct of contemporary industrial society is analysed, the *gender* stereotype so constructed is in fact found to be a *sexual* stereotype. Thus descriptors like docile, soft, passive, nurturant, vulnerable, weak, narcissistic, childlike, incompetent, masochistic, and domestic that are generally used for women, gain their validity only in apposition to 'male' activities. Socially, femaleness means femininity which means attractiveness which, in turn, means sexual availability on male terms. Thus, through gender identification, women see themselves as sexual beings that exist for men (Mackinnon, 1982).

When women enter the public realm, they continue to be governed by gender stereotypes in diverse ways. Ferguson (1982) points out that the shift from patriarchal ideology based in the male-dominated family to a more diffuse masculinist ideology has resulted in a shift in power from fathers and husbands to male professionals and bosses. Michel Foucault (1979) in tracing the history of sexuality notes that the rising bourgeois class gradually creates a new ideology for itself that shifts the emphasis from control of the social process through marriage alliance to the control of sexuality as a way of maintaining class hegemony. In public, this dynamic exhibits itself as a metaphorical father–daughter relationship, with the daughter as eternally ignorant and the father as consistently knowledgeable and discursive.

It is thus difficult to agree with Jane Gallop, who complains that both psychoanalysis and feminism flounder in the familial interpretation of power relations. While psychoanalysis considers revolutionary conflict along a parent–child model, thus reassimilating larger social issues into the familial domain, feminism, with its insistence on 'men-in-power', endows men with a sort of 'unified' phallic sovereignty that characterizes an absolute monarch and which bears little resemblance to the actual power in our social, economic structures. This model reproduces the daughters' view of the father (Gallop, 1982).

We believe that Kakar and Ross (1986) come closer to enunciating the problem when they note that besides its roots in the unconscious wishes and desires of individual fantasy, the conception of the daughter as the sole creation and possession of the father also reflects the reality of the traditional Indian social structure. The creation myths which describe the birth of Saraswathi, the Goddess of learning, point out that she was the mind-daughter or *Manasaputri* of Lord Brahma. Saraswathi is depicted without a consort, but stories abound of Brahma's subsequent sexual consumption of her. If sexual consumption can be understood as intellectual control, this myth can help us understand the irreversible knowledge-giving–knowledge-taking interaction between men and women.

We will examine three public service commercials and two fiction narratives to elucidate this point. The first, to explain the proper use of telephones, was made for the government department of telephones, and features a number of disruptive women. To begin with, there is a young pretty girl, whose extended love-talk over a public phone causes a log-jam of busy, irritated men. The male authoritative voice admonishes, 'Keep love-talk to the minimum.' Never shown on screen is the male interlocutor, whose complicity made possible the long conversation. In the next scene, a man about to leave for work is obliged to call his female neighbour to his phone. As all women, she is loquacious and quite oblivious of the need to be brief. The busy man frets and fumes. In the third scene, two teenaged girls play a popular record over the phone; both dance for long minutes to the tune. Once again the male authoritative voice comes on to berate them.

A more serious problem is posed by another short film. Here a busy executive suffers a heart attack in his office. He tries in vain to reach his wife. She is busy gossiping about knitting patterns and parties. Finally, the man is taken to the hospital. This time, the woman secretary takes the wife to task, though the film ends with the mandatory male voice-over. It is not clear, however, why the man persisted in calling his wife. Surely calling his doctor, or clinic or the nearest hospital emergency ward would have been more feasible?

The third short film is set in a hospital intensive care unit and purports to educate viewers about the correct deportment to adopt in such places. A young woman patient suffering from a heart attack is considerably cared for by everyone, but (unbelievably) her own mother. The mother, evidently the last to know of her daughter's condition, is loud, brash, overdressed, and stupid. She declares she is too busy with her social rounds to visit her daughter during the specified visiting hours, and argues so loudly with the nurse that the patient suffers a relapse. Once again, the male voice evaluates the woman's reprehensible behaviour. Two stereotypes clash in this film—the nurturing mother with the loud-voiced, strident woman—and the negative one wins.

In one serial, a retired judge, distressed by the plight of women in his immediate vicinity, resolves to help them through voluntary service. Several episodes of this serial show the judge and his friend, a retired police commissioner, tackle issues of dowry, widowhood, and so on. The judge's educated, wealthy, homebound daughter-in-law is shown involved in a women's club, attempting to raise money to build a swimming pool. She is educated about the need to use the money to build public toilets for slum dwellers. In another episode, the daughter-in-law is seen begging her husband for a page of his newspaper to read at breakfast. Quite viciously, he informs her that the paper is not a deck of cards to be distributed, and anyway all she would be interested in is notices of garment sales and new face creams. Later the woman is shown with an egg mask on her face, and is again viciously baited by her husband. The metaphoric father's intelligence can be appreciated best if offset by the incredible stupidity of the metaphoric daughter.

The elements of sarcasm and subterranean violence that inform this narrative and the three commercials discussed earlier are missing from the serial on the lives of Indian freedom fighters. In the episode under review, the young freedom fighter notes his wife's restlessness. She expresses her loneliness and desire to be involved in his work. The husband takes her to meet his mentor. The mentor welcomes the idea and gives the woman a set of hand-spun clothes to wear. As befitting the followers of Gandhi, the symbolic father–daughter interaction is here imbued with gentle guidance. The woman's social and political initiation is in effect a rebirth, and to make this plain, the narrative shows her cutting off relations with her wealthy and unsympathetic father.

Thus in the public realm, whether through sarcastic coercion or sweet reasonableness, the preferred male–female interaction depicted is that of father–daughter.

One mechanism which ensures the continued subordination of women within the public realm, is the ideology of marriage as the ultimate goal for them. This results in women seeing themselves as temporary, part-time or emergency earners and seeking jobs that are extensions of their housekeeping roles and that capitalize on their socially acknowledged assets, their physical charm.

Television discourse confirms the 'woman as essentially homebound' ideal in many ways. In the commercials sampled, we did not come across a single case of young professional women endorsing any product. They were either young and unmarried, in which case they were seen in situations of leisure, or they were young and married, in which case they were seen engaged in domestic tasks. In programmes for women, interviews with women employed outside the home repeatedly stressed the effect of the woman's job on the family, and applauded her felicitous handling of both. Women entrepreneurs, women judges, women police personnel were all routinely subjected to the same set of questions which focused on their husbands' responses to their jobs and the co-operation they obtained from them. The husbands were projected as exceptional, generous, and unusually co-operative. The real message being projected through these programmes was that of exceptional women engaged in juggling two jobs and a subtle warning to female viewers that if they were not fortunate enough to enjoy family support, they had better remain within the ambit of the home.

Training for women was usually discussed at the 'skills' level, that is, women were prepared for jobs that would enable them to function as supplementary or emergency earners. The options emphasized jobs that were mechanical and routine and which did not necessitate profound changes in household structure. Jobs like stenography, fashion design, beauty culture are flexible and do not have to be pursued as vertical-growth careers, with provisions for promotions, increased status and earnings, old-age and medical benefits, dependent on unbroken stretches of service. Teaching and nursing are also women orientated and, together with other jobs mentioned earlier, are seen as task rather than policy-orientated.

Thus teaching, which in its essence is a deeply intellectual and, at the same time, a subversive activity, is approached by our society as a mechanical chore, ill-paid and ill-prospected, and, as such jobs usually are, reified. Because of these reasons, all the jobs promoted as being ideal for women, are transplantable, that is, they can be relocated according to the needs of the husband's career. The women's real career thus lies within the private realm.

Another set of exceptional women seen on screen were the participants in the political arena and the revolutionaries. Considering the high visibility of women in our freedom movement and their much-lauded participation in it, it may appear strange to label them 'exceptional' especially as they were held to be complementary to men. But this dynamic of complementarity lasted only as long as the movement lasted. Once the situation became stable, women were once again excluded from the public realm. Two fictional narratives reiterated this 'emergency' role of women. Mackinnon (1982) rightly

notes that the concern of revolutionary leadership for ending women's confinement to traditional roles arises from the need to make their labour available to the regime. Women become as free as men to work outside the home,
while men remain as free of it within. Women's labour and militancy are
both co-opted. Just as our freedom movement remained a partial revolution
(we only exchanged one set of rulers for another without disturbing the
structure of Indian society), so women's participation remained partial.
They operated within narrow, male-defined limits which did not alter the
structure of male–female relationships.

Agriculture, no less than politics, was presented as a public realm in which
women could negotiate roles only as wives or entertainers. In programmes
for farmers, women invariably appeared as entertainers, singing folk songs
or dancing. The actual work was presented as purely male activity, with hard-
working men turning to dancing and singing as a respite. Commercials
sponsoring farmers' programmes also reflected this theme, with males discussing fertilizer inputs, tractor hire, and crop prices, while the females
adorned themselves. The man-as-earner and woman-as-consumer ideology
was propagated even by public sector units.

Programmes about inputs to stimulate progress in agriculture also had
male farmers as their target. Thus the visual of a mechanical paddy trans-
plantor showed a man wielding the machine whereas in the field, this job is
women-intensive. Women's involvement in agriculture was limited to
kitchen gardens. In one programme, the camera travelled to the kitchen garden of the Vice-Chancellor of Haryana Agricultural University. His wife was
interviewed on this programme. She was asked if she popularized kitchen
gardens among her friends while her husband was asked 'technical' questions relating to fertilizers, pesticides, etc. In the background could be seen
labourers engaged in weeding and caring for the plants. The focus in this programme was on the women's role as home-maker, overseeing the home-
based production of domestically consumed articles. The man, in command
of technical expertise, was affirmed as one whose expertise was at the service
of the public at large.

Although in the programme on women artists the compère was female, two
males were invited as experts. One of them noted that the works featured exhib-
ited no tension, because in the Indian society women and men had equality of
opportunity and expression. This palpably absurd remark went unchallenged
by the compère. One woman artist, who had changed her medium from oil to
fabric collage, said that at first she felt like a housewife as she went about with
her fabric and scissors. Her self-esteem and identity as artist was validated only
when she went on to win awards for her work. We can now appreciate Barrett's
remark that the meaning of gender in patriarchal discourse is not simply 'difference' but 'division, oppression, inequality and interiorized inferiority for
women' (Barrett, 1980). With the division of social space into public and private comes the labelling of public as superior and private as inferior. When
women enter into complicity with men in devaluing work within the home,
they assist in the hegemonial process of valorizing men's work.

The construction of the public realm as male space, as we have seen, confirms male authority. This is most evident in the news bulletins, which are
records of male activity. News is information about recent events. To think

about news is to make important assumptions about time, events, and ways of informing the people. These assumptions have their roots in socially defined reality; they reflect the way a society or culture views the world (Mckinley, 1983).

On Doordarshan the news bulletin is a highly structured programme. News relating to political, economic, and developmental activities is followed by news about sports and, finally, the weather. Mckinley notes that that news sequence is one which moves from events at the centre of culture, that is problems of government, business, religion, and so on, to athletic competence, which is the cultural cultivation of natural abilities. Finally, concern is expressed over those aspects of nature not subject to human control, that is the weather.

Our findings about the structure of news programmes support the findings of similar researches. We noted that political news formed about 45 per cent of the content of every bulletin. The first 10 items of every bulletin also dealt with political news; 66 per cent of the time in the case of Hindi bulletins and 66.3 per cent in the case of English bulletins. Smith (1979) reported that in his sample, the government was the dominant subject, the primary actor, and the primary acted-upon. Government investigations, hearings, and meetings provided the single largest category of news subjects, and governments at the city, state, and federal levels were the subjects of more than half the stories in the sample.

In our sample, more than 60 per cent of the newsmakers were celebrities, more often than not political leaders of the ruling party representing the government. Of the newsmakers in our sample, 72.4 per cent were male, and 40.3 per cent of them made news in the political context. Women made news in 6.5 per cent of the cases; here, too, they were largely politicians and government functionaries. Mckinley (1983) noted that the structure of society itself provides the context for interpreting newsworthy events. Since our society is deeply androcentric and class-divided, the criteria of significance and selection of newsworthy items are determined by this framework. Thus, not only women, but the poor and the disadvantaged are also excluded. Our findings show that if women made news as individuals, they were celebrities like politicians or Wimbledon stars. In groups, they were shoppers during hours of curfew relaxation or victims of calamities. *En masse* they were featured as audiences at public rallies, passively listening to politicians. On the other hand, a report of an opposition-organized protest where women were described as participants was not supported with visuals. The collective strength of women as actors was thus rendered invisible.

Greene and Kahn (1985) help us to understand the invisibilization of women in the news when they quote Lerner (1979), who noted that as long as history (news) has as its primary focus 'the transmission and experience of power', and as long as 'war and politics are seen as more significant to the history of humankind than child rearing', women will remain marginalized or invisible.

Women and the poor featured largely in the 'deaths and disasters' and 'development news' category. Even in the case of development news, as Ignatieff (1985) has noted, the government remains the actor. The shift in focus to the disadvantaged sections of society is supposed to balance government hand-outs; instead, the inclusion of the so-called human interest stories, according to Ignatieff, has destroyed the coherence of the genre itself. While we do not completely agree with this, we hold that the inclusion of the human interest stories, embedded in the matrix of political stories, is more in the nature of providing relief from the grim business of life itself. It is a devaluation of the lived experience of the poor and the marginalized of society.

The Joshi Committee Report (1985) has strongly decried the tendency of television news to be orientated towards the activities of political and other celebrities. It notes: 'The viewers of Doordarshan live well above the poverty line and Doordarshan, through its VIP-oriented news programmes and trivial entertainment, promotes complacency, and a drugged indifference to issues of social transformation, rather than any self-questioning of their lifestyle on the part of its middle and upper class viewers.' We agree, and feel with Ignatieff that 'television (news) is worshipping state power and insisting that we do so as well. It is power itself—the sacred offices of state—that is worshipped.'

Both enrichment and sectoral programmes as well as commercials celebrate men's power to evaluate the world in general and women's activities in particular. The pattern of compèring followed by the enrichment and sectoral programmes illustrates this trend, as does the use of men as experts in all fields and on all occasions. Commenting on this disturbing trend, a media critic has pointed out that 'women lawyers, economists, women of real intellectual calibre and social conscience have been kept off the screen'. She points out that, by and large, only women sympathetic to the establishment participate in important interviews and discussion. 'One woman who was asked to participate in the *Sach ki Parchaiyan* programme on women was hastily dropped when she said she would mention Shah Bano' (Malik, 1986). The reference was to the controversial Muslim Women (Protection of Rights on Divorce) Act 1986, which most women see as a retrogressive measure. The medium thus persistently denies women's insights into what are seen as matters of public policy; their visibility is noted only at the level of tasks to be performed. Women are projected as reacting to situations, as if they never, at any point, have a dissenting voice to raise. Alternatively, they are presented as expositors, not as original thinkers. Thus, on women's programmes and health programmes, women, as doctors and citizens can be heard talking of the need to delay marriage and childbirth in terms of rise in birth-rates, and the need to give the woman time to develop into a 'better' wife and mother. But we get to hear very little about the effect of early pregnancies on the physical and mental development of the woman herself.

Compères and experts on women's programmes repeatedly stressed the need for women to use clean water for drinking and cooking purposes. Women activists and development workers, and indeed citizens who have experienced the mirage of clean water at the most personal level and who can thus ask pointed questions relating to developmental priorities, are never heard on such programmes.

What are the effects of having significantly more prominent men than women on television? On the basis of her ongoing research into sex roles on Canadian television, Williams (1986) suggested that

— There are fewer role models for females than males; this is especially important for children.
— It becomes difficult to provide variety in the portrayals of prominent females, which leads to stereotyping.
— The consistent portrayal of more men than women leads to the implicit message that females are less important than males.

She noted further that the consistency of such survey results and the apparent resistance to depicting women as important, knowledgeable, and authoritative appeared to be consistent with the 'keep men in power' viewpoint of Gerbner (1978) and Tuchman (1978). With regard to Indian television, we hold that the drive is to shore up male ideology rather than males themselves. The activities of women ministers and politicians of the ruling party are also given fairly extensive coverage. As we noted in our theoretical considerations, such apparently felicitous findings can result from the mechanical application of content analysis techniques. They need to be interpreted in the light of the Indian emphasis on the government as actor.

Women are thus allowed a precarious foothold in the public realm under certain well-defined conditions. Such conditions serve as exclusionary mechanisms. Thus, the prescription states:

— Women are temporary or emergency earners/participants. They have to go back home once the emergency is over. The temporary, unmarried state is also emergency-related.
— Their choice of jobs should be limited to spheres which do not disrupt the household and do not challenge the importance of the male.
— When women aspire to careers rather than jobs, they can do so only because they are supported by exceptionally large-hearted men.
— Women are consumers, men are producers. Hard-working men can find respite either through their sheltered caring wives, or through programmes of music and dance.
— Women understand their presence in the public realm as an intrusion into male space and express this understanding through veiling their faces, modulating their voices, and hiding their intelligence.

We need to take note of the many dissenting voices that refuse to valorize the public realm. Rogers (1978), quoted in Greene and Kahn (1985), asks why research takes no note of women's involvement as matchmakers or as sharers in wealth or higher status. Further, if women are kept away from public life, are they necessarily inferior? Why should we give priority to public life, and why devalue women's importance in less formal, private roles?

We need to seriously address ourselves to this problem. While it is true that we should not use categories (such as private and public) to challenge the ideology from within which they arise, we have to note that however important women's work is within the private realm, it still places them effectively under male control. We need to challenge, as we noted earlier, the interiorization of this control. Further, in the Indian context, women are placed under male control precisely by apportioning to them such 'important' work. If autonomy was part of women's lived experience, would we, as a nation, experience ever-rising levels of female foeticide, female infanticide, and dowry-related deaths? All these phenomena require female complicity and such complicity arises only from women's interiorized inferiority.

References   Arendt, Hannah (1958), *The Human Condition* (Chicago: Univ. of Chicago Press).

Barrett, Michele (1980), *Women's Oppression Today: Problems in Marxist Feminist Analysis* (London: Villiers Publications).

Ferguson, Ann (1982), 'On "Compulsory Hetero Sexuality and Lesbian Experience": Defining the Issues', in Keohane, Rosaldo, and Gelphi, *Feminist Theory: A Critique of Ideology* (Sussex: Harvester Press).

Foucault, Michel (1979), *The History of Sexuality* (London: Allen Lane).

Gallop, Jane (1982), *Feminism and Psychoanalysis: The Daughter's Seduction* (London: Macmillan).

Gerbner, George (1978), 'The Dynamics of Cultural Resistance', in G. Tuchman, A. K. Daniels, and J. Benet (eds.), *Hearth and Home* (New York: Oxford Univ. Press).

Greene, Gayle, and Kahn, Coppelia (1985), *Making a Difference: Feminist Literary Criticism* (London: Methuen).

Ignatieff, Michael (1985), 'Is Nothing Sacred? The Ethics of Television', *Daedalus* (Fall), 57–78.

Joshi, S. R. (1986), *Participation of Women in Higher Decision-Making Levels of Doordarshan, the Television Authority of India*, paper presented at the Conference of the International Association for Mass Communication Research, New Delhi.

Kakar, Sudhir, and Ross, John (1986), *Tales of Love, Sex and Danger* (New York: Alfred Knopf).

Keohane, Nannerlo, Rosaldo, Michelle Z., and Gelphi, Barbara C. (1982), *Feminist Theory: A Critique of Ideology* (Sussex: Harvester Press).

Lerner, Gerda (1979), *The Majority Finds its Past: Placing Women in History*, quoted in Greene and Kahn (1985).

Mckinley, Robert (1983), 'Culture Meets Nature on the Six O'Clock News: American Cosmology', *Journal of Popular Culture*, 17/3: 109–14.

Mackinnon, Catherine (1982), 'Feminism, Marxism, Method and the State: An Agenda for Theory', in Keohane, Rosaldo, and Gelphi, *Feminist Theory: A Critique of Ideology* (1982).

Malik, Amita (1986), 'We were not Amused', *Express Magazine*, 13 Apr.

O'Brien, Mary (1982), 'Feminist Theory and Dialectical Logic', in Keohane, Rosaldo, and Gelphi, *Feminist Theory: A Critique of Ideology* (1982).

Smith, Robert Rutherford (1979), 'Mythic Elements in Television News', *Journal of Communication*, 29/1: 75–82.

Tuchman, Gaye (1978), *Making News: A Study in the Construction of Reality* (New York: Free Press).

Williams, Tannis, *et al.* (1986), *The Portrayal of Sex Roles on Canadian and U.S. Television*, paper presented at the Conference of the International Association for Mass Communication Research, New Delhi.

Working Group on Software for Doordarshan—Joshi Committee Report (1985), *All Indian Personality for Television* (New Delhi: Publications Division, Ministry of Information and Broadcasting, Government of India).

4

Situation Comedy, Feminism, and Freud: Discourses of Gracie and Lucy

Patricia Mellencamp

> Since we said 'I do,' there are so many things we don't.
> *Lucy Ricardo*

> This is a battle between two different ways of life, men and
>   women.
> The battle of the sexes?
> Sex has nothing to do with it.
> *Gracie Allen and Blanche Morton*

DURING THE LATE 1940s and the 1950s, linked to or owned by the major radio networks, television recycled radio's stars, formats, and times through little proscenium screens, filling up the day. Vaudeville and movies fed both of these voracious, domestic media, each reliant on sound, and each influential in the rapidly developing suburbs. With a commercial collage of quiz, news, music, variety, wrestling/boxing, fashion/cooking, and comedy shows, both media were relatively irreverent toward well-fashioned narrative and worshipful of audiences and sponsors. Television was then (and continues to be) both an ecology—a repetition and recycling through the years—and a family affair, in the 1950s conducted collectively in the living room, with the dial dominated by Dad. A TV set was a status symbol, a roof-top economic declaration, and an invitation to other couples to watch.

Like suburban owners of TV 'sets', the four television networks were also concerned with status; thus 'the news' was made a separate category of the real and legitimate, presumably distinct from 'entertainment'. At the beginning of the 1950s, the United Nations debates were prestigiously broadcast. The proceedings of the Kefauver congressional committee, which was inves-

Originally published in Tania Modleski (ed.), *Studies in Entertainment: Critical Approaches to Mass Culture* (Bloomington: Indiana University, 1986), 80–95. This argument is further developed in Patricia Mellencamp's *High Anxiety* (Indiana University Press, 1992).

tigating organized crime, were televised by WPIX in New York; the networks carried these 'real life' dramas with good ratings. In April 1951 General Douglas MacArthur's speech to Congress was broadcast; his words attacked the 'containment' and limited warfare policies of the Truman administration, revving up the paranoiac or conspiracy interpretation of not only world but also social events. In July 1952 the GOP convention was televised, and Stevenson and Eisenhower fought part of the subsequent election on television. The Army–McCarthy hearings began on 22 April 1954 and received high ratings for the many hours during which Senator Joseph McCarthy accused the military of 'communist infiltration' and then was undone on live television.[1]

Coincident with these prestigious broadcasts of the 'real'—events of power, politics, and 'truth'—and the massive licensing of broadcast air and time, women were being urged to leave the city, work-force, and salaries; move to the suburbs, leisure, and tranquillity; raise children; and placate commuting, overworked husbands for free. In reality, of course, not all women did so. Most women over 35 remained in the paid work-force; when allowed, instead of building battleships, they took other jobs. That TV and particularly situation comedies would, like radio, both serve and support the new, imaginary, blissful domesticity of a ranch style house, backyard barbecue, and a bath and a half seems logical—it is, of course, historical. 'Containment' was not only a defensive, military strategy developed as US foreign policy in the 1950s; it was practised on the domestic front as well, and it was aimed at excluding women from the work-force and keeping them in the home.

1 Eric Goldman, *The Crucial Decade and After: America, 1945–1960* (New York: Vintage Books, 1956 and 1960).

Gracie Allen and George Burns

To argue that television was a powerful machinery for familial containment of women is hardly original. Yet the specifics of programme strategies are intriguing and complex—hardly monolithic or perfectly generic, as most discourses presume. For me, two issues are central: the importance in early 1950s comedy of idiosyncratically powerful female stars, usually in their late thirties or forties; and the gradual erosion of that power that occurred in the representation of women within comedy formats. In situation comedy, pacification of women occurred between 1950 and 1960 without a single critical mention that the genre's terrain had altered: the housewife, although still ruling the familial roost, changed from being a humorous rebel or well-dressed, wise-cracking, naïve dissenter who wanted or had a paid job—from being out of control via language (Gracie) or body (Lucy)—to being a contented, if not blissfully happy, understanding homebody (Laura Petrie). With this in mind, we need to review specific programmes, particularly in TV's early stages. This paper is based on a general analysis of forty episodes of *The George Burns and Gracie Allen Show*, which was on the air Wednesday nights from October 1950 until June 1958, when Gracie left the show; and of 170 of the 179 episodes of *I Love Lucy*, which was broadcast Monday evenings from October 1951 until May 1957. It also begins to rethink Freud's construction of the radical underpinnings and 'liberating' function of jokes, the comic, and humour—perhaps yet another 'foreign' policy of potential containment for US women.

I   In fifteen-minute segments, broadcast live three times a week in 1949, Gertrude Berg—writer, producer, and star—disguised herself as Molly Goldberg, the quintessential Jewish mother, a *mélange* of chicken soup malaprops and advice. Leaning out of her window, she would intimately confess to us: 'If Mr Goldberg did not drink Sanka decaffeinated coffee, I don't know what I would do—I don't even know if we'd still have a marriage . . . just try it once, and that's what I'm telling you.' The programme and its popularity were emblematic of the subsequent televised avalanche of situation comedies, a direct descendant of radio, vaudeville's 'husband and wife' sketches, music hall, and *commedia dell'arte*'s stereotypical scenes and characters. The elision of programme and star with sponsor was another version of television's corporate coupling/ownership.

In the 1950–1 season *The George Burns and Gracie Allen Show* debuted, continuing in this tradition. Burns and Allen funnelled their 1926 marriage, their vaudeville, radio, and film routines, and their characters/stars into an upper middle-class situation comedy—a historical agglutination suggesting that what is monolithically termed 'mass culture' is a process: a collection of discourses, scenes, or turns recycled from various media and contextualized within historical moments. Despite its similarity to the Molly Goldberg type of programme, this show represented a new version of the happily married couple, featuring the zany, fashionable Gracie of bewildering *non sequiturs* and the relaxed, dapper George of one-liners and wisecracks living in suburban, affluent Beverly Hills. Gracie was certainly unlike TV's nurturing-yet-domineering mothers who dwelled in city apartments. Yet she was familiarly different as 'Gracie'. Derailing the laws and syntax of language and logic, her technique was a referral back to either the nearest or the most unexpected referent as a comic turn on the arbitrary and conventional authority of speech (and she would continually break her own rules just when her friends and we caught on). She baffled all the male and most of the female characters, concocting improbable stories and schemes that were invariably true in amazing circumlocutions which became that week's 'plot'.

The casual narratives of each week's programme were used merely as continuity for vaudeville routines and existed primarily to be mocked by George. The scenario is often as follows: an ordinary event—shopping, going to the movies—would be 'misinterpreted' and then complicated by Gracie, who would then connect a second, random event to the first. For example, their college son, Ronnie, needs a story for the USC newspaper; Blanche Morton, her next-door neighbour and confidante, wants new dishes. Linking these two unrelated problems, Gracie contrives a fake theft of Ronnie's wealthy friend's car. When the car is initially found in the Mortons' garage, Blanche's husband is so relieved not to have to pay for this 'new' car, which he believes Blanche has bought, that he gladly buys the plates; and Ronnie scoops the story of the theft.

Adding to the shaggy dog quality of the plots were the many bewildered characters (including the postman) who would drop by the house and would then be involved by Gracie. The more unrelated the character, or innocent bystander to the plot, the better; a large measure of Gracie's comedy depended on the other characters' astonishment. Her naïve, friendly *non sequiturs* rendered them speechless, reluctantly agreeing, finally reduced to staring in reaction shots. (This is diametrically the opposite of what occurs in *I Love Lucy* where Lucy is invariably given the last word or look, the editing indicating that different mechanisms of identification and spectator positioning are operative in each show.) Then, winking, George would either join in the linguistic mayhem or sort things out. His intervention was not, however, for our understanding, but for that of the confused, speechless characters; his Aristotelian analyses of Gracie's behaviour and illogic left bystanders doubly amazed. Finally, at the end of each show, George would issue the imperative, 'Say goodnight, Gracie.'

Garbed in dressy fifties fashion, set in an upper middle-class milieu of dens, patios, and two-car garages, constantly arranging flowers or making and serving coffee but not sense, Gracie equivocally escaped order. Despite being burdened by all the clichés applied to women—illogical, crazy, nonsensical, possessing their own, peculiar bio-logic and patronized accordingly—in certain ways, she seemed to be out of (or beyond) men's control. Unlike the ever loyal and bewildered Harry VonZell, the show's and the story's announcer, and other characters in the narrative sketches, neither she nor her neighbour Blanche (who both loved and understood Gracie) revered George or were intimidated by his cleverness; in fact, Gracie rarely paid attention to him, or to any authority figure. She unmade decorum, she unravelled patriarchal laws, illustrating Jean Baudrillard's assertion through Freud: 'The witticism, which is a transgressive reversal of discourse, does not act on the basis of another code as such; it works through the instantaneous deconstruction of the dominant discursive code. It volatizes the category of the code, and that of the message.'[2] The 'dominant discursive code' of patri-archy tried, through benevolent George, to contain Gracie's volatization, her literal deconstruction of speech, and her tall tales of family. Whether or not the system won can be answered either way, depending on where the analyst is politically sitting—with George in his den, or in the kitchen with the women.

Gracie's forte was the shaggy dog story—either as verbal riff or as the very substance of the narrative: the first use led to illogical nonsense, a way of thinking definitive of Gracie's comedy; the second led to instigation and res-olution of the week's episode. Furthermore, the shaggy dog event, preposter-ous as it was, would always prove to be 'true'. Take for example the following episode. The scene is Gracie's sunny, ruffle-curtained kitchen with table in the centre, an auto-replenishing coffee-pot, and numerous exits. The initial situation is explicated in the dialogue:

GRACIE: Thanks for driving me home, Dave.

DAVE: As long as I towed your car in, I didn't mind at all Mrs Burns.

GRACIE: There's some coffee on the stove. Would you like some?

DAVE: I've been wondering, Mrs Burns. How are you going to explain this little repair job to your husband?

GRACIE: I'll just tell him what happened. I went shopping and bought a blouse and on my way home I stopped to watch them put up the tents and this elephant came along and sat on my fender and smashed it.

DAVE: He'll never believe it.

GRACIE: Of course he will. He knows a fender isn't strong enough to hold up an elephant. George is smarter than you think he is.[3]

To prove her story to George, Gracie will show him the blouse. Her idiosyn-cratic cause–effect connections have nothing (or everything) to do with physics, the arbitrary conventions of language, or common sense. In many ways, her style of speech is uncommonly funny because it is ahistorical, ignoring the speaker and the situation while obeying language's rules. Like Chico Marx, she takes language literally; unlike Chico, she is unaware of her effect on other characters.[4] Gracie delivers her deadpan lines without reac-tion or expectation, obliviously using the same expressive tone no matter what the terms of the discursive contract—which she ultimately reconstructs anyway.

The rest of this episode consists of retelling the story—first to Blanche, who then tells her husband, Harry; then to the insurance salesman, Prescott; and simultaneously to Harry VonZell and Stebbins, the circus man. George, basically a solo, narrative entrepreneur, keeps breaking and entering Gracie's dilemma of credulity with comments ('All I wanted was a little proof'), observations on life, and ironic maxims about marriage: 'Married people

2 Jean Baudrillard, 'Requiem for the Media', *For a Critique of the Political Economy of the Sign*, trans. Charles Levin (St Louis: Telos, 1981), 184.

3 The transcription was taken from tape.

4 See my 'Jokes and Their Relation to the Marx Brothers', in Stephen Heath and Patricia Mellencamp (eds.), *Cinema and Language* (Frederick, Md.: University Publications of America, 1983), for further explication of jokes and the comic within the wacky male world of the Marx brothers.

don't have to lie to each other. We've got lawyers and friends to do that for us.' George bribes Gracie with a promise of a mink coat for the 'true' story, which, of course, she has already told him. The show culminates in a final courtroom scene with all of the participants sitting in the Burns's living room validating the truth of Gracie's initial story, which is confirmed by Dave, the 'seeing is believing' mechanic. The truth of male vision verifying Gracie's words is endlessly repeated, both in the series and in this programme. Dave says, 'If I hadn't come down to the circus grounds to tow away your car, I wouldn't have believed it myself.' During the last scene, he reiterates: 'If I hadn't seen it with my own eyes, I wouldn't have believed it myself.' During this conclusive trial, presided over by George, a new character—Duffy Edwards, the furrier—enters with Gracie's newly won fur coat and says to George: 'I always watch your show. I knew you were going to lose.' Unlike Lucy, Gracie always wins in the narrative, which thereby validates her story.

However, other codes are also operative: George is centre-framed in the *mise-en-scène* and by the moving camera; he is taller than all the other characters; and he has access to the audience via his direct looks at the camera. He nods knowingly, with sidelong collusive glances at us (or perhaps at eternal husbands everywhere). In the end Gracie is frame left. She wins the narrative and the mink coat, but loses central screen space; perhaps most importantly, she never was in possession of 'the look'. Roland Barthes, placing power firmly in language, asks: 'Where is speech? In locution? In listening? In the returns of the one and the other? The problem is not to abolish the distinctions in functions . . . but to protect the instability . . . the giddying whirls of the positions of speech.'[5] The whirls are giddying; yet George Burns, the dapper entertainer as Hollywood gossip, critic, and golf partner of CBS president William Paley, presides over the show with benign resignation, a wry smile, and narrative 'logic' firmly grounded in bemused knowledge of the frothy status of the situation, comedy, and television. Throughout each programme, Gracie is blatantly dominated not only by George's looks at the camera and direct monologues to the audience, but also by his view of the programme from the TV set in his den, and by his figure matted or superimposed over the background action as his voice-over comments on marriage, Gracie, her relatives, movie stars, show business, and the 'story'.

In his analysis of Freud's *Jokes and Their Relation to the Unconscious*, Samuel Weber suggests an intriguing reading of the *Aufsitzer*, or shaggy dog jokes—nonsense jokes which create the expectation of a joke, causing one to search for concealed meaning. 'But one finds none, they really are nonsense,' writes Freud. Weber argues that the expectation rests in the desire 'to make sense of the enigmatic assertion with which the joke begins . . . such jokes "play" games with the desire of the listener. . . . By rousing this "expectation" and then leaving it unsatisfied . . . such jokes function in a manner very reminiscent of the discourse of the analyst, who refuses to engage in a meaningful dialogue with the analysand.'[6] It is, however, difficult to apply Weber's insight to Gracie, to compare *her* rather than George to the analyst. After all,

5 Roland Barthes, 'Writers, Intellectuals, Teachers', *Image-Music-Text*, ed. Stephen Heath (London: Fontana/Collins, 1977), 205–6.

6 Samuel Weber, *The Legend of Freud* (Minneapolis: Univ. of Minnesota Press, 1982), 114.

it is George with whom the listener is in collusion; it is George who hears Gracie from his tolerant, central, bemused vantage-point. It is as if he occupies the central tower in the panopticon, or the analyst's chair behind the couch, unseen, with all scenes visible to his gaze.

As Weber writes, these jokes are 'come-ons', taking us for a ride. 'For at the end of the road all we find is nonsense: "They really are nonsense," Freud states, thus seeking to reassure us, and himself as well.'[7] Perhaps *Burns and Allen* could be interpreted as a massive, male reassurance that women's lives are indeed nonsense. The *Aufsitzer* is a joke played on the expectation of a joke, and is clearly a complicated matter—in the case of Gracie Allen, it is a refusal of conventional meaning gleefully accepted and encouraged as rebellion by Blanche Morton and contained for the audience by the omniscience of George, who narcissistically strives as super/ego to 'unify, bind . . . and situate [himself] as a self-contained subject'.[8]

Nor should we be misled by the fact that George is the 'straight man' and thus seems to occupy a slightly inferior position, which he himself describes as follows:

> For the benefit of those who have never seen me, I am what is known in the business as a straight man. If you don't know what a straight man does, I'll tell you. The comedian gets a laugh. Then I look at the comedian. Then I look at the audience—like this . . . That is known as a pause . . .
>
> Another duty of a straight man is to repeat what the comedian says. If Gracie should say, 'A funny thing happened on the streetcar today,' then I say, 'A funny thing happened on the streetcar today?' And naturally her answer gets a scream. Then, I throw in one of my famous pauses . . .

But George was never *just* a straight man; the monologue continues:

> I've been a straight man for so many years that from force of habit I repeat everything. I went out fishing with a fellow the other day and he fell overboard. He yelled 'Help! Help!' So I said, 'Help? Help?' And while I was waiting for him to get his laugh, he drowned.

This gag defines quite precisely George's actions, as well as indicating their vaudeville origins. Inevitably, like the male leads in most situation comedies, he got the final and controlling look or laugh. Containment operated through laughter—a release which might have held women to their place, rather than 'liberating' them in the way Freud says jokes liberate their tellers and auditors. As radical as the nonsense joke might be (when it comes from the mouth of the male), it's different, as is the rest of life, for the female speaker. The audience too is measured and contained by George, whom both the camera and editing follow: the husband as television critic, solo stand-up comic, female psychologist, and tolerant parent/performer. Yet, unlike in most situation comedies, it was clear that George depended on Gracie, who worked both in the series' imaginary act and the programme's narratives. Thus, the contradiction of the programme and the double bind of the female

---

7 Samuel Weber, *The Legend of Freud* (Minneapolis: Univ. of Minnesota Press, 1982), 114.

8 Ibid. 116.

spectator and comedian—women as both subject and object of the comedy, rather than the mere objects that they are in the Freudian paradigm of jokes—are dilemmas which, for me, no modern critical model can resolve.

II   In its original version, *I Love Lucy* debuted on Monday, 15 October 1951, at 8 p.m. Held to the conventional domesticity of situation comedy, Lucy Ricardo was barely in control, constantly attempting to escape domesticity—her 'situation', her job, in the home—always trying to get into show business by getting into Ricky's 'act', narratively fouling it up, but brilliantly and comically performing in it. Lucy endured marriage and housewifery by transforming them into vaudeville: costumed performances and rehearsals which made staying home frustrating, yet tolerable. Her dissatisfaction, expressed as her desire for a job, show business, and stardom, was concealed by the happy endings of hug/kiss (sometimes tagged with the line, 'now we're even')/applause/titles/theme song. Her discontent and ambition, weekly stated, were the show's working premisses, its contradictions massively covered up by the audience's pleasure in her performances, her 'real' stardom. The series typified the paradox of women in comedy—the female performer caught somewhere between narrative and spectacle, historically held as a simulation between the real and the model.

As was the case with *The George Burns and Gracie Allen Show*, the entire series was biographically linked to the marriage of the two stars. Lucille Ball, movie star, and her husband Desi Arnaz, Cuban band leader, became Lucy and Ricky Ricardo; their 'friends' appeared on programmes as bit players or as 'themselves'. At the end of one episode, for instance, the voice-over

announcer said: 'Harpo Marx played himself'. Image/person/star are totally merged as 'himself', the 'real' is a replayed image, a scene, a simulation— what Jean Baudrillard calls 'the hyperreal'. The most extraordinary or bizarre example of the elision of 'fact' and fiction, or the 'real' with the simulation, marshalled by the 'formal coherency' of narrative, was Lucy's hyperreal pregnancy. In 1952, with scripts supervised by a minister, a priest, and a rabbi, seven episodes were devoted to Lucy's TV and real pregnancy (without ever mentioning the word). The first episode was aired on 8 December, timed with Lucy's scheduled caesarean delivery date of Monday, 19 January 1953. Lucy's real, nine-month baby, Desi, Jr., was simulated in a seven-week TV gestation and electronically delivered on 19 January at 8 p.m. as Little Ricky, while 44 million Americans watched. (Only 29 million tuned in to Eisenhower's swearing-in ceremony. We liked Ike. We loved Lucy.) As were all the episodes in the series, this one was given a children's book title, 'Lucy Goes to the Hospital'.[9]

But if the 'real' domestic and familial details of the star's life were so oddly mixed up with the fiction, perhaps the supreme fiction of the programme was that Lucy was not star material, and hence needed to be confined to domesticity. Thus the weekly plot concerned Lucy's thwarted attempts to break out of the home and into show business. Unlike Gracie's implausible connections and overt machinations, though, all of Lucy's schemes failed, even if failure necessitated an instant and gratuitous reversal in the end. Lucy was the rebellious child whom the husband/father Ricky endured, understood, loved, and even punished, as, for example, when he spanked her for her continual disobedience. However, if Lucy's plots for ambition and fame *narratively* failed, with the result that she was held, often gratefully, to domesticity, *performatively* they succeeded. In the elemental, repetitive narrative, Lucy never got what she wanted: a job and recognition. Weekly, for six years, she accepted domesticity, only to try to escape again the next week. During each programme, however, she not only succeeded, but demolished Ricky's act, upstaged every other performer (including John Wayne, Richard Widmark, William Holden, and even Orson Welles), and got exactly what she and the television audience wanted: Lucy the star, performing off-key, crazy, perfectly executed vaudeville turns—physical comedy as few women (particularly beautiful ones, former Goldwyn girls) have ever done.

The typical movement of this series involves Lucy performing for us, at home, the role that the narrative forbids her. She can never be a 'real' public performer, except for us: she must narratively remain a housewife. In the episode entitled 'The Ballet', for example, Ricky needs a ballerina and a burlesque clown for his nightclub act; Lucy pleads with him to use her. Of course he refuses. Lucy trains as a ballet dancer in one of her characteristic performances: dressed in a frothy tutu, she eagerly and maniacally imitates a dancer performing ballet movements which she then transforms through automatic, exaggerated repetition into a charleston. Whenever Lucy is confident that she has learned something new, no matter how difficult, she gets carried away. These are the great comic scenes, occurring after the narrative set-up:

---

9 Bart Andrews, *Lucy & Ricky & Fred & Ethel* (New York: E. P. Dutton, 1976). This book contains a synopsis of shows by air date and title which helped me to organize my textual analysis.

pure performances during which the other characters show absolutely no reactions. This is the first 'story' line, before the mid-programme 'heart break': 'curtains' as halves of a heart lovingly open/close, or frame and divide each episode. Then, the second: Lucy will now train to be a burlesque comic. Her baggy pants clown/teacher arrives at their apartment, pretends she's a man, tells his melodramatic tale of woe about Martha and betrayal; Lucy becomes involved, says the Pavlovian name, Martha, and is hit with a pig bladder, sprayed with seltzer water, and finally, gets a pie in the face. The scene ends with Lucy saying, 'Next time, you're going to be the one with the kind face'—in other words, the victim of the sketch. Then, as in all the episodes, and in this one more literally than in most, the two stories are condensed in a final, on-stage performance. At his nightclub, Ricky is romantically singing 'Martha' in Spanish. Ethel calls Lucy to inform her that Ricky needs someone in his act. She dresses up as the burlesque clown (not the needed dancer), and steps on-stage with her wrong props. When Ricky sings the refrain, the word 'Martha' is now her Pavlovian cue: she beats the male ballet dancers with the bladder; squirts the female ballerina with seltzer water; and, in a conclusion which uses up all the previous set-ups, slams a pie in the singing face of tuxedoed, romantic crooner Ricky. (The Saudi Arabian government detected an element of subversion in this series and banned it because Lucy dominated her husband.) This episode, like so many others, is a rehearsal for a performance, involving in the end a comical public upstaging of Ricky. We are simultaneously backstage and out-front in the audience, waiting for Lucy's performance and Ricky's stoic, albeit frustrated, endurance; thus, expectation is not connected to narrative, but to anticipation of the comic—a performative or proairetic expectation.

An exemplary instance of Lucy's upstaging, or humiliation, of Ricky may be seen in the episode entitled 'The Benefit', in which Ricky's attempts to be the comedian rather than the straight man are utterly foiled. In this episode Lucy, along with the audience, discovers that Ricky has re-edited their benefit duo, taking all the punchlines for himself. Fade. On-stage, in identical costumes of men's suits, straw hats, and canes, Ricky and Lucy perform a soft-shoe sketch. Ricky stops, taps his cane, and waits for Lucy to be the 'straight man'. Of course, she won't. While singing 'Under the Bamboo Tree' about marriage and happiness, Lucy, with the camera close-up as her loyal accomplice in the reaction shots, outrageously steals all of Ricky's lines, smirking and using every upstaging method in the showbiz book. Applause, exit; the heart, this time as a literal curtain, closes. Lucy gets the last word and the last laugh during this ironic 'turn' on the lyrics of the romantic song. It is interesting to compare Ricky, the would-be comedian forced by his partner/wife to be the straight man, to George, the 'straight man' who always gets the final, controlling laugh.

That Ricky can be so constantly upstaged and so readily disobeyed is not insignificant, for with his Cuban accent (constantly mimicked by Lucy), he does not fully possess language, and is not properly symbolic as is George, the joker or wielder of authoritatively funny speech. The programme's reliance on physical rather than verbal comedy, with Lucy and Ethel as the lead performers, constitutes another exclusion of Ricky. Unlike George, Ricky is not given equal, let alone superior, time. He constantly leaves the story, and his departure becomes the cue for comic mayhem and audience pleasure. Although he is 'tall, dark, and handsome', not the usual slapstick type, his representation as the Latin lover/bandleader/crooner and slapstick foil for Lucy's pies in the face suggests that Lucy's resistance to patriarchy might be more palatable because it is mediated by a racism which views Ricky as inferior.

In 'Vacation from Marriage', the underside of situation comedy's reiteration of the same is briefly revealed. Lucy, with Ethel in the kitchen, is talking about the boredom and routine of marriage. 'It isn't funny, Ethel, it's tragic.' The rest of this show and the series make marriage funny and adventurous. Week after week, the show keeps Lucy happily in her confined, domestic, sitcom place after a 23-minute *tour-de-force* struggle to escape. That neither audiences nor critics noticed Lucy's feminist strain is curious, suggesting that comedy is a powerful and unexamined weapon of subjugation. In most of the programmes' endings, the narrative policy was one of twofold containment: every week for seven years, she was wrong and duly apologetic; and while repeating discontent, her masquerades and escapades made Monday nights and marriage pleasurable. Allen, on the same network, untied legal language and the power polarities implicit in its command; Ball took over the male domain of physical comedy. Both unmade 'meaning' and overturned patriarchal assumptions, stealing the show in the process; yet neither escaped confinement and the tolerance of kindly fathers. 'That's entertainment!'— for women a massive yet benevolent containment.

III   As theorists of historiography have argued, discourses of 'truth' and the 'real' move through a cause–effect, narrative chronology to a resolute closure without gaps or discontinuities. There is something at stake in this strategy, and it is related to power and authority. Narrative embodies a political determinism in which women find a subordinate place. But narrative in situation comedy is only the merest overlay, perhaps an excuse. As George Burns said, 'more plot than a variety show and not as much as a wrestling match'. This implausible, sparse 'situation' exemplifies—in its obsessive repetition of the domestic regime, of marital bliss as crazy 'scenes' and competitive squabbles—a social plaint if not a politics.

Situation comedy, with 'gaps' of performance and discontinuities, *uses* narrative offhandedly. The hermeneutic code is not replete with expectation, not in need of decipherment, not ensnaring us or lying to us. Expectation of pleasurable performance—the workings of the comic and humour—rather than narrative suspense are currencies of audience exchange. Perhaps this system might challenge 'narrative's relation to a legal system';[10] certainly narrative is not viewed as sacred or authoritative any more than husbands are. It is necessary but not equal to performance. In trying to determine how comedy works to contain women and how successfully it does so, theories of narrative will thus be of little help to us. It is necessary to turn to theories of the comic and humour.

10 Hayden White, 'The Value of Narrativity in the Representation of Reality', *Critical Inquiry*, 7/1 (1980), 10.

I will hesitantly begin an inquiry into the consequences of Freud's assessment of the comic and humour in situations where both subject and object are women. In his study of jokes, particularly tendentious or obscene jokes, Freud assigns woman to the place of object between two male subjects. However, there must be a difference, perhaps an impossibility, when 'woman' becomes the joke-teller. Also, given that the process between spectator/auditor and joker is, according to Freud, a mutually timed, momentary slippage into the unconscious, one wonders what occurs when that 'unconscious' is labelled 'female'—without essentialist or biological simplifications, but with historical and cultural difference in mind. Yet, while the 'joke' comprises the majority of Freud's study, and while the joke is for Freud a more complicated process than is the comic, its structure is not applicable to the structure of either of these television series (with the crucial exception of the role of George Burns, for whom Freudian joke analysis works perfectly), possibly because the joke *is* such a strong male preserve.

Unlike the three-way dealings of jokes, the comic, for Freud, is a two-way process; it is not gender-defined, and it derives from the relations of human beings 'to the often over-powerful external world'.[11] We experience a pleasurable empathy with the person who is pitted against this harsh world, whereas if we were actually in the situation, 'we should be conscious only of distressing feelings'.[12] We laugh at Lucy's comic moments, yet I wonder whether women might not also have experienced a certain amount of distress, particularly given the constraints of the 1950s and the constant subtle and not-so-subtle attempts to confine women to the home. Freud notes that 'persons become comic as a result of human dependence on external events, particularly on social factors'.[13] Lucy is caught in her economic subservience to Ricky, as well as in the social mores of the fifties, a decade which covertly tried to reduce women to the status of dependent children. Lucy and Gracie are continually referred to as children; the women are 'helpless' or economically dependent on males—particularly Lucy and Ethel, who do not have jobs as Gracie does. Thus it is interesting to note that what Freud calls the 'comic of situation is mostly based on embarrassments in which we rediscover the child's helplessness'[14] (one thinks perhaps of Lucy's exaggerated crying when she is frustrated or thwarted in her desires). Moreover, just as one rediscovers the helplessness of children in the comic of situation, so too the pleasure that it affords is compared by Freud to a child's pleasure in repetition of the same story. Situation comedy endlessly repeats *mise-en-scène*, character, and story; this pleasure, like the pleasure derived from *most* television, must depend to a degree on weekly forgetting as well as on repetition of the intimately familiar. Freud concludes his meandering thoughts on the comic and its infantile sources: 'I am unable to decide whether degradation to being a child is only a special case of comic degradation, or whether everything comic is based fundamentally on degradation to being a child.'[15]

11 Sigmund Freud, *Jokes and Their Relation to the Unconscious*, trans. James Strachey (New York: Norton & Co., 1960), 196.

12 Ibid. 197.

13 Ibid. 199.

14 Ibid. 226.

15 Ibid. 227.

'Degradation' is the crucial word here. Featuring the perennially disobedient and rebelliously inventive child, *I Love Lucy* hovers somewhere between the comic of situation and what Freud calls the 'comic of movement'; or better, the 'situation' (the external world) is the problem which necessitates the comic of movement of which Lucy is the master.

An appendage ten pages before the end of *Jokes and Their Relation to the Unconscious*, and a later, brief essay by Freud entitled 'Humour', are especially interesting for our purposes. Freud's analysis of 'humour'—epitomized by 'gallows jokes', the clever, exalted diversions of the condemned victim just before the hanging—as a category distinct from either the joke or the comic better explains the female victim (both subject and object, both performer and spectator), her place in the internal and external conditions of *Lucy*'s production. Endlessly repeating that she wanted to work, to perform, humour for Lucy was 'a means of obtaining pleasure in spite of the distressing affects that interfere[d] with it'. It acted precisely 'as a substitute' for these affects.[16] Humour was 'a substitute' produced 'at the cost of anger—instead of getting angry.'[17] As Freud observes, 'the person who is the victim of the injury, pain . . . might obtain *humorous* pleasure, while the unconcerned person laughs from *comic* pleasure.'[18] Perhaps, in relation to husband and wife sketches, and audiences, the sexes split right down the middle, alternating comic with humorous pleasure depending on one's view of who the victim is; this invocation of different pleasures suggests a complexity of shifting identifications amidst gendered, historical audiences.

Trying to revive Lucy for feminism, I have suggested that throughout the overall series, and in the narrative structure of each episode, she is the victim—confined to domesticity and outward compliance with patriarchy. Yet this series is complex; Ricky is often the immediate victim of Lucy, a role more easily accepted due to his Cuban rather than Anglo-Saxon heritage. Given this perhaps crucial qualification, Lucy is, finally, rebelliously incarcerated within situation comedy's domestic regime and *mise-en-scène*, acutely frustrated, trying to escape via the 'comic of movement', while cheerfully cracking jokes along the way to her own unmasking or capture.

Importantly, humorous pleasure for Freud comes from 'an economy in expenditure upon feeling' rather than from the lifting of inhibitions that is the source of pleasure in jokes—not a slight distinction. Unlike the supposedly 'liberating' function of jokes, humorous pleasure 'saves' feeling because the reality of the situation is too painful. As Lucy poignantly declared to Ethel, 'It's not funny, Ethel. It's tragic.' Or as Freud states, 'the situation is dominated by the emotion that is to be avoided, which is of an unpleasurable character'. In *I Love Lucy*, the avoided emotion 'submitted to the control of humour'[19] is anger at the weekly frustration of Lucy's desire to escape the confinement of domesticity. This desire is caricatured by her unrealistic dreams of instant stardom in the face of her narrative lack of talent: her

16 Sigmund Freud, *Jokes and Their Relation to the Unconscious*, trans. James Strachey (New York: Norton & Co., 1960), 228.

17 Ibid. 231.

18 Ibid. 228.

19 Ibid. 235.

wretched, off-key singing, her mugging facial exaggerations, and her out-of-step dancing. Her lack of talent is paradoxically both the source of the audience's pleasure and the narrative necessity for housewifery. Using strategies of humorous displacement (the 'highest of defensive processes', says Freud—a phrase that takes on interesting connotations in light of 1950s containment policies) and of the comic, both of which are 'impossible under the glare of conscious attention',[20] situation comedy avoids the unpleasant effects of its own situations. The situation of Lucy was replicated by the female spectator—whether working as a wife or in another 'job'—moving between comic and humorous pleasure, between spectator and victim, in tandem with Lucy.

In this later essay, Freud elevates humour to a noble, heroic status:

> [Humour] is fine . . . elevating . . . the triumph of narcissism, the ego's victorious assertion of its own invulnerability. It refuses to be hurt . . . or to be compelled to suffer. It insists that it is impervious to wounds dealt by the outside world, in fact that these are merely occasions for affording it pleasure. Humour is not resigned, it is rebellious. It signifies the triumph of not only the ego but the pleasure principle . . . it [repudiates] the possibility of suffering . . . all without quitting the ground of mental sanity . . . it is a rare and precious gift.[21]

For Lucy, Gracie, and their audiences, humour was 'a rare and precious gift'. Given the repressive conditions of the 1950s, humour might have been women's weapon and tactic of survival, ensuring sanity, the triumph of the ego, and pleasure; after all, Gracie and Lucy were narcissistically rebellious, refusing 'to be hurt'. On the other hand, comedy replaced anger, if not rage, with pleasure. The double bind of the female spectator, and of the female performer, is replicated in the structure of the programmes—the shifts between narrative and comic spectacle, the latter being contained within the resolute closure of the former—and the response of the spectator is split between comic and humorous pleasure, between denial of emotion by humour and the sheer pleasure of laughter provided by the comic of movement and situation of Lucy's performances. Whether heroic or not, this pleasure/provoking cover-up/acknowledgement is not a laughing but a complex matter, posing the difficult problems of women's simulated liberation through comic containment.

20 Ibid. 233.

21 Sigmund Freud, 'Humour', *The Standard Edition of the Complete Psychological Works of Sigmund Freud*, xxi (London: Hogarth Press, 1964), 162–3.

5

Roseanne: Unruly Woman as Domestic Goddess

Kathleen K. Rowe

Sometime after I was born in Salt Lake City, Utah, all the little babies were sleeping soundly in the nursery except for me, who would scream at the top of my lungs, trying to shove my whole fist into my mouth, wearing all the skin off on the end of my nose. I was put in a tiny restraining jacket.... My mother is fond of this story because to her it illustrates what she regards as my gargantuan appetites and excess anger. I think I was probably just bored.

Roseanne: My Life As A Woman[1]

QUESTIONS ABOUT TELEVISION celebrities often centre on a comparison with cinematic stars—on whether television turns celebrities into what various critics have called 'degenerate symbols' who are 'slouching toward stardom' and engaging in 'dialogues of the living dead'.[2] This chapter examines Roseanne Barr, a television celebrity who has not only slouched but whined, wisecracked, munched, mooned, and sprawled her way to a curious and contradictory status in our culture explained only partially by the concept of stardom, either televisual or cinematic. Indeed, the metaphor of decay such critics invoke, while consistent with a strain of the grotesque associated with Barr, seems inappropriate to her equally compelling vitality and *jouissance*. In this study I shall be using the name 'Roseanne' to refer to Roseanne Barr-as-sign, a person we know only through her various roles and performances in the popular discourse. My use follows Barr's lead in effacing the lines among her roles: Her show, after all, bears her name and in interviews she describes her 'act' as 'who she is'.

Nearing the end of its second season, her sitcom securely replaced *The Cosby Show* at the top of the ratings. The readers of *People Weekly* identified her as their favourite female television star and she took similar prizes in the People's Choice award show this spring. Yet 'Roseanne', both person and show, has been snubbed by the Emmies, condescended to by media critics, and trashed by the tabloids (never mind the establishment press). Consider *Esquire*'s solution of how to contain Roseanne. In an issue on its favourite

© OUP, 1990.

Originally published in *Screen*, 31/4 (Winter 1990), 408–19.

1 Roseanne Barr, *Roseanne: My Life as a Woman* (New York: Harper and Row, 1989), 3.

2 The phrase 'slouching towards stardom' is Jeremy Butler's.

(and least favourite) women, it ran two stories by two men, side by side—one called 'Roseanne—Yay', the other 'Roseanne—Nay'. And consider this from *Star*: 'ROSEANNE'S SHOTGUN "WEDDING FROM HELL" '—'Dad refuses to give pregnant bride away—"Don't wed that druggie bum!" '; 'Maids of honor are lesbians—best man is groom's detox pal'; 'Ex-hubby makes last-ditch bid to block ceremony'; 'Rosie and Tom wolf two out of three tiers of wedding cake' (6 Feb. 1990). Granted that tabloids are *about* excess, there's often an edge of cruelty to that excess in Roseanne's case, and an effort to wrest her definition of herself from the comic to the melodramatic.

Such ambivalence is the product of several phenomena. Richard Dyer might explain it in terms of the ideological contradictions Roseanne plays upon—how, for example, the body of Roseanne-as-star magically reconciles the conflict women experience in a society that says 'consume' but look as if you don't. Janet Woollacott might discuss the clash of discourses inherent in situation comedy—how our pleasure in Roseanne's show arises not so much from narrative suspense about her actions as hero, nor from her one-liners, but from the economy or wit by which the show brings together two discourses on family life: one based on traditional liberalism and the other on feminism and social class. Patricia Mellencamp might apply Freud's analysis of wit to Roseanne as she did to Lucille Ball and Gracie Allen, suggesting that Roseanne ventures farther than her comic foremothers into the masculine terrain of the tendentious joke.[3]

All of these explanations would be apt, but none would fully explain the ambivalence surrounding Roseanne. Such an explanation demands a closer look at gender and at the historical representations of female figures similar to Roseanne. These figures, I believe, can be found in the tradition of the 'unruly woman', a topos of female outrageousness and transgression from literary and social history. Roseanne uses a 'semiotics of the unruly' to expose the gap she sees between the ideals of the New Left and the Women's Movement of the late 60s and early 70s on the one hand, and the realities of working-class family life two decades later on the other.

Because female unruliness carries a strongly ambivalent charge, Roseanne's use of it both intensifies and undermines her popularity. Perhaps her greatest unruliness lies in the presentation of herself as *author* rather than actor and, indeed, as author of a self over which she claims control. Her insistence on her 'authority' to create and control the meaning of *Roseanne* is an unruly act *par excellence*, triggering derision or dismissal much like Jane Fonda's earlier attempts to 'write' her self (but in the genre of melodrama rather than comedy). I will explain this in three parts: the first takes a brief look at the tradition of the unruly woman; the second, at the unruly qualities of *excess* and *looseness* Roseanne embodies; and the third, at an episode of her sitcom which dramatizes the conflict between female unruliness and the ideology of 'true womanhood'.

3 Janet Woollacott, 'Fictions and Ideologies: The Case of the Situation Comedy', in Tony Bennett, Colin Mercer, and Janet Woollacott, *Popular Culture and Social Relations* (Philadelphia: Open Univ. Press, 1986), 196–218; Patricia Mellencamp, 'Situation Comedy, Feminism, and Freud', in Tania Modleski (ed.), *Studies in Entertainment* (Bloomington: Indiana Univ. Press, 1986), 80–95 (Ch. 4 in this volume).

The Unruly Woman

The unruly woman is often associated with sexual inversion—'the woman on top', according to social historian Natalie Zemon Davis, who fifteen years ago first identified her in her book *Society and Culture in Early Modern France*. The sexual inversion she represents, Davis writes, is less about gender confusion than about larger issues of social and political order that come into play when what belongs 'below' (either women themselves, or their images appropriated by men in drag) usurps the position of what belongs 'above'. This topos isn't limited to Early Modern Europe, but reverberates whenever women, especially women's bodies, are considered excessive—too fat, too mouthy, too old, too dirty, too pregnant, too sexual (or not sexual enough) for the norms of conventional gender representation. For women, excessive fatness carries associations with excessive wilfulness and excessive speech ('fat texts', as Patricia Parker explains in *Literary Fat Ladies*, a study of rhetoric, gender, and property that traces literary examples of this connection from the Old Testament to the twentieth century).[4] Through body and speech, the unruly woman violates the unspoken feminine sanction against 'making a spectacle' of herself. I see the unruly woman as prototype of woman as subject—transgressive above all when she lays claim to her own desire.

The unruly woman is multivalent, her social power unclear. She has reinforced traditional structures, as Natalie Davis acknowledges.[5] But she has also helped sanction political disobedience for men and women alike by making such disobedience thinkable. She can signify the radical utopianism of undoing all hierarchy. She can also signify pollution (dirt or 'matter out of place', as Mary Douglas might explain). As such she becomes a source of danger for threatening the conceptual categories which organize our lives. For these reasons—for the power she derives from her liminality, her associations with boundaries and taboo—she evokes not only delight but disgust and fear. Her ambivalence, which is the source of her oppositional power, is usually contained within the licence accorded to the comic and the carnivalesque. But not always.

The unruly woman has gossiped and cackled in the margins of history for millennia, from Sarah of the Old Testament who laughed at God (and figures in Roseanne's tribute to her grandmother in her autobiography), to the obstinate and garrulous Mrs Noah of the medieval Miracle Plays (who would not board the Ark until she was good and ready), to the folk figure 'Mère Folle' and the subject of Erasmus' *The Praise of Folly*. Her more recent incarnations include such figures as the screwball heroine of the 1930s film, Miss Piggy, and a pantheon of current female grotesques and sacred monsters: Tammy Faye Bakker, Leona Helmsley, Imelda Marcos, and Zsa Zsa Gabor. The media discourse around these women reveals the same mixed bag of emotions I see attached to Roseanne, the same cruelty and tendency to carnivalize by pushing them into parodies of melodrama, a genre which, unlike much comedy, punishes the unruly woman for asserting her desire. Such

---

4 Patricia Parker, *Literary Fat Ladies: Rhetoric, Gender, Property* (New York: Methuen, 1987).

5 Natalie Zemon Davis, *Society and Culture in Early Modern France* (Stanford: Stanford Univ. Press, 1975), 124–51.

parodies of melodrama make the unruly woman the target of *our* laughter, while denying her the power and pleasure of her own.

The disruptive power of these women—carnivalesque and carnivalized—contains much potential for feminist appropriation. Such an appropriation could enable us to problematize two areas critical to feminist theories of spectatorship and the subject: the social and cultural norms of femininity, and our understanding of how we are constructed as gendered subjects in the language of spectacle and the visual. In her essay 'Female Grotesques', Mary Russo asks: 'In what sense can women really produce or make spectacles out of themselves? . . . The figure of female transgressor as public spectacle is still powerfully resonant, and the possibilities of redeploying this representation as a demystifying or utopian model have not been exhausted.'[6] She suggests that the parodic excesses of the unruly woman and the comic conventions surrounding her provide a space to act out the dilemmas of femininity, to *make visible* and *laughable* what Mary Ann Doane describes as the 'tropes of femininity'.

Such a sense of spectacle differs from Laura Mulvey's. It accepts the relation between power and visual pleasure but argues for an understanding of that relation as more historically determined, its terms more mutable. More Foucaldian than Freudian, it suggests that visual power flows in multiple directions and that the position of spectacle isn't entirely one of weakness. Because public power is predicated largely on visibility, men have traditionally understood the need to secure their power not only by looking but by being seen—or rather, by fashioning, as author, a spectacle of themselves. Already bound in a web of visual power, women might begin to renegotiate its terms. Such a move would be similar to what Teresa de Lauretis advocates when she calls for the strategic use of narrative to 'construct other forms of coherence, to shift the terms of representation, to produce the conditions of representability of another—and gendered—social subject'.[7] By returning the male gaze, we might expose (make a spectacle of) the gazer. And by utilizing the power already invested in us as image, we might begin to negate our own 'invisibility' in the public sphere.

Roseanne as Spectacle

The spectacle Roseanne creates is *for* herself, produced *by* herself from a consciously developed perspective on ethnicity, gender, and social class. This spectacle derives much of its power from her construction of it as her 'self'—an entity which, in turn, she has knowingly fashioned through interviews, public performances, and perhaps most unambiguously her autobiography. This book, by its very existence, enhances the potency of Roseanne-as-sign because it grants a historicity to her 'self' and a materiality to her claims for authorship. The autobiography describes key moments in the development of 'Roseanne'—how she learned about female strength when for the first time in her life she saw a woman (her grandmother) stand up to a man, her

---

6 Mary Russo, 'Female Grotesques', in Teresa de Lauretis (ed.), *Feminist Studies, Critical Studies* (Bloomington: Indiana Univ. Press, 1986), 217.

7 Teresa de Lauretis, *Technologies of Gender* (Bloomington: Indiana Univ. Press, 1987), 109.

father; how she learned about marginality and fear from her childhood as a Jew in Utah under the shadow of the Holocaust, and from her own experience of madness and institutionalization. Madness is a leitmotif both in her autobiography and in the tabloid talk about her.[8] Roseanne's eventual discovery of feminism and counter-culture politics led to disillusionment when the women's movement was taken over by women unlike her, 'handpicked', she writes, to be acceptable to the establishment.

Coexisting with the pain of her childhood and early adulthood was a love of laughter, the bizarre, a good joke. She always wanted to be a writer, not an actor. Performance, however, was the only 'place' where she felt safe. And because, since her childhood, she could always say what she wanted to as long as it was funny, *comic* performance allowed her to be a writer, to 'write' herself. While her decision to be a comedian was hampered by a difficulty in finding a female tradition in which to locate her own voice, she discovered her stance (or 'attitude') when she realized that she could take up the issue of female oppression by adopting its language. Helen Andelin's *Fascinating Womanhood* (1974) was one of the most popular manuals of femininity for the women of her mother's generation. It taught women to manipulate men by becoming 'domestic goddesses'. Yet, Roseanne discovered, such terms might also be used for 'self-definition, rebellion, truth-telling', for telling a truth that in her case is both ironic and affirmative. And so she built her act and her success on an exposure of the 'tropes of femininity' (the ideology of 'true womanhood', the perfect wife and mother) by cultivating the opposite (an image of the unruly woman).

Roseanne's disruptiveness is more clearly paradigmatic than syntagmatic, less visible in the stories her series dramatizes than in the image cultivated around her body: Roseanne-the-person who tattooed her buttocks and mooned her fans, Roseanne-the-character for whom farting and nose-picking are as much a reality as dirty dishes and obnoxious boy bosses. Both in body and speech, Roseanne is defined by *excess* and by *looseness*—qualities that mark her in opposition to bourgeois and feminine standards of decorum.

Of all of Roseanne's excesses, none seems more potent than her weight. Indeed, the very appearance of a 200-plus-pound woman in a weekly prime-time sitcom is significant in itself. Her body epitomizes the grotesque body of Bakhtin, the body which exaggerates its processes, its bulges and orifices, rather than concealing them as the monumental, static 'classical' or 'bourgeois' body does. Implicit in Bakhtin's analysis is the privileging of the female body—above all the *maternal* body which, through pregnancy and childbirth, participates uniquely in the carnivalesque drama of inside-out and outside-in, death-in-life and life-in-death. Roseanne's affinity with the grotesque body is evident in the first paragraph of *Roseanne: My Life as a Woman*, where her description of her 'gargantuan appetites' even as a newborn brings to mind Bakhtin's study of Rabelais.[9] Roseanne compounds her

---

8 For example 'Roseanne goes nuts!', in the *Enquirer*, 9 Apr. 1989, and 'My insane year', in *People Weekly*, 9 Oct. 1989: 85–6. Like other labels of deviancy, madness is often attached to the unruly woman.

9 Mikhail Bakhtin, *Rabelais and His World*, trans. Helene Iswolsky (Bloomington: Indiana Univ. Press, 1984).

fatness with a 'looseness' of body language and speech—she sprawls, slouches, flops on furniture. Her speech—even apart from its content—is loose (in its 'sloppy' enunciation and grammar) and excessive (in tone and volume). She laughs loudly, screams shrilly, and speaks in a nasal whine.

In our culture, both fatness and looseness are violations of codes of feminine posture and behaviour. Women of 'ill-repute' are described as loose, their bodies, especially their sexuality, seen as out of control. Fatness, of course, is an especially significant issue for women, and perhaps patriarchy nowhere inscribes itself more insidiously and viciously on female bodies than in the cult of thinness. Fat females are stigmatized as unfeminine, rebellious, and sexually deviant (under or over-sexed). Women who are too fat or move too loosely appropriate too much space, and femininity is gauged by how little space women take up.[10] It is also gauged by the intrusiveness of women's utterances. As Henley notes, voices in any culture that are not meant to be heard are perceived as loud when they do speak, regardless of their decibel level ('shrill' feminists, for example). Farting, belching, and nose-picking likewise betray a failure to restrain the body. Such 'extreme looseness of body-focused functions' is generally not available to women as an avenue of revolt but, as Nancy Henley suggests, 'if it should ever come into women's repertoire, it will carry great power'.[11]

Expanding that repertoire is entirely consistent with Roseanne's professed mission.[12] She writes of wanting 'to break every social norm . . . and see that it is laughed at. I chuckle with glee if I know I have offended someone, because the people I intend to insult offend me horribly.'[13] In an interview in *People Weekly*, Roseanne describes how Matt Williams, a former producer on her show, tried to get her fired: 'He compiled a list of every offensive thing I did. And I do offensive things. . . . *That's who I am. That's my act.* So Matt was in his office making a list of how gross I was, how many times I farted and belched—taking it to the network to show I was out of control' (my emphasis). Of course she was out of control—*his* control. He wanted to base the show on castration jokes, she says, recasting it from the point of view of the little boy. She wanted something else—something different from what she sees as the norm of television: a 'male point of view coming out of women's mouths . . . particularly around families'.[14]

Roseanne's ease with her body, signified by her looseness, triggers much of the *unease* surrounding her. Such ease reveals what Pierre Bourdieu describes as 'a sort of indifference to the objectifying gaze of others which neutralizes its powers' and 'appropriates its appropriation'.[15] It marks

10 Nancy M. Henley, *Body Politics: Power, Sex and Non-verbal Communication* (Englewood Cliffs: Prentice-Hall, 1977), 38.

11 Ibid. 91.

12 In 'What am I anyway, a Zoo?', *New York Times*, 31 July 1989, she enumerates the ways people have interpreted what she stands for—the regular housewife, the mother, the postfeminist, the 'Little Guy', fat people, the 'Queen of Tabloid America', 'the body politic', sex, 'angry womankind herself', 'the notorious and sensationalistic La Luna madness of an ovulating Abzugienne woman run wild', etc.

13 *Roseanne*, 51.

14 *People Weekly*, 85–6.

15 Pierre Bourdieu, *Distinction: A Social Critique of the Judgement of Taste*, trans. Richard Nice (Cambridge, Mass.: Harvard Univ. Press, 1984), 208.

Roseanne's rebellion against not only the codes of gender but of class, for ease with one's body is the prerogative of the upper classes. For the working classes, the body is more likely to be a source of embarrassment, timidity, and alienation, because the norms of the 'legitimate' body—beauty, fitness, and so on—are accepted across class boundaries while the ability to achieve them is not. In a culture which defines nature negatively as 'sloppiness', physical beauty bears value that is not only aesthetic but moral, reinforcing a sense of superiority in those who put some effort into enhancing their 'natural' beauty (p. 206).

Roseanne's indifference to conventional readings of her body exposes the ideology underlying those readings. Concerning her fatness, she resists the culture's efforts to define and judge her by her weight. Publicly celebrating the libidinal pleasure of food, she argues that women need to take up more space in the world, not less. And her comments about menstruation similarly attack the 'legitimate' female body, which does not menstruate in public. On an award show she announced that she had 'cramps that could kill a horse'. She startled Oprah Winfrey on her talk show by describing the special pleasure she took from the fact that she and her sister were 'on their period'— unclean, according to Orthodox law—when they were allowed to bear their grandmother's coffin. And in her autobiography she writes about putting a woman (her) in the White House: 'My campaign motto will be "Let's vote for Rosie and put some new blood in the White House—every 28 days" ' (p. 117). Rather than accepting the barrage of ads that tell women they can never be young, thin, or beautiful enough and that their houses—an extension of their bodies—can never be immaculate enough, she rejects the 'pollution taboos' that foster silence, shame, and self-hatred in women by urging them to keep their genitals, like their kitchen appliances, deodorized, antisepticized, and 'April fresh'. Instead she reveals the social causes of female fatness, irritability, and messiness in the strains of working-class family life, where junk food late at night may be a sensible choice for comfort after a day punching out plastic forks on an assembly line.

Demonic Desires

Roseanne sleepwalks to her long-awaited bath

The episode I'm going to talk about (7 November 1989) is in some ways atypical because of its stylistic excess and reflexivity. Yet I've chosen it because it so clearly defines female unruliness and its opposite, the ideology of the self-sacrificing wife and mother. It does so by drawing on and juxtaposing three styles: a realist sitcom style for the arena of ideology in the world of the working-class wife and mother; a surreal dream sequence for female unruliness; and a musical sequence within the dream to reconcile the 'real' with the unruly. Dream sequences invariably signal the eruption of unconscious desire. In this episode, the dream is linked clearly with the eruption of *female* desire, the defining mark of the unruly woman.

The episode begins as the show does every week, in the normal world of broken plumbing, incessant demands, job troubles. Roseanne wants ten minutes alone in a hot bath after what she describes as 'the worst week in her life' (she just quit her job at the Wellman factory). But between her husband Dan and her kids, she can't get into the bathroom. She falls asleep while she's

Flanked by the 'pec twins' and in a glamorous hairdo and robe, Roseanne flaunts her new power

Roseanne takes aim at her son D. J. before zapping him with a replica of his own toy ray gun

The pec twins prepare to boil husband Dan in a pot of creamed corn

Crystal, the perfect lady, testifies against Roseanne and praises Dan's sweaty masculine allure

'Sing? I can't sing'

'We love Roseanne'

waiting. At this point all the marks of the sitcom disappear. The music and lighting signal 'dream'. Roseanne walks into her bathroom, but it's been transformed into an opulent, Romanesque pleasure spa where she is pampered by two bare-chested male attendants ('the pec twins', as Dan later calls them). She's become a glamorous redhead.

Even within this dream, however, she's haunted by her family and the institution that stands most firmly behind it—the law. One by one, her family appears and continues to nag her for attention and interfere with her bath. And one by one, without hesitation, she kills them off with tidy and appropriate means. (In one instance, she twitches her nose before working her magic, alluding to the unruly women of the late 60s/early 70s sitcom *Bewitched*.) Revenge and revenge fantasies are of course a staple in the feminist imagination (Marleen Gorris's *A Question of Silence* (1982), Nelly Kaplan's *A Very Curious Girl* (1969), Cecilia Condit's *Possibly in Michigan* (1985), Karen Arthur's *Lady Beware* (1987)). In this case, however, Roseanne doesn't murder for revenge but for a bath.

Roseanne's unruliness is further challenged, ideology reasserts itself, and the dream threatens to become a nightmare when she is arrested for murder and brought to court. Her family really *isn't* dead, and with her friends they testify against her, implying that because of her shortcomings as a wife and mother she's been murdering them all along. Her friend Crystal says: 'She's loud, she's bossy, she talks with her mouth full. She feeds her kids frozen fish sticks and high calorie sodas. She doesn't have proper grooming habits.' And she doesn't treat her husband right even though, as Roseanne explains, 'The only way to keep a man happy is to treat him like dirt once in a while.' The trial, like the dream itself, dramatizes a struggle over interpretation of the frame story that preceded it: the court judges her desire for the bath as narcissistic and hedonistic, and her barely suppressed frustration as murderous. Such desires are taboo for good self-sacrificing mothers. For Roseanne, the bath (and the 'murders' it *requires)* are quite pleasurable for reasons both sensuous and righteous. Everyone gets what they deserve. Coincidentally, ABC was running ads during this episode for the docudrama *Small Sacrifices* (12–14 November 1989), about a real mother, Diane Downs, who murdered one of her children.

Barely into the trial, it becomes apparent that Roseanne severely strains the court's power to impose its order on her. The rigid oppositions it tries to enforce begin to blur, and alliances shift. Roseanne defends her kids when the judge—Judge Wapner from *People's Court*—yells at them. Roseanne, defended by her sister, turns the tables on the kids and they repent for the pain they've caused her. With Dan's abrupt change from prosecutor to crooner and character witness, the courtroom becomes the stage for a musical. He breaks into song, and soon the judge, jury, and entire cast are dancing and singing Roseanne's praises in a bizarre production number. Female desire *isn't* monstrous; acting on it 'ain't misbehavin'', her friend Vanda sings. This celebration of Roseanne in effect vindicates her, although the judge remains unconvinced, finding her not only guilty but in contempt of court. Dreamwork done, she awakens, the sound of the judge's gavel becoming Dan's hammer on the plumbing. Dan's job is over too, but the kids still want her attention. Dan jokes that there's no place like home but Roseanne

Roseanne basks in adoration, the star of the show

The plumbing now fixed, Roseanne's dream comes to an end

'Oh no, you're alive'

answers 'Bull'. On her way, at last, to her bath, she closes the door to the bath-room to the strains of the chorus singing 'We Love Roseanne'.

The requirements for bringing this fantasy to an end are important. First, what ultimately satisfies Roseanne isn't an escape from her family but an acknowledgement from them of *her* needs and an expression of their feeling for her—'We love you, Roseanne'. I am not suggesting that Roseanne's series miraculously transcends the limitations of prime-time television. To a cer-tain degree this ending does represent a sentimental co-opting of her power, a shift from the potentially radical to the liberal. But it also indicates a refusal to flatten contradictions. Much of Roseanne's appeal lies in the delicate bal-ance she maintains between individual and institution and in the impersonal nature of her anger and humour, which are targeted not so much at the peo-ple she lives with as at what makes them the way they are. What Roseanne *really* murders here is the ideology of 'perfect wife and mother', which she reveals to be murderous in itself.

The structuring—and limits—of Roseanne's vindication are also important. Although the law is made ludicrous, it retains its power and remains ultimately indifferent and immovable. Roseanne's 'contempt' seems her greatest crime. More important, whatever vindication Roseanne does enjoy can happen only within a dream. It cannot be sustained in real life. The realism of the frame story inevitably reasserts itself. And even within the dream, the reconciliation between unruly fantasy and ideology can be brought about only deploying the heavy artillery of the musical and its conventions. As Rick Altman has shown, few forms embody the utopian impulse of popular culture more insistently than the musical, and within musicals, contradictions difficult to resolve other-wise are acted out in production numbers. That is what happens here. The pro-duction number gives a fleeting resolution to the problem Roseanne typically plays with: representing the unrepresentable. A fat woman who is also sexual; a sloppy housewife who's a good mother; a 'loose' woman who is also tidy, who hates matrimony but loves her husband, who hates the ideology of 'true womanhood' yet considers herself a domestic goddess.

There is much more to be said about Roseanne and the unruly woman: about her fights to maintain authorial control over (and credit for) her show; her use of the grotesque in the film *She Devil* (1989); her performance as a stand-up comic; the nature of her humour, which she calls 'funny woman-ness'; her identity as a Jew and the suppression of ethnicity in her series; the series' move toward melodrama and its treatment of social class. A more sweeping look at the unruly woman would find much of interest in the Hollywood screwball comedy as well as feminist avant-garde film and video. It would take up questions about the relation between gender, anger, and Medusan laughter—about the links Hélène Cixous establishes between laughing, writing, and the body and their implications for theories of female spectatorship. And while this article has emphasized the oppositional poten-tial of female unruliness, it is equally important to expose its misogynistic uses, as in, for example, the Fox sitcom *Married . . . With Children* (1988). Unlike Roseanne, who uses female unruliness to push at the limits of accept-able female behaviour, Peg inhabits the unruly woman stereotype with little distance, embodying the 'male point of view' Roseanne sees in so much tele-vision about family.

Roseanne points to alternatives. Just as 'domestic goddess' can become a term of self-definition and rebellion, so can spectacle-making—when used to seize the visibility that is, after all, a precondition for existence in the public sphere. The ambivalence I've tried to explain regarding Roseanne is evoked above all, perhaps, because she demonstrates how the enormous apparatus of televisual star-making can be put to such a use.

With thanks to Ellen Seiter for her helpful comments on an earlier draft of this article.

6

L.A. Law and Prime-Time Feminism

THE REFERENCE TO 'prime-time feminism' in my title might seem initially to be a contradiction in terms, or at the very least a tongue-in-cheek starting-point from which, if I were speaking from the vantage-point of 'authentic' feminism, I would be expected to demonstrate that prime-time 'feminism' is not feminism at all. I am not concerned here, however, with the authenticity of representations of feminism, but rather with the significance of the fact that increasingly, feminism is being appropriated by various mass cultural forms. At a time when the crazed demands of the most famous American villainess of 1987, Glenn Close's Alex in *Fatal Attraction*, evoke striking parallels with the feminist critique of male privilege, it is important for feminist critics to continue to examine and rethink the links between feminism and mass culture.[1] If the limitations of the 'progress' model—according to which feminist pressure on the media has resulted in 'better images' of women—are fairly self-evident, there remains none the less a cynicism on the part of many feminists about the ways in which feminism has been appropriated and assumed by, or otherwise grafted onto, mass cultural forms.

My concern in this study is with the relationship between feminism and television narrative in a series that has been praised widely for its engagement with issues of gender and sexual politics. The product of a collaboration between Terry Louise Fisher, formerly of *Cagney and Lacey*, and Steven Bochco, the co-creator of *Hill Street Blues*, *L.A. Law* began its regular run in 1986. There are, of course, other television programmes in which feminist questions have been raised, and still others that feminists have found more progressive and satisfying than *L.A. Law*, from *Golden Girls* with its focus on female bonding and ageing to *Cagney and Lacey*'s female—and occasionally feminist—heroics. *L.A. Law* is distinctly interesting for the feminist questions it raises, due in large part to how those questions are given narrative shape and definition within the particular format of the multi- and overlapping-narrative and ensemble cast structure. Put another way, *L.A. Law* represents feminism not only as a thematic issue, but also as a narrative one.

That *L.A. Law* is the successor to *Hill Street Blues* is fairly obvious, not only

© The Regents of the University of Wisconsin, 1988.

Originally published in *Discourse*, 10/2 (1988), 30–47.

1 The terms of this examination and rethinking have been developed most persuasively by Tania Modleski; see *Loving with a Vengeance: Mass-Produced Fantasies for Women* (1982; New York: Methuen, 1984).

through the Bochco connection, but also through *L.A. Law*'s position in the NBC Thursday night line-up in the spot previously held by *Hill Street Blues*. Like *Hill Street Blues*, as well as other MTM productions, including *The Mary Tyler Moore Show*, *L.A. Law* focuses on the surrogate family of the workplace, where a benevolent patriarch (Leland McKenzie in *L.A. Law*, corresponding to Lou Grant in *The Mary Tyler Moore Show* and Frank Furillo in *Hill Street Blues*) presides over a family of co-workers.[2] Now it is tempting to view *L.A. Law* as the upscale, yuppie revision of *Hill Street Blues*, with some significant changes—more women in *L.A. Law*, a more distinctly heterosocial environment (as opposed to the homosocial world of *Hill Street Blues*), and less 'messiness'—that is, *L.A. Law* is much cleaner, much more straightforward, and, despite its overlapping story-lines, much easier to follow than *Hill Street Blues*. While I do not disagree that *Hill Street Blues* was a more innovative programme, the very term 'innovation' can be misleading in television criticism since, as many critics have argued, television innovation has more to do with recombining other components of television programming than with inventing startling new forms.[3] Hence, *Hill Street Blues* was innovative to the extent that it combined elements of 'live' television, soap opera, and episodic comedy and drama.[4] *L.A. Law* may thus be innovative in a different way, for it takes the 'feminism' which previously had been associated with relatively one-dimensional formats (the cop show in *Cagney and Lacey*, the sitcom in *Golden Girls*) and combined it with the multi-narrative, large cast format associated with MTM productions like *Hill Street Blues* and *St Elsewhere*. But I would argue as well that the overlapping narrative structure of *L.A. Law* is qualitatively different from its predecessors, for in *L.A. Law* the very possibility of multiple narration is predicated on the terms of gender.

In the pilot for *L.A. Law*, one of the central story-lines focuses on the relationship between Michael Kuzak, a partner in the firm of McKenzie, Brackman, Chaney, and Kuzak, and Adrienne Moore (portrayed by Alfre Woodard), who appears in court to testify against a group of young men accused of gang-raping her and throwing her in a dumpster. Kuzak is the reluctant lawyer for one of the young men, the son of a wealthy client of the firm. Adrienne Moore suffers from leukaemia, a fact which gives the defence an opportunity to pursue a peculiarly twisted logic: since she has so little time left to live, she was undoubtedly on the prowl for some wild group sex with the young men. 'Gather ye rosebuds while you may, Miss Moore,' says the lawyer who questions her. Adrienne Moore's response is not only outrage, but failure to comprehend the lawyer's turn of phrase, and genuine perplexity as to why she cannot explain *her* side of the story. When the female judge says, 'I warn you,' Adrienne Moore responds furiously: 'I warn you—this door swings both ways,' and threatens to get a gun in order to take justice into her own hands. She is then cited for contempt and temporarily removed from the courtroom until she agrees to apologize.

The image of a door swinging both ways, here a function of helpless

2 See Jane Feuer, Paul Kerr, and Tise Vahimagi (eds.), *MTM: 'Quality Television'* (London: BFI, 1984).

3 See Todd Gitlin, *Inside Prime Time* (New York: Pantheon, 1983), esp. ch. 5 ('The Triumph of the Synthetic: Spinoffs, Copies, Recombinant Culture').

4 See Gitlin's discussion of *Hill Street Blues* in *Inside Prime Time*, ch. 14.

outrage, is particularly emblematic, not only of this particular story-line, but of the overall movement and development of *L.A. Law*. For in the pilot, Michael Kuzak's manipulation of a situation he finds repugnant is also very appropriately described as swinging a door both ways, but now in a way that allows for a more decisive articulation of justice. Kuzak is identified here as he will be throughout the series as the moral centre of *L.A. Law*, the lawyer who agonizes most over what is right and wrong, and whether the law can take the human factor sufficiently into account. Adrienne Moore, recognizing that there is not only no hope for justice, but no hope for her to tell *her* story in a court of law, makes the required apologies to the court, retakes the stand, and gives the defence an obvious opportunity to dismiss her testimony. As a result, Kuzak's client—a true stereotype of the obnoxious rich boy—goes free. Kuzak, however, gives a prosecution team member a tip that leads to his client's arrest on other charges, and eventually to his conviction on the rape charge. If the law is a narrative system—and *L.A. Law* emphasizes, again and again, that the law is first and foremost about story-telling and image-making—then the stories of the Adrienne Moores of this world are hopelessly fragmented and ineffective until they are retold by master narrators like Michael Kuzak, for whom doors that swing both ways are fundamental tools of the trade.

That Michael Kuzak is a white male, and Adrienne Moore a black female, suggests yet another way in which the image of a door swinging both ways is particularly appropriate to describe *L.A. Law*. After Kuzak's client has been sentenced to prison (where, as the senior partner of the firm later puts it to Kuzak, he will 'learn more about rape than you bargained for'), Kuzak extends an offer of friendship to Adrienne Moore. In the concluding scene of the pilot, the woman comes to Kuzak's office and confesses tearfully how afraid she is. The two embrace. Now this conclusion practically begs for a critical reading, for taken at face value, it presumes that offers of 'friendship', not to mention the narrative of the law, can transcend the boundaries of race, class, and gender. Such strains on ideological credulity are common in *L.A. Law*, but they are more significant for the multiple readings that they inspire than for their more obvious melodramatic or humanistic flourish. For depending upon your point of view, *L.A. Law* may be read as a 'realistic' portrayal and critique of lawyers and the practice of the law, or as a smug portrayal of an 'us–them' dichotomy with a liberal veneer. Accordingly, critical response to the series has varied widely, from praise for its satirical and critical presentation of lawyers, to dismissal of its idealized image of the law profession.[5]

L.A. Law is by no means the first prime-time series to capitalize on the door that swings both ways. From sitcoms like *All in the Family* to prime-time soaps like *Dallas*, television narrative has relied centrally on principles of multiple identification and of narrative structure in which there is a fine line, if any line at all, between irony and rhetoric, between critique and cele-

---

5 For typical examples of critical praise for the series, see Michele Kort, 'Terry Louise Fisher: How She Dreamed Up the Women of *L.A. Law*', *Ms.*, June 1987: 38, 42, 44; and Harry F. Waters with Janet Huck, 'Lust for Law', *Newsweek*, 16 Nov. 1987: 84–91. For negative criticism of the series, see Michael McWilliams, 'The Biggest Snow Job in Prime Time', *Village Voice*, 7 Oct. 1986: 45–6.

bration.[6] Indeed, one of the most distinctive characteristics of contemporary television narrative might well be the breaking down of familiar boundaries—between fiction and non-fiction, between transparency and self-reflexivity, between progressive and reactionary vantage-points.[7] What is particular to the narrative ambiguity of *L.A. Law* is its constant return, not only to issues of gender—which is not so uncommon in television narrative—but also to the ways these issues have been raised in feminist discourse.

For the door that swings both ways in the *L.A. Law* pilot is shaped by the opposition between a woman prevented from telling her story in a court of law, and a man who—despite his own vested interest in the practice of law—is not only capable of hearing what she has to say, but of turning the law around in her favour. Michael Kuzak is one of several sensitive male lawyers in the series who are located, in different ways, in an ambiguous space between objectivity and subjectivity, between the law as institutionalized objectivity and the more subjective considerations irreducible to the law. To be sure, Michael Kuzak's narrative and legal desires have to do with his own position as subject. But even if *his* story is no adequate substitute or replacement for *her* story, it none the less assigns her a vantage-point from which some satisfaction, some resolution, is possible. If this particular story-line is any indication, then *L.A. Law* can only tell *its* stories by acknowledging, however subtly or indirectly, that men and women occupy radically different positions *vis-à-vis* the law.

The figure of the door that swings both ways reappears in the first episode of *L.A. Law*'s 1987–8 season. Arnie Becker, the resident womanizer and divorce lawyer of the firm, meets with a male client being sued for divorce by his successful and wealthy wife, a television star. Becker describes his client as a man who gave up his own career as an athletic trainer in order to be a full-time homemaker. Thus, Becker attempts to convince his client to demand alimony, arguing that 'the feminist door swings both ways'. The obvious point is that what gains women have made in the name of feminism should be available for men to enjoy as well. In other words, unlike the story-line in the pilot, *this* door evokes the sameness of men and women before the law. According to this logic, feminism guarantees the equality, thereby dispelling the fear that women might—again in the name of feminism—usurp male privileges. And while the door that swings both ways in the series pilot engages with issues of difference—gender and sexual politics as well as race and class—the door that swings both ways at the beginning of *L.A. Law*'s second season is identified explicitly and exclusively as a *feminist* door. In identifying feminism as an explicit or implicit protagonist, as it has throughout its first two seasons, the narrative of *L.A. Law* shifts constantly between the two different swinging doors—the one suggestive of the radical difference between men and women *vis-à-vis* the law, and the other of the applicability of the law to men and women alike.

---

6 For a discussion of *All in the Family* that is relevant to this discussion, see Horace Newcomb, *TV: The Most Popular Art* (New York: Anchor Books, 1974), 221–5; and for an equally relevant discussion of *Dallas*, see Ien Ang, *Watching Dallas: Soap Opera and the Melodramatic Imagination* (New York: Methuen, 1985), esp. chs. 3 and 4.

7 See John Ellis, *Visible Fictions: Cinema: Television: Video* (London: Routledge & Kegan Paul, 1982); and Jane Feuer, 'Melodrama, Serial Form and Television Today', *Screen*, 25 (1984), 4–16.

The pre-credits sequence about the feminist door concludes when Arnold Becker, having asked his client for advice about weight training, removes his shirt so that the man can examine his pectorals. Roxanne Melman, Becker's secretary, enters the office unannounced and is suitably shocked at what she sees. The mention of feminism thus serves to inflect the strategies of narration in yet another way. Few characters on *L.A. Law* have given less indication than Arnold Becker of swinging both ways. While *L.A. Law* often romanticizes excessively about heterosexuality and male–female couples, a tentative but recurrent theme in the series is gay sexuality. Sometimes the theme is explicit, as in a story-line on AIDS, or a lesbian character who rejects Becker's advances, and sometimes it is implicit—the only character whose heterosexuality was not emphasized from the outset is Victor Sifuentes, provoking some viewers to ponder whether his earring was a wandering signifier of difference, or rather a more precise sign of sexual allegiance.[8] The evocation of gay sexuality in *L.A. Law* seems to me a fairly clear example—to quote the gay lawyer who confronts Grace Van Owen in the AIDS case—of 'wanting to have it both ways'. In other words, allusions to gay sexuality are flirtations with sexual difference that assure, rather than challenge, heterosexuality as norm. Yet such allusions also suggest a destabilization of that very norm. That feminism permits a gay joke in Arnie's encounter with his client is thus symptomatic of a fundamental narrative link between the two, as simultaneous lure and threat. The lesbian character and story-line, for example, appear in an episode which was designed and widely publicized as a response to women viewers who complained that Roxanne Melman's excessive devotion to Arnold Becker was offensive.[9] In the episode, Roxanne stands firm in her demands for a raise. Her refusal to be seduced by Arnie's attempts to dissuade her is not unlike the lesbian's rejection of Arnie's sexual advances. When the two story-lines cross and Roxanne responds with shock and disgust to the lesbian's open display of affection with her lover, Roxanne—and the series—get to 'have it both ways': assertiveness is affirmed without the dreaded taint of sexual rejection of men. Yet at the same time, the lesbian represents a detachment from Arnold Becker's sexual bravado that is seductive in its own way.

In both the series pilot and the second season opener, the doors that swing both ways are defined within terms central to feminist discourse: rape as the ultimate test of whether the law is patriarchal or not; female narration as difficult and marginal; the appropriation of feminism by men to recapture those privileges challenged by feminism in the first place; the definition of feminism as a threat to the heterosexual status quo. But perhaps where *L.A. Law* is most obviously and strikingly 'feminist' is in its cast of characters, all of whom are engaged in various stages of door-swinging. The female characters on *L.A. Law* may not necessarily be identified as feminists, but all of the four major female leads—partner Ann Kelsey, District Attorney Grace Van Owen, associate Abby Perkins, and secretary Roxanne Melman—exhibit variations of two features commonly associated with a popularized view of feminism: power dressing and assertiveness training. The four characters fall

---

8 Eventually Victor's heterosexuality is established, and we learn that his earring does indeed function as a wandering signifier of difference.

9 Michele Kort, 'The Women of *L.A. Law*', *Ms.*, June 1987: 43.

into two distinct groups and offer two kinds of pleasure particularly perti-nent and interesting to female spectators: on the one hand, there are the two lawyers who have made it, and whose power and skill are measured fre-quently by their abilities to undermine, challenge, or otherwise to mock the discourse of patriarchy; and on the other, there are the devoted, underpaid secretary and the insecure, beginning lawyer, who have a more tentative rela-tionship to success, and who struggle to affirm an identity within the realm of the law.[10] L.A. Law is not, of course, the only series on television to equate 'feminism' with the styles of power dressing and assertiveness. Prime-time programmes such as Who's the Boss come to mind; and the stock figure of the villainess on both prime-time and daytime soaps has not infrequently been given such a 'feminist' inflection—witness the ruthless businesswoman Lee Halprin on the ABC daytime soap One Life to Live who runs an all-woman consulting firm called 'Dynawoman' and who frequently calls men on their sexism in between planting dead mice in punchbowls and making unscrupu-lous business deals.

However, the appropriation of feminism in L.A. Law is better described in terms of narrative structure than in terms of character per se. Put another way, the cast of characters in the series is more interesting for the ways in which different functions of narration are assigned across gender lines. Individual episodes of L.A. Law tend to include anywhere from two to four major story-lines, at least one of them a courtroom trial. The story-lines are complicated not only by the relations between them, but also by the overlap-ping personal and professional lives of the lawyers. Recurrent scenes and motifs include the staff or partners' meetings, characterized by multiple reaction shots and summary of what has preceded or exposition of what is to come; standard punctuation marks, such as the sweeping pans of the city with which each programme begins; and a poignant conclusion, always of two people, usually embracing, frequently Kuzak and Van Owen (again, shades of the bedroom scenes between Joyce Davenport and Frank Furillo that form the coda to Hill Street Blues episodes). Depending upon the kinds of cases in which they are involved, individual lawyers vary in the amount of narrative authority they possess. Three male characters possess what might be called a capacity for omniscient narration: Leland McKenzie, the patriarch of the firm and its sole remaining founding partner; Douglas Brackman, son of one of the founders who oversees the staff meetings and insists constantly on productivity and the generation of large fees; and Arnold Becker, the most overtly manipulative lawyer of the firm, largely because he recognizes each and every case he takes on as a familiar scenario to which he can, most often, predict the outcome. These three overarching perspectives are consistently mocked in the series—gently, in the case of Leland McKenzie (the partners rise up in virtual revolt when it is revealed he used an 'old boy' tactic to remove a lawyer from a case); broadly, in the case of Douglas Brackman (whose style of 'office management' is an ongoing joke); and a little of both

---

10 During L.A. Law's second season, Abby Perkins begins to make the transition from the one group to the other. Perkins is the lawyer who is most attentive to people's feelings. The case that marks her ini-tiation into the realm of success concerns a feud between former business partners, and her recom-mendation—scoffed at by virtually all of the other lawyers in the firm—is that they attempt to reconcile their differences. They do, and hire Abby as their lawyer. Abby's success thus implies that the stereotypically female preoccupation with feelings and relationships is compatible with the law.

in the case of Arnold Becker (a perpetual pleasure in the series is watching his narrative predictions backfire). The narrative centre of *L.A. Law* is occupied, rather, by those lawyers with no pretence to omniscience, and with a more limited narrative range—Ann Kelsey, Grace Van Owen, Michael Kuzak, and Victor Sifuentes in particular.

Put another way, the overarching narrative perspective of *L.A. Law* comes from juxtaposition and combination, rather than from the identification of a single narrator or a single perspective as the voice of narrative authority and cohesion. Sometimes the interconnectedness of the segments—the thematic overlap between story-lines, or an 'echo' effect, where story-lines reflect off of each other—is made quite evidently, and sometimes it is made more subtly. But almost without exception, the relationships between the different segments in an individual episode are not acknowledged or articulated by the individual lawyers themselves, giving the series its much-acclaimed quality of open-endedness.

L.A. Law has shown a particular preference for story-lines on rape. The centrality of multiple and overlapping narration in the series suggests the possibility of a more complex engagement with rape, defined as a problem of representation as well as a problem of sexual violence, than is usually the case on prime-time television. Now given that one of the most distinctive features of *L.A. Law* is this overlapping and interweaving of story-lines, any consideration of narrative must take into account the juxtaposition of segments as a narrative device in its own right. One of the appeals of the law as a framework for narrative, and for television narrative in particular, is that it engages with a multiplicity of narrative perspectives, and yet also allows sharp and clear definitions of what is right and what is wrong—in Patrice Petro's terms, television law allows a folding of the hysterical text into the criminal text.[11] If feminism, for *L.A. Law*, is a prime example of the door that swings both ways, then where the series is most provocative in feminist terms is in the ways that feminism is narrativized, situated in the context of multiple story-lines, defined as a narrative perspective in relationship to others.

I've suggested that in the *L.A. Law* pilot, a basic structure is articulated whereby the white male lawyer intervenes and manipulates the law so that a black woman's story might be told. That Kuzak's position as narrator can be read as both a form of manipulation in its own right, and as an enlightened reach across the boundaries of race, gender, and class, is typical of *L.A. Law*'s own status as a door that swings both ways. The definition of the lawyer as narrator when the lawyer in question is female raises some of the most interesting questions concerning *L.A. Law* and feminism. In the series pilot, another story-line involves a black woman who is never seen on camera, a woman who has been brutally exploited by her insurance company. In this story-line, the black woman functions as nothing more than a pretence for Ann Kelsey to fight the insurance company; indeed, Kelsey says as much herself in the conclusion of the story-line in the following episode. After she has won a large settlement for her client, Kelsey acknowledges to Leland McKenzie that she had virtually no relationship with her client and fought the case for her own sake, not for her client's. Two black women function,

11 Patrice Petro, 'Criminality or Hysteria?: Television and the Law', *Discourse,* 10/2 (1988).

then, as central narrative figures: the one—Adrienne Moore as portrayed by Alfre Woodard—very much the visible centre of the pilot, the other a most conspicuously absent and marginal figure. More central to Kelsey's case are the showdowns between her and the insurance agent, an obnoxious and somewhat pathetic sexist, who bears a strong physical resemblance to Stuart Markowitz, the lawyer who will soon become Kelsey's significant other. Kelsey's role as narrator is staked out in the pilot as calling the bluff of macho behaviour and puncturing masculine pretence, whether by icy detachment, witty repartee, or deflation of male superiority.

If Kelsey acknowledges that this particular legal battle has more to do with her male opponent than with her client, then her relationship to the law can be seen as either the opposite of Michael Kuzak's (he, the enlightened liberal; she, the ruthless one), or its repressed side (Kelsey thus making explicit the self-serving and performance-like aspects of the law displaced in Kuzak's story-line), or—more in keeping with the swinging doors of *L.A. Law*—as both simultaneously. While it is tempting to regard *L.A. Law* as one of the few truly equal opportunity programmes on prime-time, Ann Kelsey's function in this respect is remarkably evocative of a more familiar definition of woman—the feminine as a return of the repressed, the eruption of a connection not otherwise speakable.

Consider, for example, a juxtaposition of scenes in the pilot from two separate story-lines. In one scene, the insurance agent makes a settlement offer which Kelsey refuses. In response to his remark that 'Juries don't like bull-dozing, chop-busting, butch lady lawyers any better than I do,' Kelsey remains cool: 'Thank you for sharing that insight with me Mr Messman,' she says, and rejects the offer again. That scene is followed by an equally tense encounter pitting Arnold Becker and his female client against her husband and his lawyer. The husband occupies much the same position as the insuranceman in the previous scene, for he speaks the same language of sexual put-down. But here, the woman responds in kind, screaming at her husband and calling him—in what is one of the more memorable epithets in the show—an 'impotent piece of snot'. While the argument could be made that the two scenes draw parallels between what happens to women in the workplace and what happens to them in marriages, the far more immediate connection drawn is that Arnold Becker's client vents the rage suppressed in Ann Kelsey's lawyerly façade.

At stake in the strategies of undercutting, of *double entendre*, of narrative ambiguity in *L.A. Law* are the claims of feminism itself. Teresa de Lauretis defines the goal of feminist criticism as accentuating and insisting upon the gap between 'woman'—'the other-from-man (nature and Mother, site of sexuality and masculine desire, sign and object of men's social exchange)' and 'women'—'the real historical beings who cannot as yet be defined outside of those discursive formations'.[12] Indeed, *L.A. Law* draws on feminist discourse in order both to open up and to close down the analogous gap between 'feminine' and 'feminist'. Consider, for example, another episode in which overlapping story-lines, again involving Michael Kuzak and Ann

---

12 Teresa de Lauretis, *Alice Doesn't: Feminism, Semiotics, Cinema* (Bloomington: Indiana Univ. Press, 1984), 5.

Kelsey, accentuate the radical difference in narrative mode between male and female practice of the law. The principal story-line in the episode is a case of date rape, in which Kuzak defends a woman who was raped by a man after she had gone back to his room after a party. The jury makes a decision that is most ambiguous: it rules in the woman's favour but gives her a cash award of $1.00, thus suggesting that there are some rapes that are not quite so criminal as others. Although Kuzak makes a convincing case for the seriousness of date rape, it is later revealed that he is not completely convinced of his client's innocence either. Only when another woman comes to his office to tell him that she, too, was raped by the same man does the programme seem to affirm, unequivocally, the woman's point of view that she was indeed raped (note the striking narrative logic here: the man is not a real rapist until he does it twice). Yet the discourse of the date rape case slides into another story-line, almost as if there is a narrative price to be paid for the woman's vindication, a vindication virtually indistinguishable from the feminist insistence that acquaintanceship in no way mitigates the criminality of rape. The attorney for the defendant—a woman—argued in her summation that:

> Every woman in this courtroom knows it is more respectable, more femi-
> nine and sometimes more alluring to manifest the sign of resistance—at
> least initially. You know something else?—the men know it too. The sim-
> ple fact is sometimes we say no when we really mean yes, and sometimes
> we say no when we really mean no, and sometimes men can't tell which is
> which.

This narration describes with remarkable accuracy the accompanying story-line in which Ann Kelsey decides to sell her condominium, and agrees to a rather elaborate deal arranged by her lover, Stuart Markowitz. Suddenly, in an inexplicable burst of fickleness, she changes her mind and tells him and the potential buyer that the deal is off. At the conclusion of the programme, Ann apologizes to Stuart and asks if it is too late to change her mind about the sale. Stuart Markowitz, another of the legions of man who 'can't tell which is which', throws up his hands in the air in exasperation. The two kiss and make up, as if to prove the lawyer's point that sometimes it is 'more alluring' to say no. The episode thus trivializes the very issue that it attempts to present, through Kuzak's crisis of conscience, as worthy of serious legal attention. In addition, it is once again the woman upon whom the narrative contradictions are projected.

This projection of contradictions onto the body of the woman occurs in a particularly complex and interesting way in a story-line devoted to Stacy Gill (portrayed by Steven Bochco's real-life wife, Barbara Bosson), a woman television news anchor who has brought charges of sex discrimination after her firing—according to the television station, purely because of poor ratings, and according to her, because of a story she agreed to do, at the station's request, on breast cancer, during which she demonstrated the various components of cancer detection and quite literally bared her breasts for the camera. A secondary story-line during the two episodes in which the Stacy Gill trial was aired concerns Douglas Brackman's transformation from a slumlord into a concerned, responsible landlord. During his slumlord phase, Brackman meets his wife in a restaurant for her birthday and asks her to sign papers so that their property can be turned over temporarily to his mother. Sheila, his wife, mistakenly assumes that he wants a divorce and begins bemoaning her fate, making quite a spectacle of herself in the process. After telling Douglas that she 'doesn't snap back like some twenty-five-year-old with elastic breasts', she proceeds to sing 'Happy Birthday' quite loudly, while everyone in the restaurant gapes and stares. In an earlier scene in the episode, Stacy Gill and Kuzak chat in a bar about her case, and Gill cries as she describes her discomfort at being seen as a 'breast with a woman attached'. Sheila Brackman, in making a spectacle of herself, thus becomes the hysterical version of Stacy Gill.

Rarely do the characters in *L.A. Law* draw connections between individual story-lines; those connections emerge, rather, through other narrative devices, such as the principles of overlap I've described. An exception to this rule occurs during the Stacy Gill story-line. Kuzak defends Gill passionately, and as is usually the case in his arguments, emphasizes the human factor over the narrowly legal one. The station makes a generous settlement offer which Gill refuses, against Kuzak's recommendation, primarily because it would require her to drop the sex discrimination charge. Only after the jury rules in her favour, with a huge award, does Kuzak discover that Gill has an advance book contract contingent upon going through to a jury verdict. As a result, he feels exploited. Gill tells him that had she informed him of the contract, he would have been less fired up, less passionate in her defence. In a secondary story-line, Kuzak does exactly what he is miffed at Stacy Gill for doing—he gives a case to Sifuentes, tells him to ask for a continuance, and neglects to inform him that there are no more continuances to be had—so that Sifuentes has to prepare the case cold. Kuzak defends his actions with a logic that echoes Stacy Gill's. Now the more typical pattern in *L.A. Law* would be for the ironic echo to remain implicit—obvious, perhaps, but none the less not narrated or called attention to by an individual lawyer. However, in this case, Grace Van Owen confronts Kuzak with the recognition that what Stacy Gill did to him was no different than what he did to Sifuentes.

This atypical narrative development is enormously instructive, particularly given its position at the conclusion of a story-line which was introduced with the parallel between a distraught Stacy Gill and an hysterical Sheila Brackman. Grace Van Owen is given a position of narrative authority that seems initially to stand in opposition to that previous equation of a woman fighting a sex discrimination suit with a woman making a spectacle of herself. Like the juxtapositions that situate Ann Kelsey's professional behaviour in contrast with its repressed, the Stacy Gill/Sheila Brackman parallel closes down the gap between 'feminist' (the woman who agreed to expose her experience with breast cancer to the public in order to help other women, and who accuses her employer of sex discrimination) and 'feminine' (the woman who is distraught about the elasticity of her breasts, and who fears her husband is having an affair). Yet in both instances, the eruptions of the 'feminine' offer possibilities for opening *up* the gap as well, if for no other reason than the fact that the need to eliminate the distinction speaks to a narrative anxiety, a problem of representation. I am not arguing here for reading these strategies against the grain, which implies an initial coherence that might then be turned around, but rather for identifying the ambivalence central to the strategies themselves. Ambivalent or not, however, Grace Van Owen's function as a narrator could be read as an alternative strategy, an instance of female authority that is distinctly unambivalent. Van Owen affirms a principle of equality that may be somewhat cynical, but is none the less of feminist inspiration: that women and men have the same rights to exploit the law, and lawyers, to their benefit. While the position Van Owen is assigned in this episode is, as I've said, unusual for *L.A. Law*, the perspective she articulates here is one she represents fairly consistently in the series. Grace Van Owen represents the notion that the polarities of 'male' and 'female' are simply roles that men and women can adopt at their discretion and will. But Van Owen's 'feminism' is—to refer again to one of *L.A. Law*'s preferred phrases—a door that swings both ways. When an attempt is made on Van Owen's life after she has argued successfully for a death sentence, she neglects to recognize a gender component to her vulnerability, a component underscored ironically when she decides, nervously, to buy a handgun, and changes her mind after agreeing with the salesman who says to her, somewhat sleazily, 'Sexy, isn't it?' In another episode, Van Owen even appropriates the language of rape to describe her own desires. In the episode, Van Owen comes on to a man in a gorilla suit, thinking it is Michael Kuzak. When she later describes the incident, she tells Kuzak that she 'practically raped the guy'.

These two strategies—the 'echo' effect on the one hand, through which the stereotypically feminine seems, if not necessarily to undermine, then at least to complicate female challenges to male power; and on the other, female narration that theorizes the symmetry of male and female behaviour—correspond to the two types of swinging doors which I've described as symptomatic of *L.A. Law*'s engagement with feminism. The 'echo' effect represents an essential difference of men and women *vis-à-vis* the law, while the unusual identification of a female narrator suggests a more equal opportunity approach, whereby men and women are the same before the law. These options are remarkably evocative of what Catherine MacKinnon has described as the 'two routes to sex equality':[13]

> The primary avenue views women as if we were men. It measures our similarity with men to see if we are or can be men's equals. This standard is called the equality rule. . . . The second approach . . . views women as men view women: in need of special protection, help, or indulgence. To make out a case, complainants have to meet the male standard for women: femininity. . . . In other words, for purposes of sex discrimination law, to be a woman means either to be like a man or to be a lady. We have to meet either the male standard for males or the male standard for females.   (p. 74)

MacKinnon goes on to say that for a woman lawyer, both standards are applicable, simultaneously: 'Available to women in the practice of law are the same two roles as those in standards of sex discrimination law, except that women lawyers are held to both at once.' In the terms of television narrative,

13 Catherine MacKinnon, 'On Exceptionality: Women as Women in Law', *Feminism Unmodified: Discourses on Life and Law* (Cambridge, Mass.: Harvard Univ. Press, 1987), 71.

then, the woman lawyer is an emblem of ambiguity and contradiction; as MacKinnon puts it, 'Now, given that you are a woman lawyer, are you feeling a little schizoid?' (p. 75).

I don't think it inappropriate to describe *L.A. Law* as a series of endless ambiguities about the law and sexual politics, and about feminism itself. But there is something suspicious about this delight in ambiguity, both within narrative—where it can function so often as a ruse, a decoy—and within criticism—where it can harden into an idealized abstraction. However complex the desire, in *L.A. Law*, to both open up and close down the difference between femininity and feminism, the narrative strategies of the series all lead to a virtually identical point of closure: the poignant two-shot that concludes each episode. Indeed, the very regularity and consistency of closure suggest its importance within the narrative economy of the series. The most common closing shot of *L.A. Law* is an image of one of the couples—Ann Kelsey and Stuart Markowitz or, more frequently, Grace Van Owen and Michael Kuzak. Sometimes the closing shot predicts a couple-to-be, like Abby Perkins and George Handelman, a lawyer in the district attorney's office. While the closing shot does evoke, as I've suggested, the concluding images of Joyce Davenport and Frank Furillo in *Hill Street Blues*, the narrative functions are quite different. For in *Hill Street Blues*, the steamy love scenes between Davenport and Furillo often seem like reminders that the series does exist in a heterosexual world, after all. As Steven Jenkins puts it, *Hill Street Blues*, through the Furillo–Davenport relationship, 'asserts a sense of heterosexual, male–female, private/professional balance in the face of its own imbalance; it returns the spectator, after the supposed chaos, to a space where things are in their correct place, as they should be'.[14]

The comparison with *Hill Street Blues* is none the less instructive. While *L.A. Law* may have plenty of chaos of its own, it does not lack in female characters or in heterosexual interaction. Hence the final shots do not really function as tacked-on conclusions, second thoughts that represent what has been by and large repressed. Rather, the final shot of each episode reiterates what is one of *L.A. Law*'s most obvious and insistent fantasies: a utopian heterosexuality, a complementarity of men and women in the face of the massive disorder instigated, in the previous fifty-five minutes, by the intersection of the law and gender. Frequently the concluding shot assures that however tough the women of *L.A. Law* may be in their legal battles with men, their challenge to patriarchy does not extend into the realm of sexual preference or desire. The point was made strikingly in a second season episode in which Grace Van Owen was accused of being a 'humourless radical feminist' in her defence of a teenage stripper sexually molested by a group of lawyers. In the concluding shot of the episode, Van Owen and Kuzak inhale helium from a balloon and talk in funny voices as they embrace, so that at least the 'humourless' and the 'radical' parts are temporarily dispelled.

---

14 Steve Jenkins, '*Hill Street Blues*', in Jane Feuer *et al.* (eds.), *MTM: 'Quality Television'*, 192. Jenkins later suggests that the Furillo–Davenport finale can be read just as persuasively as a 'logical extension of the narrative, rather than as a kind of calming coda to it' (196). The point, of course, is that like the door that swings both ways in *L.A. Law*, both readings are encouraged simultaneously.

During the first (1986–7) season of *L.A. Law*, a few concluding images of episodes do not feature the male–female couples of the show. One is the pilot, which I've described as setting out the overlapping boundaries of the law and gender through the final embrace of Michael Kuzak and Adrienne Moore. Two episodes conclude with images suggestive of a disruption in the law: an episode featuring the story-line of a judge accused of taking a bribe concludes with the judge and Leland McKenzie in a face-to-face, and another episode in which Kuzak overidentifies with Sid Herschberg, a lawyer who cracks under pressure and eventually commits suicide, concludes with Kuzak visiting Herschberg in a mental institution and embracing him. These occasional departures from concluding shots of men and women in love focus on the law as a fraternity, a brotherhood. One is, of course, reminded of Luce Irigaray's observation that heterosexuality is a ruse, 'just an alibi for the smooth workings of man's relations with himself, of relations among men'.[15]

In the former episode, the judge calls Leland McKenzie a 'wizard of ambiguity', and takes great glee in forcing his longtime associate to answer a question 'yes' or 'no'. Now the brotherhood of the law may not erupt in quite the same way that stereotypical femininity does within individual episodes, but I would argue that this male fellowship of the law disrupts the utopian heterosexuality which provides *L.A. Law* with one of its most distinct continuous threads and certainly with its strongest sense of resolution and closure. While there is much to be said about the conspicuously ideological dimensions of this utopian heterosexuality, I am more interested in its narrative dimensions. For the feminism that is appropriated in *L.A. Law* is, at the very least, capable of making a good story. *L.A. Law* makes for an interesting comparison, in this respect, with another recent articulation of feminism and the law. In an 8 November 1987 piece on the *New York Times* editorial page, Stephen Gillers, a professor of law and a member of the board of the New York Civil Liberties Union, criticized feminism for not letting some stories be told. Gillers's piece was occasioned by the acquittal of Karen Straw for the murder of her husband on the basis of the evidence that she was a battered wife. Gillers draws a rather remarkable connection between the feminist defence of Karen Straw, and the feminist criticism of a completely unrelated case— the trial of Robert Chambers for the murder of Jennifer Levin. In the Chambers case, feminists have criticized the attempt by the defence to introduce as relevant material Jennifer Levin's supposed history of sexual 'aggression' with other men. As Gillers so strikingly puts it in a remarkable turn of convoluted narrative logic, feminists 'would permit Karen Straw but not Robert Chambers to pin blame on someone else'. Feminists are thus guilty, in Gillers's view, of 'denying Mr Chambers the right to tell his story'.[16]

If, in Gillers's view of feminism and the law, feminism threatens to block the flow of narrative and to stifle a man's right to tell his story, feminism in *L.A. Law* has the opposite effect, for it encourages and stimulates the production of narrative. To be sure, the representation of feminism in *L.A. Law*

15 Luce Irigaray, 'Women on the Market', *This Sex Which Is Not One*, trans. Catherine Porter (1977; Ithaca: Cornell Univ. Press, 1985), 172.

16 Stephen Gillers, 'Feminists vs. Civil Libertarians', *New York Times*, 8 Nov. 1987: 20.

is a function of feminism's capacity to disrupt and upset the categories of legal and narrative discourse. But if feminism, as a source of narrative tension, seems to be suspended momentarily with each concluding scene of *L.A. Law*, then the few concluding scenes that are *not* of one romantic couple or another are useful reminders that fantasies of integration and resolution, whether in male–female relations or in courts of law, are temporary and fleeting indeed.

7

Empowering Women? The *Oprah Winfrey Show*

Corinne Squire

The Oprah Winfrey Show, *the most-watched US daytime talk show, aims to empower women. This chapter examines the show's representations of gender and how images of 'race', sexuality, and class cross-cut them. It considers the show's status as television psychology. It explores the show's translation of aspects of black feminism to television, and discusses the social implications of its 'super-real' representations.*

WINFREY:	Listen . . . obviously I come from a very biased point of view here.
FEMALE GUEST:	Because you're a woman.
WINFREY:	Yes. Well, and because I—what we try to do—we do program these shows to empower women.

Oprah Winfrey Show, 1989*b*

Introduction

EVERY WEEKDAY in the USA, 20 million people watch the *Oprah Winfrey Show*, making it the most-watched daytime talk programme. Snaring an unassailable 35 per cent of the audience, it acts as a lead-in for local stations' lucrative early evening news programmes (McClellan, 1993; Boemer, 1987). The show has become a common source of information and opinions about relationships, psychopathology, and gender. It is a cultural icon, signifying at the same time lurid dilemmas, emotional intensity, fame, and black women's success. It is even a well-known chronological marker, as in 'I worked so hard I was done in time for *Oprah*', or, 'I did my shopping so quick I was home by *Oprah*'.

Winfrey, the first African American woman to host a national talk show[1] is

© Sage, 1994.

Originally published in *Feminism and Psychology*, 4/1 (1994), 63–79.

1 Another African American woman, the comedian Marsha Warfield, has had a half-hour networked morning show, and Montel Williams, the 'male Oprah', has an hour-long morning show on CBS. A new crop of *Oprah* challengers, several with African American hosts, appeared in 1993 (Freeman, 1992). The earliest African American talk-show host was Ellis Haizlip, who, in the late 1960s and early 1970s, fronted *Soul*, 'a live performance/talk show inspired by the burgeoning cultural nationalist movement' (Jones, 1991).

also well known for her television specials on self-esteem and child abuse, for her role as Sophia in the film *The Color Purple,* as an advocate for abused children, and as a philanthropist supporting programmes for poor black youth. The tabloids chronicle her fluctuating weight and self-esteem and her long-standing relationship with a businessman, Stedman Graham. She is one of the richest women in the world, with a yearly income of around $40 million, $16 million more than Madonna (Goodman, 1991). In 1989 she was voted the second most admired woman in the USA—after Nancy Reagan. The Oprah phenomenon is interesting in itself but this essay will restrict itself to considering Oprah, 'daytime queen' (Guider, 1987), in the context of the show.

In this study I will treat the television programme as a polysemous, difficult but readable text; examine its compliance with and departure from television conventions; investigate its framing by broader 'texts' of social power and history; and see it as suffused with the intensity and fragmentariness of subjectivity. While psychologists are increasingly taking on such modes of analysis, psychological studies of television generally use more traditional methods, like content analysis or the micro-analysis of speech and non-verbal communication. An exception is Valerie Walkerdine's 'Video Replay' (1989), which provides an exemplary reading of the criss-crossed narratives of gender and class that inhabit our subjective responses to the small screen.

Like other daytime talk shows, *Oprah* aims to entertain, inform, and encourage communication about difficult issues. It is a kind of popular psychology, lacing advice and catharsis with comedy and melodrama. But the show also tries, Winfrey says, to empower women: to be a televisual feminism. Not only the host but many guests and the majority of the studio and watching audiences are women, and most episodes address female-identified topics: relationships, communication, physical appearance. Host, guests, and the studio audience also spend a lot of time in animated, messy discussions of injustices that are at the centre of much contemporary feminist campaigning, like job discrimination, male violence, and sexual abuse.

While Winfrey often says the show transcends 'race', it features black guests and issues of concern to black people in the USA more than comparable shows and focuses particularly on black women's perspectives. Since the 1980s such perspectives have had a major impact on US feminism as black women activists and writers make their voices heard within the largely US women's movement (see, for instance, Butler, 1990; de Lauretis, 1986; Hill Collins, 1990; hooks, 1981, 1989; Moraga and Anzaldua, 1981; Spelman, 1990; Spivak, 1988). Differences in class and sexuality between women, which are also concerns of contemporary feminism (Lorde, 1984; Rich, 1986), have only a small place on the *Oprah* show however. Edginess characterizes *Oprah*'s occasional mentions of lesbian and gay sexuality, and class is rarely explicitly discussed.

I am going to explore the show's diverse and intricate representations of gender, 'race', sexuality, class, and subjectivity, and how the nature of television affects these representations. In the process I aim to develop an account of *Oprah*'s relationship to feminism. I am adopting a very general definition of feminism here, assuming that it is concerned, first, to understand gender relationships as fully as possible, in their interrelationships with other social differences, with history, with subjectivity, and with different representational media like television; and second, that it tries to make gender relations and relationships between women less oppressive (Coward, 1983). Does *Oprah*, much watched by women, and a secular authority on gender issues, speak to these feminist concerns? I shall argue that it does and that its most interesting contributions are first, a feminism generalized from black women's histories and writing, and second, its super-realism—an unsettling combination of emotional and empirical excess that puts common assumptions about gendered subjectivities in doubt.

Analysing *Oprah*   Western feminists were slow to pay attention to television, despite its dominant position in their culture. Television representations of gender seemed dauntingly conventional in the face of feminists' limited power to effect change. Left analyses of the media as ideological control also contributed to feminist dismissals of television as shallow, repetitive, and emotionally manipulative. Since the 1970s, however, a number of feminists have treated the pleasures and powers of television seriously, recognizing that they must pay attention to this engrossing cultural form if they are to address the realities and fantasies of gender with which we all live (Kaplan, 1987). Such analyses have to balance an awareness of feminist elements in television messages and in audience understanding of them, with a recognition of television's traditionalism and of the ways in which the television message and the power relations of television consumption constrain viewer interpretations (Brunsdon, 1989; Morris, 1988, Nightingale, 1990). Recent analyses of film and television by black writers and by theorists of queer representations start from this complexity, taking it for granted and then compounding it (Bad Object-Choices, 1991; Dent, 1992; Doty, 1992; Julien and Mercer, 1988).

   The study draws on a regular monitoring of the *Oprah Winfrey Show* from late 1988 to mid-1993 but its core is an analysis of episodes shown during two weeks in May 1990. Throughout the study, the contents of the show have been fairly constant. Episodes split evenly between 'self-help' topics—obsessions, disobedient children, and destructive relationships—and an 'all others' category which includes shows on appearance (cosmetic surgery, dieting, people who think they are ugly) and physical, mental, or behavioural abnormality (disabling allergies, multiple personality, women who murder their children) and, more rarely, shows on social issues (buying a house, education, poverty), 'cute' shows ('Alaskan men', people who can't throw anything away), and celebrity interviews (Joan Rivers, Barbara Bush). The show's form, too, is consistent. Winfrey introduces each episode by reading an outline of the day's topic to camera, talks to guests, solicits a few questions from the audience, brings in some expert opinions, and then alternates guests', experts', and audience members' comments while she roams around the audience with a mike in the style Phil Donahue brought to talk-show prominence. The representations of gender, 'race', sexuality, class, and subjectivity with which I am concerned are also highly consistent across shows. I shall go through each of these as elements in a sequential manner, but the intersections should soon become apparent.

Representations of Gender on Oprah

Sometimes the *Oprah* show seems simply to endorse traditional notions of femaleness. In the woman-dominated world of daytime television, it appears, the predominantly female audience watches the mainly female casts of the early afternoon soap operas endlessly play out relationship dilemmas—and then listens to a female talk-show host, her many female guests, and her largely female studio audience discuss how to improve your looks, marriage, and parenting. The advertisements in the breaks, like most advertisements and indeed most programming (Bretl and Cantor, 1988; Davis, 1990), show women in traditional roles, worrying about their weight and their children. While the show encourages women to speak frankly about their lives, including their sexualities, the conventional limits apply. In one episode Winfrey assured a woman who had employed a male surrogate sex therapist to teach her to reach orgasm that she could be 'explicit'. 'Well, he started by using his finger inside me, very gently. I felt a contraction . . .', the woman said, and was abruptly cut off by a commercial. During the break Winfrey said, 'I didn't mean *that* explicit' (King, 1987: 126). Conventionally, the show uses women to conjure prohibited pleasures; their transgressive, cathartic confessions become the apotheosis of television's voyeurism (Ellis, 1982).

Winfrey touches audience members a lot, cries and laughs, and they touch, laugh, and cry back. These exchanges signify an empathy that is traditionally feminine, but also feminist in its insistence on the 'personal', and that is largely free of the inflections of authority and sexuality mixed in with male hosts' touching.

The show also presents feminist arguments about women's lower economic and social status, men's difficulties in close relationships, women's difficulties in combining paid work and parenting, the suppression of women's sexuality and men's physical and sexual abuse. Moreover, since television representations often have more than one meaning, even the show's apparently conservative representations of gender can support feminist readings. The show's representations of the female body for instance are not simply incitements to female self-hatred. In one notorious episode Winfrey hauled on-stage 67 pounds of lard—the amount of weight she had lost; since then she has forsworn dieting. Today, the show routinely notes the oppressiveness and irrelevance of dominant images of the female body, explores how preoccupations with food and weight cloak depression and feelings of low self-worth and acknowledges the comforting, social and sensual nature of eating, and one episode focused exclusively on discrimination against fat people. Winfrey's own size acts as a reminder of how women's bigness can be a form of power, perhaps especially when they are black women in a field dominated by white men. As Gracie Mae Still, the narrator of Alice Walker's '1955' put it, 'fat like I is looks distinguished. You see me coming and know somebody's *there*!' (1982: 13).

The show sometimes considers motherhood with conventional reverence, but also treats it as a matter of hard work or discusses it in a more flexible way, as when Maya Angelou calls Winfrey her 'daughter-friend' *(Oprah Winfrey Show,* 1993). It has also problematized motherhood, as in an episode on maternal child abuse.

The show's feminism is most explicit, however, in its often-declared commitment to empowering women. This term has multiple meanings, indicating variously an interest in women's political, economic, and educational advancement; in women getting help for personal and relationship problems; and most generally, in women perceiving a range of individual and social choices as open to them and deciding among them. Each meaning implies a different version of feminism. The first suggests a public, the second a personal focus for feminism and the last founds feminist politics in psychological well-being. Nevertheless the show's representations of empowerment all assume a commonality between women that allows the representations to make the category 'women' their unproblematic centre. Feminism must use this category to ground its analyses and claims, but the category always has a social and historical context that gives it a specific meaning (Riley, 1988; Spelman, 1990). *Oprah,* however, represents women as sharing emotional and social qualities—communication skills, for instance—regardless of the differences between women. The show's aim is to empower this shared womanhood.

The dominant presence of women on the show is underwritten by a complementary male presence. The show continually solicits men's opinions, runs episodes on men as lovers and parents, and raises and counters the suggestion that *Oprah* is 'anti-men'. The show's 'woman-centred' talk is always, silently, about men, for gender is a relationship: one term evokes the other.

The complementariness of *Oprah*'s representations of gender raises an important question about its relationship to feminism. Might women's disempowerment, against which the show defines itself, nevertheless be its most powerful message? A narrative of empowerment structures each episode but the show's repeated accounts of victimization often seem to overwhelm them. After the daily success story of women getting their lives in order, you know that tomorrow you will start off once more with the harrowing experiences of women whose lives have been taken from them by abuse, illness, or poverty. Feminism has to describe structures of male power in order to resist them and to this degree it is complicit with them. But on the *Oprah Winfrey Show,* self-consciously complicit description often seems to collapse into a fruitless reiteration of stories of personal suffering. Domestic violence, child abuse, and eating disorders support regular episodes, each claiming to bring to light a horrible and hitherto secret oppression, each by this claim implicitly reinstating the horror and prohibitions around the topic; for talking about a forbidden subject may maintain as much as disperse a taboo. *Oprah*'s current emphasis on health and exercise at the expense of diets, for example, is undercut by a conventional subtext of the female body as subject to control (Bordo, 1989; Coward, 1989), and by the frequency with which diets are mentioned, only to be dismissed.

The show's complementary meanings have some promising feminist implications as well. The show often presents women as objects of beauty: in make-over episodes, for instance; or on the daily credits, shot when Winfrey was near her thinnest, had a Revlon modelling contract, and could operate as a powerful screen player in the cultural and psychic masquerade of femininity (Heath, 1985). The credits show Winfrey in a series of slowed, staggered close-ups and medium close-ups, listening sympathetically to guests, laughing, swinging her hair, bouncing across the screen. Beginning with Laura Mulvey, feminist film theorists have argued that such representations of femininity put the spectator in a complementarily masculine position of pleasure and desire (Mulvey, 1975, 1981). *Oprah*'s predominantly female studio and viewing audience is thus set up to look at the feminine object, Winfrey, from a patriarchal position: as men. The audience may either adopt this masculine spectatorship or abdicate spectatorship for an identification with the femininity on screen (see also de Lauretis, 1991; Doane, 1987). Such work suggests that *Oprah* offers women a variety of psychic investments, so its feminism will not be a simple matter of women watching women but will filter through the multiple subjectivities of spectatorship.

If we view *Oprah*'s multiple representations of gender in a context wider than the show, their relationship to feminism often starts to seem closer. Despite the limits the show sets on what can be said, for instance, and its tendency to present talk as a cure-all, its stress on 'explicit' speech seems oppositional in the broader context of US pro-censorship campaigns, especially since explicit talk on *Oprah* is often talk about a common censorship target, female sexuality. The show's representations of men also appear more resistant if they are read against the power relationships generally obtaining between women and men. Episodes shift from description to prescription, from problems with men or men's problems, to women's solutions. Even if a similar move will be made all over again in the very next episode, the move cuts against the cultural grain. Viewed historically, too, *Oprah*'s repeated and apparently unchanging considerations of some sensational topics may indicate not just unsated voyeurism or stalled feminism but a series of historically distinct concerns. A show about rape survivors, for example, means something different after the Palm Beach case, in which William Smith, a nephew of Edward Kennedy, was acquitted of raping a lower middle-class white woman, than it does after the Central Park case, in which black youths were convicted of beating and raping a white woman stockbroker who was running in the park.

'Race' and Racism   Henry Louis Gates (1989) describes how, in the 1950s, his family would rush to see African Americans on television, and how concerned they were that the performers be good. More African Americans are on television now but blacks are still under-represented and appear mainly as a set of sitcom and drama clichés or as news anchors. The concern of people of colour about their television representation remains strong (Fife, 1987; Grey, 1989; Ziegler and White, 1990). Shows like *Oprah* generate big expectations and concomitant criticism. *Oprah* has been said to absolve white guilt by presenting a rags-to-riches black, unthreatening female, who hugs whites in the audience more than people of colour. The show has also been accused of being negative about African American men, having few minorities on the production team, and giving racist white organizations air-time rather than confronting more subtle and pervasive racisms. Winfrey ridicules calls for her to be more black, asking, 'How black do you have to be?' (King, 1987: 187). The demand that she 'represent' African Americans is indeed a sign of her token status on television. As Isaac Julien and Kobena Mercer have written of film, the notion that one instance 'could "speak for" an entire community of interests reinforces the perceived secondariness of that community' (1988: 4).

The *Oprah* show is, in any case, permeated with 'race' as much as it is with gender. Winfrey's own Chicago-based production company, the first owned by an African American, makes it. This, together with her ratings, gives her Cosby-like powers—to determine topics and how to treat them, for instance—that black people rarely have in television. The show itself consistently addresses racism, explicitly, by calling for equal opportunities and recruiting people of colour for the production team and, implicitly, by challenging casual instances of racism. In an episode on interracial relationships, Winfrey ironizes a white male guest's history of dating only black women, saying, 'It's that melanin that got you . . . that melanin count just overwhelmed him.' *Oprah* avoids overt racial politics but towards the end this episode featured audience members' political analyses of interracial relationships:

> FEMALE AUDIENCE MEMBER: . . . the reason people are taking it so terribly is that we are part of a racist society period, and that has to change for anything to change.
> FEMALE GUEST: That's right.   (*Oprah Winfrey Show*, 1989a)

Less overtly, the show often features visual representations of racial difference without verbal comment, a silence that may be the result of television's caution about 'race' but that may work, as Kum-Kum Bhavnani (1990) has described, as anti-racist empowerment. In one segment of the '1991 Follow-up Show' (*Oprah Winfrey Show*, 1992), for instance, an African American family, identified simply as a 'family' living in a project, got a 'dream house'. Two other segments showed dramatic reunions between adopted children and birth parents. In both cases children of mixed parentage met previously unknown white or black parents, while 'race' went unmentioned. These silences allowed racial differences to appear but refused them legitimacy in the narratives. In the silences, the cultural mythology of a de-raced all-American 'family' achieved a tactical defeat of other more clearly racist mythologies of black welfare mothers and tragic mulatto children.

The show's representations of black America are also telling. It regularly features successful African American business people, professionals, and entertainers, generating a picture of black culture and achievement rare in mainstream media. After a long absence, rappers now appear on the show occasionally; there are indeed parallels between *Oprah*'s woman-empowering aims and those some women rappers express (Rose, 1990). The show regularly considers issues that are important and controversial among blacks: education, self-esteem, class tensions, conflicts between black women and men over black women's alleged disrespectful and money-grabbing, 'ain't nothing going on but the rent' approach to black men and black men's claimed irresponsibility, black discrimination against dark-skinned black people, interracial adoption and relationships, and black hair and skin care. Black-orientated advertisements and public service announcements are more frequent than on most other network shows. More generally, Winfrey's and her black guests' stories of their lives combine with the show's references to black struggles, especially those of strong black women, to provide a perpetually renewed and reformulated television history of African America, not as comprehensive as those produced during Black History Month, but there all year round.

Winfrey sometimes talks black American, usually to make a joke. Television conventionally allows such language for comedic purposes but it remains language infrequently heard outside sitcoms, dramas, and documentary representations of inner cities. Winfrey even induces similar speech in others. Once, trailing one of her specials on the early evening news after her show, she talked with the black newsreader Roz Abrams, and the somewhat formal Abrams called her 'girlfriend'. For a hallucinatorily brief moment black women's acquaintanceship and talk displaced the bland chumminess and linguistics common in such exchanges.

Occasionally Winfrey addresses whites in the studio audience to explain some aspect of black life. This move homogenizes both the life and the audience, and can seem to offer a quasi-anthropological supplement to talk shows' usual peeping-tom pleasures. But it gives a public voice to marginalized phenomena and acknowledges an ignorance and distance that usually goes unspoken, while Winfrey's blunt pedagogy circumvents voyeurism.

Finally, black feminism seems, as much as woman-centred feminism, to define the show. This black feminism recognizes the different history of patriarchy among African Americans (Gaines, 1988), writes the history of black women's resistance in the anti-slavery and civil rights movements and in every family, and celebrates the strength and creativity of black women (Walker, 1983). Winfrey often invokes the film *The Color Purple*, the writing of Gloria Naylor (1982), and the work of Maya Angelou (1970), whose account of growing up in the black South she says describes her own life and whom she calls her mentor (*Oprah Winfrey Show*, 1993). Men's abuse, which Patricia Hill Collins (1990: 185) says needs to be the object of black feminist analysis, implicitly receives this attention through the host's and black audience members' repeated engagements with it. Angelou and Walker are often said to ignore the history and problematic of black masculinity, and in the process collude with white racism. *Oprah* is subject to similar criticisms but tackles the issues by presenting positive images of African American fatherhood and male mentoring. Winfrey still Signifies on black men though, as Gloria-Jean Masciarotte (1991), citing Gates (1988) citing Hurston, says; and other African American women on the show do the same. This Signifyin(g) is, as Gates says, both a verbal game and a serious cultural engagement. A black woman in the audience raised a laugh when she admonished a black male guest, a Lothario vacillating between two white women, one with dark, one with light hair, 'She over there on the light side, she over there on the dark side, you in the middle on the *grey* side' (*Oprah Winfrey Show*, 1992). The show itself also Signifies, in Gates's broad sense of textual revision, on the texts of African American women writers, rewriting them in a different medium and for a larger racially diverse audience. For many of the white and black viewers of *Oprah*, the show's enduring canon of these writers—along with the more variable set of female self-help gurus and high-achieving women who guest—must constitute the dominant cultural representation of feminism.

Sexualities

In common with the rest of television, the *Oprah Winfrey Show* is heterosexist. Openly lesbian or gay guests appear rarely, the show carefully establishes the heterosexuality of well-known guests, and when it addresses homosexuality directly it tends either to problematize it or to mainstream it as a human issue, distanced from sex and politics (Gross, 1989). Bisexuality is a special problem. In an episode presented jointly with the hunt-the-criminal programme *America's Most Wanted*, a man's bisexuality became the emblem of his ability to elude the criminal justice system: 'The problem with John Hawkins is he's a very good-looking guy, he's a very good con, and he's bisexual, so he has the ability to basically adapt into any community or any type of social structure', said a police officer (reshown on *Oprah Winfrey Show*, 1992).

Sometimes *Oprah* gives screen time to camp men who function briefly and conventionally as jesters. More of a challenge to dominant assumptions about sexuality is the show's marking of differences within heterosexuality, for instance the line it draws between abusive and non-abusive heterosexual relationships. This acknowledgement of plural heterosexualities coexists with the show's more traditional representations of sexual relationships between women and men either as always involving the same desires and social patterns, as in episodes along the lines of 'Save Your Marriage' and 'Best Husband Contest' or as infinitely various, as in 'Men Who Married Their Divorced Wives' and 'Women Who Married Their Stepsons'. Finally, the show's overwhelmingly female spectacle and spectatorship might conceivably be read as a kind of televisual lesbianism but the link between female spectatorship, sexuality, and sexual politics is very unclear (de Lauretis, 1991; Stacey, 1988).

Class

Despite a late-1980s' burst of class-conscious sitcoms, television is not very interested in class relationships. On *Oprah* though the all-American narrative of Winfrey's progress from poverty to wealth is often invoked, and her riches legitimized as the rightful reward of her struggle for a piece of the pie. The wealth is frequently represented as exuberant consumption by references to Winfrey's restaurant, her condo, her farm, and her furs. In a study of women's reactions to *Dynasty*, Andrea Press (1990) writes that working-class women have a particular affinity with such representations; the *Oprah* show's periodic ditchings of gritty emotion in favour of glitz may then be a part of its success. But the show represents Winfrey's good works and her dispensations of wealth to the poor too. Taken together, these representations turn wealth into something new, strange, and full of responsibilities. The show also refers often and unromantically to poverty, in episodes on project life for instance, and points up class differences in values and lifestyles. At the start of a show on 'Stressed-out Dads', Winfrey showed two clips from *thirtysomething* of yuppie fathers caring for their children and then said, laughing and sarcastic, 'I know that happens in y'all's house every night' (*Oprah Winfrey Show*, 1990*b*).

The show may present Winfrey as a de-raced all-American success story but it gives a strong presence to middle-class African Americans and pays attention to the responsibilities and close historical relationships middle-class blacks have with and for poorer blacks, especially young people. Many issues debated between black women and men on the show involve class: the averred paucity of suitable black men available to educated black women; these women's alleged prejudices about ordinary working black men, and whether black women or men, especially those in the middle class, should have interracial relationships. No other networked shows give these topics the acrimonious airings they get on *Oprah*; the other daytime talk shows seem unable to see their contentiousness. *Oprah* is indeed at times better able to recognize the shifting and intersecting agendas of class, gender, and 'race' than is much feminist theory.

Oprah as Psychology

Alongside the show's investment in social relationships runs a much more explicit preoccupation with psychological issues and explanations. The daytime talk show is a psychological genre (Carbaugh, 1988). Most *Oprah* episodes focus on overtly psychological phenomena like 'obsessions' and 'negotiation skills', psychologists are the show's commonest 'expert' guests, Winfrey's interventions and those of audience members are mostly directed at clarifying experiences and emotions, and interpersonal communication is presented as a cathartic and enabling solution to social as well as personal problems. The show gives almost all the problems it addresses, even those like unemployment, some psychological content, usually in terms of 'feelings'. Each episode's narrative moves towards psychological closure: people end up 'feeling' better because they have 'expressed themselves' or 'started to think about what they really want'. Winfrey's psychological democracy, her representation as a person just like the audience members, is also very powerful. Showing an extreme version of the usual perception of television as the mass medium closest to interpersonal communication (Ellis, 1982; Pfau, 1990), women in *Oprah*'s audience frequently preface their contributions by telling Winfrey how much they like her and the show, and how they feel they know her almost as a friend (Waldron, 1987: 182).

The ubiquity of psychological discourse on *Oprah* is important to recognize at a time when psychology has wide-ranging social power in the overdeveloped world, and in view of the female-identified and often feminist-approved status of explanations in 'personal' terms. Psychologism has been indicted as the failing of talk shows generally. Aaron Fogel (1986) describes the genre as a collective psychological reaction to Puritanism, and Giuseppe Minnini (1989) characterizes it as pure ego, a 'talk-showman' [*sic*] holding forth in a way that does not allow dialogue, let alone productive engagement with issues. Less moralistically, it could be argued that *Oprah*'s psychologism sometimes drowns out its, at times, more complicated representations of power relationships. In an episode on obsessional jealousy, one woman's account of how her youth had facilitated her husband's manipulation of her was invalidated and replaced by Winfrey's, a psychologist's, and audience members' declarations that people can only do things to you if you let them.

The show mirrors psychologists' professional confidence in their ability to improve things with a relentless optimism that leaves little room for persistent problems or imperfect solutions. Psychologists do not however have an easy ride on the show. They are often drowned out by audience members' and Winfrey's own floods of psychological pronouncements and Winfrey jokes about these appropriations of expertise. The show steers its audience towards self-help groups or books written by its guest rather than towards professional help. In an episode that featured women living with men who would not marry them, first the audience, and then Winfrey made restrained fun of the guest psychologists' zeal:

PSYCHOLOGIST 1: ... counseling would really be appropriate (audience laughter starts) for a couple who seems to be, stuck, no, I'm talking about together, and together with a counselor establishing an agenda for themselves as a couple ...

WINFREY: All therapists want everybody to go to counseling, yeah (laughs).

PSYCHOLOGIST 2: Oprah it helps ... it helps a lot.

WINFREY: Oh I know it does, I know it helps a lot. (*Oprah Winfrey Show*, 1990*a*)

Antiprofessionalism is a common stance in the USA but *Oprah*'s lay psychology has other connotations too. Its emphasis on getting people to communicate is part of a utopian picture of a viewing community and a world in which everyone knows they are not alone. Often the stress on communication recalls a religious commitment to testifying (see also Masciarotte, 1991), and this convergence of talk show with worship (Fogel, 1986) takes on a specific resonance in *Oprah* from the history of black churches as places where African American women's voices could be raised and heard. The show's persistent focus on self-esteem ties into an implicit liberal democratic politics of rights, responsibilities, and choice, and, through the non-specific spirituality the show attaches to self-worth, to New Ageism. *Oprah*'s optimism about psychological improvement is associated with beliefs in religious redemption and in social progress, for which redemption is itself a metaphor. Andrea Stuart (1988; see also Bobo, 1988) has suggested that black women watching *The Color Purple* read its happy ending not within the film narrative, where it seems inconsistent and sentimental, but within broader religious, social, and historical narratives where it offers an important antidote to hopelessness. Perhaps *Oprah*'s daily psychological resolutions of dramatic suffering support a similar reading.

An individual woman may be represented on *Oprah* as shaped by social forces like racism and male violence but also as fully and only responsible for her own actions. An odd *mélange* can result, of growth psychology, religious devotion, political analysis, and personal hubris. An emblematic example on *Oprah* itself was Angelou's presentation of herself and her work. Describing her composition of a poem for Clinton's inauguration, she said she was not nervous: all she had to do was 'get centred' and write. No false humility was required: after all, 'I come from the Creator trailing wisps of glory'. And telling of her own overcoming of abuse, poverty, and racism she recalled the key realization: 'God loves *me*. Oprah, Oprah, the skies opened up. I can do *anything*' (*Oprah Winfrey Show*, 1993). Winfrey looked deeply touched, they clasped hands, and the show broke for commercials. The show's loose concatenations of ideas are easy to deride but they build up a complicated picture of psychological, as well as social and historical relationships, relationships which the show does not try to resolve. Some might see the ambiguities as disabling and claim television audiences cannot cope with them. But I think it is productive for a talk show to display, as *Oprah* does, the contradictions that traverse our subjectivities, rather than to opt for social determinist explanations of problems, victimologies that allow subjectivity no clear place, or to invoke an unproblematic human agency as the general solution, as talk shows usually do. *Oprah*'s infusion by black feminism seems to be what generates this complexity.

Oprah, Television, and Super-Realism

Oprah's reflexivity about being television calls attention to how the characteristics of television, and of the daytime talk show in particular, shape it. More than most television (see Ellis, 1982), the daytime talk show is a casual form, not watched continuously. To compensate, it is made eye-catching, with clear, immediate images and plenty of camera movement and cutting to offset the slowness of talk. Daytime viewers may be attending to things other than television or just passing through a room where the television is on, so the shows favour sound bites: punchy questions; short, clear encapsulations of arguments and feelings; brief passages of incoherent speech, tears, or silence to signal deep emotion; bursts of laughter and applause, snatches of theme music bracketing breaks and the programme itself, and enticing cliffhanger trails before each break: 'when we get back, are strong-thinking, decisive women a threat to you men?' (*Oprah Winfrey Show*, 1989b). These characteristics produce a currency of rapid, intense, simple, and repetitive aural and visual representations, from the six-note sequence that means *Oprah*, to the screwed-up, crying faces of incest survivors asked 'How did it feel?' These fragmented representations are always breaking up the coherence and continuity of the talk show's narrative of psychological improvement.

It might be said of *Oprah*, as is often argued of talk shows and television in general, that its dispersed, atomistic representations do not disturb but only support the cultural consensus (Ellis, 1982; Fogel, 1986; Miller, 1990; Minnini, 1989). From this perspective, *Oprah* is too frivolous to be feminist. Some feminists have, however, interpreted television representations that reach *Oprah*'s level of disruption as carnivalesque or melodramatic challenges to television's conventional representations of gender (Ang, 1985; Brown, 1990; Deming, 1990). I am going to argue that *Oprah*'s televisual characteristics produce rather a *super-realism* that has some modest feminist value.

Daytime talk shows like *Oprah* try to reach a realist truth by interleaving information and entertainment, and deploying narratives of psychological growth to pull this 'infotainment' together. Sometimes, they do not manage the integration and super-realism, a realism torn out of shape by excesses of emotion or empiricism, disrupts the explanatory framework. On *Oprah*, this disruption happens in one of two ways. First, super-realism may take over when a 'psychological' truth recurs so often on the show that it begins to shed its individual psychological character and starts to look more like a social, political, or religious fact. The narratives of sexual abuse on *Oprah*, for example, very similar and endlessly repeated, seem to go beyond psychological understanding to become facts about gender relationships that demand explanation in other, social terms. It is the televisual superficiality and facility of the show that allows this super-real excess to register.

Oprah's second type of super-realism appears when the emotions in the show get so intense that the show forgoes any claim to provide information and simply displays an extreme effect—accessible to psychoanalytic interpretation, perhaps, but not to the kinds of psychological explanations most of us are familiar with and use. For instance, when the show featured an abused woman with 92 personalities, it could not provide a coherent account of her subjectivity. Abuse started to seem utterly idiosyncratic and affectively overwhelming. Again, this registering of excess relied on the show's super-real televisual character: on snappy formulations of monstrous feelings and quick moves to commercial breaks ('back in a moment') that left the unspeakable and the unimaginable resounding around American living rooms.

I would argue that *Oprah* owes its cultural effects largely to its super-realist emotional and empirical excesses, which rework or Signify on television and culture, something talk shows' more conventional psychological explanations are unlikely to do. Its contribution to US debates about the education of black children or the relationships between black women and black men comes not so much from its explicit consideration of these debates as from their unannounced, unasked for, and unmarked recurrence within the show, so frequently and pervasively that they become super-real facts, uncontainable within the show's psychological narratives.

Henry Louis Gates (1989) wrote that he hopes 'blacks will stop looking to tv for (their) social liberation'. Feminists of colour and white feminists rarely look to television for social liberation. But television can achieve what feminist writing finds difficult: *Oprah*'s interwoven explorations of 'race', class, and gender and its popularization of aspects of black feminist thought are examples. And feminists may discover something about how to deal with the complex connections between subjectivity, gender, and other social relationships from the suspension of the *Oprah Winfrey Show* between fluff and gravity; psychology, social analysis, and emotions; realism and super-realism; and from their own difficulties in addressing this mixture.

I would like to thank Ann Phoenix, Kum-Kum Bhavnani, Chris Griffin, and an unnamed reviewer for their helpful comments and encouragement.

References   Ang, I. (1985), *Watching Dallas: Soap Opera and the Melodramatic Imagination* (London: Methuen).

Angelou, M. (1970), *I Know Why The Caged Bird Sings* (New York: Random House).

Bad Object-Choices (1991) (ed.), *How Do I Look? Queer Film and Video* (Seattle: Bay Press).

Bhavnani, K.-K. (1990), 'What's Power Got To Do With It?', in I. Parker and J. Shotter (eds.), *Deconstructing Social Psychology* (London: Routledge).

Bobo, J. (1988), '*The Color Purple*: Black Women as Cultural Readers', in D. Pribram (ed.), *Female Spectators Looking at Film and Television* (London: Verso).

Boemer, M. (1987), 'Correlating Lead-in Show Ratings with Local Television News Ratings', *Journal of Broadcasting and Electronic Media*, 31: 89–94.

Bordo, S. (1989), 'Reading the Slender Body', in M. Jacobus, E. Foxkeller, and S. Shuttleworth (eds.), *Body/Politics* (New York: Routledge).

Bretl, D., and Cantor, J. (1988), 'The Portrayal of Men and Women in US Television Commercials: A Recent Content Analysis and Trends over 15 Years', *Sex Roles*, 18: 595–609.

Brown, M. E. (1990), 'Motley Moments: Soap Operas, Carnival, Gossip and the Power of the Utterance', in M. E. Brown (ed.), *Television and Women's Culture: The Politics of the Popular* (London: Sage).

Brunsdon, C. (1989), 'Text and Audience', in E. Seiter, H. Borchers, G. Kreutzner, and E. Warth (eds.), *Remote Control* (New York: Routledge).

Butler, J. (1990), *Gender Trouble* (New York: Routledge).

Carbaugh, D. (1988), *Talking American: Cultural Discourses on Donahue* (Norwood, NJ: Ablex).

Coward, R. (1983), *Patriarchal Precedents* (London: Routledge & Kegan Paul).

—— (1989), *The Whole Truth* (London: Faber & Faber).

Davis, D. (1990), 'Portrayals of Women in Prime-time Network Television: Some Demographic Characteristics', *Sex Roles*, 23: 325–32.

de Lauretis, T. (1986) (ed.), *Feminist Studies/Critical Studies* (Bloomington: Indiana Univ. Press).

—— (1991), 'Film and the Visible', in Bad Object-Choices (1991).

Deming, C. (1990), 'For Television-Centred Television Criticism: Lessons from Feminism', in M. E. Brown (ed.), *Television and Women's Culture: The Politics of the Popular* (London: Sage).

Dent, G. (1992) (ed.), *Black Popular Culture* (Seattle: Bay Press).

Doane, M. A. (1987), *The Desire to Desire* (Bloomington: Indiana Univ. Press).

Doty, A. (1992), *Making Things Perfectly Queer* (Minneapolis: Univ. of Minnesota Press).

Ellis, J. (1982), *Visible Fictions* (London: Routledge & Kegan Paul).

Fife, M. (1987), 'Promoting Racial Diversity in US Broadcasting: Federal Policies Versus Social Realities', *Media, Culture and Society*, 9: 481–505.

Fogel, A. (1986), 'Talk Shows: On Reading Television', in S. Donadio, S. Railton, and S. Ormond (eds.), *Emerson and His Legacy* (Carbondale: Southern Illinois Univ. Press).

Freeman, M. (1992), 'Can We Talk? New for 1993', *Broadcasting and Cable* (Dec.), 14.

Gaines, J. (1988), 'White Privilege and Looking Relations: Race and Gender in Feminist Film Theory', Last Special Issue on 'Race', *Screen*, 29: 12–27.

Gates, H. L. (1988), *The Signifying Monkey* (New York: Oxford Univ. Press).

—— (1989), 'TV's Black World Turns—But Stays Unreal', *New York Times* (Nov.), 12.

Goodman, F. (1991), 'Madonna and Oprah: The Companies They Keep', *Working Women*, 16: 52–5.

Grey, H. (1989), 'Television, Black Americans, and the American Dream', *Critical Studies in Mass Communication*, 6: 376–86.

Gross, L (1989), 'Out of the Mainstream: Sexual Minorities and the Mass Media', in E. Seiter, H. Borchers, G. Kreutzner, and E. Warth (eds.), *Remote Control* (New York: Routledge).

Guider, E. (1987), 'Katz Advises How to Handle Daytime Queen', *Variety* (July), 8.

Harrison, B. (1989), 'The Importance of Being Oprah', *New York Times Magazine* (June), 11.

Heath, S. (1985), 'Joan Riviere and the Masquerade', in V. Burgin, J. Donald, and C. Kaplan (eds.), *Formations of Fantasy* (London: Methuen).

Hill Collins, P. (1990), *Black Feminist Thought* (Cambridge, Mass.: Unwin Hyman).

hooks, b. (1981), *Ain't I A Woman? Black Women and Feminism* (Boston: South End Press).

—— (1989), *Talking Back: Thinking Feminist, Thinking Black* (Boston: South End Press).

Jones, L. (1991), 'Hot Buttered "Soul" ', *Village Voice* (Mar.), 12.

Julien, I., and Mercer, K. (1988), 'Introduction: De Margin and De Center', Last Special Issue on 'Race', *Screen*, 29: 2–10.

Kaplan, E. A. (1987), 'Feminism Criticism and Television', in R. Allen (ed.), *Channels of Discourse* (Chapel Hill: Univ. of North Carolina Press).

King, N. (1987), *Everybody Loves Oprah* (New York: Morrow).

Lorde, A. (1984), *Sister Outsider: Essays and Speeches* (Trumansburg, NY: Crossing Press).

McClellan, S. (1993), 'Freshman "Deep Space Nine" Records Stellar Sweep Debut', *Broadcasting and Cable* (Apr.), 24–6.

Masciarotte, G.-J. (1991), 'C'mon Girl: Oprah Winfrey and the Discourse of Feminine Talk', *Genders*, 11: 81–110.

Miller, M. C. (1990), *Boxed In: The Culture of Television* (Evanston, Ill.: Northwestern Univ. Press).

Minnini, G. (1989), 'Genres de discours et types de dialogue: Le "Talk-show" ', in E. Weigand and F. Hundnurscher (eds.), *Dialoganalyse*, ii (Tübingen: Niemeyer).

Moraga, C., and Anzaldua, G. (1981), *This Bridge Called My Back* (Watertown, Mass.: Persephone Press).

Morris, M. (1988), 'Banality in Cultural Studies', *Block*, 14: 15–26.

Mulvey, L. (1975), 'Visual Pleasure and Narrative Cinema', *Screen*, 16: 6–18.

—— (1981), 'Afterthoughts on "Visual Pleasure and Narrative Cinema" Inspired by "Duel in the Sun" ', *Framework*, 15/16/17: 12–15.

Naylor, G. (1982), *The Women of Brewster Place* (New York: Viking).

Nightingale, V. (1990), 'Women as Audiences', in M. E. Brown (ed.), *Television and Women's Culture: The Politics of the Popular* (London: Sage).

Oprah Winfrey Show (1989*a*), 'Blacks and Whites Dating' (New York: Journal Graphics, 1 Mar.).

—— (1989*b*), 'Home Fights' (New York: Journal Graphics, 25 Apr.).

—— (1990*a*), 'A Mother's Plea: Marry My Daughter' (23 May, author's transcript).

—— (1990*b*), 'Stressed-Out Dads' (30 May, author's transcript).

—— (1992), '1991 Follow-up Show' (8 Jan., Channel 4, Britain, author's transcript).

—— (1993), 'Maya Angelou Interview' (13 July, author's transcript).

Pfau, M. (1990), 'A Channel Approach to Television Influence', *Journal of Broadcasting and Electronic Media*, 34: 195–214.

Press, A. (1990), 'Class, Gender and the Female Viewer: Women's Responses to *Dynasty*', in M. E. Brown (ed.), *Television and Women's Culture: The Politics of the Popular* (London: Sage).

Rich, A. (1986), 'Compulsory Heterosexuality and Lesbian Existence', in *Blood, Bread and Poetry* (New York: Norton).

Riley, D. (1988), *Am I That Name? Feminism and the Category of 'Women' in History* (Minneapolis: Univ. of Minnesota Press).

Rose, T. (1990), 'Never Trust a Big Butt and a Smile', *Camera Obscura*, 23: 109–32 (in this volume).

Spelman, E. (1990), *Inessential Woman* (London: Women's Press).

Spivak, G. (1988), *In Other Worlds* (New York: Routledge, Chapman and Hall).

Stacey, J. (1988), 'Desperately Seeking Difference', in L. Gamman and M. Marshment (eds.), *The Female Gaze* (London: Women's Press).

Stuart, A. (1988), ' "The Color Purple": In Defence of Happy Endings', in L. Gamman and M. Marshment (eds.), *The Female Gaze* (London: Women's Press).

Waldron, R. (1987), *Oprah!* (New York: St Martin's Press).

Walker, A. (1982), *You Can't Keep A Good Woman Down* (London: Women's Press).

—— (1983), *In Search of Our Mothers' Gardens* (New York: Harcourt Brace Jovanovich).

Walkerdine, V. (1989), 'Video Replay', in V. Burgin (ed.), *Formations of Pleasure* (London: Methuen).

Ziegler, D., and White, A. (1990), 'Women and Minorities on Network Television News: An Examination of Correspondents and Newsmakers', *Journal of Broadcasting and Electronic Media*, 34: 215–23.

8

Identity in Feminist Television Criticism

Charlotte Brunsdon

Introduction

T IS ABOUT fifteen years since the first feminist television criticism began to appear in Britain and the US, and it is now possible to begin to construct a history of this criticism, and particularly, a history of its personae, of the characters who are specific to feminist television criticism: the feminist television critic and the female viewer. This pair, and the drama of their identity and difference, seem one of the most interesting productions of feminist television criticism, and in the contours of their relationships I think we can see patterns of feminist intellectual work which are not specific to the criticism of television.

My argument is briefly, that the formative stage of feminist television criticism extends from about 1976 to the mid-1980s, and that the key feature of this formative stage is the move from outside to inside the academy. While in 1976 the feminist critic writes with a primary address to her movement sisters, in a tone quite hostile to the 'mass media', yet concerned to justify her attention to television, by the mid-1980s she inhabits a more academic position, tends to address other scholars, and is beginning to be anthologized in books used on both Communications and Women's Studies courses (*Spare Rib*, 1972 onwards; Butcher *et al.*, 1974; King and Stott, 1977; Tuchman *et al.*, 1978; Kaplan, 1983; Masterman, 1984; MacCabe, 1986). There are a series of journal special issues in the 1980s through which it is also possible to chart a rather more confident engagement with television specifically.[1] Thus occasions such as the 'Console-ing Passions' conference held at the University of Iowa in 1992 and billed, correctly, as 'The first feminist conference on television and video', can properly be understood as one manifestation of the more academic second period of feminist television criticism, as can the recent rash of 'woman and television' books such as Mary Ellen Brown's *Television and Women's Culture* (1990), Christine Geraghty's *Women and Soap Opera* (1991), Andrea Press's *Women Watching Television* (1991), Lynn Spigel's *Make Room for TV* (1992), Ann Gray's *Video Playtime* (1992), and Julie D'Acci's *Defining Women: Television and the Case of* Cagney and Lacey (1993). If the formative period is marked, as I have suggested, at an institu-

© Sage, 1993.

Originally published in *Media, Culture and Society*, **15/2 (Apr. 1993)**, 309–20.

1 For example: *Women's Studies International Quarterly*, 3/1 (1980); *Communication*, 9/3–4 (1987); *Journal of Communication Inquiry*, 11/1 (1987); *Camera Obscura*, 16 (1988).

tional level, by a move from outside to inside the academy, it is also characterized, or perhaps I should say experienced, through the constitution of a new and as we shall see, contradictory, kind of individual, the feminist intellectual.

Feminist Television Criticism and the Academy

One of the reasons for the shift from outside to inside the academy is that feminist concerns have had a particular impact in two critical areas in the study of television: first in relation to the study of a genre, soap opera, and second in relation to the study of the audience, a perennial concern for media studies and mass communications. This is not to suggest that there hasn't been substantial feminist work in other genres/fields (for example: Mellencamp, 1986; Skirrow, 1987; Holland, 1991; or work collected in Mellencamp, 1990; Tuchman and Daniels, 1978; Creedon, 1989) nor to underestimate the attention to audiences and serial drama in existing research on television (Arnheim, 1944; Herzog, 1944), but to argue that it is in relation to soap opera and audience that feminist critical work on television has made a distinctive contribution which is recognized as such in the wider arena.

Thus Ien Ang (1985), Dorothy Hobson (1982), Michèle Mattelart (1986), Tania Modleski (1979), Ellen Seiter (1981), and the London Women and Film Group (Dyer *et al.*, 1981) all conducted research on soap opera in the late 1970s and 1980s, work which either hypothesized about the female audience or, in Ien Ang's case, actually investigated it. All this work forms part of a much larger body of feminist research, begun in the late 1970s, which re-evaluates traditional feminine genres and forms, like the women's picture, romantic fiction, the diary, and the magazine, and, either by implication or directly, investigates audience engagement (Radway, 1984; Gledhill, 1987; Taylor, 1989; Winship, 1987).

Soap opera, as a genre, including US prime-time shows as well as much more localized national serials, has moved from being a ridiculed object of study to a mainstay of many syllabuses. Thus, in addition to the pioneering work mentioned above, there has been—and this is not an exhaustive list—the long Liebes and Katz *Dallas* project (1990), Robert Allen's *Speaking of Soap Operas* (1985), Sandy Flitterman-Lewis's work on commercials and seriality (1983, 1988), David Buckingham's study of *EastEnders* (1987), Christine Geraghty's comprehensive analysis of the genre (1991), Sonia Livingstone's psychological study of audiences (1989), and the work of Kim Christian Schrøder (1988), Jostein Gripsrud (1990), Jane Feuer (1984), and Mark Finch (1986) on the prime-time soap *Dynasty*.

In the same period, there has been a general shift, across a whole range of social science and humanities disciplines, from a focus on the study of the text to an increased interest in the audience. In the study of television there has been a noticeable—if controversial—embrace of the virtues of qualitative methodology, a vogue for the work associated with the Centre for Contemporary Cultural Studies, and a series of detailed studies of particular audiences or audience sectors (Fiske, 1987, 1990; Gillespie, 1989; Grossberg *et al.*, 1992; Seiter *et al.*, 1989).

From its inception, this 'new' media ethnography has been marked by the problematic of gender in one of two ways. Either it has been mainly women who were the subject of the inquiry—as with the work of Hobson (1980), Ang (1985), Bobo (1988), and Radway (1984) or, because the focus of the work is domestic, as with the work of Morley (1986), Gray (1987), Moores (1991), and Spigel (1992), gender (and generation) have been significant analytic and interpretative categories. Thus we could identify the feminist contribution to television research in the last fifteen years, in its most widely accepted form, to be the gendering of two key concepts, that of genre and that of audience. We now have gendered genres, and we also have gendered audiences. This shift can be exemplified quite simply in the differences between early textbooks of television studies, such as Fiske and Hartley's *Reading Television* (1978) and Len Masterman's *Teaching About Television* (1980), or textbook collections in communications such as Curran *et al.* (1977), and later books such as John Fiske's *Television Culture* (1987), Robert Allen's *Channels of Discourse* (1987), and Curran and Gurevitch's *Mass Media and Society* (1991), which pay more specific attention to issues of gender both as an analytic category and object of study.

Existing Accounts of Feminist Television Criticism

There are several surveys of feminist media criticism, only one of which, by Ann Kaplan (1987), is specifically concerned with the study of television, although the introductions to the three collections on women and television—Baehr and Dyer (1987), Brown (1990), and Spigel and Mann (1992)—also offer some mapping of the field. What is striking about the more general surveys of feminism and the media such as those offered by Leslie Steeves (1987) and Liesbet van Zoonen (1991) is the similarity of the typologies used by both these authors and Kaplan (1987). In each case, the typologies are a variant of the familiar political distinctions between liberal, radical, and socialist feminism. Thus Kaplan combines 'bourgeois, Marxist, radical and post-structuralist' feminism with the distinction between essentialist and non-essentialist approaches, while van Zoonen distinguishes between liberal, radical, and socialist feminism in her analysis of the range of feminist media research. Both authors, with slightly different emphases and inflections, argue for the methodological and analytic significance of the tradition of British cultural studies to the feminist analysis of television, seeing this as one way of avoiding essentialism. The value of these typologies—the way in which they point to the differentiations within feminist thought, and the connection between media analyses and the analyses of wider social issues—should not obscure the fact that, as the authors themselves suggest, and Margaret Gallagher (1992) points out, very little criticism fits into only one category, and some work, such as Gallagher's own, is categorized differently in different schemas. Van Zoonen however, in a suggestive section entitled 'The Audience and "US" ' (1991: 43–4) raises issues about feminist research on popular culture which recur across all feminist work, and it is these ideas which I wish to explore in my own typology.

A Different Typology

I want to construct a typology which is based on the conceptualization of the relationship between *feminism* and *women*, or the feminist and other women as inscribed within the critical text. I offer this categorization most immediately as an heuristic, rather than an historical typology. That is, I am not suggesting that feminist criticism has moved from stage one to stage three, although I would argue that there are discernible historical shifts in the type of paradigms that are dominant at any one moment. My three categories would be the following:

(*a*) Transparent—no others;
(*b*) Hegemonic—non-feminist women others;
(*c*) Fragmented—everyone an other.

Each of these categories is defined through the relationship between the feminist and her other, the ordinary woman, the non-feminist woman, the housewife, the television viewer. It is this relationship, the way in which feminism constructs and has constructed itself in relation to the category 'woman', rather than the way in which women's subordination is theorized, which is essential to an understanding of feminist cultural criticism. That is, I am suggesting that feminist critical discourse itself constructs and produces, rather than simply analyses, a series of positions for 'women'.

■ **Transparent**

The positing of a transparent relationship between feminism and women is characteristic of the utopian, activist—and I think we could properly say formative—phase of post-1960s feminism. Although very rarely found without some articulation with the second 'hegemonic' relation, this utopian moment posits a shared sisterhood between all women, a consciousness of women as a gender group who are subject to a global patriarchal subordination and who thus have gender specific experiences in common. The dream, and the frequently asserted reality, of this moment is that all women are sisters, there is no 'otherness' between feminism and women, and that the appropriate pronoun of criticism is 'we'.

It is this consciousness that dominates media reviews in, for example, early British movement magazines like *Spare Rib* in the 1970s, and it is this consciousness, this 'we', which has been most vulnerable to attack for its political exclusions (which women?) and its epistemological assumptions (do women know differently?).

It is also, however, this notion of a shared gender experience which underpins part of the challenge that feminist work has offered to sociological and ethnographic research. Thus Dorothy Hobson's early research—which was scrupulous in its understanding of the complexity of the relationship between interviewer and interviewee, and which was consistently cautious about the class assumptions of the feminist 'we'—was not initially about the media, but about the experience of *being* a young working-class housewife/mother, and she insists on the way in which reference to shared experience increased the richness of her interviews (Hobson, 1978). Similarly, the work of the distinguished sociologist Ann Oakley offers some of its most radical challenges to existing social science methodologies in her consistent refusal to occupy conventional positions of neutrality in response to the questions of her 'interviewee mothers' (Oakley, 1981). She adopts this strategy as a specific response to what she calls 'the dilemma of a feminist interviewer interviewing women' (Oakley, 1981: 47), when the topic of the interviews is the frightening, but eagerly anticipated experience of a first baby.

Ironically, given that it has partly been the political attacks on the unthinking exclusions of this feminist 'we' that have marginalized it as an enunciative position, it is currently in response to the writing of women of colour that we most often find the assumption of transparency. Thus we find Jacqueline Bobo's work often characterized as 'what black women think' and as the site for the investigation of ethnicity—as if all those white audiences were without ethnic identity—and as if the articulation of ethnicity and gender here is not also historical, contradictory, and sometimes provisional (Bobo, 1988). Indeed, in less academic feminism, it could be argued that the acceptance of the political critique of the transparency of the straight white Western feminist 'we' has led to a multiplication of special category, transparent, representative identities—older lesbians, working-class women, etc.—who are perhaps enabled to speak as a 'we', but also imprisoned by the inflexible demands of this identity fixing. This tendency is clearly represented by the British collection on women in the media, *Out of Focus* (Davies *et al.*, 1987).

■ **Hegemonic**   What I am calling the hegemonic relationship between the feminist and the woman has been the most common position within feminist television criticism. It would also be possible to call this structure of relationship 'recruitist' to use Angela McRobbie's term (McRobbie, 1982), the impulse to transform the feminine identifications of women to feminist ones. The construction of feminist identity through this relation involves the differentiation of the feminist from her other, the ordinary woman, the housewife, the woman she might have become, but at the same time, a compulsive engagement with this figure. The position is often profoundly contradictory, involving both the repudiation and defence of traditional femininity. In psychoanalytic terms, we could hypothesize that the encounter between the feminist and the housewife—a very clear arena for early and proto-feminist work from the 1960s on (Friedan, 1963; Gavron, 1966; Oakley, 1974; Hall, 1980; Lowry, 1980)—involves not just the construction of an identity 'independent woman' against another possible one 'dependent woman', but, specifically, an engagement with the mother.[2] In terms of feminist television criticism, this usually meant the television viewer, in relation to whom much of the early writing is profoundly ambivalent.

A key rhetorical device here, one with which we are familiar from other traditions of anthropological and sociological work, is the introduction of a guide or intermediary, who gives instruction to the researcher about the pleasures and procedures of television viewing. These figures are often to be found in acknowledgements—for example, Carol Lopate, in one of the first

2 Janice Winship, whose work van Zoonen selects as not producing a tension between 'us' feminists and 'them', makes this point explicit in her dedication of her book on women's magazines to 'My mother and . . . myself' (Winship, 1987: v).

feminist discussions of soap opera: 'I should like to thank Irena Kleinbort, whose insights were invaluable in helping me develop some of the ideas in this paper, and who furnished me with examples from her more extensive soap opera watching' (1977: 51). This disclaimer about soap expertise was anticipated by her earlier comment about learning how to watch, 'Until I got to know the stories, the afternoon felt like one long, complicated saga . . .' (1977: 41). It is almost as if the researcher must prove herself not too competent within the sphere of popular culture to retain credibility within the sphere of analysis.

Tania Modleski's influential essay, 'The Search for Tomorrow in Today's Soap Operas', is marked by a similar ambivalence, particularly in its early version. For example:

> Clearly, women find soap operas eminently entertaining, and an analysis of the pleasure that soaps afford can provide clues not only about how feminists can challenge this pleasure, but also how they can incorporate it. For, outrageous as this assertion may at first appear, I would suggest that soap operas are not altogether at odds with a possible feminist aesthetics.   (1979: 18)

This passage displays a clear separation between the author and 'women', with the author explicitly addressing herself to 'feminists', a category in some ways opposed to 'women'. The key words are 'clues' and 'outrageous'. 'Clues' reveals that this is an evangelical enterprise of detection, the analysis of soap opera will render information about other pleasures—pleasures that must be challenged. So the justification of the academic enterprise to other feminists is through its gathering of politically useful knowledge. However, within this address to an imagined sceptical feminist audience, Modleski is also making a polemical point: 'outrageous as this assertion may at first appear'. This 'outrageous' marks the other element in what I am calling the hegemonic relationship, the defence of 'women's culture'. In 1979 this insistence is made against the grain of feminist attitudes to popular television, insisting that there is something here to be taken seriously. Both 'clues' and 'outrageous' disappear from the rewritten book version of the essay, where the two sentences are split.

> Clearly, women find soap operas eminently entertaining, and an analysis of the pleasure these programs afford can provide feminists with ways not only to challenge this pleasure but to incorporate it into their own artistic practices.   (Modleski, 1982: 104)

and a page later

> Indeed, I would like to argue that soap operas are not altogether at odds with an already developing, though still embryonic, feminist aesthetics. (Modleski, 1982: 105)

These rewritten versions, smoother, more confident, less embattled, also give much less sense of that author as caught between the positions of 'woman', 'feminist', and 'intellectual'.

What we find, over and over again, in early feminist television criticism, is the complicated negotiation of the position from which the author writes.

There is a fleeting and fluctuating identification with a gender group (the residue of 'we women') which is at the same time a disavowal of many of the attributes of conventional femininity, crossed with the contradictory demands of intellectual credibility, which is of course conventionally ungendered. The identity of the feminist intellectual, which strains to combine these identities, is—necessarily—at this stage, profoundly unstable. What I have called the hegemonic impulse within feminist criticism, apart from its straightforward desire for a political mobilization around the inequities of gender, is also I think, an attempt to make the femininity/feminism relationship less contradictory by recruiting the one to the other.

■ **Fragmented**

The third way of thinking about the relationship between feminism and women I am calling 'fragmented' because it is founded on the possibility that there is no necessary relationship between these two categories. This moment is constituted by the force of the critiques directed at what I have called the 'transparent' moment both politically and theoretically as the implications of what is normally called the 'essentialism' debate percolate through the academy. 'Woman' becomes a profoundly problematic category—and arguably and ironically—'feminist' becomes rather more stable (Riley, 1988; Haraway, 1985; Spivak, 1987). Franklin *et al.* (1991) have already offered one survey of the more general issues at stake here for cultural analysis in this journal. I want to sketch briefly two distinct directions in current research work which share a radical particularism. One is towards 'historical autobiography', the other towards a stress on the contingency of gender identifications, and the significance of the articulation of these identifications with the whole range of other formative identifications. Valerie Walkerdine's work (1990) on the video-viewing of the *Rocky* films in the home of a working-class family can be understood in the context of a growing body of very sophisticated feminist autobiography (Heron, 1985; Steedman, 1986; Trinh, 1989; Kuhn, 1991; Lury, 1991; Wallace, 1990; Ware, 1992), all of which can be understood as contributing to, or commenting on, the fragmentation of the 'transparent' relationship between feminism and women in their exploration of the constitutive dynamics of class, ethnicity, migration, and gender in the story of each self. All of these accounts suggest the impossibility of telling stories in which individuals are 'just' gendered. The other thread, best exemplified by Ang and Hermes's radical review of the use of gender as an explanatory category in recent ethnographic projects, argues for the radical contingency of gender identifications, and against a research agenda which concentrates on 'women's culture' to the neglect of an articulation with ethnicity and class. The logic of Ang and Hermes's position is to jettison 'some fixed figure of "women"', and to argue that 'any feminist standpoint will necessarily have to present itself as partial, based upon the knowledge that while some women sometimes share some common interests and face some common enemies, such commonalities are by no means universal' (Ang and Hermes, 1991: 324).

Conclusion   In summary, I have offered a typology of feminist television criticism in which the varying inscriptions of the relative identities 'feminist critic' and 'ordinary woman viewer' are seen as distinctive. I have suggested that the period (1975–84) of the institutional acceptance and development of feminist television criticism in the white anglophone academy (Britain, USA, Australia) is a period in which we see the professionalization of the enunciative identity 'feminist critic'. I have tried to stress that I am offering an analytic, rather than an historical, typology, although Raymond Williams's distinction between residual, dominant, and emergent modes of production might allow some mapping of these modes of feminist identity over both institutional changes in the academy and political changes in the feminist movements. I can offer here only the most blunt hypotheses. I could thus characterize the utopian, transparent moment, as dominant within the early days of second-wave feminism. There are also at this stage no scholars appointed to teach 'Feminist Theory' or 'Gender Studies' in universities and colleges. The unconscious class and ethnic identity of the 'we' of this moment has been extensively documented elsewhere. I suggest that the dominant mode of feminist critique in the period of academic institutionalization is an hegemonic/recruitist one, hegemonic in the sense that this feminism has aspirations to dominate all accounts of the feminine. In this mode, the feminist critic is distinguished from her other, the ordinary woman, and the complicated defence and repudiation of conventional feminine culture which characterizes much feminist criticism of popular culture begins to be institutionalized. The pronouns here are 'we' and 'they', with the shifting referent of the 'we' being both 'feminists' and 'women', although the 'they' is always 'women'. The third moment is that in which the epistemological grounding of the political category 'woman' is thrown into crisis—engulfed in a sea of what Dick Hebdige has called 'the Posts' (Hebdige, 1988). Here we have the confluence of the political critique of the 1970s with post-structuralist thought and the theorization of the post-modern. Everyone here is an other—and there are no pronouns beyond the 'I'—but there are, relatively, lots of women teaching and writing books about these ideas.

It is customary, in typologies of this type, for the approach or position being advocated to come at the end. However, I am not sure that this type of theoretical clean get-away is either possible or desirable. First, the logic of my own argument so far compels me to observe that my theoretically chic third category is itself dependent on its otherness from the first two categories. It too involves a repudiation of earlier femininities—in this case, feminisms. Indeed I would even venture that the fierce debate about essentialism which dominated feminist academic work in the later 1980s could be understood symptomatically as the repudiation of the 'transparent' and 'hegemonic' moments (de Lauretis, 1990). Second—and this is a point which I can only make most tentatively—I think the apparent intellectual autonomy of the third category would reward sociological scrutiny. That is, I am interested by arguments made by feminist scholars such as Meaghan Morris that post-structuralism/postmodernism should partly be understood as responses to the political and epistemological challenges of feminism—and, one should add, post-colonial movements (Morris, 1988). However, I also think this last position may be a much less conflictual one for *women* to inhabit *as intellectuals,* and it is to this end that I would, very crudely, point to the increasing dominance of this position as feminism becomes more academically visible outside the specialist enclaves of Women's Studies.

So if there are no theoretical clean get-aways, how can we reinterrogate this typology? Perhaps with the humility and sense of history that Christine Geraghty shows in the following passage which comes at the end of her book on soap opera:

> In marking a change in the experience of writing about *Coronation Street* in the mid-seventies and in writing about soap opera now, I am conscious of my own ambiguities about the project. What then was a desire to re-evaluate a cultural form which was denigrated, at least in part, because it was associated with women, now runs the risk of celebrating an illusion—the assertion of a common sensibility between women and a set of values sustaining us simply because we are women. In this context even to write 'we' rather than 'they' becomes problematic in its assumption and smacks of a community of interest which needs to be constructed rather than asserted.   (1990: 197)

Geraghty here gives an account of the historicity of identities and identifications, a micro-history of the identity 'woman' during the brief period of feminist work on television with which I have been concerned. She rejects the assumptions of shared interest—but she is still interested in sharing interests. The logic of her argument is a recognition of the difficulties of any move outside the potential solipsism of a 'fragmented' feminist identity—but not an abandonment of the project. She did finish the book.

References   Adams, P., and Cowie, E. (1990) (eds.), *The Woman in Question*, m/f (London: Verso).
Allen, R. C. (1985), *Speaking of Soap Operas* (Chapel Hill: Univ. of North Carolina Press).
—— (1987) (ed.), *Channels of Discourse* (London: Methuen).
Ang, I. (1985), *Watching Dallas: Soap Opera and the Melodramatic Imagination* (London: Methuen).
—— and Hermes, J. (1991), 'Gender and/in Media Consumption', in J. Curran and M. Gurevitch (eds.), *Mass Media and Society*, 307–28.
Arnheim, R. (1944), 'The World of the Daytime Serial', in P. Lazarsfeld and F. Stanton (eds.), *Radio Research 1942–3* (New York: Duell, Sloan, and Pearce), 34–85.
Baehr, H., and Dyer, G. (1987) (eds.) *Boxed-In* (London: Pandora).
Bobo, J. (1988), '*The Color Purple*: Black Women as Cultural Readers', in E. D. Pribram (ed.), *Female Spectators* (London: Verso), 90–109.
Brown, M. E. (1990), *Television and Women's Culture* (London, Newbury Park, New Delhi: Sage).
Buckingham, D. (1987), *Public Secrets: EastEnders and its Audience* (London: British Film Institute).
Butcher, H., *et al.* (1974), 'Images of Women in the Media', stencilled occasional paper, Centre for Contemporary Cultural Studies, University of Birmingham.
Carby, H. (1982), 'White Woman Listen!', in Centre for Contemporary Cultural Studies, *The Empire Strikes Back* (London: Hutchinson), 212–36.
Creedon, P. (1989) (ed.), *Women in Mass Communication* (Newbury Park: Sage).
Curran, J., *et al.* (1977) (eds.), *Mass Communication and Society* (London: Edward Arnold).

—— and Gurevitch, M. (1991), *Mass Media and Society* (Sevenoaks: Edward Arnold).

D'Acci, J. (1994), *Defining Women: Television and the Case of* Cagney and Lacey (Chapel Hill: Univ. of North Carolina Press).

Davies, K., *et al.* (1987) (eds.), *Out of Focus* (London: The Women's Press).

de Lauretis, T. (1990), 'Upping the Anti (sic) in Feminist Theory', in M. Hirsh and E. Fox Keller (eds.), *Conflicts in Feminism* (New York: Routledge), 255–70.

Dyer, R., *et al.* (1981), *Coronation Street* (London: British Film Institute).

Feuer, J. (1984), 'Melodrama, Serial Form and Television Today', *Screen*, 25/1: 4–16.

Finch, M. (1986), 'Sex and Address in *Dynasty*', *Screen*, 27/6: 24–42.

Fiske, J. (1987), *Television Culture* (London: Routledge).

—— (1990), 'Ethnosemiotics: Some Personal and Theoretical Reflections', *Cultural Studies*, 4/1: 85–99.

—— and Hartley, J. (1978), *Reading Television* (London: Methuen).

Flitterman, S. (1983), 'The Real Soap Opera: TV Commercials', in E. A. Kaplan (ed.), *Regarding Television*, 84–96.

Flitterman-Lewis, S. (1988), 'All's Well that Doesn't End', *Camera Obscura*, 16: 119–29.

Franklin, S., *et al.* (1991), 'Feminism and Cultural Studies: Pasts, Presents and Futures', *Media, Culture and Society*, 13/2: 171–92.

Friedan, B. (1963), *The Feminine Mystique* (New York: Dell).

Gallagher, M. (1992), 'Women and Men in the Media', *Communication Research Trends*, 12/1: 1–15.

Gavron, H. (1966), *The Captive Houswife* (London: Routledge & Kegan Paul).

Geraghty, C. (1991), *Women and Soap Opera* (Oxford: Polity).

Gillespie, M. (1989), 'Technology and Tradition: Audio-Visual Culture among South Asian Families in West London', *Cultural Studies*, 3/2: 226–39.

Gledhill, C. (1987), *Home is Where the Heart is: Studies in Melodrama and the Woman's Film* (London: British Film Institute).

Gray, A. (1987), 'Behind Closed Doors: Video Recorders in the Home', in H. Baehr and G. Dyer (eds.), *Boxed-In*, 38–54 (in this volume).

—— (1992), *Video Playtime* (London: Comedia/Routledge).

Gripsrud, J. (1990), 'Towards a Flexible Methodology in Studying Media-Meaning: *Dynasty* in Norway', *Critical Studies in Mass Communication*, 7: 117–28.

Grossberg, L., *et al.* (1992) (eds.), *Cultural Studies* (New York: Routledge).

Hall, C. (1980), 'The History of the Housewife', in Ellen Malos (ed.), *The Politics of Housework* (London: Allison and Busby), 44–71.

Haraway, D. (1985), 'A Manifesto for Cyborgs', *Socialist Review*, 15/80: 65–107.

Hebdige, D. (1988), *Hiding in the Light* (London: Comedia/Routledge).

Heron, L. (1985), *Truth, Dare or Promise* (London: Virago).

Herzog, H. (1944), 'What Do We Really Know about Daytime Serial Listeners?', in P. Lazarsfeld and F. Stanton (eds.), *Radio Research 1942–3* (New York: Duell, Sloan, and Pearce), 3–33.

Hobson, D. (1978), 'Housewives: Isolation as Oppression', in Women's Studies Group (ed.), *Women Take Issue* (London: Hutchinson), 79–95.

—— (1980), 'Housewives and the Mass Media', in Stuart Hall *et al.* (eds.), *Culture, Media, Language* (London: Hutchinson), 105–14.

—— (1982), *Crossroads: The Drama of a Soap Opera* (London: Methuen).

Holland, P. (1991), '*This Week*: Moments of Crisis', paper to the 1991 International Television Studies Conference, London.

Kaplan, E. A. (1983) (ed.), *Regarding Television* (Los Angeles: American Film Institute).

—— (1987), 'Feminist Criticism and Television', in R. C. Allen (ed.), *Channels of Discourse*, 211–53.

King, J., and Stott, M. (1977) (eds.), *Is This Your Life?: Images of Women in the Media* (London: Virago).

Kuhn, A. (1991), 'Remembrance', in Jo Spence and Patricia Holland (eds.), *Family Snaps* (London: Virago), 17–25.

—— (1992), '*Mandy* and Possibility', *Screen*, 33/3: 233–43.

Liebes, T., and Katz, E. (1990), *The Export of Meaning* (Oxford: Oxford Univ. Press).

Livingstone, S. (1989), *Making Sense of Television: The Psychology of Audience Interpretation* (Oxford: Pergamon).

Lopate, C. (1977), 'Daytime Television: You'll Never Want to Leave Home', *Radical America*, 11/1 (1977), 32–51.

Lowry, S. (1980), *The Guilt Cage* (London: Elm Tree Books).

Lury, C. (1991), 'Reading the Self: Autobiography, Gender and the Institution of the Literary', in S. Franklin *et al.* (eds.), *Off-Centre* (London: Harper Collins), 97–108.

MacCabe, C. (1986), *High Theory, Low Culture* (Manchester: Manchester Univ. Press).

McRobbie, A. (1982), 'The Politics of Feminist Research', *Feminist Review*, 12: 46–57.

Masterman, L. (1980), *Teaching About Television* (London: Macmillan).

—— (1984), (ed.) *Television Mythologies* (London: Comedia).

Mattelart, M. (1986), *Women/Media/Crisis* (London: Comedia).

Mellencamp, P. (1986), 'Situation Comedy, Feminism and Freud', in T. Modleski (ed.), *Studies in Entertainment* (Bloomington: Indiana Univ. Press), 80–95 (in this volume).

—— (1990) (ed.), *Logics of Television* (Bloomington and London: Indiana Univ. Press and the British Film Institute).

Modleski, T. (1979), 'The Search for Tomorrow in Today's Soap Operas', *Film Quarterly*, 33/1: 12–21 (in this volume).

—— (1982), *Loving with a Vengeance* (Hamden, Conn.: Shoestring Press).

Moores, S. (1991), 'Dishes and Domestic Cultures: Satellite TV as Household Technology', paper to International Television Studies Conference, London.

Morley, D. (1986), *Family Television* (London: Comedia).

Morris, M. (1988), *The Pirate's Fiancée* (London: Verso).

Oakley, A. (1974), *Housewife* (London: Allen Lane).

—— (1981), 'Interviewing Women: A Contradiction in Terms', in Helen Roberts (ed.), *Doing Feminist Research* (London: Routledge & Kegan Paul), 30–61.

Press, A. L. (1991), *Women Watching Television* (Philadelphia: Univ. of Pennsylvania Press).

Radway, J. (1984), *Reading the Romance* (Chapel Hill: Univ. of North Carolina Press).

Rakow, L. F. (1992) (ed.), *Women Making Meaning: New Feminist Directions in Communication* (New York: Routledge).

Riley, D. (1988), '*Am I that Name?*' *Feminism and the Category of 'Women' in History* (London: Macmillan).

Schrøder, K. C. (1988), 'The Pleasure of *Dynasty*: The Weekly Reconstruction of Self-confidence', in P. Drummond and R. Paterson (eds.), *Television and its Audience* (London: British Film Institute), 61–82.

Seiter, E. (1981), 'The Role of the Woman Reader: Eco's Narrative Theory and Soap Opera', *Tabloid*, 6: 35–43.

—— *et al.* (1989) (eds.), *Remote Control* (London: Routledge).

Skirrow, G. (1987), 'Women/Acting/Power', in H. Baehr and G. Dyer (eds.), *Boxed-In*, 164–83.

Spigel, L. (1992), *Make Room for TV* (Chicago: Univ. of Chicago Press).

—— and Mann, D. (1992) (eds.), *Private Screenings* (Minneapolis: Univ. of Minnesota Press).

Spivak, G. (1987), *In Other Worlds* (London: Methuen).

Steedman, C. (1986), *Landscape for a Good Woman* (London: Virago).

Steeves, H. L. (1987), 'Feminist Theories and Media Studies', *Critical Studies in Mass Communication*, 4/2: 95–135.

Taylor, H. (1989), *Scarlett's Women* (London: Virago).

Trinh, T. Minh-ha (1989), *Woman, Native, Other* (Bloomington: Indiana Univ. Press).

Tuchman, G., *et al.* (1978) (eds.), *Hearth and Home* (New York: Oxford Univ. Press).

van Zoonen, L. (1991), 'Feminist Perspectives on the Media', in J. Curran and M. Gurevitch (eds.), *Mass Media and Society*, 33–54.

Walkerdine, V. (1990), *Schoolgirl Fictions* (London: Verso).

Wallace, M. (1973), *Black Macho and the Myth of Superwoman* (New York: The Dial Press).
—— (1990), *Invisibility Blues* (London: Verso).
Ware, V. (1992), *Beyond the Pale* (London: Verso).
Winship, J. (1987), *Inside Women's Magazines* (London: Pandora).

9

New Traditionalism and Post-Feminism: TV Does the Home

Elspeth Probyn

IN THE RECENT Canadian film *A Winter Tan* (Burroughs, Clark, Frizzell, Walker, Weissman, 1988) the protagonist says that she is taking a vacation from feminism. This holiday ends with her death. While this independent and communally written, directed, and produced film explores and deconstructs the very image of 'woman' as it offers seemingly uncaptured moments of one woman pleasing herself with young Mexican boys, it none the less left me somewhat uneasy. In part my unease stemmed from the ways in which the film self-consciously winked at feminism, the ways in which feminism is held at a distance—in the air but not quite there. The film positions itself as coming, quite literally, after feminism (Maryse Holder, the character played by Jackie Burroughs has left behind the college where she taught feminist literary criticism). For Maryse 'there is feminism and then there's fucking',[1] and in line with a certain understanding of what comes after feminism, the film gives us the experienced mind and body of a woman now out for herself. As she talks to us, to the camera, as she waits for the last return of her lover and presumed killer, we are to understand that she inhabits and controls the excess that she lives. But in the end she does die, leaving behind the literary traces which have enabled the film (this is, after all, a true story).

One question that *A Winter Tan* immediately raises is: What happens when you take a break from feminism? Implicit to the film is the construction of feminism as a moral discourse—as Maryse puts it: 'It must have been to curb my natural sluttishness that I became a feminist in the first place.'[2] The film gives us feminism as a coherent political line, if not a secure home. And when women leave this safe place, when they step off the line, they're in trouble: for all her freedom, Maryse is represented as quite painfully bulimic—a fact that becomes a metaphor for her sexual binges. The conclusion seems to be that women can be either feminists or in Maryse's words, 'a thing to plug', but if you try to be both (like Maryse) you die. And indeed, if one digs a little

Originally published in *Screen*, 31 (1988), 147–59.

1 Quoted in Jane Weinstock, 'Out of her Mind: Fantasies of the 26th New York Film Festival', *Camera Obscura*, 19 (1989), 138.

2 Cited in Weinstock, ibid.

A Winter Tan
(courtesy of Films Transit
Inc., Canada/Institute of
Contemporary Arts,
London)

deeper into the logic which motivates this, one finds a fairly old moral: 'seemingly self-sufficient women in their thirties and forties pay dearly for their independence'.[3]

In a review of several current films, Jane Weinstock states: 'It would seem, then, that we are facing a historical condition: women everywhere are falling apart. Not that this is anything new, but this disintegration is now being presented as an insidious effect of feminism.'[4] While I'm not sure that women are actually falling apart at the moment, what we can see is an interesting conjuncture of discourses that are re-positioning women in the home. On any Tuesday night in North America you can see at least four different versions of the home and each one of them has an indirect relation to the discursive articulation of women and the home. Thus the premiss of the humour of *Who's the Boss?* is that women can have full-time jobs while the husband stays at home. *Wonder Years* uses its mid-60s location to replay the suburban home as safe haven. It is, however, a home that both the audience and the programme know will be soon disturbed. In this scenario Mom is the warden and wet blanket; the grown-up voice-over of the 13-year-old protagonist tells us that 'it's hard struggling for manhood when your Mom weighs fifty pounds more than you'. *Roseanne* opens with outside shots of the warmly lit house. Once inside, however, it becomes clear that Roseanne Barr rules the home with high irony. From irony we move to truth with the mythic realism of *thirtysomething*'s home as moral sanctity.

In many ways these homes correspond to different visions of generations of feminism, a sort of 'vulgarization' of feminist discourses. Thus, underlying *Who's the Boss?* is a seventies liberal feminism insisting on women's rights to equality of employment; underneath *Wonder Years* lies Betty Friedan's articulation of the suburban home housing the 'problem which has no name'; *Roseanne* updates the seventies line and gives the wife and mother all

3 Ibid. 140–1.

4 Ibid. 140.

Roseanne
(courtesy of C4 television)

power: economic, social, as well as affective control over her family; and then with *thirtysomething* we have a post-feminist vision of the home to which women have 'freely' chosen to return. Of course, the word 'feminism' is never mentioned in any of these shows; it's not even there as what Judith Mayne calls, 'an echo effect'.[5] Rather, feminism and feminist ideas are totally submerged—it is the word that cannot be said. However, feminism can also be seen as the Other to these versions of women and home. And it is feminism as Other which articulates the discourses of 'post-feminism' and 'the new traditionalism'.

The questions I want to raise here have to do with the ways in which that Other is suppressed in order to allow for a new generation of television programmes commonly called 'female-centred'. This recentring of women in the family and the home constitutes an important conjunctural moment. In situating the reappearance of the home as conjunctural I want to recall Althusser's description of the 'backwardnesses, forwardnesses, survivals and unevenness of development which *co-exist* in the structure of the real histor-

---

5 Judith Mayne, '*L.A. Law* and Prime-Time Feminism', *Discourse*, 10/2 (Spring–Summer, 1988), 42 (Ch. 6 in this volume).

ical present'.[6] In other words, prime-time's re-articulation of women and the home cannot be seen as hermetically or hermeneutically sealed—to a certain extent, its meanings are up for grabs. If indeed these visions of home have an affective purchase (which seems to be the case in terms of audience loyalties and the network's strategic use of these shows) then we have to start thinking about the positivity of discourses that focus on the home; discourses framed in terms like new traditionalism and post-feminism.

However, I should also state that my interest in, and understanding of, the circulation of post-feminism as a public discourse is a local one—or at least, a North American one. Thus while British feminist theorists like Angela McRobbie can convincingly argue that post-feminism also represents a political and semiotic playfulness,[7] and others, like John Caughie,[8] can present the positivity of the new slew of North American television drama series, my approach will be a little warier. While I do want to think about how we can theorize the post-fem/new trad trend without losing sight of its affectivity, I do speak from a political situation which is now ruled by what Ad Man of the Year, Richard Wirthlin (the brain behind Reagan's image), characterizes as one where 'the language of values is the language of emotions'.[9] That language is currently articulating Reagan's project to protect ('*they're* going to steal our symbols and slogans: words like community and the family') with Bush's aim to guide America into a kinder, gentler family ('a thousand points of light, that is my mission'). On the other side of the 'longest undefended border', in Canada the language of Real Women has gained more and more ground. This summer the language of the family allowed for two slighted boyfriends to gain injunctions prohibiting their former girlfriends from obtaining abortions in Canada. While I am not going to construct any strict equivalence between political realities and television fiction, I do think that the discourses of the family, of new traditionalism, and post-feminism are in the air and need to be addressed by feminists.

At the very least, the currency of these discourses recalls with some force the postmodern refusal of representation: in other words, can we still maintain that feminism can represent, or stand in for, all women? The terms of the new family are indeed a challenge to feminism. Nevertheless, I think that they can be used positively to question certain current trends within cultural interpretation. Thus, the post-feminist trend in television raises in my mind aspects of cultural criticism which revolve around the figure of the feminine. Later on I will turn to a certain tendency I see in some cultural studies criticism to collapse feminism into the post in the name of feminine.

However, the first question to be dealt with is where and what is 'post-feminism' and the 'new traditionalism'? During its brief glory the film *A Winter Tan* was, for example, immediately labelled by reviewers as 'post-feminist'. While to my mind the rather depressing ending disqualifies this film as

6 Louis Althusser, 'The Object of *Capital*', in Louis Althusser and Etienne Balibar, *Reading Capital*, trans. Brewster (London: NLB, 1975), 106.

7 Angela McRobbie, paper presented at the conference, 'Communications and Cultural Studies: Convergences and Divergences', Carleton University, Ottawa, April 1989.

8 John Caughie, 'The Problem of being Thirtysomething', *New Statesman and Society*, 19 May 1989: 43.

9 Bill Moyers, *Bill Moyers: The Public Mind* (PBS, Nov. 1989).

post-feminist, one needn't look far to find other examples of the boom. For instance, the new women now populating prime-time were recently sanctioned by being *Newsweek*'s cover story. Across the smiling face of Murphy Brown, the headline read: 'How Women are Changing TV'. The authors state that 'The feminization of television has surprisingly little to do with feminism'[10] and go on to list 'the unprecedented number of series featuring virtually all-female casts': *China Beach, Heartbeat* (recently deceased), and *Nightingale*, as well as *Designing Women* and *Golden Girls*. The authors also coined the term 'female-centred' to describe shows like *Murder, She Wrote*. Surprisingly enough, this term wasn't stretched to include the hottest shows of the season: *thirtysomething, Roseanne,* or *L.A. Law*. While Murphy describes herself as feeling like 'June Cleaver on acid', *thirtysomething* has Hope, the serene mother, surrounded by several women in various stages of distress. The large figure of Roseanne Barr embraces both the traditional family as well as her scathing and funny critiques of the very notion of motherhood. Meanwhile, *L.A. Law* combines the workplace as family with Stuart and Anne's real life and television marriage and their search for a child. In these instances and others, we can see that there is a new and active articulation of successful women who want something more. As that noted post-feminist Madonna puts it: 'Life is a mystery | Everyone must stand alone | I hear you call my name and it feels like home . . .'. In their ambiguity these words can be used to sum up the two principles that frame a post-feminist ontology: the world's a crazy place and you have to fight for yourself but at the end of the day you can always go home. In television terms, this means that you can be a top corporate lawyer and be pregnant (*L.A. Law*); a hot-shot current affairs anchor and consider single parenthood (*Murphy Brown*); or you can just *choose* to stay home, and indeed *be* home (*thirtysomething*).

In other words, you can have your post-feminism at the same time as your new traditionalism. In fact, the two go so handily together that it's hard to have one without the other. The ad executives who 'discovered' New Traditionalism are succinct in their estimation of its appeal:

> It was never an issue except among feminists who felt that we were telling women to stay home and have babies. We're saying that's okay. But that's not all we're saying. We're saying they have a choice. It's a tough world out there.[11]

As Leslie Savan has pointed out, new traditionalism has become synonymous with a new age of 'choiceoisie' and it is precisely this ideology of choice that articulates new traditionalism and post-feminism. According to *Good Housekeeping*, new traditionalism marks a 'reaffirmation of family values unmatched in recent history'.[12] *Good Housekeeping*'s magazine ads feature happily reformed women returned to the family home and flanked by children. Seemingly contrary to the ad agency's *laissez-faire* attitude to kids or not ('hey, we're saying that's okay') the television spot for *Good Housekeeping* bluntly tells us that:

10 'How Women are Changing TV', *Newsweek*, 13 Mar. 1989: 48.

11 Cited in Leslie Savan, 'Op Ad', *Village Voice*, 7 Mar. 1989: 49.

12 Ibid.

> Mother's haven't changed. Kids haven't changed. Families haven't
> changed. Love hasn't changed. What is fundamental to our lives, what
> really matters . . . hasn't changed.[13]

In the best logic of advertising, new traditionalism both symbolizes and
reproduces the solid nature of the status quo as it urges women to get on the
bandwagon, to buy into the old as new (as Savan says 'the old-fashioned as
fashion'). Thus the material world is portrayed as unchanging. It stays the
same; it's just that the articulations have to be reformed with that flighty and
eminently unstable group: women. The categories of 'mother's', 'kids',
'love', and even 'life' are presented as immutable truths which only those
feminist 'changelies' would not choose. In other words, the ideology of
choiceoisie operates not on choice but as a reaffirmation of what has supposedly always been there, always already there for the right women. Thus, in an
age of ironies, it is not surprising that the *Good Housekeeping* seal of approval
rewards those who already have been given it and reproves those who don't
(those who can't, in any number of currencies, afford this type of choice).
Quite simply, new traditionalism hawks the home as the 'natural choice'—
which means, of course, no choice.

If new traditionalism naturalizes the home into a fundamental and
unchanging site of love and fulfilment, the discourse of post-feminism turns
on a re-articulation of that choice. Post-feminism then returns a sense of difference to the rather flat landscape of new traditionalism. After all, if the new
trad home is the 'natural' option, why or how would anyone even consider
anything else? Post-feminism thus allows choiceoisie to be posed as the possibility of choosing between the home or the career, the family or the successful job. Thus in television terms, *thirtysomething* gives us a new
traditionalist home complete with Dads getting in touch with their kids, and
at the same time post-feminism lends piquance as, in the background, we
hear the ticking of the omnipresent biological clock. In one episode of
thirtysomething the repressed returns with a vengeance as we see Melissa (the
carefree but increasingly anxiously *single* artist) in a dream sequence. She is
pinned down on an enormous clock in the shape of an ovary while possible
sperm donors appear. In a simple twist of fate, American television has gone
from the coyness of Lucille Ball's on-air pregnancy (where the P word was
never mentioned) to *Maude*'s confrontation with abortion, to the panic of
the ticking of the biological clock in the same time-frame as the woman who
is now thirty something years old. Of course the battles to get the networks to
allow certain words to be spoken (like abortion) are forgotten even in the
most self-reflexively intertextual of programmes like *thirtysomething*. Rather
the attention is turned to novel ways of presenting birth scenes, as in a recent
episode which telescoped the whole affair from end to beginning.

The ticking of the clock and the search for a mate reproduces an individual urgency masked as an historical one. One of the ways in which post-
feminism is effective is precisely this marking of urgency as 'the problem' for
women in the late eighties. Indeed the representation of women in gynaeco-
logical terms (as a limited number of eggs and a dwindling bunch of hor-
mones) has become (or re-emerged as) the subject of popular humour. One

13 Ibid.

thirtysomething
(courtesy of C4 television)

instance of this particular hailing can be seen in the rather smug comic strip *Cathy*. Recently the strip had Cathy and her friend reading a book entitled 'How to Flirt'. Above them the text reads: 'Some call it "The New Traditionalism". Some call it "Retrofeminism". Some call it a bad joke.' The text continues with a genealogy of the 'post-feminist woman' and tells us that, 'many women who postponed marriage for careers are now trying to discover the delicate, feminine art of wooing a man's heart'. Cathy's friend then greets a strange man with, 'Hello. I want your baby.'

Smoking guns and descriptions aside, it's now time to turn on the theory. I want to do this in two ways: first, by asking what can be said about these popular discourses; and second, to use these images to show up some weak spots in current theorizing.

Two of the most important terms and horizons in feminist criticism are the concepts of gender and sexuality. Projects of interpreting representations (whether filmic, televisual, photographic, or literary) have involved questions of how gendered subjects are constructed as sexed objects and positioned by images. While I am not now going to attempt to give a history of feminist theories of representation, I hope that we can take certain major interpretative paradigms for granted. In other words, I am thinking of feminist psychoanalytic film theory as a condition of possibility for any present theorizing. However, at the same time, I will insist that the 'thirty something' generation of television shows requires different analytic tools than did the classic Hollywood genres. I also think we can acknowledge that there are now different generations of feminists; what Rosi Braidotti calls 'discursive generation gaps . . . [with] each generation [having to] reckon with its own problematics'.[14] The emergence of the discourse of 'choiceoisie' strikes me as one of the problematic objects of my generation. While it would be easy to state, as I have already intimated, that this choiceoisie is no choice, there are aspects of the post-feminist discourse that hit home. As a woman in my early thirtysomething, newly in a tenure-track university job that promises retirement thirty years from now, I am a ripe candidate for the kids and home hype. While I am certainly not saying that the post-feminist discourse *describes* my life or my options, it does, none the less, provide a public language to talk about me and other similar women—it may even provide women with words to talk about themselves. And it is precisely this aspect, this function of discourses that has to be dealt with. It is also this analytic level of the work of discourse (what Michèle Le Dœuff calls '*le faire*' of the discourse) that is ignored in much contemporary television criticism.

Meaghan Morris has recently argued that cultural studies is currently going through a 'banal' moment. The banalities are especially clear for Morris in the extreme positions of Jean Baudrillard and John Fiske. While it is clear that Morris is not rejecting either postmodernism or cultural studies, she does question the limitations of our critical vocabulary and 'the level of "enunciative" practice'.[15] It is the way in which certain 'solutions' are repeatedly trundled out that bothers Morris. As she says, 'the critical vocabulary available to people wanting to theorize the discriminations that they make in relation to their own experience of popular culture . . . is today extraordinarily depleted'.[16] In other words, what happens if you like some post-feminist trappings but still find the discourse problematic? The cultural studies' dictum that the masses are not cultural dupes remains important but the largess with which some terms are handed out sometimes can get slightly silly. Brought down to the specificities of oneself, it is unlikely that one could proudly say, 'well, I'm a resisting reader'. Arthur Kroker likes to call this approach 'theory as life insurance', and while there's nothing really wrong with having an insurance (an optimism of the will) do we really need such blanket policies? As Morris puts it: 'the vox pop style of cultural studies . . . offer[s] us the sanitized world of a deodorant commercial where there's always a way to redemption'.[17]

Recently redemption has taken on a feminine form. Whether it is due to a more widespread acceptance of feminism as a critical discourse, or whether it is thanks to post-structuralist and postmodern articulations of the feminine as disruption, resistance is now gendered. While there are positive aspects to this move, the currency of the feminine can also be seen as an example of the current poverty of critical vocabulary. An instance of this can be seen in John Fiske's recent turn to 'the feminine'. While Fiske is not alone in the appropriation of the feminine, his recent work does reveal the limitations of condensing a 'vox-pop' style with a mode of textual analysis that posits sexuality as the redemptive horizon. His use of the feminine as a

14 Rosi Braidotti, 'The Politics of Ontological Difference', in Teresa Brennan (ed.), *Between Feminism and Psychoanalysis* (London: Routledge, 1989), 91.

15 Meaghan Morris, 'Banality in Cultural Studies', *Discourse*, 10/2 (Spring–Summer, 1988), 19.

16 Ibid.

17 Ibid. 21

critical figure merits some consideration because of the way in which he constructs a category of feminine sexuality which then serves to guarantee his textual reading of television. In his book *Television Culture*, Fiske posits a series of equivalences between practices and an ontological category of femininity: 'Feminine work, feminine viewing practices, and feminine texts combine to produce decentred, flexible, multifocused feminine subjectivities'. [18] Fiske gets his model of the feminine from the quite particular work of Shere Hite and Nancy Chodorow. He then uses this construction of feminine sexuality to guarantee his reading of how (and why) women watch soap operas. While men 'come', women, according to Fiske,

> have no such final achievement. The emphasis on seduction and on its continuous pleasure and power is appropriate to a contemporary feminine subjectivity, for that subjectivity has necessarily been formed through a constant experience of powerlessness and subordination. [19]

To state the obvious, there are problems here. Apart from his implicit heterosexual bounds, Fiske has turned a hypostasized model of sexuality into the grounds for resistance. Fiske argues that soap operas constitute a 'feminine aesthetic' because of their 'lack of narrative closure and the multiplicity of ... plots'.[20] This form is then made to accord with a feminine sensibility: 'It can be seen more positively as an articulation of a specific feminine definition of desire and pleasure that is contrasted with the male pleasure of final success.'[21] So in Fiske's account, the feminine can be used as what Mayne calls a 'swinging door': genres are defined as feminine and then correspond to what he has defined as a feminine sexuality and subjectivity. These feminine genres can even allow women to learn and practise their feminine 'skills': 'they provide training in the feminine skills of "reading people", and are the means of exercising the feminine ability to understand the gap between what is meant and what is said'.[22]

It seems to me that one of the things that the discourse of post-feminism is saying is that the question of 'what do women want' (*Was will das Weib?*) has been answered. The answer is that they want 'choice'. This is perfectly in keeping with the kind of liberal feminism that floats through post-feminism and new traditionalism. It is, however, a liberal feminism shorn of its political programme—it is choice freed of the necessity of thinking about the political and social ramifications of the act of choosing. It also closes that gap that Fiske mentions. As George Bush puts it: 'read my lips'—what is meant is what is said.

One of the positivities that this offers is that it reveals Fiske's enigmatic feminine as outdated. It also confirms the limitations of a text-based analysis of the *thirtysomething* generation of television. In other words, the cultural importance of these programmes can not be read off their surfaces. In the programmes that I've mentioned, the feminine is not an enigma to be

---

18 John Fiske, *Television Culture* (London: Methuen, 1987), 196.

19 Ibid. 187–8.

20 Ibid. 180.

21 Ibid. 181.

22 Ibid. 183.

thirtysomething
(courtesy of C4 television)

discovered or interpreted (by men); she is the site of prime-time television. As Sasha Torres has recently argued, 'the unanswered and persistent question . . . is masculinity, not femininity. *thirtysomething* knows, or at least thinks it knows, where women's "place", spatially and affectively, is'.[23] Thus, the feminine as a hermeneutic horizon will not tell you much. The question is outside of the text, in the larger discursive re-articulation of the feminine and the home in the name of post-feminism. The postmodern devices employed in these programmes (such as extensive quotation from television's and popular culture's past) already has interpreted itself as text. Thus, the project of the critic in front of isolated texts becomes rather redundant. We (the audience, the text) know what it 'means'.

The interpretative task of the feminist critic, therefore, lies elsewhere. This is to say that the politics of these programmes can no longer be identified solely at the level of the textual system. After all, shows like *thirtysomething* are quite upfront about what they represent (in both senses of the word): As Ken Olin/Michael Steedman put it:

> Nobody on this show is presuming that the problems of these characters are as serious as the problems of the homeless and the mentally ill and the tragedy of war . . . [b]ut that is not to say that this generation doesn't face a set of issues that is valid too.[24]

Of course, this type of statement doesn't guarantee any particular shade of politics either, but it does push us outside of the text—it begs the question of what these discourses do extratextually.

23 Sasha Torres, 'Melodrama, Masculinity and the Family: *thirtysomething* as Therapy', *Camera Obscura*, 19 (1989), 92.

24 Cited in Torres, ibid. 91.

Taking from the French feminist philosopher Michèle Le Dœuff, we can begin to ask what the work of a discourse is. While the discourses of the family and on post-feminism are being re-produced in *thirtysomething* etc., they are also producing and re-positioning lived relations in regard to 'women's places' and the home. Le Dœuff argues that we can take discourses as 'points of view'. Instead of discourses replicating reality, the discourse as a point of view can be trained on itself or what it is supposed to represent. In Le Dœuff's terms: 'it can construct questions and modes of analysis about the patch of reality that it is drawn from'.[25] While, of course, Le Dœuff is talking about philosophical systems and not television shows, her analysis of the functions of discourse can be used to pose epistemological questions about how television makes sense. In other words, this is to look at the ways in which the discourse of post-feminism both circulates in television programmes and is lodged elsewhere—within what Le Dœuff calls 'the primacy of the real'. However, let me specify that 'a primacy of the real' is not over and beyond television. As a level of abstraction, 'the primacy of the real' describes the articulations that are made between television's representations and those we live: self-representations. Thus the prime-time discourses of the family or of the home or of women are affective precisely because they lodge in the real; they are attached to other ideological frameworks. These discourses also connect people together in different ways. They draw actual women to conversations about actual families and homes. The *thirtysomething* generation of programmes, including their regional offspring such as the Canadian shows *Street Legal* and *ENG*, also can be seen as articulating a sameness, bringing us all into a family, a home. They want to create a happy sameness in all of our everyday lives.

However, that point of sameness when the discourses catch up with each other (as one reviewer asked himself after watching *thirtysomething*: 'good lord, are my problems so common that even *television* can pick up on them?'),[26] is also the point when the discourse can be used to question itself. Simply put, we begin to question the differences between the currency of the family, etc., on television and the family as an institutional discourse. To take a recent example, one of this season's *thirtysomething* episodes actually introduced a gay character, Russell. The story-line explicitly drew a parallel between Russell getting together with one of Michael and Elliott's colleagues and the representation of Melissa's affair with a younger man as problematic. In alternating scenes we see Melissa's nightmarish version of Lee (the younger man) meeting the 'family' (Hope *et al.*), and Russell and Peter lying in bed discussing the loss of their friends through AIDS. Now the reading of this episode can go in any direction: from 'about time that they actually broke up the heterosexual contract that rules the show', to disgust at the way in which AIDS is trivialized and pathologized in the context of Melissa's angst over age-difference, to inside ironic laughter because the actress who plays Melissa is thought to be gay. Meanwhile, the most widely read agony column, *Ann Landers*, had that week come out in favour of same-sex couples. While these two discursive moments don't guarantee a thing, they do point

25 Michèle Le Dœuff, *L'Étude et le Rouet* (Paris: Éditions du Seuil, 1989), 105–6.

26 Jay Rosen, 'thirtysomething', *Tikkun*, 4/4 (1989), 31.

to ways in which the discourse of the family also raises its own problematic: does the family have to be heterosexual? In other words, there is a positivity in the ways in which discourses circulate on television that allows for questions to be raised about how they are also lodged in 'the real'. In a very local way, *Roseanne*'s gripes against motherhood and children are being heard at the same time as the introduction of a Quebec policy to give (not pay) women $3000 for their third child. The recognition by most of Quebec society that this was a paltry amount coincided with a wide condemnation of the Quebec Court ruling that the foetus had rights.

Now again, these examples don't prove anything except that the different articulations of post-feminism and the family are hard to gauge in advance. However, instead of reifying the *thirtysomething* generation of television as 'quality television' or writing it off as mere ideological replay, I suggest that we use these discourses to focus upon the changing social climate which we live and watch. This obviously means that the work of the post-feminist and new traditionalist discourses will be very different in Quebec than in Scotland. It also means that the positivity of post-feminism has to be judged according to its conjunctural work. However, far from initiating a break from feminism, I think that the current discursive landscape is a condition of possibility for generations of feminist analysis. And in the midst of the reborn family and the refurbished home, it is more important than ever that we make the personal political and theoretical (Braidotti).

2

Audiences and Reception Contexts

2

Introduction to Part 2

OVER THE PAST two decades feminist critics have contributed to and often shaped debates about the public's relationship with and reception of television. As is more generally true of the increased interest in audiences and reception studies during this period, feminist criticism in this area has been interdisciplinary in nature—mixing models from literary and film theory with those drawn from sociology and anthropology. From literary and film criticism, feminists inherited an interest in the ways texts encourage women to identify with a 'subject position' or what is often also called a 'spectator position', 'reading position', 'implied reader', and the like. From the social sciences, feminist critics inherited a focus on the empirical audience. For example, how do women viewers use television programmes like *Star Trek* to form female fan communities? How are soap operas like *Coronation Street* and *EastEnders* used for the stuff of everyday conversation in the workplace?[1] Or how do Korean women living in the United States use Korean soaps to recall a sense of 'home' while faced with the alienation of post-colonial urban life?[2] Or as some other critics ask, how have women integrated television and video into the context of their daily lives and family rituals? Rather than being either text-based or context-based by design, feminist research and method in this area are often both at once. The hybrid quality of this research can be seen in many articles featured in this part, which collects together a range of essays investigating and theorizing the reception of television.

Part 2 starts with Annette Kuhn's much-cited 1984 essay, 'Women's Genres', in which she investigates the disciplinary origins of what was then

---

1 See Constance Penley, 'Brownian Motion: Women, Tactics, and Technology', in Constance Penley and Andrew Ross (eds.), *Technoculture* (Minneapolis: Univ. of Minnesota Press, 1991), 135–61; Henry Jenkins, '*Star Trek*: Rerun, Reread, Rewritten: Fan Writings as Textual Poaching', *Critical Studies* in *Mass Communication*, 5/2 (1988), 85–107; Camille Bacon-Smith, *Enterprising Women: Television, Fandom and the Creation of Popular Myth* (Philadelphia: Univ. of Pennsylvania Press, 1992); Dorothy Hobson, 'Soap Operas at Work', in Ellen Seiter *et al.* (eds.), *Remote Control: Television, Audiences, and Cultural Power* (London, Routledge, 1989), 150–67.

2 See Minu Lee and Chong Heup Cho, 'Women Watching Together: An Ethnographic Study of Korean Soap Opera Fans in the United States', *Cultural Studies*, 4/1 (1990), 30–44.

the emerging feminist scholarship on television and cinema genres—such as soap opera and the 'weepie'—aimed at female audiences. Kuhn points to the expansion of research in these fields in the 1970s and early 1980s, showing that although these 'gynocentric' genres may appear to have their appeal to female audiences in common, this appeal is conceptualized very differently in different studies. She suggests that research which comes from film studies tends to use a notion of a spectator implied by the text, while work in television studies emphasizes the contexts of a social audience. Kuhn goes on to argue that attention to both—a subject/spectator and a social audience—is important to any sophisticated understanding of the popularity of these genres with women, and that therefore we must look at both text and context in our analyses.

Similarly concerned with texts, contexts, and interpretation, Ien Ang, in 'Melodramatic Identifications', reprises some of the findings of her study of *Dallas* fans conducted in the early 1980s in the Netherlands.[3] In this study, Ang had used ideas of fantasy more commonly associated with film melo-drama to help her empirical investigation of viewers' letters about the television programme *Dallas*. In the article reprinted here, in addition to speculation on the attractions of a *Dallas* character like Sue-Ellen for women, Ang considers the appeal of the tougher Christine Cagney (from *Cagney and Lacey*). She suggests that the often tearful identification women feel with these characters testifies to the complexity of the task of 'being a woman', while also pointing out that not all, and not *only*, women like melodrama. She begins to develop the point into an argument that identification is less stereotypically gender-divided than much feminist criticism assumes, an argument she expands in work later than that reproduced here.[4]

The assumptions of feminist criticism are probed in a slightly different way by Jacqueline Bobo and Ellen Seiter in their article, 'Black Feminism and Media Criticism: *The Women of Brewster Place*'. They commence with a more general survey of the patterns of exclusion practised by white feminism, but then signal the very particular resonances of differential historical access to privacy for black and white families in relation to the 'turn to the domestic' in current audience and ethnographic work. Bobo and Seiter point out that most of the 'new' small-scale ethnographic studies are with white audiences.[5] This they see as partly a result of who gets the academic support and who gets to do the research—particularly in a context where a white 'investigator' might be extremely unwelcome in black domestic and neigh-bourhood space. Thus, although they defend the increased interest in the domestic sphere in shaping media consumption as 'theoretically sound', they point to the importance of continually scrutinizing the structural exclu-

---

3 First published as *Het Geval Dallas* by Uitgeverij SUA (Amsterdam, 1982) and as *Watching Dallas: Soap Opera and the Melodramatic Imagination* (London: Methuen, 1985).

4 Ien Ang and Joke Hermes, 'Gender and/in Media Consumption', in *Mass Media and Society* (Sevenoaks: Edward Arnold, 1991), 307–28.

5 Some exceptions to this are Evelyn Cauleta Reid, 'Viewdata', *Screen*, 30/1–2 (1989), 114–21; Jacqueline Bobo, *Black Women as Cultural Readers* (New York: Columbia Univ. Press, 1994); Marie Gillespie, *Television, Ethnicity and Cultural Change* (London: Routledge, 1995); Gloria Abernathy-Lear, *African American Viewers and Daytime Serials* (Philadelphia: Univ. of Pennsylvania Press, forth-coming).

sions of some groups of participants in this research. The second part of their article attempts to put into practice one of their own demands, which is for greater attention to the increasingly aggressive adaptation of black women's literature for film and television. They offer a reading of the television version of *The Women of Brewster Place*, taken from Gloria Naylor's novel. They stress the ways this work offers a very different understanding of the family and its psychological dynamic from that explored by white feminists in previous discussions of family melodrama and soap opera, demonstrating their argument about the different historical meanings of the family for different groups.

Lyn Thomas's research returns to the investigation of a particular programme's group of fans. She investigates some Londoners who self-identified as fans of the internationally successful 'quality' British crime drama *Inspector Morse*. Her original research design attempted to reach a broader group of *Morse* fans but, as she discusses, it was white women with whom she shared many subcultural codes who dominated the discussions on which she here reports. She thus points to the way in which, at least in Britain, there is a recognizable class and ethnically specific heterosexual feminist subculture taking its pleasures from widely exported 'quality' television. Her analysis illuminates the structuring role of this subculture in informing her discussants' responses to *Inspector Morse*, and indeed the way the adaptations exclude some obvious misogynies in the passage from novel to television. She also underscores that many fans—research subjects—might never want to appear duped by television, and discusses the considerable ironies for these women of being in 'love with *Inspector Morse*'.

Hilary Hinds addresses the issues of text and context in an extract from her case study of the reception of *Oranges Are Not the Only Fruit*.[6] The text Hinds discusses is of overdetermined interest to feminists in that, like *The Women of Brewster Place*, it was produced by a mainly female team from the work of a woman writer and has lesbianism as one of its concerns. Bobo and Seiter discuss the rather thin critical response to *The Women of Brewster Place*. Hinds, in contrast, is able to point to the very considerable, favourable response to *Oranges* in Britain. This response, she argues, had very particular contextual determinations in January 1990. She points to two important news events of the time as creating a climate of discussion which affected the critical response to *Oranges*. First, the Conservative government's new law, passed in 1988, which made it illegal for any group or body in receipt of local government funding to 'promote homosexuality'. Secondly, the widely publicized condemnation to death of author Salman Rushdie, for blasphemy against Islam in his book *The Satanic Verses*. Hinds argues that the reverberating debates around these issues created a context in which *Oranges*, which is largely an account of a lesbian girlhood in a fierce Christian fundamentalist home and sect in northern Britain, was read in a way that decentred its lesbianism. Hinds argues that 'bad' fundamentalism at that particular time was worse than normally taboo lesbianism.

6 See also Margaret Marshment and Julia Hallem's essay on *Oranges Are Not the Only Fruit*, 'From String of Knots to Orange Box: Lesbianism on Prime Time', in Diane Hamer and Belinda Budge (eds.), *The Good, the Bad, and the Gorgeous: Popular Culture's Romance with Lesbianism* (London: Pandora, 1994), 142–65.

Another set of essays in this part considers the relationship between technological innovation and the culture of everyday lives at home. Lynn Spigel's 'The Suburban Home Companion: Television and the Neighbourhood Ideal in Post-War America' charts the contextual territory and domestic space of early US television reception. She examines television's integration into post-war culture and the suburban home in relation to the overall reorganization of social space at the time. She draws on advertisements, popular press articles, social scientific journals, television programmes, films, and comic strips to document post-war culture's portrayal of television as the 'ideal companion' to suburban lifestyles of the 1950s. This new 'electrical space', she suggests, provided a window out to the world and into the home, and in doing so, balanced the contradictory ideals of privatization and community involvement that were clashing at the time. Spigel analyses such contradictions in post-war representations of television and details the gender and racial dynamics that formed US suburbia—television's domestic context—both on television and off.

Ann Gray's research also focuses on the domestic environment in which television and video are viewed, but her investigation is ethnographic in nature. The research project reported on here was conducted in Britain in the mid-1980s when the video cassette recorder was first becoming established as a familiar feature of the domestic environment.[7] Gray is interested in the video recorder as domestic technology, and the differential relations to it of different household members, but she is also interested in the extent to which the VCR changes the context of choice about viewing. The article reproduced here addresses the gendering of a technology and the gendering of genre. Gray reports on the long semi-structured interviews she employed to try to understand who used the video recorder, with what expertise, and how these usages and possibilities affected viewing practices. She points to a discernible gendering of aesthetic judgement, an issue that recurs in many articles in this book. In this instance, she shows how the women she interviewed often represented themselves as choosing and preferring to watch material which they simultaneously think of as 'rubbish'.

---

7 The full research report can be found in Ann Gray, *Video Playtime: The Gendering of a Leisure Technology* (London: Routledge, 1992).

10

Women's Genres

Melodrama, Soap Opera, and Theory

Annette Kuhn

TELEVISION SOAP OPERA and film melodrama, popular narrative forms aimed at female audiences, are currently attracting a good deal of critical and theoretical attention. Not surprisingly, most of the work on these 'gynocentric' genres is informed by various strands of feminist thought on visual representation. Less obviously, perhaps, such work has also prompted a series of questions which relate to representation and cultural production in a more wide-ranging and thoroughgoing manner than a specifically feminist interest might suggest. Not only are film melodrama (and more particularly its subtype the 'woman's picture') and soap opera directed at female audiences, they are also actually enjoyed by millions of women. What is it that sets these genres apart from representations which possess a less gender-specific mass appeal?

One of the defining generic features of the woman's picture as a textual system is its construction of narratives motivated by female desire and processes of spectator identification governed by female point of view. Soap opera constructs woman-centred narratives and identifications, too, but it differs textually from its cinematic counterpart in certain other respects: not only do soaps never end, but their beginnings are soon lost sight of. And whereas in the woman's picture the narrative process is characteristically governed by the enigma-retardation-resolution structure which marks the classic narrative, soap opera narratives propose

> competing and intertwining plot lines introduced as the serial progresses. Each plot . . . develops at a different pace, thus preventing any clear resolution of conflict. The completion of one story generally leads into others, and ongoing plots often incorporate parts of semi-resolved conflicts.[1]

Recent work on soap opera and melodrama has drawn on existing theories, methods, and perspectives in the study of film and television, including the structural analysis of narratives, textual semiotics and psychoanalysis, audience research, and the political economy of cultural institutions. At the

© OUP, 1984.

Originally published in *Screen*, 25/1 (1984), 18–28.

[1] Muriel G. Cantor and Suzanne Pingree, *The Soap Opera* (Beverly Hills: Sage, 1983), 22. Here 'soap opera' refers to daytime (US) or early evening (UK) serials . . . not prime-time serials like *Dallas* and *Dynasty*.

same time, though, some of this work has exposed the limitations of existing approaches, and in consequence been forced if not actually to abandon them, at least to challenge their characteristic problematics. Indeed, it may be contended that the most significant developments in film and TV theory in general are currently taking place precisely within such areas of feminist concern as critical work on soap opera and melodrama.

In examining some of this work, I shall begin by looking at three areas in which particularly pertinent questions are being directed at theories of representation and cultural production. These are, first, the problem of gendered spectatorship; secondly, questions concerning the universalism as against the historical specificity of conceptualizations of gendered spectatorship; and thirdly, the relationship between film and television texts and their social, historical, and institutional contexts. Each of these concerns articulates in particular ways with what seems to be the central issue here—the question of the audience, or audiences, for certain types of cinematic and televisual representation.

Film theory's appropriation to its own project of Freudian and post-Freudian psychoanalysis places the question of the relationship between text and spectator firmly on the agenda. Given the preoccupation of psychoanalysis with sexuality and gender, a move from conceptualizing the spectator as a homogeneous and androgynous effect of textual operations[2] to regarding her or him as a gendered subject constituted in representation seems in retrospect inevitable. At the same time, the interests of feminist film theory and film theory in general converge at this point in a shared concern with sexual difference. Psychoanalytic accounts of the formation of gendered subjectivity raise the question, if only indirectly, of representation and feminine subjectivity. This in turn permits the spectator to be considered as a gendered subject position, masculine or feminine: and theoretical work on soap opera and the woman's picture may take this as a starting-point for its inquiry into spectator–text relations. Do these 'gynocentric' forms address, or construct, a female or a feminine spectator? If so, how?

On the question of film melodrama, Laura Mulvey, commenting on King Vidor's *Duel in the Sun*,[3] argues that when, as in this film, a woman is at the centre of the narrative, the question of female desire structures the hermeneutic: 'what does *she* want?' This, says Mulvey, does not guarantee the constitution of the spectator as feminine so much as it implies a contradictory, and in the final instance impossible, 'phantasy of masculinisation' for the female spectator. This is in line with the author's earlier suggestion that cinema spectatorship involves masculine identification for spectators of either gender.[4] If cinema does thus construct a masculine subject, there can be no unproblematic feminine subject position for any spectator. Pam Cook, on the other hand, writing about a group of melodramas produced during the 1940s at the Gainsborough Studios, evinces greater optimism about the

2 See Jean-Louis Baudry, 'Ideological Effects of the Basic Cinematographic Apparatus', *Film Quarterly*, 28/2 (1974–5), 39–47; Christian Metz, 'The Imaginary Signifier', *Screen*, 16/2 (1975), 14–76.

3 Laura Mulvey, 'Afterthoughts on "Visual Pleasure and Narrative Cinema" ', *Framework*, 15/16/17 (1981), 12–15.

4 Laura Mulvey, 'Visual Pleasure and Narrative Cinema', *Screen*, 16/3 (1975), 6–18.

possibility of a feminine subject of classic cinema. She does acknowledge, though, that in a patriarchal society female desire and female point of view are highly contradictory, even if they have the potential to subvert culturally dominant modes of spectator–text relation. The characteristic 'excess' of the woman's melodrama, for example, is explained by Cook in terms of the genre's tendency to '[pose] problems for itself which it can scarcely contain'.[5]

Writers on TV soap opera tend to take views on gender and spectatorship rather different from those advanced by film theorists. Tania Modleski, for example, argues with regard to soaps that their characteristic narrative patterns, their foregrounding of 'female' skills in dealing with personal and domestic crises, and the capacity of their programme formats and scheduling to key into the rhythms of women's work in the home, all address a female spectator. Furthermore, she goes as far as to argue that the textual processes of soaps are in some respects similar to those of certain 'feminine' texts which speak to a decentred subject, and so are 'not altogether at odds with . . . feminist aesthetics'.[6] Modleski's view is that soaps not only address female spectators, but in so doing construct feminine subject positions which transcend patriarchal modes of subjectivity.

Different though their respective approaches and conclusions might be, however, Mulvey, Cook, and Modleski are all interested in the problem of gendered spectatorship. The fact, too, that this common concern is informed by a shared interest in assessing the progressive or transformative potential of soaps and melodramas is significant in light of the broad appeal of both genres to the mass audiences of women at which they are aimed.

But what precisely does it mean to say that certain representations are aimed at a female audience? However well theorized they may be, existing conceptualizations of gendered spectatorship are unable to deal with this question. This is because spectator and audience are distinct concepts which cannot—as they frequently are—be reduced to one another. Although I shall be considering some of its consequences more fully below (pp. 151–3), it is important to note a further problem for film and television theory, posed in this case by the distinction between spectator and audience. Critical work on the woman's picture and on soap opera has necessarily, and most productively, emphasized the question of gendered spectatorship. In doing this, film theory in particular has taken on board a conceptualization of the spectator derived from psychoanalytic accounts of the formation of human subjectivity.

Such accounts, however, have been widely criticized for their universalism. Beyond, perhaps, associating certain variants of the Oedipus complex with family forms characteristic of a patriarchal society and offering a theory of the constructions of gender, psychoanalysis seems to offer little scope for theorizing subjectivity in its cultural or historical specificity. Although in relation to the specific issues of spectatorship and representation there may, as I shall argue, be a way around this apparent impasse, virtually all film and

5 Pam Cook, 'Melodrama and the Woman's Picture', in Sue Aspinall and Robert Murphy (eds.), *Gainsborough Melodrama* (London: BFI, 1983), 17.

6 Tania Modleski, *Loving with a Vengeance: Mass Produced Fantasies for Women* (Hamden, Conn.: Archon Books, 1982), 105. See also Tania Modleski, 'The Search for Tomorrow in Today's Soap Operas', *Film Quarterly*, 33/1 (1979), 12–21 (Ch. 2 in this volume).

TV theory—its feminist variants included—is marked by the dualism of universalism and specificity.

Nowhere is this more evident than in the gulf between textual analysis and contextual inquiry. Each is done according to different rules and procedures, distinct methods of investigation and theoretical perspectives. In bringing to the fore the question of spectator–text relations, theories deriving from psychoanalysis may claim—to the extent that the spectatorial apparatus is held to be conterminous with the cinematic or televisual institution—to address the relationship between text and context. But as soon as any attempt is made to combine textual analysis with analysis of the concrete social, historical, and institutional conditions of production and reception of texts, it becomes clear that the context of the spectator/subject of psychoanalytic theory is rather different from the context of production and reception constructed by conjunctural analyses of cultural institutions.

The disparity between these two 'contexts' structures Pam Cook's article on the Gainsborough melodrama, which sets out to combine an analysis of the characteristic textual operations and modes of address of a genre with an examination of the historical conditions of a particular expression of it. Gainsborough melodrama, says Cook, emerges from a complex of determinants, including certain features of the British film industry of the 1940s, the nature of the female cinema audience in the post-World War II period, and the textual characteristics of the woman's picture itself.[7] While Cook is correct in pointing to the various levels of determination at work in this sentence, her lengthy preliminary discussion of spectator–text relations and the woman's picture rather outbalances her subsequent investigation of the social and industrial contexts of the Gainsborough melodrama. The fact, too, that analysis of the woman's picture in terms of its interpellation of a female/feminine spectator is simply placed alongside a conjunctural analysis tends to vitiate any attempt to reconcile the two approaches, and so to deal with the broader issue of universalism as against historical specificity. But although the initial problem remains, Cook's article constitutes an important intervention in the debate because, in tackling the text–context split head-on, it necessarily exposes a key weakness of current film theory.

In work on television soap opera as opposed to film melodrama, the dualism of text and context manifests itself rather differently, if only because—unlike film theory—theoretical work on television has tended to emphasize the determining character of the contextual level, particularly the structure and organization of television institutions. Since this has often been at the expense of attention to the operation of TV texts, television theory may perhaps be regarded as innovative in the extent to which it attempts to deal specifically with texts as well as contexts. Some feminist critical work has in fact already begun to address the question of TV as text, though always with characteristic emphasis on the issue of gendered spectatorship. This emphasis constitutes a common concern of work on both TV soaps and the woman's picture, but a point of contact between text and context in either medium emerges only when the concept of social audience is considered in distinction from that of spectator.

7 Cook, 'Melodrama and the Woman's Picture'.

Each term—spectator and social audience—presupposes a different set of relations to representations and to the contexts in which they are received. Looking at spectators and at audiences demands different methodologies and theoretical frameworks, distinct discourses which construct distinct subjectivities and social relations. The *spectator*, for example, is a subject constituted in signification, interpellated by the film or TV text. This does not necessarily mean that the spectator is merely an effect of the text, however, because modes of subjectivity which also operate outside spectator–text relations in film or TV are activated in the relationship between spectators and texts.

This model of the spectator/subject is useful in correcting more deterministic communication models which might, say, pose the spectator not as actively constructing meaning but simply as a receiver and decoder of pre-constituted 'messages'. In emphasizing spectatorship as a set of psychic relations and focusing on the relationship between spectator and text, however, such a model does disregard the broader social implications of filmgoing or televiewing. It is the social act of going to the cinema, for instance, that makes the individual cinemagoer part of an audience. Viewing television may involve social relations rather different from filmgoing, but in its own ways TV does depend on individual viewers being part of an audience, even if its members are never in one place at the same time. A group of people seated in a single auditorium looking at a film, or scattered across thousands of homes watching the same television programme, is a *social audience*. The concept of social audience, as against that of spectator, emphasizes the status of cinema and television as social and economic institutions.

Constructed by discursive practices both of cinema and TV and of social science, the social audience is a group of people who buy tickets at the box office, or who switch on their TV sets; people who can be surveyed, counted, and categorized according to age, sex, and socio-economic status.[8] The cost of a cinema ticket or TV licence fee, or a readiness to tolerate commercial breaks, earns audiences the right to look at films and TV programmes, and so to be spectators. Social audiences become spectators in the moment they engage in the processes and pleasures of meaning-making attendant on watching a film or TV programme. The anticipated pleasure of spectatorship is perhaps a necessary condition of existence of audiences. In taking part in the social act of consuming representations, a group of spectators becomes a social audience.

The consumer of representations as audience member and spectator is involved in a particular kind of psychic and social relationship: at this point, a conceptualization of the cinematic or televisual apparatus as a regime of pleasure intersects with sociological and economic understandings of film and TV as institutions. Because each term describes a distinct set of relationships, though, it is important not to conflate social audience with spectators. At the same time, since each is necessary to the other, it is equally important to remain aware of the points of continuity between the two sets of relations.

These conceptualizations of spectator and social audience have particular

---

8 Methods and findings of social science research on the social audience for American daytime soap operas are discussed in Cantor and Pingree, *The Soap Opera*, ch. 7.

implications when it comes to a consideration of popular 'gynocentric' forms such as soap opera and melodrama. Most obviously, perhaps, these centre on the issue of gender, which prompts again the question: what does 'aimed at a female audience' mean? What exactly is being signalled in this reference to a gendered audience? Are women to be understood as a subgroup of the social audience, distinguishable through discourses which construct a priori gender categories? Or does the reference to a female audience allude rather to gendered spectatorship, to sexual difference constructed in relations between spectators and texts? Most likely, it condenses the two meanings; but an examination of the distinction between them may nevertheless be illuminating in relation to the broader theoretical issues of texts, contexts, social audiences, and spectators.

The notion of a female social audience, certainly as it is constructed in the discursive practices through which it is investigated, presupposes a group of individuals already formed as female. For the sociologist interested in such matters as gender and lifestyles, certain people bring a pre-existent femaleness to their viewing of film and TV. For the business executive interested in selling commodities, TV programmes and films are marketed to individuals already constructed as female. Both, however, are interested in the same kind of woman. On one level, then, soap operas and women's melodrama address themselves to a social audience of women. But they may at the same time be regarded as speaking to a female, or a feminine, spectator. If soaps and melodramas inscribe femininity in their address, women—as well as being already formed *for* such representations—are in a sense also formed *by* them.

In making this point, however, I intend no reduction of femaleness to femininity: on the contrary, I would hold to a distinction between femaleness as social gender and femininity as subject position. For example, it is possible for a female spectator to be addressed, as it were, 'in the masculine', and the converse is presumably also true. Nevertheless, in a culturally pervasive operation of ideology, femininity is routinely identified with femaleness and masculinity with maleness. Thus, for example, an address 'in the feminine' may be regarded in ideological terms as privileging, if not necessitating, a socially constructed female gender identity.

The constitutive character of both the woman's picture and the soap opera has in fact been noted by a number of feminist commentators. Tania Modleski, for instance, suggests that the characteristic narrative structures and textual operations of soap operas both address the viewer as an 'ideal mother'—ever-understanding, ever-tolerant of the weaknesses and foibles of others—and also posit states of expectation and passivity as pleasurable:

> the narrative, by placing ever more complex obstacles between desire and fulfilment, makes anticipation of an end an end in itself.[9]

In our culture, tolerance and passivity are regarded as feminine attributes, and consequently as qualities proper in women but not in men.

Charlotte Brunsdon extends Modleski's line of argument to the extra-textual level: in constructing its viewers as competent within the ideological and moral frameworks of marriage and family life, soap opera, she implies,

---

9 Modleski, *Loving with a Vengeance*, 88.

addresses both a feminine spectator and female audience.[10] Pointing to the centrality of intuition and emotion in the construction of the woman's point of view, Pam Cook regards the construction of a feminine spectator as a highly problematic and contradictory process: so that in the film melodrama's construction of female point of view, the validity of femininity as a subject position is necessarily laid open to question.[11]

This divergence on the question of gendered spectatorship within feminist theory is significant. Does it perhaps indicate fundamental differences between film and television in the spectator–text relations privileged by each? Do soaps and melodramas really construct different relations of gendered spectatorship, with melodrama constructing contradictory identifications in ways that soap opera does not? Or do these different positions on spectatorship rather signal an unevenness of theoretical development—or, to put it less teleologically, reflect the different intellectual histories and epistemological groundings of film theory and television theory?

Any differences in the spectator–text relations proposed respectively by soap opera and by film melodrama must be contingent to some extent on more general disparities in address between television and cinema. Thus film spectatorship, it may be argued, involves the pleasures evoked by looking in a more pristine way than does watching television. Whereas in classic cinema the concentration and involvement proposed by structures of the look, identification, and point of view tend to be paramount, television spectatorship is more likely to be characterized by distraction and diversion.[12] This would suggest that each medium constructs sexual difference through spectatorship in rather different ways: cinema through the look and spectacle, and television—perhaps less evidently—through a capacity to insert its flow, its characteristic modes of address, and the textual operations of different kinds of programmes into the rhythms and routines of domestic activities and sexual divisions of labour in the household at various times of day.

It would be a mistake, however, simply to equate current thinking on spectator–text relations in each medium. This is not only because theoretical work on spectatorship as it is defined here is newer and perhaps not so developed for television as it has been for cinema, but also because conceptualizations of spectatorship in film theory and TV theory emerge from quite distinct perspectives. When feminist writers on soap opera and on film melodrama discuss spectatorship, therefore, they are usually talking about different things. This has partly to do with the different intellectual histories and methodological groundings of theoretical work on film and on television. Whereas most TV theory has until fairly recently existed under the sociological rubric of media studies, film theory has on the whole been based in the criticism-orientated tradition of literary studies. In consequence, while the one tends to privilege contexts over texts, the other usually privileges texts over contexts.

However, some recent critical work on soap opera, notably work produced within a cultural studies context, does attempt a *rapprochement* of text

10 Charlotte Brunsdon, '*Crossroads*: Notes on Soap Opera', *Screen*, 22/4 (1981), 32–7.

11 Cook, 'Melodrama and the Woman's Picture', 19.

12 John Ellis, *Visible Fictions* (London: Routledge & Kegan Paul, 1982).

and context. Charlotte Brunsdon, writing about the British soap opera *Crossroads*, draws a distinction between subject positions proposed by texts and a 'social subject' who may or may not take up these positions.[13] In considering the interplay of 'social reader and social text', Brunsdon attempts to come to terms with problems posed by the universalism of the psychoanalytic model of the spectator/subject as against the descriptiveness and limited analytical scope of studies of specific instances and conjunctures. In taking up the instance of soap opera, then, one of Brunsdon's broader objectives is to resolve the dualism of text and context.

'Successful' spectatorship of a soap like *Crossroads*, it is argued, demands a certain cultural capital: familiarity with the plots and characters of a particular serial as well as with soap opera as a genre. It also demands wider cultural competence, especially in the codes of conduct of personal and family life. For Brunsdon, then, the spectator addressed by soap opera is constructed within culture rather than by representation. This, however, would indicate that such a spectator, a 'social subject', might—rather than being a subject in process of gender positioning—belong after all to a social audience already divided by gender.

The 'social subject' of this cultural model produces meaning by decoding messages or communications, an activity which is always socially situated.[14] Thus although such a model may move some way towards reconciling text and context, the balance of Brunsdon's argument remains weighted in favour of context: spectator–text relations are apparently regarded virtually as an effect of socio-cultural contexts. Is there a way in which spectator/subjects of film and television texts can be thought of in a historically specific manner, or indeed a way for the social audience to be rescued from social/historical determinism?

Although none of the feminist criticism of soap opera and melodrama reviewed here has come up with any solution to these problems, it all attempts, in some degree and with greater or lesser success, to engage with them. Brunsdon's essay possibly comes closest to an answer, paradoxically because its very failure to resolve the dualism which ordains that spectators are constructed by texts while audiences have their place in contexts begins to hint at a way around the problem. Although the hybrid 'social subject' may turn out to be more a social audience member than a spectator, this concept does suggest that a move into theories of discourse could prove to be productive.

Both spectators and social audience may accordingly be regarded as discursive constructs. Representations, contexts, audiences, and spectators would then be seen as a series of interconnected social discourses, certain discourses possessing greater constitutive authority at specific moments than others. Such a model permits relative autonomy for the operations of texts, readings, and contexts, and also allows for contradictions, oppositional readings, and varying degrees of discursive authority. Since the state of a discursive formation is not constant, it can be apprehended only by means of

---

13 Brunsdon, '*Crossroads*: Notes on Soap Opera', 32.

14 A similar model is also adopted by Dorothy Hobson in Crossroads: *The Drama of a Soap Opera* (London: Methuen, 1982).

inquiry into specific instances or conjunctures. In attempting to deal with the text–context split and to address the relationship between spectators and social audiences, therefore, theories of representation may have to come to terms with discursive formations of the social, cultural, and textual.

One of the impulses generating feminist critical and theoretical work on soap opera and the woman's picture is a desire to examine genres which are popular, and popular in particular with women. The assumption is usually that such popularity has to do mainly with the social audience: TV soaps attract large numbers of viewers, many of them women, and in its heyday the woman's picture also drew in a mass female audience. But when the nature of this appeal is sought in the texts themselves or in relations between spectators and texts, the argument becomes rather more complex. In what specific ways do soaps and melodramas address or construct female/feminine spectators?

To some extent, they offer the spectator a position of mastery: this is certainly true as regards the hermeneutic of the melodrama's classic narrative, though perhaps less obviously so in relation to the soap's infinite process of narrativity. At the same time, they also place the spectator in a masochistic position of either—in the case of the woman's picture—identifying with a female character's renunciation or, as in soap opera, forever anticipating an endlessly held-off resolution. Culturally speaking, this combination of mastery and masochism in the reading competence constructed by soaps and melodramas suggests an interplay of masculine and feminine subject positions. Culturally dominant codes inscribe the masculine, while the feminine bespeaks a 'return of the repressed' in the form of codes which may well transgress culturally dominant subject positions, though only at the expense of proposing a position of subjection for the spectator.

At the same time, it is sometimes argued on behalf of both soap opera and film melodrama that in a society whose representations of itself are governed by the masculine, these genres at least raise the possibility of female desire and female point of view. Pam Cook advances such a view in relation to the woman's picture, for example.[15] But how is the oppositional potential of this to be assessed? Tania Modleski suggests that soap opera is 'in the vanguard not just of TV art but of all popular narrative art'.[16] But such a statement begs the question: under what circumstances can popular narrative art itself be regarded as transgressive? Because texts do not operate in isolation from contexts, any answer to these questions must take into account the ways in which popular narratives are read, the conditions under which they are produced and consumed, and the ends to which they are appropriated. As most feminist writing on soap opera and the woman's melodrama implies, there is ample space in the articulation of these various instances for contradiction and for struggles over meaning.

The popularity of television soap opera and film melodrama with women raises the question of how it is that sizeable audiences of women relate to

---

15 Cook, 'Melodrama and the Woman's Picture'. E. Ann Kaplan takes a contrary position in 'Theories of Melodrama: A Feminist Perspective', *Women and Performance: A Journal of Feminist Theory*, 1/1 (1983), 40–8.

16 Modleski, *Loving with a Vengeance*, 87.

these representations and the institutional practices of which they form part. It provokes, too, a consideration of the continuity between women's interpellation as spectators and their status as a social audience. In turn, the distinction between social audience and spectator/subject, and attempts to explore the relationship between the two, are part of a broader theoretical endeavour: to deal in tandem with texts and contexts. The distinction between social audience and spectator must also inform debates and practices around cultural production, in which questions of context and reception are always paramount. For anyone interested in feminist cultural politics, such considerations will necessarily inform any assessment of the place and the political usefulness of popular genres aimed at, and consumed by, mass audiences of women.

11

Melodramatic Identifications: Television Fiction and Women's Fantasy

Ien Ang

CONTEMPORARY POPULAR TELEVISION fiction offers an array of strong and independent female heroines, who seem to defy—not without conflicts and contradictions, to be sure—stereotypical definitions of femininity. Heroines such as Maddie Hayes (*Moonlighting*) and Christine Cagney (*Cagney and Lacey*) do not fit into the traditional ways in which female characters have generally been represented in prime-time television fiction: passive and powerless on the one hand, and sexual objects for men on the other.

Christine Cagney, especially, and her partner Mary-Beth Lacey, are the kind of heroines who have mobilized approval from feminists.[1] *Cagney and Lacey* can be called a 'socialist realist' series, in which the personal and professional dilemmas of modern working women are dealt with in a serious and 'realistic' way. Cagney explicitly resists sexual objectification by her male colleagues, forcefully challenges the male hierarchy at work, and entertains an adult, respectful, and caring friendship with her 'buddy' Lacey.

Maddie Hayes is a little more difficult to evaluate in straightforward feminist terms. However, while she often has to cope with the all-but-abusive, but ever-so-magnetic machismo of her recalcitrant partner David Addison, *Moonlighting*, as a typical example of postmodernist television, self-consciously addresses, enacts, and acknowledges metonymically the pleasures and pains of the ongoing 'battle between the sexes' in the context of the series' characteristic penchant for hilarious absurdism and teasing parody.[2] In that battle, Maddie is neither passive nor always the loser: she fights and gains respect (and love) in the process.

© Ien Ang, 1990.

Originally published in Mary Ellen Brown (ed.), *Television and Women's Culture: The Politics of the Popular* (London: Sage, 1990), 75–88.

1 See J. D'Acci, 'The Case of *Cagney and Lacey*', in H. Baehr and G. Dyer (eds.), *Boxed-In: Women and Television* (London: Pandora Press, 1987); also D. Clark, '*Cagney and Lacey*: Feminist Strategies of Detection', in M. E. Brown (ed.), *Television and Women's Culture: The Politics of the Popular* (London: Sage, 1990), 116–33.

2 See S. R. Olson, 'Meta-Television: Popular Postmodernism', *Cultural Studies in Mass Communication*, 4 (1987), 284–300.

Many women enjoy watching series such as *Cagney and Lacey* and *Moonlighting*, and it is likely that at least part of their pleasure is related to the 'positive' representations of women that both series offer. But this does not mean that other, more traditional television fictions are less pleasurable for large numbers of women. On the contrary, as is well known, soap operas have traditionally been *the* female television genre, while prime-time soaps such as *Dallas* and *Dynasty* have always had a significantly larger female audience than a male one.

Personally, I have often been moved by Sue Ellen of *Dallas* as much as I am at times by Christine Cagney. And yet, Sue Ellen is a radically different heroine from Cagney: she displays no (will for) independence whatsoever, she derives her identity almost entirely from being the wife of the unscrupulous and power-obsessed J. R. Ewing, whom she detests because he is never faithful, but whom she does not have the strength to leave.[3] As a consequence, Sue Ellen's life is dominated by constant frustration and suffering—apparently a very negative representation of 'woman' indeed. Despite this, the Sue Ellen character seems to be a source of identification and pleasure for many women viewers of *Dallas*: they seem not so much to love to hate J.R. but to suffer with Sue Ellen.

An indication of this can be derived from the results of a small-scale research that I conducted a few years ago.[4] Through an advertisement in a Dutch weekly magazine, I asked people to send me their views about *Dallas*. From the letters, it was clear that Sue Ellen stood out as a character whom many women viewers were emotionally involved with. One of the respondents wrote:

> I can sit very happy and fascinated watching someone like Sue Ellen. That woman can really get round us, with her problems and troubles. She is really human. I could be someone like her too. In a manner of speaking.

Another wrote:

> Sue Ellen is definitely my favourite. She has a psychologically believable character. As she is, I am myself to a lesser degree ('knocking one's head against a wall once too often') and I want to be (attractive).

It is interesting to note that another *Dallas* character whose structural position in the narrative is similar to Sue Ellen's has not elicited such committed responses at all. Pamela Ewing (married to J.R.'s brother, Bobby) is described rather blandly as 'a nice girl', or is seen as 'too sweet'. In fact, the difference of appeal between the two characters becomes even more pronounced in the light of the findings of a representative Dutch survey conducted in 1982 (around the time that the popularity of *Dallas* was at its height). While 21.7 per cent of female viewers between 15 and 39 years mentioned Sue Ellen as their favourite *Dallas* character (as against only 5.9 per

---

3 At one point, Sue Ellen decided to become a businesswoman—and with great success. However, even this major structural change in her life was motivated by a wish to mess up J.R.'s schemes and plans. She started her business (Valentine Lingerie) as a shrewd tactic to get rid of J.R.'s mistress.

4 See I. Ang, *Watching* Dallas: *Soap Opera and the Melodramatic Imagination*, trans. D. Couling (London and New York: Methuen, 1985).

cent of the men), only 5.1 per cent named Pamela as their favourite (and 4.2 per cent of the men).[5]

Clearly Sue Ellen has a special significance for a large number of women viewers. Two things stand out in the quotes above. Not only do these viewers assert that the appeal of Sue Ellen is related to a form of realism (in the sense of psychological believability and recognizability); more importantly, this realism is connected with a somewhat tragic reading of Sue Ellen's life, emphasizing her problems and troubles. In other words, the position from which Sue Ellen fans seem to give meaning to, and derive pleasure from, their favourite *Dallas* character seems to be a rather melancholic and sentimental structure of feeling which stresses the down-side of life rather than its happy highlights; frustration, desperation, and anger rather than euphoria and cheerfulness.

To interpret this seemingly rather despondent form of female pleasure, I shall examine the position which the Sue Ellen character occupies in the *Dallas* narrative, and unravel the meaning of that position in the context of the specific fictional genre to which *Dallas* belongs: the melodramatic soap opera. The tragic structure of feeling embodied by Sue Ellen as a fictional figure must be understood in the context of the genre characteristics of the *Dallas* drama: just as Christine Cagney is a social-realist heroine and Maddie Hayes a postmodern one, so is Sue Ellen a melodramatic heroine. In other words, articulated and materialized in Sue Ellen's identity is what in 1976 American critic Peter Brooks called a melodramatic imagination.

Of course, fictional characters may be polysemic just as they can take on a plurality of meanings depending on the ways in which diverse viewers read them. Thus, Sue Ellen's melodramatic persona can be interpreted and evaluated in several ways. Whilst her fans tend to empathize with her and live through her problems and troubles vicariously, others stress her bitchiness and take a stance against her. In the words of one *Dallas* viewer:

> Sue Ellen has had bad luck with J.R., but she makes up for it by being a flirt. I don't like her much. And she's too sharp-tongued.

Others have called her a frustrated lady. One of my respondents was especially harsh in her critique:

> Take Sue Ellen. She acts as though she's very brave and can put up a fight, but she daren't make the step of divorce. What I mean is that in spite of her good intentions she lets people walk over her, because (as J.R. wants) for the outside world they have to form a perfect family.

According to Herta Herzog, who interviewed German viewers about *Dallas* in 1987, older viewers tend to see in Sue Ellen the woman ruined by her husband, while younger ones tend to see her as a somewhat unstable person who is her own problem.[6] However, despite the variation in emphasis in the different readings of Sue Ellen, a basic agreement seems to exist that her situation is an extremely contentious and frustrating one, and her

---

5 These figures come from a survey of the Department of Viewing and Listening Research, NOS, Hilversum, May 1982.

6 See M. H. Herzog, 'Decoding *Dallas*: Comparing German and American Viewers', in A. A. Berger (ed.), *Television in Society* (New Brunswick, NJ: Transaction Books, 1987).

personality is rather tormented. This is the core of the melodramatic heroine. But while many viewers are put off by this type of character, some are fascinated, a response evoked not only by the dramatic content of the role, but by the melodramatic style of the actress, Linda Gray. As one fan discloses,

> Sue Ellen (is) just *fantastic*, tremendous how that woman acts, the movements of her mouth, hands, etc. That woman really enters into her role, looking for love, snobbish, in short a real woman.

As a contrast, the same viewer describes Pamela as a Barbie doll with no feelings!

It is not my intention to offer an exhaustive analysis of the Sue Ellen character as melodramatic heroine. Nor do I want to make a sociological examination of which segment of the audience is attracted to characters like her. Rather, I use her as a point of departure to explore women's pleasure in popular fiction in general, and melodramatic fiction in particular. Women who use Sue Ellen as a source of identification while watching *Dallas* do that by taking up, in fantasy, a subject position which inhabits the melodramatic imagination.[7] The pleasure of such imaginary identification can be seen as a form of excess in some women's mode of experiencing everyday life in our culture: the act of surrendering to the melodramatic imagination may signify a recognition of the complexity and conflict fundamental to living in the modern world.

Soap Opera and the Melodramatic Imagination

I now move to summing up some of the structural soap opera characteristics of *Dallas* which contribute to its melodramatic content.[8] It should first be noted, however, that because *Dallas* is a prime-time programme, some of its features are different from those of the traditional daytime soaps. Most importantly, because the programme must attract a heterogeneous audience it will include a wider range of themes, scenes, and plots. For example, male characters, as well as themes, scenes, and plots which traditionally are mainly appreciated by male audiences, such as the wheelings and dealings of the oil business, and the cowboy/Western elements of the show, occupy a much more prominent place in the fictional world of *Dallas* than in regular daytime soap. Nevertheless, the general formal characteristics of *Dallas* do remain true to the soap opera genre, and are very important for the construction of melodramatic meanings and feelings in the text.[9]

First of all, as in all melodrama, personal life is the core problematic of the narrative. Personal life must be understood here as constituted by its every-

---

7 It should be noted, however, that watching a television programme does not necessarily involve identification with only one character. On the contrary, numerous subject positions can be taken up by viewers while reading a television text. Consequently, a *Dallas* viewer may alternate between positions of identification and positions of distance, and thus inhabit several, sometimes contradictory imaginary structures at the same time.

8 See R. C. Allen, *Speaking of Soap Operas* (Chapel Hill: Univ. of North Carolina Press, 1985).

9 See Ang, *Watching* Dallas; J. Feuer, 'Enterprises: An Overview', in J. Feuer, P. Kerr, and T. Vahimagi (eds.), *MTM: 'Quality Television'* (London: BFI, 1984); also for melodrama in general see P. Brooks, *The Melodramatic Imagination: Balzac, Henry James, Melodrama and the Mode of Excess* (New Haven: Yale Univ. Press, 1976); C. Gledhill (ed.), *Home is Where the Heart is* (London: BFI, 1987).

day realization through personal relationships. In soap operas, the evolution of personal relationships is marked out through the representation of significant family rituals and events such as births, romances, engagements, marriages, divorces, deaths, and so on. It is the experience of these rituals and events (and all the attendant complications and disputes) on which soap opera narratives centre. This does not imply that non-personal issues are not addressed. However the way in which they are treated and take on meaning is always from the standpoint of personal life:

> the action of soap opera is not restricted to the familial, or quasi-familial institutions, but everything is told from the point of view of the personal.[10]

Thus, while J.R.'s business intrigues form a focal narrative concern in *Dallas*, they are always shown with an eye to their consequences for the well-being of the Ewing family members, not least his wife Sue Ellen.

A second major melodramatic feature of soap opera is its excessive plot structure. If family life is the main focus of the *Dallas* narrative, the life of the Ewings is presented as one replete with extraordinary conflicts and catastrophes. To the critical outsider this may appear as a purely sensationalist tendency to cliché and exaggeration—a common objection levelled at melodrama since the late nineteenth century. It is important to note, however, that *within* the fictional world of the soap opera all those extreme story-lines such as kidnappings, bribery, extramarital affairs, obscure illnesses, and so on, which succeed each other at such a breathtaking pace, are not treated in a sensational manner, but are taken entirely seriously.[11] The parameters of melodrama require that such clichés be regarded and assessed not for their literal, referential value—that is, their realism—but as meaningful in so far as they solicit a highly charged, emotional impact. Their role is metaphorical, and their appeal stems from the enlarged emotional impact they evoke: it is the feelings being mobilized here that matter. An excess of events and intensity of emotions are inextricably intertwined in the melodramatic imagination.

Sue Ellen's recurrent alcoholism is a case in point. Even though she has stayed away from alcohol for a long time loyal viewers are reminded of this dark side of her past every time she is shown refusing a drink. Do we detect a slight moment of hesitation there? Alcoholism is a very effective narrative motif that, in a condensed way, enables the devoted viewer to empathize with her feelings of desperation. She is married to a man she loathes but who has her almost completely in his power. In other words, Sue Ellen's propensity for alcoholism functions as a metaphor for her enduring state of crisis.

Such a state of crisis is not at all exceptional or uncommon in the context of the soap opera genre. On the contrary, crisis can be said to be endemic to it. As a result, Sue Ellen's predicament, as it is constructed, is basically

---

10 C. Brundson, '*Crossroads*: Notes on Soap Opera', *Screen*, 22/4 (1981), 34.

11 The moment a soap opera becomes self-conscious about its own excess, which is sometimes the case with *Dynasty*, and no longer takes its own story seriously, it presents itself as a parody of the genre, as it were, accentuating its status as discourse through stylization and formalism (such as slow-motion techniques). Sections of the *Dynasty* audience that read the show as a form of camp, for instance, are responding to this aspect of the *Dynasty* text.

unsolvable unless she leaves the *Dallas* community and disappears from the serial altogether. Here, a third structural characteristic of the soap opera makes its impact: its lack of narrative progress. *Dallas*, like all soap operas, is a never-ending story: contrary to classic narratives, which are typically structured according to the logic of order/disorder/restoration of order, soap opera narratives never reach completion. They represent process without progression and as such do not offer the prospect of a conclusion of final denouement, in which all problems are solved. Thus, soap operas are fundamentally anti-utopian: an ending, happy or unhappy, is unimaginable. This does not mean, of course, that there are no moments of climax in soap operas. But, as Tania Modleski has observed, 'the "mini-climaxes" of soap opera function to introduce difficulties and to complicate rather than simplify the characters' lives'.[12] Here, a basic melodramatic idea is conveyed: the sense that life is marked by eternal contradiction, by unsolvable emotional and moral conflicts, by the ultimate impossibility, as it were, of reconciling desire and reality. As Laura Mulvey has put it,

> The melodrama recognises this gap by raising problems, known and recognisable, and offering a personal escape similar to that of a day-dream: a chance to work through inescapable frustrations by positing an alternative ideal never seen as more than a momentary illusion.[13]

The life of the Sue Ellen character in *Dallas* exemplifies and dramatizes this melodramatic scenario. She even expresses an awareness of its painfully contradictory nature. In one dialogue with Pamela, for example, she states:

> The difference [between you and me] is that you're a strong woman, Pam. I used to think I was, but I know differently now. I need Southfork. On my own, I don't amount to much. As much as I hate J.R., I really need to be Mrs J.R. Ewing. And I need him to be the father of John Ross [her son]. So I guess I just have to lead a married life without a husband.

In general then, it could be said that the soap operatic structure of *Dallas* opens up a narrative space in which melodramatic characters can come to life symbolically—characters who ultimately are constructed as victims of forces that lie beyond their control. A heroine like Sue Ellen will never be able to make her own history: no matter how hard she tries, eventually the force of circumstances will be too overwhelming. She lives in the prison of an eternally conflictual present. No wonder that she reacts with frustration, bitterness, resignation, and cynical ruthlessness on the rebound. As she neatly summarizes her own life philosophy:

> If J.R. seeks sex and affection somewhere else, so why shouldn't I? All Ewing men are the same. And for you to survive you have two choices. You can either get out, or you can play by their rules!

In fact, this frame of mind has led her to give up all attempts to find true happiness for herself: although she has her occasional moments of joy (a new

---

12 T. Modleski, 'The Rhythms of Reception: Daytime Television and Women's Work', in E. A. Kaplan (ed.), *Regarding Television* (Los Angeles: American Film Institute, 1983), 107.

13 L. Mulvey, 'Notes on Sirk and Melodrama', *Movie*, 25 (1978), 30.

lover, for example), they are futile in the face of her biggest self-imposed passion: to use all the power she has to undermine J.R.'s projects, to ruin his life just as he has ruined hers. She even refuses him a divorce to keep him from marrying another woman (by which he expects to win an extremely advantageous business deal). It is such small victories which make her feel strong at times. But they are ultimately self-destructive and will never allow her to break out of her cage.

Against this background, identifying with Sue Ellen implies a recognition of the fact that Sue Ellen's crisis is a permanent one: there seems to be no real way out. She may experience happy moments, but as viewers we know that those moments are bound to be merely temporary and inevitably followed by new problems and difficulties. At stake, then, must be a rather curious form of pleasure for these viewers. Whereas in other narratives pleasure comes from the assurance and confirmation of a happy end—as with the romantic union of a man and a woman in the formulaic 'they live happily ever after', involvement with a character like Sue Ellen is conditioned by the prior knowledge that no such happy ending will ever occur. Instead, pleasure must come from living through and negotiating with the crisis itself. To put it more precisely, many female Sue Ellen fans tend to identify with a subject position characterized by a sense of entrapment: a sense in which survival is, in the words of television critic Horace Newcomb, 'complicated by ambiguity and blurred with pain even in its most sought-after moments'.[14]

If this is true (and I have already given some indications that this is indeed the case) how do we interpret this kind of identification, this form of pleasure in popular fiction?

Pleasure, Fantasy, and the Negotiation of Femininity

One could assert that melodramatic heroines like Sue Ellen should be evaluated negatively because they attest to an outlook on life that stresses resignation and despair. Isn't the melodramatic imagination a particularly damaging way of making sense of life because it affirms tendencies of individualistic fatalism and pessimism? And isn't such an impact especially harmful for women as it reinforces and legitimizes masochistic feelings of powerlessness? Wouldn't it be much better for women and girls to choose identification figures that represent strong, powerful, and independent women who are able and determined to change and improve their lives, such as Christine Cagney?

Such concerns are, of course, often heard in feminist accounts of popular fiction, but it is important to note here that they are often based upon a theoretical approach—what could be called a role/image approach, or more conventionally, 'images of women' approach—which analyses images of women in the media and in fiction by setting them against real women. Fictional female heroines are then seen as images of women functioning as role models for female audiences.[15] From such a perspective, it is only logical

---

14 H. Newcomb, *TV: The Most Popular Art* (New York: Anchor Books, 1974), 178.

15 T. Moi, *Sexual/Textual Politics: Feminist Literary Theory* (London: Methuen, 1986); L. F. Rakow, 'Feminist Approaches to Popular Culture: Giving Patriarchy its Due', *Communication*, 9 (1986), 19–41.

to claim that one should strive to offer positive role models by supplying positive images of women. And from this perspective, feminist common sense would undoubtedly ascribe the Sue Ellen character to the realm of negative images, reflecting a traditional, stereotyped, or trivialized model of womanhood.

However, this approach contains both theoretical and political problems. Most importantly here, because it implies a rationalistic view of the relationship between image and viewer (whereby it is assumed that the image is seen by the viewer as a more or less adequate model of reality), it can only account for the popularity of soap operas among women as something irrational. In other words, what the role/image approach tends to overlook is the large *emotional involvement* which is invested in identification with characters of popular fiction.

To counteract this attitude, we first of all need to acknowledge that these characters are products of *fiction*, and that fiction is not a mere set of images to be read referentially, but an ensemble of textual devices for engaging the viewer at the level of fantasy.[16] As a result, female fictional characters such as Sue Ellen Ewing or Christine Cagney cannot be conceptualized as realistic images of women, but as textual constructions of possible *modes of femininity*: as embodying versions of gendered subjectivity endowed with specific forms of psychical and emotional satisfaction and dissatisfaction, and specific ways of dealing with conflicts and dilemmas. In relation to this, they do not function as role models but are symbolic realizations of feminine subject positions with which viewers can identify *in fantasy*.

Fantasy is central here. In line with psychoanalytic theory, fantasy should not be seen as mere illusion, an unreality, but as a reality in itself, a fundamental aspect of human existence: a necessary and unerasable dimension of psychical reality. Fantasy is an imagined scene in which the fantasizing subject is the protagonist, and in which alternative scenarios for the subject's real life are evoked. Fantasizing obviously affords the subject pleasure, which, according to the psychoanalysts, has to do with the fulfilment of a conscious or unconscious wish. Here I would suggest more generally that the pleasure of fantasy lies in its offering the subject an opportunity to take up positions which she could not do in real life: through fantasy she can move beyond the structural constraints of everyday life and explore other situations, other identities, other lives. It is totally unimportant here whether these are realistic or not. As Lesley Stern has remarked, 'gratification is to be achieved not through acting out the fantasies, but through the activity of fantasising itself'.[17]

Fantasies, and the act of fantasizing, are usually a private practice in which we can engage at any time and the content of which we generally keep to ourselves. Fictions, on the other hand, are collective and public fantasies; they are textual elaborations, in narrative form, of fantastic scenarios which,

16 V. Walkerdine, 'Some Day my Prince will Come: Young Girls and the Preparation for Adolescent Sexuality', in A. McRobbie and M. Nava (eds.), *Gender and Generation* (London: Macmillan, 1983), 168. See also E. Cowie, 'Fantasia', *m/f* 9 (1984), 71–105; C. Kaplan, '*The Thornbirds*: Fiction, Fantasy, Femininity', in V. Burgin, J. Donald, and C. Kaplan (eds.), *Formations of Fantasy* (London and New York: Methuen, 1986).

17 L. Stern, 'The Body as Evidence', *Screen*, 23/5 (1982), 56.

being mass-produced, are offered ready-made to audiences. We are not the originators of the public fantasies offered to us in fiction. This explains, of course, why we are not attracted to all the fictions available to us: most of them are irrelevant. Despite this, the pleasure of consuming fictions that do attract us may still relate to that of fantasy: that is, it still involves the imaginary occupation of other subject positions which are outside the scope of our everyday social and cultural identities.

Implicit in the theoretical perspective I have outlined so far is a poststructuralist theory on subjectivity.[18] Central to this is the idea that subjectivity is not the essence or the source from which the individual acts and thinks and feels; on the contrary, subjectivity should be seen as a product of the society and culture in which we live: it is through the meaning systems or discourses circulating in society and culture that subjectivity is constituted and individual identities are formed. Each individual is the site of a multiplicity of subject positions proposed to her by the discourses with which she is confronted; her identity is the precarious and contradictory result of the specific set of subject positions she inhabits at any moment in history.

Just as the fictional character is not a unitary image of womanhood, then, so is the individual viewer not a person whose identity is something static and coherent. If a woman is a social subject whose identity is at least partially marked out by her being a person of a certain sex, it is by no means certain that she will always inhabit the same mode of feminine subjectivity. On the contrary, many different and sometimes contradictory sets of femininities or feminine subject positions (ways of being a woman) are in principle available to her, although it is likely that she will be drawn to adopt some of those more than others. Certain modes of femininity are culturally more legitimate than others; and every woman knows subject positions she is best able to handle. This does not mean, however, that her identity as a woman is something determined in the process of socialization. On the contrary, the adoption of a feminine subjectivity is never definitive but always partial and shaky: in other words, being a woman implies a never-ending *process* of becoming a feminine subject: no one subject position can ever cover satisfactorily all the problems and desires an individual woman encounters.

All too often women (and men too, of course, but their relationship to constructions of masculinity is not at issue here) have to negotiate in all sorts of situations in their lives—at home, at work, in relationships, in larger social settings. In this women are constantly confronted with the cultural task of finding out what it means to be a woman, of marking out the boundaries between the feminine and the unfeminine. This task is not a simple one, especially in the case of modern societies where cultural rules and roles are no longer imposed authoritatively, but allow individualistic notions such as autonomy, personal choice, will, responsibility, and rationality. In this context, a framework of living has been created in which every individual woman is faced with the task of actively reinventing and redefining her femininity as required. The emergence of the modern feminist movement has intensified this situation: now women have become much more conscious about their position in society, and consequently are encouraged to take

---

18 See C. Weedon, *Feminist Practice and Poststructuralist Theory* (Oxford: Basil Blackwell, 1987).

control over their own lives by rejecting the traditional dictum that anatomy is destiny. Being a woman, in other words, can now mean the adoption of many different identities, composed of a whole range of subject positions, not predetermined by immovable definitions of femininity. It would stretch beyond the purpose of this article to explore and explain in more detail how women construct and reconstruct their feminine identities in everyday life. What is important to conclude at this point then is that being a woman involves *work*, work of constant self-(re)construction. (The ever-growing array of different women's magazines is a case in point: in all of them the central problematic is 'how to be a true woman', while the meanings of 'true' are subject to constant negotiation.) At the same time, however, the energy women must put in this fundamental work of self-(re)construction is suppressed: women are expected to find the right identity effortlessly. (Women's magazines always assume an enthusiastic, 'you-can-do-it!' mode of address: work is represented as pleasure.)

It is in this constellation that fantasy and fiction can play a distinctive role. They offer a private and unconstrained space in which socially impossible or unacceptable subject positions, or those which are in some way too dangerous or too risky to be acted out in real life, can be adopted. In real life, the choice for this or that subject position is never without consequences. Contrary to what women's magazines tell us, it is often *not* easy to know what it means to be a 'true' woman. For example, the social display of forms of traditional femininity—dependence, passivity, submissiveness—can have quite detrimental and self-destructive consequences for women when strength, independence, or decisiveness are called for. In fantasy and fiction, however, there is no punishment for whatever identity one takes up, no matter how headstrong or destructive: there will be no retribution, no defeat will ensue. Fantasy and fiction then, are the safe spaces of excess in the interstices of ordered social life where one has to keep oneself strategically under control.

From this perspective identification with melodramatic heroines can be viewed in a new way. The position ascribed to Sue Ellen by those identifying with her is one of masochism and powerlessness: a self-destructive mode of femininity which, in social and political terms, could only be rejected as regressive and unproductive. But rather than condemn this identification, it is possible to observe the gratification such imaginary subject positions provide for the women concerned. What can be so pleasurable in imagining a fantastic scenario in which one is a self-destructive and frustrated bitch?

In the context of the discussion above, I can suggest two meanings of melodramatic identifications. On the one hand, sentimental and melancholic feelings of masochism and powerlessness, which are the core of the melodramatic imagination, are an implicit recognition, in their surrender to some power outside the subject, of the fact that one can never have everything under control all the time, and that consequently identity is not a question of free and conscious choice but always acquires its shape under circumstances not of one's own making. Identification with these feelings is connected with a basic, if not articulated, awareness of the weighty pressure of reality on one's subjectivity, one's wishes, one's desires. On the other hand, identification with a melodramatic character like Sue Ellen also validates those feelings by offering women some room to indulge in them, to let go as it were, in a moment of intense, self-centred abandon—a moment of giving up to the force of circumstances, just like Sue Ellen has done, so that the work of self-(re)construction is no longer needed. I would argue that such moments, however fleeting, can be experienced as moments of peace, of truth, of redemption, a moment in which the complexity of the task of being a woman is fully realized and accepted. In short, whilst indulgence in a melo-dramatic identity in real life will generally only signify pathetic weakness and may have paralysing effects, fantasy and fiction constitute a secure space in which one can be excessively melodramatic without suffering the conse-quences. No wonder melodrama is often accompanied with tears.

Final Remarks This interpretation of the appeal of melodramatic characters among women must, of course, be contextualized and refined in several ways. First of all, by trying to explain what it means for women to identify with a melodramatic fictional character, I have by no means intended to justify or endorse it. I have tried to make it understandable, in the face of the ridicule and rejection that crying over melodramatic fiction (as if it were irrational) continues to receive. However, my analysis does not extend to any further impact upon the subjects concerned. Whether the release of melodramatic feelings through fantasy or fiction has an empowering or paralysing effect upon the subject is an open question and can probably not be answered without analysing the context of the fantasizing.

Secondly, we should not overlook the fact that not all women are attracted to melodrama, and that some men can be moved by melodrama too. If any-thing, this fact suggests that femininity and masculinity are not positions inhabited inevitably by biological women and men, but that identity is tran-sitory, the temporary result of dynamic identifications. Further research and analysis could give us more insight into the conditions, social, cultural, psy-chological, under which a surrender to the melodramatic imagination exerts its greatest appeal. Melodrama has been consistently popular among women in the modern period, but this does not have to be explained exclusively in terms of constants. The fundamental chasm between desire and reality, which forms the deepest 'truth' of the melodramatic imagination, may be an eternal aspect of female experience, but how that chasm is bridged symboli-cally and in practice is historically variable. In fact, there is a fundamentally melodramatic edge to feminism too. After all, are not the suffering and frus-tration so eminently materialized in melodramatic heroines the basis for the anger conveyed in feminism? And does not feminism stand for the over-whelming desire to transcend reality—which is bound to be a struggle, full of frustrations and moments of despair? While the melodramatic heroine is someone who is forced to give up, leaving a yawning gap between desire and reality, the feminist is someone who refuses to give up, no matter how hard the struggle to close that gap might be.

Christine Cagney, too, shares more with Sue Ellen than we might expect. Of course, the manifest dramatic content of *Cagney and Lacey* is more in line with feminist ideals and concerns, and as such the Cagney and Lacey characters can provide an outlet for identification with fantasies of liberation for women viewers.[19] Despite the fact that Christine Cagney is an independent career woman who knows where she stands, she too must at times face the unsolvable dilemmas inherent in the lives of modern women: how to combine love and work; how to compete with the boys; how to deal with growing older . . . Often enough, she encounters frustration and displays a kind of cynical bitchiness not unlike Sue Ellen's. I would argue that some of the most moving moments of *Cagney and Lacey* are those in which Cagney gives in to the sense of powerlessness so characteristic of the melodramatic heroine.

19 G. Dyer, 'Women and Television: An Overview', in H. Baehr and G. Dyer (eds.), *Boxed-In: Women and Television* (London: Pandora Press, 1987), 10.

12

Black Feminism and Media Criticism: *The Women of Brewster Place*

Jacqueline Bobo and Ellen Seiter

THAT BLACK WOMEN are writing and talking about their history, their politics, and their socio-economic status is not a recent occurrence, though it has sometimes been treated as if it is a 1980s phenomenon. Hazel Carby, in *Reconstructing Womanhood,* documents the fact that black women have long used the mechanisms available to them to attain a 'public voice'. Whether in writing, public speaking, or establishing national networks among a wide spectrum of black women, black feminists have worked diligently to comment upon and improve their social condition.[1] Other recent research by black women has recovered a wealth of literary and political work written by black women and used this as the basis for formalizing a body of thought concerning black feminist theory.[2] This archaeological work was necessary, notes Valerie Smith, because black women had been structured out of the writings of others.[3] The consequences of this neglect were that black women were misrepresented in the theoretical writings of others, if not omitted entirely. For cultural critics this was a particularly vexing problem, in that one of its consequences has been a limited access to works created by black women: now, however, the groundwork has been laid by literary scholars for an analysis of a range of cultural products. No longer can a text constructed by a black woman be considered in isolation from the context of its creation, from its connection with other works within the tradition of black women's creativity, and from its impact not just on cultural critics but on cultural consumers. As we witness the aggressive move towards

© OUP, 1991.

Originally published in *Screen*, 32/3 (Autumn 1991), 286–302.

1 Hazel Carby, *Reconstructing Womanhood: The Emergence of the Afro-American Woman Novelist* (New York: Oxford Univ. Press, 1987).

2 Examples are Barbara Christian, *Black Women Novelists: The Development of a Tradition 1892–1976* (Westport, Conn.: Greenwood Press, 1980); Mary Helen Washington, *Invented Lives: Narratives of Black Women 1860–1960* (New York: Anchor Press, 1987); and more recent essays about black feminist theory in Cheryl Wall (ed.), *Changing Our Own Words: Essays on Criticism, Theory, and Writing by Black Women* (New Brunswick, NJ: Rutgers Univ. Press, 1989); and Joanne Braxton and Andree Nicola McLaughlin (eds.), *Wild Women in the Whirlwind: Afro-American Culture and the Contemporary Literary Renaissance* (New Brunswick, NJ: Rutgers Univ. Press, 1990).

3 Valerie Smith, 'Black Feminist Theory and the Representation of the "Other" ', in Cheryl A. Wall (ed.), *Changing Our Own Words*, 38–57; 'Gender and Afro-Americanist Literary Theory and Criticism', in Elaine Showalter (ed.), *Speaking of Gender* (New York: Routledge, Chapman and Hall, 1989), 56–70.

adapting black women's literature for film and television, a similar effort directed at film and television criticism is now needed. Of course, different considerations must be brought to bear on a work of literature and on its media transformation; which suggests that some theoretical work needs to be done. Film studies has in large part shunned the study of adaptations as too literary, too traditional, and too uninformed by developments in film theory. But, in the case of black women's fiction, adaptations to film and television are the primary, if not the only, source of black feminist thought available to a large audience.[4] Works such as *The Color Purple* (Steven Spielberg, Warner Bros, 1985) and *The Women of Brewster Place* (Donna Deitch, ABC, 1989) represent a particularly vital area of popular narrative film and television today, and have the potential to challenge existing conventions of representation and characterization of women in ways that can also attract a broad, mass audience.

This chapter begins with a consideration of the ways in which black women and other women of colour have been either neglected or only selectively included in the writings of feminist cultural analysts: we consider the responses by women of colour to this omission, the ramifications for feminist studies, and some ways in which this neglect might be redressed. We then turn to an analysis of the television version of *The Women of Brewster Place*, which was based upon the novel by the black American writer Gloria Naylor. Examining the insertion of *The Women of Brewster Place* within a range of political and social appropriations can provide a necessary intervention in the struggle over the meaning of black women's artistic work. This analysis assesses the programme from the perspective of its usefulness for feminist cultural criticism in general and of its position within the politics of popular cultural representations.[5]

The Politics of Feminist Cultural Criticism

The problematic relationship between the feminism of middle-class white women and issues affecting other women, in particular women of colour, has been documented in several well-known works which examine differences between women from historical and social perspectives.[6] For example, Hazel Carby, a black feminist cultural critic, has looked at the historical, social, and economic conditions governing the lives of black and white women, emphasizing that oppression manifests itself differently in black and white women's lives. A crucial difference arose from women's roles during the slavocracy: white women were used (in part) to produce heirs to an oppressive system;

---

4 This point is made by Barbara Christian in 'The Race for Theory', *Feminist Studies*, 14/1 (1988), 67–79. This is a revision and update of an article first published in *Cultural Critique*, 6 (1987), 51–63.

5 Although much of what is written in this article concerns women of colour in the United States, we would like to think it can be more broadly applicable and useful for feminists in other countries. For a more specific detailing of black women's cultural activities throughout the world see the entry on 'Black Cinema', in Annette Kuhn (ed.), *Women in Film: An International Guide* (New York: Ballantine, 1991).

6 See e.g. bell hooks, *Ain't I a Woman? Black Women and Feminism* (Boston: South End Press, 1981); Gloria I. Joseph and Jill Lewis (eds.), *Common Differences: Conflict in Black and White Feminists' Perspectives* (New York: Anchor, 1981).

black women functioned as breeders to produce property that added to the capital accumulation of the plantation system. The continuing divergent material circumstances would later affect the production of black and white women's texts about the status of their various oppressions.[7]

Aïda Hurtado, writing about the different ways patriarchy has affected white women and women of colour, notes that white women in the US have responded with the notion that the personal is political. Hurtado stresses that the political consciousness of women of colour 'stems from an awareness that the public is *personally* political'.[8] Her conclusion that the public sphere contains the elements of political thought and activity for women of colour is especially important for white feminist critics to recognize:

> the public/private distinction is relevant only for the white middle and upper classes since historically the American state has intervened constantly in the private lives and domestic arrangements of the working class. Women of Color have not had the benefit of the economic conditions that underlie the public/private distinction. White feminists' concerns about the unhealthy consequences of standards for feminine beauty, their focus on the unequal division of household labor, and their attention to childhood identity formation stem from a political consciousness that seeks to project private sphere issues into the public arena. Feminists of Color focus instead on public issues such as affirmative action, racism, school desegregation, prison reform and voter registration—issues that cultivate an awareness of the distinction between public policy and private choice.[9]

White feminist film and video critics can learn from the writings and experiences that have characterized fiction and literary criticism by women of colour. However, greater effort needs to be devoted to making this work available. Michele Wallace—a black feminist cultural critic who has taken some difficult stands against impediments to black women's progress— addresses a significant aspect of the problem. Her book *Black Macho and the Myth of the Superwoman* (1979), along with Ntozake Shange's choreopoem *for colored girls who have considered suicide when the rainbow is enuf* (1978), are considered pivotal works in contemporary debates about the racial 'correctness' of black women's cultural works. Wallace has criticized Adrienne Rich in her role as an intermediary between black women's writing and the public dissemination of their work. In her review of Rich's *Blood, Bread, and Poetry* (1986) for the *New York Times Book Review*, she chronicles Rich's political evolution, noting that when Rich won the National Book Award for poetry in 1974, she insisted that the honour be shared between herself and the black women who were also nominated, Alice Walker and Audre Lorde.[10]

---

7 See Carby's *Reconstructing Womanhood*, and also her earlier assessment of the relationship of white feminism to the actual lives of women of colour in 'White Woman Listen: Black Feminism and the Boundaries of Sisterhood', in Centre for Contemporary Cultural Studies, *The Empire Strikes Back: Race and Racism in Seventies* Britain (London: Hutchinson, 1982), 212–35.

8 Aïda Hurtado, 'Relating to Privilege: Seduction and Rejection in the Subordination of White Women and Women of Color', *Signs: Journal of Women in Culture and Society*, 14/4 (1989), 849.

9 Ibid. 850.

10 Michele Wallace, 'Sexism is the Least of it', *New York Times Book Review*, 17 Mar. 1987: 18.

Wallace writes that even though Rich might have the best of intentions, she 'pretends to sponsor that which is not in her power to sponsor, that which she can only silence: a Black feminist voice and/or theory'. Wallace explains that Rich exercises control over the works of black women and other women of colour in that she is a gatekeeper for those works that will appear on the 'essential reading list'. She adds: 'When I say reading list, that's a euphemistic way of referring to book contracts, book sales, teaching jobs, tenure, publication in anthologies and journals, without which it is now impossible to be a writer, much less a black feminist writer.'[11]

The gatekeeping function of certain strains of white feminist thought extends beyond being a filter through which designated works are sifted: it limits the kinds of issues that can be written or thought about. Because much of the creative and theoretical work written by black women is available only through alternative outlets, some mainstream critics remain ignorant of, and uneducated in, black feminist thought. Wallace writes that the problem at present represents

> a critical juncture at the crossroads of a white mainstream academic feminism, which is well paid, abundantly sponsored and self-consciously articulate, and a marginalised, activist-oriented Black feminism, which is not well-paid, virtually unsubsidized and generally inarticulate, unwritten, unpublished and unread.[12]

In the face of these shortcomings, feminists working within cultural studies need to rethink their writing. Jane Gaines, a white feminist cultural critic, has assessed the inadequacies of contemporary feminist criticism (Lacanian psychoanalysis and Marxist feminism) in its practice of examining creative works only for their significance to white, middle-class heterosexual women. Gaines chastises mainstream feminists for their token gestures towards the inclusion of different perspectives, stating 'our political etiquette is correct, but our theory is not so perfect'.[13]

In a similar critique, Coco Fusco details the political expediency within the current 'crisis of conscience'. Fusco criticizes avant-garde art institutions and the individuals who operate them for their selective inclusion of works by people of colour and for the assumption that a 'single event' series can serve as a corrective to decades of racism and sexism. Since these serve as mediators between works by people of colour and public knowledge of their existence, Fusco feels that the avant-garde needs to look to its own practices and re-examine its perspective on 'the other'.[14]

A survey of the opinions of many feminist media analysts in the recent special issue of *Camera Obscura* on 'the spectatrix' makes clear the lack of sub-

11 Michele Wallace, 'The Politics of Location: cinema/theory/literature/ethnicity/sexuality/me', *Framework*, 36 (1989), 42–55.

12 Ibid. 48.

13 Jane Gaines, 'White Privilege and Looking Relations: Race and Gender in Feminist Film Theory', *Screen*, 29/4 (1988), 12–26. Gaines succinctly assesses the difficulties of theorizing about 'the other' using traditional feminist analysis.

14 Coco Fusco, 'Fantasies of Oppositionality: Reflections on Recent Conferences in Boston and New York', *Screen*, 29/4 (1988), 80–93. A rebuttal to Fusco's article was presented in a later issue of *Screen*: Berenice Reynaud and Yvonne Rainer, 'Responses to Coco Fusco's "Fantasies of Oppositionality"', with reply from Coco Fusco, *Screen*, 30/3 (1989), 79–100.

stantial theorizing about issues around class or race and cinema. After summarizing the terrain of female spectatorship, the editors admit that there is a difficulty in redressing this omission: it is easier, they say, to recognize that spectator positions involving race, class, age, and so on need to be taken into account than it is 'to arrive at satisfactory methods for doing so, or even more simply, to understand what it is that we want to know, and why'.[15]

What we want to know and why we as cultural commentators need to know it is exemplified in the problem of sampling currently confronting researchers in cultural studies, audience studies, and ethnographic work. Recently there has been a surge in empirical work in reader/audience studies, especially relating to women's genres such as romance, melodrama, and soap opera. In cultural studies work on audiences (as in much of the mass communications research it seeks to oppose), samples have tended overwhelmingly to be white. This fact deserves a closer look: it is too frequent an occurrence to be shunted aside or excused by the brief apologies which attribute white samples to limited funding or scope. It is not something that 'just happens', not simply a case of sampling error, nor of the failure of individual researchers to be sufficiently diligent in making contacts, although these are certainly factors that contribute to the problem.

This situation has partly to do with the demographics of the academy in the United States: who the researchers are (predominantly white), where they live (in segregated white neighbourhoods), and where they work. Occupational segregation has been durably established in US universities: whites filling professorial ranks and senior positions, and people of colour relegated to service and clerical positions, or assuming faculty positions in small numbers and at untenured, junior levels. This structure remains in place even as many institutions pay fashionable lip-service to their efforts toward diversity in faculty and student population. It also, and less obviously, has to do with the trend towards interviewing respondents in their homes. Women of colour will probably be less likely to welcome white researchers into their homes than will white women. As long as the state so often interferes in their private sphere under the guise of a range of seemingly innocuous ventures, women of colour will be wary of intrusions into their domestic space by white middle-class professionals. Thus, while theoretically sound, the increased emphasis of late on the crucial role of the domestic sphere in shaping media consumption must be scrutinized in terms of the limitations it may set on the kinds of participants available for studies involving the home as both site and object of research.[16]

James Clifford, among others, has called attention to the unequal power relations inherent in the ethnographic enterprise and to the 'objectification' of the subject in ethnographic discourse.[17] While many white social scientists

---

15 Janet Bergstrom and Mary Ann Doane, 'The Female Spectator: Contexts and Directions', *Camera Obscura*, 20–1 (1989), 5–27.

16 See e.g. David Morley, *Family Television: Cultural Power and Domestic Leisure* (London: Comedia, 1986); Janice Radway, *Reading the Romance: Women, Patriarchy and Popular Literature* (Chapel Hill: Univ. of North Carolina Press, 1984); and studies such as those by Rogge, Tulloch, and Seiter, in Ellen Seiter *et al.* (eds.), *Remote Control: Television, Audiences, and Cultural Power* (London: Routledge, 1989).

17 An early influential article on this topic is James Clifford, 'On Ethnographic Authority', *Representations*, 1/2 (1983), 118–46.

are only now considering these issues, people of colour have long been aware of the possibilities of being ripped off by researchers, and of the ways in which academic studies are often used in the long run to legitimate various forms of oppression. While it would be wrong to dismiss ethnography as a valuable method, it has to be recognized that it produces knowledge which circulates in influential ways within the disciplines in which it is used. Thus, for example, many of the notions of gender difference deriving from ethnographic work with all-white samples in current circulation are reified and ethnocentric: the experiences of women of colour with the media remain unheard, unstudied, untheorized.

Nevertheless, some recently published research by women of colour promises to change the way researchers consider media audiences. Jacqueline Bobo's work with black women's responses to the film *The Color Purple* has demonstrated how black women, because of their low expectations of the media (and their expectation of encountering racism) can read around and through a Hollywood text.[18] Minu Lee and Chong Heup Cho's work with middle-class Korean soap opera fans in the United States similarly points to a much wider range of reactions and uses than has been imagined in theorizing the (white) spectator.[19] It can be predicted with certainty that other work by women of colour will not only alter the pool of empirical findings in cultural studies, but also challenge, redefine, and renovate the theoretical agenda in ways white academics cannot at present imagine. White researchers must work harder to consider the problems of racial and ethnic difference, scrutinize their research designs and their methods of contacting respondents, and bring to their work a high degree of self-consciousness about racism and the power relations inherent in research.

Ultimately, however, substantial improvement in the situation awaits bringing more women of colour into the field of cultural studies and its descriptions of media audiences. There is an unfortunate tendency to consider as a separate agenda—one set apart from theoretical work—issues of affirmative action, diversification of academic faculties, recruitment of students, and equitable entrance requirements. Experience also demonstrates that far too often graduate students of colour lack academic advisers who are strong advocates for them or for their course of study. It is no accident that there are few black, latino, native-born Asian, and native American doctoral students or Ph.D.s in the United States—and with numbers especially small in media studies. Problems range from a curriculum and canon which are overwhelmingly white to a lack of precedent for students to do research relating to their experience—and a lack of encouragement from advisers.[20] A rewriting of the canon and the curriculum must take into account popular films and television programmes, as well as independent and experimental

18 Jacqueline Bobo, '*The Color Purple*: Black Women as Cultural Readers', in E. Deidre Pribram (ed.), *Female Spectators: Looking at Film and Television* (London: Verso, 1988), 90–109.

19 Minu Lee and Chong Heup Cho, 'Women Watching Together: An Ethnographic Study of Korean Soap Opera Fans in the US', *Cultural Studies*, 4/1 (1990), 30–44.

20 For specific examples of this problem for students of colour in graduate programmes, see Yolanda T. Moses, *Black Women in Academe: Issues and Strategies* (Washington, DC: Project on the Status and Education of Women/Association of American Colleges, 1989). An especially frank and insightful look at the issue is given by Karen J. Winkler, 'Minority Students, Professors Tell of Isolation, Anger in Graduate School', *Chronicle of Higher Education*, 9 Nov. 1988: A15, A17.

work by black film-makers. White feminists must recognize that, as an area of academic interest, feminist cultural studies is likely to appear trivial to women of colour until white academics connect more strongly with the politics of the public sphere and the university.

The Women of Brewster Place

The Women of Brewster Place is the story of seven women who live in the run-down black neighbourhood of Brewster Place, located in an unnamed American city. A brick wall at the end of the block, erected as a result of political and economic machinations, separates the residents from the rest of the world. It comes to stand for racism, and its effects are felt daily in the women's lives. Both Gloria Naylor's novel and the television programme are composed of six interconnected stories which detail the lives of seven women. This structure gives characters an individuality that rescues them from the fate of being viewed as anonymous 'female heads of households'. At the same time, according to Barbara Christian, the interrelationships of the women's lives is given full play, establishing 'Brewster Place as a community with its own mores, strengths and weaknesses'.[21]

The first and longest story follows Mattie Michael from her parents' home in the rural South, through her struggles to survive on her own in a northern city with her young son Basil and finally as a middle-aged woman forced to move to Brewster Place after losing her home to bailbondsmen when her son is accused of murder. Etta Mae Johnson is an ageing *femme fatale* who has existed by her ability to attach herself to successful men: she comes to live with her lifelong friend Mattie when she runs out of men to take care of her. Ciel, Mattie's 'adopted' daughter, lives a desperate life waiting for the father of her child to return after each of his abrupt departures: during an argument about his current exodus, their child accidentally dies. Kiswana Browne is a starry-eyed civil rights activist from a financially secure family, now living in Brewster Place because she feels the need to be close to 'the people'. She organizes the residents of the neighbourhood for a rent strike against the owners of the squalid buildings in which they live. Cora Lee, the poorest and most isolated character, is a young woman with seven children: her children are the terror of the neighbourhood and everyone tries to persuade her to stop having more. Lorraine and Theresa have arrived in Brewster Place after living in other, better, neighbourhoods around the city. They have been forced to move on when the other residents have learned they are lesbians, because Lorraine is fearful she will lose her job as a schoolteacher. Theresa refuses to move again because, as she puts it, there is no place left to run; Brewster Place is the end of the line: she does not care how their neighbours on Brewster Place treat them. Lorraine, on the other hand, ostracized by her family and fired from a teaching job, yearns to be part of the community. She wants to be embraced within it, but encounters cruel rejection when she tries to participate in the newly formed block organization. Alienated from the other women, Lorraine ventures out alone one night and is raped in an alley by a

21 Barbara Christian, 'Gloria Naylor's Geography: Community, Class, and Patriarchy in *The Women of Brewster Place* and *Linden Hills*', in Henry Louis Gates, Jr (ed.), *Reading Black, Reading Feminist* (New York: Meridian, 1990), 353.

group of young black men (in the television version there is only one rapist).

The Women of Brewster Place was heavily promoted on US network television, on early morning talk shows, and in magazine articles about Oprah Winfrey, its prime mover, star, and executive producer: it was only on Winfrey's insistence that ABC executives agreed to air the programme. In spite of all the advance publicity, it generated a conspicuous lack of critical attention. Those publications which did review it made the now obligatory observation that the novel was yet another written by a black woman with an unflattering depiction of black men: but even these comments lacked the fervour or bite of those directed against *The Color Purple*. More forceful were reviewers' complaints that the programme was simply a black soap opera, that it was formulaic melodrama at its worst, and that it had the look of a situation comedy.

Audience response, however, was phenomenal: over its two-part broadcast the programme easily outdistanced competing offerings. Given the current decline in audience for network television, the Nielsen ratings (23.5/36 the first night; 24.5/38 the second) also indicate that people who normally do not watch network television tuned in specifically to watch this programme.[22] The series was given a full rerun during prime time within a year of its original broadcast—a privilege reserved for only the most popular mini-series. A double VHS cassette of *The Women of Brewster Place* is currently available for rental in most large video stores in the United States.

Although it has received little critical attention, *The Women of Brewster Place* was quite unlike anything on commercial network television in the US. This obviously had to do with the unique set of circumstances enabling its production: Oprah Winfrey has made productive use of her stardom as a talk show host to gain economic and creative control over her own television projects, which she sees through many different phases. (Winfrey has also been the subject of an extraordinary amount of negative publicity from many sources, from the *National Enquirer* to the *New York Times*, which cast her acquisition of production facilities, capital, and so on in the melodramatic light of neurotic greed and obsession with power.)[23]

An additional element which helped distinguish *The Women of Brewster Place* was its maker, Donna Deitch, an independent director best known for the feature film *Desert Hearts* (1985), a lesbian love story. Deitch produced *Desert Hearts* on a shoe-string, and the film went on to enjoy a moderate success on the art cinema circuit in the United States. Deitch was probably selected to direct *The Women of Brewster Place* because of her past focus on relationships between women and her handling of the lesbian romance using the techniques of commercial mainstream cinema: it is in fact precisely on this point that Deitch has been criticized—for her prettification of the *Desert Hearts* story and its treatment as conventional Hollywood romance.[24]

---

22 These numbers represent the rating and share for the two nights the programme was broadcast. This means that approximately forty-seven million viewers watched the programme the first night and approximately forty-nine million the second. The share numbers indicate that more than one-third of the viewing audience was tuned in to *The Women of Brewster Place*.

23 Barbara Grizzuti Harrison, 'The Importance of being Oprah', *New York Times Magazine*, 11 June 1989: 28–30.

24 See the entry on 'Lesbian Independent Cinema', in Annette Kuhn (ed.), *Women in Film: An International Guide*.

Deitch's work on *Brewster Place* could similarly be criticized for its glamorous visual treatment of the character Lorraine. However, the television series, like the novel, does focus on the violence of homophobia and its far-reaching and destructive effects on the everyday lives of the characters.

The selection of Deitch as director is noteworthy also in that it marks the first time a woman has directed a media adaptation of the work of a black woman author; a vastly more promising situation than Steven Spielberg's self-selection as director of Alice Walker's *The Color Purple*. Deitch and screenwriter Karen Hall said they attempted to remain very faithful to the original novel and to Naylor's vision of the lives of the black characters, in order to compensate for the fact that they themselves are white.[25] Naylor herself, who lost control of the screen rights for the book in her publishing contract, had originally envisaged an adaptation of her novel for the non-commercial Public Broadcasting Service—circumstances which might have made more likely the hiring of a black woman as director. With the exception of Euzhan Palcy (*A Dry White Season*, 1989), no black women directors have succeeded in making commercial feature films in the US, although independent film-makers such as Julie Dash, Debra Robinson, and Zeinabu irene Davis, or television directors such as Caroll Parrott Blue, M. Neema Barnette, and Debbie Allen certainly had the qualifications to take on such a project.

Significantly, the novel probes subject areas similar to those explored in other works from black women writers, such as Toni Morrison, Paule Marshall, Alice Walker, and others, through the 1970s and 1980s. A few of these topics—a sense of community, female bonding, overcoming adversity—are especially significant because they brought to the project elements not normally found in television plots. *The Women of Brewster Place* runs close to the codes of the television melodrama (especially of soap operas and made-for-television movies), but at the same time is very different. There are three notable features appearing in the television adaptation that the novel *The Women of Brewster Place* shares with other works by black women writers and which are critical to the present analysis: an exploration of the sense of community among black women, an indictment of sexism, and an emphasis on the importance of black women supporting each other. In *The Women of Brewster Place*, the black community is used for survival rather than individual advancement and upward mobility. Although the programme tells the story of seven women, the first and longest story establishes Mattie Michael (the Oprah Winfrey character) as a pivotal figure—functioning much as the 'tentpole character' does in soap opera. Mattie's story covers about eighteen years, beginning with her first and only pregnancy. Through good fortune, hard work, and the friendship of an older woman, Mattie achieves one of her dreams of success: she becomes a home owner. Miss Eva's and Mattie's house is represented neither as a cold and alienating bourgeois prison in the tradition of family melodrama on film (and of avant-garde feminist films such as *Jeanne Dielmann* (Chantal Akerman, 1975)), nor as the flimsy, obviously artificial, temporary set of American soap operas. Rather, the characters' aspirations to the comforts and the aesthetics of cosy domestic space are dignified with many lingering takes of interiors in which an absence of dialogue focuses attention on the sounds and the rhythms of life within the home. These images contrast sharply with the cramped rooms without views on Brewster Place. At the end of the first episode, Mattie loses the house when her son, on a murder charge, skips bail and disappears. The rest of the story traces Mattie's descent, her fall from economic grace and her arrival at Brewster Place. By the end of the programme, we realize that Mattie's personal fall has permitted her move into a nexus of women friends and neighbours, and thus the beginning of the community—troubled though it may be—of Brewster Place.

This is a strikingly different structure from that of most Hollywood film narratives, in which images of community are for the most part entirely lacking, and narrative conventions are typically based on the autonomous, unconnected individual.[26] *The Women of Brewster Place*, though, does not offer a utopian image of community: poverty, violence, and bigotry are permanent features, and these are shown to deform personal relationships and threaten women. Yet it contains striking instances of deeply held values that are starkly opposed to the values of the mainstream white culture and economy. For example, after Mattie has left her rat-infested apartment and searched futilely for another place to live, she and her infant son are taken in by Miss Eva to share her home. Miss Eva rejects the money that Mattie offers her for board, refusing to translate into market relations her gesture of help to a woman in need. Mattie, bewildered by this generosity, puts money in the cookie jar every week, but Miss Eva never takes it. Miss Eva shares all her material wealth and comfort with Mattie—literally a stranger off the street—without hesitation. It is almost impossible to conceive of this kind of act towards a person unrelated by blood in the universe of the white family melodrama. Miss Eva also shares her home with her granddaughter Ciel, and cares for and raises Mattie's son Basil just as though he were a member of her own family.

A second feature *The Women of Brewster Place* shares with the work of other writers in its tradition is a scrutiny of sexism and of violence against black women by black men. Novels such as *Brown Girl Brownstones* (1959), *The Color Purple*, and *Beloved* (1987) often explore the meaning of violence in everyday life, and the costs of survival. Their frank confrontation of incest, rape, and wife- and child-beating has been the most controversial aspect of these works. Although there is an attempt to put sexism in the context of the continual humiliation of black men by white people and the desperation caused by the massive denial of economic opportunities, there is at the same time a vehement rejection of violence. For example, in the television version of *The Women of Brewster Place*, Mattie's father, Sam, is played sympathetically by veteran black actor Paul Winfield. Dialogue stresses that Mattie is his pride and joy. Yet on discovering that Mattie is pregnant and will not reveal the name of the child's father, he explodes in a violent rage and beats her to the ground with a stick. In both novel and television programme, there is a graphic portrayal of the blows falling on her pregnant body. Mattie's mother

---

26 See David Bordwell, Janet Staiger, and Kristin Thompson, *The Classical Hollywood Cinema: Film Style and Mode of Production to 1960* (New York: Columbia Univ. Press, 1985).

(Mary Alice) a mild woman and devoted wife, picks up a rifle, points it at her husband and says: 'So help me Jesus, Sam, hit my child again and I'll meet your soul in hell!' Thus, while feelings of rage and frustration are acknowledged—in this case, a father's disappointment that his dreams for his daughter's future are ruined—the violence is uncompromisingly condemned.

In the face of both domestic violence and the multiple circumstances of oppression facing black women (the triple jeopardy of sex discrimination, race discrimination, and poverty), the heroines of these novels by black women emerge as exceptionally strong and able to fight for survival. *The Women of Brewster Place*, like other novels by black women, offers distinctive portrayals of black women, in that these women fight back, get out, leave the abuse behind. They are usually assisted in this by another black woman. As Barbara Christian has argued, this process often involves a new feeling of self-worth and identity, forged through identification with another woman.[27] In *The Women of Brewster Place*, the characters are paired in ways that reveal the tensions and contradictions of their positions: Mattie (celibate) and Etta Mae (lusty); Mattie (a single mother) and Ciel (struggling to keep her marriage together); Kiswana (privileged, single, do-gooder) and Cora Lee (poor, uneducated, mother of seven); Theresa (out as a lesbian) and Lorraine (in the closet to protect her job).

A third feature characteristic of much of black women's fiction, and which is developed in the television version of *The Women of Brewster Place*, with its reordering of the conventions of the television melodrama, is an exploration of a range of relationships between women: as friends, room-mates, lovers, mothers, and daughters. All these relationships take place outside of the nuclear family: Mattie and Ciel, for example, have one of the strongest bonds of love in the story, and they have adopted each other as mother and daughter, in much the same way Mattie and Miss Eva adopted one another. The white family melodrama has been preoccupied with ties of blood—the relentless interest in ascertaining paternity, for example, a staple of the woman's film and the soap opera—and with intense mother–daughter conflicts within the family. In novels in the black woman's writing tradition, these kinds of issues do not appear, and a more encompassing view of family takes their place.

Like *The Color Purple*, *The Women of Brewster Place* deals explicitly with sexual love between women. Its final story concerns Lorraine and Theresa, a middle-class couple who have just moved into the neighbourhood. The narrative explores in detail the persecution and hostility from black women and men that lesbians face. As in *The Color Purple*, *The Women of Brewster Place* places sexual love between women on a continuum of sexual experience which includes heterosexuality and celibacy. In a key scene towards the end of the television programme, Mattie and Etta Mae discuss the relationship of Lorraine and Theresa and the vicious gossip that is circulating about them. They have witnessed the disapproval of people in the neighbourhood, especially from a busybody named Miss Sophie. Miss Sophie senses before anyone else that there is 'something funny' going on between 'those two'. When

27 Barbara Christian, 'Trajectories of Self-Definition: Placing Contemporary Afro-American Women's Fiction', in Marjorie Pryse and Hortense J. Spillers (eds.), *Conjuring: Black Women, Fiction, and Literary Tradition* (Bloomington: Indiana Univ. Press, 1985), 233–48.

she figures out what it is, she spreads the word 'like a scent', as it is described in the novel. While Mattie does Etta's hair, she is working through her own feelings about how 'the two' feel about each other. She asks Etta how 'they get that way' and if they are that way from birth. Etta says categorically that women like that are just different: 'they love each other the way you would a man'. Mattie, still uncertain, talks about her love for the women in her life, including her best friend Etta: 'Ornery as you can get, I've loved you practically all my life.' She tells Etta that she has loved some women more deeply than she has loved any man, 'and there have been some women who loved me more and did more for me than any man ever did'. There is a pause before Mattie finally adds 'maybe it's not so different. Maybe that's why some women get so riled up about it, 'cause they know deep down it's not so different at all.'

The idea of sisterhood as a sustaining element for black women has been discussed frequently in an abstract sense in political writing, but it became widely visible for the first time with the popularity of *The Color Purple*. For all the discussion about the novel and the film, one of the most enduring memories of that work is its portrait of the bonds that exist between the black women. In black women's writings there is a rich legacy of depictions of women supporting women: it is vividly portrayed in Harriet Jacobs's *Incidents in the Life of a Slave Girl* (1861), Zora Neale Hurston's *Their Eyes Were Watching God* (1937), and more recently in Toni Morrison's *Sula* (1972) and *Beloved* (1987). The novel *The Women of Brewster Place* looks at the ways in which black women support each other, and the potentially tragic repercussions when that support is lacking: Lorraine's rape occurs after she has been rejected from the community of Brewster Place. Gloria Naylor comments that her intent was to demonstrate how black people's survival depends on mutual support and that when this fails, the community can collapse.[28]

Barbara Christian argues that Naylor both acknowledges the remarkable achievements of writers such as Walker, Morrison, and Marshall, and at the same time criticizes 'women-centred communities'. Along with a celebration of black women's survival instincts, Naylor feels that black women should also look towards political power. For although the community of Brewster Place holds its residents together for a time, at the end they are again displaced women.

> By presenting a community in which strong women-bonds do not break the cycle of powerlessness in which so many poor black women are imprisoned, Naylor points to a theoretical dilemma with which feminist thinkers have been wrestling. For while the values of nurturing and communality are central to a just society, they often preclude the type of behavior necessary to achieve power in this world, behavior such as competitiveness, extreme individualism, the desire to conquer. How does one break the cycle of powerlessness without giving up the values of caring so necessary to the achievement of a just society?[29]

---

28 Quoted in William Goldstein, 'A Talk with Gloria Naylor', *Publisher's Weekly*, 9 Sept. 1983: 35–6.

29 Barbara Christian, 'Gloria Naylor's Geography', 366.

Christian discusses two sections of Naylor's novel which offer resolutions to this question. The first is the dream-like sequence at the end of the book: in the novel, Lorraine's rape is followed by a subjective account of the thoughts, fears, and nightmares, over an entire week, of each of the other women on the block. The women are haunted by the violence against another woman and their failure to stop it. After the week has passed, the block party takes place, and Mattie dreams that the women tear down the wall blocking the street as a protest against the forces that led to Lorraine's death. As Christian states: 'Even as the women in the final scene of the novel chip away at the wall that imprisons them, we are aware that this is someone's dream, for such an act would be the prelude to a community rebellion, a step these nurturing, restricted women cannot take if they are to survive as they have.'[30]

Much of this subtlety is lost in the television version of the novel—indicating some of the limitations of the adaptation of literature to the small screen. In the television version, the action is compressed into a single night—in which Lorraine is raped during the block party and the women turn from discovery of the crime to an attempt to tear down the wall. The final shots of the programme are medium shots of the women from the other side of the wall. Drenched by rain and flooded by coloured lights, they tear at the wall with their hands. The strange lights, the rain, and the odd camera angle represent a complete stylistic break with what has gone before. But the tendency is to take the image literally rather than as suggesting a dream state; so that the women look bedraggled and desperate, their attempts to dismantle the wall pitiful and hysterical. Earlier, Mattie's first-person voice-over had offered a reflection on the events of her life. In this final scene, however, there is no visual, active equivalent to her and the other women's earlier contemplative, intersubjective reactions. The women are not seen as reflecting on the violence; rather they erupt into a burst of collective action, puzzling in its futility, on the spot. A 'naturalistic' television style can render Naylor's symbolic action—the tearing down of a brick wall—only with great difficulty, and at the cost of a complete stylistic break.

The character Kiswana represents a second resolution to the question posed by Naylor about avenues to power for black women. Kiswana grew up in the upper-middle-class black neighbourhood of Linden Hills. The segment of the story devoted to Kiswana focuses on her psychological conflict with her mother and her struggle for a separate identity, placing her political activity in the light of youthful rebellion (a story familiar enough in the bourgeois family melodrama). This segment also establishes that, unlike the other women on Brewster Place, Kiswana lives there by choice and can leave whenever she wants to. It is her privileged background and the fact that she has other options that enable Kiswana to organize the residents as a united political entity to work against the landlord and the city government. As Christian aptly analyses the character, Kiswana is the only one of the women who can rebel because

> she does not risk survival, as the others would if they rebelled; nor has she yet been worn down by the unceasing cycle of displacement that the others have experienced. And she has a sense of how power operates

---

30 Ibid. 358.

(*front row*) Ceil (Lynn Whitfield), Mattie Michael (Oprah Winfrey), Etta Mae (Jackée), Cora Lee (Phyllis Yvonne Stickney) (*back row*) Lorraine (Lonette McKee). Kiswana (Robin Givens), Theresa (Paula Kelly)

Publicity still for *The Women of Brewster Place* (ABC)

precisely because she comes from Linden Hills, a place she leaves *precisely* because it is so focused on money and power.[31]

As Naylor constructs a range of class positions for black women, from the impoverished Cora Lee to the privileged Kiswana, she presents the need for those who struggle for survival also to develop an ability to understand and use political power. This aspect of the novel is translated with some difficulty to television. Cora Lee is reduced to an object of Kiswana's reformist zeal—Kiswana wants to get Cora Lee and her children out to see her boyfriend's staging of *A Midsummer Night's Dream*. Cora Lee seems rather too easily converted, through her one-time exposure to black people performing in a work of 'high art', into a better mother: tidying up her apartment, keeping the kids clean, encouraging them to work harder at school. In the novel, Cora Lee's story is written from a point of view which allows her to react with silent suspicion and resentment to the intrusions of Kiswana, a single, middle-class woman who is unfamiliar with her problems. (This ambivalence towards Kiswana is expressed most strongly in the casting of Robin Givens, who had

31 Barbara Christian, 'Gloria Naylor's Geography', 367.

received a large amount of unfavourable publicity accusing her of opportunism in her marriage to boxing champion Mike Tyson. Givens's performance is broader than that of most of the other main characters, being more in the style of the situation comedy *Head of the Class*, in which she had gained most of her previous screen experience.)

In the novel, Cora Lee's segment is used as a sort of reverie on the sensual aspects of mothering infants: Cora Lee loves babies, but seems unable to understand children when they grow older and create responsibilities other than nurturing. Here, the juxtaposition of Cora Lee's sensuality with creative expression (the theatrical performance) appears to be a commentary on the consequences of oppression. But on television, where we are denied her account of her own childhood and her relationship with the men who 'give' her the adored babies, Cora Lee's characterization is rendered rather simplistically: she appears a creature of pure sensuality and a confused welfare recipient. She is never included in the community as an active member, and takes no part in the interplay of personal and public dramas in which the other characters are involved. In the novel, while the other women feel Cora Lee should stop having so many kids, she is still considered an integral part of the community.

Conclusion

As a novel and as a television programme, *The Women of Brewster Place* makes a strong contribution to black feminist thought as well as to feminist criticism in general. Black feminist theory has criticized, corrected, and improved the understanding of feminism put forward by white critics. Novels such as *The Women of Brewster Place*, as well as *The Color Purple*, have made an admirable attempt to dramatize into an explicitly feminist narrative black feminist commentary on the material, historical, social, economic, and symbolic status of black women. If the media versions fall short of the novels, their popularity with audiences—especially with black women—shows that much more work needs to be done by feminist critics on considerations of audience and on the analysis of all works by women of colour, in whatever medium.

The Women of Brewster Place would make a productive addition to the canon of films by and about women represented in courses on melodrama, women directors, and women's representation in film and television. As a popular work written by a black woman author, adapted for the screen by a white director and screenwriter, it opens up questions around the nature of women's experience and of differences stemming from race and class. The television version of *The Women of Brewster Place* in particular violates expectations about representations of black women long familiar from movies and television series. Within the narrow range employed by the media in showing black women, three features are familiar: the black woman tends to be defined by a 'natural' connection to sexuality, by her relationship to white people as domestic servant, and by her role in the nuclear family as a domineering or restraining force. The television adaptation of *The Women of Brewster Place* situates its characters in ways that challenge, complicate and politicize our understanding of these types. As in the novel, it continually violates expectations of characters' sexuality: one of the most lascivious characters is Miss Eva, a woman in her seventies; one of the most glamorous is Lorraine, a lesbian. The scarlet woman, Etta Mae, is perfectly happy to settle down with Mattie, her best friend. Mattie, who is involved in the programme's only extended love scene—a scene unusual for American television in its length and eroticism—remains celibate after her teenage pregnancy. As with the sexuality of all the characters, Mattie's celibacy is shown to be the result of a confluence of different factors—fatigue, limited time, fear of pregnancy, fear of men, lack of opportunity, enjoyment of motherhood. For each character there are costs as well as gains from the lifestyle she has adopted.

The maternal melodrama, which has inspired important critical work by white feminists such as Linda Williams and E. Ann Kaplan, takes on an entirely new aspect when considered in terms of black women's experiences with motherhood and childrearing. *The Women of Brewster Place*, which includes a number of figures who are strong black mothers, is careful to portray the crushing limitations these women face in daily life in a racist society and to investigate the hostility and resentment they incur from others who are threatened by their strength. As such, it could usefully assume a place alongside films like *Blonde Venus* (Josef von Sternberg, 1932), *Stella Dallas* (King Vidor, 1937), and *Mildred Pierce* (Michael Curtiz, 1945) as a point of comparison and as a corrective, stemming largely from the insights of black feminist sociology, to the dominance of psychoanalysis as a critical method in film theory's treatment of the figure of the mother. Black feminist sociologists offer a perspective on black women's lives which has particular relevance for commentators on 'women's genres'. In *The Women of Brewster Place*, the black mother's suffering cannot be located internally, because the role of the public sphere in determining the fate of mother and children is abundantly, incessantly, clear. Patricia Hill Collins notes that as black women researchers provide more information on the ways black women perceive their own mothering, a different view of motherhood emerges.[32] Black women are very connected to their biological children, as well as to those in their extended families and within the wider black community. They are also well aware of the choices available to them in 'historically specific political economies'. Collins directs us to Janice Hale's work, which demonstrates that black mothers see their roles in part as intermediaries between their children and institutional intervention. As Collins puts it: 'Black mothers are sophisticated mediators between the competing offerings of an oppressive dominant culture and a nurturing Black value-structure.'[33]

It can be seen, then, that a cultural product such as *The Women of Brewster Place* is dramatizing a psychological dynamic very different from that of the white family melodrama or soap opera. There is an emphasis on the process and survival of grief, on community and on family ties not defined exclusively by blood relation, and on women's lifelong friendships as a survival mechanism. All of these are issues missing from mainstream feminist con-

---

32 Patricia Hill Collins, 'Learning from the Outsider Within: The Sociological Significance of Black Feminist Thought', *Social Problems*, 33/6 (1986), 17.

33 Collins's reference is to Janice Hale's 1980 work 'The Black Woman and Child Rearing', in LaFrances Rodgers-Rose (ed.), *The Black Woman* (Beverly Hills, Calif.: Sage, 1980), 79–88.

siderations and prominent in the recent work of black feminist cultural critics. There is a pressing need for feminist media critics to acquaint themselves
with the work of black feminist theorists and creative writers, and to understand the relevance of this work to ongoing considerations of female representation, melodrama, and relations between domestic and public space.
Here the work of black feminist literary critics, sociologists, and historians
may offer a better and richer perspective on media representations and the
interplay of race and gender. Finally, the creative work of black women
writers, and the success of that work when adapted to small and large screens,
can revitalize an interest among feminists in identifying and producing
television and film which is both popular and politically challenging.

13

In Love with *Inspector Morse*

Feminist Subculture and Quality Television

Lyn Thomas

Abstract

THIS CHAPTER CONSISTS of textual analysis of a highly successful television series, *Inspector Morse*, combined with qualitative audience study. The study of *Morse* and the fan culture surrounding it is presented in the context of a discussion of recent feminist work on the texts and audiences of popular culture. The textual analysis focuses on those elements of the programmes which contribute to its success as 'quality' television, and particularly on *Morse* as an example of the role played by nostalgic representations of Englishness in 'quality' media texts of the 1980s. The chapter goes on to discuss whether the presence of such representations in these programmes leads inevitably to a convergence of 'quality' and conservative ideology. The discussion of the ideological subtexts of the programmes then focuses on the area of gender representation, and on the extent to which feminist influences are discernible in this example of quality popular culture, particularly in its representations of masculinity. The second part of the chapter presents an analysis of a discussion group involving fans of the series, which was organized as part of a larger qualitative study of the fan culture surrounding the programmes. There is a detailed discussion of the impact of the social dynamics of the group on their readings of *Morse*. The analysis also focuses on the ways in which the discourses identified in the textual analysis, such as gender representation, quality, and Englishness, are mobilized in talk about the programmes. Finally, the nature of the group made it possible to discuss the construction of a feminist subcultural identity in talk about a mainstream media text, and to identify irony and critical distance as key components of that identity, particularly in the discussion of the pleasures offered by the romance narratives of the programmes.

Keywords   feminism; audiences; television; Englishness; identity; masculinity

Originally published in *Feminist Review*, 51 (Autumn 1995), 1–25.

Introduction   *Inspector Morse* (Zenith, 1987–93), a conventional crime fiction series with two male heroes, may seem an unlikely starting-point for a discussion of feminism, but it is precisely this apparent incompatibility which renders *Morse* a suitable vehicle for the exploration of the relationship between feminism and contemporary British popular culture. *Morse*, perhaps more than any other television series, has become synonymous both with quality and mass popularity; if *Morse* can represent the often contradictory obsessions with economic success and high cultural value of the new Conservative era, then in this study they are juxtaposed with a social movement often regarded as having little to contribute in either sphere, relegated to a cultural Jurassic Park. This juxtaposition poses questions about the nature of subcultures and their relation to more dominant cultural forms generally, and about the extent to which, in the late 1980s and early 1990s, feminism can be seen as incorporated in the mainstream or surviving in the margins. Here these questions arise in the context of analysis of a popular television programme and of some aspects of the fan culture surrounding it. My approach combines analysis both of the text, and of a group discussion taken from a larger study of *Morse* fans. This study is part of a now established feminist tradition of academic writing on popular culture, and some critical reflection on this phenomenon forms part of the project: to what extent, for example, can the term 'post-feminist' be used to describe changes in the texts and audiences of contemporary popular culture? What is the nature of the relationships between researcher and researched, between text and audience, or text and researcher in this and similar projects? First, however, I will explore the place and significance of *Morse* in contemporary British culture: how mainstream is *Morse*?

The Escape from Enterprise: Englishness and Cultural Value   Audience ratings are not enough to give cultural status to a television programme, as the fate of any number of soap operas will attest. *Morse* has succeeded both in terms of audience size and as a cultural icon which can be invoked to illustrate and epitomize the term 'quality television'. Before considering any subcultural or subversive readings of *Morse*, it is important to investigate its place in the mainstream, its relation to the dominant culture of the period and the possible reasons for its adoption as icon of quality.

The discourse of quality, despite its literary background, has always been prevalent in discussion of television, which as a medium still struggles for respectability. It could indeed be argued that the definition of certain programmes as quality productions has played a vital role in increasing the cultural status of television, and in countering arguments about its nefarious influence. The recent revival of this debate hardly seems surprising given the new Conservatives' self-appointed role as guardians of British traditions and morality, and Charlotte Brunsdon has described the impact of the White Paper of 1988 on definitions of quality television (Brunsdon, 1990). According to Brunsdon, the quality discourse, for example in newspaper previews, can comprise traditional aesthetic criteria, professional codes, realist paradigms, entertainment and leisure codes, and moral paradigms, though in the White Paper, significantly, mainly moral and realist criteria are used. In her work on the American organization 'Viewers for quality television', Sue Brower has similarly identified a combination of aesthetic concerns and moral values in the organization's definitions of quality; she describes the moral values as '"enlightened", middle-class, liberal, feminist', and argues that the members of the organization use quality as a mask for fan behaviour, and as a way of acquiring status by association (Brower, 1992: 172).

In Britain, both the aesthetic and moral aspects of the discourse are given a particular inflection by the association of quality with Englishness, which furthermore is diametrically opposed to all things American. In the context of crime fiction, this differentiation seems to hinge on factors such as the absence of violent struggles or car chases, a detective who uses his or her intellect rather than physical strength in the fight against crime, and a rural or small-town rather than big-city setting. Even before the first broadcast in January 1987 *Morse* was described in a *Sight and Sound* preview as part of a crusade to reclaim a quintessentially English tradition:

> With this crew, one feels that the English detective story is safe on its home ground with no hankering to convert the middle-aged, edgy maverick of the Thames Valley force into something more chic and Californian.   (Kockenlocker, 1986: 240)

In her use of the term 'Brideshead/Jewel' to define a particular type of quality TV, characterized by its 'heritage export value', Charlotte Brunsdon describes this association of nostalgic nationalism with cultural quality (Brunsdon, 1990: 86). *Morse* shares with the two programmes cited by Brunsdon an iconography of Englishness which became a commonplace of film and television culture in the 1980s, and which can be seen in part as a response to the pressures on British broadcasters to produce exportable television. This visual expression of Englishness requires village greens and gardens, medieval lanes and churches, and wood-panelled interiors where log fires burn even in high summer. In *Morse* none of this is denied us; the tragedy and violence of English middle-class life are revealed and deplored by Morse, and yet the secure routines of tea and dinner, the aesthetic pleasures of a country residence, remain undisturbed. The reviewers frequently seem to have absorbed this aspect of the series so completely that its pleasures are described using the same cosy and domestic imagery of Englishness which the programmes themselves abound in:

> The plots have a nice comfortable ring to them like Agatha Christie stories re-written by Iris Murdoch. They remind one of sensible shoes and unchilled sherry, toasted crumpets and the triumph of good over evil. (Naughton, 1987: 36)

In his discussion of Merchant/Ivory films, Cairns Craig has linked such images of Englishness to a national crisis of identity and to the materialism of the Thatcher years; he reads them both as a search for stability in a period of radical and destructive change, and as 'conspicuous consumption' colluding with Thatcherite values (Craig, 1991: 10). The narrative structure of *Morse* certainly seems typical of the crime genre in its playing out and eventual containment of political and psychic anxieties (Neale, 1980). However, Craig's reading of the Thatcherite values implicit in Merchant/Ivory should not be grafted on to *Morse*. While there is no denying the nostalgic nationalism identified by Brunsdon, the very size of the *Morse* audience suggests an appeal to a wider political and social spectrum, and the feminine and domestic tone of the programmes can be seen as out of tune with the more bellicose utterances of Thatcherism.

In general, characters who seem to represent the 'enterprise' culture of the 1980s receive short shrift from Morse and from the plots in which they are enmeshed. The yuppie Maguire in *Last Seen Wearing* (Zenith, 1988) may not be implicated in any crime but he is guilty of working as a 'negotiator' for a Docklands luxury development, and of owning a flat whose black, white, and chrome décor and car-shaped telephone are sufficient grounds for arrest as far as Morse is concerned. Almost inevitably a house with a swimming pool indicates foul play, or at the very least, an unhappy marriage. The conditions of production of *Inspector Morse* seem ironically typical of a 1980s scenario; it is made by Zenith, a company originally owned by Central, who initiated the project, and subsequently taken over by Carlton Communications and Paramount (Sanderson, 1991: 26). In series six, the credits announced that *Morse* was now 'in association' with Beamish Stout, thus making an uncomfortable link between the textual resistance to enterprise, and the reality of the text as commercial product. If *Morse* has succeeded commercially without completely espousing the political ethos of its time, it seems relevant to ask whether the depiction of the private sphere maintains a similarly delicate balance between conservative and radical elements. Before turning to the gender politics of the texts I will attempt to place the discussion in the context of other feminist writing on popular culture.

Feminist Readings of Popular Culture

If generally the term 'post-feminism' implies that gender equality has been achieved, or was a misguided aim in the first place, in the field of cultural studies it can be used positively to denote a more sophisticated and multi-faceted women's movement, or more often negatively, to describe a recent tendency in the media to put 'liberated' women firmly in their place. Susan Faludi, for instance, has argued that popular culture in the 1980s is characterized by violent reactions against the women's movement. She surveys the press, popular film and television, as well as the fashion and beauty industries in both America and Britain in order to conclude that the positive representations of women of the 1970s have been followed by a cultural backlash, epitomized by the film *Fatal Attraction*, and by 1980s neologisms such as 'cocooning', 'nesting', or 'the mummy track' (Faludi, 1992). Meanwhile, in *The Female Gaze* (Gamman and Marshment, 1988) researchers in Britain give accounts of a struggle to find feminist meanings in popular texts, such as *Cagney and Lacey* or *Desperately Seeking Susan*. Although individual contributions vary, the general trend of this volume is to reject earlier, more pessimistic theories of women's relation to popular culture (Mulvey, 1975), and to claim that feminism has had a significant impact. Even though much of the volume is in fact concerned with political assessment of representations of women, men, and sexuality, the articles often conclude that a single polit-ically correct line is to be rejected in favour of resistance through a variety and range of readings. In both cases the choice of texts is crucial, and perhaps dictates the diametrically opposed conclusions reached by the two works: Faludi skims through media and genres in two cultures selecting texts which contain negative representations of single women and lesbians. Texts in *The Female Gaze* are chosen for more detailed study because of their feminist content or potential, thus attention is focused on 'women's' genres, such as blockbuster romance, the film versions of feminist works such as *The Color Purple*, or advertising directed at women.

These two tendencies could be seen as an instance of the conflict between earlier traditions of critique of popular culture by the left, and the more recent desire to celebrate its possibilities for cultural resistance. If the pro-duction of meaning is rarely uniform or monolithic, then selections can be made by cultural researchers according to the tendency they wish to support. The only possible conclusion would seem to be that feminism continues to have a profound, if complicated, impact on anglophone popular culture, and that in both the academic and the popular spheres it is out of fashion. The pages of *The Female Gaze* are haunted by the spectre of 'the drab, dungareed dyke' (Gamman and Marshment, 1988: 178), and by tension between the desire both to keep up with these celebratory post-feminist times, and to be critical of negative representations of women.

Although historical genre study would be one way of avoiding the dangers of selectivity, here I have chosen to concentrate on one series, which with audiences of around 15 million is arguably the most resounding television success of the late 1980s and early 1990s. *Morse* does not belong to a 'women's' genre, the main characters are men, and with some exceptions, such as scriptwriter Alma Cullen and producer Deirdre Keir, the production team was predominantly male. If in this sense *Morse* does not belong to the category of text usually subjected to feminist scrutiny, it is all the more sig-nificant that the gender politics of the original novels were not thought suit-able for television. The analysis of feminist elements within the programmes which follows may therefore provide a case study of the influence of femi-nism on an exceptionally popular television series, chosen neither specifi-cally for its appeal to women, nor for its negative representations.

Feminism in the Text

■ From Novel to Screen

The principal difference between the six *Morse* programmes closely based on the novels by Colin Dexter and the original texts is the relative absence of sex-ual objectification in the portrayal of the women characters in the TV ver-sion. The requirements of quality television in the late 1980s clearly demanded a more subtle approach, and Morse's character has been substan-tially changed so that the sexually predatory element is replaced by romantic yearning. In *Last Bus to Woodstock* (Zenith, 1988), for example, the television Morse reprimands Lewis for his use of sexist and proprietorial language about his wife and children, while in the novel, Morse leers at the barmaid in the pub where the murder has taken place, and eventually succumbs to the charms of the murderer herself. Whereas in the television version Sylvia

Kane's death results from an accidental combination of circumstances, in which the don, Crowther, and his mistress are implicated, in the novel Sylvia's death is caused by a vicious blow from the jealous woman. A similar pattern can be observed in *Last Seen Wearing*; in Dexter's original version the Headmaster is guilty of no major crime, the Deputy Head, Baines, is not even female, let alone lesbian, and the murderer is Valerie, the missing girl herself. In the television version the Headmaster is indirectly responsible for Valerie's disappearance, and directly responsible for the death of Baines, while Valerie is guilty only of adolescent confusion.

The effect of these reversals may be to return women to the traditional status of victim, but Dexter's image of women using their sexuality against men, and showing no qualms in resorting to violence, would be more likely to cause offence or at least the charge of implausibility. The positive representation of a lesbian character in the TV version of *Last Seen Wearing* is only marginally useful to the plot and seems to emphasize the corruption and emptiness of the heterosexual relationships which lead to her death. Although the representation of women generally in the television series is far from radical, characters such as Baines do indicate some acknowledgement that if the TV Morse is a reformed character, the women he encounters need to be more than objects of desire. However, the feminist agenda is perhaps most apparent in those programmes which were written for television. In *Fat Chance* (Zenith, 1991), scripted, significantly, by a woman, Alma Cullen, we see a narrative based on feminist concerns: the ordination of women in the Church of England, and the impact of oppressive stereotypes of female beauty on adolescent girls. Zoë Wanamaker plays a character exemplifying the conventionally irreconcilable—a penchant for Italian designer suits and feminist politics. When Morse receives her seal of approval, having championed the feminist cause throughout, we are inclined to agree with her that he really is 'one of the good guys'.

Single Virtue versus Married Vice

All around Morse, heterosexuality, particularly of the married kind, wreaks havoc. It is unremarkable that *Morse*, along with a great deal of crime fiction, should manifest the deeply rooted cultural association of death and sexuality, but the repeated castigation of the morals of married men lends added significance to the emotional purity of Morse's single life, or even, though to a lesser extent, to Lewis's cosily asexual conjugal bliss. With Lewis as the notable exception, married men deceive their bored and frustrated wives and exploit the vulnerability of the single women they seduce, sometimes, as in *The Dead of Jericho* (Zenith, 1987), leading them to degradation, despair, and death. Morse oscillates between the generic requirement of celibacy (see Wilson, 1988), and the strong romantic tendencies of the character and the plots. His singleness is obsessively referred to in lines such as: 'Chastity and continence, when did I ever have anything else?' from *Service of All the Dead* (Zenith, 1987), and the contrast between Morse and the happily married Lewis is fundamental to the structure of the programmes. Murderers, potential victims, and the relatives of victims all take the opportunity, on encountering Morse, to enquire after his marital status, and to contrast his singleness with their own entanglements. In general, the family is a vipers'

Photograph by Central ITV shows John Thaw as Chief Inspector Morse and Kevin Whately as Sergeant Lewis. Photograph © Central ITV

nest, and symbols of affluence almost always guarantee the deadliness of its occupants.

It is presumably safe to assume, none the less, that the writers and producers of the television series are not *engagés* in the fight against Thatcherite family values, and that these negative images of married and family life have come to perform some crucial function in the development of the character and charisma of Morse. If Morse is surrounded by examples of male perfidy, they serve to highlight the idealized masculinity which he represents. Lewis also has his part to play in the depiction of an acceptable masculinity, but while his ability to cope with the modern demands of companionate marriage, shared childcare, and DIY are admirable, unlike our hero he cannot sustain the emotional limelight. In the first instance, Morse is deeply moral; he plays the traditional role of the detective as representative and upholder of the Law and is always on the right side in the universal battle between good and evil, which the crimes of passion he investigates often seem to invoke. Morse expresses righteous anger on the victims' behalf, and the programmes frequently end with a soliloquy on the wicked ways of men, which may include a quotation from a work of literature, and is often set against shots of Oxford's awe-inspiring architectural beauty. Morse can never resist the opportunity to point out who is the real villain of the piece, and as, for example, in *Deadly Slumber* (Zenith, 1993), is particularly enraged by the prioritization of money-making over human life. In this sense Morse is out of tune with the times, simultaneously liberal rebel and avenging patriarch, but above all passionate in his pursuit of justice.

■ **A New/Old
Masculinity**

The difference between Morse and ordinary men does not, however, lie solely in his stern righteousness, and there are indeed times when his involvement with a guilty party clouds his judgement. Perhaps it is the combination of the traditionally paternal qualities described above with an ability to nurture which makes Morse blessed among men. Morse willingly provides a shoulder to cry on and is a sensitive and perceptive listener. At times the tasks of nurturing others and punishing crime are in conflict, as in *Deadly Slumber,* where Morse's sensitivity to the tragedy of Michael Steppings's daughter makes him rather too willing to cross Steppings off the list of suspects. If this ability to give emotionally renders Morse a less effective policeman, it may do a lot for the audience ratings. In her analysis of the appeal of romantic fiction, based on Freud, Amal Treacher has argued that the romantic hero nurtures as well as dominates the heroine, and that it is in this representation of a hero who is both ideal mother and ideal father that the emotional satisfactions of such works lie for their largely female readership (Treacher, 1988). Something of this kind may be in play here; without doubt parenting is a theme in *Morse,* and it is a theme which was not present in the original novels. If the 1980s 'new man' of the advertisements has failed as an icon of anything more than a hollow self-sufficiency, perhaps Morse's attempts to father and mother are a more resonant fantasy for male and female viewers.

But what of Morse's own needs? We return again to romance, and to the appeal of Morse's own vulnerability. Morse, like the operas he immerses himself in, is a vehicle for the expression of grand emotion. Unlike other male detectives, or for that matter the Morse of the Dexter novels, emotion rather than intellect is his true medium. Although the Inspector goes through the motions of thinking, it is increasingly Lewis who has the brainwaves, while Morse relies on that most feminine of skills, intuition. In this sense Morse, despite his traditional appearance, is breaking through boundaries, both of gender and genre. In *Dead on Time* (Zenith, 1992), Morse's new/old masculinity may have strayed even beyond its own parameters; the sight of Morse sobbing over the corpse of his former fiancée and the provision of an 'explanation' for his moodiness were dangerous developments. But *Dead on Time* allowed Lewis to make his contribution to the image of caring manhood, and it seemed fortunate that a sensitive soul such as Morse should have Lewis to watch over him. While the programmes continually depict the secure and civilized pleasures of Morse's home-life—the music, good wine, and tranquil lounging on the sofa—an encounter with an attractive woman 'd'un certain âge' inevitably rekindles a poignant and disorientating longing for intimacy. Morse does all those old-fashioned things which are eschewed by the new man or irrelevant in the more prosaic world of Lewis; he sends flowers, asks women out, and pays touching if clumsy compliments. The fact that none of this ever leads to anything remotely resembling a relationship is a further enhancement of his charms. Morse remains the ideal lover, always more involved than the woman in question, and not afraid to admit it. Detection and romance thus combine admirably, since the requirement for celibacy in the former creates an enticing lack, the ultimate romance narrative where the threat of satisfaction, and hence of the loss of desire is removed (see Neale, 1980).

Introducing the
Audience

■ Quality
Television and Fan
Culture

The popularity of *Morse*, and the amount of media attention which the audience itself has received, indicate that textual analysis in isolation would be to reduce to text alone a cultural phenomenon which also encompasses secondary literature, consumer goods such as audio and video tapes, experiences such as '*Morse* tours', and the fan culture generated by, and generating, such ephemera. The *Morse* audience is variously represented in the reviews as object of statistical analysis or as subject, with the reviewer identifying as a fan and meditating on the pleasures of the programmes. In the first case the audience tends to be described as middle class and middle-aged, or more technically as 'ABC1 adults aged 35+' (MacArthur, 1990: 25). In the second, humour is a protection from the excesses of mindless fandom:

> Morse is back! There was, I think, a fresh spring in my step. I spent the day in anxious reverie. What would it be like? After months of youthful repeats, would the new series simply confirm that nothing stands the test of time? Or could the old red Jaguar still do two hours in what always seemed a mere 40 minutes?   (Newnham, 1992: 29)

If the statistics produce an image too general to be of interest outside the advertising world, the self-reflective irony of the article quoted above suggests that being a fan of a quality series is not without its complexities. Jensen has argued that fandom is often represented as an irrational and excessive cult of a low-status cultural form (Jensen, 1992). It is therefore not surprising that despite the evidence of 'fan' behaviour, the popularity of *Morse* is rarely discussed in such terms. In contrast to the low status of television as a medium, *Morse* aspires to cultural respectability, and to be a devotee of the series may therefore have altogether different connotations from those usually associated with TV fandom. The audience research described in the final part of this piece was particularly concerned to investigate how these contradictions might be experienced and expressed by fans of the series.

■ Feminism and
Audience Study

Perhaps the danger of selecting texts and reading them according to a pre-set agenda can be avoided, at least to some extent, by combining textual analysis with audience study. It would seem likely that here, if anywhere, the frequently invoked polysemy might be found. If feminism has a role, then its presence will be felt not only in texts, but also in the talk about texts which it could be argued is the place where popular culture 'happens'. One aim of this research was to explore how feminism might inform such talk, and how feminist elements in the text are taken up in particular social contexts, in this case discussion groups and telephone interviews. Although I did not attempt to recruit feminist fans specifically, gender politics emerged as the main preoccupation in one of the discussion groups, and some telephone interviews. As a result I was able to explore questions about the nature of a particular subculture which seemed to be expressing itself in the discussion of *Morse*, the kinds of subject positions which were adopted within it, the reading strategies and discourses which it generated. I was also concerned with the paradox of a subcultural adoption of a highly conventional mainstream text. Inevitably, if I was exploring how talk about television in the 1990s might be influenced by feminism, I was doing so in the era of 'post-feminism', and although impossible to prove, it seemed likely that such talk would differ significantly from similar conversations in the early years of the women's movement. Finally, my research is small-scale and can only claim to have investigated a few instances of feminist subculture, or *Morse* fan culture; its limitations and the peculiarities of the social events I am analysing are discussed in detail below.

The Research Process

If my own reading had identified the critique of heterosexuality and the search for an acceptable masculinity as instances of textual engagement with feminist issues, it remained to be seen whether this would be recognized by other regular viewers, and how they might negotiate the polarities quality/fandom or feminism/traditionalism. In audience work by feminist researchers, a cultural gulf may develop between the researcher and the researched, whose tastes are secretly disapproved of. The researcher may express ambivalence resulting from the conflict between identification with a women's genre such as romantic fiction and with the women who are the subjects of the research, and feminist political correctness. These issues have been raised by Janice Radway in a critique of her earlier work on readers of romantic fiction, in which she describes how despite intending to affirm the romance readers' culture, she in the end distanced herself as 'knowing analyst' from them (Radway, 1994: 214). Although my desire to write about *Morse* was dictated initially more by my own involvement with the series than by academic considerations, I have inevitably acquired a certain status as researcher and cannot claim to be free of these contradictions. Throughout the discussion, I have therefore attempted to reflect on, and wherever possible to clarify, my own role and position.

An answer to the question of how to contact *Morse* fans was provided by the NFT's decision to screen a John Thaw season in September 1991, including one episode of *Morse*. I distributed questionnaires at the screening (*The Dead of Jericho*) which asked people who might be willing to participate in a discussion group or telephone interview to give their name, address, occupation, age group, and reason for attending the screening. Out of an audience of about 100, 30 completed questionnaires were collected. The sample was white, predominantly though not exclusively middle class, and young (75 per cent under 35). Some months later, in April 1992, while a new series of *Morse* was being screened on ITV, this sample of 30 were contacted again, and asked whether they would be willing to participate in a telephone interview. Thirteen responded positively and nine interviews ranging from 10 to 40 minutes in length were carried out. These were followed by two discussion evenings at the then Polytechnic of North London.

Here I will concentrate on the second of the two groups, where the content of the discussion developed in such a way as to be highly relevant to the theme of this article. By this stage it seemed likely that the participants, who by now had responded to two further approaches, were keen *Morse* fans, rather than just cinemagoers who happened to be at the NFT that evening. None the less, the culture of both discussion groups was very clearly white and metropolitan, and a geographical location outside London or a greater ethnic diversity may well have produced very different results. The composition of the group was as follows:

Lisa: mid-twenties, postgraduate psychology student
Sarah: late twenties, postgraduate psychology student
Sue: late thirties, civil servant
Joan: late fifties, unemployed
Jim: early thirties, civil servant.

An interested colleague, Karen, attended the session as an observer; Karen and I were both lecturers at the then Polytechnic of North London, in our late thirties, and Karen is German. Food and wine were provided, and four extracts from *Inspector Morse* (chosen for their relevance to the issues of gender representation discussed on pp. 189–91) were screened, with time for discussion after each one. The extracts were:

1. The last five minutes of *The Dead of Jericho* (first broadcast on 6 January 1987).
2. Morse and Lewis interviewing the Headmaster and his family in *Last Seen Wearing* (first broadcast on 8 March 1988).
3. From the same programme, Morse interviewing the Deputy Headmistress, Miss Baines, in her house late at night, immediately prior to her death during a row with the Head, who pushes her downstairs.
4. The scene from *Dead on Time* (first broadcast on 26 April 1992), when Morse entertains Susan, his former fiancée.

Morse as 'Lived Experience'

■ The Social Context

Adopting the categories proposed by Fairclough (1989), and already applied to the analysis of children's talk about television by Buckingham (1993), I have analysed the discussions in terms of *relations* between group members and *subject positions* adopted, as well as content. This approach aims to avoid the danger of assuming that people say what they mean in any simple sense, and to counteract the tendency of much previous work in this area to divorce meaning from the social context in which it is produced. In practice it was difficult to separate subject positions from relations, since the adoption of the former is a crucial part of the latter. In the section below, therefore, a consideration of the groups' relationships with each other leads into a discussion of subject positions adopted by group members, and the dividing line is inevitably blurred.

Despite the food and wine provided, the setting for the discussions was unmistakably educational, and it is possible to identify a tension between the 'party' connotations of the plentiful supplies of food and wine and the far from luxurious classroom setting. The slightly guilty tones, or suggestions that I should switch off the tape recorder when someone asked for more wine suggest that the event was perceived more as a class than a party, though particularly in this case, where at least half the group was likely to be very at home in an educational context, the atmosphere became increasingly relaxed as the evening progressed, and there were many occasions for laughter. A detailed analysis of my interventions shows that I was mainly in 'teacher' mode. Seventy per cent of my interventions had functions such as:

— introducing new subjects/asking questions
— addressing a named person
— following up a point
— summarizing or reflecting back
— giving information about the programmes
— structuring/organizing the event.

The fact that for 30 per cent of the time I participated as a fan, recounting the plot, telling jokes, or occasionally commenting on programmes, none the less indicates that I was split between my conscious intention to behave as a neutral facilitator of the discussion, and the desire to participate in the group, and switch to 'fellow fan' mode. The implications of this for the discussion are analysed more fully below. Here, it is sufficient to note that the combination of being one of the group some of the time and in the powerful position of teacher/researcher the rest means that the cultural agenda which I set is likely to play a significant role in the development of the discussion.

The group dynamics in this discussion seem particularly influenced by gender difference. The fact of being the only man in the group seems to have elicited certain types of response from Jim, who seems concerned to make an impression on the others and even to obtain a dominant position. This behaviour was met with opposition, at times verging on hostility, both from the group members and from myself. I certainly saw keeping Jim under control and sabotaging his attempts at dominance as an important part of my role as discussion facilitator. After the discussion Karen commented that it had been a women-dominated group, and I felt rather guilty about treating Jim unfairly. When the tape was played to a (mixed) group of fellow researchers they commented that Jim had had a hard time, and it was indeed the case that I silenced him on several occasions during this short extract. It is therefore interesting that counting the number of lines spoken by each person reveals that Jim spoke more than anyone other than Sarah, and that he introduced more new subjects than anyone other than myself. The fact that the representation of women in *Inspector Morse* became a major theme in this group, whereas this was not the case in the other discussion group, has to be seen in the context of this gender-based power struggle. There is no doubt that this theme was a common area of interest uniting Sarah, Lisa, Sue, and myself, but the fact that it was taken up with such energy, and returned to so repeatedly, must to some extent be the result of these rather particular group dynamics.

The discussion was analysed both by means of a simple line count and a 'map' of the introduction of new topics. This information revealed that in this group, the participant most involved in the representation of women theme, Sarah, is also the dominant member of the group. She introduces relatively few new topics, but she speaks most, is most responsible for the fact that certain areas are developed, and is most frequently the first to respond to questions which I asked. The fact that she was sitting opposite me and that empathy was expressed through eye contact and laughing loudly at each other's jokes meant that Sarah assumed a 'star pupil' role, and that to some extent a new and particularly powerful friendship pair was formed within the group. Given that Sarah and Lisa, and Joan and Sue had come as pairs of friends, it would be possible to comment that the all-female couple was a subtext for the group, and that this provides an interesting context for the discussion of the images of heterosexual couples presented in the *Morse* extracts. The agenda set by these friendship pairs, and by my role, was undoubtedly that of educated, white, middle-class feminism. Sarah, Lisa, Sue, Karen, and I were all in our twenties or thirties, and our class position was broadly similar, even if the trajectory we had followed to arrive at it may well have been different, and was not the subject of this research. The common culture which operated in this subgroup is perhaps most evident in the intertextual references, particularly to soap opera, where in the form of jokes there was a certain amount of feminist 'reclaiming' of apparently conventional texts such as *The Archers* (BBC Radio, 1951–). The subject position which I and these group members adopted seemed to be that of critical reader, whose status in feminist alternative culture gives her permission to enjoy 'ideologically unsound' popular texts.

Jim was excluded from this position by gender, and perhaps by educational background, and seemed more concerned to establish himself as critical reader in terms of knowledge of the programmes and the production process, and ability to evaluate quality. Joan's position was more complex, in that she participated very little in the discussion and in that sense could be seen as far more excluded than Jim. This may be attributable to her age (over 55) and employment status, which differentiated her from the other women present. Perhaps because of these factors my attempts to bring her into the discussion were unsuccessful. Although Joan spoke very little, she introduced one entirely new area to the discussion (the theme of 'pastness' in *Morse*), and at times adopted an oppositional position in relation to Jim:

JIM:　But the story is about a male detective and his male sidekick

SUE:　Yeah but I bet the audience is mostly women

JIM:　Well I mean OK you know I don't go for middle-aged grey-haired men er I mean I'm outnumbered here

JOAN:　I might

(General laughter).

As this extract shows, Joan is very much part of the oppositional 'women's culture' of the group, and here she introduces the topic of 'fancying' Morse which is developed later by other group members. She is also involved in subverting Jim's overtly masculine point of view. At the same time she is perhaps differentiating herself from the younger women. Despite this, and the fact that the ages in this group range from early twenties to late fifties, some kind of a consensus emerged from the discussion of the representation of youth culture in *Cherubim and Seraphim* (Zenith, 1992); Sue was instrumental in this in referring to herself as 'an old fart' and thus making the only overt statement about age. The subject position adopted by Sue was clearly approved of by the women in the group, who laughed loudly at this point, and despite the presence of two very young women, being older and listening to Radio 4 rather than Acidhouse seemed to form part of the feminist cultural identity being constructed in the discussion. This older identity may result from the fact that many 'second-wave' feminists are now in their late thirties or forties, and this may therefore be a more culturally established position than 'young feminist'. The feminist construction of younger women as 'other' exemplified in the last lines of Shelagh Young's piece in *The Female Gaze*, may contribute to this:

> We could start by listening to the views of those wayward daughters who seem to be so actively resisting, rather than conforming to, any simple feminist model of the New Woman. After all, there must be that little bit of a feminist subject lurking in there somewhere, mustn't there? And if there is, I suspect she's looking back at me.   (Young, 1988: 188)

In this case the younger women manifested a desire to contribute to a group identity based on gender and feminist politics, rather than gazing critically on the latter. The youth theme also led to a heated discussion of class, as Jim's mis-recognition of the youth subculture provoked an indignant response:

JIM:	I think you can tell I'm middle class. I've never had any experience of that but from what I know and from what you read in the papers and what you hear I think all that sort of underclass culture I think it was toned down
LISA:	I don't think it was underclass culture
LYN:	They were middle class
	(All talk at once)
LISA:	It was a youth culture
SEVERAL VOICES:	Yes.

In educational terms, it may well be that Jim is less middle class than most of the women present, and his claim may be an expression of resulting feelings of insecurity. The almost angry response of the other group members perhaps also denotes an anxiety in this area. Mis-recognition of a middle-class person as working class may be particularly threatening to an insecure subject position resulting either from a move from working class to middle class, or from a middle-class person's political empathy with less privileged groups. In general the subject position in relation to class adopted by Sarah, Lisa, and Sue is certainly a long way from Jim's statement, and they refer repeatedly to the rich people on *Morse*, who are outside their normal experience. Another heated argument erupts when Lisa accuses the programme-makers of ignoring working-class Oxford, and Jim explains their financial motivations for this to her:

> JIM: But what the Oxford City Council or whoever it is wants to portray, they want to portray sort of dreaming spires and punting down the river, things like that, you know to get the tourists in . . . (Passage omitted)
>
> LISA: (angrily) But I expect it's not the people who need the money that are getting it.

In this instance, and in the repeated distancing from wealthy characters, an oppositional position in relation to 'middle-classness' is being adopted, as part of the alternative feminist culture which pervaded the discussion. It is therefore not surprising that Jim's more aspirational statement was met with disapproval.

■ **Critical Reading and Emotional Involvement**

The discussion of *Morse* is perhaps unlike talk about other television programmes less obviously stamped with the quality label; because the programmes themselves, and all the literature surrounding them, are concerned to differentiate *Morse* from less polished products, it may be the case that to be a *Morse* fan is in some sense to associate oneself with this cultural superiority, negotiating fandom in the same way as members of 'Viewers for quality television' in Sue Brower's account (see p. 186 above). Given the oppositional position in relation to 'middle-classness' discussed above, the negotiation of this area in this group was likely to be a complex matter. Although quality was a less dominant theme than gender representation, it was referred to in the discussion, which made conventional associations of quality with high production values, realism, the intellectual challenge of the plots, and the character of Morse himself:

> SUE: It's supposed to be, you know this is an intellectual
> SARAH: It's extremely, he's not listening to 'Right Said Fred' and drinking brown ale here
> LISA: He can't possibly understand the wide real world [ ]
> JIM: Good stuff that. I don't see why he shouldn't do that. I'm not a particular fan of classical music but a lot of [what] Morse listens to, is a darned sight better than what you get on television nowadays
> SARAH: He is a sort of cultured man, he doesn't spend his evening with his feet up watching *EastEnders*. He is listening to that particularly good recording of Verdi with a nice bottle of wine or something. The way whenever he goes to a pub he doesn't just go to a pub he goes in one that's got good draught ale. It's always very quality.

As this extract shows, there are at least two kinds of relation to the concept of quality in this discussion: while Jim is anxious to claim the ability to differentiate Morse from lower-quality texts, in this case popular as opposed to classical music, Sarah and Sue are taking up a position of critical distance, able to appreciate the connotations of Morse's 'quality' tastes, without necessarily associating themselves with them. For them what is at stake is the demonstration of the ability to read the signs, rather than the capacity to be impressed by them. Jim, on the other hand, is anxious to affirm his middle-class status, by claiming the ability to appreciate classical music, which according to Pierre Bourdieu is a particularly significant cultural marker:

> For a bourgeois world which conceives its relation to the populace in terms of the relationship of the soul to the body, 'insensitivity to music' doubtless represents a particularly unavowable form of materialist coarseness.   (Bourdieu, 1979: 19)

Whereas Jim attempts to align himself with Morse's musical superiority, the other members of the group are reading off precisely the meaning defined by Bourdieu, and thus demonstrating their ability to interpret the significant elements of the Morse character, and hence to be aware of its constructed nature. Jim's attempts to acquire 'cultural capital' in this context, where he does not belong to the critical subculture being developed, consist partly, as here, in recognizing the quality aspects of the programmes, and partly in explaining *how* and *why* things are done. Ellen Seiter has described how in an interview with two men about soap opera, one of the men seemed most concerned to impress the 'high status' academics doing the interview by showing off his factual knowledge. Seiter uses Bourdieu to explain why such attempts are doomed to failure, and to position herself and her colleague as 'legitimate autodidacts' who have a stake in the maintenance of this particular cultural and social divide (Seiter, 1990: 65–6). Seiter's discussion seems particularly pertinent to the analysis of Jim's position in this group, where his knowledge is constantly rejected as illegitimate, or inappropriate to the academic setting and cultural agenda set by the other group members and myself. Jim's concern is to demonstrate that he knows how television programmes are put together, and while he expresses cynicism about the programme-makers' intentions the tone of his discussion is one of acceptance, that this is how things of necessity have to be. In this again, he is at odds with the rest of the group, who are questioning precisely this inevitability:

JIM: You've got to remember that it's rich people that make sort of interesting characters. I mean sort of people that do boring mundane jobs and sort of come home in the evening and watch telly and go to bed, I mean where's the interest in that?
SUE: What about *Coronation Street*?
(Laughter).

Although the high production standards of *Morse* are referred to in this group, criticism is more prevalent than praise. This of course does not mean that the group members are indifferent to this aspect of the programmes, merely that in this context they feel that it is more appropriate to be critical:

LISA: It's still compelling viewing it really is. It's compelling sort of viewing. I would do anything not to miss, I mean most things I don't bother videoing it if I'm going to be out, but Morse definitely you know. I've even learnt how to set the video to do it. But yes OK you can be critical, but then I think you're partly asking us to be critical.

This sense of being asked to be critical may be a response to the educational setting, and it is significant that those most used to operating in this context felt this.

The association of quality with Englishness discussed on pp. 185–6 above was introduced here by the oldest participant, Joan, indicating perhaps that her silence may be the result of a different range of interests from the rest of the group; at this point there is a departure from the predominant feminist critique, and Sarah, who is extremely active in the rest of the discussion, is significantly silent:

JOAN: *Morse* to me never seems to be current. It seems to be in the past. I don't know how far back in the past, not that far back [ ]

LISA: It's the whole thing about Oxford and the setting as well isn't it?

JOAN: Yes

LISA: I mean it's a very sort of antiquated setting in a way and when you hear the word sort of Oxford you assume that you're talking about you know the university and [the sort of buildings

JIM: [Too much dreaming spires and students on pushbikes.

Lisa seems able to recognize and identify with what Joan is saying and she later returns to this theme in one of the rare moments where an emotional, as opposed to intellectual pleasure is discussed:

LISA: The trouble with all these little digressions into Australia and Italy and subcultures or whatever, I don't know I actually like the old formula and the sort of almost the predictability of the Oxford and the car and you know all these little things.

The sense of reassurance and security described here is reminiscent of the reviews, and may be an expression of the process of containment of anxiety by a television narrative (see pp. 186–7 above). The satisfactions afforded by familiarity are, however, more frequently disavowed, displaced by critique of the repetitiveness of the plots or the stereotyping of the characters, just as in general critical distance rather than emotional involvement is the predominant mode of talking about the programmes in this discussion.

■ **Feminism and Popular Romance**

It is in the area of romance that the tension between the expression of pleasure and the establishment of status as critical reader is most marked. The romance plot seems to be the aspect of the programmes which this group finds most fascinating, since it is introduced early in the discussion of each extract, and occupies more time than any other single topic. To some extent the choice of extracts set this particular agenda. However, in the other discussion group the topic is not developed to the same extent. On the contrary, in several of the telephone interviews, which were of course independent of this screening, romance again emerged as a preoccupation. Although I chose the extracts because of their relevance to my own reading of the negative representation of the family and the heterosexual couple (see p. 189 above), this may not be obvious to spectators who are not specifically trained to be aware of issues of representation, as the first discussion group would seem to attest. Even in this group, where the representation issue was addressed, the theme which I saw as the common thread linking the extracts did not emerge as significant, and it was the related but distinct question of the representation of women which became an almost obsessive concern. Here a great deal of critical energy was generated, as Sarah, Sue, and Lisa poured scorn on the 'pathetic' women characters:

LISA: They're very peripheral to the stories I think if they're not actually involved with Morse directly

JIM: But the story is about a male detective and his male sidekick

SUE: Yeah but I would think its audience is mostly women.

This extract amply illustrates how critique is functioning as a way of acquiring and expressing solidarity as women, culminating in the view that 'we are the audience'. It is also interesting that the presence of the romance plot in the programmes and this group's preoccupation with it leads to a reversal of the conventional association of crime fiction with masculinity. It would, however, be wrong to conflate criticism of this kind with the absence of emotion, for while distance from the text is certainly expressed, usually in the form of irony, emotions such as anger, or indignation as here, do surface, indicating a passionate engagement with the programmes. The more positive feelings usually associated with romance do none the less seem incompatible with the feminist persona who haunts this discussion. The talk about one of the most romantic episodes, *Dead on Time*, is dominated by criticism of the episode's implausibility, the cliché of the romantic dinner à deux, Morse's besottedness, and the heroine's coy femininity, but immediately after the screening, before the critical mood gains momentum, Lisa expresses her feelings about the extract:

LISA: [ ] It was so sort of touching, wasn't it, Lewis sort of protecting him from the knowledge right the way through to the end and he never told him right at the end and considering the hard time Morse always gives Lewis and you know the barking at him in the office and for getting things wrong and when he has actually got something right he only, because it's too painful for Morse he doesn't tell him. I thought that was such a sweet thing for Lewis to do.

It is significant that this rare instance of emotional response to the text is focused on the Morse/Lewis relationship rather than on the romance plot itself. None the less, some of the identifications and readings proposed as possible sources of pleasure (see pp. 191–2), do seem to operate in some form here. Early in the discussion awareness of the narrative necessity of Morse's unsuccessful romantic life was evident:

JIM: I mean if he hadn't stuck his oar in or whatever she'd still be alive and perhaps Morse would be enjoying a successful love life
SUE: Can't have that
(Loud laughter).

This was repeated later when Jim's suggestion—'The Sergeant Lewis Show'— was greeted with horror, on the grounds that since Lewis is happily married, there could be 'no development'. The opportunities for identification provided by the gap in the text left by Morse's inconclusive affairs could not be embraced wholeheartedly in this context, but the use of irony did permit the expression of the fantasy. In this way it was possible simultaneously to remain outside the text, and to enter into it, by filling the gap in the narrative:

SARAH: You imagine you know that he would say 'take off your glasses, why Miss Smith you're beautiful'
(Loud laughter)
SARAH: He noticed me *yes*. I think that's the secret of it, he's so involved in his work, that if he does notice someone it's something special
(More laughter).

The energy of the female laughter here indicates partly that Sarah has achieved exactly the right balance—moderating the image of starry-eyed fan by her subtle and ironic intertextual reference, and partly it may be releasing any anxiety generated by Sarah's crossing of the diegetic boundary. Immediately before this section, the fantasy of being the woman with whom Morse would at last be happy was linked to the combination of vulnerability and ability to nurture also discussed in p. 191 above:

JIM: You know do the women here [.] you know do you like John Thaw?
SUE:] Oh yes
LISA:] He's terribly attractive
SUE: Yeah you know because the idea is that you're the person who understands him and he's had a really shitty life
SARAH: He's a sad man, who'd love you.

Ann Rosalind Jones has analysed the impact of feminism on contemporary romantic fiction in terms of a transformed power relationship between hero and heroine, based on textual evidence of his vulnerability (Jones, 1986). Here Morse's vulnerability may be attractive to these feminist critical readers in a similar way, seeming to offer a reversal of the pattern common both in fiction and in women's experience of heterosexuality, where male emotional needs are often masked by projection on to the woman. Wendy Hollway has analysed how the positioning of the woman as the subject of what she describes as the 'have/hold discourse' results in emotional inequality, with the woman always needier than her male partner (Hollway, 1992). This syndrome was already transparent to Simone de Beauvoir in the 1940s; in *Le Deuxième Sexe* she provides a detailed analysis of the process whereby women's prioritization of relationships leads them to a dependent role where they are forever trying to ensnare the man into spending more of his precious time with them, while he is anxious to escape in order to realize his many projects in life (de Beauvoir, 1949). With Morse masculinity has come full circle, and the closing images of *Promised Land* (Zenith, 1991) demonstrate the penalties of the avoidance of intimacy: Morse stands alone and desolate on the steps of the Sydney opera house, while Lewis goes off to fill in time before the impending arrival of Mrs Lewis. Like de Beauvoir the women in this group feel that the problem of femininity or at least of these representations of it is the lack of projects, of something to do in life:

SARAH: You know if somewhere in Oxford it was not just entirely populated with attractive 45-year-old women
SUE: Blonde (laughter)
SARAH: (laughs) All blonde
JIM: Yeah but]
LISA:] They're incompetent. I mean there are competent women around aren't there]
SARAH:] Yes and they're always]
SUE:] Who do jobs rather than hanging around waiting to be screwed by Morse.

However, unlike de Beauvoir they seem aware of the limitations of traditional masculinity; the appeal of *Morse* is that despite Morse's evident devotion to duty, the programmes present the inadequacies of a work-orientated existence. Morse's neediness, his constant pursuit of 'attractive 45-year-old women' seems here to be providing the beginnings of a feminist fantasy where female power can be combined with romance.

Conclusion The first part of this chapter illustrates the complex balancing of conservative and more radical elements in a 'quality' television series of the late 1980s and early 1990s. The programmes oscillate between critique of the status quo and visual affirmation of the securities of English middle-class life, between castigation of heterosexual behaviour and pure romance and, in the case of the hero himself, between the ability to nurture others and his own neediness. The existence of these tensions in the text creates the possibility for a range of readings and identifications, and may be one of the aspects of the series which has ensured its success in winning large audiences. The analysis of the discussion group in the second part of the chapter indicates how the image of a uniform, mass audience perpetuated by statistical research, masks the range and subtlety of readings and specific fan cultures which a programme such as this may generate. Two aspects of this research, at least, have also been identified in other audience studies (see Buckingham, 1993). First, the readings produced here are specific to this particular social interaction and, in this sense, the social dynamics are at least as significant a factor as the text itself in defining the discourses within which the programme may be discussed. Secondly, participants in this kind of research are understandably anxious to demonstrate that they are not duped by the media. Although this tendency may be heightened in the research situation, it seems likely, given the low status attributed to television as a medium, and to 'fan' behaviour, that presenting oneself as not 'taken in' by the media may be a general feature of talk of this kind.

In this case, the particular versions of this distanced position were 'feminist critical reader' for most of the women present, and 'well-informed cynic about the media' in Jim's case. In the case of the former, the women in the group, including myself, were united by educational level, and by feminist politics, and middle-class, educated feminism became the dominant discourse. As a result of his inability to participate in this discourse, Jim became the least powerful member of the group. While recognizing the small scale of this research, I would guess that the feminist culture expressed in this discussion is not an isolated phenomenon. It seems unlikely that the women in the group could have mobilized discourses such as critique of the representation of women with such alacrity if such discourses were not already well established in some middle-class, educated circles. In this sense, the analysis of feminist influences at work in the text, and of feminism as dominant discourse in this particular discussion suggests that a certain kind of feminism, at least, has a significant, if at times uneasy place in mainstream popular culture in 1990s Britain. The complex position of feminism as both oppositional culture and part of the mainstream is indicated here by the group members' subtle negotiation of such issues as the conflict between feminist critique and romance as a conventionally 'feminine' pleasure. Perhaps most significant are the sense of a feminist identity espousing the 'middle-aged' pleasures of Radio 4 or quality television drama, and the role of irony in this identity, whether directed at the romantic excesses of the text, or at the 'boring old fart' herself.

I would like to thank Betty and Terry Doonan for their invaluable help in transcribing the tapes.

References   Beauvoir, Simone de (1949), *Le Deuxième Sexe* (Paris: Éditions Gallimard).

Bourdieu, Pierre (1979), *Distinction: A Social Critique of the Judgement of Taste*, trans. 1984 by Richard Nice (London: Routledge & Kegan Paul).

Brower, Sue (1992), 'Fans as Tastemakers: Viewers for Quality Television', in Lewis (1992).

Brunsdon, Charlotte (1990), 'Problems with Quality', *Screen*, 31/1: 67–90.

Buckingham, David (1993), *Children Talking Television* (London: The Falmer Press).

Craig, Cairns (1991), 'Rooms without a View', *Sight and Sound*, 1/2, June 1991: 10–13.

Cruz, Jon, and Lewis, Justin (1994) (eds.), *Viewing, Reading, Listening: Audiences and Cultural Reception* (Boulder and Oxford: Westview Press).

Fairclough, Norman (1989), *Language and Power* (London: Longman).

Faludi, Susan (1992), *Backlash: The Undeclared War Against Women* (London: Vintage).

Gamman, Lorraine, and Marshment, Margaret (1988) (eds.), *The Female Gaze: Women as Viewers of Popular Culture* (London: The Women's Press).

Hollway, Wendy (1992), 'Gender Difference and the Production of Subjectivity', in Helen Crowley and Susan Himmelweit (eds.), *Knowing Women: Feminism and Knowledge* (London: Polity Press and The Open University).

Jensen, Joli (1992), 'Fandom as Pathology: The Consequences of Characterization', in Lewis (1992).

Jones, Ann Rosalind (1986), 'Mills and Boon meets Feminism', in Jean Radford (ed.), *The Politics of Popular Fiction* (London: Routledge & Kegan Paul).

Kockenlocker (1986), 'High Tecs', *Sight and Sound*, 55/4: 240–1.

Lewis, Lisa (1992) (ed.), *The Adoring Audience: Fan Culture and Popular Media* (London and New York: Routledge).

MacArthur, Brian (1990), 'Watching the Detectives', *Guardian*, 10 Dec.: 25.

Mulvey, Laura (1975), 'Visual Pleasure and Narrative Cinema', *Screen*, 16/3: 6–18.

Naughton, John (1987), 'Ahead of the Pack', *Listener*, 117/2995, 22 Jan.: 36.

Neale, Stephen (1980), *Genre* (London: British Film Institute).

Newnham, David (1992), 'Goofy over Mickey Morse', *Guardian*, 27 Feb.: 29.

Potter, Jonathan, and Wetherell, Margaret (1987), *Discourse and Social Psychology: Beyond Attitudes and Behaviour* (London: Sage Publications) (see pp. 188–9 for transcription conventions).

Radway, Janice (1994), 'Romance and the Work of Fantasy: Struggles over Feminine Sexuality and Subjectivity at Century's End', in Cruz and Lewis (1994).

Sanderson, Mark (1991), *The Making of Inspector Morse* (London: Macmillan).

Seiter, Ellen (1990), 'Making Distinctions in TV Audience Research: Case Study of a Troubling Interview', *Cultural Studies*, 4/1: 61–84.

Treacher, Amal (1988), 'What is Life without My Love: Desire and Romantic Fiction', in Susannah Radstone (ed.), *Sweet Dreams: Sexuality, Gender and Popular Fiction* (London: Lawrence & Wishart).

Wilson, Elizabeth (1988), 'The Counterfeit Detective', in *Hallucinations: Life in the Post-Modern City* (London: Radius).

Young, Shelagh (1988), 'Feminism and the Politics of Power: Whose Gaze is it anyway?', in Gamman and Marshment (1988).

14

Fruitful Investigations: The Case of the Successful Lesbian Text

Hilary Hinds

This extract is drawn from a longer study examining the rather puzzling cultural phenomenon of Jeanette Winterson's enormously successful Oranges Are Not The Only Fruit. *This text, centrally concerned with representations of lesbianism, has been extraordinarily well received, not only within a lesbian subcultural context but also by mainstream critics and audiences. Winner of Whitbread, BAFTA, and Cannes film festival awards, hailed as a major new literary figure by, amongst others, Gore Vidal, fêted by publications as diverse as the* Daily Mail, *the* Financial Times, *and* Marxism Today, *celebrated and adored by lesbian audiences, author, novel, and TV adaptation have succeeded in an unlikely combination of cultural contexts.*

The full-length article from which this is drawn offers a detailed investigation of some of the ways in which this text achieved both literary and popular success. In particular, it analyses the discourses which shaped its media reception. In the extract which follows, I contextualize the reception of Oranges *in order to investigate how and why a generally homophobic mainstream press reacted so positively to the representation of lesbianism in the TV adaptation of* Oranges.[1]

EANETTE WINTERSON'S ADAPTATION for television of her novel *Oranges Are Not The Only Fruit* was first broadcast in January 1990. Particularly significant for the reception of the text at this time were the repercussions from arguments that had circulated in relation to two events of 1988 and 1989 respectively: the passing of Section 28 of the Local Government Act, which aimed to ban the 'promotion of homosexuality' by any bodies funded by local authorities, and the death threat made against Salman Rushdie on the publication of his novel *The Satanic Verses.* These two events had elements in common, most significantly in the responses and opposition that they elicited: the liberal arts establishment saw each as undermining the principle of free speech. One of the most successful

© OUP, 1991.

Originally published in *Women: A Cultural Review*, 2/2 (1991), 128–33.

1 The full version of this article was published in Sally Munt (ed.), *New Lesbian Criticism: Literary and Cultural Readings* (New York: Columbia Univ. Press, 1992), 153–72.

counter-arguments made in opposition to Section 28 was that posed by the arts lobby, who saw 'great works', either by lesbian and gay writers or concerning lesbian and gay issues, as being under threat from this legislation.[2] This argument carried the implication that lesbianism and homosexuality were to be understood differently in this context: they necessitated a response in keeping with their status as art, rather than in relation to their sexual/political status. Concerning Rushdie, the arguments were similar: the novel may be offensive to Islam, but this was no justification for trying to stop the mouth of an artist, who should be allowed to function free from outside political or religious constraints. In both instances, then, the issue of 'art' was seen to be paramount: a text's status as art should protect it from the crudities of political critique. As became the case with *Oranges*, the concerns of art were to take precedence over values and beliefs that might hold sway in other contexts. Thus *Oranges* was read in a cultural context where high-cultural 'art' had been established as having a meaning separable from questions of politics, sexual or otherwise.

Significant, too, in relation to Rushdie and to *Oranges* is the way that religious fundamentalism was represented in the media: not only was freedom of speech being threatened, but it was being threatened by religious extremists, who were characterized as repressive, violent, and alien to the traditions of their 'host' country.[3] Although this related specifically to the Muslim faith, it fed into and fortified a pre-existing climate of opinion regarding so-called fundamentalism fuelled by news stories from the USA exposing financial corruption and sexual intrigues within the ranks of high-profile evangelical groups. 'Fundamentalism', then, came to be characterized as being, on the one hand, a violent threat (namely Rushdie) and, on the other, an object for our superior laughter, as its essential hypocrisy was exposed (namely US groups). Both these elements can be seen to have played their part in the TV representation and media reception of the evangelical group so central to Jess's childhood in *Oranges*.

In addition to these historically very specific phenomena was the question of the status of *Oranges* as a 'quality' television drama—an example of 'art television'.[4] Mandy Merck has argued that there is a particular relationship between art cinema and the representation of lesbianism,[5] and this argument offers an important perspective on the critics' reception of the lesbianism in *Oranges*. Merck aphoristically suggests that 'if lesbianism hadn't existed, art cinema might have invented it' (p. 166): by this, she means that the representation of lesbianism in art cinema is sufficiently 'different' from dominant (more popular) cinematic representations of sex and sexuality to be

2 See Jackie Stacey, 'Promoting Normality: Section 28 and the Regulation of Sexuality', in Sarah Franklin, Celia Lury, and Jackie Stacey (eds.), *Off Centre: Feminism and Cultural Studies* (London: Harper Collins Academic, 1991).

3 This chapter was written before the Gulf War; since then these associations have developed and intensified. See Kevin Robbins, 'The Mirror of Unreason', *Marxism Today*, Mar. 1991: 42–4.

4 'Art television' remains a tentative concept within critical work; see John Caughie, 'Rhetoric, Pleasure and "Art Television"—*Dreams of Leaving*', *Screen*, 22/4 (1981), 9–31. On 'quality' television, see Paul Kerr, 'Classic Serials—To Be Continued', *Screen*, 23/1 (1982), 6–19, and Charlotte Brunsdon, 'Problems with Quality', *Screen*, 31/1 (1990), 67–90.

5 Mandy Merck, '*Lianna* and the Lesbians of Art Cinema', in Charlotte Brunsdon (ed.), *Films for Women* (London: BFI Publishing, 1986), 166–75.

seen as courageous and challenging, and yet, in fact, it simply offers more of the same: that is, it works with the familiar equation: 'woman = sexuality' (p. 166). Merck concludes that 'it is the legitimisation of the female spectacle which makes lesbianism such a gift to art cinema' (p. 173). Thus what is at stake is not only *what* is represented, but *where* it is represented: the underlying equation of women with sexuality may be the same in all kinds of representation, but none the less lesbianism is read as 'meaning' something different in art cinema from in other contexts; similarly, it was read as meaning something different in 'art television' than it would have done elsewhere in television.

Oranges was read in a tradition of other 'quality' dramas that had occupied the Wednesday night 'controversy slot',[6] the controversy being seen to arise primarily from the explicit representation of sex in these previous productions. Certain of these acted as sexual reference points for *Oranges*:

> A lesbian love scene between two adolescent girls on BBC2 next week could mark a new stage in the passage of television from the kitchen sink to the boudoir.
>
> This new challenge to viewers comes after the explicit straight sex of David Lodge's *Nice Work* and Dennis Potter's *Blackeyes*.[7]

The representation of sex in *Oranges*, then, was seen as an advance on the work of Potter and Lodge because it shows lesbian rather than 'straight sex', which of necessity represents something more challenging, risky and 'adult'. This seems to confirm that for 'art television', as for art cinema, there is a strong association with and expectation of 'adult' and 'realistic' representations of sex. The scheduling of *Oranges* in the 'controversy slot', with its dual associations of sex and high quality, then, was of significance for its reception. The representation of sex here could be seen as risky and challenging, rather than merely titillating; its 'quality' acted as a guard against 'those dreary public outbursts of British prudishness'.[8] Together, these two elements contributed to the production of a context in which lesbianism could be read as something positive.

A second possible reason for the acceptability of the lesbianism in *Oranges* follows from Merck's claim that another of the features of art cinema is that it 'characteristically solicits essential humanist readings' (p. 170); it has some kind of universal human relevance with which we can all identify. In relation to *Oranges*, then, this would imply that the adaptation's success rested on the critics' ability to read it as being essentially about something other than its lesbianism. If this is the case, it is working against Winterson's own assertion that her text was framed as a challenge:

> I know that *Oranges* challenges the virtues of the home, the power of the church and the supposed normality of heterosexuality. I was always clear that it would do. I would rather not have embarked on the project than see it toned down in any way. That all this should be the case and that it should still have been so overwhelmingly well received cheers me up.[9]

6 e.g. David Lodge's *Nice Work* and Dennis Potter's *Blackeyes*.

7 *Sunday Times*, 7 Jan. 1990.

8 *Birmingham Post*, 18 Jan. 1990.

Did the critics, in the mainstream press at least, pick up the gauntlet that she had thrown down, or did they read around this challenge, read it, as Merck suggests, as having above all else an allegorical, essentially humanist, meaning?

Overwhelmingly, the latter seems to have been the case: the lesbianism is decentred and the critics present us with a drama 'about' all sorts of other things. The three-part series, we are told, 'is fundamentally about a young person looking for love';[10] it is 'a wonderfully witty, bitter-sweet celebration of the miracle that more children do not murder their parents';[11] it 'follows Jess in a voyage of self-discovery from her intense religious background, via a friendship with another girl';[12] it is 'a vengeful satire on Protestant fundamentalism'.[13] Most critics find the universality that they perceive, the opportunity to sympathize with the heroine despite her peculiar circumstances, to be in the programme's favour. *Time Out* (18 January 1990), it is true, complains about 'the author's own use of that hoary liberal cop-out about *Oranges* being about "two people in love"—who wants to see that tedious story again?' Most, however, welcome the opportunity to read *Oranges* as essentially about all (or other) human relationships, rather than about the specificities of lesbian ones.

The decentring of the lesbianism, however, does not involve its denial: in most reviews it is mentioned, but nearly always in relation to something else, generally the ensuing rejection and exorcism of Jess by members of the evangelical group. In this context, lesbianism is seen either as comic comeuppance for her mother's repressive childrearing methods—'Warned off boys by this hell-fire freak, Jess turns instead to girls'[14]—or as a source of pathos: 'a bitter-sweet tragedy, the tale of how a young woman tries and fails to reconcile her religion with her lesbianism'.[15] Lesbianism, then, is always seen in relation to other issues, be they religion, the family, or simply 'growing up'.

However, as well as being read from a broadly humanist perspective, as a story about young love, there is another element of this decentring of lesbianism that is significant: the emphasis that is placed on the representation of religion. This is important not only as an example of this decentring, but also because, contrary to what most previewers predicted, it was this, rather than the representation of lesbianism, that became the focus for viewers' and reviewers' anger. So, as well as the evangelical group being seen as one of the main sources of the humour of the series, its members are written about as ridiculous ('prattling, eye-rolling, God-fearing women'),[16] and as potentially violent ('each and every one . . . looked as though she could kill with a blow

---

9 Jeanette Winterson, *Oranges Are Not The Only Fruit—The Script* (London: Pandora, 1990), p. xvii.

10 *Today*, 10 Jan. 1990.

11 *Observer*, 14 Jan. 1990.

12 *Todmorden News*, 18 Aug. 1989.

13 *Listener*, 18 Jan. 1990.

14 *Financial Times*, 10 Jan. 1990.

15 Uncredited review for 11 Jan. 1990.

16 *Daily Express*, 11 Jan. 1990.

of her nose').[17] Moreover, the Christian fundamentalism of *Oranges* is explicitly linked to Muslim fundamentalism, overwhelmingly associated with repression and violence in the press reviews: we are told that Jess is brought up 'in a provincial family whose fundamentalist religious beliefs make the Ayatollah Khomeini, by contrast, seem a model of polite tolerance'.[18] This association of the two fundamentalisms, Christian and Muslim, with repression, is further reinforced when *Television Today* (18 January 1990) expresses the hope that the 'small, if vocal, number of objectors' to the serial will not 'turn writer Jeanette Winterson into the nineties Salman Rushdie'.

Subject to the most anger, however, was the exorcism of Jess carried out by the pastor and assorted members of the congregation when Jess is found to have been having a sexual relationship with Melanie. Critics commented on the 'brutal' nature of this scene, noted that it is 'sexually-charged', and suggested that:

if anybody was disturbed by the scene in which the pastor—armed with rope, gag and pulsating neck—straddled the young Jess to exorcise the demon of illicit love, then so they should have been.[19]

Hilary Kingsley in the *Mirror* (15 January 1990) concurred: the headline announced that the scene was 'Brutal, Shocking, Horrifying. But You Mustn't Miss It'. Anger and disgust are not only legitimate—they are to be actively sought as the 'correct' response; thus emotions that many expected to be directed towards the lesbian scenes are actually located instead with the representation of this repressive religious group. Perhaps it was possible for so much sympathy to be shown to the plight of Jess and Melanie not only because of the way their relationship was interpreted, but also because we witness—and abhor—the punishment that they undergo. Their persecutors have already been established as outmoded, repressive, and anti-sex, and it is a small step to add violence to this list. This, indeed, is facilitated by the pre-existing links between fundamentalism and violence that I have outlined above. Christopher Dunkley writes:

Jess . . . is promptly subjected by her mother's fundamentalist sect to the sort of persecution and torture so dear to the hearts of religious fanatics throughout the ages.[20]

Here he clearly suggests that the punishment tells us more about religious fundamentalists than it does about the status of lesbianism in our society. The liberal viewer, then, can feel distanced from the punishment meted out to Jess because these people are not 'normal' members of our society. This sympathy, then, can be seen to rest on two mutually reinforcing bases: first, it is a response to the punitive, anti-sex attitudes of the evangelical group—and even gay and lesbian sexual rights have increasingly become the objects of liberal championing since the passing of Section 28; and secondly, it is

17 *The Times*, 11 Jan. 1990.
18 *Evening Standard*, 22 Jan. 1990.
19 *Sunday Times*, 21 Jan. 1990.
20 *Financial Times*, 10 Jan. 1990.

responding to the representation of fundamentalism, which has become so prominent a liberal target in the wake of the Rushdie affair. Thus, it appears that the yoking of the lesbianism with the fundamentalism was itself crucial for the favourable mainstream liberal response: lesbianism became an 'otherness' preferable to the unacceptable otherness of fundamentalism.

I would like to thank the following people for their help, and for their perceptive and encouraging comments on earlier drafts of this chapter: Richard Dyer, Lynne Pearce, Martin Pumphrey, Margaret Reynolds, Fiona Terry and, especially, Jackie Stacey.

15

The Suburban Home Companion: Television and the Neighbourhood Ideal in Post-War America

Lynn Spigel

IN **DECEMBER 1949** the popular radio comedy *Easy Aces* made its television debut on the DuMont network. The episode was comprised entirely of Goodman Ace and his wife Jane sitting in their living room, watching TV. The interest stemmed solely from the couple's witty commentary on the programme they watched. Aside from that, there was no plot. This was television, pure and simple. It was just the sense of being with the Aces, of watching them watch, and of watching TV with them, that gave this programme its peculiar appeal.

The fantasy of social experience that this programme provided is a heightened instance of a more general set of cultural meanings and practices sur-

1. 'Let's go, Mr Dreamer, that television set won't help you shovel the walk'

© Princeton Architectural Press, 1992.

Originally published in Beatrix Columbia (ed.), *Sexuality and Space* (Princeton: Princeton Architectural Press, 1992), 185–217.

rounding television's arrival in post-war America. It is a truism among cultural historians and media scholars that television's growth after World War II was part of a general return to family values. Less attention has been devoted to the question of another, at times contradictory, ideal in post-war ideology—that of neighbourhood bonding and community participation. During the 1950s millions of Americans—particularly young white couples of the middle class—responded to a severe housing shortage in the cities by fleeing to new mass-produced suburbs. In both scholarly studies and popular literature from the period, suburbia emerges as a conformist-orientated society where belonging to the neighbourhood network was just as important as the return to family life. Indeed, the new domesticity was not simply experienced as a retreat from the public sphere; it also gave people a sense of belonging to the community. By purchasing their detached suburban homes, the young couples of the middle class participated in the construction of a new community of values; in magazines, in films, and on the airwaves they became the cultural representatives of the 'good life'. Furthermore, the rapid growth of family-based community organizations like the PTA suggests that these neo-suburbanites did not barricade their doors, nor did they simply 'drop out'. Instead, these people secured a position of meaning in the *public* sphere through their new-found social identities as *private* landowners.

In this sense, the fascination with family life was not merely a nostalgic return to the Victorian cult of domesticity. Rather, the central preoccupation in the new suburban culture was the construction of a particular *discursive space* through which the family could mediate the contradictory impulses for a private haven on the one hand, and community participation on the other. By lining up individual housing units on connecting plots of land, the suburban tract was itself the ideal articulation of this discursive space; the dual goals of separation from and integration into the larger community was the basis of tract design. Moreover, as I have shown elsewhere, the domestic architecture of the period mediated the twin goals of separation from and integration into the outside world.[1] Applying principles of modernist architecture to the mass-produced housing of middle-class America, housing experts of the period agreed that the modern home should blur distinctions between inside and outside spaces. As Katherine Morrow Ford and Thomas H. Creighton claimed in *The American House Today* (1951), 'the most noticeable innovation in domestic architecture in the past decade or two has been the increasingly close relationship of indoors to outdoors'.[2] By far, the central design element used to create an illusion of the outside world was the picture window or 'window wall' (what we now call sliding glass doors), which became increasingly popular in the post-war period. As Daniel Boorstin has argued, the widespread dissemination of large plate-glass windows for both domestic and commercial use 'leveled the environment' by

---

1 See my article 'Installing the Television Set: Popular Discourses on Television and Domestic Space, 1948–55', *Camera Obscura*, 16 (Mar. 1988), 11–47; and my dissertation, 'Installing the Television Set: The Social Construction of Television's Place in the American Home' (Univ. of California-Los Angeles, 1988).

2 Katherine Morrow Ford and Thomas H. Creighton, *The American House Today* (New York: Reinhold Publishing Co., 1951), 139.

encouraging the 'removal of sharp distinctions between indoors and out-doors' and thus created an 'ambiguity' between public and private space.[3] This kind of spatial ambiguity was a reigning aesthetic in post-war home magazines which repeatedly suggested that windows and window walls would establish a continuity of interior and exterior worlds. As the editors of *Sunset* remarked in 1946, 'Of all improved materials, glass made the greatest change in the Western home. To those who found that open porches around the house or . . . even [the] large window did not bring in enough of the out-doors, the answer was glass—the invisible separation between indoors and out.'[4]

Given its ability to merge private with public spaces, television was the ideal companion for these suburban homes. In 1946 Thomas H. Hutchin-son, an early experimenter in television programming, published a popular book designed to introduce television to the general public, *Here is Television, Your Window on the World*.[5] As I have shown elsewhere, com-mentators in the popular press used this window metaphor over and over again, claiming that television would let people imaginatively travel to dis-tant places while remaining in the comfort of their homes.[6]

Indeed, the integration of television into post-war culture both precipi-tated and was symptomatic of a profound reorganization of social space. Leisure time was significantly altered as spectator amusements—including movies, sports, and concert attendance—were increasingly incorporated into the home. While in 1950 only 9 per cent of all American homes had a television set, by the end of the decade that figure rose to nearly 90 per cent, and the average American watched about five hours of television per day.[7] Television's privatization of spectator amusements and its possible disinte-gration of the public sphere were constant topics of debate in popular media of the period. Television was caught in a contradictory movement between private and public worlds, and it often became a rhetorical figure for that contradiction. In the following pages, I examine the way post-war cul-ture balanced these contradictory ideals of privatization and community

3 Daniel J. Boorstin, *The Americans: The Democratic Experience* (New York: Vintage Books, 1973), 336–45. Boorstin sees this 'leveling of place' as part of a wider 'ambiguity' symptomatic of the demo-cratic experience.

4 *Sunset Homes for Western Living* (San Francisco: Lane Publishing Co., 1946), 14.

5 Thomas H. Hutchinson, *Here is Television, Your Window on the World* (1946; New York: Hastings House, 1948), p. ix.

6 For more on this, see my article 'Installing the Television Set: Popular Discourses on Television and Domestic Space, 1948–55' and my dissertation, 'Installing the Television Set: The Social Construction of Television's Place in the American Home'.

7 The data on installation rates vary slightly from one source to another. These estimations are based on Cobbett S. Steinberg, *TV Facts* (New York: Facts on File, 1980), 142; 'Sales of Home Appliances', and 'Dwelling Units', *Statistical Abstract of the United States* (Washington, DC, 1951–6); Lawrence W. Lichty and Malachi C. Topping, *American Broadcasting: A Source Book on the History of Radio and Television* (New York: Hastings House, 1975), 521–2. Note, too, that there were significant regional differences in installation rates. Television was installed most rapidly in the north-east; next were the central and western states, which had relatively similar installation rates; the south and south-west mountain areas were considerably behind the rest of the country. See 'Communications', in *Statistical Abstract of the United States* (Washington, DC, 1959); *US Bureau of the Census, Housing and Construction Reports*, Series H-121, nos. 1–5 (Washington, DC, 1955–8). Average hours of television watched is based on a 1957 estimate from the A. C. Nielsen Company printed in Leo Bogart, *The Age of Television: A Study of Viewing Habits and the Impact of Television on American Life* (1956; New York: Frederick Unger, 1958), 70.

involvement through its fascination with the new electrical space that television provided.

Post-war America witnessed a significant shift in traditional notions of neighbourhood. Mass-produced suburbs like Levittown and Park Forest replaced previous forms of public space with a newly defined aesthetic of pre-fabrication. At the centre of suburban space was the young, upwardly mobile middle-class family; the suburban community was, in its spatial articulations, designed to correspond with and reproduce patterns of nuclear family life. Playgrounds, yards, schools, churches, and synagogues provided town centres for community involvement based on discrete stages of family development. Older people, gay and lesbian people, homeless people, unmarried people, and people of colour were simply written out of these community spaces—relegated back to the cities. The construction and 'red-lining' policies of the Federal Housing Administration gave an official stamp of approval to these exclusionary practices by ensuring that homes were built for nuclear families and that 'undesirables' would be 'zoned' out of the neighbourhoods. Suburban space was thus designed to purify communal spaces, to sweep away urban clutter, while at the same time preserving the populist ideal of neighbourliness that carried America through the Depression.

Although the attempt to zone out 'undesirables' was never totally successful, this antiseptic model of space was the reigning aesthetic at the heart of the post-war suburb. Not coincidentally, it had also been central to utopian ideals for electrical communication since the mid-1800s. As James Carey and John Quirk have shown, American intellectuals of the nineteenth century foresaw an 'electrical revolution' in which the grime and noise of industrialization would be purified through electrical power.[8] Electricity, it was assumed, would replace the pollution caused by factory machines with a new, cleaner environment. Through their ability to merge remote spaces, electrical communications like the telephone and telegraph would add to this sanitized environment by allowing people to occupy faraway places while remaining in the familiar and safe locales of the office or the home. Ultimately, this new electrical environment was linked to larger concerns about social decadence in the cities. In both intellectual and popular culture, electricity became a rhetorical figure through which people imagined ways to cleanse urban space of social pollutants; immigrants and class conflict might vanish through the magical powers of electricity. As Carolyn Marvin has suggested, nineteenth-century thinkers hoped that electrical communications would defuse the threat of cultural difference by limiting experiences and placing social encounters into safe, familiar, and predictable contexts. In 1846, for example, *Mercury* published the utopian fantasies of one Professor Alonzo Jackman, who imagined a transcontinental telegraph line through which 'all the inhabitants of the earth would be brought into one intellectual

---

8 James W. Carey and John J. Quirk, 'The Mythos of the Electronic Revolution', in James W. Carey (ed.), *Communication as Culture* (Boston: Unwin Hyman, 1989), 113–41. For related issues, see Leo Marx, *The Machine in the Garden: Technology and the Pastoral Ideal in America* (New York: Oxford Univ. Press, 1964); John F. Kasson, *Civilizing the Machine: Technology and Republican Values in America, 1776–1900* (New York: Penguin, 1977); Wolfgang Schivelbusch, *Disenchanted Night: The Industrialization of Light in the Nineteenth Century*, trans. Angela Davies (Berkeley: Univ. of California Press, 1988).

neighborhood and be at the same time perfectly freed from those contaminations which might under other circumstances be received'. Moreover, as Marvin suggests, this xenophobic fantasy extended to the more everyday, local uses of communication technology: 'With long-distance communication, those who were suspect and unwelcome even in one's neighborhood could be banished in the name of progress.' Through telecommunications it was possible to make one's family and neighbourhood into the 'stable center of the universe', eliminating the need even to consider cultural differences in the outside world.[9]

Although Marvin is writing about nineteenth-century communication technology, the utopian fantasy that she describes is also part and parcel of the twentieth-century imagination. Indeed, the connections between electrical communications and the purification of social space sound like a prototype for the mass-produced suburbs. Throughout the twentieth century, these connections would be forged by utility companies and electrical manufacturers who hoped to persuade the public of the link between electricity and a cleaner social environment. Then too, the dream of filtering social differences through the magical power of the 'ether' was a reigning fantasy in the popular press when radio was introduced in the early 1920s. As Susan Douglas has shown, popular critics praised radio's ability to join the nation together into a homogeneous community where class divisions were blurred by a unifying voice. This democratic utopia was, however, imbricated in the more exclusionary hope that radio would 'insulate its listeners from heterogeneous crowds of unknown, different, and potentially unrestrained individuals'.[10] Thus, broadcasting, like the telephone and telegraph before it, was seen as an instrument of social sanitation.

In the post-war era, the fantasy of antiseptic electrical space was transposed onto television. Numerous commentators extolled the virtues of television's antiseptic spaces, showing how the medium would allow people to travel from their homes while remaining untouched by the actual social contexts to which they imaginatively ventured. Television was particularly hailed for its ability to keep youngsters out of sinful public spaces, away from the countless contaminations of everyday life. At a time when juvenile delinquency was considered a number one social disease, audience research showed that parents believed television would keep their children off the streets.[11] A mother from a Southern California survey claimed, 'Our boy was always watching television, so we got him a set just to keep him home.' Another mother from an Atlanta study stated, 'We are closer together. . . . Don and her boyfriend sit here instead of going out, now.'[12] Women's home

---

9 Carolyn Marvin, *When Old Technologies Were New: Thinking About Communications in the Late Nineteenth Century* (New York: Oxford Univ. Press, 1988), 200–1.

10 For discussions about electricity see Carey and Quirk, 'The Mythos of the Electronic Revolution' and 'The History of the Future', in *Communication as Culture*, 173–200; Andrew Feldman, 'Selling the "Electrical Idea" in the 1920s: A Case Study in the Manipulation of Consciousness' (Master's Thesis, Univ. of Wisconsin-Madison, 1989); Susan J. Douglas, *Inventing American Broadcasting, 1899–1922* (Baltimore: Johns Hopkins Univ. Press, 1987), 308.

11 For a detailed study of the widespread concern about juvenile delinquency, see James Gilbert, *A Cycle of Outrage: America's Reaction to the Juvenile Delinquent in the 1950s* (New York: Oxford Univ. Press, 1986).

12 Edward C. McDonagh *et al.*, 'Television and the Family', *Sociology and Social Research*, 40/4 (Mar.–Apr. 1956), 116; and Raymond Stewart cited in Bogart, *The Age of Television*, 100.

magazines promoted and reinforced these attitudes by showing parents how television could limit and purify their children's experiences. *House Beautiful* told parents that if they built a TV fun room for their teenage daughters they would find 'peace of mind because teenagers are away from [the] house but still at home'.[13] Television thus promised to keep children away from unsupervised, heterogeneous spaces.

But television technology promised more than just familial bliss and 'wholesome' heterosexuality. Like its predecessors, it offered the possibility of an intellectual neighbourhood, purified of social unrest and human misunderstanding. As NBC's president Sylvester 'Pat' Weaver declared, television would make the 'entire world into a small town, instantly available, with the leading actors on the world stage known on sight or by voice to all within it'. Television, in Weaver's view, would encourage world peace by presenting diverse people with homogeneous forms of knowledge and modes of experience. Television, he argued, created 'a situation new in human history in that children can no longer be raised within a family or group belief that narrows the horizons of the child to any belief pattern. There can no longer be a We-Group, They Group under this condition. Children cannot be brought up to laugh at strangers, to hate foreigners, to live as man has always lived before.' But for Weaver, this democratic utopian world was in fact a very small town, a place where different cultural practices were homogenized and channelled through a medium whose messages were truly American. As he continued, 'it [is] most important for us in our stewardship of broadcasting to remain within the "area of American agreement," with all the implications of that statement, including however some acknowledgement in our programming of the American heritage of dissent.' Thus, in Weaver's view, broadcasting would be a cultural filter that purified the essence of an 'American' experience, relegating social and ideological differences (what he must have meant by the 'American heritage of dissent') to a kind of programming ghetto. Moreover, he went on to say that 'those families who do not wish to participate fully in the American area of agreement' would simply have to screen out undesirable programming content by overseeing their children's use of television.[14]

The strange mix of democracy and cultural hegemony that ran through Weaver's prose was symptomatic of a more general set of contradictions at the heart of utopian dreams for the new antiseptic electrical space. Some social critics even suggested that television's ability to sanitize social space would be desirable to the very people who were considered dirty and diseased. They applauded television for its ability to enhance the lives of disenfranchised groups by bringing them into contact with the public spaces in which they were typically unwelcome. In a 1951 study of Atlanta viewers,

---

13 *House Beautiful* (Oct. 1951), 168.

14 Sylvester L. (Pat) Weaver, 'The Task Ahead: Making TV the "Shining Center of the Home" and Helping Create a New Society of Adults', *Variety*, 6 Jan. 1954: 91. The hope for a new democratic global village was also expressed by other industry executives. David Sarnoff, chairman of the board of RCA, claimed, 'When Television has fulfilled its destiny, man's sense of physical limitation will be swept away, and his boundaries of sight and hearing will be the limits of the earth itself. With this may come a new horizon, a new philosophy, a new sense of freedom and greatest of all, perhaps, a finer and broader understanding between all the peoples of the world.' Cited in William I. Kaufman, *Your Career in Television* (New York: Merlin Press, 1950), p. vii.

Raymond Stewart found that television 'has a very special meaning for invalids, or for Southern Negroes who are similarly barred from public entertainments'.[15] One black respondent in the study claimed:

> It [television] permits us to see things in an uncompromising manner. Ordinarily to see these things would require that we be segregated and occupy the least desirable seats or vantage point. With television we're on the level with everyone else. Before television, radio provided the little bit of equality we were able to get. We never wanted to see any show or athletic event bad enough to be segregated in attending it.[16]

Rather than blaming the social system that produced this kind of degradation for African Americans, social scientists such as Stewart celebrated the technological solution. Television, or more specifically, the private form of reception that it offered, was applauded for its ability to dress the wounds of an ailing social system. As sociologist David Riesman claimed, 'The social worker may feel it is extravagant for a slum family to buy a TV set on time, and fail to appreciate that the set is exactly the compensation for substandard housing the family can best appreciate—and in the case of Negroes or poorly dressed people, or the sick, an escape from being embarrassed in public amusement places.'[17] Riesman thus evoked images of social disease to suggest that disempowered groups willed their own exclusion from the public sphere through the miraculous benefits of television.

Although social critics hailed television's ability to merge public and private domains, this utopian fantasy of space-binding revealed a dystopian under-side. Here, television's antiseptic spaces were themselves subject to pollution as new social diseases spread through the wires and into the citizen's home. Metaphors of disease were continually used to discuss television's unwelcome presence in domestic life. In 1951 *American Mercury* asked if television 'would make us sick . . . or just what?' Meanwhile, psychologists considered television's relation to the human psyche. Dr Eugene Glynn, for example, claimed that certain types of adult psychoses could be relieved by watching television, but that 'those traits that sick adults now satisfy by television can be presumed to be those traits which children, exposed to television from childhood . . . may be expected to develop'.[18] More generally, magazine writers worried about the unhealthy psychological and physical effects that television might have on children. Indeed, even if television was hailed by some as a way to keep children out of dangerous public spaces, others saw the electrical environment as a threatening extension of the public sphere.[19] Most typically, television was said to cause passive and addictive

15 Stewart's findings are summarized here by Bogart, *The Age of Television*, 98.

16 Respondent to Stewart's study is cited in Bogart, *The Age of Television*, 98.

17 David Riesman, 'Recreation and the Recreationist', *Marriage and Family Living*, 16/1 (Feb. 1954), 23.

18 Eugene David Glynn, MD, 'Television and the American Character—A Psychiatrist Looks at Television', in William Y. Elliot (ed.), *Television's Impact on American Culture* (East Lansing, Mich.: Michigan State Univ. Press, 1956), 177.

19 Following along the trail of other mass media aimed at youth (e.g. dime novels, comic books, radio, and film), television became a particular concern of parents, educators, clergy, and government officials. The classic tirade against mass culture during the period was Frederic Wertham's *Seduction of the Innocent* (1953; New York: Rinehart and Company, 1954), the eighth chapter of which was entitled, 'Homicide at Home: Television and the Child'.

2

behaviour which would in turn disrupt good habits of nutrition, hygiene, social behaviour, and education. In 1951 *Better Homes and Gardens* claimed that television's 'synthetic environment' produced children who refused to sleep, eat, or talk as they sat passively 'glued' to the set. Similarly, in 1950 *Ladies' Home Journal* depicted a little girl slumped on an ottoman and suffering from a new disease called 'telebugeye' (Fig. 2). The caption described the child as a 'pale, weak, stupid-looking creature' who grew 'bugeyed by looking at television too long'. As the popular wisdom often suggested, the child's passive addiction to television might itself lead to the opposite effect of increased aggression. In 1955, for example, *Newsweek* reported on young Frank Stretch, an 11-year-old who had become so entranced by a television western that 'with one shot of his trusty BB gun [he] demolished both villain and picture tube'.[20]

Metaphors of disease went beyond these hyperbolic debates on human contamination to the more mundane considerations of set repair. Discussions of technology went hand in hand with a medical discourse which attributed to television a biological (rather than technological) logic. A 1953 Zenith ad declared, 'We test TV blood pressure so you'll have a better picture.' In that same year *American Home* suggested that readers 'learn to

20 William Porter, 'Is Your Child Glued to TV, Radio, Movies, or Comics?', *Better Homes and Gardens* (Oct. 1951), 125; *Ladies' Home Journal* (Apr. 1950), 237; 'Bang! You're Dead', *Newsweek*, 21 Mar. 1955: 35. For more information on this, see my dissertation 'Installing the Television Set' and my article 'Television in the Family Circle: The Popular Reception of a New Medium', in Patricia Mellencamp (ed.), *Logics of Television* (Bloomington: Indiana Univ. Press, 1990), 73–97.

diagnose and cure common TV troubles', listing symptoms, causes, treatments, and ways to 'examine' the set. Thus the television set was itself represented as a human body, capable of being returned to 'health' through proper medical procedures.[21]

Anxieties about television's contaminating effects were based on a larger set of confusions about the spaces that broadcast technology brought to the home. Even before television's innovation in the post-war period, popular media expressed uncertainty about the distinction between real and electrical space and suggested that electrical pollutants might infiltrate the physical environment. *Murder By Television*, a decidedly B film of 1935, considered the problems entailed when the boundaries between the television universe and the real world collapsed. The film featured Bela Lugosi in a nightmarish tale about a mad corporate scientist who transmits death rays over electrical wires. In an early scene, Professor Houghland, the benevolent inventor of television, goes on the air to broadcast pictures from around the world. But as he marvels at the medium's ability to bring faraway places into the home, his evil competitor, Dr Scofield, kills him by sending 'radiated waves' through the telephone wires and into the physical space of the television studio where the unfortunate Professor Houghland dies an agonizing death.

While less extreme in their representation of threatening technology, film comedies of the thirties and forties contained humorous scenes that depicted confusion over boundaries between electrical and real space. In the farcical *International House* (1933), for example, businessmen from around the globe meet at a Chinese hotel to witness a demonstration of the first fully operating television set. When Dr Wong presents his rather primitive contraption to the conventioneers, television is shown to be a two-way communication system that not only features entertainment but can also respond to its audiences. After a spectator (played by W. C. Fields) ridicules the televised performance of crooner Rudy Vallee, Vallee stops singing, looks into the television camera, and tells Fields, 'Don't interrupt my number. Hold your tongue and sit down.' Later, when watching a naval battle on Wong's interactive television set, Fields even shoots down one of the ships in the scene. Similarly, in the popular film comedy serial *The Naggers*, Mrs Nagger and her mother-in-law confuse the boundaries between real and electrical space in a scene that works as a humorous speculation about television ('The Naggers Go Ritzy', 1932). After the Naggers move into a new luxury apartment, Mr Nagger discovers that there is a hole in the wall adjacent to his neighbour's apartment. To camouflage the hole, he places a radio in front of it. When Mrs Nagger turns on the radio, she peers through the speaker in the receiver, noticing a man in the next apartment. Fooled into thinking that the radio receiver is really a television, she instructs her mother-in-law to look into the set. A commercial for mineral water comes on the air, claiming, 'The Cascade Spring Company eliminates the middle-man. You get your water direct from the spring into your home.' Meanwhile, Mrs Nagger and her mother-in-law gaze into the radio speaker hoping to see a televised image. Instead, they find

21 *Better Homes and Gardens* (Sept. 1953), 154; John L. Springer, 'How to Care for Your TV Set', *American Home* (June 1953), 44.

themselves drenched by a stream of water. Since a prior scene in the film shows that the next-door neighbour is actually squirting water at the Naggers through the hole in the adjacent wall, the joke is on the technically illiterate women who can't distinguish between electrical and real space.[22]

By the late 1940s the confusion between spatial boundaries at the heart of these cinematic jokes was less pronounced. People were learning ways to incorporate television's spectacles within the contours of their homes. As I have shown elsewhere, post-war home magazines and handbooks on interior décor presented an endless stream of advice on how to make the home into a comfortable theatre.[23] In 1949, for example, *House Beautiful* advised its readers that 'conventional living room groupings need to be slightly altered because televiewers look in the same direction and not at each other'. *Good Housekeeping* seconded the motion in 1951 when it claimed that 'television is theatre; and to succeed, theatre requires a comfortably placed audience with a clear view of the stage'.[24] Advertisements for television sets variously referred to the 'chairside theatre', the 'video theatre', the 'family theatre', and so forth. Taken to its logical extreme, this theatricalization of the home transformed domestic space into a private pleasure dome. In 1951 *American Home* displayed 'A Room that Does Everything' which included a television set, radio, phonograph, movie projector, movie screen, loud speakers, and even a barbecue pit. As the magazine said of the proud owners of this total theatre, 'The Lanzes do all those things in *The Room*'.[25] In fact, the ideal home theatre was precisely 'the room' which one need never leave, a perfectly controlled environment of wall-to-wall mechanized pleasures.

But more than just offering family fun, these new home theatres provided post-war Americans with a way to mediate relations between public and private spheres. By turning one's home into a theatre, it was possible to make outside spaces part of a safe and predictable experience. In other words, the theatricalization of the home allowed people to draw a line between the public and the private sphere—or, in more theatrical terms, a line between the proscenium space where the spectacle took place and the reception space in which the audience observed the scene.

Indeed, as Lawrence Levine has shown, the construction of that division was central to the formation of twentieth-century theatres.[26] Whereas theatre audiences in the early 1800s tended to participate in the show through hissing, singing, and other forms of interaction, by the turn of the century theatres increasingly attempted to keep audiences detached from the performance. The silent, well-mannered audience became a mandate of 'good taste', and people were instructed to behave in this manner in legitimate

---

22 A similar scene is found in *The Three Stooges* comedy short 'Scheming Schemers' (c.1946) when the Stooges, posing as plumbers, mistakenly squirt a gush of water through the television set of a wealthy matron who is showing her guests a scene of Niagara Falls on TV.

23 See my 'Installing the Television Set: Popular Discourses on Television and Domestic Space, 1948–55' and my dissertation 'Installing the Television Set: The Social Construction of Television's Place in the American Home'.

24 *House Beautiful*, 91 (Aug. 1949), 66; 'Where Shall We Put the Television Set?', *Good Housekeeping* (Aug. 1951), 107.

25 *American Home* (May 1951), 40.

26 Lawrence W. Levine, *Highbrow/Lowbrow: The Emergence of Cultural Hierarchy in America* (Cambridge, Mass.: Harvard Univ. Press, 1988).

theatres and, later, in nickelodeons and movie palaces. In practice, the gen-
teel experiences that theatres encouraged often seem to have had the somewhat less 'tasteful' effect of permitting what George Lipsitz (following John
Kasson) has called a kind of 'privacy in public'.[27] Within the safely controlled
environment of the nickelodeon, audiences—especially youth audiences—
engaged in illicit flirtation. At a time of huge population increases in urban
centres, theatres and other forms of public amusements (most notably, as
Kasson has shown, the amusement park) offered people the fantastic possibility of being alone while in the midst of a crowd. Theatres thus helped construct imaginary separations between people by making individual
contemplation of mass spectacles possible.

In the post-war era, this theatrical experience was being reformulated in
terms of the television experience. People were shown how to construct an
exhibition space that replicated the general design of the theatre. However, in
this case, the relationship between public/spectacle and private/spectator
was inverted. The spectator was now physically isolated from the crowd, and
the fantasy was now one of imaginary unity with 'absent' others. This inversion gave rise to a set of contradictions that weren't easily solved. According
to the popular wisdom, television had to recreate the sense of social proximity that the public theatre offered; it had to make the viewer feel as if he or she
were taking part in a public event. At the same time, however, it had to maintain the necessary distance between the public sphere and private individual
upon which middle-class ideals of reception were based.

The impossibility of maintaining these competing ideals gave rise to a
series of debates as people weighed the ultimate merits of bringing theatrical
experiences indoors. Even if television promised the fantastic possibility of
social interconnection through electrical means, this new form of social life
wasn't always seen as an improvement over real community experiences.
The inclusion of public spectacles in domestic space always carried with it the
unpleasant possibility that the social ills of the outside world would invade
the private home. The more that the home included aspects of the public
sphere, the more it was seen as subject to unwelcome intrusions.

This was especially true in the early years of innovation when the purchase
of a television set quite literally decreased privacy in the home. Numerous
social scientific studies showed that people who owned television receivers
were inundated with guests who came to watch the new set.[28] But this
increased social life was not always seen as a positive effect by the families
surveyed. As one woman in a Southern California study complained,

---

27 George Lipsitz, *Time Passages: Collective Memory and American Popular Culture* (Minneapolis: Univ.
of Minnesota Press, 1990), 8. Also see John F. Kasson, *Amusing the Million: Coney Island at the Turn
of the Century* (New York: Hill and Wang, 1978) and Kathy Peiss, *Cheap Amusements: Working
Women and Leisure in Turn-of-the-Century New York* (Philadelphia: Temple Univ. Press, 1986).

28 After reviewing numerous studies from the fifties, Bogart claims in *The Age of Television*, 'In the early
days, "guest viewing" was a common practice' (p. 102). For a summary of the actual studies, see
Bogart, pp. 101–7. For additional studies that show the importance of guest viewing in the early
period, see John W. Riley *et al.*, 'Some Observations on the Social Effects of Television', *Public Opinion
Quarterly*, 13/2 (Summer 1949), 233 (this article was an early report of the CBS–Rutgers Univ. studies
begun in the summer of 1948); McDonagh *et al.*, 'Television and the Family', 116; 'When TV Moves
In', *Televiser*, 7/8 (Oct. 1950), 17 (a summary of the Univ. of Oklahoma surveys of Oklahoma City and
Norman, Oklahoma); Philip F. Frank, 'The Facts of the Medium', *Televiser* (Apr. 1951), 14; and 'TV
Bonus Audience in the New York Area', *Televiser* (Nov. 1950), 24–5.

'Sometimes I get tired of the house being used as a semiprivate theater. I have almost turned the set off when some people visit us.'[29] Popular media were also critical of the new 'TV parties'. In 1953 *Esquire* published a cartoon that highlighted the problem entailed by making one's home into a TV theatre. The sketch pictures a living room with chairs lined up in front of a television set in movie theatre fashion. The residents of this home theatre, dressed in pyjamas and bathrobes with hair uncombed and feet unshod, are taken by surprise when the neighbours drop in—a bit too soon—to watch a wrestling match on television. Speaking in the voice of the intruders, the caption reads, 'We decided to come over early and make sure we get good seats for tonight's fight.' In that same year, a cartoon in *TV Guide* suggested a remedy for the troublesome neighbours which took the form of a hand-held mechanical device known as 'Fritzy'. The caption read, 'If your neighbor won't buy his own set, try "Fritzy". One squeeze puts your set on the fritz.'[30]

Such popular anxieties are better understood when we recognize the changing structure of social relationships encountered by the new suburban middle class. These people often left their families and lifelong friends in the city to find instant neighbourhoods in pre-planned communities. Blocks composed of total strangers represented friendships only at the abstract level of demographic similarities in age, income, family size, and occupation. This homogeneity quickly became a central cause for anxiety in the suburban nightmares described by sociologists and popular critics. In *The Organization Man* (1957), William H. Whyte argued that a sense of community was especially important for the newcomers who experienced a feeling of 'rootlessness' when they left their old neighbourhoods for new suburban homes. As Whyte showed, the developers of the mass-produced suburbs tried to smooth the tensions caused by this sense of rootlessness by promising increased community life in their advertisements. For example, Park Forest, a Chicago suburb, assured consumers that 'Coffeepots bubble all day long in Park Forest. This sign of friendliness tells you how much neighbors enjoy each other's company—feel glad that they can share their daily joys— yes, and troubles, too.'[31] But when newcomers arrived in their suburban communities, they were likely to find something different from the ideal that the magazines and advertisements suggested. Tiny homes were typically sandwiched together so that the Smiths' picture window looked not onto rambling green acres, but rather into the Jones' living room—a dilemma commonly referred to as the 'goldfish bowl' effect. In addition to this sense of claustrophobia, the neighbourhood ideal brought with it an enormous amount of pressure to conform to the group. As Harry Henderson suggested in his study of Levittown (1953), the residents of this mass-produced suburb were under constant 'pressure to "keep up with the Joneses" ', a situation that led to a 'kind of superconformity' in which everyone desired the same luxury goods and consumer lifestyles. In his popular critique of the new suburbia, aptly entitled *The Crack in the Picture Window* (1956), John Keats con-

29 McDonagh *et al.*, 'Television and the Family', 116.

30 *Esquire* (July 1953), 110; Bob Taylor, 'Let's Make Those Sets Functional', *TV Guide*, 21–7 Aug. 1953: 10.

31 William H. Whyte, *The Organization Man* (Garden City, NY: Doubleday, 1957), 314.

sidered the tedium of this superconformity, describing the life of Mary and
John Drone who lived among a mob of equally unappealing neighbours. And
in *The Split-Level Trap* (1960), Richard Gordon and others used eight case
studies to paint an unsettling picture of the anxieties of social dislocation
experienced in a suburban town they called 'Disturbia'.[32]

These nightmarish visions of the pre-planned community served as an
impetus for the arrival of a surrogate community on television. Television
provided an illusion of the ideal neighbourhood—the way it was supposed to
be. Just when people had left their lifelong companions in the city, television
sitcoms pictured romanticized versions of neighbour and family bonding.
When promoting the early domestic comedy *Ethel and Albert*, NBC told
viewers to tune into 'a delightful situation comedy that is returning this
weekend . . . Yes, this Saturday night, *Ethel and Albert* come into view once
again to keep you laughing at the typical foibles of the kind of people who
might be living right next door to you.' The idea that television families were
neighbours was also found in critical commentary. In 1953 *Saturday Review*
claimed, 'The first thing you notice about these sketches [*The Goldbergs, The
Adventures of Ozzie and Harriet, Ethel and Albert,* and the live *Honeymooners*
skits] is that they are incidents; they are told as they might be told when
neighbors visit (in the Midwest sense of the word) on the front porch or the
back fence.' Indeed, since many of the comedies had been on radio in the
thirties and forties, the characters and stars must have seemed like old friends
to many viewers. Then too, several of the most popular sitcoms were set in
urban and ethnic locales, presenting viewers with a nostalgic vision of neighbourhood experiences among immigrant families.[33] Even the sitcoms set in
suburban towns externalized the private world by including neighbour characters who functioned as lifelong friends to the principal characters.[34] The
opening credits of fifties sitcoms further encouraged audiences to perceive
television's families as neighbours, linked through electrical wires to their
own homes. Typically, the credit sequences depicted families exiting their
front doors (*Donna Reed, Leave It to Beaver, Make Room for Daddy, Ozzie and
Harriet*) or greeting viewers in a neighbourly fashion by leaning out their
windows (*The Goldbergs*), and the programmes often used establishing shots
of the surrounding neighbourhoods (*Father Knows Best, Ozzie and Harriet,
Leave It to Beaver, Make Room for Daddy, The Goldbergs*).

Early television's most popular situation comedy, *I Love Lucy*, is a perfect—and typical—example of the importance attached to the theme of
neighbourhood bonding in the programmes. The primary characters, Lucy
and Ricky Ricardo, and their downstairs landlords, Ethel and Fred Mertz,

32 Harry Henderson, 'The Mass-Produced Suburbs', *Harper's* (Nov. 1953), 25–32, and 'Rugged
American Collectivism', *Harper's* (Dec. 1953), 80–6; John Keats, *The Crack in the Picture Window*
(1956; Boston: Houghton Mifflin, 1957); Richard E. Gordon, MD, *et al.*, *The Split-Level Trap* (New
York: Dell, 1960).

33 'NBC Promo for *Ethel and Albert* for use on *The Golden Windows*', Clyde Clem's Office, 31 Aug.
1954, NBC Records box 136: folder 15, State Historical Society, Madison, Wis.; Gilbert Seldes,
'Domestic Life in the Forty-Ninth State', *Saturday Review*, 22 Aug. 1953: 28. For a fascinating discussion of nostalgia in early ethnic situation comedies see Lipsitz, 'The Meaning of Memory: Family, Class
and Ethnicity in Early Network Television', in *Time Passages*, 39–76.

34 *I Married Joan*'s Aunt Vera, *My Favorite Husband*'s Gilmore and Myra Cobbs, *Burns and Allen*'s Harry
and Blanch Morton, and *Ozzie and Harriet*'s Thorny Thornberry were faithful companions to the central characters of the series.

were constantly together, and the more mature Mertzes served a quasi-parental role so that neighbours appeared as a family unit. In 1956, when the Ricardos moved from their Manhattan apartment to an idyllic Connecticut suburb, Lucy and Ricky re-enacted the painful separation anxieties that many viewers must have experienced over the previous decade. In an episode entitled 'Lucy Wants to Move to the Country', Lucy has misgivings about leaving the Mertzes behind and the Ricardos decide to break their contract on their new home. But at the episode's end, they realize that the fresh air and beauty of suburban life will compensate for their friendships in the city. After learning their 'lesson', the Ricardos are rewarded in a subsequent episode ('Lucy Gets Chummy With the Neighbors') when they meet their new next-door neighbours, Ralph and Betty Ramsey, who were regularly featured in the following programmes. While the inclusion of these neighbour characters provided an instant remedy for the painful move to the suburbs, the series went on to present even more potent cures. The next episode, 'Lucy Raises Chickens', brings Ethel and Fred back into the fold when the older couple sell their Manhattan apartment to become chicken farmers in the Connecticut suburb—and of course, the Mertzes rent the house next door to the Ricardos. Thus, according to this fantasy scenario, the move from the city would not be painful because it was possible to maintain traditional friendships in the new suburban world.

The burgeoning television culture extended these metaphors of neighbourhood bonding by consistently blurring the lines between electrical and real space. Television families were typically presented as 'real families' who just happened to live their lives on TV. Ricky and Lucy, Ozzie and Harriet, Jane and Goodman Ace, George and Gracie, and a host of others crossed the boundaries between fiction and reality on a weekly basis. Promotional and critical discourses further encouraged audiences to think that television characters lived the life of the stars who played them. For example, when writing about the *Adventures of Ozzie and Harriet*, a critic for a 1953 issue of *Time* claimed that the 'Nelson children apparently accept their double life as completely natural.' In that same year, the *Saturday Review* commented, 'The Nelsons are apparently living their lives in weekly installments on the air . . .'. In a 1952 interview with the Nelsons, *Newsweek* explained how 'Ricky Nelson kicks his shoes off during the filming, just as he does at home, and both boys work in front of the cameras in their regular clothes. In fact, says Harriet, they don't even know the cameras are there.' Even those sitcoms that did not include real-life families were publicized in this fashion. In 1954 *Newsweek* assured its readers that Danny Thomas was a 'Two Family Man', and that 'Danny's TV family acts like . . . Danny's Own Family.' One photograph showed Danny in a family portrait with his television cast while another depicted Danny at his swimming pool with his real family. The reviewer even suggested that Danny Williams (the character) resembled Danny Thomas (the star) more than Gracie Allen resembled herself on *The Burns and Allen Show*.[35]

---

35 'The Great Competitor', *Time*, 14 Dec. 1953: 62; Seldes, 'Domestic Life in the Forty-Ninth State', 28; 'Normality and $300,000', *Newsweek*, 17 Nov. 1952: 66; 'Two-Family Man', *Newsweek*, 5 Apr. 1954: 86.

These televised neighbours seemed to suture the 'crack' in the picture window. They helped ease what must have been for many Americans a painful transition from the city to the suburb. But more than simply supplying a tonic for displaced suburbanites, television promised something better: it promised modes of spectator pleasure premised upon the sense of an illusory—rather than a real—community of friends. It held out a new possibility for being alone in the home, away from the troublesome busybody neighbours in the next house. But it also maintained ideals of community togetherness and social interconnection by placing the community *at a fictional distance.* Television allowed people to enter into an imaginary social life, one which was shared not in the neighbourhood networks of bridge clubs and mahjong gatherings, but on the national networks of CBS, NBC, and ABC.

Perhaps this was best suggested by Motorola television in a 1951 advertisement (Fig. 3). The sketch at the top of the ad shows a businessman on his way home from work who meets a friend while waiting at a bus stop. Upon hearing that his friend's set is on the blink, the businessman invites him home for an evening of television on his 'dependable' Motorola console. A large photograph further down on the page shows a social scene where two couples, gathered around the television set, share in the joys of a TV party (Fig. 4).[36] Thus, according to the narrative sequence of events, television promises to increase social contacts. What is most significant about this advertisement, however, is that the representation of the TV party suggests something slightly different from the story told by the ad's narrative structure. In fact, the couples in the room do not appear to relate to one another; rather they interact *with and through* the television set. The picture emanating from the screen includes a third couple, the television stars George Burns and Gracie Allen. The couple on the left of the frame stare at the screen, gesturing towards George and Gracie as if they were involved in conversation with the celebrities. While the husband on the right of the frame stares at the television set, his wife looks at the man gesturing towards George and Gracie. In short, the social relationship between couples in the room appears to depend upon the presence of an illusion. Moreover, the illusion itself seems to come alive in so far as the televised couple, George and Gracie, appear to be interacting with the real couples in the room. Television, thus, promises a new kind of social experience, one which replicates the logic of real friendship (as told by the sequence of events in the advertisement's narrative), but which transforms it into an imaginary social relationship shared between the home audience and the television image (as represented in the social scene). In this advertisement as elsewhere, it is this idea of simulated social life which is shown to be the crux of pleasure in television.

Indeed, television—at its most ideal—promised to bring to audiences not merely an illusion of reality as in the cinema, but a sense of 'being there', a kind of *hyperrealism.* Television producers and executives devised schemes by which to merge public and private worlds into a new electrical neighbourhood. One of the central architects of this new electrical space was NBC's Pat Weaver, who saw television as an extension of traditional

36 *Better Homes and Gardens* (Nov. 1951), 162.

3 4

community experiences. As he claimed, 'In our entertainment, we . . . start with television as a communications medium, not bringing shows into the living room of the nation, but taking people from their living rooms to other places—theaters, arenas, ball parks, movie houses, skating rinks, and so forth.'[37] Implementing these ideals in 1949, Weaver conceived *The Saturday Night Review*, a three-hour programme designed to 'present a panorama of Americans at play on Saturday night'. The programme took the segmented format of variety acts and film features, but it presented the segments as a community experience shared by people just like the viewers at home. As *Variety* explained, 'For a film, the cameras may depict a family going to their neighborhood theatre and dissolve from there into the feature.'[38] Thus, television would mediate the cultural transition from public to private entertainment by presenting an imaginary night at the movies.

While Weaver's plan was the most elaborate, the basic idea was employed by various other programmes, particularly by television shows aimed at women. In 1952 New York's local station, WOR, aired *TV Dinner Date*, a variety programme that was designed to give 'viewers a solid two-and-a-half hours of a "night out at home" '.[39] CBS even promised female viewers an imaginary date in its fifteen-minute programme *The Continental*. Sponsored by Cameo Hosiery, the show began by telling women, 'And now it's time for your date with the Continental.' Host Renza Cesana (whom *Variety* described as Carl Brisson, Ezio Pinza, and Charles Boyer all rolled into one) used a vampire-like Transylvanian accent to court women in the late night hours. Cesana addressed his romantic dialogue to an off-camera character as he navigated his way through his lushly furnished den, a situation designed to create the illusion that Cesana's date for the night was the

37 Sylvester L. Weaver, 'Thoughts on the Revolution: Or, TV Is a Fad, Like Breathing', *Variety*, 11 July 1951: 42.

38 'NBC to Project "American Family" in 3-Hour Saturday Night Showcase', *Variety*, 3 Aug. 1949: 31.

39 *Variety*, 6 Aug. 1952: 26.

home viewer.[40] Meanwhile, during daytime hours, numerous programmes were set in public spaces such as hotels or cafés with the direct intention of making women feel as if they were part of the outside world. One of the first network shows, *Shoppers Matinee*, used a subjective camera that was intended to take 'the place of the woman shopper, making the home viewer feel as if she were in the store in person'.[41] In 1952 CBS introduced the daytime show *Everywhere I Go*, boasting of its 'studio without walls' that was designed to 'create the illusion of taking viewers to the actual scene' of presentation. One segment, for example, used rear-screen projection to depict hostess Jane Edwards and her 9-year-old daughter against a backdrop of their actual living room.[42] More generally, locally produced 'Mr and Mrs' shows invited female viewers into the homes of local celebrities, providing women with opportunities imaginatively to convene in familiar family settings with stars that exuded the warmth and intimacy of the people next door.

Television's promise of social interconnection has provided numerous post-war intellectuals—from Marshall McCluhan to Joshua Meyrowitz—with their own utopian fantasies. Meyrowitz is particularly interesting in this context because he has claimed that television helped foster women's liberation in the 1960s by bringing traditionally male spaces into the home, thus allowing women to 'observe and experience the larger world, including all male interactions and behaviors'. 'Television's first and strongest impact', he concludes, 'is on the perception that women have of the public male world and the place, or lack of place, they have in it. Television is an especially potent force for integrating women because television brings the public domain to women . . .'.[43] But Meyrowitz bases this claim on an essentialist notion of space. In other words, he assumes that public space is male and private space is female. However, public spaces like the office or the theatre are not simply male; they are organized according to categories of sexual difference. In these spaces certain social positions and subjectivities are produced according to the placement of furniture, the organization of entrances and exits, the separation of washrooms, the construction of partial walls, and so forth. Thus, television's incorporation of the public sphere into the home did not bring 'male' space into female space; instead it transposed one system of sexually organized space onto another.

Not surprisingly in this regard, post-war media often suggested that television would increase women's social isolation from public life by reinforcing spatial hierarchies that had already defined their everyday experiences in patriarchal cultures. The new family theatres were typically shown to limit opportunities for social encounters that women traditionally had at movie

40 For a review of the show, see *Variety*, 30 Jan. 1952: 31. Note that the particular episode I have seen clearly is aimed at a female audience with its pitch for women's stockings and its promise of a date with Cesana; however, Cesana addresses the home viewer as if she were a man, specifically his pal who has been stood up for a double date. Also note that there was a radio version of this programme in which a female host courted male viewers in the late night hours. Entitled *Two at Midnight*, the programme was aired locally on WPTR in Albany and is reviewed in *Variety*, 22 Oct. 1952: 28.

41 'DuMont Daytime', *Telecasting*, 12 Dec. 1949: 5.

42 'CBS-TV's "Studio Without Walls" New Gitlin Entry', *Variety*, 24 Sept. 1952: 43.

43 Joshua Meyrowitz, *No Sense of Place: The Impact of Electronic Media on Social Behavior* (New York: Oxford Univ. Press, 1985), 223–4.

theatres and other forms of public entertainment. In 1951 a cartoon in *Better Homes and Gardens* stated the problem in humorous terms. On his way home from work, a husband imagines a night of TV wrestling while his kitchen-bound wife, taking her freshly baked pie from the oven, dreams of a night out at the movies (Fig. 5).[44] Colgate dental cream used this dilemma of female isolation as a way to sell its product. A 1952 advertisement that ran in *Ladies' Home Journal* showed a young woman sitting at home watching a love scene on her television set, complaining to her sister, 'All I do is sit and view. You have dates any time you want them, Sis! All I get is what TV has to offer.'[45] Of course, after she purchased the Colgate dental cream, she found her handsome dream date. Thus, as the Colgate company so well understood, the imaginary universe that television offered posed its own set of female troubles. Even if television programmes promised to transport women into the outside world, it seems likely that women were critical of this, that they understood television's electrical space would never adequately connect them to the public sphere.

5

In 1955 the working-class comedy *The Honeymooners* dramatized this problem in the first episode of the series, 'TV or Not TV'.[46] The narrative was structured upon the contradiction between television's utopian promise of increased social life and the dystopian outcome of domestic seclusion. In

---

[44] *Better Homes and Gardens* (Nov. 1951), 218.

[45] *Ladies' Home Journal* (Jan. 1952), 64.

[46] *The Honeymooners* was first seen in 1951 as a skit in the live variety show *Cavalcade of Stars* on the DuMont network. The filmed half-hour series to which I refer aired during the 1955–6 season.

an early scene Alice Kramden begs her husband Ralph to buy a television set:

> I . . . want a television set. Now look around you, Ralph. We don't have any electric appliances. Do you know what our electric bill was last month? Thirty-nine cents! We haven't blown a fuse, Ralph, in ten years. . . . I want a television set and I'm going to get a television set. I have lived in this place for fourteen years without a stick of furniture being changed. Not one. I am sick and tired of this. . . . And what do you care about it? You're out all day long. And at night what are you doing? Spending money playing pool, spending money bowling, or paying dues to that crazy lodge you belong to. And I'm left here to look at that icebox, that stove, that sink, and these four walls. Well I don't want to look at that icebox, that stove, that sink and these four walls. I want to look at Liberace!

Significantly, in this exchange, Alice relates her spatial confinement in the home to her more general exclusion from the modern world of electrical technologies (as exemplified by her low utility bills). But her wish to inter-connect with television's electrical spaces soon becomes a nightmare because the purchase of the set further engenders her domestic isolation. When her husband Ralph and neighbour Ed Norton chip in for a new TV console, the men agree to place the set in the Kramden's two-room apartment where Norton is given visitation privileges. Thus, the installation of the set also means the intrusion of a neighbour into the home on a nightly basis, an intrusion that serves to take away rather than to multiply the spaces which Alice can occupy. In order to avoid the men who watch TV in the central living space of the apartment, Alice retreats to her bedroom, a prisoner in a house taken over by television.

Social scientific studies from the period show that the anxieties expressed in popular representations were also voiced by women of the period. One woman in a Southern California study confessed that all her husband 'wants to do is to sit and watch television—I would like to go out more often'. Another woman complained, 'I would like to go for a drive in the evening, but my husband has been out all day and would prefer to watch a wrestling match on television.'[47]

A nationwide survey suggested that this sense of domestic confinement was even experienced by teenagers. As one respondent complained, 'Instead of taking us out on date nights, the free-loading fellas park in our homes and stare at the boxing on TV.' For reasons such as these, 80 per cent of the girls admitted they would rather go to a B movie than stay home and watch television.[48]

If television was considered to be a source of problems for women, it also became a central trope for the crisis of masculinity in post-war culture. According to the popular wisdom, television threatened to contaminate masculinity, to make men sick with the 'disease' of femininity. As other scholars have observed, this fear of feminization has characterized the

---

47 McDonagh *et al.*, 'Television and the Family', 117, 119.

48 Cited in Betty Betz, 'Teens and TV', *Variety*, 7 Jan. 1953: 97.

debates on mass culture since the nineteenth century. Culture critics have continually paired mass culture with patriarchal assumptions about femininity. Mass amusements are typically thought to encourage passivity, and they have often been represented in terms of penetration, consumption, and escape. As Andreas Huyssen has argued, this link between women and mass culture has, since the nineteenth century, served to valorize the dichotomy between 'low' and 'high' art (or modernism). Mass culture, Huyssen claims, 'is somehow associated with women while real, authentic culture remains the prerogative of men'.[49] The case of broadcasting is especially interesting because the threat of feminization was particularly aimed at men. Broadcasting quite literally was shown to disrupt the normative structures of patriarchal (high) culture and to turn 'real men' into passive homebodies.

In the early 1940s this connection between broadcast technology and emasculation came to a dramatic pitch when Philip Wylie wrote his bitter attack on American women, *Generation of Vipers*. In this widely read book, Wylie maintained that American society was suffering from an ailment that he called 'momism'. American women, according to Wylie, had become overbearing, domineering mothers who turned their sons and husbands into weak-kneed fools. The book was replete with imagery of apocalypse through technology, imagery that Wylie tied to the figure of the woman. As he saw it, an unholy alliance between women and big business had turned the world into an industrial nightmare where men were slaves both to the machines of production in the factory and to the machines of reproduction—that is, women—in the home.

In his most bitter chapter, entitled 'Common Women', Wylie argued that women had somehow gained control of the airwaves. Women, he suggested, made radio listening into a passive activity that threatened manhood, and in fact, civilization. As Wylie wrote,

> The radio is mom's final tool, for it stamps everyone who listens to it with the matriarchal brand—its superstitions, prejudices, devotional rules, taboos, musts, and all other qualifications needful to its maintenance. Just as Goebbels has revealed what can be done with such a mass-stamping of the public psyche in his nation, so our land is a living representation of the same fact worked out in matriarchal sentimentality, goo, slop, hidden cruelty, and the foreshadow of national death. . . .[50]

In the annotated notes of the 1955 edition, Wylie updated these fears, claiming that television would soon take the place of radio and turn men into female-dominated dupes. Women, he wrote, 'will not rest until every electronic moment has been bought to sell suds and every bought program censored to the last decibel and syllable according to her self-adulation—along with that (to the degree the mom-indoctrinated pops are permitted access to the dials) of her de-sexed, de-souled, de-cerebrated mate.'[51] The mixture of misogyny and 'telephobia' which ran through this passage was clearly hyper-

49 Andreas Huyssen, *After the Great Divide: Modernism, Mass Culture, Postmodernism* (Bloomington: Indiana Univ. Press, 1986), 47.

50 Philip Wylie, *Generation of Vipers* (New York: Holt, Rinehart and Winston, 1955), 214–15.

51 Ibid. 213–14.

bolic; still, the basic idea was repeated in more sober representations of everyday life during the post-war period.

As popular media often suggested, television threatened to rob men of their powers, to usurp their authority over the image, and to turn them into passive spectators. This threat materialized in numerous representations that showed women controlling their husbands through television. Here, television's blurring of private and public space became a powerful tool in the hands of housewives who could use the technology to invert the sexist hierarchies at the heart of the separation of spheres. In this topsy-turvy world, women policed men's access to the public sphere and confined them to the home through the clever manipulation of television technology. An emblematic example is a 1955 advertisement for *TV Guide* that conspires with women by giving them tips on ways to 'Keep a Husband Home'. As the ad suggests, 'You might try drugging his coffee . . . or hiding all his clean shirts. But by far the best persuader since the ball and chain is the TV set . . . and a copy of *TV Guide*.'[52]

This inversion of the gendered separation of spheres was repeated in other representations that suggested ways for women to control their husbands' sexual desires through television. A typical example is a 1952 advertisement for Motorola television that showed a man staring at a bathing beauty on television while neglecting his real-life mate. The dilemma of 'the other woman', however, was countered by the enunciative control that the housewife had in the representation. While the man is shown to be a passive spectator sprawled in his easy chair, his wife (who is holding a shovel) dominates the foreground of the image, and the caption, which speaks from her point of view, reads, 'Let's go, Mr Dreamer, that television set won't help you shovel the walk' (Fig. 1). Similarly, a 1953 RCA advertisement for a set with 'rotomatic tuning' shows a male spectator seated in an easy chair while watching a glamorous woman on the screen. But the housewife literally controls and sanctions her husband's gaze at the televised woman because she operates the tuning dials.[53] Then too, numerous advertisements and illustrations depicted women who censored male desire by standing in front of the set, blocking the man's view of the screen (Figs. 6, 7).[54] Similarly, a cartoon in a 1949 issue of the *New York Times* magazine showed how a housewife could dim her husband's view of televised bathing beauties by making him wear sunglasses, while a cartoon in a 1953 issue of *TV Guide* suggested that the same form of censorship could be accomplished by putting window curtains on the screen in order to hide the more erotic parts of the female body.[55] Television, in this regard, was shown to contain men's pleasure by circumscribing it within the confines of domestic space and placing it under the auspices of women. Representations of television thus presented a position for

52 *TV Guide*, 29 Jan. 1955: back cover.

53 *Better Homes and Gardens* (Feb. 1952), 154; *Better Homes and Gardens* (Sept. 1953), 177.

54 See e.g. an advertisement for Durall window screens that shows a housewife blocking her husband's view of a bathing beauty on the television set in *Good Housekeeping* (May 1954), 187. A similar illustration appears in *Popular Science* (Mar. 1953), 179. And an advertisement for Kotex sanitary napkins shows how a woman, by wearing the feminine hygiene product, can distract her husband's gaze at the screen; *Ladies' Home Journal* (May 1949), 30.

55 *New York Times*, 11 Dec. 1949: magazine, p. 20; *TV Guide*, 6 Nov. 1953: 14.

"I think it's time you gave a little of your attention to these forty-two-inch screens"

GLENN R. BERNHARDT

COLLIER'S

male spectators that can best be described as passive aggression. Structures of sadistic and fetishistic pleasure common to the Hollywood cinema were still operative, but they were sanitized and neutralized through their incorporation into the home.

In contemporary culture, the dream of social interconnection through antiseptic electrical space is still a potent fantasy. In 1989, in an issue entitled 'The Future and You', *Life* magazine considered the new electronic space that the home laser holographic movie might offer in the twenty-first century. Not coincidentally, this holographic space was defined by male desire. As Marilyn Monroe emerged from the screen in her costume from *The Seven Year Itch*, a male spectator watched her materialize in the room. With his remote control aimed at the set, he policed her image from his futuristic La-Z-Boy Lounger. Although the scene was clearly coded as a science-fiction fantasy, this form of home entertainment was just the latest version of the older wish to control and purify public space. Sexual desire, transported to the home from the Hollywood cinema, was made possible by transfiguring the celluloid image into an electrical space where aggressive and sadistic forms of cinematic pleasure were now sanitized and made into 'passive' home entertainment. The aggression entailed in watching Monroe was clearly marked as passive aggression, as a form of desire that could be contained within domestic space. But just in case the desire for this electronic fantasy woman could not be properly contained, the article warned readers to 'fasten the seatbelt on your La-Z-Boy'.[56]

As this example shows, the utopian dreams of space-binding and social sanitation that characterized television's introduction in the fifties is still a dominant cultural ideal. Electronic communications offer an extension of those plans as private and public spaces become increasingly intertwined

56 *Life* (Feb. 1989), 67.

Those with an itch for Marilyn high-stepping right out of the tube need only get up the scratch: home laser holographic movies are on their way.

8

through such media as home computers, fax machines, message units, and car phones. Before considering these social changes as a necessary part of an impending 'electronic revolution' or 'information age', we need to remember the racist and sexist principles upon which these electrical utopias have often depended. The loss of neighbourhood networks and the rise of electronic networks is a complex social phenomenon based on a series of contradictions that plague post-war life. Perhaps being nostalgic for an older, more 'real' form of community is itself a historical fantasy. But the dreams of a world united by telecommunications seem dangerous enough to warrant closer examination. The global village, after all, is the fantasy of the colonizer, not the colonized.

16

Behind Closed Doors: Video Recorders in the Home

Ann Gray

THE VIDEO CASSETTE recorder is arguably the major innovation in home entertainment in Britain since television. When we address questions of how women watch television and video we inevitably raise a complex set of issues which relate to women and their everyday lives. In talking to women about home video cassette recorders (VCR) and television use, I have identified some of the determining factors surrounding these activities which take place within the domestic environment.[1] With the development of VCRs and other products such as home computers and cable services, the 1980s is seeing an ever-increasing trend towards home-centred leisure and entertainment. New technology in the home has to be understood within a context of structures of power and authority relationships between household members, with gender emerging as one of the most significant differentiations. This far from neutral environment influences the ways in which women use popular texts in general and television and video in particular, and the pleasures and meanings which these have for them.

The Video Revolution Although it is a relatively recent phenomenon, home video arrived as long ago as 1972 with Philips VCR and Sony U-matic. But it wasn't until Sony Betamax and VHS (video home system), both of which use 19 mm tape, brought the cost down significantly, that the stage was set for a consumer boom. In 1983 15 per cent of households in the United Kingdom had access to a VCR, by 1986 the figure had reached 40 per cent. An important factor in the British VCR experience is that the distribution of recorders operates through the already existing television rental networks, thereby making it

© Pandora, 1987.

Originally published in Helen Baehr and Gillian Dyer (eds.), *Boxed-In: Women and Television* (London: Pandora Press, 1987), 38–54.

1 This research was initially funded by the Economic and Social Research Council and has taken the form of long, open-ended discussions with women whose age, social position, employment, and family circumstances differ (race is a variable which has not been introduced). Part of my strategy has been to encourage open discussion and allow the women themselves to introduce topics which are of importance to them. By keeping the discussions open they can take pleasure in having the opportunity to explore and express their own ideas and feelings on these matters. For discussions on feminist research methods see Roberts (ed.), 1981; Stanley and Wise, 1983; Bell and Roberts, 1984.

possible to rent a VCR on a monthly basis, without the necessity for large capital investment. This results in video recorders being made available to a much wider range of socio-economic groups than might at first be imagined. We are not, in the British case, considering a 'luxury' item which graces the affluent household, rather, a widely available home entertainment facility which has rapidly become an accepted and essential part of everyday life, cutting across economic and class boundaries.

The development and marketing of entertainment consumer hardware can often outpace the provision of 'software' or 'content'. Raymond Williams points out that when domestic radio receivers were first marketed there was very little to receive in terms of programming content, 'It is not only that the supply of broadcasting facilities preceded the demand; it is that the means of communication preceded their content' (Williams, 1974: 25).

There are two major uses for VCRs: time-shift, which involves recording off-broadcast television in order to view at a different time, and the playing of pre-recorded tapes.[2] These can be purchased, though the majority are hired through video rental 'libraries'. Although off-air recording is an attractive proposition, it has become obvious to a few entrepreneurs that there is a large potential market for the hiring of pre-recorded tape. In Britain during the early 1980s one feature of almost every high street was a new phenomenon known as the 'video library'. These were often hastily converted small shops offering tapes, mainly of movies, for hire. In these early days, in order to finance their purchase of new material, the libraries demanded a membership fee, often as high as £40, as well as a nightly fee for the hiring of tapes. Nowadays it is possible to join a video library free of charge, with a nightly rental fee of £1.00–1.50 per tape. There are now upwards of 6,500 movies[3] available for hire on video tape and at a rough estimate four million tapes are hired a week. Indeed, 97 per cent of film watching is now done outside the cinema, mainly on broadcast television, but the hiring of films accounts for a significant proportion of this viewership (Howkins, 1983).

The video library industry—and I use this term to describe the distributors and retailers of pre-recorded tapes for purchase or hire—has experienced major change. Many of the smaller retail outlets have gone by the board, forced out by the larger and well-established distributors who moved in once the market had been tested. The industry has established its own quasi-professional organizations in order to protect itself against 'video piracy' and to professionalize and improve its image, which has not been good. The 'moral panic' which resulted in the Video Recordings Bill of 1984, providing for every film on hire to be censored for home viewing, had a devastating effect on the public image of the video libraries. This was fuelled enthusiastically by the popular press (Petley, 1984; Kuhn, 1984a; Barker, 1984). On 1 September 1982 the *Sun* carried the headline 'Fury over video nasties' and referred to the video distributors and retailers as 'the merchants of menace' who were threatening the well-being of our children. This kind of response to a new development in mass cultural production is similar to

---

2 VCRs can also be used in conjunction with a video camera to produce home video tapes.

3 'Movies' in this context include films made specially for video distribution, films made for TV, both British and American, as well as 'feature' films which are produced primarily for the cinema.

those precipitated by the novel in the nineteenth century, cinema in the 1920s, and television in the 1950s. The moral reformers were then, as now, fearful for the effects of these new mass-produced cultural forms on those 'weaker' members of society—women, children, and the 'lower orders' in general—whom they sought to protect.

Video and Family Life

Although there are many aspects of the video phenomenon which are worthy of study, my research initially focuses on the potential choice which the VCR offers for viewing within the domestic and family context. The major reason for this is that, until recently, attention to the context of viewing seems to have been largely neglected in media and cultural studies.[4] The relationship between the viewer and television, the reader and text, is often a relationship which has to be negotiated, struggled for, won or lost, in the dynamic and often chaotic processes of family life. As video recorders offer, above all, extended choice of content and time management for viewing within the home, research into its use has to be focused within that very context. The context of 'the family' is, for my purposes, conceived of as a site of constant social negotiation within a highly routinized framework of material dependency and normative constraint,[5] and all these elements enter into the negotiations which surround viewing decisions. This family setting, with its power relationships and authority structures across gender, is an extremely important factor in thinking more generally of 'leisure' and, specifically, home-based leisure. The home has increasingly become the site for entertainment, and we can see VCRs as yet one more commodity which reduces the necessity for household members to seek entertainment outside the home, a situation reinforced by the present economic climate in Britain:

> js: Well, we can't really afford to go out to the pictures, not any more. If we all go and have ice-creams, you're talking about eight or nine pounds. It's a lot of money.

What is especially important for women is that the domestic sphere is increasingly becoming defined as their only leisure space. Many married women are in paid work outside the home, but women are still largely responsible for the domestic labour in the home. Childcare, food provision, laundry, shopping, and cleaning the living space, are ultimately women's responsibility even if their male partners help. While men in paid employment come home to a non-work environment, women who either work in the home all day or go out to paid employment still have to work at home in the evenings and at weekends:

> as: Him? Oh, he sits on his backside all night, from coming in from work to going to bed.

Indeed, many women do not consider themselves as having any leisure at all (Deem, 1984). And many certainly would not allow themselves the luxury of

---

4 There are notable exceptions (Hobson, 1981 and 1982; Morley, 1986; Collett, 1986).

5 I am grateful to Elizabeth Shove and Andrew Tudor for this working definition.

sitting down to watch television until the children are fed and put to bed and the household chores have been completed:

JK: I'd feel guilty, I'd feel I was cheating. It's my job and if I'm sat, I'm not doing my job.

This is a context which, at the most basic and practical level, positions women in relation to the whole area of leisure, but particularly in relation to television and video viewing:

AS: Like, if he comes in and he's rented a video, straight after tea he wants to put it on. I say 'well let me finish the washing-up first'. I mean, I just wouldn't enjoy it if I knew it was all to do.

Video as Technology

Women and men have differential access to technology in general and to domestic technology in particular. The relations between domestic technology and gender are relatively unexplored,[6] though there is more work on gender and technology in the workplace, where, as Jan Zimmerman notes, new technology is entering existing and traditional sets of relations. Old values in this way become encoded in new technologies (Zimmerman, 1981; Cockburn, 1983, 1985). It is interesting to note that American researchers discovered that in the early 1970s the full-time housewife was spending as much time on housework as her grandmother had done fifty years earlier. Domestic technology may be labour-saving, replacing the drudgery of household work, but it is time-consuming in that each piece of equipment requires work if it is to fulfil its advertised potential. Rothschild argues that far from liberating women from housework, new technology, embedded as it is in ideological assumptions about the sexual division of labour, has further entrenched women in the home and in the role of housewife (Rothschild, 1983).

When a new piece of technology is purchased or rented, it is often already inscribed with gender expectations. The gender specificity of pieces of domestic technology is deeply implanted in the 'commonsense' of households, operating almost at an unconscious level. As such it is difficult for the researcher to unearth. One strategy I have employed which throws the gender of domestic technology into high relief is to ask the women to imagine pieces of equipment as coloured either pink or blue.[7] This produces almost uniformly pink irons and blue electric drills, with many interesting mixtures along the spectrum. The washing machine, for example, is most usually pink on the outside, but the motor is almost always blue. VCRs and, indeed, all home entertainment technology would seem to be a potentially lilac area, but my research has shown that we must break down the VCR into its different modes in our colour-coding. The 'record', 'rewind', and 'play' modes are usually lilac, but the timer switch is nearly always blue, with women having

---

6 However a recent publication by W. Faulkner and E. Arnold (eds.), *Smothered by Invention: Technology in Women's Lives* (Pluto Press, 1985), does address issues of domestic technology and gender.

7 These were ideas discussed at a seminar given by Cynthia Cockburn at York University, June 1985. See also Cockburn, 1985.

to depend on their male partners or their children to set the timer for them. The blueness of the timer is exceeded only by the deep indigo of the remote control switch which in all cases is held by the man:

> sw: Oh, yes, that's definitely blue in our house. He flicks from channel to channel, I never know what I'm watching—it drives me mad.

It does appear that the male of the household is generally assumed to have knowledge of this kind of technology when it enters the household, or at least he will quickly gain the knowledge. And certain knowledges can, of course, be withheld and used to maintain authority and control:

> as: Well, at first he was the only one who knew how to record things, but then me and my young son sat down one day and worked it out. That meant we didn't have to keep asking him to record something for us.

Although women routinely operate extremely sophisticated pieces of domestic technology, often requiring, in the first instance, the study and application of a manual of instructions, they often feel alienated from operating the VCR. The reasons for this are manifold and have been brought about by positioning within the family, the education system, and the institutionalized sexism with regard to the division of appropriate activities and knowledges in terms of gender. Or there may be, as I discovered, 'calculated ignorance':

> ch: If I learnt how to do the video it would become my job just like everything else.

If women do not feel confident or easy in approaching and operating the recorders, let alone in setting the timer for advance recording, they are at an immediate and real disadvantage in terms of exercising the apparent choices which the VCR offers. This, combined with constraints in the hiring of video tapes, either financial or simply normative, means that for women the idea of increased freedom and choice of viewing may well be spurious.

Genre and Gender

If women are 'positioned' within the context of consumption, it seems that they are also positioned, or even structured in absence, by the video industry itself in terms of the kind of audience it seems to be addressing. To enter a video library is to be visually bombarded by 'covers' depicting scenes of horror, action adventure, war, westerns, and 'soft' pornography, traditionally considered to be 'male' genres.[8] Is it therefore mainly men who are hiring video tapes, and if so, what do women feel about the kinds of tapes they are watching at home? Do women ever hire tapes themselves, or do they feel alienated from both the outlets and what they have to offer? In other words,

---

8 It is interesting to note that video tapes are now being distributed which are specifically aimed at a female audience; IPC and Videospace combined magazine and video to market their *Woman's Own Selection*, along with their more recent label *Images of Love*, while Polygram Video are offering a label, *Women's Choice*. However, in the North of England certainly, these have a very limited distribution.

what are the circumstances surrounding the use of video libraries and what is the sexual division of labour associated with the hiring and viewing of tapes? I have already made reference to the so-called 'male' genres which imply that certain kinds of films address themselves to and are enjoyed by a male audience and the same, of course, could be said for 'female' genres. But why do certain kinds of texts or genres appeal to women and not to men and vice versa and how should we conceive of the audience for these texts made up of women and men?

The 'gendered audience' has a theoretical history which, as Annette Kuhn usefully points out, has developed within two different perspectives, one emerging from media studies and the other from film theory (Kuhn, 1984b). This has resulted in two quite different notions of the gendered audience. The sociological emphasis of media studies has tended to conceive of a 'social audience', that is, an audience made up of already constituted male and female persons who bring (among other things) maleness or femaleness to a text, and who decode the text within that particular frame of reference. Film theory on the other hand, has conceived of a 'psychological audience', a collection of individual spectators who do not read the text, but rather the text 'reads' them. In other words, the film offers a masculine or feminine subject position and the spectator occupies that position. Of course, this is not automatic and there is nothing to prevent, for example, a female spectator taking up a masculine subject position. However, the construction of masculinity and femininity across the institutions within society is so powerfully aligned to the social categories 'male' and 'female' that the two usually coincide apparently seamlessly. But, as Kuhn points out, what is suggested by these two perspectives is a distinction between femaleness as a social gender and femininity as a subject position. The problem here is that neither of these two perspectives is sufficient in themselves to gain a full understanding of what happens when men and women watch films. In the former case, context is emphasized over text and in the latter text over context. The spectator–text relationships suggested by the psychoanalytic models used in film theory tend to disregard those important factors of social context involved in film and TV watching. Also, they find it difficult to allow for the subject constituted outside the text, across other discourses, such as class, race, age, and general social environment. The social audience approach, conversely, sees the response to texts as a socially predetermined one, and in this way does not allow for consideration of how the texts themselves work on the viewers/readers.

There have been some attempts to link text with context by examining the particular features of 'women's genres'. Soap operas, for example, have been looked at in terms of their distinctive narrative pattern, which is open-ended and continuous; their concern with so-called 'female' skills; their scheduling on television which fits into the rhythm of women's work at home, all of which can be seen as specifically addressing a social audience of women (Brunsdon, 1981; Modleski, 1982). However, this would still seem to stress context over text and in this area the film theory perspective has certainly been limited by its implicit assumption of an intense and concentrated relationship between spectator and text in a darkened cinema. For television this relationship is more likely to be characterized by distinction and diversion. As Kuhn points out:

This would suggest that each medium constructs sexual difference through spectatorship in rather different ways: cinema through the look and spectacle, and TV—perhaps less evidently—through a capacity to insert its flow, its characteristic modes of address and the textual operations of different kinds of programmes into the rhythms and routines of domestic activities and sexual divisions of labour in the household at various times of day.   (Kuhn, 1984*b*: 25)

This distinction is important and useful, but when thinking about the use of VCRs the two media are viewed in the same context. Movies have long been a part of television's nightly 'flow' as well as part of daytime viewing. But in video recording movies off television for watching at a later date, and in hiring movies, we have a discrete 'event' which disrupts the flow of television and its insertive scheduling:

AC: Oh yes, we all sit down and watch—'we've got a video, let's sit down'—TV's different, that's just on.

Concepts of the psychological audience and the social audience are not sufficient in themselves to explore the whole complexity of text, subject, and context and the ways in which they intersect. But both are necessary, representing as they do different instances within the process of consumption of popular texts. While the psychological model posits an unacceptably homogeneous and 'universal' audience, it does allow us to consider the importance of how texts work, not only in terms of subject positioning and interpellation, but also in terms of pleasure and desire. The social model demands that the audience is heterogeneous and requires us to explore those other differences and contexts which, to a greater or lesser extent, determine the ways in which women and men read those texts. It seems clear that the problem of the relationship between text and gendered audience cannot be resolved at the theoretical level, but rather must be kept in play and, if possible, problematized throughout the research enterprise.

Viewing Contexts

It would seem that women do have certain preconceptions about what constitutes a 'film for men' as against a 'film for women', and furthermore, a typology of viewing contexts is beginning to emerge, along with appropriate associated texts (see Table 1).

I wish to focus mainly on Context (Female alone), but before I do it is worth mentioning the difference between the negotiations around Contexts (Male alone) and (Female alone). For the latter to exist, the male partner must normally be out of the house, either at work or at leisure, whereas Context (Male alone) would be likely to exist when both male and female were in the house together. The women simply wouldn't watch:

BA: If he's watching something I'm not enjoying, I'll either knit or read.

JS: Well, I can read when the telly's on if it's something I don't like.

DS: I usually go to bed with a book, or sometimes I'll watch the portable in the kitchen, but it's damned uncomfortable in there.

CH: Well, when he's in, Father has priority over what's on. Yes, he does, but I can go in the other room if I don't want to watch it.

TABLE 1: *Typology of viewing contexts*[9]

	CONTEXT	FILM	TV
1	Family together	*Superman* Walt Disney *Jaws* Comedy	Children's TV Quiz shows Comedy *EastEnders*
2	Male and female partners together	*An Officer and a Gentleman* *Kramer v. Kramer* The Rockys Any Clint Eastwood	*Auf Wiedersehen Pet* *Minder* Shows *Coronation Street* *EastEnders*
3	Male alone	War Action adventure* Horror* Adults*	Sport News Documentaries
4	Female alone	*Who Will Love My Children?* *Evergreen* Romance	*Coronation Street* *Crossroads* *Dallas* *Dynasty* *A Woman of Substance* *Princess Daisy*

* These are the category headings used by many video libraries.

Women Only

For women who are at home all day, either with very small children or children of school age, and whose husbands are out at work, there are obvious opportunities for them to view alone. However, most of the women I have talked to are constrained by guilt, often referring to daytime viewing as some kind of drug:

> SW: No, I've got too many things to do during the daytime, I couldn't do it to myself, I'd be a total addict.
>
> JK: Well, I watch *Falcon Crest*—it's a treat, when I've done my work, then I sit down and it's my treat. But I'm not one to get videos during the day because I think you can get really addicted, then everything else suffers.

The second woman quoted indicates what is a fairly common strategy—that of using daytime television programmes to establish some time for herself as a reward to which completion of household tasks will lead. This assuages the

9 These are the names which the women themselves gave to the different texts and genres.

guilt to a certain extent and the pleasure afforded by this particular viewing context seems to go far beyond the pleasures of the text itself. What it represents is a breathing space when the busy mother can resist the demands of her children and domestic labour for a brief period of time. One of the most popular daytime programmes cited was *Sons & Daughters*, an Australian imported soap opera, transmitted three afternoons a week in the Yorkshire region. Most of the women preferred to watch this alone, some taking the telephone off the hook to ensure uninterrupted concentration, but they would watch it with a friend if they happened to be in each other's houses at the time. Janice Radway in her study of women and romantic fiction talks with regret of the isolated context within which popular romances are consumed by women (Radway, 1984). The next viewing context I wish to discuss reveals a more optimistic state of affairs for women.

This context is again female only, but is one in which several women get together to watch a video which they have hired jointly. This would normally happen during the day when their children are at school. Far from being instrumental in isolating women, it would seem that there is a tendency to communal use of hired videos, mainly on economic grounds, but also on the grounds that the women can watch what they want together without the guilt or the distraction of children:

BS: There are three of us, and we hire two or three films a week and watch them together, usually at Joyce's house when the kids are at school. We can choose what we want then.

JK: Yes, if there's something we want to see we wait 'til the kids have gone back to school so's we can sit and watch it without them coming in saying 'can I have . . . can I have . . .' it makes it difficult.

The idea of viewing together during the day for this particular network of women living on the same street came when one of them found herself continually returning the video tapes which her husband had hired the night before. She discovered that there were films which she would like to watch but which her husband never hired. A good relationship was established with the woman who worked in the video library who would look out for good films:

BS: She comes into the shop where I work and I go 'have any new videos come out?' She tells me. She knows what we like.

One favoured form for this viewing network is that of the long family saga, often running to two or three tapes:

JK: We like something in two or three parts; something with a really good story to it so's you can get involved.

BS: Mm . . . the other week we had a Clint Eastwood and Burt Reynolds film because she [MD] likes Clint Eastwood but we talked all the way through that, didn't we?

When the group views sagas which extend over two or three tapes there is obvious pleasure in anticipating both the outcome of the narrative and the viewing of the following tape. A considerable amount of discussion and speculation ensues and a day for the next viewing is fixed:

> MD: We like to spread them out—every other day, it helps to break the week up. Sometimes we have them on an evening, if our husbands are away or out. We'll have a bottle of wine then, then we don't even have to get up to make a cup of tea.

These women are also devotees of the American soap operas and operate a 'failsafe' network of video recording for each other, refusing to discuss each episode until they have all seen it. These popular texts form an important part of their friendship and association in their everyday lives and give a focus to an almost separate female culture which they can share together within the constraints of their positions as wives and mothers. Furthermore, they are able to take up the feminine subject positions offered by these texts comfortably and pleasurably. In contrast, the films which their husbands hire for viewing Context (Male and female partners together) mainly offer a masculine subject position which the women seem to take up through their male partners, who in turn give their approval to such texts.

The major impetus for a viewing group like this is that films which women enjoy watching are rarely, if ever, hired by their male partners for viewing together because they consider such films to be 'trivial' and 'silly' and women are laughed at for enjoying them:

> BA: I sit there with tears running down my face and he comes in and says 'you daft thing.'

This derision also applies to soap operas, and is reproduced in male children:

> JK: Oh, my son thinks I'm stupid because I won't miss *Dallas*—perhaps I am.

It is the most powerful member within the household who defines this hierarchy of 'serious' and 'silly', 'important' and 'trivial'. This leaves women and their pleasures in films downgraded, objects and subjects of fun and derision, having to consume them almost in secret. But the kinds of films and television soap operas which women enjoy watching alone deal with things of importance to them, highlighting so-called 'female' concerns—care of children, concern for members of one's own family, consideration for one's own sexual partner, selflessness in character—all of which are the skills of competence, the thought and caring which husbands and children expect of women and assume as a matter of natural course.[10] This is a deeply contradictory position for women, lying between the realities of their day-to-day lives and the pleasures and gratifications that they seek to find in texts that their partners, and very often their children, look upon as so much rubbish:

> JS: I think a lot of story-lines in soap operas are very weak and I think a man needs something to keep his interest more than a woman. That makes a man sound more intelligent, but that's not what I mean. It's got to be something worth watching before he'll sit down and actually

---

10 Charlotte Brunsdon has made this point in relation to *Crossroads*, but we can see that it can apply to other 'women's genres' (Brunsdon, 1981).

watch it, but I'd watch anything. I think he thinks it's unmanly to watch them.

sw: All the soap operas are rubbish for men, fantasy for women.

ag: *Do you think men need fantasy?*

sw: They need fantasy in a different way, detectives and wars, that's their fantasy world, and science fiction, a tough, strong world. Not sloppy, who's fallen in love with who, who's shot JR—it's rubbish. Men know it's rubbish, that's the difference.

Here are two women talking about a genre they love in relation to their male partners, giving us a sense of the 'power of definition' within the partnerships, but also the ways in which the women themselves think of their own pleasures.

Conclusion

Theories of the gendered audience as they have been developed are useful, but when women and men watch movies and television they become that hybrid, the *social spectator* (Kuhn, ibid.) and, in understanding the subject–text–context relationship, the social and the psychological have to be kept in play to a proportionately greater or lesser degree. This allows us to consider how texts and contexts (both the specific and the wider social context) combine together in producing the gendered reading subject. Charlotte Brunsdon, writing on *Crossroads*, has attempted to resolve this dualism and suggests that, 'The relation of the audience to the text will not be determined solely by that text, but also by positionalities in relation to a whole range of other discourses—discourses of motherhood, romance and sexuality for example' (Brunsdon, 1981: 32). This enables us to think of the subject in the social context occupying different positions in relation to different discourses which change across time. As particular discourses become central issues, they will affect the ways in which the social subject occupies, or resists, the subject position constructed by a text.

The viewing and reading of texts takes place, for the majority of people, within the domestic context. However, this is a context which is not singular and unchanging, but plural and open to different permutations, dependent upon the negotiations between members of the household and the particular texts involved. The VCR offers the potential for extended choice of viewing in terms of text and context. But in order to explore how this potential is being used the particular conditions of its consumption must be addressed. The viewing contexts and their associated texts which I have outlined here have emerged from my discussions with women who occupy different social positions and there are remarkable similarities in the ways in which all the women have spoken about their domestic viewing practices. However, it is simply not sufficient to have identified these similarities, and my analysis of the interview 'texts' continues in an attempt to make visible the important differences between the women's accounts of these practices. These differences must be seen in relation to their particular social positioning and the various specific discourses which they inhabit. The interview material I have gathered demands a framework of analysis which uses theories and concepts developed within different disciplines and will, I am sure, test their relative strengths and weaknesses in revealing the complexity of how women relate to television and video in their everyday lives.

I am grateful to Andrew Tudor for his thorough reading of an early draft of this article, and indebted to the women who gave me much more than their time.

References

Barker, M. (1984) (ed.), *The Video Nasties* (London: Pluto Press).

Bell, C., and Roberts, H. (1984) (eds.), *Social Researching* (London: Routledge & Kegan Paul).

Brunsdon, C. (1981), '*Crossroads*: Notes on a Soap Opera', *Screen*, 22/4: 32–7.

Cockburn, C. (1983), *Brothers* (London: Pluto Press).

—— (1985), *Machinery of Dominance* (London: Pluto Press).

Collett, P. (1986), 'Watching the TV Audience', paper presented to International Television Studies conference 1986.

Deem, R. (1984), 'Paid Work, Leisure and Non-Employment: Shifting Boundaries and Gender Differences', paper presented to British Sociological Association conference 1984.

Faulkner, W., and Arnold, E. (1985) (eds.), *Smothered by Invention* (London: Pluto Press).

Hobson, D. (1981), 'Housewives and the Mass Media', in S. Hall *et al.* (eds.), *Culture, Media, Language* (London: Hutchinson).

—— (1982), '*Crossroads*': The Drama of a Soap Opera (London: Methuen).

Howkins, J. (1983), 'Mr Baker: A Challenge', *Sight & Sound* (autumn), 227–9.

Kuhn, A. (1984*a*), 'Reply to Julian Petley', *Screen*, 25/3 (May/June), 116–17.

—— (1984*b*), 'Women's Genres', *Screen*, 25/1 (Jan./Feb.), 18–28.

Modleski, T. (1982), *Loving With a Vengeance* (Hamden, Conn.: Shoe String Press).

Morley, D. (1986), *Family Television: Cultural Power and Domestic Leisure* (London: Comedia).

Petley, J. (1984), 'A Nasty Story', *Screen*, 25/2 (Mar./Apr.), 68–74.

Radway, J. A. (1984), *Reading the Romance* (Chapel Hill: Univ. of North Carolina Press).

Roberts, H. (1981) (ed.), *Doing Feminist Research* (London: Routledge & Kegan Paul).

Rothschild, J. (1983), *Machina ex Dea* (New York: Pergamon Press).

Stanley, L., and Wise, S. (1983), *Breaking Out* (London: Routledge & Kegan Paul).

Williams, R. (1974), *Television Technology and Cultural Form* (London: Fontana).

Zimmerman, J. (1981), 'Technology and the Future of Women: Haven't we Met Somewhere Before?', *Women's Studies International Quarterly*, 4/3: 355.

3

Private Bodies,
Public Figures

3

Introduction to Part 3

THE FINAL PART OF the book returns to the public/private opposition that has been of interest to so many feminist critics. Each article in this topically diverse section has a thematic concern with the way women's bodies, which are ideologically represented as personal and private, can be sites on which wider, public meanings are contested. These meanings and ideologies that are 'written on the body' are, of course, not only ideologies about gender and sexual identity. The body is the primary site on which, and through which, 'racial' difference is constructed and made natural, and scholarship in this area has, of necessity, to recognize that bodies are never *just* gendered. This has not always been the case in feminist television scholarship. The articles in this section, then, articulate concerns about the control, reproduction, maintenance, and desire for female bodies within different configurations of power. These range from the US personal hygiene system to diplomatic exchanges between Australia and Malaysia. By collecting this group of articles together we are not suggesting that they necessarily deal with equivalent matters, but we are arguing that through each runs the representational trope of the woman's body which is made to stand for *something else*. Sometimes this something else is explicit—for example, a particular version of national identity clearly symbolized in the narrative by a specific female character. Sometimes, as is the case in the battle over reproductive politics, not only are women's bodies contested sites in terms of who—in national, class, and 'racial' terms—should be allowed to reproduce, and who should make these choices, but feminists themselves internationally have disagreed strongly. In calling the part 'Private Bodies, Public Figures', we propose that the woman's body, which has often been seen as a kind of baseline for feminist unity, is in fact always differently experienced and regulated through different dynamics of state, social, and cultural power. Some bodies, historically, are more private than others.

The section opens with an article that bridges the concerns of the preceding section, 'Audiences and Reception Contexts', with those of this third part. Purnima Mankekar's 'Television Tales and a Woman's Rage' is one of two published reports on her research project on the role television plays in constructing ideas about 'Indian Womanhood'—a project in which she worked with twenty-five families in New Delhi.[1] The first discussion of Doordarshan (the state-run Indian television station) in our collection involved an overview of the channel's output during the period of the study. Mankekar, in contrast, bases her research on interpretations of a particular scene in the 1990 television version of the *Mahabharata*, which, with the *Ramayama*, is one of the two Hindu 'sacred serials' recently shown on Indian television and internationally.[2] The scene on which Mankekar concentrates is that of the humiliating, public 'disrobing' of the central female character, Draupadi. Mankekar's study explores the extent to which Draupadi was interpreted symbolically by both production crew and viewers. She examines the ways women viewers both accepted Draupadi as a symbol of Indian womanhood and used her disrobing to reflect on their own lives. Although her study involved Hindu, Muslim, and Sikh families, in this essay Mankekar reports only on work with Hindu families. She is particularly concerned to trace the way in which Draupadi comes to symbolize not Hindu, but Indian womanhood, just as, she argues, the Indian nation-state is constructing itself as a Hindu state. Thus Mankekar's article offers an example of the very complex relations of gender and national identity that viewers mobilize in their responses to the humiliation of a female character in a widely viewed epic of origins.

The second article in this section addresses the woman's body in different ways but with many tacit implications for the notion of national identity. In 'Leading up to *Roe* v. *Wade*: Television Documentaries in the Abortion Debate', Julie D'Acci focuses on four US 'reality' programmes dealing with abortion in the 1960s and early 1970s. She argues that documentary television's imperative to produce 'balance', to offer competing sides of a controversial public issue, ended up establishing a binary pro/con territory for the abortion debates. In this binary, the complexities of the 'pro' side were effaced, and feminist voices (from both predominantly white and predominantly African American feminist groups) were completely muffled. She shows how the Supreme Court's decision decriminalizing abortion was ushered in amidst the discourses of the population control movement, a movement with a history rooted in racist, classist, and imperialist agendas—in controlling the bodies and reproductive freedoms of women of colour, poor women, and 'Third World' women. D'Acci is concerned to demonstrate television documentary's specific participation in this overall phenomenon.

In an article that keeps the focus on women's bodies, Kate Kane trains a critical eye on the ubiquitous television commercials for 'feminine hygiene' products. She takes on one of the taboo areas of US culture—female bodily secretions. Kane uses the anthropological research of Mary Douglas, which investigates the way different societies maintain boundaries between the 'pure' and the 'unclean', to suggest that US hygiene commercials are a set of contemporary secular pollution beliefs that regulate the female body. Kane argues that feminine hygiene commercials are part of, and contribute to, an 'ideology of freshness' which maintains the 'fresh' female body in the

---

1 See Purnima Mankekar, 'National Texts and Gendered Lives: An Ethnography of Television Viewers in a North Indian City', *American Ethnologist*, 20/3 (1993), 543–63.

2 Marie Gillespie, *Television, Ethnicity and Cultural Change* (London: Routledge, 1995), offers another ethnography of the viewing of these serials in Southall, West London.

deodorized home, while tying both into essential commodity consumption. She uses a distinction elaborated in the work of another anthropologist, Claude Lévi-Strauss, between the 'raw' and the 'cooked' to argue that the ideology of freshness demands the use of feminine hygiene products to transform raw (rotten) femaleness into fresh femininity. Kane develops these ideas in the detailed textual analysis of an advertisement for Carefree panty pads, showing the way in which the ideology of freshness is articulated through what she describes as a 'pseudo-feminist' discourse, thus taking us back to some of the concerns of authors in the first part of the book.

Tricia Rose, in 'Never Trust a Big Butt and a Smile', analyses the lyrics and music videos of female rap artists MC Lyte, Salt-N-Pepa, and Queen Latifa, and conducts interviews with the performers themselves. She conceives of rap music as a 'relatively safe free-play zone' where young African Americans can creatively address 'questions of sexual power, the reality of truncated economic opportunity, the pain of racism and sexism'. Rose takes great care to demonstrate how African American women rappers have understood the widespread fear of feminine sexuality, expressed their own sexuality openly, and challenged men to take them seriously by saying, 'we've got plenty of sexual power and integrity, but don't mess with us'. She furthermore challenges 'feminists'—specifically white feminists—to systematically re-evaluate how feminism is conceptualized and how ethnicity, class, and race fracture gender as a category.

Writing from Australia, Rosanne Kennedy returns us to a widely exported, liberal US series which has already been discussed in Part 1 by Judith Mayne. In 'The Gorgeous Lesbian in *L.A. Law*: The Present Absence?' Kennedy uses Australian source material—a feature in the magazine *Australian Cleo*—to explore the politics involving the representation of the programme's 'gorgeous' sexually 'flexible' character, CJ. She argues that *L.A. Law* became cult viewing for lesbian audiences because CJ is the most attractive female character on the show for women, whether they want to be like her, or just want her. However, she points out that CJ's sexuality is both a public issue in the show and strangely absent from it. CJ's lesbian relationship is used to air the issue of lesbian custody cases, but the relationship itself takes place behind doors much more firmly closed than those of the programme's heterosexual couples. Similarly, CJ can be used to signal the importance of HIV awareness for the sexually active; but her lesbian sex life never really gets past a kiss. Kennedy goes on to discuss the extent to which CJ can be seen as *queer*, thus exposing the hypocrisy of the programme's 'liberalism' by disturbing taken-for-granted binaries of difference like 'being lesbian' and 'being straight'. By introducing the idea of queerness (that queerness is something everyone finds pleasurable), Kennedy's article signals one of the directions from which new challenges to the second-wave feminism which dominates the history collected in this book have come in the 1990s.[3]

3 See Alexander Doty, *Making Things Perfectly Queer* (Minneapolis: Univ. of Minnesota Press, 1993); Mandy Merck, *Perversions: Deviant Readings* (New York: Routledge, 1993); Larry Gross, 'Out of the Mainstream: Sexual Minorities and the Mass Media', in Ellen Seiter *et al.* (eds.), *Remote Control: Televisions, Audiences, and Cultural Power* (New York: Routledge, 1989), 130–49; Diane Hamer and Belinda Budge, *The Good, the Bad and the Gorgeous: Popular Culture's Romance with Lesbianism* (London: Pandora, 1994); Victoria Johnson, 'The Politics of Morphing: Michael Jackson as Science Fiction Border Text', *Velvet Light Trap*, 32 (1993), 58–65.

In 'Reproducing Reality: Murphy Brown and Illegitimate Politics', Rebecca L. Walkowitz exposes yet another threatening female body as she confronts the brouhaha surrounding the 'real-life' US Vice-President Dan Quayle and the 'fictional' Murphy Brown. The single woman television character, according to Quayle, promoted the 'poverty of values' in the United States by having a child 'out of wedlock'. Walkowitz details how the entire phenomenon centred around the blurring of boundaries—representation/ reality, fiction/news, popular culture/politics, and especially real/bogus journalism and real/beyond-the-pale Americans. She uncovers the conservative moral premises undergirding both 'real' journalism and 'real' Americans and demonstrates how both are challenged and undermined by female sexuality and reproduction.

In 'Representation Wars: Malaysia, *Embassy*, and Australia's *Corps Diplomatique*', Suvendrini Perera discusses the complexity of representations—and especially the representations of women—in a neo- or post-colonial world. Opening with an account of how representation was legitimized as an item of formal diplomatic concern by the prime ministers of Malaysia and Australia in 1991, she goes on to examine the representation of Malaysia (the fictional Ragaan) and its relationship to the Australian diplomatic corps on the Australian television programme *Embassy*. She argues that such representations must be analysed from the point of view of their reception by 'ethnic' spectators, and offers her own (Sri Lankan) viewing of an episode as an example. Perera shows how the stereotyped figure of the Asian woman in the programme produces two constructions of cultural difference—an accommodation or incorporation of difference on the one hand, and a frantic, hysterical, untranslatable, ethnic excess on the other. She goes on to show that in addition to analysing how neo-colonial imperialist powers generate discourses of 'orientalism' (such as those produced on *Embassy*), we must also attend to the ways post-colonial states and subjects have been shaped (de-formed) by histories of these same discourses and may themselves continue to participate in them. She thus concludes by analysing the representation of 'oriental femininity' in a Malaysian government trade publication that seeks to attract world-wide industries by invoking 'the manual dexterity of the oriental female'. Perera makes this move in order to foreground the complexities involved in the redeployment of orientalist discourse by those previously colonized, and to insist on the need for carefully examining 'local stories and local conditions and . . . how these intersect and are intersected by global discourses'.

Taken together, these essays begin to expose the ways the female body becomes a narrative vehicle for a set of social, political, and national problems—the ways 'woman' becomes a trope for something else and is made to signify things that have nothing to do with 'femininity'. Their arguments make crushingly clear the myriad ways that women's bodies are made to bear the burdens of the whole body politic.

17

Television Tales and a Woman's Rage: A Nationalist Recasting of Draupadi's 'Disrobing'

Purnima Mankekar

THE *MAHABHARATA* IS an 'ancient tale' told anew by Indian television.[1] Like all tales, its meanings acquire new valence with every telling. The readings I am about to present derive from the unfolding and reception of this megadramatization, enabled by the contemporary Indian nation-state both discursively and technologically. The scene under discussion here is the story of the public disrobing (*vastraharan*) of one of the epic's most important female characters, Draupadi, the wife of the five Pandava brothers.

Discourses of nation, sexuality, and gender overlap in the divergent readings of the televisual experience provided by women viewers who watched the *Mahabharata*, which was serialized on state-owned television over the course of the ninety-three weeks from September 1988 to July 1990. The divergent interpretations of the drama drawn from Hindu, lower middle-class, and working-class women, and the producers of the televised epic, reconstitute Draupadi as a symbol of 'Indian Womanhood'.

The creators of the televised *Mahabharata* saw Draupadi as an index of the position of 'woman' in Indian society and, more foundationally, as a marker of (Hindu) Indian 'civilization'. For both the producers of Draupadi's disrobing as well as its female viewers, Draupadi also embodied woman's rage, in particular, the rage of a woman wronged. An analysis of Draupadi-as-sign reveals how this aspect of her personality has been appropriated in nationalist ideologies and practices both during the period of anti-colonial struggles,

Originally published in *Public Culture*, 5/3 (1993), 469–92.

1 This paper is a part of a larger project on the role of television in the construction of discourses of 'Indian Womanhood'. On the basis of twenty months of fieldwork with twenty-five lower middle-class and upwardly mobile working-class families living in multi-ethnic neighbourhoods in New Delhi, I have explored the production and interpretation of ideologies of gender and nationhood. About three-quarters of the families I worked with were Hindus; the remainder were equally divided among Muslims and Sikhs. However, because my purpose is to foreground slippages and ruptures within majority discourses rather than to engage in sociological comparisons of the interpretations of viewers of different religions, this article focuses on the responses of Hindu women.

and, with different referents, in the present post-colonial conjuncture.[2] We will see how both the producers and Hindu viewers of Draupadi's disrobing are interpellated by discourses of nationhood; how, in their retelling of the tale, Draupadi comes to embody the reconfiguration of discourses not just of Hindu womanhood, but of Indian Womanhood, thereby conflating and equating 'Hindu' with the 'nation'.

Viewers, especially women, also perceived Draupadi as an icon of women's vulnerability.[3] The imaginative connections viewers made between themselves and Draupadi, between her experiences and theirs, show that she was *more than* just a symbol of Indian Womanhood. While producers' and viewers' perceptions overlapped in their construction of Draupadi as a palimpsest for ideologies of gender and nationhood, the lack of closure in these interpretations is inescapable. While women viewers accepted Draupadi as a symbol of Indian Womanhood, they used her disrobing to critique their own lives, and to theorize gender relations in the worlds they inhabited. Such appropriations disrupted the reading of Hindu womanhood as Indian Womanhood and provided a moment of rupture in which their affective interaction with what they watched opened spaces and possibilities for social critique. The coexistence of these multiple interpretations thus illustrates the manner in which viewers sometimes *appropriate* hegemonic discourses to critique existing systems of power.

Some of the early theorizations of mass media, such as that of Laura Mulvey (1975) and Tania Modleski (1979, 1983), analysed the ways in which film and television texts created spectator positions. But, drawing from structuralism and Lacanian semiotics, these theorists neglected the ways in which film and television programmes could be interpreted by heterogeneous audiences. Reception theory interrogated and extended these perspectives by situating texts in broader ideological frameworks and by anticipating the ways in which their meanings could be interpreted. Again, however, the focus remained on the limitations and possibilities contained within *texts* rather than on the active engagement of *viewers*.[4] By foregrounding the spectator's role in the production of meanings, I diverge from textualist analyses of mass media: I have focused on the manner in which viewers, living in specific socio-cultural contexts, actively interpret cultural texts. By locating these interpretations in viewers' daily lives and practices, I will show how

---

2 For a detailed explication of the genealogical method see Foucault (1982).

3 For an elegant and remarkably lucid explication of the indexicality and iconicity of signs, see Daniel (1984).

4 In the late 1970s, this approach, loosely termed 'Screen Theory', was questioned by several critics who challenged the manner in which subject positions created by film and television texts were conflated with those assumed by historical and social subjects. An extensive discussion of some of these debates is provided in the introduction to my dissertation, 'Television and the Reconstitution of Indian Womanhood: An Ethnography of Viewers in a North Indian City' (in progress) and in an abridged form in Mankekar (n.d.). See also Mulvey (1981), Penley's review essay on feminist film theory (1988), and Kaplan's (1987) excellent discussion of feminist critiques of television. Reception theory extended the premises of 'Screen Theory' by situating film and television texts in particular sociohistorical conjunctures (see Jeffords (1989) and Taylor (1989) for brilliant examples of such work). However, apart from Morley's (1980) pioneering study of families watching 'Nationwide' television, Bobo (1988), Seiter *et al.* (1989), and Ang's work with Dutch viewers of *Dallas* (1991), there are relatively few analyses of how viewers actively interpret what they watch. Some of the political implications of ignoring the ways in which viewers engage with television and film texts are forcefully argued by Gledhill (1988).

ethnographically investigating viewers' active engagement with television's tales enables us to construct a more nuanced understanding of popular narratives. My objective, therefore, is to theorize popular culture as a contested space in which subjectivities are constituted.

Televised Epics and the Politics of Nationalism

The serialization of the *Mahabharata* followed and overlapped the televising of another Hindu epic, the *Ramayana*. This period was marked by Hindu revivalist activities, the escalation of tension between Hindus on the one hand, and Sikhs and Muslims on the other, and finally, the 'ethnicization' of nationalism with the consolidation of what is now commonly referred to as Hindu nationalism. Television's version of the *Ramayana* was unequivocal in its attempt to depict the 'glorious Hindu past' often invoked by Hindu revivalists, and journalists and scholars have frequently pointed to the ways in which it may have, in part, facilitated the growth of Hindu nationalism (Philipose, 1990; Thapar, 1990). In serving to promote a Hindu consciousness nationwide, the mounting of the *Ramayana* as a televisual extravaganza is the most recent variant on a historical theme: the *Ramayana* has long served as an ideological vehicle for articulating a theocratic polity in which 'outsiders' are marginalized, even demonized. As a template for a sacral politics, it stages a dichotomized vision of us and them, and by extension, 'us' (Hindus) and 'them' (Muslims).

Though the *Mahabharata* did not historically foreground the *Ramayana*'s ideological vision of a homogeneous polity that resists difference, it is this communalized interpretative context that we must hold in view as we examine women's reception of the *Mahabharata* with its more nuanced messages. Thus, though the televisation of the *Mahabharata* is likely to have reinforced prevailing currents of Hindu chauvinism, it was also possible for it to be 'heard' by a more inclusive audience. The Hindu, Muslim, and Sikh viewers I worked with engaged with the *Mahabharata* in more complex ways than they did with the *Ramayana*. While many felt that watching the *Ramayana* was comparable to participating in a Hindu ritual, the tales of blood and gore, romance and family politics, conspiracy and deception contained in the *Mahabharata* made for a multitextual viewing experience (Bipan Chandra, 1991; R.G.K. 1990; Padgaonkar, 1990; Dethe and Sharma, 1990; Sherif, 1991).[5] Although the Muslim and Sikh viewers I interviewed saw it as a Hindu epic (rather than an Indian one), they felt it was less of a transgression, less intrusive than the *Ramayana*.[6] Muslim and Sikh women, along with their Hindu counterparts, were moved by Draupadi's disrobing:

5 One viewer compared the *Mahabharata* with the *Ramayana* in the following manner: 'The *Ramayana* story is straight, like a palm tree. The *Mahabharat* [sic] story is like a banyan tree with spreading stems full of rich sub-plots and vivid characters' (quoted in Kala, 1990). Significantly, some Hindu right-wing commentators were upset that Lord Krishna was portrayed as Machiavellian and felt that television's *Mahabharata* presented a 'distorted' picture of Hinduism. The controversy spilled into op-ed pages and letters to the editor in several national dailies. See e.g. an essay written by Damodar Agrawal (1990), and the response it elicited from Khair and Nath (1990) and from several readers who participated in these debates in their letters to the newspapers (e.g. Parthasarathy, 1990; Kumar, 1990; Hoskote, 1990).

6 For reports on the popularity of the *Mahabharata* with Muslim viewers in india and Pakistan, see Dethe and Sharma (1990) and Das (1990).

temporarily abstracting this episode from the rest of the televisual drama, they saw it as yet another gripping tale of the oppressions (*zulm*) perpetrated on women. A moment of suture was created when Draupadi stares into the camera to confront audiences, and to question a husband's right to 'do what he wants with his wife'. This moment moved the Muslim and Sikh women I worked with to see in Draupadi's disrobing a reflection of their own vulnerabilities as women living in a 'man's world'.

In insisting upon the fundamentally 'incomplete' nature of hegemonic discourses underscored by moments of rupture, I have another objective driven by my concern to position myself as a feminist critic of the Indian nation-state.[7] I hope to create possibilities for a counter-hegemonic space that can potentially subvert majority discourses. Thus, although I interviewed viewers from different religious communities, in this chapter I have chosen to strategically highlight the slippages and ruptures in the interpretations of Hindu women. In these troubled times when the Indian nation-state is becoming increasingly fascist, and when religious identities are being forged through violence and bloodshed, I believe that those of us committed to feminist and secularist praxis need to foreground and consolidate our critiques precisely on such moments of rupture.

Draupadi's Disrobing

The *Mahabharata* was produced for state-run Indian television by one of the most successful film-makers of the Bombay film industry, B. R. Chopra. One of the reasons the *Mahabharata* held the attention of viewers from different communities and drew ratings unsurpassed in Indian television history was its deployment of a combination of techniques to narrate the story for an audio-visual medium.[8] My objective in this section, then, is not merely to describe the sequence of events surrounding Draupadi's disrobing but to call attention to some of the techniques used in television's rendition of the story. Like many other serials shown on Indian television these techniques ranged from the modes of address and performative traditions of Hindi film melodrama, the use of background music and song, the narrative rhythms of US soap operas, and the iconography of popular calendar art.[9]

The core narrative of television's version of the *Mahabharata* focused on the relations between two branches of the Kuru dynasty: the five Pandava brothers, their wife Draupadi, and their mother on the one hand, and the Kaurava clan, consisting of the blind King Dhritarashtra and his family on the other. The main story to this point has been King Dhritarashtra's son Duryodhana's attempts to destroy the Pandavas. The disrobing of Draupadi, in the presence of her five husbands, her in-laws, and the Kaurava court forms a turning-point in the narrative.

---

7 See Williams (1977) for an important discussion of the intrinsically incomplete nature of hegemony.

8 See Thomas (1985) for an excellent analysis of the importance of the 'balanced' formula (the *masala*) required for the success of popular Hindi films.

9 The most cursory study of Indian popular culture reveals an old history of the dependence of mass entertainment on mythological material. The phenomenal success of mythological material on television should thus come as no surprise. What needs to be explored, however, are the political implications of the depiction of religious epics on state-controlled television.

Like all episodes, this one begins with an introduction by a commentator (*sutradhaar*), in this case Kaal, who is none other than Time himself. In a booming, if disembodied, voice Kaal announces that this episode is about 'appropriate conduct' (*maryada*). In a flashback from a previous episode we see Yudhishtra, the eldest Pandava brother, gambling with Duryodhana in the presence of King Dhritarashtra and the Kaurava elders. Through visual metaphors drawn from popular iconography, the Pandava brothers are resplendent in white, the colour of purity; Duryodhana's wicked uncle Shakuni, the instigator of all evil, wears black and red, the colours of anger and envy.

After losing his kingdom and his wealth, Yudhishtra gambles and loses each of his brothers. The drama inherent in this situation is heightened by melodramatic conventions borrowed from Hindi film (e.g. the use of close-ups and loud music) and histrionic traditions typical of some forms of North Indian folk theatre (such as the stylized, exaggeratedly raucous laughter of 'villains', in this case Duryodhana and his cronies).

When Yudhishtra tries to stop the game by saying that he has lost everything, Duryodhana's friend Karna suggests that he stake his wife Draupadi. Yudhishtra's brothers (who all 'share' Draupadi in a polyandrous marriage) look on in horror and despair. Duryodhana taunts Yudhishtra into staking Draupadi. Yudhishtra loses her, to the loud, derisive laughter of his opponents. Duryodhana then sends a sentry to bring Draupadi to the gaming house. Draupadi is in seclusion because she is menstruating. She sends the sentry back to the court with a question for Yudhishtra: Did he stake her before or after he lost himself? Duryodhana is furious when the sentry returns without Draupadi. He commands: 'Tell that woman with five husbands to come here immediately!' Draupadi, rendered nameless, becomes the 'woman with five husbands', a woman of deviant sexuality. Draupadi once again refuses to accompany the sentry; this time she says she will come only at the behest of her elders. Duryodhana is further enraged by her defiance. He now asks his younger brother Dushasana to bring 'that woman with five husbands' to the court. Dushasana grasps her hair and starts to drag her to the court.

After giving us an aerial view of Draupadi being dragged down the steps of the court, the camera swings to provide us with close-ups of the men: the leering faces of Duryodhana and his accomplices, the impotent fury of her husbands who sit with their heads bowed, their backs to her as she is dragged in, and the distress and shock of the Kaurava elders.

Draupadi manages to break away from Dushasana's clutches, and she runs toward the kind. The camera follows her gaze to the faces of her elders who bow their heads in shame. Relentless, she tells them that they are responsible for this *adharma* (in this context, 'misconduct') because they did not prevent it from occurring. 'Is a wife her husband's property?' she demands, 'Is she an object that can be gambled? And if she is, what right did Yudhishtra have to stake me once he lost all he owned?'

The Kaurava elder Bheeshma replies that, although it was 'improper' for Yudhishtra to use Draupadi as a stake, 'the fact is that a man has the right to do what he wants with his wife'. Draupadi whirls around to confront Bheeshma. So doing, she stares directly into the camera and addresses the audience, thus creating a moment of suture with viewers. 'How is this "right" to be interpreted?' she demands, 'What are its limits? Isn't it a man's fore-most duty to protect his wife?'

But instead of Bheeshma it is Duryodhana's friend Karna who responds, saying that, since none of her five husbands could protect her, she should sit on Duryodhana's lap. Speechless, Draupadi snarls at him in rage. Karna continues: 'You are already the wife of five husbands. She what harm is there in holding the hand of a sixth? A woman who lives with five husbands is not a wife but a whore. What honour can a whore have? If Draupadi had been brought here naked, it would not have been inappropriate.' In a manner reminiscent of Hindi film villains, Duryodhana sneers: 'My friend is telling the truth. What is honour or dishonour for a whore?' He asks Dushasana to disrobe her so he can see what the woman he has won 'looks like'.

Dushasana lunges toward her and pulls at her sari. The camera lingers voyeuristically on her trembling, perspiring body. She struggles, then pauses with her sari between her teeth and, with her hands folded, starts to pray to Lord Krishna. Dushasana, to the loud contemptuous laughter of Duryodhana and his supporters, continues to pull her sari. But the sounds of their laughter are soon drowned by background music consisting of the ringing of temple bells and the blowing of conches.[10] Lord Krishna has intervened: we see his face in the upper-left corner of the frame. He smiles down at Draupadi beatifically, reassuringly; saris begin to flow from his palm, which he raises in blessing. As Dushasana pulls off one sari another drapes Draupadi's body. All we hear for a while is Draupadi's voice praying to Krishna and the music of temple bells, conches, and drums (*tablas*). The conches begin to sound increasingly martial and the beat of the drums picks up. These are the sounds of war. The disrobing of Draupadi has started a chain of events that can only culminate in war, the war of Kurukshetra that her men will fight to avenge the dishonour done to them.

The camera swings rhythmically between the figure of Draupadi, her perspiring body the battlefield for forces of good (*dharma*, represented by the righteousness of Krishna) and evil (*adharma*, signified by the envy and lust of Duryodhana and his accomplices), and the faces of the men as they realize that Draupadi cannot be disrobed. We are provided with close-ups of their faces and we see their expressions change: Duryodhana's, Dushasana's, and Karna's from lust and glee to incomprehension; the Pandava brothers' from pain and defeat to relief; the Kaurava elders' from helplessness and frustration to awe, the recognition that they are in the presence of a supernatural force. Suddenly the music turns upbeat. The drums, temple bells, and conches reach a crescendo: they are still martial but now express the music of victor. And above all these sounds, we hear the strains of a flute, perhaps that of Lord Krishna.[11]

Exhausted from his efforts to strip Draupadi, Dushasana falls to the floor. Draupadi also collapses, and the background music comes to a halt. The ensuing silence is shattered by her husband Bhima's vow that he will not rest until he has drunk Dushasana's blood in the battlefield. Draupadi then

---

10 To many Hindus in the audience the blowing of conches will signify both the beginning of prayers (*pooja*) as well as the commencement of war (Krishna's *panchjanya*).

11 In devotional literature and popular iconography Lord Krishna is often depicted playing a flute.

stands to face the court again. We are made fully aware of her power as we see her standing before the men, her tense body upright and trembling with fury, her waist-length hair loose and dishevelled, her eyes blazing—perhaps to some in the audience the image will be reminiscent of that of Goddess Kali, the incarnation of woman's rage.

And as she begins to put a curse on the 'shameless and cowardly' assembly she is interrupted mid-sentence by Gandhari, Duryodhana's mother, who pleads with her to stop. The episode ends with a freeze shot of Gandhari begging Draupadi to stop, a 'cliff-hanger' typical of soap opera (will Gandhari succeed in preventing Draupadi from cursing her men?). We hear the strains of a song informing us that 'he who insults womankind | will be destroyed by god'. In the following episode Draupadi tells her husbands that she will leave her hair loose until she has washed it with the blood of Duryodhana and Dushasana that they bring for her from the battlefield.

A Nationalist Recasting of Draupadi's Disrobing

In what follows I show how interpretations of Draupadi's disrobing at once overlap and diverge. In investigating the emergence of Draupadi as a palimpsest for discourses on Indian womanhood, I foreground the ways in which hegemonic ideologies, in this case those pertaining to gender and nationhood, mediate the processes by which viewers negotiate, appropriate, and sometimes reject subject positions created by cultural texts.

■ The Interpretations of the *Mahabharata* Crew

My purpose here is not to privilege 'authorial intention' but to illuminate the discursive framework within which Draupadi's disrobing was conceived. When I arrived at director Chopra's studio in Bombay, also present were researcher Satish Bhatnagar and scriptwriter Rahi Masoom Raza, a Muslim and a former member of the Communist Party of India. While their individual interpretations of the disrobing varied, they seemed to agree that Draupadi indexed the position of 'Woman' in Indian society and hence the degree to which Indian society is 'civilized'. Further, while they believed that Draupadi's rage reflects the power of Woman, they were unequivocal in their insistence that this power must be contained in the interests of the integrity of the family and, more importantly, the unity of the nation.

■ The Disrobing as Index

When Draupadi questions her husband's right to use her as a stake in his game of dice, she claims that these questions are being asked not merely by her but by all Indian women and describes herself as a representative of all of Indian womanhood. It hence came as no surprise to me that for Chopra, Raza, and their colleagues Draupadi's disrobing showed that the status of women is the most revealing index of how 'enlightened' a particular society is. He and his colleagues agreed that 'Woman's position' is a marker of 'civilization and culture'. But, they pointed out, instead of being respected as 'mother earth', Draupadi is humiliated. Her disrobing thus indexes what Chopra described as 'the extent to which the rot has seeped into her society'.

Indeed, he and his colleagues conceived of Draupadi not just as an index of the 'state of Indian society' but, more fundamentally, of ideal-typical

Indian Womanhood. For instead of critically analysing gender relations in particular historical conjunctures, by speaking of 'Woman' as 'mother earth' and as the 'focal point of evolution' Chopra and his colleagues conceived of Indian Womanhood in essentialist categories. For Raza, Woman had to be conceived of in terms of power (*shakti*), as 'mother earth', as the 'focal point of evolution': only then can we give 'due respect' to her. Further, Woman was also fire (*agni*) and energy. The specific location of Draupadi, or indeed that of the multitude of Indian women in particular socio-historical contexts, was thus displaced by an ahistorical discourse on Draupadi as an index of the position of 'Woman' in not just 'Hindu culture' but 'Indian culture'.

■ **'Woman's Power' and the Unity of the Nation**

But in the discourse of Chopra and his colleagues, although Draupadi is vulnerable, her anger, her refusal to be passive, reveals the fire in her. She is the personification of power and energy. However, the creators of the disrobing episode insisted that Woman's power must be contained within the parameters of family and nation. They had no doubts that, notwithstanding her creative potential, Woman's place is with (and in) her family.[12] More significantly, Chopra and Raza made explicit connections between the family and the nation by insisting that the family is the 'corner-stone' of a 'civilized' society and, above all, of a strong nation. This crucial link between the unity of the family and the unity of the nation was particularly clear when Raza claimed that the *Mahabharata* 'is about how the family is rooted in society. How the rot in the family spreads to the society to the country to the political system.'

Internecine conflict in the family is reflective of, analogous to, and symptomatic of internecine conflict in the nation. For Chopra and Raza, the 'contemporary relevance' of the *Mahabharata* lay precisely in the fact that it revealed the importance of the unity of the family to the integrity of the nation. Further, according to Chopra, one of the 'perpetual truths inherent in the epic', what made the *Mahabharata* particularly pertinent to contemporary times, was that it spoke so forcefully about the importance of national integration, that it emphasized that the unity and integrity of the nation must always be protected.

This point came up several times in our discussion but was most overt when I asked them why their *Mahabharata* ended earlier than other versions. Unlike other renditions that describe the aftermath of the war of Kurukshetra, Chopra's *Mahabharata* ended with the death of Bheeshma, the venerable Kaurava elder, on the battlefield. In this version, Bheeshma gives a long speech on patriotism, the importance of fighting against the division of one's country (significantly, the term Bheeshma used was *vibhajan*, a Hindi word for the partition of the subcontinent into India and Pakistan). Watching this scene in the context of the separatist movements threatening the unity of the Indian nation, I had found this speech particularly significant. When I first brought it up, Chopra claimed that they ended their serial at that point because they had conceived of Bheeshma as the hero of their

---

12 These interpretations are particularly significant in the presence of feminist interpretations of the *Mahabharata* and, in particular, of Draupadi. See e.g. Irawati Karve's depiction of Draupadi in *Yuganta* (1974).

story and felt that, as far as they were concerned, the climax of the story came with his death. But the political undertones of Bheeshma's speech had been to plain to me that I pursued my line of questioning. Raza responded that the last scene did indeed have 'contemporary relevance' because it was about how the country must never be divided: the *Mahabharata*, he said, showed how attempts to divide the kingdom led to destruction on a massive scale in the battle of Kurukshetra.

The primacy they gave to national integration and their views on women's location in the nation were even more forcefully evident in their description of Draupadi's desire for vengeance. According to Chopra, when Draupadi complains to Lord Krishna he first listens to her sympathetically. But when she persists in venting her anger, he 'snubs Draupadi: "What is this all the time, with your hair loose. Your personal hurt cannot engulf the political divide. The state is more important than your personal hurt. Your personal problems should not be allowed to overshadow the national problem." '

This then is the discursive framework in which Draupadi's disrobing was conceived. On the one hand, Draupadi indexes the place of Woman in not just Hindu society but in Indian society: at the same time that she is vulnerable, she also represents the creative power, resilience, fire, and energy of Indian Womanhood. Articulated at a historical moment when the Indian nation-state is becoming increasingly fascist, their insistence that Draupadi's rage though justified must be contained and that the family and, more importantly, the nation must remain unscathed and 'supreme' is particularly significant.

■ **Viewers'**
Interpretations
The Hindu women I describe below belong to working-class and lower middle-class households and live in multi-ethnic neighbourhoods in New Delhi. The confluence of ideologies of gender and sexuality, viewers' precarious class positions, and their locations in the politics of their families account for some of the differences between their responses and those of the producers. Here I focus on women viewers because they, more than men, seemed profoundly moved by the disrobing and could narrate the episode and their responses to it in vivid detail and with astonishing emotional intensity for months after its telecast. The disrobing frequently surfaced in conversations not just about television but also about their experiences as women. In fact, I found that Draupadi's disrobing enabled these viewers to confront and critique their own positions in their family, community, and class.

While the producers had claimed that the climax of their story was the death of the Kaurava elder Bheeshma, women viewers unequivocally believed that the disrobing was the climax. Even as their responses were embedded in their own life narratives, some common themes emerged in their interpretations of what they watched. For all the women that I spoke with, Draupadi was an icon of women's vulnerability; for many of them she evoked the power of women's rage; and for some, intimate engagement with Draupadi's disrobing enabled them to rupture hegemonic constructions of Indian Womanhood.

Threats to their physical safety in the public spaces of New Delhi; sexual harassment at work; economic, sexual, and emotional exploitation in the family: these were the realities the women I describe here strived to cope with. Watching Draupadi's disrobing compelled them to confront and theorize their emotional, financial, and sexual vulnerabilities. The disrobing episode seemed to affect young, unmarried women particularly profoundly. What struck them with great intensity was the fact that Draupadi was disrobed by her brother-in-law, at the behest of her husband's kinsmen, in her in-laws' court, in front of the elders of her clan, in front of her husbands.

Sushmita Dasgupta was in her early thirties when I first met her. Sushmita worked as a junior clerk in the Education Ministry. She lived with her large family (consisting of her parents, her elder brother, his wife and little daughter, her younger brother, and her two younger sisters) in a one-room, eight-by-ten-feet flat. She and her father were the primary breadwinners. But her father was about to retire. And Sushmita seemed to be the financial and emotional mainstay of her family, a fact that often overwhelmed her. She frequently spoke to me of her loneliness. Her cousin once told me that Sushmita desperately wanted to get married, to escape the claustrophobia of her family and start a life of her own. But her father and elder brother had become so dependent on her salary that every time a proposal came for her marriage, they would find an excuse to turn it down. This, along with persistent financial anxiety, resulted in considerable tension in the family. For the most part, Sushmita appeared to take her family politics in her stride. But every now and then she would slip into a depression that would last for weeks, sometimes months.

Sushmita, apprehensive about whether her father would ever allow her to get married, terrified that she would be mistreated if she entered her in-laws' home without a dowry, told me on two different occasions that what shocked her most was the failure of Draupadi's elders to protect their daughter-in-law. But I didn't realize how deeply shaken Sushmita had been by the disrobing until her mother described her response to me: 'My daughter, when she saw [what happened], cried and cried. She cried all morning. Imagine what happened to Draupadi! And in public, in front of her in-laws! A feeling came to my daughter: what will happen to me when I get married and go to my in-laws' home?'

Evidently, Sushmita intimately identified with Draupadi. She saw in the disrobing her own vulnerability. For not only did she feel isolated in her parents' house, she was also extremely anxious about what would happen if she ever did get married. She was acutely conscious of the fact that her precariously lower middle-class family did not have the resources for a dowry. How would she protect herself if her in-laws humiliated her for not bringing a dowry? All her insecurities and fears surfaced when she saw Draupadi's disrobing: her precarious class position and her tenuous location in the politics of her family inflected her response to it.

Indeed, the vulnerability of women was discussed by every single woman that I interviewed on Draupadi's disrobing: this happened without exception, across classes, across generations, across communities. Draupadi embodied what seemed to be a crucial aspect of their understanding of what it meant to be a woman, an Indian woman, living in a man's world. Take, for

instance, the following exchange between Uma and her mother Jayanthi
Chandran:

JAYANTHI: Draupadi, [in] that scene in which her hair was pulled,
               showed that things have been this way since the olden times.
               Now of course it's this way anyway. But this shows how a man
               shows his 'manpower'. It's been going on since then.

UMA: I didn't realize that this is not a new thing. You suddenly real-
               ize that in every situation it's the same thing that's happen-
               ing—a man has the power to put a woman down simply
               because he has physical superiority. It's we that get stuck in
               the 'hot water', nothing happens to him.

JAYANTHI: No matter how many associations or institutions you have for
               women, there is nothing you can do about this. [*pointing to
               Uma*] . . . see how much I have educated her? I've sent her to a
               coeducational school. Still, if she's a little late, I worry about
               her. It's natural, it comes from within [to worry].

I agreed with her and described how, when I was a student in India, my
mother would wait for me at our gate every time I was a little late coming
home from Delhi University. Jayanthi Chandran added that, if Uma had
been a boy, she would not have worried as much. She said: 'That's the basic
difference, the natural thing, it can never change, no matter how many
women's organizations you might have.' Returning to Draupadi's disrobing,
she added, 'If you ever have to really insult a woman, this is what you'll do.'
This, according to her, was the worst thing a man could do to a woman.
When I asked if similar things still happened to women, Uma replied: 'It
won't be as dramatic that someone pulls a woman by the hair. But they'll find
a thousand and one things. Like in buses, they'll pinch you, they'll treat you
as if you have no dignity at all. You're just there as their plaything.'

JAYANTHI: Inside all of us, there is a shard of fear. You can't see it, you
               can't explain it.

UMA: This is very true. It's like a reflex action. Like if someone stares
               at you for a long time.

Most of the women I spoke with were convinced that their vulnerability
stemmed from their sexuality. Many young women told me that when they
watched Draupadi's disrobing they learned, to their surprise, that women
have been the target of sexual violence since the days of the epics (as Uma put
it: 'I didn't realize that this is not a new thing.'). For Uma and her mother,
and for many other women that I spoke with, women's sexual vulnerability
is what distinguishes girls from boys, women from men: this is a fact that all
the women's organizations in the world cannot erase, the source of the fear
that resides 'inside all of us'.

Although I do not for a moment wish to imply that the home is a haven of
protection, where women are safe from predatory males, this exchange needs
to be considered in light of New Delhi's legendary hostility to women.
For example, taking public transportation in New Delhi has always
been extremely humiliating for women (myself included) who have to constantly deal with men trying to push, paw, and pinch them. I have seen (and

experienced) the way in which the memory of previous brushes with the sexual aggression of strangers is inscribed on women's bodies as they sit hunched in buses, their arms wrapped tightly across their breasts; the warning flashed in a mother's glance when her daughter's *chunni*, the scarf covering the upper body, accidentally slips off her shoulders; the knot that forms in the pit of one's stomach when, in Uma's words, a strange man 'stares at you for a long time'. These and other experiences reinforce women's sense of insecurity as they go about their daily lives.

■ **Draupadi and Women's Rage**

But if Draupadi served as an icon of women's vulnerability, her figure also evoked the power of women's rage. When Sushmita described Draupadi's rage, her voice became shrill with emotion: 'After what happened with her, any girl would become that angry. The way she was insulted! In front of a court full of men! It is not an ordinary thing to tolerate that kind of insult. If any woman gets that angry, she can burn to ashes!'

When I asked her to explain what she meant, she replied: 'The anger and grief in her mind will turn her to ashes.'

I next wanted to know if she felt that Draupadi had been depicted in a 'strong light'. Sushmita replied, 'Yes. She showed that a woman has power too ... we have Mother Kali. We see that even a mother won't tolerate sin. She too will kill the culprit.'

I then asked her if she thought that Draupadi was like the Goddess Kali. She replied: 'Draupadi was a woman. She wasn't a goddess. That is why she needed her husbands' help. Mother Kali is a goddess, she can come in any form. . . . [When I saw Draupadi] I thought, women are so weak.'

'I thought, women are so weak.' Time and again I heard these words from women as they discussed Draupadi's disrobing. But although her plight made them relive their humiliation at the hands of men, many of them also felt that the rage of a woman who has been wronged can be all-consuming. Yet, although 'a woman has power too', she is *not* as powerful as a goddess. Sushmita eloquently pointed to the difference between goddesses and lesser mortals, between idealizations of 'Woman's power' in Hindu revivalism and the vulnerability of women like her. A goddess can, in her wrath, destroy the world. But women must keep their rage on a leash. Hence, even though in Hindu mythology women's anger has a legitimate place in restoring moral order, the rage of ordinary women, however righteous, must be contained. It cannot be permitted to overflow and threaten the family or, as we will see shortly, the nation.

Discourses about women's rage surfaced most vividly when Draupadi was compared with one of the ideals of Hindu womanhood, Sita of the *Ramayana*, the other Hindu epic telecast on Indian television. Draupadi has never been considered a role model for Hindu women in the same way as Sita or Savitri. In fact, all the viewers I spoke with *contrasted* Draupadi with Sita. As Sushmita pointed out, 'Draupadi did not hesitate to take revenge'; unlike Sita she 'didn't bow her head'. But most women were also ambivalent about the power of women's rage. For instance, although Draupadi iconicized the traits she associated with contemporary Indian Womanhood, Sushmita admired Sita's humility (as opposed to Draupadi's fire) and Sita's respect for her elders (unlike Draupadi, who did not flinch at challenging her in-laws, thus transgressing her role as a daughter-in-law). If Sita represented an ideal model of Hindu womanhood, Draupadi mirrored the reality of contemporary Indian Womanhood. Sushmita told me that her mother claimed that tolerance, rather than anger, was a source of strength for women. But she felt confused as to how far she could rebel against the injustice meted out to her by her family: 'For us, we can't tell what path we should take. Should we tolerate or not?' Should she aspire to Sita's tolerance rather than Draupadi's rage? What is the appropriate conduct for her as a woman, as a modern Indian woman? If Sushmita considered Draupadi a more appropriate symbol of Indian Womanhood perhaps it was because her own life experience as a contemporary woman led her to feel that, far from empowering women, tolerance made them weak. More important, implicit in her dilemma was an ambivalence toward the valorization of Hindu womanhood exemplified in the idealization of Sita and emphasized in the discourses of Hindu revivalists.

Despite their ambivalence toward the different models of womanhood represented by Sita and Draupadi, respectively, several women seemed to believe that 'tolerance' (*sahansheelta*) was not just unique but fundamental to Indian womanhood. Poonam Sharma and her mother Shakuntala differed in their conceptions of the appropriate behaviour for Indian women: once again, these differences surfaced in their discussion of Draupadi's disrobing. Once, when Poonam expressed her outrage at what happened to Draupadi, Shakuntala turned to me and said that she was terribly worried that Poonam was 'too sharp-tongued'. Poonam's views on dowry terrified her even more: she frequently told her parents that she would refuse to marry anybody who asked for a dowry. And if her in-laws harassed her for a dowry after the wedding she would defy all social conventions and leave their home in anger. Shakuntala admitted that to give and take dowry was to participate in and endorse an evil that humiliated women. But if giving or taking dowry was bad, leaving one's husband and in-laws' home in rage was worse. She said: 'This is not something women in my family do; this is not something Indian women do.'

■ **Draupadi as a Symbol of Indian Womanhood**

While notions of Indian Womanhood are neither homogeneous nor monolithic, the foregoing statements reveal how notions of appropriate behaviour for women are circumscribed by cultural nationalism. The women described her encountered discourses of Indian Womanhood (epitomized by the ideal of the *bhartiya naari*), not as an abstract construct but as a material reality that inflected everyday practice: as girls, growing into womanhood, when they negotiated and participated in discourses on the family, the community, and the nation; in discourses on appropriate behaviour for Indian women; most commonly, in popular texts such as the cinema and in literature of different genres; and now, in television serials. I found that for many women, the self-recognition of what it means to be a woman was mediated by a sense of being a particular type of woman, an *Indian* woman, essentially different from, say, 'Western' women. For although concepts of Indian Womanhood pre-date the contemporary nation-state, they acquire particular significance in the light of the manner in which ideologies of gender and nationhood have come to coimplicate each other in the post-colonial era.[13]

Despite the fact that her figure had multiple resonances, Draupadi seemed to symbolize Indian Womanhood for both producers and viewers. Producers as well as viewers felt, to varying degrees, that 'Woman's power' needs to be contained within the parameters of nation and family. Draupadi, for all her rage against her husbands, will follow them to the forest when they go into exile: it is clear that her place is with them. Her rage, and that of the contemporary Indian woman, is valid as long as it is contained within meta-narratives of family and nation. For the director and his colleagues, the family was sacrosanct because it is the corner-stone of the nation. And for viewers like Shakuntala Sharma, who rebuked her daughter for being outspoken, metanarratives of family and nation slid into one another ('This is not something women in my family do; this is not something Indian women do.').

By highlighting the coimplication of discourses of gender and nationalism, these interpretations reveal the power of nationalist ideologies as they percolate, through popular culture, into the everyday lives of ordinary women. To understand why nationalist readings acquire such potency, why certain readings, more than others, seem the most 'natural', the most 'commonsensical' (Hall, 1977), it is essential that we undertake a genealogical analysis of the production of Draupadi as a symbol of Indian womanhood in recent Indian history. For like other discursive practices, semiotic processes are not synchronic: signs have lives, trajectories, and genealogies as well.

■ The Coimplication of Gender and Nationhood

As argued above, unlike other symbols of Indian womanhood (such as Sita, who is invoked for her loyalty to her husband and his clan), the mythic figure of Draupadi is polysemic.[14] However, no singular model of Indian womanhood has ever existed—either at different moments of the nationalist struggle or at any given moment. Nor is the invocation of oppressed womanhood to symbolize the nation new to Indian nationalism. Studies of debates on sati and widow remarriage describe some of the contexts in which nationalist thought emerged and took shape. At the hands of colonialists and nationalists, the status of women in India came to symbolize the status of 'Indian culture'. Emblematic of tradition, women became the 'ground' for discourses on sati (Mani, 1987), on what constituted 'authentic tradition', and on how 'civilized' India was (Chakravarti, 1989). The attribution of a superior morality to colonial rulers, as opposed to the inferior morality of their subjects, was discussed primarily in terms of the condition of Indian women. Although these constructs were neither static, nor homogeneous, nor

---

13 In another article (Mankekar, n.d.), I describe the proliferation of discourses on womanhood that have emerged within the nationalist framework advocated by the state and discuss the manner in which they reflect the productive aspects of power (cf. Foucault, 1982).

14 The dependence of Indian nationalists on figures drawn from Hindu mythology and iconography points to the elision between Hindu cultural nationalism and mainstream Indian nationalism from the outset.

universal with regard to class and region, they constituted a material force that individual women had to contend with in their daily lives.[15]

Draupadi's rage was first invoked by early nationalists as a call to action to Indian *men*. It is not surprising that the mythic figure of Draupadi fired the imagination of many nationalist poets. For instance, the nationalist Tamil littérateur Subramania Bharati wrote a poem on Draupadi entitled 'Panchali's Vow' in which he compared her disrobing to colonial domination and chided Indian men for not avenging the insult to their country. But later, Gandhi and his contemporaries focused on her agency to encourage Hindu *women* to participate in the freedom struggle.

Thus, neither the pre-Independence nationalist representation of Draupadi nor the 1990 television version has depicted her as either passive or defeated. In fact, it is Draupadi's anger that attracted nationalists, who appropriated this facet of her image to symbolize first, the subjugated nation, and, after independence, the fledgeling nation-state. As the focus of nationalism changed from national liberation to the consolidation of the post-colonial nation-state, this uneasy relationship between discourses of gender and nationalism was to leave an enduring legacy. For, as the discourses of those involved in the production of the *Mahabharata* show us, at the same time that they continue to be markers of tradition and nationhood, there is also an attempt to invoke, in however essentialist a fashion, women's agency and power.

Much work remains to be done with regard to the trajectories followed by post-colonial nationalism; this study is merely a part of a larger project on the different ways in which television's representations of Indian Womanhood are interpreted by men and women in heterogeneous audiences. But the foregoing analysis of the interpretations by the *Mahabharata*'s creators and viewers reveals some of the gendered subject positions created by discursive practices like nationalism. For although discourses on Indian Womanhood have been neither static nor unchanging, mainstream nationalist ideologies, by constituting discourses on Indian Womanhood and by conflating their construct of Woman with individual women, have attempted to deny women a complex subjectivity. It is especially critical that we foreground the slippage from Hindu womanhood to Indian Womanhood at a time when nationalist ideologies are being consolidated in response to the challenges faced by the beleaguered and fragile Indian nation-state. As we have seen, these discursive practices have profound consequences for the lives of ordinary women—a testimony to the materiality of a discursive practice that engenders national subjects even as it constitutes them.

Conclusion This focus on viewers' active negotiation of hegemonic discourses represents important conceptual and polemical gains for several reasons. As mentioned above, in emphasizing the ways in which viewers interpret the texts of television I diverge from constructions of monolithic accounts of 'the meaning' of

---

15 Different discussions of how women nationalists negotiated nationalist discourses are to be found in Chakravarti (1989), Forbes (1981), and Visweswaran (1990).

popular narratives. For, by insisting on a more nuanced understanding of the place of popular narratives in the construction of subjectivity, I foreground the ways in which mass media like film and television interpellate viewers in multiple, sometimes contradictory, ways. Further, viewers bring a whole range of experiences to their encounters with film and television texts: thus, their interpretations of what they watch are contingent not just on the subject positions created by these texts but also those constructed by a multitude of discursive practices. In this study I have described the way in which class consciousness and discourses of sexuality refract women's responses to nationalist ideologies.

In addition, the multiplicity of interpretations I have described above exemplify the overlaps and disjunctures between the formulation of dominant ideologies and their appropriation by viewers in positions of subalternity (similar discussions are to be found in Amin's analysis of the appropriation of Gandhi's discourses by peasants in Gorakhpur (1989), and Bhabha's elegant theorization of the rupture between the 'pedagogic' and 'performative' aspects of nationalist ideology (1990)). Instead of assuming that viewers unproblematically accept the subject positions created by dominant ideologies such as those of Hindu/Indian nationalism, I have tried to foreground some of the fissures intrinsic to hegemonic discourses. This is crucial to creating a space for the construction of feminist and secularist praxis. Given the attempts on behalf of the Indian nation-state to deploy television's discourses toward the construction of a hegemonic, pan-Indian 'national culture' on the one hand and a tendency to perceive 'Third World' women as passive victims of totalizing systems of oppression on the other, this conceptualization of viewers as active subjects has significant theoretical and political implications.

If the overlaps in the interpretations analysed above are significant, equally telling are the points at which they diverge. While for both the presenters of Draupadi's disrobing and its viewers Draupadi symbolized Indian Womanhood, it is equally evident that there were points of rupture, moments that forestalled ideological closure. Unlike the *Mahabharata* crew, who spoke of Draupadi in terms of abstract conceptions of gender and nationhood, women viewers intimately identified with Draupadi. They saw in her disrobing a reflection of their own struggles to negotiate a hostile environment. In this sense, Draupadi was more than just a symbol of Indian Womanhood: she became an icon of their vulnerability as women.

In these moments of epiphany, Draupadi's disrobing enabled women viewers to introspect about, and often critique, their own positions in their family, class, and community. Thus, while Uma and Jayanthi Chandran felt that women's vulnerability stems largely from their sexuality, the biological, essential 'difference' between men and women, Sushmita Dasgupta was acutely aware of her position as a lower middle-class woman in an acquisitive, consumerist society. Fear of prospective in-laws and anxieties surrounding issues of dowry also surfaced in Poonam and Shakuntala's responses to Draupadi's disrobing. Even when they were uncertain about the extent to which they could express their anger, Draupadi's rage encouraged women like Uma, Jayanthi, Sushmita, and Poonam to confront what they saw as the injustices perpetrated on women like them.

What do these interpretations of Draupadi's disrobing tell us about the relationship between contexts, texts, and lives? As mentioned above, many interpretations of televisual texts fall into one of the following traps: as in some television theory inspired by Lacanian semiotics they are either purely textual, with no interest in the manner in which audiences actively interpret what they watch, or, at the other extreme, accounts of individual responses that ignore the wider societal discourses that mediate viewers' interpretations. One way to avoid these positions is to ethnographically investigate the ways in which communicative codes and their interpretations are mediated by larger ideological practices. Viewers' responses to spectacles like Draupadi's disrobing are mediated by the discursive contexts in which they live. Thus, although televisual signs, like many other signs, are polysemous, this polysemy cannot be equated with pluralism. The connotations of these signs are not 'equal' among themselves but are mediated by hegemonic discourses. And audiences are not always in a position to 'choose' the meanings they attribute to what they watch. Instead, preferred readings emerge from specific discursive frameworks.

According to Stuart Hall (1980), when viewers interpret texts in terms of the reference code in which it has been encoded they operate from the 'dominant position'. At first glance, the viewers I have described above seem to occupy this position when they interpret Draupadi as a symbol of Indian Womanhood.

However, it is clear that this apparent convergence of interpretations in no way entails closure. These viewers seem to occupy what Hall labels the 'negotiated position'. Interpreting texts from within the negotiated position enables viewers to accept hegemonic discourses, in this case nationalism, while simultaneously formulating their own 'ground rules'. The negotiated position accepts some dominant definitions while making a 'more negotiated application to "local conditions" ' (Hall, 1980: 338). Negotiated readings of dominant ideology are therefore 'shot through' with contradictions.[16] Hence, it seems most fruitful to conceptualize the points of rupture in viewers' engagement with dominant discourses in terms of active negotiation. The moments of epiphany underlying Sushmita's tears, Poonam's outrage, and Uma's fears at watching Draupadi's disrobing reveal how processes of intimate engagement with the texts of television open spaces and opportunities for women to understand as well as critique their own lives and destinies.

But, as mentioned earlier, pointing to viewers' multiple interpretations serves another purpose: that of foregrounding the slippages and, equally important, the ruptures within nationalist hegemony. Nationalism attempts to create unified subject positions (Visweswaran, 1990). But the semiotic excess surrounding the figure of Draupadi as she gets disrobed in front of her family, the range of emotions and memories sparked by her predicament, enabled the Hindu viewers I describe here to confront and theorize their own

---

16 Thus, concepts such as 'compliance' and 'resistance' are, in and of themselves, inadequate to understand the processes by which viewers engage with television texts. 'Compliance' neglects the place of interpretation on the part of heterogeneous viewers who, variably located in specific socio-cultural contexts, actively interact with television texts. Similarly, as an analytical construct 'resistance' is too totalizing to capture the ephemeral, yet profound, nature of the interactions between texts and viewers: it fails to concede the multiple, and sometimes contradictory, subject positions offered by texts and negotiated by viewers.

vulnerabilities as women. For even as they accepted her as a symbol of Indian womanhood, they appropriated Draupadi's disrobing, the moment when she is at her most vulnerable, to reflect on and to critique their own positions in their family, community, and nation.[17]

Finally, I want to close by recalling Uma's horror that sexual violence toward women is not a 'modern' phenomenon but was inflicted upon women even in what Hindu revivalists have called 'the glorious Hindu past'. Similarly, let us remember Sushmita's eloquent description of the difference between idealizations of womanhood in orthodox Hindu ideology and what she calls the 'reality of women's lives'. I write at a time when the violence of the Indian state and rising Hindu chauvinism leaves me very few spaces, either for critique or for constructive intervention. Hence, Uma's and Sushmita's words are particularly heartening. Not only do they rupture nationalist master narratives, they also counter nostalgic, right-wing Hindu invocations of 'ancient Hindu civilization' as an egalitarian era when women not only had equal rights but were revered for their power. It is these counter-narratives, these moments of slippage and rupture that secular feminists need to strategically seize upon and consolidate if we are to ever construct a counter-hegemonic praxis, if we are to ever progress from deconstruction to construction.

Fieldwork for this chapter was funded by a Fulbright–Hays Doctoral Dissertation Award (1990–1) and an American Institute for Indian Studies grant (1992). I am grateful to families in Vikas Nagar and Basti, New Delhi, and to Satish Bhatnagar, B. R. Chopra, Gufi Paintal, and the late Rahi Masoom Raza for sharing with me their interpretations of Draupadi's 'disrobing'. Finally, I would like to thank Lila Abu-Lughod, Ann Anagnost, Ruth Frankenberg, Beth Gerstein, Inderpal Grewal, Akhil Gupta, Susan Jeffords, Lorna Rhodes, Edgar Winans, and Sylvia Yanagisako for their comments.

References

Agrawal, Damodar (1990), 'Agenda', *Times of India*, 20 June 1990: 11.

Amin, Shahid (1989), 'Gandhi as Mahatma: Gorakhpur District, Eastern UP, 1921–2', in Ranajit Guha (ed.), *Subaltern Studies III: Writings on South Asian History and Society* (Delhi: Oxford Univ. Press), 1–61.

Ang, Ien (1991), *Watching Dallas: Soap Opera and the Melodramatic Imagination* (London: Routledge).

Bhabha, Homi (1990), 'DissemiNation: Time, Narrative and the Margins of the Modern Nation', in Homi Bhabha (ed.), *Nation and Narration* (London: Routledge), 291–322.

Bharati, Subramania (1977), 'Panchali's Vow', in *Poems of Subramania Bharati*, trans. Prema Nandakumar (New Delhi: Sahitya Akademi), 151–84.

Bobo, Jacqueline (1988), 'The *Color Purple*: Black Women as Cultural Readers', in E. Deirdre Pribram (ed.), *Female Spectators* (London: Verso), 90–109.

Chakravarti, Uma (1989), 'Whatever Happened to the Vedic *Dasi*? Orientalism, Nationalism and a Script for the Past', in Kumkum Sangari and Sudesh Vaid (eds.), *Recasting Women* (New Delhi: Kali for Women), 27–87.

Chandra, Bipan (1991), 'Communalism and the State: Some Issues in India', in K. N.

---

17 Hall also speaks of 'oppositional positions', in which viewers resist hegemonic discourses and interpret messages in terms of alternative frameworks of reference, e.g. if a viewer reads 'class interest' into every mention of 'national interest' (1980). I find this hypothetical position unconvincing because it assumes that subjects can somehow stand outside the discursive formation to which they belong to engage in alternative readings.

Panikkar (ed.), *Communalism in India: History, Politics and Culture* (New Delhi: Manohar), 132–41.

Daniel, E. Valentine (1984), *Fluid Signs: Being a Person the Tamil Way* (Berkeley and Los Angeles: Univ. of California Press).

Das, Indira (1990), 'An Epic Transcends the Border', *Sunday Mail*, 8 July 1990: 1, 3.

Dethe, V. K., and Sharma, L. K. (1990), 'Pakistanis Love it!', *Times of India*, 17 June 1990: 11.

Forbes, Geraldine (1981), 'The Indian Women's Movement: A Struggle for Women's Rights or National Liberation?', in Gail Minault (ed.), *The Extended Family: Women and Political Participation in India and Pakistan* (Columbia, Mo.: South Asia Books), 49–82.

Foucault, Michel (1982), 'Afterword: The Subject and Power', in Hubert J. Dreyfus and Paul Rabinow (eds.) *Michel Foucault: Beyond Structuralism and Hermeneutics* (Chicago: Univ. of Chicago Press), 208–26.

Gledhill, Christine (1988), 'Pleasurable Negotiations', in E. Deirdre Pribram (ed.), *Female Spectators* (London: Verso), 64–89.

Hall, Stuart (1977), 'Culture, the Media and the Ideological Effect', in Michael Gurevitch *et al.* (eds.), *Culture, Society and the Media* (London: Methuen), 315–48.

—— (1980), 'Encoding/Decoding', in Stuart Hall *et al.* (eds.), *Culture, Media, Language* (Birmingham, England: Centre for Contemporary Cultural Studies), 128–38.

Hoskote, Ranjit (1990), 'Vyasa's Krishna: Letter to the Editor', *Times of India*, 27 July 1990: 7.

Jeffords, Susan (1989), *The Remasculinization of America: Gender and the Vietnam War* (Bloomington: Indiana Univ. Press).

Kala, Arvind (1990), 'Mahabharata: The Mad Rush', *Sunday Mail*, 1 July 1990: 15–16.

Kaplan, E. Ann (1987), 'Feminist Criticism and Television', in Robert C. Allen (ed.), *Channels of Discourse* (Chapel Hill: Univ. of North Carolina Press), 247–83.

Karve, Irawati (1974), *Yuganta* (New Delhi: Disha).

Khair, Tabish, and Nath, Gyanendra (1990), 'Mahabharata's Krishna: A Machiavelli or a God?', *Times of India*, 10 July 1990: 11.

Kumar, Kanti (1990), 'Vyasa's Krishna: Letter to the Editor', *Times of India*, 27 July 1990: 7.

Mani, Lata (1987), 'Contentious Traditions: The Debate on Sati in Colonial India', *Cultural Critique*, 7: 119–56.

Mankekar, Purnima (n.d.), 'National Texts and Gendered Lives: An Ethnography of Television Viewers in India', *American Ethnologist*, forthcoming.

Modleski, Tania (1979), 'The Search for Tomorrow in Today's Soap Operas', *Film Quarterly*, 32/1: 226–78 (in this volume).

—— (1983), 'The Rhythms of Reception: Daytime Television and Women's Work', in E. Ann Kaplan (ed.), *Regarding Television: Critical Approaches—An Anthology* (Los Angeles: American Film Institute Monographs Series), 67–75.

Morley, David (1980), *Everyday Television: The 'Nationwide' Audience* (London: British Film Institute Monograph).

Mulvey, Laura (1975), 'Visual Pleasure and Narrative Cinema', *Screen*, 16/3: 6–18.

—— (1981), 'Afterthoughts on "Visual Pleasure and Narrative Cinema" Inspired by *Duel in the Sun*', *Framework*, 15/16/17: 12–15.

Padgaonkar, Dileep (1990), 'A "Republican" Epic', *Times of India*, 17 June 1990: 11.

Parthasarathy, R. J. (1990), 'Vyasa's Krishna: Letter to the Editor', *Times of India*, 27 July 1990: 7.

Penley, Constance (1988), 'Introduction—The Lady Doesn't Vanish: Feminism and Film Theory', in Constance Penley (ed.), *Feminism and Film Theory* (New York: Routledge), 1–24.

Philipose, Pamela (1990), 'An Epic Mistake?', *Observer*, Nov. 1990: 13.

R.G.K. (1990), 'The Nowness of the Mahabharata', *Times of India*, 24 June 1990: 1, 3.

Seiter, Ellen, Borchers, Hans, Kreutzner, Gabriele, and Warth, Eva-Maria (1989) (eds.), *Remote Control: Television, Audiences, and Cultural Power* (London: Routledge).

Sherif, Shameem Akhtar (1991), 'Krishna: To Chant or Not', *Times of India*, 15 Sept. 1991: 18.

Taylor, Ella (1989), *Prime Time Families: Television Culture in Postwar America* (Berkeley and Los Angeles: Univ. of California Press).

Thapar, Romila (1990), 'The Ramayana', *India Magazine*, June 1990: 30–43.

Thomas, Rosie (1985), 'Indian Cinema: Pleasures and Popularity', *Screen*, 26/3–4: 123–35.

Visweswaran, Kamala (1990), 'Family Subjects: An Ethnography of the "Woman Question" in Indian Nationalism', Ph.D. diss. Department of Anthropology, Stanford University.

Williams, Raymond (1977), *Marxism and Literature* (Oxford: Oxford Univ. Press).

18

Leading up to *Roe* v. *Wade*: Television Documentaries in the Abortion Debate

Julie D'Acci

SOCIAL UPHEAVALS, LEGAL battles, and judicial rulings involving abortion have rocked the United States since abortion was decriminalized in 1973; rather than abating, such tumult has intensified, reaching horrendous proportions in the brutal murders of healthcare professionals and aides at US clinics.[1] Recent Supreme Court decisions and legislative amendments have curtailed women's ability to get abortions in public hospitals, constrained publicly employed doctors from performing the procedure, promoted the recognition of foetuses as persons, and declared that neither federal nor state governments must pay for abortions (even if medically necessary) for women on welfare.[2] It seems astonishing that the fury over abortion rages more heatedly now than it did in 1973 when the Supreme Court handed down the *Roe* v. *Wade* decision decriminalizing abortion in the United States. But a closer look at the vested interests and pressures that helped shape the decision (as well as the decriminalization of abortion in seventeen states prior to *Roe*) makes it clear that fury and mounting struggle would be its most certain legacies.[3] The medical and legal

© Julie D'Acci

In Mary Beth Haralovich and Lauren Rabinovitz (eds.), *Feminism, History and Television* (Durham, NC: Duke University Press, forthcoming).

1 See Sarah Franklin, Celia Ury, and Jackie Stacey (eds.), 'part 3: Science and Technology', *Off-Centre: Feminism and Cultural Studies* (London: Harper Collins Academic, 1991), 129–218, for articles on abortion and reproductive politics. See also Linda Gordon, *Woman's Body, Woman's Right: Birth Control in America* (New York: Penguin, 1990); Rosalind Petchesky, *Abortion and Woman's Choice: The State, Sexuality, and Reproductive Freedom*, rev. edn. (Boston: Northeastern Univ. Press, 1990); Kristin Luker, *Abortion and the Politics of Motherhood* (Los Angeles: Univ. of California Press, 1984); Marlene Gerber Fried (ed.), *From Abortion to Reproductive Freedom: Transforming a Movement* (Boston: South End Press, 1990); Rhonda Copelon, 'From Privacy to Autonomy: The Conditions for Sexual and Reproductive Freedom', in Fried (ed.), *From Abortion to Reproductive Freedom*, 27–43; Sarah Weddington, *A Question of Choice* (New York: Penguin, 1993); Ruth Bader Ginsburg, 'Some Thoughts on Autonomy and Equality in Relation to *Roe* v. *Wade*', *North Carolina Law Review*, 63 (Jan. 1985), 375–86; Dawn E. Johnsen, 'The Creation of Fetal Rights: Conflicts with Women's Constitutional Rights to Liberty, Privacy, and Equal Protection', *Yale Law Journal*, 95 (Jan. 1986), 599–625; Wendy Brown, 'Reproductive Freedom and the Right to Privacy: A Paradox for Feminists', in Irene Diamond (ed.), *Families, Politics and Public Policy* (New York: Longman, 1983), 322–88; Meera Werth, 'Spousal Notification and the Right of Privacy', *Chicago Kent Law Review*, 59 (Fall 1983), 1129–51; Laura Grindstaff, 'Abortion and the Popular Press: Mapping Media Discourse from *Roe* to *Webster*', unpublished paper, 1993.

2 See Gordon, *Woman's Body, Woman's Right*, 397–488; Petchesky, *Abortion and Woman's Choice*, 241–329; Weddington, *A Question of Choice*, 197, 211–25.

3 Gordon, *Woman's Body, Woman's Right*, 403.

establishments, the women's movement including pro-abortion Black feminist groups and individuals, and population-control organizations (some with clear histories of racist, sexist, and imperialist policies), were among the odd bedfellows that actively struggled for liberalized abortion during the late 1960s and early 1970s. They formed the coalitions that advocated decriminalization. But the muting of feminist voices and women's movement demands, in both these coalitions and the final legislation, contributed to a public policy that situated abortion not as a woman's *absolute* right but one contained under the right to privacy, governed by a physician's discretion, and subject to state intervention after the first trimester.[4] This muting is all the more troubling because, as Linda Gordon and Rosalind Petchesky demonstrate, it was these feminist voices that by and large forced the issue onto the US public scene.[5]

Struggles over abortion in the United States during the years leading up to *Roe* involved four television documentaries that illuminate the medium's part in establishing the terms of the abortion debate and its 'officially' legitimated players. These programmes bring a number of crucial questions to light: How did TV's attempts to achieve 'balance' shape the abortion debate?[6] How did institutional conceptions of television news and documentary cast the debate as a 'democratic' struggle among 'legitimate' competing voices? How did the combination of participants and pressures intersect with the conventions of television documentaries to help frame abortion policy? How did TV participate in defining abortion as a government- and medically controlled practice, and a moral, ethical, and medical quandary, rather than an unequivocal and socially based right of women?

Television's imperative to produce 'balance'—to present what it deemed as 'both' sides of a controversial public issue—had grave political consequences for the women's movement and for feminist objectives regarding abortion. Its effacement of the women's movement and ultimate framing of the 'pro' side within the discourses of population control clarifies (in retrospect) but obfuscated (at the time) the racism, classism, and sexism that undergirded part of the reform movement and helped make *Roe* a possibility. On the one hand, the documentaries and their production histories show how television brought a controversial social issue to a mass audience of diverse classes, races, and ages. In some ways this fulfilled TV's stated ideals of educating and informing. On the other hand, television distorted the terms in which abortion was discussed, maintaining social hegemony and

---

4 Gordon, *Woman's Body, Woman's Right*, 405. As Rhonda Copelon points out, it was not until 1977 that the court actually extended the right to decide about abortion to the woman herself—*Roe* had technically assigned it to physicians. See Copelon, 'From Privacy to Autonomy', in Fried (ed.), 35.

5 Gordon, *Woman's Body, Woman's Right*, 397–416; Petchesky, *Abortion and Woman's Choice*, 125–32.

6 The issue of 'balance' that is so central to the history of the television documentaries presented here pivots on what came to be called the US Federal Communication Commission's 'Fairness Doctrine'. At the time of the documentaries under discussion, the Fairness Doctrine stated that the public had the right to an 'uninhibited marketplace of ideas' and that broadcasters were obliged to 'afford reasonable opportunity for the discussion of conflicting views on issues of public importance'. Achieving representations of 'conflicting views' led to the many struggles over the notion of 'balance' and 'balanced programming'. The Fairness Doctrine was abandoned with the deregulation of US broadcasting in the 1980s. See Christopher H. Sterling and John M. Kitross, *Stay Tuned: A Concise History of American Broadcasting*, 2nd edn. (Belmont, Calif.: Wadsworth Publishing, 1990), 426–7.

constraining the medium's more emancipatory possibilities. TV's first two documentaries on abortion illustrate how 'balance' was determined, how particular spokespeople in the abortion debate were invested with authority and approbation and others—specifically women and feminists (both white and women of colour)—were not. The second two documentaries make eminently clear how national policy on abortion was ushered in under the auspices of population control rather than that of a feminist vision of reproductive rights. Each of the documentaries coincided with turning-points in the history of abortion debates in the United States and brought out and defined the opposing sides as never before.

The Historical Context

Abortions in the US (following British Common Law) were by and large legal until the later 1800s. However, between 1850 and 1890, physicians agitated for bans on the practice and by 1900 every state in the union had passed anti-abortion laws. For a range of reasons, the medical and legal establishments tried to relax these laws during the 1950s, and in the second half of that decade, continuing into the 1960s, public exposés of abortion rackets and unsafe illegal procedures were common.[7]

Linda Gordon and Rosalind Petchesky have documented the ways the women's movements of the late 1960s forced the abortion issue onto the stage of public policy and have analysed the many complications involved in battling over legislation. While specifying that she is not diagnosing a failure of tactics, Gordon describes how some segments of the women's movement retreated from the early 'abortion on demand' slogan to one of an individual's 'right to choose'. This shift occurred amid fierce oppositional pressures, a philosophy of individualism that underpinned much of the women's movement, and a lack of focus on the *social* aspects of abortion.[8] Furthermore, Gordon attributes important influence to the population control movements and traces how they 'clouded the vision of reproductive freedom' that feminism upheld.[9] Under the aegis of population control, public policy on abortion became increasingly dissociated from the women's movement. Petchesky argues,

> the state—and the population policy establishment that had become the architect of state policy on fertility—carefully avoided concessions to feminist ideology about reproductive freedom. To accommodate popular pressures without legitimating feminism—or acknowledging the true causes of the need for abortion—state and population planners subsumed abortion politics under the rubric of population control.[10]

The slogan 'right to choose', in sharp contrast to 'abortion on demand', better fitted the rhetoric of population control and the growing desire to situate abortion policy within the individual's right to privacy.

7 Gordon, *Woman's Body, Woman's Right*, 34–40, 400–16; Petchesky, *Abortion and Woman's Choice*, 49–137; Luker, *Abortion and the Politics of Motherhood*, 11–15.

8 Gordon, *Woman's Body, Woman's Right*, 396–400.

9 Ibid. 396.

10 Petchesky, *Abortion and Woman's Choice*, 117.

Prime-Time
Abortion

The first US television programme on abortion was a fifteen-minute dramatic recreation, entitled 'Abortions: A Look into the Illegal Abortion
Racket', on the 1955 syndicated programme *Confidential File*. But the first
actual *network* documentary appeared ten years later on the critically
acclaimed *CBS Reports*. Called 'Abortion and the Law', it was written and
produced by progressive journalist/film-maker David Lowe and narrated by
newsman Walter Cronkite. In 1969 ABC filmed the second documentary,
'Abortion', written and produced by the equally progressive, though less well
known, Ernest Pendrell, and broadcast on the *Summer Focus* series.

There is no question that each of these documentaries strongly advocated
legalization. There is also little doubt that the networks and producers were
willing to put themselves on the line to do the programmes.[11] (The 1965 *CBS
Reports* team, however, had the benefit of working during the Lyndon B.
Johnson administration which was itself urging at least the widespread dissemination of birth control information, while the Pendrell team faced a
more restrictive Richard Nixon White House.)[12] But despite the producers'
and networks' support of decriminalization, it was the way the dimensions of
the struggle got *defined* and its participants determined that has proved so
problematic for US abortion policy. These first two documentaries established the groundwork for how the debate would be framed and handled on
American television and for deciding which players would be selected for air
time and which shunted to the sidelines. The notion of 'balance' that
grounded these decisions was tied to the liberalism that marginalized and
muffled feminist and female spokespeople.

In 'Abortion and the Law', most of the legitimated players were enumer-
ated in Cronkite's opening statement: 'Only recently have our abortion laws
been openly questioned, has a dialogue begun among *doctors, lawyers and
clergymen*' [emphasis mine].[13] Indeed, the documentary, which presented a
complex and well-researched case for decriminalization, included an array
of *male* experts in favour of liberalizing the law—nine physicians, a lawyer,
an Episcopal priest, and a state legislator; and four speaking against liberalization—a physician (speaking from a religious position), an attorney (representing the US Catholic bishops), and two Catholic priests.

In the course of the documentary, five women tell stories of traumatic illegal abortions in the US or ones obtained by travelling to Puerto Rico or
Mexico; another tells of qualifying for a legal US procedure because she had
contracted rubella; another (who currently wants to terminate her pregnancy) speaks of the fear of a 'back alley' abortion; and a final one (the

11 Thomas Wolf to Martin Rubenstein, ABC Interdepartment Correspondence, 6 Feb. 1969, Ernest
Pendrell Collection, Wisconsin Center for Film and Theater Research, State Historical Society of
Wisconsin, box 7, folder 2: 'this series [about ABC's *Summer Focus*] is being undertaken with or without the support of sponsors, as part of our continuing obligation to bring to the American people the
major concerns of the day—many of them involving considerable difference of opinion'. References
to this collection henceforth cited as 'Pendrell', followed by box and folder numbers.

12 *Business Week*, 13 Feb. 1965, David Lowe Collection, Wisconsin Center for Film and Theater
Research, State Historical Society of Wisconsin, box 1, folder 6: Clipping describes President Lyndon
Johnson's state of the union message which urged that birth control information should be made
available to more people. References to this collection henceforth cited as 'Lowe', followed by box
and folder numbers.

13 From 'Abortion and the Law', script, Lowe, box 1, folder 5, 1.

mother of a young woman who endured an illegal and badly executed treatment without telling her parents) speaks about the horrors her daughter faced.[14] Although their testimonies provided the ground for the documentary's discussion—giving bodily evidence to the need for legal reform—the women were not seen as legitimate participants in the 'dialogue' which had begun among those openly questioning abortion laws. The women were taking enormous risks and displaying personal and political courage. Yet, they were not afforded positions in the debate *per se*, were not cast as active subjects of the documentary's argument. They were presented as its cause and its objects, its victims, and, on some level, its physical spectacle.

Four years later, in 'Abortion', the sanctioned players included two male physicians and a Catholic priest. However, mothers of rubella babies and politicians also became 'rightful' participants in the dialogue. In this documentary, two white, middle-class women who had contracted rubella speak out for abortion—one was able to terminate her pregnancy legally, and the other gave birth to a child with multiple and severe disabilities. The president of the Borough of Manhattan speaks fervently about the class injustices in the present situation, and seven New York state legislators (six male and one female) debate the New York bill for decriminalization. In 'Abortion', therefore, a few women emerge as more active participants in the debate. But they draw their authority primarily from their status as mothers, presenting cases for legal abortions in the face of potential 'birth defects'. Two other white, middle-class women who give personal testimonies of abortions (one illegal in the US and one in Puerto Rico), are handled in ways similar to the women in 'Abortion and the Law'—not as active players but as objects and ground of the controversy.

The Quest for 'Balance'

The production files of producer-writer Ernest Pendrell for 'Abortion' offer a fascinating glimpse into how the various participants and positions in the documentary were actually determined and selected, and how the 'balance' required by the network was adjudicated and achieved. At the project's outset, ABC's lawyers advised,

> while we can argue for a liberalization of existing laws, we should not advocate that anybody deliberately violate existing state statutes, no matter how outmoded they be. And if we do take a 'position' on a controversial subject like this, should we not outline conflicting attitudes in this self-same program—so as to avoid 'fairness' problems to the network and to each of its affiliates?[15]

As the research and writing went forward, network executives grew increasingly worried about the achievement of this fairness and the exercise of

---

14 Since with 'Abortion and the Law' I am working from a script only (rather than the film itself or a videotape), I am unable to specify the races or classes of the women presented.

15 Vernon L. Wilkinson, McKenna & Wilkinson Law Offices, to Martin Rubenstein, ABC, 20 Feb. 1969, Pendrell, box 7, folder 2.

'balance'.[16] The show's executive producer, Lester Cooper, wrote to Pendrell calling for script revisions and admonishing that there was 'a danger in the point-of-view. The slant is so obvious; the sympathies so definite. It ceases to be a report and becomes a tract . . . I feel this shouldn't be a "horror" story but a *balanced* report on the issue, the problem and the various attitudes toward them' [emphasis mine].[17]

The network's vice-president for news and public affairs, Thomas Wolf, although supportive of the documentary's 'slant' and 'sympathies', began firing off memos urging Pendrell to achieve balance by incorporating particular spokespeople and opposing positions. Attached to one memo was a copy of a letter to ABC President Elton Rule from a fundamentalist anti-abortion attorney, Robert Sassone:

> I am a member of a Right to Life committee interested in protecting the rights of infants and unborn babies. I would like to insure that you have access to all of our committee's arguments favoring strict abortion laws. If you wish, I will send you a six page summary of the medical, psychological, and sociological arguments favoring strict abortion laws.

Wolf notes on the letter's margin that Pendrell should 'be sure to get his material'.[18] But Pendrell's response to Wolf, while stopping short of insubordination, suggests that he had adequate representation of that perspective: 're: Your note on the letter from Robert Sassone of the Right to Life Committee sent you from Mr. Rule. We have done an extensive sound piece on Mrs. Valerie Dillon, spokesman for this committee in New Jersey at her home in Somerset. . . . This was the lead you had sent me, if you recall. I will, of course, write him [Sassone] and get his material.'[19]

Vice-President Wolf also solicited material from the women's movement. A letter to Wolf from Joanna Martin of the Chicago National Organization for Women (NOW) reads: 'Enclosed is a tape of the keynote address which Betty Friedan delivered at the recent national conference on abortion laws. Mrs. Friedan told me that you had asked for tapes of her speech . . .'.[20] The final documentary, however, included no spokespeople from *either* the women's movement (not even its reform-orientated, rather than radical, wing represented by Friedan) or fundamentalist anti-abortion groups.[21]

---

16 This was the case even though ABC, through its owned and operated New York station, had already taken a publicly televised stand in favour of liberalizing existing laws: on 3, 4, and 5 Feb. 1969, WABC-TV, New York, broadcast an editorial urging such liberalization. See 'WABC-TV Editorial Favors Proposals For More Moderate Abortion Law in New York', Pendrell, box 7, folder 2. This was rebutted by Mrs Valerie Dillon for the Respect for Life Committee; see 'WABC-TV Editorial Rebuttal', Pendrell, box 7, folder 3.

17 Lester Cooper to Ernest Pendrell, ABC Interdepartment Correspondence, 17 Mar. 1969, Subject: Abortion, Pendrell, box 7, folder 2.

18 Robert Sassone to Elton Rule, 2 Apr. 1969, Pendrell, box 7, folder 2. It is clear from Thomas Wolf's letters, memos, and actions dealing with this and the Marlene Sanders's documentary in 1973, that he was supporting liberalization of abortion laws.

19 Pendrell to Tom Wolf, typed note, 14 Apr. 1969, Pendrell, box 7, folder 2.

20 (Mrs) Joanna Martin, Public Relations, Chicago NOW to Thomas Wolf, ABC, 10 Mar. 1969, Pendrell, box 7, folder 2.

21 The omission of non-Catholic, anti-abortion spokespeople raised ire in both the religious press and viewer responses to the programme. Russell Faist's 'ABC's of Abortion', in 'The Catholic Universe

So in 1969, a couple of years before the voices of the population control movement would come to exert a truly widespread discursive authority over the pro side of US abortion debates, network documentary declined to offer representation to women's movement spokespeople. It appears that at the time *both* the women's movement and the fundamentalist anti-abortion groups were too far outside the mainstream—outside the hegemony of officially warranted interests—to be included in the television debate. Even after seeking out Friedan's speech and directing Pendrell's attention to fundamentalist anti-abortionists, the network ultimately allowed the documentary's 'fairness' and 'balance' to be achieved without their representation.

Prime-Time and the Path to *Roe*

On the heels of 'Abortion', in July of 1969, President Nixon appointed a commission to examine population growth and its impact on the country. Chaired by John D. Rockefeller III, the Commission on Population and the American Future included twenty-three other participants from medicine, academia, the corporate and religious worlds, élite foundations, Congress, students, and members listed as 'housewife-volunteers'.[22] The Commission's work also spawned the next two television documentaries about abortion.

A number of contextual factors must be foregrounded at this point: Rockefeller and the Rockefeller Foundation had a long history of work in eugenics and population control, some of which involved attempts to control populations in Third World countries during the height of the Cold War and African Americans, other US people of colour, and the poor during the 1950s and 1960s.[23] As Petchesky demonstrates, in 1968 Rockefeller had laid out a rationale for a pro-abortion consensus among population groups, family planners, medical organizations, and government officials. This underscored the growing need for medically controlled and medically adjudicated abortions, the fact that women were skirting the law, and that children had the right to be born into families that wanted them.[24] The rationale never mentioned the needs or rights of women. However, it was the women's movement's actions that provoked the issues and the very need for

Bulletin', a diocesan paper of the Cleveland Catholic diocese with accompanying letter from Faist, 13 June 1969, Pendrell, box 7, folder 2.

Although Betty Friedan and NOW's position were not included, the documentary itself opened with a strong analysis and *implicitly* feminist indictment of the anti-abortion position from a young, white, middle-class woman identified simply as 'Mary': 'I do feel that on a level maybe that isn't conscious that most people, that society in general feels that girls who get themselves pregnant are bad girls, they aren't nice girls, and they've been careless and wayward, and promiscuous, and that they should get punished. You know, this is the only way to teach them, because if you let girls get abortions, then they're going to run around and have sex all the time, and the whole society will fall apart.' 'Abortion' script, Pendrell, box 7, folder 3, 1. See also the film, 'Abortion', Pendrell Collection, Film Archives of the Wisconsin Center for Film and Theater Research, State Historical Society of Wisconsin.

22 'Population and the American Future', Report of the Commission on Population Growth and the American Future, Washington, DC: US Government Printing Office (1972), 5.

23 Gordon, *Woman's Body, Woman's Right*, 386–96; Petchesky, *Abortion and Woman's Choice*, 116–25; Angela Davis, 'Racism, Birth Control, and Reproductive Rights', in Fried (ed.), *From Abortion to Reproductive Freedom*, 15–26. Linda Gordon warns that we must be careful to recognize that not all participants in the population control movement were working with racist or imperialist agendas: Gordon, 389.

24 Petchesky, *Abortion and Woman's Choice*, 122–3.

consensus: women in large numbers were refusing to abide by federal and state law, they illegally continued to terminate pregnancies, and set up women-run services in which safe, inexpensive abortions were provided.[25]

Nixon certainly knew Rockefeller's background in the population control movement and his position on abortion when he appointed him to chair the Commission.[26] But Nixon always took a *public* position against abortion and supported the Catholic Church which, in the late 1960s and early 1970s, was abortion's most outspoken opponent.[27] Petchesky argues that Nixon wished *to appear* to oppose abortion in order to preserve the political support of the Church. But at the same time he wanted to go along with the corporate-backed population control movement which, by the late 1960s, favoured not only government-sponsored family planning but legalized abortion as well.[28] All these factors contributed to shaping the work of the Nixon-appointed Commission, its report, its aftermath, and the next two documentaries to deal with abortion.[29]

In March 1972, almost three years after its establishment, the Commission issued a 186-page, 1.6-million-dollar report called 'Population and the American Future'. It delineated 47 recommendations for sex education, abortion, voluntary sterilization, family planning, immigration, racial minorities and the poor, and equal rights for women—advocating the passage of the Equal Rights Amendment (ERA). Several members of the Commission issued separate dissenting statements that repudiated the report's sections on abortion and reproductive control.[30] In May, Nixon publicly reacted to the document and unequivocally rejected the recommendations for liberalized abortion and birth control education for minors. The report, followed by the President's remarks, touched off the first major mobilization of the newly configured fundamentalist and Catholic right-to-life coalitions. The *New York Times* reported that letters came in five to one in opposition to the Commission's findings, many from organized religious groups, with at least one letter-writer recounting that sample protest forms were handed out to congregations from church pulpits.[31]

The Commission itself, unwilling to let its work be rebuffed and go unimplemented, was spurred by Rockefeller to form what it called the Citizens' Committee on Population and the American Future.[32] The Committee was

25 Gordon, *Woman's Body, Woman's Right*, 400–9; Petchesky, *Abortion and Woman's Choice*, 122–32.

26 It is worth noting that Nixon's own message while creating the Commission spoke of the specific need to get reproductive information to lower-income women. See Production Research Document, 18 July 1969, Marlene Sanders Collection, Wisconsin Center for Film and Theater Research, State Historical Society of Wisconsin, box 2, folder 1. References to this collection henceforth cited as 'Sanders', followed by box and folder numbers.

27 Petchesky, *Abortion and Woman's Choice*, 122.

28 Ibid. 122. It is also important to note here that the population control movement shifted from not advocating abortions (favouring instead sterilization) to supporting them when it became clear that women would continue to obtain them illegally: ibid. 118–25.

29 Ibid. 120.

30 'Population and the American Future', 141–69.

31 'Pro Abortion Policy of Population Panel Opposed 5–1 in Mail', *New York Times*, 11 May 1972.

32 See 'ABC Report on the population show', undated, Sanders, box 1, folder 1, 3–4, which states that in order to avoid oblivion, John D. Rockefeller III insisted on establishing a Citizens' Committee on Population and the American Future which would be privately funded and exist for a year to push the Commission's findings.

funded with private foundation moneys and co-chaired by former *Today* host Hugh Downs and African American feminist lawyer-activist—now congressional delegate from Washington, DC—Eleanor Holmes Norton. (That Holmes Norton and John D. Rockefeller III were working together graphically underscores the contradictory character of some of the movement's coalitions at the time.) The Citizens' Committee's main tasks were to complete a filmed documentary of the Commission's report, to get it aired on television, and to circulate it throughout the nation's high schools with accompanying teaching materials. A corporation called Population Education, Inc., also financed by private corporate money, was formed to produce the film.

This documentary was conceived as a straightforward filmed version of the Commission's report, and shooting had begun while the Commission was completing its work. Once Nixon nixed what many Commission members considered their most important recommendations, the completion and broadcast of the documentary became an urgent imperative. What the President rejected was, in fact, the most important section for the Committee; as the Committee's Executive Director put it, human reproduction 'is the subject which we feel is the key'.[33]

The Importance of Television

Rockefeller, many of the original Commission members, and the newly formed Citizens' Committee saw television as the medium that would bring their message to those they most wanted to reach. They spoke of the power of TV to do for this Commission report what no other report had ever achieved—widespread dissemination of its ideas to the American public.[34] The Citizens' Committee took the film to the three major networks and tried to buy air time. The various players, of course, had mixed and conflicting investments in pursuing television so wholeheartedly.

Part of the motivation for Rockefeller and some of the other population control-orientated members of the Commission was at least to some degree rooted in their belief that TV was one of the best ways to reach people of colour and the poor with birth control and abortion information. Although the Commission's report attempted to defuse what had become widely publicized worries about the eugenics and racist undertones to population control, racist and classist discourses were none the less evident. For example, although it explicitly stated that 'despite their high fertility rates, minorities—precisely because of their smaller numbers—contribute less to population growth than does the rest of the population', it also repeatedly, and somewhat contradictorily, linked 'high fertility' and even 'excess fertility' to families of colour and poor people.[35]

33 Carol Foreman, Executive Director of the Citizens' Committee on Population and the American Future, to Marlene Sanders, 9 Jan. 1973, Sanders, box 2, folder 5.

34 David K. Lelewar of Rockefeller's office to ABC President Elton Rule, 29 July 1971, Sanders, box 1, folder 1. Lelewar writes, 'Because of the report's importance and its wide interest to Americans generally, we feel that it should be presented not only as a written document but via TV as well.' See also Jeannette Smyth, 'Getting It Down on Film', *Washington Post*, 22 Nov. 1972. Such reports are known for falling into oblivion.

35 'Population and the American Future', 72–3.

For progressives on both the Commission and the Citizens' Committee, television may have been conceived as simply the best way to reach the greatest number of people, especially women and teenage girls, with alternative views on reproductive technologies and issues.[36] For many of the medical doctors involved, it might have been a way to go broadly public with a view of abortion that would guarantee not only the procedure's safety and respectability, but also its control by the medical establishment. For the Nixon White House, it may have been a way to allow the views of the corporate-backed and administration-friendly population movement to get widespread airing but at the same time be cast as views which Nixon himself explicitly opposed.[37]

For an African American feminist such as Eleanor Holmes Norton, co-chairing the Citizens' Committee and pushing for the television documentary most likely involved a number of intricate negotiations. Many African American leaders at the time were speaking out against government-sponsored reproductive control and family planning policies as disguised attempts to weaken and contain the Black population; they were urging Black women to produce *more*, not fewer children.[38] Despite this, African American feminists such as Toni Cade Bambara, Shirley Chisholm, and the Black Women's Liberation Group of Mt. Vernon New York, were publicly opposing *both* population control and the notion that Black women should produce more children. They supported legal abortions for women of colour and birth control education.[39]

Eleanor Holmes Norton's advocacy for a televised version of the Commission's report seems to have been rooted in a unique combination of positions. She vociferously championed the belief that women of colour and poor women should have the same exposure to reproductive control options as white and middle-class women. However, in an article on reproductive rights for women of colour, she also invoked the need for population control and so seems to have forged a position in which advocacy for both population control and birth control (including abortion) was a possibility for African Americans at the time.[40]

---

36 Articles in family planning pamphlets were describing the success of TV spots in, for example, generating 'a 7-fold increase in calls to family planning information services'. See 'The Family Planner', May 1970, Sanders, box 2, folder 1.

37 According to the film's producer, Craig Fisher, Nixon had asked Rockefeller to put a halt to the filming very early on, but Rockefeller threatened to resign from the Commission, and Nixon had backed down agreeing that shooting could continue. Craig Fisher, interview by author, telephone, August 1992.

38 Petchesky, *Abortion and Woman's Choice*, 130. Gordon, *Woman's Body, Woman's Right*, 441, writes that, 'Birth control and abortion advocates were insensitive to black fears about population control—51 per cent of black women surveyed in the early 1970s believed that the survival of black people depended on increasing black births, and 37 per cent believed that birth-control programs were genocidal in intent. (Black men were even more suspicious.) Indeed, throughout the 1960s and 1970s, fears of genocide were prominent in black commentary on all forms of birth control . . .'.

39 Gordon, *Woman's Body, Woman's Right*, 441–2; Petchesky, *Abortion and Woman's Choice*, 130; Toni Cade, 'The Pill: Genocide or Liberation?', in Toni Cade (ed.), *The Black Woman* (New York: Signet, 1970), 162–9; Shirley Chisholm, 'Facing the Abortion Question', in Gerda Lerner (ed.), *Black Women in White America: A Documentary History* (New York: Vintage, 1972), 602–6; Black Women's Liberation Group, Mt. Vernon, New York, 'Statement on Birth Control', in Robin Morgan (ed.), *Sisterhood is Powerful* (New York: Random House, 1970), 360–1.

40 Eleanor Holmes Norton, 'For Sadie and Maude', in Morgan (ed.), *Sisterhood is Powerful*, 353–9.

With these numerous and sometimes conflicting motivations tacitly churning within its own membership, the Citizens' Committee approached all three networks with the proposed documentary.[41] According to Craig Fisher, the film's producer/director, Rockefeller was convinced that CBS would air the film because of his friendship with network president William Paley and because, as Rockefeller said to Fisher, 'Paley got whatever he wanted'. After a lunch with Paley, however, Rockefeller reported that CBS, like the other networks, retained complete control over its editorial material and would not broadcast the film because it had been produced by an out-of-house film-maker—one not part of the CBS staff.[42] ABC and NBC also declined the project for the same reasons.[43] Most articles in the mainstream press claimed that the networks had declined because they did not want to touch such a politically and socially controversial package, and some reporters even speculated that the networks were afraid of the power of the Catholic Church.[44] Fisher, who had been hired away from NBC by Rockefeller to work on the project, truly believed the networks would not take news or documentary material that did not originate with their own news divisions. He states he had warned Rockefeller about this policy from the outset.[45] The Public Broadcasting Service (PBS), however, agreed to broadcast the film. Several months later, ABC, under the supervision of producer Marlene Sanders, began production on its own self-generated documentary of the Commission's report.[46]

41 Frank Getlein, 'Television Report with Bite', *Evening Star News*, 29 Nov. 1972; David K. Lelewar to Elton Rule, 29 July 1971, Sanders, box 1, folder 1.

42 Getlein; Fisher interview.

43 Ibid.

44 Getlein; and John Carmody, 'PBS: Focus on Overpopulation', *Washington Post*, 29 Nov. 1972.

45 Fisher interview; Smyth, 'Getting It Down'.

46 Marlene Sanders to Tom Wolf, Memo, 6 July 1972, Sanders, box 1, folder 1. Sanders tells Wolf about the Fisher film that is well under way, and an unnamed ABC executive writes back on the margins telling Sanders to 'go ahead', 'try to break some new ground'; Tom Wolf writes in the margins, 'it's important to us for reasons you know'.
It is important to consider the institutional conditions that accompanied the undertaking of these potentially incendiary documentaries at this particular time. As Charles Hammond points out in his book on television documentary, during the late 1960s and early 1970s TV had become the US's primary news source. The air was glutted with news from Civil Rights to Black Power coverage, and the networks began, increasingly, to conceive of this information function as part of their corporate mission. Although there was a drop-off in traditional news and theme documentaries between 1968 and 1975, the documentaries actually produced during this time became fairly bold and hard-hitting (ABC's 'Abortion' falls within this category). By 1972 and 1973 such documentaries began to come under attack by the FCC for alleged lack of fairness and balance. Charles Hammond, *The Image Decade: Television Documentary: 1965–1975* (New York: Hastings House, 1981), 106–7, 70, 224–7.
Each of these conditions is evident in the ways that PBS and ABC proceeded with their programmes. Both networks seemed to conceive of their efforts under the aegis of providing the country at large with what it needed to know. Furthermore, the documents in Marlene Sanders's production files indicate that, as with the Pendrell film a few years before, ABC's news division (with Tom Wolf still vice-president of News and Public Affairs) wanted to take what it considered to be an aggressive approach to the subject matter. The division was, in fact, both angry yet unshaken by what was reported as lack of co-operation, an implied threat, and intimidation from the White House. But at the same time both PBS and ABC, as we saw with ABC in 1969, tried to present what they determined to be the sanctioned opposing sides and 'balanced' presentations. Marlene Sanders to Tom Wolf, Memo, undated, Sanders, box 1, folder 1.

'Population and the American Future'

The Commission's official one-hour documentary, called 'Population and the American Future' (bearing the same name as the Commission's report), was produced by Craig Fisher, co-written and co-directed by Fisher and John Martin, narrated by Hugh Downs, and broadcast from PBS station WGBH Boston on 29 November 1972. Prior to airing, Catholic and fundamentalist right-to-life groups (considerably more organized than when 'Abortion' was broadcast in 1969) protested about the film to Congress, the Federal Communication Commission, PBS, and the Xerox Corporation, which had contributed $250,000 to its production. The Executive Director of the US Coalition for Life threatened to take PBS to court and to seek an injunction that would delay the programme.[47] The Public Affairs Coordinator for PBS fired back: 'Population control, regardless of how you feel about it, is a burning national issue and deserves an airing on national television.'[48]

The 57-minute film basically comprises footage with voice-over or on-screen narration by Hugh Downs. Unlike the first two television documentaries dealing with abortion, there are no interviews or spokespeople for different sides of the issues. In addition, this documentary and the Marlene Sanders one after it, is not only about abortion. The first half of 'Population and the American Future' reviews population statistics and the effects of these statistics on the economy, the environment, housing, transportation, poverty, cities, and national security. It also deals briefly with the Commission's recommendations on immigration. The second half focuses on human reproduction, recommending a range of progressive social policies, such as comprehensive health care for mothers and children, day care, widespread sex education, freedom of choice in all reproductive matters, the elimination of laws restricting contraceptive information and services to anyone, including teenagers.

The section on abortion occupies seven minutes and reviews the different options considered by the Commission, ranging from fairly strict prohibition to the repeal of all restrictions without ever mentioning the women's movement. It discusses the Commission's choice of a middle ground: that abortions up to the twenty-fourth week should be left to the 'conscience of the woman concerned in consultation with her physician' and that abortion should be liberalized along the lines of the 1971 New York state law. One segment opens with a large banner that is difficult to read in the shot: 'Stop religious oppression! Abortion . . . freedom of choice!' But that is quickly followed with shots that make clearly legible more than twenty signs carrying such slogans as 'Christ was a fetus', 'I love life', 'Forgive Them Father for They Know not What They Do', and 'What if you had been aborted?' Other signs also bear drawings of foetuses, and footage includes shots of large anti-abortion rallies with clerics and laypeople praying on the steps of public buildings and picketing in front of clinics. At the end of the documentary, there is a one-minute segment urging the passage of the Equal Rights Amendment that includes footage of a women's movement march replete

---

47 Jack Rosenthal, 'TV Film of Population Report Fought by Anti-Abortion Groups', *New York Times*, 28 Nov. 1972.

48 Ibid.

with signs declaring 'Equal Rights' and 'Sisterhood is Powerful'. But at no point is feminism, or any feminist spokesperson, tied to the documentary's advocacy of abortion or other reproductive rights.

Furthermore, like the report before it, the film is troubling with regard to issues of race and class. Although it takes care to report that 70 per cent of the growth in the American population comes from white middle-class families, it also reproduces subtle and not-so-subtle stereotypes and innuendoes. In the section in which it ties poverty to over-population, virtually all the shots are of African Americans or other people of colour. The section on sex education also claims, 'Couples in all age and socio-economic groups experience unwanted pregnancy but they *occur most often and have the most serious effects among the low income couples*' [emphasis mine]. The image at this point is a shot of a young African American woman. Finally and most disturbing, a segment recommending surgical sterilization for contraception focuses and lingers on a young Black woman, an image that overwhelms the following quick shots of two white men and a white woman.[49]

PBS deemed that 'balance' was missing from the documentary, especially regarding abortion and birth control matters. In order to provide a forum for opposing views, it scheduled an hour following the documentary for people to challenge the documentary's pro-abortion stance. Revd Jesse Jackson spoke against abortion and population control as racist. Marjory Mecklenberg, president of Minnesota Citizens Concerned for Life, displayed slides of foetuses and played a recording of a 14-week-old heartbeat. Valerie Dillon of the Respect for Life Committee quipped, 'Shall we sell [contraceptive technologies to teenagers] in school vending machines?' Conservative Ben Wattenberg argued for *more* births. After the programme, at least one newspaper article remarked that this hour was significantly more effective television than the documentary itself.[50] The discussion touched off a huge letter-writing campaign co-ordinated by fundamentalist groups and the Catholic Church that resulted in the shelving of the documentary which was to have been distributed to schools and colleges by the US Office of Education.[51]

Feminist representatives, who would have articulated pro-abortion arguments associated with women's rights and distinct from those of population control, were not included in the group of invited challengers or in the documentary. Because particular spokespeople were ordained and others were not, because women's movement voices were so completely silenced, the terms in which the pro-abortion position could be cast were severely limited.

| 'Population: Boom or Doom' | Two weeks before *Roe* v. *Wade* on 6 January 1973, Marlene Sanders's ABC documentary 'Population: Boom or Doom' was broadcast. Like the Fisher film, it intended to be a documentary version of the Commission's report, |

49 Craig Fisher and John Martin, *Population and the American Future*, film in possession of author on loan from Fisher.

50 John Archibald, 'More-People People Steal Population Show', *St. Louis Post Dispatch*, 1 Dec. 1972.

51 Nancy Ross, 'Television: Shelving a Film', *Washington Post*, 11 Jan. 1973.

but Sanders included interviews with many Commission members as well as with numerous others. The documentary was divided into three parts: a short introduction to population statistics and issues, a long segment on reproductive matters, and a short segment on immigration. The segment on reproduction included sections on birth control technologies, sex education, and abortion. The only participants speaking against the Commission's recommendations on these matters were Commission member Paul Cornely (an African American physician) and James T. McHugh (a Catholic priest from the US Catholic Conference), both of whom opposed the recommendations on contraceptives for minors and on abortion. (Dr Paul Cornely's objections, it should be noted, were articulated in religious rather than race-based arguments.)

In the section on sex education, the racist implications of population control surface momentarily. During a question and answer session at the University of North Carolina, an African American male student asks Rockefeller, 'How do you rationalize with a Black person that for them to stop having a certain number of kids is not genocide but is indeed helping their race as well as helping society as a whole?' Rockefeller replies that he believes in 'voluntarism' and 'freedom of choice' and that 'every citizen should have the same knowledge and availability of services'.

The seven-minute section on abortion includes: footage at a Planned Parenthood clinic where abortions were performed and an interview with the clinic's director, Cornely and McHugh objecting to the Commission's stand, and Commission member Carol Foreman defending the report's conclusions. Like the Fisher documentary, no women's movement spokesperson is presented. The sole feminist-orientated statement—'women should have the freedom to control their own fertility and the freedom from the burdens of unwanted childbearing'—is framed and embedded in almost an hour of population-control discourse.[52]

ABC encountered active protest prior to its airing of the documentary, and it received much pro and con correspondence after the broadcast. As with the 1969 'Abortion', many letters from fundamentalist spokespeople complained that the documentary misled viewers by having a Catholic priest articulate the only opposing view. (While preparing the documentary, Sanders had inquired of her bosses if having a 'Protestant' spokesperson was necessary for 'fairness' considerations. Obviously, she and ABC ultimately decided—as did Pendrell and the network in 1969—that it was not.)[53] Other letters congratulated ABC and the documentary for living up to television's responsibility to inform and educate.[54] Rockefeller wrote to ABC president Elton Rule praising the film. The Executive Director of the Citizens' Committee wrote that three people had called her office 'wondering why we wasted time making an independent film of the Commission Report when you were obviously able to do it so much better. Ah, that hurts.'[55]

52 Fisher and Martin, *Population and the American Future*.

53 See Sanders, 'ABC Report on the "population show" ', undated, box 1, folder 1; Sanders inquires, 'If we interview McHugh [the Catholic priest] does fairness dictate that a Protestant leader who supports the proposal be included? Please advise.'

54 See Sanders, box 2, folder 5, for examples of letters.

55 Carol Foreman, Executive Director of the Citizens' Committee on Population and the American Future, to Marlene Sanders, 9 Jan. 1973, Sanders, box 2, folder 5.

Considering the Ramifications

The struggle over these two abortion documentaries prior to the *Roe* v. *Wade* decision illuminates some of the ways that the original feminist perspective—abortion as a woman's unequivocal right, having nothing to do with population control—was silenced in what became official public policy. Television's quest for 'balance', more fervidly enacted as the Federal Communication Commission began to crack down on documentaries that they felt provided a biased view of topics under discussion, shaped the public debate by giving recognition to what it deemed the *legitimated* voices struggling over abortion.[56] TV allowed population control advocates (some with legacies of blatant racism and classism) and the medical establishment to speak the pro-abortion view. This turned a complex, multifaceted battle into a two-sided contest—those who were *for* and those who were *against* legalized abortion. Those against were the Catholic Church, the having-it-both-ways Nixon White House, the fundamentalist New Right, African American abortion and birth control opponents, and individual politicians. Those who were for were the population-control groups, the medical and legal establishments, and other politicians. The women's movement, including African American feminist groups, was totally suppressed.

This suppression happened at various levels of the fight, and the shift of part of the women's movement to a 'choice' framework for abortion rights, a framework that was commensurate with that of the population control movement, ended up exacerbating the dilemma. For example, Sarah Weddington, the young liberal feminist lawyer who argued *Roe*, has discussed the ways she received help from the population control establishment in researching the case and how she welcomed the Commission's report 'Population and the American Future' as a support and groundwork for her own preparation of *Roe*.[57]

My aim is not to assign 'blame' to abortion proponents such as David Lowe, Ernest Pendrell, Marlene Sanders, Craig Fisher, Thomas Wolf, or even ABC and CBS for not attending to the ways in which they chose to apportion 'balance'; or to players like Sarah Weddington for pleading the case within the terms of privacy—as opposed, for example, to those of equal rights and protections; or to feminists who moved the terms from 'abortion on demand' to 'freedom to choose'. I am simply arguing that trouble followed for this coalition on abortion rights which included liberal views in its legitimated 'pro' position, but which strategically decided to ignore, minimize, or subsume radical (delegitimated) ones in order to secure its goals—goals that were inflected with many different meanings for different 'pro' participants. That this is the case seems abundantly clear not only from the aftermath of *Roe* but from the ways TV documentaries with generally liberal and progressive viewpoints on abortion played out the struggles over these rights.

For television, the ideology of documentary production practices got inflected repeatedly by how 'balance' was conceived.[58] In this case, US TV

56 Hammond, *The Image Decade*, 224–7.

57 Weddington, *A Question of Choice*, 91–3, 135.

58 Stuart Hall, Ian Connell, and Lidia Curti wrote in 1976 that although political news programmes in Great Britain may have offered different 'party sides' to issues, they essentially worked to buttress and fortify the very notion of parliamentary democracy. Stuart Hall, Ian Connell, and Lidia Curti, 'The

documentary's conception and enactment of 'balance' shored up the notion of liberal pluralism—that competing voices contribute equally to fashioning public policy on difficult social issues. What gets repressed is the incontrovertible fact that some voices are given legitimacy through representation and others are not: some get air time and others get stifled. The ways TV chose to incarnate the abortion debate reduced its complexities to a particular 'pro' and 'con' binary and then went on to situate the terms of public discourse around that binary. Decisions about 'balance' had the effect of pulling the 'pro' sides of the debate into the vortex of the population control discourses on abortion, rather than those of feminism, because that became the rational, sanctioned position in favour of liberalizing the law.

Among many other things, this analysis reveals the ongoing and remarkable disparities between the lived social and the officially represented—represented in terms of having sanctioned and recognized positions from which to speak, and in terms of gaining places on US documentary television. The vast array of women who participated in the battle for legal abortions, who marched and protested, argued the issue, spoke out at state legislatures, worked as physicians, nurses, and lawyers, performed abortions, and secured for themselves illegal and sometimes traumatic treatment, found very little place as active subjects on America's home-screen documentaries. This contrasts to the way anti-abortion groups and individuals (as we saw with the PBS forum) ultimately gained representation in the pre-*Roe* period.

The policy that ensued in *Roe* v. *Wade* fell short of situating abortion as an absolute right conceived in terms of women's socially constructed and socially situated position. It therefore invited an array of other opposing rights to rise up and challenge women's ability to secure legal abortions. The rights of the foetus (pitted, in fact, more and more, in the 1980s and 1990s, against the selfish and immoral mother), the rights of the husband, of the father, the rights of the state, the rights of a pregnant teenager's parents, were some of the many challengers that sought to erode the permanence of the 1973 decision.

Although Celeste Condit has argued, in a rhetorical study of abortion discourse, that it was not the essentially liberal social system but the barrage of competing voices that resulted in a compromising of the women's movement's full goals, I am arguing that US television documentaries' liberal democratic character contributed to shaping a troubled US abortion policy and understanding that will most likely be up for renegotiation in the not too distant future.[59] The history presented here makes plain that feminist abortion supporters should be prepared to articulate clearly formulated demands for judicially protected abortion rights which, in my opinion, should be reframed around terms of equal rights and protections rather than privacy, and the *social* rather than the individualistic dimensions of abortion.[60]

"Unity" of Current Affairs Television', *Cultural Studies 9: Working Papers in Cultural Studies* (Birmingham: Centre for Contemporary Cultural Studies, 1976), 51–93.

59 Celeste Michelle Condit, *Decoding Abortion Rhetoric: Communicating Social Change* (Urbana: Univ. of Illinois Press, 1990).

60 For a delineation of the equal rights and protection v. the privacy justifications for abortion law, see Frances Olsen, 'Unraveling Compromise', *Harvard Law Review*, 103 (1989), 105–35; Reva Siegel, 'Reasoning from the Body: A Historical Perspective on Abortion Regulation and Questions of Equal Protection', *Stanford Law Review*, 44 (1992), 261–381; Catharine MacKinnon, 'Privacy v. Equality:

Thanks to Charlotte Brunsdon, Mary Beth Haralovich, Michele Hilmes, Laura Stempel Mumford, Lauren Rabinovitz, and Jane Schacter for many astute suggestions on various drafts of this chapter.

Beyond *Roe v Wade*', in MacKinnon, *Feminism Unmodified* (Cambridge: Harvard Univ. Press, 1987), 93; Ruth Bader Ginsburg, 'Some Thoughts on Autonomy and Equality in Relation to *Roe v. Wade*', *North Carolina Law Review*, 63: 375–86; Dawn E. Johnsen, 'The Creation of Fetal Rights', *Yale Law Journal*, 95: 599–625; Wendy Brown, 'Reproductive Freedom and the Right to Privacy', in Diamond (ed.), *Families, Politics and Public Policy*, 322–88; Rhonda Copelon, 'From Privacy to Autonomy', in Fried (ed.), *From Abortion to Reproductive Freedom*, 27–43.

19

The Ideology of Freshness in Feminine Hygiene Commercials

Kate Kane

EVERYBODY HATES FEMININE hygiene commercials. An *Advertising Age* survey found them at the top of both women's and men's most-hated lists (Hume, 1988: 3). This hatred, I believe, goes beyond taboos about menstruation, because the category includes more than just tampons and menstrual pads—it encompasses douches, sprays, and washes. In social discourse, matters of hygiene flirt with the limits of good taste; *feminine* hygiene transgresses those limits, evoking (but never showing) images of blood and forbidden smells. There is, I shall argue, more at work here than the 'bad taste' of popular culture. Feminine hygiene commercials are powerful weapons in an ideological battle for control of women's sexuality. The ideology of freshness is crucial to that battle.

This chapter focuses on how American television commercials for feminine hygiene products define the female body, construe its polluting effect, and prescribe rituals of purification. Feminine hygiene commercials participate in an overdetermined discourse on femininity that relies on beliefs about the body common in post-industrial society. As Michèle Mattelart has argued, the media in liberal democracies represent a range of possibilities for feminine identity, but insist fundamentally on an 'eternal' feminine specificity (Mattelart, 1986: 23). The implied assertion that women are biologically determined naturalizes male dominance and corporate social control.

In part one I discuss the cultural context of body beliefs and pollution avoidance in which feminine hygiene commercials participate. First I discuss commercial discourse on cleanliness in general (household and physical) and its importance to social control. Then I examine one element common to house and body cleanliness—freshness—for its ideological value in regard to femininity. In part two, I illustrate the ideology of freshness with an analysis of one commercial.

■ Control of the Body, Social Control, and Ideology

This analysis is inspired by the work of anthropologist Mary Douglas on pollution beliefs and social order. She argues that cultures have rules about how things may leave or enter the body, as well as to whom the bodily emission

© *JCI*, 1990.

Originally published in *Journal of Communication Inquiry*, 14/1 (Winter 1990), 82–92.

might be dangerous (Douglas, 1966). While Douglas discusses traditional cultures that use ritual to restore the social and religious imbalance that pollution causes, her insights on the function of social and personal boundaries illuminate modern cultural beliefs as well.

> With us pollution is a matter of aesthetics, hygiene or etiquette, which only becomes grave in so far as it may create social embarrassment. The sanctions are social sanctions, contempt, ostracism, gossip, perhaps even police action. But in another large group of human societies the effects of pollution are much more wide ranging. A grave pollution is a religious offence.   (Douglas, 1966: 73)

While beliefs about hygiene in American culture may well be secular and mundane, their ideological significance goes beyond mere 'social sanctions'. The problematic of the female body is rooted in Judaeo-Christian mythology: in the temptation of Eve, and in the proscriptions of Leviticus (ch. 12, uncleanness of childbirth, and ch. 15, verses 19–33, uncleanness of menstrual flow). So hygiene beliefs resonate from religious rules, although admittedly without the threat of death as a sanction.

In *The Curse: A Cultural History of Menstruation*, the authors (Delaney *et al.*, 1988) find that menstrual taboos are alive and well in 'modern' culture. As we shall see, the menstrual taboo extends to all vaginal secretions. It thus incorporates sexuality into the taboo. Feminine hygiene commercials constitute a sort of secular sacramentality.

Second, in secular post-industrial culture, the commercial mass media have a voice at least equal to that of other ideological institutions. Displacing the authority of church, school, and family, corporate-controlled public discourse exploits the terms of traditional authority for its own ends (see Ewen, 1976). The importance of corporate social control as a correlate to economic hegemony cannot be underestimated.

Advertising's ability to evoke unconscious response is part of its ideological power (see Schwartz, 1974). As Foucault argues, discursive power in relation to sexuality and the body resides in dominant institutions (Foucault, 1980). Television is not only the most pervasive and mundane of ideological institutions; its raison d'être is advertising. Television uses its discursive power to define the body as a site of multiple pollution possibilities. The human body, as written in American television commercials, is a composite of potential emissions that threaten to disrupt social order.

Hygiene commercials situate the body in a complex of pollution beliefs that reconcile the individual body to society:

> rituals of purity and impurity create unity in experience. . . . By their means, symbolic patterns are worked out and publicly displayed. Within these patterns disparate elements are related and disparate experience is given meaning.   (Douglas, 1966: 2–3)

By following the rules of body culture, we render ourselves acceptable to society. We exchange our self-control (in whatever permutations our society dictates) for access to others. Hygiene commercials of all types prey on fear of rejection by intimates, or fear of not achieving physical proximity with others (breath and mouth products, for example: 'Want love? Get Closeup.').

Taken together, these commercials form a picture of a people obsessed with physical intimacy, yet unable to achieve it without performing many elaborate, expensive daily purifications.

In so many words, hygiene commercials warn constantly that body odours are repulsive to others. They claim to be able to restore a natural odour ('freshness') or at least a neutral one (de-odorant), but actually they overlay body odour with another smell. We may smell like something other than a human body, but we think we smell OK because everybody else smells the same way we do—or almost everybody. The way we smell, as much as the way we dress and speak, indicates our social status.

■ **Bodily Pollution and How to Avoid it**

According to American commercials, the best way to avoid pollution is prophylaxis, or prevention. Because it is social subjects themselves who are at risk from bodily emissions, individual bodies are responsible for containing their own fluids. Sweat, for example, should be stopped at the body's boundary ('Never let them see you sweat' (antiperspirant commercial)). If by chance (usually through some appropriately masculine activity) sweat does befoul your clothes, a deodorizing detergent will purify it (Surf). Plastic diapers are another example of prophylaxis as the dominant mode of pollution control. Their 'leak-proof' quality protects others, not the baby.

Note that pollution control is an individual responsibility, focusing on the private sphere and not the public one. According to Douglas, pollution beliefs flourish amid contradiction: 'when moral rules are obscure or contradictory there is a tendency for pollution beliefs to simplify or clarify the point at issue' (Douglas, 1966: 142). She does not discuss who makes the clarification, but in this case it is clearly in the interests of corporate control to locate pollution in the home. The illusion of personal control masks corporate culpability for environmental/public pollution.

American television commercials seem obsessed with sanitation, particularly in the domestic sphere, which includes the body. In addition to the numerous body products that promise to repress odour, many household products are required to maintain a pure home. 'Air fresheners', floor cleaners, bathroom and toilet-scrubbing solutions are only part of the picture. For what cannot be sprayed away must be contained, as indicated by many types and sizes (one might say 'styles') of plastic garbage bags, including deodorant ones. In the kitchen, it is particularly important to safeguard food against the decaying effect of air and other foods, as the abundance of plastic wraps, bags, and marvellously specialized plastic containers attest. Throughout all these examples, the ideal state is 'freshness'. 'Freshness' is the way the subject/consumer (coded more often than not as female) attains/maintains a position in the social order, whether by satisfying her family or the standards of female attractiveness.

The very existence of a special category, feminine hygiene, indicates that female bodies require specific cleansing rituals. Television's prescription for menstrual pollution-avoidance is historically and culturally specific. Feminine hygiene commercials must be seen as positioned on the continuum of American body beliefs, at a point of intersection with the iconography of gender difference.

The ideology of freshness conjoins women's bodies and the domestic sphere, correlating the self and the home. Consider, for example, that douches come in the same scents as room deodorants (floral, herbal, baby-powder). It is a long-standing common belief that a woman's house and her body reflect her image of herself and indicate her worth. Hygiene commercials implicate women's bodies in the system of commodity consumption.

■ **The Ideology of Freshness**

The work of another cultural anthropologist, Claude Lévi-Strauss, suggests a line of thinking that illuminates the problematic of 'freshness'. Lévi-Strauss deduced a set of underlying oppositions concerning nature and culture in their symbolic associations with the raw and the cooked (Lévi-Strauss, 1969). His schema is useful to this study because it identifies culture as the mediator of natural conditions and social relations.

According to Lévi-Strauss, the raw and the cooked are symbolic opposites, associated with nature and culture, respectively. In nature, the raw will become rotten without the intervention of cooking, which represents culture (Lévi-Strauss, 1969: 294). These structural relationships are played out in myth and ritual and refer to people as well as to plant and animal foods. The socialized individual is a 'cooked' person (Lévi-Strauss, 1969: 336).

'Fresh' is like and unlike raw. Freshness opposes rottenness. As such, freshness implies a natural pristine condition that, like rawness, is temporary, given the tendency of natural objects to decay. In post-industrial culture, however, 'natural' is not raw. It is a particular kind of cooked. When commercials or products invoke freshness they frequently refer to nature: pine forests (Pine-Sol cleaner), summer days (Snuggle fabric softener), mountain herbs, country flowers, and particular flowers such as daisies (Massengill douche), fruits such as lemon-scented dish soap, and spice-flavoured room deodorants. This artificial naturalness is a post-industrial category with symbolic purchase across many categories of advertising (food, for example: all-natural chocolate-covered granola bars). It indicates that there is a distance between unspoiled nature and polluted civilization (Williamson, 1978: 103–37). Corporate consciousness-makers would like to obscure that distance while simultaneously exploiting it by selling nature-substitutes, and conflating Mother Earth with synthetic imitations under the umbrella term 'freshness'.

'Freshness' generates a field of meanings that contains women's sexuality within phallocentric parameters. If women are seen as 'naturally' more self-polluting, feminine hygiene products represent a masculine/cultural intervention. Lévi-Strauss notes that 'the individuals who are [ritually] "cooked" are those deeply involved in a physiological process' (Lévi-Strauss, 1969: 336). That is, those who are dangerously close to natural functions, such as babies being born and women who are menstruating, require rituals to recuperate them into culture. It would seem that the sexually marked (menstrual-age) American woman is perpetually close to nature. As the woman in the Carefree Panty Shields (which are meant for daily use) commercial puts it, 'I'm a woman every day.' Cultural intervention, or 'cooking', renders the dangerous individual 'edible', or perhaps more appropriately in this case, consumable.

While they are not rituals or myths in the strict sense, feminine hygiene commercials are like rituals in that they seek to define and mediate experi-ence. They establish a danger and offer salvation. They further define gender difference, indicating how to transform a potentially rotten female into an acculturated 'fresh' feminine person.

The importance of culture as a mediator of charged natural objects is evi-dent in hygiene commercials. That is the value of the Lévi-Straussian analy-sis. The raw–cooked–rotten model does not fully account for 'freshness', but it does suggest that cultured naturalness might be a central and fruitful con-tradiction in the term's cultural baggage.

■ **Femininity and** While this fear of bodily dirt and domestic pollution is discernible in many
Pollution categories of television advertising, feminine hygiene commercials occupy a special place in the discourse:

> when the principle of male dominance is applied to the ordering of social life but is contradicted by other principles such as that of female indepen-dence, or the inherent right of women as the weaker sex to be more pro-tected from violence than men, then sex pollution is likely to flourish. (Douglas, 1966: 142)

Because they speak directly to biological difference, feminine hygiene commercials are in a unique position to articulate this culture's conception of femininity. Their basic ideological assumptions illuminate the foundation on which the TV woman is culturally constructed. Female hygiene commer-cials posit that women are biologically more self-polluting than men are. While this is also the case in some other cultures, what is at issue here is not only the pollution itself, but more important, who defines pollution and what must be done to avoid it. By containing polluting bodily fluids, women become socially acceptable and potentially desirable. Desirability, which represents the ultimate achievement for the late-industrial woman, is predi-cated on a specific kind of femininity which has freshness at its core.

While the lines drawn by feminine hygiene commercials indicate appro-priate femininity, they also imply outlaw sexuality. Because they define the boundary in terms of bodily emission, it is clear that unchecked vaginal emis-sion marks the 'bad woman'. That is, the freely sexual woman, such as Mae West represents, is an abomination to polite society. William Randolph Hearst's characterization of West as 'a monster of lubricity' (Anger, 1975: 264) exposes the bodily fluid basis of his disapprobation. The woman who acts on her wetness (i.e. is sexually self-determined), rather than keeping it under wraps, breaks social taboos as well as hygienic ones.

This construction of acceptable female sexuality is unmistakably bour-geois, whether in the 1930s or in the present day. Although public sexual standards may seem to have progressed since Mae West scandalized right-thinking folk, contemporary popular culture provides many examples that the freely sexual woman is a social menace (*Fatal Attraction, Body Heat*). I return to Mattelart's discussion of modernity:

> In women's magazines, their constant renewal and search for variety is related to consumption, based on the principle of obsolescence and the 'dynamism' of newness. This cult of the ephemeral reveals the essence of

modernity, but as a class strategy: this periodic system of renewal, which in most cases is no more than a simple readjustment of units which themselves remain unchanged, is rich in mythical significance. . . . Women are imprisoned within the symbols of modernity, just as they were imprisoned, not long ago, within the symbols of the bourgeoisie: piano lessons and education in convent schools.   (Mattelart, 1986: 43)

'Freshness' represents the particular form of control over women's sexuality in the present historical circumstances; the underlying misogyny remains.

Rituals of Purification

The following Carefree Panty Shields commercial exemplifies many strategies common to feminine hygiene commercials. It equates freshness and femininity. It peddles a regressive pseudo-feminism as a mask for its celebration of the 'eternal' feminine. It uses repression and display as textual mechanisms. And it promotes appearance over desire as the appropriate expression of female/'feminine' sexuality.

■ Description of the Commercial

A woman addresses the camera directly from her casual seat on the front steps of a brownstone. Her testimony is intercut with pictures of her in various settings wearing different costumes.

CAREFREE PANTY SHIELDS

Shot	Soundtrack	Visual
1	Who am I? Well, some days I'm	Wide shot woman on front steps.
2	silk, and some days	Wide shot, woman in suit walks down steps.
3	I'm denim	Wide shot, woman in jeans on park bench with bicycle next to her.
4	but underneath it all, I'm a woman every day	Wide shot, woman in underwear sits on her bed, tosses her hair, walks out of frame.
5	and I always want to be feminine	American shot, woman walks to dresser, opens drawer.
6	so I start each day fresh with Carefree	Close-up, package in drawer with underwear.
7	Carefree's something I do for me	Close-up, hand holding package, takes one pad out.
8	'cause when I'm fresh dressed I feel more feminine. So even though some days	Shoulder shot, woman on porch with hand on chin.
9	I'm cashmere	Wide shot, woman in red coat runs across street to taxi.
10	and some days I'm cotton	American shot, woman in skirt walks across bridge, pushes up sleeve.

11 I'm a woman every day, so underneath it all I use Carefree every day.	Wide shot, woman on steps Super in bottom of frame: Carefree every day because you're a woman every day.

■ **Freshness and Femininity**

While many commercials imply a relationship between freshness and femininity, this one spells out the connection. The last shot demonstrates the tautological nature of the fresh–feminine equation. The character says 'I'm a woman every day, so underneath it all I use Carefree every day.' At the bottom of the frame is a superimposition: 'Carefree every day because you're a woman every day.'

Another bit of ideological magic in the freshness bag of tricks works to perpetuate what Mattelart calls 'the myth of modernity' (Mattelart, 1986: 33–56). By appealing to freshness, commercials participate in the paradoxical commodification of newness, in which products, fashion, and other consumables change their style but not their substance. By using Carefree, the woman makes her self fresh—new—every day.

That femaleness and femininity are not the same is evident in the line 'I'm a woman every day and I always want to be feminine.' Femaleness is the raw condition, femininity is the cooked. Although it is important that femininity have the aura of being natural, it is clearly an acculturated state.

This commercial also demonstrates the feminine specificity inherent in the range of possible roles for the 'modern' woman. The speaker's dress reflects her latitude of choice: she can be businesslike (silk), athletic (denim), romantic (cashmere), or casual (cotton). 'But, underneath it all, I'm a woman every day and I always want to be feminine.' That is, no matter whether she is professional or playful, her essential being is female/raw-rotten; in order to be feminine/fresh, she must perform the daily Carefree ritual.

■ **The Eternal Feminine**

Another way to read the multiple possibilities she asserts for her identity is as the capricious, inconstant, moody woman of the 'eternal' feminine. Temporal indicators such as 'some days' are part of the traditional association of women with natural cycles. Lévi-Strauss characterizes nature as continuous time, and culture as discontinuous. Culture interrupts nature, which, like woman, is unchanging (Lévi-Strauss, 1969: 279). Mattelart identifies the bourgeois ideology of change as a paradox. Change, she says, is 'one of the most sensitive areas of bourgeois mystification', because

> [t]he bourgeois regime interprets capitalist order not as a transitory phase of the historical process, but rather as the absolute form of social production. (Mattelart, 1986: 33)

This static notion of time requires some ideological sleight-of-hand and centres on women as the locus of artificial change. Mattelart sees this artifice in fashion, for example, and particularly in advertising (Mattelart, 1986: 35).

'Some days' could also be a coy indicator for menstrual period. With repetition, 'some days' takes in the whole month, correlating Carefree with menstrual pads, and vaginal wetness with menstrual blood. 'I'm a woman every day' underscores this point by including—without mentioning—those 'special days' marked by more dramatic evidence of femaleness.

■ Pseudo-
Liberation

'Carefree's something I do for me' helps this character partake of 'me-generation' self-help pop psychology. It asserts a pseudo-feminist stance, in which standing up for one's rights is conflated with spending money on feeling good, which is defined as feeling good about oneself. Feeling good about oneself is predicated on having a particular kind of appearance, rather than on personal growth or power or any such non-purchasable quality.

It is also pseudo-feminist because it asserts a false independence, the freedom to choose fetishized femininity over politics. As an advertisement for *Being a Woman: Fulfilling Your Femininity and Finding Love* (Grant, 1987) puts it, 'If we've come so far, then why aren't we married?' (*Chicago Tribune*, 1988). Marriage and children represent the only real satisfaction women can achieve, all else is transitory. The feminine mystique is still at work, albeit in a power suit.

The brand name Carefree partakes of a post-liberation discourse apparent in other sanitary pads that feature 'freedom', Stayfree and New Freedom. Freedom itself is narrowly confined within cosmetic boundaries, although its possible meanings include liberation and democracy. But in the world of television commercials, democracy means the equality of purchasing power. Of what care is she free? Ostensibly these pads free women from 'old-fashioned' belts and non-adhesive pads. Explicitly, they purport to free women from worrying about leakage. Implicitly, moreover, the commercials evoke sexual freedom while at the same time working against it.

The Carefree woman moves freely through public space, but as an object to be seen. Her pleasure ('Carefree's something I do for me') derives not from her own desire but from her ability to achieve femininity ('when I'm fresh dressed I *feel* more feminine' (my emphasis)). She tacitly acknowledges that femininity is an artificial condition, but embraces it none the less and positions herself as object of display (her pose on the front porch recalls pin-up images).

■ Textual
Operations:
Repression and
Display

Simultaneous repression and display are the hallmark of feminine hygiene commercials. Several factors constrain these commercials: network standards (or, in pre-deregulation days, the National Association of Broadcasters code); public 'taste'; convention. The central problematic is how to represent something that cannot be shown, how to say what cannot be spoken. In settling for euphemism and coyness, advertisers circumlocute the problem by positioning their products as cosmetic or medical or both. None the less they must deal with the real identity of their products while never actually evoking 'dirt'. They find many ways to do that.

In most cases, advertisers show only the box, not the actual product. Commercials for pads and tampons rarely have any red in them; white compositions are much more frequent. A Massengill commercial, in which a mother and daughter have an intimate talk, takes place on a beach with the ocean in the background. It displays the source of an identifiable odour (the subject of many jokes about the smell of women) while the dialogue describes how to get rid of it, but never overtly refers to smell. An overnight pad commercial features a woman who just found the right colour sheets to go with her décor. She stops short of saying the unspeakable: 'and wouldn't you know . . .', but summons an image of blood-stained sheets in classic film dialectic—the next shot is the overnight pad.

The Carefree commercial uses repression and display in several ways. It never states what exactly it is about being a woman that requires a pad every day, but intimates it via 'freshness' and 'underneath it all' (this phrase appears twice). I noted above the tautology, 'I'm a woman every day, so underneath it all I use Carefree every day', which appears reversed on the screen in the last shot. Like an enthymeme (an argument with a premiss or conclusion left out), the statement leaves unspoken the premiss implied by the earlier disjunction of woman and feminine ('I'm a woman every day and I always want to be feminine'): female bodies are naturally polluted.

Narratively, the commercial uses repression and display in its structuring of public and private space. The shots of the woman wearing lingerie in her bedroom are embedded between the silk/denim shots and the cashmere/cotton shots, which all occur on the street. The bedroom shots display her more sexually than the other shots do, but the voice-over doesn't say 'I'm lingerie', it says 'I'm a woman'. So while it displays her in undergarments, the commercial's word-picture speaks of proximity to genitals ('underneath it all'), repressing the slippage between the genital specificity of 'woman' and undergarments' proximity to the genitals, thereby creating the space to insert the product.

■ **Appearance versus Desire**

This archetypal woman identifies herself ('Who am I?') so closely with her appearance that she is what she wears ('I'm silk . . . I'm denim . . . I'm cashmere . . . I'm cotton . . .'). In this, the commercial follows conventional representations of the female image as to-be-looked-at rather than as looking, active subject (see Mulvey, 1985). Moreover, it defines her pleasure in her appearance as the essence of her identity as a feminine being, contained in culture by her devotion to the rites of freshness.

The ideology of freshness works to contain feminine sexuality within phallocentric boundaries. By defining any type of vaginal wetness as a pollution inimical to nice-girl femininity, these commercials displace the physiological sign of sexual arousal from the vagina to the face (red, wet lips, moist skin) and outward appearance. They repress the actual internal experience of one's own sexuality in favour of an external display of feminine codes. Thus feminine hygiene commercials reiterate the sexist imperative that appropriate female sexuality is constituted in appearance rather than in desire or action. Being seen by others precedes existing for oneself.

The manufacture of feminine hygiene products is dominated by a few transnational corporations (Procter and Gamble, Johnson and Johnson, Kimberly-Clark, Tambrands). It is their interests that drive the proliferation of discourse on the female body. As they export capitalist modes of production, we should bear in mind that they also export an ideology that works to keep women 'in their place' while pretending to offer them liberation.

References
Anger, Kenneth (1975), *Hollywood Babylon* (New York: Dell Publishing Co.).

Chicago Tribune (1988: 15 May), sect. 14, p. 10.

Delaney, Janice, Lupton, Mary Jane, and Toth, Emily (1988), *The Curse: A Cultural History of Menstruation*, rev. edn. (Urbana, Ill.: Univ. of Illinois Press).

Douglas, Mary (1966), *Purity and Danger: An Analysis of the Concepts of Pollution and Taboo* (London: Routledge & Kegan Paul).

Ewen, Stuart (1976), *Captains of Consciousness: Advertising and the Social Roots of the Consumer Culture* (New York: McGraw-Hill).

Foucault, Michel (1980), *The History of Sexuality*, vol. 1, trans. R. Hurley (New York: Vintage).

Grant, Toni (1987), *Being a Woman: Fulfilling Your Femininity and Finding Love* (New York: Random House).

Hume, Scott (1988: 18 July), ' "Most hated" ads: feminine hygiene', *Advertising Age.*

Lévi-Strauss, Claude (1969), *The Raw and the Cooked: Introduction to a Science of Mythology*, vol. 1, trans. J. and D. Weightman (Chicago: Univ. of Chicago Press).

Mattelart, Michèle (1986), *Women/Media/Crisis: Femininity and Disorder* (London: Comedia).

Mulvey, Laura (1985), 'Visual pleasure and narrative cinema', in G. Mast and M. Cohen (eds.), *Film Theory and Criticism*, 3rd edn. (New York: Oxford Univ. Press), 803–16; repr. from *Screen*, 16/3.

Schwartz, Tony (1974), *The Responsive Chord* (Garden City, NY: Anchor/Doubleday).

Williamson, Judith (1978), *Decoding Advertisements: Ideology and Meaning in Advertising* (London: Marion Boyars).

20
Never Trust a Big Butt and a Smile

Tricia Rose

IF **YOU WERE** to construct an image of rap music via accounts of rap in the established press, you would (besides betraying limited critical instincts about popular culture) probably perceive rap to reflect the violent, brutally sexist reality of a pack of wilding 'little Willie Hortons'.[1] Consequently, you would wonder what a group of young black women rappers was doing fraternizing with these male rappers and why they seemed to be having such a good time. If I were to suggest that their participation in rap music produced some of the most important contemporary black feminist cultural criticism, you would surely bemoan the death of sexual equality. As Public Enemy's Chuck D has warned regarding the mainstream press, 'Don't believe the hype.' Sexism in rap has been gravely exaggerated by the mainstream press. Rap is a rich, complex multifaceted African American popular form whose male practitioners' style and subject matter includes the obsessive sexism of a 2 Live Crew, the wacky parody of Biz Markie, the 'edutainment' of Boogie Down Productions, the gangster-style story-telling of Ice Cube, the gritty and intelligent speed rapping of Kool Moe Dee, and the explicit black nationalism of X-Clan. Women rappers are vocal and respected members of the Hip Hop community, and they have quite a handle on what they are doing.

Fortunately or unfortunately (I'm not sure which), most academics concerned with contemporary popular culture and music have avoided sustained critical analysis of rap. A few literary scholars and theorists have explained the historical and cultural heritage of rap as an African American from, while others have made passing reference to it as an important site of postmodernist impulses or as the prophetic voice of an angry disenfranchised group of young African Americans.[2] The work on women rappers

Originally published in *Camera Obscura*, 23 (May 1990), 109–31 and subsequently published as *Black Noise*.

1 For a particularly malicious misreading of rap music see David Gates, 'The Rap Attitude', *Newsweek Magazine*, 19 Mar. 1990: 56–63. While 'The Rap Attitude' is an outrageous example, the assumptions made about the use and intent of rap are quite common. Exceptions to misreadings of this nature include Michael Dyson, 'The Culture of Hip Hop', *Zeta Magazine* (June 1989), 45–50 and the works of Greg Tate, a *Village Voice* staff writer, who has been covering rap music for almost a decade.

2 See Henry Louis Gates, Jr., 'Two Live Crew De-Coded', *New York Times*, 19 June 1990: 31; Bruce Tucker, 'Tell Tchaikovsky the News: Postmodernism, Popular Culture and the Emergence of Rock n Roll', *Black Music Research Journal* (Fall 1989), 271–95; Anders Stephanson, 'Interview with Cornell West', in Andrew Ross (ed.), *Universal Abandon?: The Politics of Postmodernism* (Minneapolis: Univ. of Minnesota Press, 1989), 269–86.

(while making claims that women rappers are pro-women artists) has been published in popular monthly periodicals and consequently has been limited to short but provocative inquiries.[3]

While any positive, critical attention to rap comes as a welcome relief, almost all of these accounts observe rap music outside of its socio-historical framework, as texts suspended in time. Such distanced readings, especially of a musical form to which it is difficult to gain direct and sustained access, leave open the possibility of grave misreadings regarding meanings and context. Women rappers are especially vulnerable to such misreadings precisely because their presence in rap has been consistently ignored or marginalized, even by those social critics who have published some of the most insightful analyses of rap. This essay, which is part of an extended project on rap music, will try to correct some of these misunderstandings, or as Chuck D states, 'give you something that I knew you lacked. So consider me a new jack'.[4] Better yet, here's Queen Latifah:

> Some think that we can't flow (can't flow)
> Stereotypes they got to go (got to go)
> I'm gonna mess around and flip the scene into reverse
> With what?
> With a little touch of ladies first.[5]

The summer of 1989 marked the tenth anniversary of rap music's explosive début in the recording industry. In honour of its unexpected longevity, Nelson George, a pro-Hip Hop music critic and *Village Voice* columnist, published a sentimental rap retrospective in which he mourned rap's movement from a street subculture into the cold, sterile world of commercial record production. George points out that, until recently, music industry powers have maintained a studied indifference to rap music, but now that rap's 'commercial viability has been proven' many major recording companies are signing any half-way decent act they can find. What worries George, and rightly so, is that corporate influence on black music has led, in the past, to the dissolution of vibrant black cultural forms and that rap may become the latest victim. The problem is complex, real, and requires analysis. However, Nelson George, like media critics generally, imbeds his descriptions of 'authentic rap' and fears of recent corporate influence on it in gender-coded language that mischaracterizes rap and silences women rappers and consumers. In his tenth anniversary piece, George traces major shifts in rap, naming titles, artists, and producers. He weaves over twenty rap groups into his piece and names not a single female rapper. His retrospective is chock-full of prideful, urban black youth (read men), whose contributions to rap reflect 'the thoughts of city kids more deeply than the likes of Michael Jackson, Oprah Winfrey et al.' His concluding remarks make apparent his underlying perception of rap:

3 See the special issue entitled 'The Women of Rap!', *Rappin Magazine* (July 1990); Dominique Di Prima and Lisa Kennedy, 'Beat the Rap', *Mother Jones* (Sept./Oct. 1990), 32–5; Jill Pearlman, 'Rap's Gender Gap', *Option* (Fall 1988), 32–6; Marisa Fox, 'From the Belly of the Blues to the Cradle of Rap', *Details* (July 1989), 118–24.

4 Public Enemy, 'Don't Believe The Hype', *It Takes a Nation of Millions to Hold Us Back*, Def Jam Records, 1988.

5 Queen Latifah, 'Ladies First', *All Hail the Queen*, Tommy Boy Records, 1989.

To proclaim the death of rap, is to be sure, premature. But the farther the control of rap gets from its street corner constituency and the more corporations grasp it—record conglomerates, Burger King, Minute Maid, Yo! MTV Raps, etc.—the more vulnerable it becomes to cultural emasculation.

For George, corporate meddling not only dilutes cultural forms, it also reduces strapping testosterone-packed men into women! Could we imagine anything worse? Nelson George's analysis is not unusual; his is merely the latest example of media critics' consistent coding of rap music as male in the face of significant and sustained female presence.

Many social critics who have neglected to make separate mention of women rappers would probably claim that these women are in many ways just 'one of the boys'. Since they are as tough as male rappers, women rappers fit into George's mind-boggling yet emblematic definition of rap as an 'ultra-urban, unromantic, hyperrealistic, neo-nationalist, antiassimilationist, aggressive Afrocentric impulse'. For George, and for media critics generally, it is far easier to re-gender women rappers than to revise their own gender-coded analysis of rap music.[6]

Since the summer of 1989 there has been a marked increase in media attention to women rappers. Most of the articles have been written by women and have tried to shed some light on female rappers and offer a feminist analysis of their contributions. I would like to extend some of the themes presented in these pieces by showing how women rappers participate in a dialogue with male rappers and by revising some of the commonly held assumptions about what constitutes 'feminist' expression.

As Nancy Guevara notes, the 'exclusion and/or trivialization of women's role in Hip Hop' is no mere oversight.[7] The marginalization, deletion, and mischaracterization of women's role in black cultural production is routine practice. Angela Davis extends this criticism by stating that this is 'an omission that must be attributed to the influence of sexism'. In her article 'Black Women and Music: An Historical Legacy of Struggle', Davis makes three related arguments that are of particular importance here. First, she contests the marginal representation of black women in the documentation of African American cultural developments and suggests that these representations do not adequately reflect women's participation. Second, she suggests that music (song and dance) are especially productive sites for examining the collective consciousness of black Americans. And third, she calls for a close re-examination of black women's musical legacy as a way to understand black women's consciousness. She writes:

Music has long permeated the daily life of most African-Americans; it has played a central role in the normal socialization process; and during moments characterized by intense movements for social change, it has helped to shape the necessary political consciousness. Any attempt, therefore, to understand in depth the evolution of women's consciousness within the Black community requires a serious examination of the

---

6 Nelson George, 'Rap's Tenth Birthday', *Village Voice*, 24 Oct. 1989: 40.

7 Nancy Guevara, 'Women, Writin', Rappin', Breakin'', in Mike Davis *et al.* (eds.), *The Year Left*, 2 (New York: Verso, 1987), 160–75.

music which has influenced them—particularly that which they them-selves have created.[8]

She continues by offering a close reading of Gertrude 'Ma' Rainey's music as a step toward redressing such absences. Dealing with similar issues, Hazel Carby charges that white-dominated feminist discourse has marginalized (and I would add often ignored) non-white women and questions of black sexuality. She further argues that representations of black women's sexuality in African American literature differ significantly from representations of sexuality in black women's blues.[9]

Carby and Davis, while concerning themselves specifically with women's blues, are calling for a multifaceted analysis of black women's identity and sexuality as represented by their musical production. Stating that 'different cultural forms negotiate and resolve different sets of social contradictions', Carby suggests that black women writers have been encouraged to speak on behalf of a large group of black women whose daily lives and material conditions may not be adequately reflected in black women's fiction. For example, the consumption patterns and social context of popular music differ significantly from those of fiction. The dialogic capacity of popular music, especially that of rap music, engages many of the social contradictions and ambiguities that pertain specifically to contemporary urban, working-class black life.

George Lipsitz, applying Mikhail Bakhtin's concept of 'dialogic' criticism to popular music, argues that:

> Popular music is nothing if not dialogic, the product of an ongoing his-torical conversation in which no one has the first or last word. The traces of the past that pervade the popular music of the present amount to more than mere chance: they are not simply juxtapositions of incompatible realities. They reflect a dialogic process, one embedded in collective his-tory and nurtured by the ingenuity of artists interested in fashioning icons of opposition.

Lipsitz's interpretation of popular music as a social and historical dialogue is an extremely important break from traditional, formalist interpretations of music. By grounding cultural production historically and avoiding the appli-cation of a fixed inventory of core structures, dialogic criticism as employed by Lipsitz is concerned with how popular music 'arbitrates tensions between opposition and co-optation at any given historical moment'.[10]

This notion of dialogism is especially productive in the context of African American music. The history of African American music and culture has been defined in large measure by a history of the art of signifying, recontex-tualization, collective memory, and resistance. 'Fashioning icons of opposi-tion' that speak to diverse communities is part of a rich black American

---

8 Angela Davis, 'Black Women and Music: An Historical Legacy of Struggle', *Wild Women in the Whirlwind: Afro-American Culture and the Contemporary Literary Renaissance* (New Jersey: Rutgers Univ. Press, 1990), 3.

9 Hazel V. Carby, 'It Jus Be's Dat Way Sometime: The Sexual Politics of Women's Blues', *Radical America*, 20/4 (1986), 9–22.

10 George Lipsitz, *Time Passages: Collective Memory and American Popular Culture* (Minneapolis: Univ. of Minnesota Press, 1990), 99.

musical tradition to which rappers make a significant contribution. Negotiating multiple boundaries, black women rappers are in dialogue with each other, male rappers, other popular musicians (through sampling and other revisionary practices), and with Hip Hop fans.

Black women rappers are integral and resistant voices in Hip Hop and in popular music generally. They sustain an ongoing dialogue with their audiences and male rappers about sexual promiscuity, emotional commitment, infidelity, the drug trade, racial politics, and black cultural history. Rappers interpret and articulate the fears, pleasures, and promises of young black women and men whose voices have been relegated to the silent margins of public discourse. By paying close attention to rap music, we can gain some insight into how young African Americans provide for themselves a relatively safe free-play zone where they creatively address questions of sexual power, the reality of truncated economic opportunity, the pain of racism and sexism and, through physical expressions of freedom, relieve the anxieties of day-to-day oppression.

If you have been following the commercial success of rap music, it is difficult to ignore the massive increase in record deals for women rappers following Salt-N-Pepa's double platinum (two million) 1986 début album *Hot, Cool and Vicious*. Such album sales, even for a rap album by a male artist, were virtually unprecedented in 1986. Since then, several female rappers, many of whom have been rapping for years (some since the mid-1970s), have finally been recorded and promoted.[11] Says female rapper Ms Melodie:

> It wasn't that the male started rap, the male was just the first to be put on wax. Females were always into rap, and females always had their little crews and were always known for rockin' house parties and streets or whatever, school yards, the corner, the park, whatever it was.[12]

In the early stages, women's participation in rap was hindered by gender considerations. M. C. Lady 'D' notes that because she didn't put a female crew together for regular performances, she 'didn't have to worry about getting [her] equipment ripped off, coming up with the cash to get it in the first place, or hauling it around on the subways to gigs—problems that kept a lot of other women out of rap in the early days'.[13] For a number of reasons (including increased institutional support and more demand for both male and female rappers), such stumbling-blocks have been reduced.

MC Lyte's 1988 release 'Paper Thin' sold over 125,000 copies in the first six months with virtually no radio play. Lady B, who became the first recorded female rapper in 1978, was Philadelphia's top rated DJ on WUSL and is founder and editor-in-chief of *Word Up!*, a tabloid devoted to Hip Hop.[14] Salt-N-Pepa's first single, 'Expressions', from their latest album release *Black's Magic*, went gold in the first week and stayed in the number one position on *Billboard*'s Rap Chart for over two months.

---

11 Roxanne Shante was the first commercial breakthrough female artist. Her basement-produced single was 'Roxanne's Revenge' (1985).

12 Pearlman, 'Rap's Gender Gap', 34.

13 Di Prima and Kennedy, 'Beat the Rap', 34.

14 Pearlman, 'Rap's Gender Gap', 34.

But these industry success-markers are not the primary focus here. I intend to show that the subject matter and perspectives presented in many women's rap lyrics challenge dominant notions of sexuality, heterosexual courtship, and aesthetic constructions of the body. In addition, music videos and live performances display exuberant communities of women occupying public space while exhibiting sexual freedom, independence, and, occasionally, explicit domination over men. Women's raps grow more and more complex each year and, with audience support, many rappers have taken risks (regarding imagery and subject matter) that a few years ago would have been unthinkable. Through their lyrics and video images, black women rappers—especially Queen Latifah, MC Lyte, and Salt-N-Pepa—form a dialogue with working-class black women and men, offering young black women a small but potent culturally reflexive public space.

In order to understand the oppositional nature of these women rappers, it is important to have at least a sketch of some of the politics behind rap's battle of the sexes. Popular raps by both men and women have covered many issues and social situations that pertain to the lives of young, black working-class teens in urban America. Racism, drugs, police brutality, sex, crime, poverty, education, and prison have been popular themes in rap for a number of years. But raps about celebration, dance, styling, boasting, and just 'gittin' funky' (in Kid-N-Play's words) have been equally popular. Raps about style and prestige sometimes involve the possession of women as evidence of male power. Predictably, these raps define women as commodities, objects, and ornaments. Others are defensive and aggressive raps that describe women solely as objects of male pleasure. In rap music, as in other popular genres, women are divided into at least two categories—the 'kind to take home to mother' and the 'kind you meet at three o'clock in the morning'. In Hip Hop discourse, the former is honest and loyal—but extremely rare (decidedly not the girl next door). The latter is not simply an unpaid prostitute, but a woman who only wants you for your money, cars, and cash, will trap you (via pregnancy or other forms of manipulation), and move on to another man (probably your best friend). It would be an understatement to suggest that there is little in the way of traditional notions of romance in rap. Sexist raps articulate the profound fear of female sexuality felt by these young rappers and by many young men.

In a recent *Village Voice* interview with ex-NWA member Ice Cube, notorious not only for harsh sexist raps but for brilliant chilling stories of ghetto life, Greg Tate (one of the best Hip Hop social critics) tries to get 'some understanding' about the hostility toward women expressed in Ice Cube's raps:

TATE: Do you think rap is hostile toward women?

ICE CUBE: The whole damn world is hostile toward women.

TATE: What do you mean by that?

ICE CUBE: I mean the power of sex is more powerful than the motherfuckers in Saudi Arabia. A girl that you want to get with can make you do damn near anything. If she knows how to do her shit right, she can make you buy cigarettes you never wanted to buy in life. . . . Look at all my boys out here on this video shoot, all these motherfuckers sitting out here trying to look fly, hot as a motherfucker, ready to go home. But there's too many women here for them to just get up and leave. They out here since eight o'clock in the morning and ain't getting paid. They came for the girls.[15]

Ice Cube's answer may appear to be a non sequitur, but his remarks address what I believe is the subtext in rap's symbolic male domination over women. Ice Cube suggests that many men are hostile toward women because the fulfilment of male heterosexual desire is significantly checked by women's capacity for sexual rejection and/or manipulation of men. Ice Cube acknowledges the reckless boundaries of his desire as well as the power women can exercise in this sexual struggle. In 'The Bomb', Ice Cube warns men to 'especially watch the ones with the big derriers' because the greater your desire, the more likely you are to be blinded by it, and consequently the more vulnerable you are likely to be to female domination. From the perspective of a young man, such female power is probably more palpable than any woman realizes. Obviously, Ice Cube is not addressing the institutional manifestations of patriarchy and its effects on the social construction of desire. However, he and many black male rappers speak to men's fears and the realities of the struggle for power in teenage heterosexual courtship in a sexist society.

During the summer of 1990 Bell Biv Divoe, a popular R&B/Rap crossover group, raced up the charts with 'Poison', a song about women whose chorus warns men not to 'trust a big butt and a smile'. The song cautions men about giving in to their sexual weaknesses and then being taken advantage of by a sexy woman whose motives might be equally insincere. The degree of anxiety expressed is striking. 'Poison' explains both their intense desire for and profound distrust of women. The capacity of a woman to use her sexuality to manipulate *his* desire for *her* purposes is an important facet of the sexual politics of male raps about women. Bell Biv Divoe are telling men: 'You may not know what a big butt and a smile really means. It might not mean pleasure; it might mean danger—poison.'

All of this probably seems gravely sexist—so much so that any good feminist would reject it out of hand. However, I would like to suggest that women rappers effectively engage with male rappers on this level. By expressing their sexuality openly and in their own language, yet distinguishing themselves from poisonous and insincere women, black women rappers challenge men to take women more seriously. Black women rappers might respond by saying: 'That's right, don't automatically trust a big butt and a smile. We've got plenty of sexual power and integrity, but don't mess with us.' I am not suggesting that women have untapped power that once accessed will lead the way to the dismantling of patriarchy. Ice Cube and Bell Biv Divoe's expressions of fear must be understood in the context of their status as men and the inherent social power such a gender assignment affords. But, understanding the fear of female sexuality helps explain the consistent sexual domination

15 Greg Tate, 'Manchild at Large: One on One with Ice Cube, Hip Hop's Most Wanted', *Village Voice*, 11 Sept. 1990: 78.

men attempt to sustain over women. Without such fears, their efforts would be unnecessary.

Women's raps and my interviews with female rappers display similar fears of manipulation, loss of control, and betrayal at the hands of men. What is especially interesting about women rappers is the way in which they shift the focus of the debate. Male rappers focus on sexually promiscuous women who 'want their money' (in rap lingo they are called skeezers) and almost never offer a depiction of a sincere woman. Female rappers focus on dishonest men who seek sex from women (much like the women who seek money from men), and they represent themselves as seasoned women with sexual confidence and financial independence.

During my interview with Salt (one half of the female rap duo Salt-N-Pepa), I pressed her about how she could envision a committed relationship without some degree of emotional dependence. She replied:

> I just want to depend on myself. I feel like a relationship shouldn't be emotional dependence. I, myself, am more comfortable when I do not depend on hugs and kisses from somebody that I possibly won't get. If I don't get them then I'll be disappointed. So if I get them, I'll appreciate them.[16]

Salt's lyrics reflect much of how she feels personally: 'You know I don't want to for your money'; 'I'm independent, I make my own money, so don't tell me how to spend it'; 'You can't disguise the lies in your eyes, you're not a heartbreaker'; 'You need me and I don't need you.'[17]

Women rappers employ many of the aesthetic and culturally specific elements present in male rap lyrics while offering an alternative vision of similar social conditions. Raps written by women which specifically concern male/female relationships almost always confront the tension between trust and savvy, between vulnerability and control. Women rappers celebrate their sisters for 'getting over' on men. Some raps by women such as Icey Jaye's 'It's a Girl Thang' mock the men who fall for their tricks. But for the most part, women rappers promote self-reliance and challenge the depictions of women in male raps, addressing the fears about male dishonesty and infidelity that most women share.

Raps written and performed by women regarding male/female relationships can be divided into at least three categories: (1) raps that challenge male dominance over women within the sexual arena, (2) raps, that by virtue of their authoritative stance, challenge men as representatives of Hip Hop, and (3) raps that explicitly discuss women's identity and celebrate women's physical and sexual power. Across these three categories, several popular female rappers and their music videos can serve as illuminating examples.[18]

---

16 Salt (Cheryl James from Salt-N-Pepa), personal interview, 17 Aug. 1990.

17 Salt-N-Pepa, *Black's Magic*, Next Plateau Records, 1990.

18 Salt-N-Pepa, 'Tramp', *Cool, Hot and Vicious*, Next Plateau Records, 1986; Salt-N-Pepa, 'Shake Your Thang', *A Salt With a Deadly Pepa*, Next Plateau Records, 1988; Queen Latifah, 'Ladies First', *All Hail the Queen*, Tommy Boy Records, 1989. As you will see, none of my analysis will involve the music itself. The music is a very important aspect of rap's power and aesthetics, but given my space limitations here and the focus of my argument, I have decided to leave it out rather than throw in 'samples' of my own. For an extended cultural analysis of rap's music see Tricia Rose, 'Orality and Technology: Rap Music and Afro-American Cultural Theory and Practice', *Popular Music and Society*, 13/4 (1989), 35–44.

MC Lyte and Salt-N-Pepa have reputations for biting raps that criticize men who manipulate and abuse women. Their lyrics tell the story of men taking advantage of women, cheating on them, abusing them, taking their money, and then leaving them for other unsuspecting female victims. These raps are not mournful ballads about the trials and tribulations of being a woman. Similar to women's blues, they are caustic, witty, and aggressive warnings directed at men and at other women who might be seduced by men in the future. By offering a woman's interpretation of the terms of heterosexual courtship, these raps cast a new light on male/female sexual power relations and depict women as resistant, aggressive participants.

Salt-N-Pepa's 1986 single 'Tramp' speaks specifically to black women, warning us that 'Tramp' is not a 'simple rhyme', but a parable about relationships between men and women:

> Homegirls attention you must pay to what I say
> Don't take this as a simple rhyme
> 'Cause this type of thing happens all the time
> Now what would you do if a stranger said 'Hi'
> Would you dis him or would you reply?
> If you'd answer, there is a chance
> That you'd become a victim of circumstance
> Am I right fellas? Tell the truth
> Or else I'll have to show and prove
> You are what you are I am what I am
> It just so happens that most men are TRAMPS.

In the absence of any response to 'Am I right fellas?' Salt-N-Pepa 'show and prove' the trampings of several men who 'undress you with their eyeballs', 'think you're a dummy', and 'on the first date, had the nerve to tell me he loves me'. Salt-N-Pepa's parable, by defining promiscuous *men* as tramps, inverts the social construction of male sexual promiscuity as a status symbol. This reversal undermines the degrading 'woman as tramp' image by stigmatizing male promiscuity. Salt-N-Pepa suggest that women who respond to sexual advances are victims of circumstance. It is the predatory, disingenuous men who are the tramps.

The music video for 'Tramp' is a comic rendering of a series of social club scenes that highlight tramps on the make, mouth freshener in hand, testing their lines on the nearest woman. Dressed in Hip Hop street gear, Salt-N-Pepa perform the song on television, on a monitor perched above the bar. Since they appear on the television screen, they seem to be surveying and critiquing the club action, but the club members cannot see them. There are people dancing and talking together (including likeable men who are coded as 'non-tramps'), who seem unaware of the television monitor. Salt-N-Pepa are also shown in the club, dressed in very stylish, sexy outfits. They act as decoys, talking and flirting with the tramps to flesh out the dramatization of tramps on the prowl, and they make several knowing gestures at the camera to reassure the viewer that they are unswayed by the tramps' efforts.

The club scenes have no dialogue. The tramps and their victims interact only with body language. Along with the music for 'Tramp', we hear Salt-N-Pepa's lyrics, which serve respectively as the club's dance music and the video's voice-over narration. Viewing much of the club action from Salt-N-Pepa's authoritative position through the television monitor, we can safely observe the playful but cautionary dramatization of heterosexual courtship. Rapping to a woman, one tramp postures and struts, appearing to ask the stock pick-up line, 'What is your zodiac sign, baby?' When she shows disgust and leaves her seat, he repeats the same body motions on the next woman who happens to sit down. Near the end of the video a frustrated 'wife' enters the club and drags one of the tramps home, smacking him in the head with her pocketbook. Salt-N-Pepa stand next to the wife's tramp in the club, shaking their heads as if to say 'what a shame'. Simultaneously, they point and laugh at him from the television monitor. At the end of the video, a still frame of each man is stamped 'tramp', while Salt-N-Pepa revel in having identified and exposed them. They leave the club together without men, seemingly enjoying their skill at exposing the real intentions of these tramps.

Salt-N-Pepa are clearly 'schooling' women about the sexual politics of the club scene. They are engaged in and critiquing the drama of heterosexual courtship. The privileged viewer is a woman who is directly addressed in the lyrics and can fully empathize with the visual depiction and interpretation of the scenes. The video's resolution is a warning to both men and women. Women: Don't fall for these men either by talking to them in the clubs or believing the lies they'll tell you when they come home. Men: You will get caught eventually and you'll be embarrassed. The 'Tramp' video also tells women that they can go to these clubs and successfully play along with the game as long as the power of female sexuality and the terms of male desire are understood.

In her video, MC Lyte has a far less playful response to her boyfriend Sam, whom she catches in the act of flirting with another woman. MC Lyte's underground hit 'Paper Thin' is one of the most scathing raps about male dishonesty/infidelity and the tensions between trust and vulnerability. Lyte has been burned by Sam, but she has turned her experience into a black woman's anthem that sustains an uncomfortable balance between brutal cynicism and honest vulnerability:

> When you say you love me it doesn't matter
> It goes into my head as just chit chatter
> You may think it's egotistical or just very free
> But what you say, I take none of it seriously.

> I'm not the kind of girl to try to play a man out
> They take the money and then they break the hell out
> No that's not my strategy, not the game I play
> I admit I play a game, but it's not done that way
> Truly when I get involved I give it my heart
> I mean my mind, my soul, my body I mean every part
> But if it doesn't work out—yo, it just doesn't
> It wasn't meant to be, you know it just wasn't
> So, I treat all of you like I treat all of them
> What you say to me is just paper thin.

Lyte's public acknowledgement that Sam's expressions of love were paper thin is not a source of embarrassment for her, but a means of empowerment.

She plays a brutal game of the dozens on Sam while wearing her past commitment to him as a badge of honour and sign of character. Lyte presents commitment, vulnerability, and sensitivity as assets, not indicators of female weakness. In 'Paper Thin' emotional and sexual commitment are not romantic Victorian concepts tied to honourable but dependent women; they are a part of her strategy, part of the game she plays in heterosexual courtship.

The high energy video for 'Paper Thin' contains many elements present in Hip Hop. The video opens with Lyte (dressed in sweatsuit and sneakers) abandoning her new Jetta because she wants to take the subway. A few members of her male posse follow along behind her, down the steps to the subway tracks. Once in the subway car, her DJ K-Rock, doubling as the conductor, announces that the train will be held in the station due to crossed signals. While they wait, Milk Boy (her body guard) spots Sam at the other end of the car, rapping heavily to two stylish women. Lyte, momentarily surprised, begins her rhyme as she stalks toward Sam. Sam's attempts to escape fail; he is left to face MC Lyte's wrath. Eventually, she throws him off the train to the tune of Ray Charles's R&B classic, 'Hit the Road Jack', and locks Sam out of the subway station, symbolically jailing him. The subway car is filled with young black teenagers, typical working New Yorkers and street people, many of whom join Lyte in signifying on Sam while they groove on K-Rock's music. MC Lyte's powerful voice and no-nonsense image dominate Sam. The tense, driving music—which is punctuated by sampled guitar and drum sections as well as an Earth Wind and Fire horn section—complement Lyte's hard, expressive rapping style.

It is important that 'Paper Thin' is set in public and on the subway, the quintessential mode of urban transportation. Lyte is drawn to the subway and obviously feels comfortable there. She is also comfortable with the subway riders in her video; they are her community. By setting her confrontation with Sam in the subway, in front of their peers, Lyte moves a private problem between lovers into the public arena and effectively dominates both spaces.

When her DJ, the musical and mechanical conductor, announces that crossed signals are holding the train in the station, he frames the video in a moment of communication crisis. The notion of crossed signals represents the inability of Sam and Lyte to communicate with one another, an inability that is primarily the function of the fact that they communicate on different frequencies. Sam thinks he can read Lyte's mind to see what she is thinking and then feed her all the right lines. But what he says carries no weight, no meaning. His words are light, they're paper thin. Lyte, who understands courtship as a game, confesses to being a player, yet expresses how she feels honestly and in simple language. What she says has integrity, weight, and substance.

After throwing Sam from the train, she nods her head toward a young man standing against the subway door, and he follows her off the train. She will not allow her experiences with Sam to paralyse her, but she does have a new perspective on dating. As she and her new male friend walk down the street, she raps the final stanza for 'Paper Thin', which sets down the ground rules:

> So, now I take precautions when choosing my mate
> I do not touch until the third or fourth date

Then maybe we'll kiss on the fifth or sixth time that we meet
'Cause a date without a kiss is so incomplete
And then maybe, I'll let you play with my feet
You can suck the big toe and play with the middle
It's so simple unlike a riddle....

MC Lyte and Salt-N-Pepa are not alone in their critique of men's treatment of women. Neneh Cherry's 'Buffalo Stance' tells men: 'You better watch, don't mess with me | No money man can buy my love | It's sweetness that I'm thinkin' of'; Oaktown 3-5-7's 'Say That Then' lashes out at 'Finger poppin', hip hoppin', wanna be bed rockin'' men; Ice Cream Tee's 'All Wrong' chastises women who allow men to abuse them; and MC Lyte's 'I Cram to Understand U', 'Please Understand', and 'I'm Not Havin' It' are companion pieces to 'Paper Thin'.

Women rappers also challenge the popular conception that male rappers are the only MCs who can 'move the crowd', a skill that ultimately determines your status as a successful rapper. Black women rappers compete head-to-head with male rappers for status as the pre-eminent MC. Consequently, rhymes that boast, signify, and toast are an important part of women's repertoire. Antoinnete's 'Who's The Boss', Ice Cream Tee's 'Let's Work', MC Lyte's 'Lyte as a Rock', Salt-N-Pepa's 'Everybody Get Up', and Queen Latifah's 'Dance For Me' and 'Come into My House' establish black women rappers as Hip Hop MCs who can move the crowd, a talent that is as important as writing 'dope' rhymes. Latifah's 'Come into My House' features Latifah as the dance master, the hostess of physical release and pleasure:

Welcome into my Queendom
Come one, come all
'Cause when it comes to lyrics I bring them
In Spring I sing, in Fall I call
Out to those who had a hard day
I've prepared a place on my dance floor
The time is now for you to party....
I'm on fire the flames too high to douse
The pool is open
Come Into My House.[19]

As rap's territory expands, so does the material of female rappers. Subjects ranging from racism, black politics, Afrocentrism, and nationalism to homelessness, physical abuse of women and children, drug addiction, AIDS, and teen pregnancy can all be found in female rappers' repertoire. 'Ladies First', Queen Latifah's second release from her début album, *All Hail The Queen*, is a landmark example of such expansions. Taken together, the video and lyrics for 'Ladies First' is a statement for black female unity, independence, and power, as well as an anti-colonial statement concerning Africa's southern region. The rap recognizes the importance of black female political activists, offering hope for the development of a pro-female, pro-black, diasporatic political consciousness. A rapid-fire and powerful rap duet between Queen Latifah and her 'European sister' Monie Love, 'Ladies First' is thus a recital

---

19 Queen Latifah, 'Come into My House', *All Hail the Queen*, Tommy Boy Records, 1989.

on the significance and diversity of black women. Latifah's assertive, measured voice in the opening rhyme sets the tone:

> The ladies will kick it, the rhyme it is wicked
> Those who don't know how to be pros get evicted
> A woman can bear you, break you, take you
> Now it's time to rhyme, can you relate to
> A sister dope enough to make you holler and scream?

In her almost double-time verse, Monie Love responds:

> Eh, Yo! Let me take it from here Queen
> Excuse me but I think I am about due
> To get into precisely what I am about to do
> I'm conversatin' to the folks who have no whatsoever clue
> So, listen very carefully as I break it down to you
> Merrily merrily, hyper happy overjoyed
> Pleased with all the beats and rhymes my sisters have employed
> Slick and smooth—throwing down the sound totally, a yes
> Let me state the position: Ladies First, Yes?

Latifah responds, 'YES!'

Without attacking black men, 'Ladies First' is a wonderful rewriting of the contributions of black women into the history of black struggles. Opening with slides of black female political activists Sojourner Truth, Angela Davis, and Winnie Mandela, the video's predominant theme features Latifah as Third World military strategist. She stalks an illuminated, conference table-size map of Southern Africa and, with a long pointer, shoves large chess-like pieces of briefcase carrying white men off white-dominated countries, replacing them with large black power style fists. In between these scenes, Latifah and Monie Love rap in front of and between more photos of politically prominent black women and footage of black struggles that shows protests and acts of military violence against protestors. Latifah positions herself as part of a rich legacy of black women's activism, racial commitment, and cultural pride.

Given the fact that protest footage rap videos (which have become quite popular over the last few years) have all but excluded scenes of black women leaders or foot soldiers, the centrality of black women's political protest in 'Ladies First' is refreshing. Scenes of dozens of rural African women running with sticks raised above their heads toward armed oppressors, holding their ground alongside men in equal numbers and dying in struggle, are rare media images. As Latifah explains:

> I wanted to show the strength of black women in history. Strong black women. Those were good examples. I wanted to show what we've done. We've done a lot; it's just that people don't know it. Sisters have been in the midst of these things for a long time, but we just don't get to see it that much.[20]

---

20 Queen Latifah (Dana Owens), personal interview, 6 Feb. 1990.

After placing a black power fist on each country in Southern Africa, Latifah surveys the map, nodding contentedly. The video ends with a still frame of the region's new political order.

Latifah's self-possession and independence is an important facet of the new cultural nationalism in rap. The powerful, level-headed and black feminist character of her lyrics calls into question the historically cosy relationship between nationalism and patriarchy. The legendary Malcolm X phrase 'There are going to be some changes made here' is strategically sampled throughout 'Ladies First'. When Malcolm's voice is introduced, the camera pans the faces of some of the more prominent female rappers and DJs including Ms Melodie, Ice Cream Tee, and Shelley Thunder. The next sample of Malcolm's memorable line is dubbed over South African protest footage. Latifah evokes Malcolm as part of a collective African American historical memory and recontextualizes him not only as a leader who supports contemporary struggles in South Africa, but also as someone who encourages the imminent changes regarding the degraded status of black women and specifically black women rappers. Latifah's use of the dialogic processes of naming, claiming, and recontextualizing is not random; nor is it simply a 'juxtaposition of incompatible realities'. 'Ladies First' is a cumulative product that, as Lipsitz would say, 'enters a dialogue already in progress'. It affirms and revises African American traditions at the same time that it stakes out new territory.

Black women rappers' public displays of physical and sexual freedom challenge male notions of female sexuality and pleasure. Salt-N-Pepa's rap duet 'Shake Your Thang', which they perform with the prominent go-go band E.U., is a wonderful verbal and visual display of black women's sexual resistance. The rap lyrics and video are about Salt-N-Pepa's sexual dancing and others' responses to them. The first stanza sets them in a club 'shakin' [their] thang to a funky beat with a go-go swing' and captures the shock on the faces of other patrons. With attitude to spare, Salt-N-Pepa chant: 'It's my thang and I'll swing it the way that I feel, with a little seduction and some sex appeal.' The chorus, sung by the male lead in E.U., chants: 'Shake your thang, do what you want to do, I can't tell you how to catch a groove. It's your thang, do what you wanna do, I won't tell you how to catch a groove.'[21]

The video is framed by Salt-N-Pepa's interrogation after they have been arrested for lewd dancing. New York police cars pull up in front of the studio where their music video is being shot, and mock policemen (played by Kid-N-Play and their producer Herbie Luv Bug) cart the women away in handcuffs. When their mug shots are being taken, Salt-N-Pepa blow kisses to the cameraman as each holds up her arrest placard. Once in the interrogation room, Kid-N-Play and Herbie ask authoritatively, 'What we gonna do about this dirty dancing?' Pepa reaches across the table, grabs Herbie by the tie and growls, 'We gonna do what we wanna do.' Outdone by her confidence, Herbie looks into the camera with an expression of shock.

The mildly slapstick interrogation scenes bind a number of other subplots. Scenes in which Salt-N-Pepa are part of groups of women dancing and

---

21 The melody and rhythm section for 'Shake Your Thang' is taken from the Iseley Brothers single 'It's Your Thang', which was on *Billboard*'s Top Forty charts in the winter of 1969.

playing are interspersed with separate scenes of male dancers, co-ed dance segments with Kid-N-Play, E.U.'s lead singer acting as a spokesman for a 'free Salt-N-Pepa' movement, and picketers in front of the police station calling for Salt-N-Pepa's release. When he is not gathering signatures for his petition, E.U. chants the chorus from a press conference podium. The camera angles for the dance segments give the effect of a series of park or block parties. Salt-N-Pepa shake their butts for the cameras and for each other while rapping, 'My jeans fit nice, they show off my butt' and 'I like Hip Hop mixed with a go-go baby, it's my thang and I'll shake it crazy. Don't tell me how to party, it's my dance, yep, and it's my body.'

A primary source of the video's power is Salt-N-Pepa's irreverence toward the morally based sexual constrictions placed on them as women. They mock moral claims about the proper modes of women's expression and enjoy every minute of it. Their defiance of the moral, sexual restrictions on women is to be distinguished from challenges to the seemingly gender neutral laws against public nudity. Salt-N-Pepa are eventually released because their dancing isn't against the law (as they say, 'We could get loose, but we can't get naked'). But their 'dirty dancing' also teases the male viewer who would misinterpret their sexual freedom as an open sexual invitation. The rappers make it clear that their expression is no such thing: 'A guy touch my body? I just put him in check.' Salt-N-Pepa thus force a wedge between overt female sexual expression and the presumption that such expressions are intended to attract men. 'Shaking your thang' can create a stir, but that should not prevent women from doing it when and how they choose.

At the video's close, we return to the interrogation scene a final time. Herbie receives a call, after which he announces that they have to release the women. The charges will not stick. Prancing out of the police station, Salt-N-Pepa laughingly say, 'I told you so.' The police raid and arrests make explicit the real, informal, yet institutionally based policing of female sexual expression. The video speaks to black women, calls for open, public displays of female expression, assumes a community-based support for their freedom, and focuses directly on the sexual desirability and beauty of black women's bodies. Salt-N-Pepa's recent video for 'Expression' covers similar ground but focuses more on fostering individuality in young women.

Salt-N-Pepa's physical freedom, exemplified by focusing on their butts, is no coincidence. The distinctly black, physical and sexual pride that these women (and other black female rappers) exude serves as a rejection of the aesthetic hierarchy in American culture that marginalizes black women. There is a long black folk history of dances and songs that celebrate big behinds for men and women (e.g. the Bump, the Dookey Butt, and most recently E.U. and Spike Lee's black chart topper, 'Da Butt'). Such explicit focus on the behind counters mainstream definitions of what constitutes a sexually attractive female body. American culture, in defining its female sex symbols, places a high premium on long thin legs, narrow hips, and relatively small behinds. The vast majority of white female television and film actresses, musicians, and even the occasional black model fits this description. The aesthetic hierarchy of the female body in mainstream American culture, with particular reference to the behind and hips, positions many black women somewhere near the bottom. When viewed in this context,

Salt-N-Pepa's rap and video become an inversion of the aesthetic hierarchy that renders black women's bodies sexually unattractive.

Obviously, the common practice of objectifying all women's bodies complicates the way some might interpret Salt-N-Pepa shaking their collective thangs. For some, Salt-N-Pepa's sexual freedom could be considered dangerously close to self-inflicted exploitation. Such misunderstanding of the racial and sexual significance of black women's sexual expression may explain the surprisingly cautious responses I have received from some white feminists regarding the importance of female rappers. However, as Hortense Spillers and other prominent black feminists have argued, a history of silence has surrounded African American women's sexuality.[22] Spillers argues that this silence has at least two faces; either black women are creatures of male sexual possession, or else they are reified into the status of non-being. Room for self-defined sexual identity exists in neither alternative. The resistant nature of black women's participation in rap is better understood when we take the historical silence, sexual and otherwise, of black women into consideration. Salt-N-Pepa are carving out a female-dominated space in which black women's sexuality is openly expressed. Black women rappers sport Hip Hop clothing and jewellery as well as distinctively black hair-styles. They affirm a black, female, working-class cultural aesthetic that is rarely depicted in American popular culture. Black women rappers resist patterns of sexual objectification and cultural invisibility, and they also resist academic reification and mainstream, hegemonic, white feminist discourse.

Given the identities these women rappers have fashioned for themselves, it is not surprising that they want to avoid being labelled feminists. During my conversations with Salt, MC Lyte, and Queen Latifah, it became clear that these women saw feminism as a signifier for a movement that related specifically to white women. They also thought feminism involved adopting an anti-male position, and they did not want to be considered or want their work to be interpreted as anti-black male.

In MC Lyte's case, she remarked that she was often labelled a feminist even though she did not think of herself as one. Yet, after she asked for my working definition of feminist, she wholeheartedly agreed with my description, which was as follows:

> I would say that a feminist believed that there was sexism in society, wanted to change and worked toward change. [She] either wrote, spoke or behaved in a way that was pro-woman, in that she supported situations [organizations] that were trying to better the lives of women. A feminist feels that women are more disadvantaged than men in many situations and would want to stop that kind of inequality.

MC Lyte responded, 'Under your definition, I would say I am.' We talked further about what she imagined a feminist to be and it became clear that once feminism was understood as a mode of analysis rather than as a label for a group of women associated with a particular social movement, MC Lyte was much more comfortable discussing the importance of black women's

---

22 Hortense Spillers, 'Interstices: A Small Drama of Words', in Carol Vance (ed.), *Pleasure and Danger: Exploring Female Sexuality* (Boston: Routledge & Kegan Paul, 1984), 73–100.

independence: 'Yes, I am very independent and I feel that women should be independent, but so should men. Both of us need each other and we're just coming to a realization that we do.'[23] For MC Lyte, feminists were equivalent to devoutly anti-male, white middle-class members of the National Organization of Women.

Queen Latifah was sympathetic to the issues associated with feminism, but preferred to be considered pro-woman. She was unable to articulate why she was uncomfortable with the term 'feminist' and preferred instead to talk about her admiration for Faye Wattleton, the black president of Planned Parenthood, and the need to support the pro-choice movement. As she told me:

> Faye Wattleton, I like her. I look up to her. I'm pro-choice, but I love God. But I think [abortion] is a woman's decision. In a world like we live in today you can't use [God] as an excuse all the time. They want to make abortion illegal, but they don't want to educate you in school.[24]

Salt was the least resistant to the term feminism yet made explicit her limits:

> I guess you could say that [I'm a feminist] in a way. Not in a strong sense where I'd want to go to war or anything like that [laughter]. . . . But I preach a lot about women depending on men for everything, for their mental stability, for their financial status, for their happiness. Women have brains, and I hate to see them walking in the shadow of a man.[25]

For these women rappers, and many other black women, feminism is the label for members of a white woman's social movement, which has no concrete link to black women or the black community. Feminism signifies allegiance to historically specific movements whose histories have long been the source of frustration for women of colour. Similar criticisms of women's social movements have been made vociferously by many black feminists who have argued that race and gender are inextricably linked for black women— and I would add, this is the case for both black and white women.[26] However, in the case of black women, the realities of racism link black women to black men in a way that challenges cross-racial sisterhood. If a cross-racial sisterhood is to be forged, serious attention must be paid to issues of racial difference, racism within the movement, and the racial blind spots that inform coalition building. In the meantime, the desire for sisterhood among and between black and white women cannot be achieved at the expense of black women's racial identity.

If feminist scholars want to contribute to the development of a women's movement that has relevance to the lives of women of colour (which also means working-class and poor women), then we must be concerned with young women's reluctance to be associated with feminism. We should be less

---

23 MC Lyte, personal interview, 7 Sept. 1990.

24 Queen Latifah, personal interview.

25 Salt, personal interview.

26 See Carby, Davis, and Spillers cited above. Also see bell hooks, *Ain't I A Woman: Black Women and Feminism* (Boston: South End Press, 1982) and *Feminist Theory: From Margins to Center* (Boston: South End Press, 1984); Barbara Smith (ed.), *Home Girls: A Black Feminist Anthology* (New York: Kitchen Table, 1983); Cheryl A. Wall (ed.), *Changing Our Own Words: Essays on Criticism, Theory and Writing By Black Women* (New Jersey: Rutgers Univ. Press, 1989).

concerned with producing theoretically referential feminist theories and more concerned with linking these theories to practices, thereby creating new concrete ways to interpret feminist activity. This will involve broadening the scope of investigations in our search for black women's voices. This will involve attending to the day-to-day conflicts and pressures that young, black working-class women face and focusing more of our attention on the cultural practices that are most important to their lives. Academic work that links feminist theory to feminist practice should be wholeheartedly encouraged, and an emphasis on making such findings widely available should be made. For feminist theorists, this will not simply entail 'letting the other speak', but will also involve a systematic re-evaluation of how feminism is conceptualized and how ethnicity, class, and race seriously fracture gender as a conceptual category. Until this kind of analysis takes place a great deal more often than it does, what any of us say to MC Lyte will remain paper thin.

One of the remarkable talents black women rappers have is their capacity to attract a large male following and consistently perform their explicitly pro-woman material. They are able to sustain dialogue with and consequently encourage dialogue between young men and women that supports black women and challenges some sexist male behaviour. For these women rappers, feminism is a movement that does not speak to men; while on the other hand, they are engaged in constant communication with black male audiences and rappers, and they simultaneously support and offer advice to their young, black female audiences. As MC Lyte explains, 'When I do a show, the women are like, "Go ahead Lyte, tell em!" And the guys are like, "Oh, shit. She's right." '[27] Obviously, such instances may not lead directly to a widespread black feminist male/female alliance. However, the dialogues facilitated by these female rappers may well contribute to its groundwork.

In a world of worst possibilities, where no such movements can be imagined, these black female rappers provide young black women with a small, culturally reflexive public space. Rap can no longer be imagined without women rappers' contributions. They have expanded rap's territory and have effectively changed the interpretative framework regarding the work of male rappers. As women who challenge the sexist discourse expressed by male rappers yet sustain dialogue with them, who reject the racially coded aesthetic hierarchies in American popular culture, who support black women and black culture, black female rappers constitute an important voice in Hip Hop and contemporary black women's cultural production generally. As Salt says:

> The women look up to us. They take us dead seriously. It's not a fan type of thing; it's more like a movement. When we shout, 'The year 1989 is for the ladies', they go crazy. It's the highlight of the show. It makes you realize that you have a voice as far as women go.[28]

I would especially like to thank MC Lyte, Queen Latifah, and Salt for their generosity and for their incredible talents. I would also like to thank Stuart Clarke for his thoughtful comments and criticism on earlier versions of this chapter and its title.

27 MC Lyte, personal interview.

28 Salt, personal interview.

21

The Gorgeous Lesbian in *L.A. Law*: The Present Absence?

Rosanne Kennedy

THAT THE POPULAR North American television series *L.A. Law* should have a female bisexual character—the gorgeous, sexy C. J. Lamb—is in no way surprising. In fact, C.J.'s bisexuality is wholly in keeping with the programme's progressive image. Despite its predominantly white, heterosexual, upwardly mobile orientation, it has distinguished itself by its range of ethnic, sexual, and class identities, and by its liberal treatment of controversial issues. The real surprise is that the show has achieved so much credibility, in terms of maintaining a 'lesbian' presence, with so little representation of lesbian sexuality, or even of lesbian issues. Amanda Donohoe, who plays C. J. Lamb, only joined the show in its fifth season, and by the end of the sixth season, she, along with several others, had left the show. Out of the forty or so episodes from those two seasons, she appears as a main character in only eight, and only five of those concern her sexuality. None of those five episodes shows C.J. erotically engaged with another woman. All we see is the disappointingly chaste three-second kiss between C.J. and Abby, the heterosexual wallflower at McKenzie Brackman, and a good deal of titillation and suggestiveness. Indeed, C.J.'s sexiest moments occur in her last two episodes, when she becomes romantically involved with a *man*. On the basis of this track record, how has *L.A. Law* managed to achieve a cult status among lesbian viewers? And what indeed has *L.A. Law* achieved? Should we take C.J.'s character as a sign of television's increasing openness and maturity towards, to paraphrase C.J., sexual 'flexibility'? Can C.J., who identifies as neither lesbian nor straight, be regarded as a representation of queer sexuality?

The Bisexual Case   C.J.'s sexuality is first signified as 'an issue' in the programme's fifth season, in the context of her deepening friendship with Abby. Their friendship reaches a crisis point in the famous 'kiss' episode, when, on parting one evening, C.J. kisses Abby on the lips. Abby, surprised, returns the kiss and

Originally published in Diane Hamer and Belinda Budge (eds.), *The Good, the Bad and the Gorgeous* (London: Pandora Press, 1994), 132–41.

scurries away. Timid Abby obsesses over the meaning of this kiss, and later confronts C.J., asking why she kissed her. C.J. returns the question and they declare their sexual cards: straight/flexible—C.J. declining to be categorized. When Abby finally indicates that she's ready to become involved, C.J., playing the sexual pedagogue, tells Abby that she's not an experiment, that she's not available on Abby's terms. Happily for all, they agree to be 'just friends'.

This kiss episode undoubtedly attracted a lesbian spectatorship by signifying C.J. as bisexual, and thereby holding out the promise that future episodes would see her involved with women. Yet the episodes between C.J. and Abby are ultimately disappointing, represent a missed opportunity, and reveal the limits of the programme's politics. In comparison with erotic scenes between the straight characters, the kiss between C.J. and Abby is restrained to the point of being asexual. Apparently, in the heterosexual world of *L.A. Law* a potentially sexual relationship between C.J. and Abby can only be represented as *an issue,* at the cost of eliminating the sex. What is worse is that this sexual restraint seems to follow naturally from the status of lesbianism as an outsider sexuality rather than from any deliberate strategy on the part of the producers. According to the logic of compulsory heterosexuality, it is only natural that Abby should obsess about what a kiss with C.J. means, rather than plunge in and think later. Yet, her response is obviously an effect of a number of choices by the programme producers that limit what could occur between the two women. For instance, the kiss takes place in public, where C.J. and Abby can hardly get carried away. More significant, the programme's choice of Abby herself, an unlikely erotic object for C.J., and its liberal commitment to the notion of an essential self-identity, limits the story-line by virtue of what would be in keeping with her character. *L.A. Law* could have clinched its status as queer rather than liberal by developing the relationship between spunky C.J. and timid Abby—that would have been queer!

Fortuitously, an innocent 'mistake' in a recent issue of *Australian Cleo* (October 1993) reveals the limits of *L.A. Law*'s sexual politics, and suggests how we as viewers might queer the plot. In an article on 'Hollywood's Hottest Lesbians', the author mistakenly identifies a photograph of Donohoe and Cecil Hoffmann, who plays Zoey on *L.A. Law*, as a photograph of Donohoe and Michelle Green, who plays Abby. While all of *Cleo*'s other shots of Hollywood's famous lesbians show them in an erotic entanglement, C.J. and Zoey are shown grinning on front of a camera, C.J.'s head next to Zoey's, in a clownish gesture of friendship. Ironically, the mistakenly identified photograph of Donohoe and Hoffmann signifies the level of lesbian content in *L.A. Law*. Zoey can substitute for Abby precisely because nothing happened between C.J. and Abby; consequently, a photograph of C.J. and *any* woman from *L.A. Law* would do, because the photo, like the friendship between Abby and C.J., only represents a potential lesbian relationship rather than an actualized one. Indeed, *Cleo*'s substitution of Zoey for Abby is an easy mistake to make given the opening credits in series six, in which C.J. and Zoey are shown together in a poolside scene, clad in bikinis, looking at each other and laughing as they do an aerobic dance routine.

The Lesbian Custody Case

The treatment of bisexuality in the Abby episode, as an issue rather than an embodied sexual practice, sets the pattern for other episodes dealing with homosexuality. The next episode involving C.J.'s sexuality occurs in the middle of the sixth season. C.J. has asked her colleague, divorce lawyer Arnie Becker, to represent her friend, Maggie Barnes, in a custody case. C.J. tells Arnie that Maggie's ex-husband has found out that she has been having an affair, since before their divorce two years earlier, with a woman. In response, the husband sues for custody of their two children. At the firm's morning meeting, when Arnie reports that he is representing a client in a lesbian custody case, C.J. acknowledges, to the firm's hushed embarrassment, that she is the client's lover. None of the partners knows quite how to respond, and the moment passes. During the trial, the father is revealed to be an undesirable character—a reformed alcoholic who mistreated his children, and visited them only twice during the first year of separation. His own masculinity on the line, he testifies that his fights with his wife were about sex rather than about his drinking, and that his wife deceived him about her sexual preference. The opposing attorney, James Pavlik, questions Maggie about her lesbian relationships and their effect on her children. A psychologist testifies that a mother's homosexuality can adversely affect her children, but admits that there is no proof that a gay parent produces a gay child. When Pavlik calls C.J. to the stand, she acknowledges that during her relationship with Maggie she had other sexual relationships, and that, like all responsible, sexually active people, she had an AIDS test, which was negative. The question about AIDS seems designed to portray C.J. as sexually 'loose'; however, she gains credibility by answering frankly. Then Maggie's 8-year-old daughter, Jenny, takes the stand, says she misses C.J., and that her father is jealous because Mommy loves C.J. rather than him. In the final scene, C.J. turns up at Maggie's house with a Christmas gift, they exchange loving looks, Maggie invites C.J. in and closes the door. End of story. The message: lesbian sex must stay behind closed doors.

On one level, the lesbian custody episode could be read as queering the mother body, by insisting that mothers are sexual beings whose sexuality will not be limited to reproductive heterosexuality. As in the Abby episode, the programme promotes the liberal message that the issues lesbianism raises, such as whether lesbians can be good mothers, or whether the sexuality of the parent will affect the sexuality of the child, should be discussed. However, two women must not be shown making-out together; graphic visual representation of lesbian sexuality must remain outside the frame of liberal television. In addition, whereas relationships between the programme's heterosexual couples are developed over a number of programmes, C.J.'s relationship with Maggie, supposedly over two years old, has no television history. Chronologically, it doesn't fit in with series five: when C.J. was becoming involved with Abby she never mentioned her relationship with Maggie, which, given her characteristic honesty, seems odd.

The Heterosexual Case

While, in the Abby and Maggie Barnes episodes, the producers can be accused of representing lesbianism only as a political or moral issue rather than a performative practice, the real twist comes in the last two episodes of series six, when C.J. becomes involved with David McCoy. McCoy, an opposing attorney in a trial in which C.J. is involved, is not the first man on the series to show an interest in her. Mikhail, Susan Bloom's husband, makes a pass at C.J., which she refuses. But McCoy is man with a twist: he's blind. Given the symbolic value of blindness as one of the most conventional signifiers of castration, C.J.'s involvement with the blind McCoy cannot be innocent. In terms of the programme's history, it has a logic and an imaginary investment. While McCoy's blindness does not signify him as literally impotent, it does indeed mark him off from the mainstream heterosexual male population. His blindness means he has not participated in a whole series of rituals of masculinity, such as playing contact sports, fighting with other boys, joining the army, viewing pornography; it also means that C.J. is not objectified by the male gaze. For her part, C.J. demonstrates her openness—it does not matter to her that McCoy is blind. In terms of the sexual logic of *L.A. Law*, it is appropriate for C.J. to go off with a man only if he, too, is in some way an outsider to normative heterosexuality. In sum, two of the three episodes dealing with 'lesbian issues' seem designed to reassure the heterosexual population that they will not be 'contaminated' by bisexuality (both Abby and Maggie's children remain, for the present at least, 'uncontaminated'), while the final episode with McCoy recuperates C.J. for some version of heterosexuality. What we never see, however, is C.J. involved in a committed relationship with a woman.

Given that C.J. is rarely ever shown engaging in explicitly sexual behaviour, how is it that she is signified as the sexiest woman and the queerest character on the show? C.J.'s sexy image is created largely in the opening credits—those short, snappy images of each character in an allegedly typical pose or memorable moment. As her character became more established and popular with audiences, her image was more overtly sexualized. In series five, C.J. appears in the opening credits three times, and each time she is dressed in appropriately professional attire which masks her sexuality. In series six, however, she appears in a suit, but she also appears poolside in a fluorescent-green and black bikini, and sexiest of all, in a short, plunging neckline, off the shoulder, black Lycra dress. In this image, she is literally performing camp, posing her hands and body in a stylized way and looking knowingly at someone off-screen. Indeed, I would maintain that C.J.'s success as a character lies in her appeal to all women, regardless of sexuality. C.J. is simply the sexiest, spunkiest, and most liberated woman on the show. But what really distinguishes her from the other female characters is her cheekiness, wit, and sense of fun. If male viewers desire the woman they want to have, and female viewers desire the woman they want to be, C.J. would win, hands down, the woman's vote. I, for one, would much rather be C.J. than Grace Van Owen, who is so busy doing what she thinks is right that she doesn't know what would make her happy, or Ann Kelsey, the picture of happy heterosexuality in a strait-jacket. Zoey, like Grace, is uptight and so worn down by life in the DA's office that she seems to be in a perpetual crisis. In comparison with these women, C.J. is hip, sexy, smart, confident, and enjoys life. Consequently, even viewers who do not identify as lesbians may find themselves identifying with C.J. And although C.J.'s bisexuality marks her out as different, it also marks her as less earnest and righteous than the other characters. C.J.'s sexuality is not the reason for her popularity with audiences. Rather, her character appeals to the majority of female viewers, regardless of the sexuality, while simultaneously appealing to lesbian viewers by holding out the promise of a lesbian relationship. But the fact that lesbians can get excited about C.J.'s character is more a testament to the absence of lesbianism on television than it is a tribute to *L.A. Law*'s radicality.

Lesbian vs Queer

So, in the final analysis, how should we evaluate C.J.'s character in *L.A. Law*? And *L.A. Law*'s score-card on issues of sexuality? Paradoxically, the episodes which are signified as having overt lesbian content are inherently conservative, because the performance of lesbian sexuality is repeatedly displaced onto a series of political and ethical issues. For instance, Maggie and C.J.'s sexual relationship is simply a backdrop for the political issue of lesbian custody. The same logic of displacement occurs in the episodes dealing with gay issues, such as the AIDS and gay cop episodes. Gay sexuality is turned into a matter of politics or ethics; lesbian and gay practices can be referred to and can even be discussed, but, unlike heterosexuality, they cannot be shown. Similarly, the Abby episode can hardly be considered a lesbian or bisexual issue; it's about heterosexual panic, the fear of discovering that the boundaries of heterosexuality are permeable. In fact, rather than giving proportional representation to bisexual women, the Abby episode sets out to disprove the lesbian version of the *When Harry Met Sally* proposition that 'a man and a woman can never be just friends, because sex always gets in the way'. It argues that a straight woman and a lesbian can be just friends, thereby affirming bisexuality as a legitimate sexual identity while reassuring straight viewers that there is no need to worry about the contamination of their own heterosexuality. Abby's heterosexuality remains securely intact, and the firm remains uncontaminated by any suspect liaisons. The representation of lesbian and gay sexuality as an 'issue' confirms the 'normality' of heterosexuality; heterosexuality only becomes an issue when it is excessive and transgressive, as in cases of incest and rape. Ordinarily, however, it is the very essence of everyday lived reality. *L.A. Law* achieves political points for representing gay and lesbian issues without, however, doing anything to revolutionize, or even create a space for, the visual representation of gay, lesbian, or queer sexuality on mainstream television. This is, of course, a classic liberal strategy that allows a heterosexual audience to tolerate difference without ever challenging the complacency of its own heterosexuality.

The above analysis does not, however, explain why *L.A. Law* created such a potentially queer character in C.J., and then limited so dramatically what she could be shown doing. Let me explain what I mean by calling C.J. queer. Queer politics is against identity politics; it rejects the notion of a gay or lesbian identity because identities inadvertently support the binary logic of compulsory heterosexuality; in opposition to a binary logic of homosexuality/heterosexuality, queer emphasizes that which disturbs the complacency of the opposition itself. Queer shifts the focus from sexual identity to sexual performativity, and claims that queers are everywhere rather than on the margins. Consequently, queer would rather find sex between women in an unexpected place—in Zoey and C.J.'s friendship—rather than in a relationship between two self-identified lesbians. Queer cannot confront the logic of heterosexuality by being another kind of identity. Queer should disturb all sexual boundaries, and create sexual mayhem, so that any individual may occupy or perform any sexual or gender identity, rather than have a true identity; in this way, queer undermines the very notion of a truth of sexuality. C.J. embodies queer by refusing to be identified as heterosexual, lesbian, or bisexual; she refuses to identify herself, to pin herself down, choosing simply to say she is sexually 'flexible'. Abby, embodying heterosexual logic, mis-takes 'flexibility' as bisexuality, and hence tries to pin down C.J.'s sexuality as an identity rather than a performance.

This analysis does not, however, explain why *L.A. Law*, having created a character who could be read as either queer or bisexual, did not take the relatively safe alternative of developing a lesbian relationship, which would have confirmed *L.A. Law*'s liberal tolerance, without challenging heterosexuality. The answer, I think, is that C.J.'s character can be read as either queer or bisexual. However, she can only be queer to the extent that she is not overtly sexualized, and she can only be shown engaging in explicit sexual behaviour that is not queer—i.e. when she is shown being heterosexual with McCoy. C.J.'s queerness must be contained; otherwise it would risk queering the show as a whole. So while as a character C.J. resists being pigeon-holed into a sexual identity, she functions, in terms of the logic of the show, as the site of a sexual identity—bisexuality.

Consequently, her queerness is rendered as an identity, parallel to heterosexuality in every way, without challenging heterosexuality. By making C.J. the locus of bisexuality, the programme gives fair representation to sexual orientations other than heterosexuality, while at the same time suggesting that both bisexuality and heterosexuality are sexual identities. Hence, none of the straight characters needs to investigate their own sexual identities. C.J.'s sexual otherness is doubly signified through her Englishness—acceptable as long as it is elsewhere, something that does not contaminate the wholesome heterosexuality of America. In addition, by making C.J. the site of bisexuality, viewers are less likely to queer other characters and situations. We are distracted from imagining a lesbian subtext between C.J. and Zoey by the implied but undeveloped relationship between C.J. and Maggie. The liberal earnestness of *L.A. Law* means that anything other than heterosexuality can only be represented as the object of compassion, rather than fun. C.J. is queer and cheeky; consequently, she can't be represented having sex, having fun, being camp, because that would be subversive.

L.A. Law could have had a lesbian relationship only if C.J. were identified as lesbian rather than queer. C.J.'s queerness could not, however, be contained in the kind of boundaried lesbian relationship that would be acceptable to the liberal world of *L.A. Law*, thereby revealing the limits of *L.A. Law*'s sexual politics. C.J. can only be queer to the extent that her sexuality takes place off-screen. Thus, her sexuality is an absent presence: it functions as a

raison d'être for raising issues, but it cannot be represented. The only characters who can be camp, oddly enough, are the very straight Brackman and his
ex-wife. When they decide to get back together they engage in silly, romantic, over-the-top behaviour—making sexual puns, ear-licking, acting
randy—which is very unlike the earnest sex we usually get on *L.A. Law*. But
that behaviour from Brackman and his wife is acceptable because it does not
threaten heterosexual monogamy. However, to substitute C.J. and Zoey for
Brackman and his wife in these scenes would be subversive and titillating.
Finally, then, we have to say that in terms of the sexual politics of contemporary television, C.J. is a great character, but she represents a lost opportunity.

I would like to thank Judith Ion, Lissa O'Neil, and Emma Partridge for discussing their
reactions to *L.A. Law* with me.

22

Reproducing Reality: Murphy Brown and Illegitimate Politics

Rebecca L. Walkowitz

It doesn't help matters when prime-time TV has Murphy Brown, a character who supposedly epitomizes today's intelligent, highly paid, professional woman, mocking the importance of fathers by bearing a child and calling it 'just another lifestyle choice'.

Vice President Dan Quayle[1]

My complaint is that Hollywood thinks it's cute to glamorize illegitimacy; Hollywood doesn't get it. . . . They ought to come with me out to where the real America is.

Vice President Dan Quayle[2]

THROWING DOWN THE first gauntlet in what the *New York Times* came to describe as a 'cultural war' of politics, Vice President Dan Quayle launched the 1992 Republican campaign for 'family values' with an attack on the popular fictional television news anchor, Murphy Brown.[3] Brown, played by Candice Bergen in a top-rated CBS sitcom called *Murphy Brown*, became unexpectedly pregnant in the 1991–2 season, and gave birth as a single parent in the last episode, which was broadcast on 18 May. Quayle's speech, delivered before a club gathering in California only two days later, followed shortly on the heels of the Rodney King riots in Los Angeles. The vice president attributed the 'lawless social anarchy' of the King riots to a broader 'poverty of values', encouraged and exemplified by the Murphy Brown story-line.[4] In an impressive rhetorical manœuvre, Quayle

© Garber, Matlock, and Walkowitz, 1993

Reprinted by permission of Routledge and the authors from Marjorie Garber, Jann Matlock, and Rebecca Walkowitz (eds.), *Media Spectacles* (New York: Routledge, 1993), 40–56.

1 Dan Quayle, quoted in John E. Yang and Ann Devroy, 'Quayle: "Hollywood Doesn't Get It" ', *Washington Post*, 21 May 1992: A17.

2 Dan Quayle, quoted in Michael Wines, 'Views on Single Motherhood Are Multiple at White House', *New York Times*, 21 May 1992: B16.

3 Maureen Dowd and Frank Rich, 'Taking No Prisoners in a Cultural War', *New York Times*, 21 Aug. 1992: A11.

4 Douglas Jehl, 'Quayle Deplores Eroding Values; Cites TV Show', *Los Angeles Times*, 20 May 1992: A1.

blithely exchanged 'poverty' in Los Angeles for a 'poverty of values' in prime-time television, and thus moved from the material to the abstract, ideological, and fictional. Moreover, through this displacement, Quayle avoided discussing either race or the urban environment, but rather universalized his topic and his analysis, making race, class, and geography inadmissible to the contest over 'real America' and its constituency.

Despite the instant and widespread attention given Quayle's remarks, the vice president's team swiftly retreated from its derision of Murphy Brown, ever mindful of the sitcom's high ratings share (the network estimated 70 million viewers for the fall 1992 season première).[5] And in any case, Quayle's advisers told the media, Murphy Brown wasn't the issue: 'The Vice President wanted to give a serious speech about the urban problem and focus on the poverty of values', William Kristol, Quayle's chief-of-staff, told Andrew Rosenthal of the *New York Times*.[6] Another aide insisted, 'It was a pop-culture cite to make [the speech] interesting.'[7]

Meanwhile, back at the White House, Quayle damage control was working overtime. Murphy Brown, White House spokesman Marlin Fitzwater soon found, was pregnant with unruly signification; with the spectacle of 'illegitimacy' came an excess of additional political baggage. Brown, after all, had chosen motherhood over abortion, and the conservative spin doctors couldn't figure out whether to embrace her decision as 'pro-life' or reject it for its affirmation of unwed motherhood.[8] On one level, the vice president might have chosen any popular cultural reference to draw attention to his speech and to create a segue from urban to moral poverty. Yet it is the argument of this essay that Quayle's choice made a difference; Murphy Brown's body—a distinctly gendered body—and her reproductive decisions mobilized the vice president's argument. The woman and the journalist, as middle terms, as media, cannot be merely looked through, but must also be looked at, as integral to the news spectacle itself.

The vice president's reference glanced specific and controversial issues—abortion, motherhood, families—both in the news and in the newsroom, a division that is dissolved to his discomfort in the *Murphy Brown* programme. For the breakdown of barriers between politics *in* the media and politics *of* the media in the content of the sitcom is mirrored by an ironic and often titillating play between fictional and real-life news in its formal design; *Murphy Brown* prides itself on the very confusion of fiction and real life. 'Just mixing the real people with the fictional people is a real kick for us', sitcom creator Diane English has said.[9] And according to reports from the Quayle camp, the commingling of real and fictional women newscasters in a sitcom baby shower for Murphy prompted the reference to *Murphy Brown* in the vice president's speech.[10] Quayle chose a television programme about the news

5 A CBS estimation reported in *New York Times*, 23 Sept. 1992: C20.

6 Andrew Rosenthal, 'Quayle's Moment', *New York Times Magazine*, 5 July 1992: 33.

7 John E. Yang and Ann Devroy, 'Quayle', A17.

8 Michael Wines, 'Views on Single Motherhood', A1.

9 Neal Koch, 'Everyone Has Advice for Murphy, Especially Real-Life TV Journalists', *New York Times*, 29 Sept. 1991: H33.

10 Andrew Rosenthal, 'Quayle's Moment', 34.

media as his medium, locating the institution of journalism, the power of journalists, and their authority in the anxiety that provoked his attack. Thus the media's reproduction and representation of political rhetoric in the content of the news became intricately tied to debates about the sexual reproductive choices of newscasters in particular and the politics of women's reproductive choice more broadly. In this sense, Dan Quayle's attack on Murphy Brown, I will argue, points to a debate about the position of journalists within a news media that produces and patrols individual personality only to reinforce the fiction of universal authority.

Real pregnant newscasters, married or unmarried, have been a topic of some gossip and occasional serious concern in the national press.[11] Indeed, Diane English freely admits that a number of episodes related to Murphy Brown's pregnancy were inspired by conflicts and stories from real newsrooms. In one programme, a news executive suggests that public scandal may force him to take Murphy off the air; this interchange was not unrelated, English says, to a run-in between *60 Minutes* executive producer Don Hewitt and his correspondent Merideth Vieira, who was expecting her second child.[12] Vieira in fact was removed from *60 Minutes*.

The hiring and firing of women newscasters, their circulation and exchange from network to network, is evident enough. Jane Pauley, Deborah Norville, Paula Zahn, Connie Chung, Diane Sawyer, Mary Alice Williams, among others, have all been shifted on and off news programmes. The reasons for these shifts vary from the specific quest for the 'younger and blonder' to the more ambiguous reasons of 'charisma' or 'how settled a person feels' to the television audience.[13] Women newscasters must be sexy, but not stray to sexual, and the boundaries are not always clear. 'If you were an anchor, they expected you to be glamorous and appear on the cover of *Vogue*', said one former news correspondent.[14] In September 1987 Diane Sawyer graced the cover of *Vanity Fair*, with an accompanying article about her entitled 'Diane Sawyer: The Glamour and the Mystery'. Maria Shriver has appeared, complete with strapless gown, frolicking with husband Arnold Schwarzenegger also in *Vanity Fair*, and in a photo sequence in *Harper's Bazaar*. Yet these women must be careful not to transgress the boundaries of what *Time* magazine has termed 'propriety and professionalism'. When Merideth Vieira, then correspondent for CBS's *West 57th Street*, posed in *Esquire*, she was criticized for showing too much thigh. *60 Minutes* star Mike Wallace, later to be (if only momentarily) Vieira's colleague, damned the *Esquire* spread as 'about as appropriate as anchormen appearing in beefcake pictures'.[15]

It may be beside the point for Wallace that anchormen never happen to be in beefcake pictures, but the comparative surveillance of women newscasters,

11 For general stories, see e.g. Susan Bickelhaupt, 'TV Makes Room for Motherhood', *Boston Globe*, 13 Apr. 1991: 8, and Jennet Conant, 'Broadcast Networking', *Working Woman*, Aug. 1990: 58–61.

12 Neal Koch, 'Everyone Has Advice for Murphy', H33.

13 Jennet Conant, 'Broadcast Networking', 58–61; Richard Zoglin, 'Star Wars at the Networks', *Time*, 3 Apr. 1992: 70–1.

14 Jennet Conant, 'Broadcast Networking', 59.

15 Anastasia Toufexis, 'The Girls of Network News', *Time*, 7 Mar. 1988: 85.

whether fictional or real, is not without consequence. Many of the critics and journalists who tout 'journalism', by definition, as an ungendered, objective, and universal mediation of truth are also those, such as Wallace, who delineate the very boundaries of what gets mediated. As a visual medium, television news anchors the authority of its journalism in personality and persons. The anchoring comes as much from behind the scenes as from the anchors themselves. Don Brown, executive vice president of NBC News, has said that his network has become more flexible as its 'talent' base has diversified to include more women. 'Talent . . . is more critical than ever, and if that talent happens to be a woman who happens to be pregnant', Brown says, the network must make sure 'talent' stays, whoever he or she may be.[16] Although he may have the best of intentions toward progressive work policies for women and families, Brown's attempts to universalize the interests of the network and his 'happens to be' grammar undermine the extent to which the regulation of various kinds of reproduction, in media form (women newscasters) and media content (the news), is never quite so accidental.

Murphy Brown was condemned by Quayle as a bad example for urban America, presumably for unwed girls who might become pregnant, who might 'get in trouble', influenced by Murphy's impoverished values. The danger, then, was not just unwanted pregnancy, but unruly behaviour, a sexual autonomy unrestricted by marriage or conservative morality. Indeed, top news anchor Connie Chung caused particular controversy not for getting pregnant, but for *trying* to get pregnant, which doesn't quite fit into the ABC executive's euphemistic 'happens to be' formulation. In 1990 Chung and her husband, news correspondent Maury Povich, announced that they would begin taking an 'aggressive approach to having a baby'.[17] *Working Woman* described Chung's decision as a 'retreat to the bedroom'. Other journalists at a convention in New York chanted 'Ovulate! Ovulate!' at a video apology when she cancelled a speech as a result of her new relation to reproduction.[18] The spectacle of Chung's sexual reproductive choices thus demeaned her status as a serious journalist, a status that had up to then been confirmed as properly sexy and respectable in a series of *People* magazine interviews over the years.[19] Chung's fault, and the fault attributed to many of her women colleagues, does not reside in the spectacle of journalists and their sexualities—which the news media, on their own terms, create all the time—but in a spectacle that threatens to uncover its own boundaries and constructions.

Chung's troubles with reproduction don't end, of course, with her personal life. Her 1989 prime-time television programme *Saturday Night with Connie Chung* upset many critics and journalists for mixing fact and fiction to confusion. Chung initially described *Saturday Night* as a 'new genre in television news': it mingled dramatic re-creations of events with eyewitness

16 Susan Bickelhaupt, 'TV Makes Room for Motherhood', 8.

17 Ibid.

18 Gail Collins, 'Chung's Choice', *Working Woman*, Dec. 1990.

19 Gail Buchalter, 'To Wake Up Its Sluggish *Early Today* Show, NBC Anchors Its Hopes on Connie Chung', *People*, 13 June 1983: 34–5; Carol Wallace, 'D.C. Newsman Maury Povich Anchors NBC's Connie Chung after a Longtime Cross-Country Romance', *People*, 10 June 1985: 150–5; Kristin McMurran, 'Two Hearts, Beating in Prime Time', *People*, 10 Apr. 1989: 116–21.

accounts and talk-show analysis. The programme's producers said they saw these techniques as a way to bring viewers closer to reality, to what they would not ordinarily be able to see: 'I saw this as a way to get to the big events that happened off camera', said executive producer Andrew Lack in the *New York Times*.[20]

Saturday Night with Connie Chung sparked heated reactions from both its critics and its defenders. Some journalists complained that it brought together too many different and conflicting visual cues from documentary, Hollywood film, television news, and political analysis. Moreover, the participation and headlining of Chung added the authority of a news anchor to what was often not considered real journalism. The *Los Angeles Times* argued in an editorial criticizing the programme that 'In good journalism there is no room—and certainly no need—for recourse to the bogus, the dishonest, the illusionary.'[21] Such methods are not necessary nor suitable, the newspaper asserted, yet again invoking language of worth and stability. On the other hand, but along the same rhetorical lines, an unidentified CBS executive supported the use of Chung's dramatic re-creations with the assertion that they are 'at least classy, not sleazy'.[22]

The most serious complaint against *Saturday Night with Connie Chung* and other information news programmes of this sort is that they shift between various degrees of documentation and re-creation, between actors and witnesses, without giving viewers signals to let them know that the rules are changing. This anxiety is not unlike the one that fuelled Dan Quayle's political and rhetorical slippage from 'poverty' to the 'poverty of values'; his transition from families to family morality, according to Quayle aides, was motivated by the sight of unseemly fiction (Murphy Brown as single mother) flirting with proper reality—namely other, real news anchors visiting the programme. It is indeed true that these programmes may confuse viewers about how they should understand and interpret the value of what they are seeing. This confusion, however, stems more from unfulfilled expectations about news and what it looks like than from a recent rash of visual manipulation. 'Journalism' and 'America'—whether we call them real or not—depend upon a 'grounding' that is constructed by the very manipulations that journalists and politicians have come to decry.[23]

Saturday Night was not the first time that Chung was attacked for participating in unworthy journalism. In 1987 Chung hosted a programme that *Washington Post* reviewer Tom Shales deemed excessively flashy for 'crossing the documentary form with the Hollywood Squares'. In the show, Chung discussed AIDS and its effect on sexual mores by running clips from popular television shows and rock videos. 'Chung sullies her good name in the

20 Bill Carter, 'Stars to Re-Enact News on Chung Program', *New York Times*, 19 Sept. 1989: C22.

21 'Just the Facts, Please', *Los Angeles Times*, 24 Nov. 1989: B10.

22 Kevin Goldman, 'TV Network News Is Making Re-Creation a Form of Recreation', *Wall Street Journal*, 30 Oct. 1989: A1, A4.

23 A television reviewer for the *Wall Street Journal*, responding to criticism of *Saturday Night* that the use of actor James Earl Jones in a re-creation alongside interviews with historical witnesses constituted the show as entertainment, not documentary, wrote, 'So maybe it's not traditional news. . . . James Earl Jones's portrait is wonderfully subtle . . . and the witnesses interject a solid grounding of fact.' Robert Goldberg, 'America's Sweetheart Nets Marlon', *Wall Street Journal*, 9 Oct. 1989: A12.

process. It will be hard to take her seriously for a while', Shales added.[24] This threat of minimized journalistic authority came with the *Saturday Night* programme as well. Reviewers in the *Boston Globe* and the *New York Times* focused on a spread of glamorous portraits of Chung that appeared in the opening credits, which, according to the *Globe*, prompted one network executive to ask, 'Is this a news programme or a date?'[25] Yet the very photos that lowered Chung's programme into the blatantly sexual for the *Globe* became evidence for 'stardom in accord with network fashion' in the *Times*. What makes a woman news anchor a star, a spectacle, is also what, it seems, reduces her very authority in and about the news.[26] Robert Goldberg in the *Wall Street Journal* lauded Chung for the 'warm glow' she brought her programme, but he too wondered whether 'America's sweetheart' could command enough screen presence and seriousness to attract audiences to a prime-time news show.[27]

As the conflated debates about Chung's appearance, lifestyle, and work suggest, in television journalism the personalities of news correspondents come to stand metonymically for the form and content of their news programmes. The policing of news anchors often implies and includes a critique of the kind of news they represent and how they represent it. Former Watergate reporter Carl Bernstein, writing about the state of journalism on the twentieth anniversary of the Watergate burglary and scandal, complained that the news media have 'been moving away from real journalism toward the creation of a sleazoid info-tainment culture in which the lines between Oprah and Phil and Geraldo and Diane and even Ted, between the *New York Post* and *Newsday*, are too often indistinguishable.'[28] Television personalities, on a first-name basis with American culture, occupy in Bernstein's description the same institutional authority as entire newspapers in the print medium. 'Even Ted', presumably Ted Koppel of ABC, no longer upholds the boundary between 'real journalism' and the 'sleazoid'. What has declined is not just the people ('even Ted') but also the form and content of what they represent. Thus Bernstein decries a 'lack of information, misinformation, disinformation, and a contempt for the truth or reality of most people's lives' in the same sweep as he condemns coverage of 'the weird and the stupid and coarse' in television programmes about 'cross-dressing in the marketplace; skinheads at your corner luncheonette; pop psychologists rhapsodizing over the airways about the minds of serial killers and sex offenders'.[29]

Certainly, this connection between those who report, what they report, and what is reported about them is not restricted to television news, even if it is most visually obvious in that medium. Carl Bernstein, himself the subject

24 Tom Shales quoted in 'Connie Chung', in Charles Moritz (ed.), *Current Biography Yearbook (1989)* (New York: H. W. Wilson, 1989), 107.

25 Bruce McCabe, 'Looking for Redemption', *Boston Globe*, 22 July 1990: 2.

26 Walter Goodman, 'Connie Chung's "Saturday" Features James Earl Jones', *New York Times*, 25 Sept. 1989: C18.

27 Robert Goldberg, 'America's Sweetheart Nets Marlon', A12.

28 Carl Bernstein, 'The Idiot Culture', *New Republic*, 8 June 1992: 24.

29 Ibid. 25.

of various kinds of personal public attention over the years, with Bob Woodward was catapulted to professional fame through the popularity of their best-selling book *All the President's Men*, and the subsequent film, starring Robert Redford and Dustin Hoffman.[30] The mythology surrounding Watergate—its glorification as journalism's 'finest hour' and the sense, true or false, that it paved the way for a 'permanently more powerful, more celebrated, and more aggressive press'—no doubt has contributed to Bernstein's stature.[31] Given his position as a presumed source of accurate information compared to, say, Dan Quayle, Bernstein and his definition of 'real journalism' carries the power to authorize representation among journalists and politicians alike.

Yet Bernstein's rhetoric of 'real' and 'sleazoid' journalism, of proper and improper newscasters, operates along terms not so unlike Quayle's boundaries of representable reproductive behaviour. News can be provocative, attract attention, even be 'popular culture', Bernstein explains, but it has to be earned culture, 'popular culture that stretches and informs its consumers'.[32] Some manipulations in the course of journalism are deemed by him worse than others, depending on the value of the fictions produced. Bernstein himself reconstructed fact in *All the President's Men*, using dramatic, fictional narratives.[33] 'Real journalism' and 'real America' are not just about what's true, but what's true to whom. In the media, the right to define 'news', to term an issue 'fit to print', presumes the right to identify not just what viewers or readers *should* know, but what they *need* know.[34] 'Real journalism' is a conflation, in Carl Bernstein's account, of the suitable and the necessary. Similarly, in political terms, 'real America' refers to the individuals and experiences that need be counted, considered, deemed representative, true, as opposed to those, in Vice President Dan Quayle's estimation, that are irrelevant, 'glamorized'.

Bernstein defines his 'real journalism' as a narrative about untrustworthy politics, with Watergate as the example *par excellence*, as opposed to narratives of impure sensationalism and celebrity, which, he argues, do not reveal 'society's real condition'.[35] The notion of discovering what others have hidden or cannot see is central to Bernstein's logic of investigative journalism, and similar to Quayle's geography of the 'real America'. The 'real America' is, according to the vice president, what the media don't get, what he must discover, what those who sit in 'newsrooms, and sitcom studios and faculty

30 Speculation about Carl Bernstein's personal life ran rampant after the publication of *Heartburn*, a novel by his ex-wife Nora Ephron, which portrayed a fictionalized Bernstein as an adulterous husband. *All the President's Men*, when it appeared in 1974, was the fastest-selling non-fiction hardback in the history of American publishing. Michael Schudson, 'Watergate: A Study in Mythology', *Columbia Journalism Review*, May/June 1992: 31.

31 Larry Martz, 'For the Media, A Pyrrhic Victory', *Newsweek*, 22 June 1992: 32; Tom Mathews, 'Watergate Blues', *Newsweek*, 22 June 1992: 24; Michael Schudson, 'Watergate: A Study in Mythology', 30; James Mann, 'Deep Throat: An Institutional Analysis', *The Atlantic*, May 1992: 106–12.

32 Carl Bernstein, 'Idiot Culture', 25.

33 Michiko Kakutani, 'Fiction and Reality: Blurring the Edges', *New York Times*, 25 Sept. 1992: C1, C31.

34 Every *New York Times* banner is underwritten by the motto, 'All the news that's fit to print.'

35 Carl Bernstein, 'Idiot Culture', 25.

lounges' have distorted and 'mock'.[36] Indeed, the 'real journalism' and the 'real America', while here defined by traditionally opposed critics, one a journalist and one a politician, both emanate from the same set of fairly conservative moral gestures, whereby boundaries of fact and fiction, reality and fantasy, worthiness and unworthiness are used to regulate the authorization of individual experience.

The challenges to these regulations, to Bernstein's and to Quayle's, manifest themselves as undisciplined sexuality and reproduction in the media and in politics. Whether as 'cross-dressing' and other 'sleazoid' topics, or as Murphy Brown, what was once 'journalism' or 'America' is being infiltrated by what should not be represented. If the gender politics of the real television newsroom has not always been a sustained topic of the national mainstream media, certainly the spectacle of Murphy Brown's fictional newsroom and its interchanges with Vice President Dan Quayle made it so. Murphy's unmarried pregnant body, alongside the bodies of real newscasters, confuses what is most dangerous and disruptive here. It's not so much the presence of real women newscasters, or the pregnant, but fictional, Murphy Brown, but the combination of the two in the same space. They begin to take on the same authority, and one category seeps into the next.

This confusion, not surprisingly, prompted many to wonder, after all, who's Murphy Brown? Most famously, Prime Minister Brian Mulroney of Canada, at a press conference to discuss a trade pact with President Bush, turned to his colleague to query the very same: 'Who's Murphy Brown?'[37] Bush, only one day after Quayle's speech, was exasperated by the controversy, particularly when he had presumably 'real' business to discuss. He finally told the press corps, 'O.K., everybody give me a *Murphy Brown* question. I've got one answer right here for you. What's your *Murphy Brown* question?'[38]

This unruly spectacle in the news made, as I have suggested, for unruly representation. Was it Murphy Brown or *Murphy Brown*? The character, the woman, or the television show by the same name? Journalists, even 'real journalists' from major newspapers, the guardians of fact, couldn't seem to make up their minds. In an early article, the *New York Times* described Quayle's target as *Murphy Brown* on first reference, a polite 'fictional Ms Brown' on the second, and 'actress Candice Bergen' on the third. 'Ms Brown' seemed to be the favourite for all future references—she was a new mother after all. In a *New York Times* article later that summer about President Bush's attacks on the cartoon programme *The Simpsons*, Bart Simpson is merely 'Bart' on second reference, not a more formal 'Mr Simpson', as is the newspaper's usual honorific for men.[39] One wonders whether the com-

---

36 In a cover story in the *New York Times Magazine*, Dan Quayle equates and conflates 'newsrooms, sitcom studios and faculty lounges', opposing them to 'the heart of America', the real America, where, he seems to argue, his 'family values' are to be found. Andrew Rosenthal, 'Quayle's Moment', 13.

37 Prime Minister Mulroney quoted in John E. Yang and Ann Devroy, 'Quayle', A1.

38 Michael Wines, 'Views on Single Motherhood', B16.

39 At the Republican National Convention in Houston, Bush called for an America that looks a lot more 'like the Waltons and a lot less like the Simpsons'. In a following episode of the Simpsons, young Bart Simpson responded: 'We're just like the Waltons. We're praying for the depression to end, too.' This falls right along the 'family values'-through-pop-culture strategy that Quayle began in May. Interestingly, the fictional television insists on its own relevance to reality, thus disrupting Bush's dis-

parative respect shown Murphy Brown reflects deference to age or to beauty; perhaps it merely indicates the value with which the newspaper invested the Murphy Brown debate.

The displacement from fact to fiction mobilized a confusion of names, but also a confusion of category. Journalists were unsure whether this was entertainment news, or political news, or merely 'information' news—not 'real journalism', in Carl Bernstein's formulation, but true in any case. For politicians, if Dan Quayle wasn't talking about real single mothers, and he insisted he wasn't, then they had to come to terms with the policy implications of 'family values'. Quayle defined 'family values' as those that the 'real America' already possessed; they were universal, understood. Like the 'real America', 'family values' as an ideology was predicated on its stability and its precise definition, a definition Quayle and his compatriots claimed to possess. He knew, he told the Southern Baptist Convention in Indianapolis, what was 'in the heart of America', where 'the real America is'.[40] It was this claim for 'values', however, that allowed Quayle to disclaim responsibility for families and for the experience of families in urban America.

'Family values' as an ambiguous ideology was a blueprint for an equally ambiguous policy as well: 'Marriage is probably the best anti-poverty program there is', the vice president asserted in the Murphy Brown speech.[41] Focusing on ideological and moral institutions, Quayle stressed in his comments to the press that he was attacking the 'glamorization' of unwed motherhood, and not unwed mothers themselves: he was attacking a thing, an idea, a value, and not a person.[42] Indeed, Quayle's language suggests that he objected not just to the presentation of an impoverished value—single motherhood—but to the excess of attention given it, to its glorification. It wasn't worthy, and it certainly wasn't worthy of a newscaster or news. Thus the conservative argument here adopted a logic much like that used to condemn artists in the censorship debates over pornography and sexuality: even as the attack on fictional television presumed to evaluate the accuracy and effect of representation, its rhetoric also condemned the value of such representation, deeming it dangerous fantasy and fiction, and thus not part of the 'real America' that is authorized to exist. Murphy Brown was judged by Quayle at once empty of right values and overflowing in wrong influence.

On the season première of *Murphy Brown* in September 1992, the first episode to follow Quayle's remarks in May, the real producers of the sitcom took the opportunity to turn the tables. The sitcom characters were shown watching May's news clips of Dan Quayle discussing their very real Murphy Brown, as if the debate had taken place entirely within the sitcom world. Characters walked into their newsroom carrying copies of both real and fictional national newspapers from the spring controversy, headlined with the

placement away from reality and his control over fiction. Maureen Dowd and Frank Rich, 'Taking No Prisoners', A11.

40 First reference from speech to Southern Baptist Convention in Indianapolis, quoted in Andrew Rosenthal, 'Quayle's Moment', 13. Second reference to Michael Wines, 'Views on Single Motherhood', B16.

41 Douglas Jehl, 'Quayle Deplores Eroding Values', A1.

42 John E. Yang and Ann Devroy, 'Quayle', A17.

Murphy Brown story, disrupting boundaries of representation all the more. 'Quayle to Murphy Brown: You Tramp', read a massive front-page headline in the *New York Daily News*. Where Dan Quayle used fiction to displace reality and to authorize his 'family values', Murphy Brown manipulated her authority as a newscaster—as a journalist—and the titillation of real-life fiction to produce a sharp retort to the vice president's condemnation.

In her return, Murphy Brown made fiction look like fact; her persona as sitcom television anchorwoman took on all the cues of broadcast journalism. Certainly, in both literature and visual media, including television, fact has always been rendered through the manipulation of fictional narrative structures. Some journalists have argued that re-creation or docudrama is at times more mimetic than documentary because such genres often present a better overall sense of reality, a contiguity that is more 'accurate' than a reproduction, such as a video eyewitness account would be. Writing in the *Christian Science Monitor*, one critic has insisted that television programmes that use only documentary footage are often more manipulative than those that mix re-created fact with description and analysis. The best of these programmes, he concluded, may or may not use 'real' clips, but rather concentrate on 'something truer than facts', what he termed putting realism 'in the right context'.[43] This is just the kind of reproduction that got Connie Chung in trouble.

It should come as no surprise, then, that Quayle's comments on Murphy Brown seemed more 'real', easier to reconcile, placed within the television sitcom world than they did outside of it. Toward the end of the programme, Murphy Brown, in her news anchor clothes, with pristine hairstyle and careful make-up, sits behind a news desk, poised for a programme on 'the American family and family values' to answer Quayle's attacks on single motherhood. Murphy Brown looks straight at the television audience, and the camera tightens to a familiar head-and-shoulder shot. She has become the authority, and she is telling the truth: 'In searching for the causes to our social ills, we could blame the media, or the Congress, or an administration that has been in power for 12 years. Or, we could blame me.'[44] Murphy Brown ends her report with the suggestion that the vice president 'expand his definition' of families, and then she introduces several non-traditional real and diverse families gathered on set. The news broadcast breaks as Murphy Brown rises to stand next to the families, who are thanked in the sitcom credits for appearing on the programme. Is Murphy Brown a real news anchor, or does she just function as one? 'Fact or fiction?' asked Boston's local news anchor Liz Walker that night on the 11 o'clock broadcast. 'Hard to tell', her co-anchor responded.[45]

'Fact or fiction?' The irony of Liz Walker's question comes with the 'fact' that she was the target of much criticism only five years earlier when she announced that she was to become a single mother. Walker, Boston's first black female co-anchor, was accused of setting a bad example for urban

43 Alan Bunce, 'Can TV Tell Us What Is Real?', *Christian Science Monitor*, 10 Oct. 1991: 14.

44 *Murphy Brown*, CBS-TV, 21 Sept. 1992.

45 Thanks to Jann Matlock who tracked this piece of Boston news banter. WBZ-TV, 21 Sept. 1992.

teenagers, among whom pregnancy was increasing.[46] Walker's story re-emerged after the Murphy Brown incident, with speculation that it had formed the basis for the sitcom plot—speculation that the programme's creators declined to confirm.[47] Asked the difference between her story and the one portrayed by Candice Bergen on *Murphy Brown*, Walker aptly responded: 'I didn't have a laugh track in my life.' What Walker clearly articulates is the distance between her subjective experience and our own as spectators in a media culture that blurs our ability to distinguish what we see, and to remember that there is a difference—particularly for Walker.[48] These real attacks on Liz Walker's morality recover and uncover the ground of Quayle's original displacement from race and class conflict to a vague 'poverty of values'. Walker's critics suggested that her actions would provide a bad model for minority youth, and thus the reproductive choices of a single woman journalist were, again, deemed responsible for the problems of urban poverty.

This *mise en abîme* of media, of network newscasters, women, and various kinds of reproduction, was just what made Quayle's reference to Murphy Brown so titillating for the spectator and so dangerous for conservative strategists. It becomes difficult to identify the origin of reproduction, when, for instance, real women news anchors begin copying Murphy Brown's clothing style.[49] After the fact, *Murphy Brown*, the programme, became if anything more popular and more invested with real authority than ever before. In the mainstream press, this investment in a fictional news anchor as an example of a single professional mother sparked an array of news stories about the diversity of real families. The *New York Times*, which a few months earlier had topped its front page with a photograph of Murphy Brown as new mother, ran a four-part cover series soon after the sitcom retort to Quayle entitled 'The Good Mother'.[50] Favourably, these articles restored real bodies and real lives to Quayle's empty discourse of values. But these articles also indicate the media's own interest in recouping the authoritative ground of real news and proper mediation. 'The political morality play . . . does not begin to suggest the complexity, diversity and confusion of being a mother in 1992', the first paragraph of the opening article argued.[51] Although sitcom warfare no doubt simplified and distorted the experience of women, such performances, I would argue, are integral to the cultural and political

46 Robert A. Jordan, 'A Personal Decision', *Boston Globe*, 27 June 1987: 19; Marian Christy, 'Liz Walker Talks about Her "Real Riches" ', *Boston Globe*, 22 Mar. 1989: 75.

47 Elizabeth Mehren, 'Just like "Murphy Brown" ', *Los Angeles Times*, 22 June 1992: F1.

48 In another angle on the 'fact or fiction' question, one might look to the career of Candice Bergen herself, who portrays Murphy Brown. Apparently, Don Hewitt, executive producer of the highly successful news programme *60 Minutes*, had been trying to convince Bergen to become a correspondent on his show, joining such well-known journalists as Mike Wallace and Diane Sawyer. She declined, the *New York Times* reports, to continue her acting career. Neil Koch, 'Everyone Has Advice for Murphy', H34.

49 In addition, when *W* magazine did a fashion spread on women anchors, it combined Jane Pauley, Kathleen Sullivan, and Murphy Brown. Harry F. Waters and Janet Huck, 'Networking Women', *Newsweek*, 13 Mar. 1989: 49.

50 Susan Chira, 'New Realities Fight Old Images of Mother', *New York Times*, 4 Oct. 1992: 1; Tamar Lewin, 'Rise in Single Parenthood Is Reshaping U.S.', *New York Times*, 4 Oct. 1992: 1; Erik Eckholm, 'Finding Out What Happens When Mothers Go to Work', *New York Times*, 6 Oct. 1992: 1; Felicity Barringer, 'In Family-Leave Debate, a Profound Ambivalence', *New York Times*, 7 Oct. 1992: 1.

51 Susan Chira, 'New Realities', 1.

landscape that they mediate and that inform them. The media, as a middle, will always, if only implicitly invoke itself in the spectacle. With great irony, Murphy Brown told her colleague, fielding a call from the *Washington Post*, 'Tell them to go find a real story.'[52] What she knew, what Liz Walker and Connie Chung knew, and what Dan Quayle was to find out, was that the story was already there.

This essay could not have been completed but for timely transatlantic research provided by Brian Martin. For generous support, my thanks to Sheila Allen, Hannah Feldman, Becky Hall, Susan Glasser, Henry Turner, Daniel J. Walkowitz, Judith R. Walkowitz, and Jamie Zelermyer. For varied and, indeed, pregnant counsel, thanks to Marjorie Garber, who suggested the essay's title, and Jann Matlock.

52 Murphy Brown, played by Candice Bergen, on *Murphy Brown*, CBS-TV, 21 Sept. 1992.

23

Representation Wars: Malaysia, *Embassy*, and Australia's *Corps Diplomatique*

Suvendrini Perera

AT THE **1991** Commonwealth Summit the Prime Ministers of Australia and Malaysia signed into existence a pact now known as 'the Harare agreement', a document legitimizing representation as an item of formal diplomatic concern.[1] In a statement which incorporated many of the questions currently circulating in the debates around postmodernism, post-colonialism, and representation, the then Australian Prime Minister acknowledged the cause of the dispute as the Australian Broadcasting Corporation's television series *Embassy*:

> Mr Hawke said yesterday that it was clear, based on internal evidence, that although *Embassy* was fictional 'the Malaysians were entitled to draw the conclusion that Malaysia was being referred to' [in that production]. (*Australian*, 19 Oct. 1991)

This essay situates the high-level diplomatic attempt to negotiate issues of referentiality, textuality, and the crisis of meaning, of authenticity and simulacra, of national and popular subjectivities, within a mesh of cultural economies. At the same time it examines how a television show such as *Embassy* can have come to figure so prominently—so publicly to be privileged and canvassed over a year or more—in the transactions over security, environmental policy, trade, and, above all, regional hegemony that are clearly at stake in current relations between the governments of Australia and Malaysia.[2]

Originally published in John Frow and Meaghan Morris (eds.), *Australian Cultural Studies: A Reader* (Sydney: Allen and Unwin, 1993), 15–29.

1 The *Sydney Morning Herald* (26 Feb. 1992) reported that the agreement 'commits both Governments to dissociating themselves from inaccurate and distorted media reports about each other's affairs', and was first invoked by Australian Foreign Affairs Minister Gareth Evans in his condemnation of the film *Turtle Beach*.

2 The struggle for regional hegemony, evident in the conflict over a number of issues including the Commonwealth Games, relations with Fiji, and UN candidates, is detailed in an article by Greg Sheridan revealingly titled 'One Perfect Whipping-Boy for Malaysia'. Reinforcing the *Australian*'s preoccupation with postures of physical subjection and sadomasochism, the article attributes a number of reasons for the direction of Malaysia's foreign policy, ranging from personal snubs to a general sense that Australia is an outsider in the Pacific (6 Nov. 1991).

As Bob Hawke's comments bear out, the entire exchange is distinctly post-modernist in its engagement with both the mechanisms and the principles of representational power. More than any other, representation figures as *the* issue in this international dispute: whatever disguised anxieties and aggressions patrol the border fence, representation seems to have been agreed upon by both parties as the ground of contestation. How does Australia represent Malaysia? Whether in Prime Ministerial denunciations—for example, Hawke's much-reported description of Malaysia as 'barbaric' for imposing the death penalty on two Australians convicted for drug smuggling—or in what both sides characterize as Australia's free press, are these representations acceptable?[3] In turn, how do the Australian media represent this dispute over representation? What are the relations between these representations and official Australian rhetoric? What are the relations between these representations and Australian political *practice*? How are these in turn re-represented in Australian media?

In posing these questions this essay is concerned also with another set of questions that have come up repeatedly in the aftermath of decolonization and will, I suspect, come up with increasing frequency during the next few years: what is involved in the representation of another culture, when interaction between the cultures concerned has been structured at every level by colonial and imperialist histories? This question has been raised most often as a diplomatic issue in the context of the Middle East—the Saudi reaction to the BBC screening of the film *Death of a Princess* in the late 1970s, the representations of Iran and Islam on US television throughout the 1980s and, most recently, the widespread and even more widely publicized furore over the publication of Salman Rushdie's *The Satanic Verses*. Regionally, however, the question of representation continues to be staged as a local dispute between Australia and Malaysia, and as one that can be adequately explained at the level of anecdote and autobiography—the Malaysian Premier's 'sulks' or his resentment over his unhappy college years in Australia—or as so much diplomatic by-play, a smokescreen for really important concerns like trade and security.[4] To historicize the diplomatic wrangle over *Embassy*, I want to begin by outlining Australia's complicated contemporary positioning within contradictory regional and cultural economies.

Precarious Postures I: The Diplomatic Position

The claim authoritatively to represent, and therefore to *know* Malaysia cannot be separated from the various kinds of authority that are combined in orientalism, the cluster of knowledges about 'oriental' cultures that has underwritten Western colonialism and imperialism. In Australia recent

3 Although the Malaysian government has argued that the ABC's official status suggests implicit government sanction of *Embassy*, Hawke and Evans have insisted on the ABC's freedom from governmental pressure. This assurance is complicated by the government's highly visible attempt to direct ABC content during the Gulf War. An official inquiry was recently announced into the ABC's bias in featuring supposedly 'pro-Iraq' commentators like Dr Robert Springborg during the war. Springborg's fitness to appear as an impartial Middle East 'expert' (or 'orientalist' as they are still called in some circles) was formally challenged by the federal government. So the ABC's attempt, in that particular instance, to represent an alternative and less demonized—a less *orientalized*—Middle East, did in fact lead to public intervention by members of the Hawke government.

4 See Greg Sheridan, 'One Perfect Whipping Boy', *Australian*, 6 Nov. 1991.

recognitions of—and celebratory explorations into—a new-found 'post-colonial' condition often pass over the problems posed by an older national self-image of Australia as regional heir to the colonizer's discarded mantle. This history positions Australia in an unequal and uneasy triangle with Europe (and especially Britain) at one end, and 'Asia' on the other—a relationship perceived as a set of continuing hierarchical rearrangements based on current conditions of military, economic, and cultural (which also at times includes 'racial') superiority.

This heritage of anxiety about place has produced its own complement of orientalist texts in Australia, representations examined in detail by Alison Broinowski in a highly publicized recent study, *The Yellow Lady*. Written by a career diplomat and launched by Governor-General Bill Hayden (who used the occasion to make a speech widely perceived as pro-republican and therefore 'anti-British'), Broinowski's book has been acclaimed for its contribution to regional understanding and the promotion of closer ties with Asia. Like *Embassy*, *The Yellow Lady* produces (and is a product of) Australian knowledge about Asia; for this reason it needs serious consideration as a text which at once critiques and reinscribes Australian orientalism (a process already enacted in its title). In spite of its careful cataloguing of orientalist representations of Asia by Australians, Broinowski's text simultaneously participates in the long history of cultural and economic panic over relations with Asia. The Foreword (by Professor James Mackie) warns ominously:

> Soon, very soon, we will have to be capable of meeting them [Asians] on their terms . . . If we continue to turn our backs on them . . . we are doomed to isolation and insignificance as a nation.[5]

Mackie represents the threat of 'Asia' as an overturning of given hierarchies, an anxiety couched in the language of an inversion of physical and spatial relations of dominance.

Similar anxieties about location and place also underlie a somewhat different group of texts, those popular cultural productions that rewrite Australian–Asian relations within an already available cultural and geographical scheme. This group includes the novel and film versions of *The Year of Living Dangerously*, the recent *Turtle Beach*, and, of course, *Embassy*. In these texts South-East Asia is produced as a surrogate Middle East of Islam, despotism, violence, oil, and sex, a storehouse where young boys as well as women circulate as endlessly accessible objects of desire and of destruction. Such a localizing of wider international tensions is reproduced at yet another level in recent attempts to construct Malaysian Prime Minister Mahathir Mohamad as a new Saddam Hussein, a construction evident, for example, in a cartoon in the *Australian* portraying Mahathir as a swaggering bully-boy in boxing gloves while an Australia-shaped punching bag hangs limply in the background.[6]

---

5 Alison Broinowski, *The Yellow Lady* (Melbourne: Oxford Univ. Press, 1992), p. v.

6 Löbbecke, *Australian*, 6 Nov. 1991. (The cartoon accompanied Greg Sheridan's article—see n. 4.) This is not to evade the valid criticisms of Mahathir's regime that have emerged from a range of Malaysian and non-Malaysian sources. I am interested here only in how such critiques tend to be posed and reposed in orientalist terms in Australian media. A similar problem was apparent during the Gulf War,

Increasingly, however, such representations are contested. The evolving power relations between Australia and the region that C. J. Koch (in *The Year of Living Dangerously*) calls Australia's Middle East, but which we might perhaps describe as Australia's Orient—South-East Asia and the Pacific—mean that these nations can now officially challenge their own orientalization, for reasons that include not only decolonization and its aftermath, but also the whole complex of specific outcomes that make up what Andrew Milner has detailed so persuasively as 'Australia's own distinctively postmodern condition':

> So Australia has been catapulted towards post-industrialism at a speed possible only in a society that had never fully industrialized; towards consumerism in a fashion barely imaginable in historically less affluent and egalitarian societies . . . towards an integration into multinational capitalism easily facilitated by longstanding, pre-existing patterns of economic dependence; towards a sense of 'being after', and of being post-European, entirely apposite to a colony of European settlement suddenly set adrift, in intellectually and imaginatively uncharted Asian waters . . . Postcolonialism—or better, perhaps, post-imperialism—is . . . Australia's own distinctively postmodern condition.[7]

As Australian economic and cultural assurance drains, nations like Malaysia and Indonesia, no longer subjected or voiceless in regional or international affairs, can—and do—actively contest representations of primitivism, barbarity, and underdevelopment.[8] While on the one hand the sense of post-imperial *malaise* is only highlighted by the increasingly desperate ring of official assertions of republicanism and regional affiliation, on the other, the energy expended in sustaining an older self-representation of regional dominance and racial superiority is correspondingly increased.

Embassy provides a charged instance for articulating this complicated cultural positioning, inflected as it is by a range of historical experience. The *Sydney Morning Herald*'s recent banner headline of 29 July 1991, 'Malaysia renews attack', is only the most obvious in a series of news reports to represent Malaysian–Australian relations as a battleground where bilateral negotiation and the language of diplomatic interchange are figured as absolute victories and absolute surrenders. In July 1991, when Foreign Minister Gareth Evans visited Malaysia and made some rather awkward efforts to distance himself from *Embassy* after more than a year of strained relations, Richard Ackland, ABC Radio National's coyly unctuous announcer on the current affairs programme *Daybreak*, repeatedly described Evans's behaviour as 'grovelling'. This is a term that draws on a set of long-establish associ-

---

when the Western peace movement deployed an older rhetoric of 'oriental despotism' in its denunciations of the anti-democratic rule of the Emir of Kuwait. My focus is on the continuing availability of the cultural lexicon of orientalism for mobilization in any kind of political criticism of the region.

7 Andrew Milner, 'Postmodernism and Popular Culture', *Meanjin*, 49/1 (1990), 35–42, at p. 39.

8 The anthropologist Johannes Fabian has described the peculiar cultural relativism and the denial he calls 'allochronism'—the differentiation between so-called 'traditional' or 'primitive' societies on the one hand and 'developed' or 'modern' societies on the other, in a way that denies coevalness or co-temporality between them. As power relations change, the observers and observed in these exercises have begun to face each other across the same time, in positions of co-temporality and contemporaneousness. See Fabian, *Time and the Other* (New York: Columbia Univ. Press, 1983).

ations to achieve a startling consciousness of reversal: in the archive of orientalism it is the orientals who grovel. Of course Australia, as a former colony, also possesses a historical memory of 'grovelling' to its colonial overlords, a memory that resonated in Prime Minister Paul Keating's denunciations of 'forelock-tugging' during Queen Elizabeth II's last visit. This complicated triangular relationship between Britain, Australia, and an increasingly powerful 'Asia', I would argue, only intensifies the emotional impact produced by the rhetoric of physical mastery and dominance.[9]

In an article in the *Australian* that plays throughout on images of physical submission and humiliation—complemented by the cartoonist Löbbecke's bizarre illustration of Evans attempting to polish a sandalled (presumably Malaysian) foot with the Australian flag—Tony Parkinson wrote even more pointedly that Evans had approached the Malaysian government 'on bended knee' and warned, 'Evans is in danger of going down as the foreign minister who rolled over for Mahathir'.[10] Next to the illustration, the *Australian* printed a quotation from Evans that said: 'Diplomacy should be conducted not on one's back or belly but on one's two feet . . . I think I know, and I think the majority of Australians know, which is the more dignified posture.' Drawing on the same set of associations evoked by the representation of Australia as Mahathir's punching bag, the grotesque absurdity of this illustration of Evans can be unpacked as a range of echoes of verbal and physical abasement. Images of boot licking, the adult man transformed into a shoeshine *boy*, the grovelling and prostration imagery provocatively invoked in Parkinson's characterization of 'the foreign minister who rolled over for Mahathir', combine with the iconography of the cramped and constricted body (even Evans's face is contorted and twisted) as it fits itself into a new posture of deference. Against the detail of Evans's representation—hairy legs in sagging socks, the paraphernalia of brush, stool, and flag-rag—the smooth, sandalled foot metonymically invoking Malaysia is curiously disembodied. The sandal, the one obvious clue to the foot's identity, makes nonsense of the shoeshine analogy: we are left with a representation of cultural accommodation that is at once violent, incomplete, and absurd.

In the public interchange between Australia and Malaysia on recognition, reciprocity, and representation, all signalled in the struggle for proper posture, *Embassy* functions, then, at once as agent and object. But having placed the series locally, so to speak, in a regional–historical frame, there emerge some implicit, but I think inescapable, questions about cultural status and authority that need to be rearticulated within a number of global discursive fields. These intersect with and sustain one another in uneven and uncertain ways: I will isolate them here by labelling them, quite arbitrarily and inconsistently, the Gulf War, the Rushdie Affair, and postmodernism.

This selection calls for immediate explanation in its lumping together of the Gulf War and the Rushdie Affair, distinct if complex public events, with something as murky and indeterminate as postmodernism. I can explain myself most directly by saying that all three seem to restate questions of nationalism and ethnicity in particularly troublesome ways. They generate

9 I am grateful to Meaghan Morris and Joseph Pugliese for discussing this point with me.

10 Tony Parkinson, 'Gareth's Malaise', *Weekend Australian*, 3–4 Aug. 1991: 25.

an anxiety, at very different political and ideological positions, about affirmations of cultural or ethnic identity and about assertions of nationhood, either by privileging unstable and variable subjectivities or, as in the Gulf War, by a universalist insistence on a common human condition.

If 'the new world order' and 'the end of history', perhaps the most characteristic locutions of the Reagan–Bush years leading up to the Gulf War, frighteningly foreshadow the dangers to locally based and localized forms of resistance, in the course of the Rushdie Affair the once liberatory properties of nationalism and culturalism often appeared to be dispersed or to be remobilized in the service of fundamentalism and essentialism. The story of the opposition to *The Satanic Verses* is much more complicated than this allows for, but that is not the story I want to tell here; my reason for introducing it is only to suggest how the Rushdie Affair might be available to be read as a confrontation between the master narratives of nationalism or cultural identity, on the one hand, and postmodernism on the other. In this version of the story, Rushdie, as literary lion of the West, could be seen as a key supplier of the sceptical, problematized metafictions of empire so highly prized by postmodernist theorists like Linda Hutcheon, while on the other side, mobs of intractable and incurably literal cultural nationalists shout, equally reprehensibly, for just representation and for blood.[11] This is not to trivialize even for a moment the enormity of the imposition made on Rushdie; rather, I am asking about two divergent strategies—those of *The Satanic Verses* and those of its opponents—for inscribing cultural identity and difference within a global culture that unfailingly produces for every media bogy of a Khomeini or Qaddafi, its Le Pen or Kahane; for each new world order, its Saddam Hussein.

Where the Gulf War held out a scenario that was simultaneously a threat and a bribe in its proposed new world order, postmodernism seems to put forth, for some of us at least, no less expansive or exhaustive a programme. To quote from Kumkum Sangari's influential essay of 1987:

> On the one hand the world contracts into the West . . . a 'specialized' scepticism is carried everywhere as cultural paraphernalia and epistemological apparatus . . . and the postmodern problematic becomes the frame through which the cultural products of the rest of the world are seen. On the other hand, the West expands into the world; late capitalism muffles the globe and homogenizes (or threatens to) all cultural production—this, for some reason, is one 'master narrative' that is seldom dismantled . . . The writing that emerges from this position, however critical it may be of colonial discourses, gloomily disempowers the 'nation' as an enabling idea and relocates the impulses for change as everywhere and nowhere.[12]

---

11 In his article 'Cosmopolitans and Celebrities' (published before *The Satanic Verses*) Tim Brennan remarks on the political ambiguity of the proliferating figure of the 'Third World Cosmopolitan Celebrity': 'Propelled and defined by media and market, cosmopolitanism today involves not so much an elite *at home*, as it does spokespersons for a kind of perennial immigration, valorised by a rhetoric of wandering, and rife with allusions to the all-seeing eye of nomadic sensibility.' Brennan, 'Cosmopolitans and Celebrities', *Race and Class*, 31/1 (1989), 1–19, at p. 2.

12 Kumkum Sangari, 'The Politics of the Possible', *Cultural Critique*, 7 (1987), 157–86, at pp. 183–4.

While the postmodernist suspicion of nationalism and ethnicity has been valuable in helping us break out of the conceptual prisonhouses of authenticity and essence, that same scepticism is often unable to distinguish between a strategic and shifting *process* of identity and difference among peoples and what Christopher Miller describes as the 'Western myth of tribalism, a metaphysical, essentialized means of segmentation'.[13] Before dismantling and demystifying concepts like nationalism and ethnicity, the specific histories which continually constitute and reconstitute these modes of resistance in their changing, even contradictory, configurations need to be acknowledged and examined. This is *not* to reinstall nation, 'race', or ethnicity as absolute, unified, and given categories, but to see them as strategic and provisional responses produced at both international and local levels by a range of needs and practices.

If post-structuralism and postmodernist theory have promoted a number of concepts such as alterity, deferral, difference, and the non-unified subject that have refined and extended our thinking of national and cultural identity, they have at the same time foreclosed *other* ways of thinking these constructs—those ways, for instance, that locate them within *worldly*, historical frames. It is possible then to identify two complementary moves: on the one hand, a celebration and even fetishization of difference at the levels of language, narrative, and representation; on the other, a failure to engage with disturbingly challenging, uncompromisingly oppositional expressions of difference by colonized and post-colonized peoples whose languages and self-representations are either dismissed as naïvely referential or delegitimized, and even demonized, by being labelled essentialist, totalizing, or plain fanatic.

Precarious Postures II: The *Corps Diplomatique*

This section examines an episode of *Embassy* drawing on a strategy suggested by Rey Chow in *Woman and Chinese Modernity*.[14] Chow's starting-point is the question I raised before: '[W]hat is involved in the representation of another culture, especially when that representation is seen by members of that culture[?]' (p. 19). What is important in such an instance, Chow argues, is not the correction or revision of a particular text by a set of competing 'facts' authorized by a different history; what matters rather is how this (often occluded or denied) history 'should be reintroduced materially as a specific way of reading—not ... "reality" ... but cultural artifacts such as films and narratives. The task involves not only the formalist analysis of the *producing* apparatus. It also involves rematerialising such formalist analysis with a pregazing ... that has always already begun.' 'Pregazing' then is Chow's term for the historical understanding brought to a film; to rematerialize this pregazing, she continues, 'we need to shift our attention away from the moment of production to the moment of reception' (p. 19).

Extending the insights of feminist film theory developed by Laura Mulvey,

13 Christopher Miller, *Theories of Africans* (Univ. of Chicago Press, 1990), 34.

14 Rey Chow, *Woman and Chinese Modernity* (Univ. of Minnesota Press, 1991). Further page references appear in the text in parentheses.

Kaja Silverman, and Teresa de Lauretis, Chow examines Bernardo Bertolucci's film *The Last Emperor* and its effects on viewers produced as 'Chinese' by 'rearguing the relationship between image and spectator and by foregrounding the cultural components that are specific to an *imaged spectatorship*' (p. 23). Examining a film like *The Last Emperor* at its point of reception by viewers interpellated by specific cultural processes, for Chow, turns what she calls ethnic spectatorship into 'a site of productive relations' (p. 23).

In what follows I consider a particular episode of *Embassy* from one possible site of ethnic or ethnicized spectatorship before going on to ask some questions about representation, particularly the role of representation in oppositional assertions of ethnicity and cultural difference.

In 'White Panic',[15] her lecture on the recent Australian backlash against multiculturalism, Meaghan Morris discusses Ella Shohat's concept of the ethnically embarrassed text:[16] in recent Hollywood-style productions, Shohat and Morris propose, ethnicity is epidermically ubiquitous on the screen although as a question it is usually textually submerged. In a curious way, *Embassy* participates in this verbal avoidance of difference although its intertexts also evidently include the older, more imperially assured narratives of Kipling, Conrad, and Maugham. In its anxiety at once to invite and evade the spectre of referentiality, the series conjures an Orient simultaneously anonymous and exhaustive, contemporary yet effectively unchanged in its implied relations of domination, where questions of racism, imperialism, and power are both always present and almost always unasked.

Filmed in Pacific locations from Melbourne to Fiji, with its shifting cast of non-white actors (all the main regulars are Anglo-Australians) spanning the spectrum of visible Asian ethnicities and speaking interchangeably in the less familiar regional languages, *Embassy* recalls in some ways that mad project of cartography described by Baudrillard of an ideal coextensivity between colonizers' map and colonized territory; or is it a perfect simulacrum, 'the generation by models of a real without origins or reality: a hyperreal'?[17] Is it both? Indubitably, *Embassy* is an assemblage of orientalism's most familiar constructs and practices. If, as Edward Said puts it, 'the Orient is the stage on which the whole East is confined',[18] *Embassy* tries hard to pack the whole Orient into the few seconds of its opening montage alone. From palm trees to black-chadored women, from minarets to sinister armed guards, the paraphernalia of orientalism clutter the screen, the found objects of old and new adventures; quickly and efficiently, these define a familiar border and survey the affective landscape of what is to follow.

The episode I discuss is titled 'Hanky Panky' and deals with a classic situation: in a characteristic inversion of the sexual relations of imperialism, an Australian diplomat, Michael, lets himself succumb to a seductive Asian

15 Meaghan Morris, 'White Panic or *Max* and the Sublime (The Costs of Multiculturalism)', Mari Kuttna Lecture on Film, University of Sydney, 17 Sept. 1991 (publication forthcoming: The Power Institute, Univ. of Sydney).

16 Ella Shohat, 'Ethnicities in Relation: Toward a Multicultural Reading of American Cinema', in Lester D. Friedman (ed.), *Unspeakable Images: Ethnicity and the American Cinema* (Chicago: Univ. of Illinois Press, 1991), 215–50.

17 Jean Baudrillard, 'Simulacra and Simulations', in *Selected Writings*, ed. Mark Poster (Cambridge: Polity Press, 1988), 166.

18 Edward Said, *Orientalism* (New York: Vintage, 1978), 63.

'housegirl' named Katut, the mistress of another Australian who is just leaving the country. The seduction is figured coyly as a massage scene; Michael, tired and vulnerable after a day of negotiating an international trade deal and arguing with Canberra over staff cuts, yields to Katut's entreaties to let her make him feel better. His friend, already half-way to the door, invites Michael to become Katut's next employer, assuring him, 'She's a Christian; no problem about the religious laws.'

The sequence brings into play two discourses that are understated but pivotal throughout this episode and in the series as a whole: first, what is always constructed as a characteristic Australian discourse of mateship, unionism, and (masculine) solidarity and—intersecting that in a somewhat ambiguous and contradictory way—the discourse of national interest and national security, figured in what is referred to throughout the series as 'the trade deal'. One of *Embassy*'s ongoing interests is the fiction that this fictional Muslim country, Ragaan, possesses its own oil deposits and that the fictional Australians are interested in ensuring a stable government in the region— even if it means supporting an anti-democratic General as ruler—so that access to the oil is regulated in a way acceptable to Australia. The 'trade deal' is put at risk when the episode of 'hankee pankee', as Katut has learned to call it, becomes a public issue; talk show hosts and tabloids all over Australia pick up the story when Katut's parents, predictably, discover her pregnancy and turn up at the embassy accusing the innocent Michael of being responsible. Since Michael cannot, of course, tell on his mate, his promising diplomatic future also hangs in the balance . . .

I will return to the discourse of mateship in this episode, but first I want to consider the seduction/rape sequence in which Katut beguiles the reluctant Michael into submitting to her handmaidenly ministrations. Katut occupies here the role of what has been positioned traditionally as a source of local knowledge for different kinds of Western (male) observers in a range of orientalist narratives: as the 'housegirl' she is the domesticated, sexually available, and faithful native informant. But, Katut, as Michael discovers later when he hires her to work as a 'cleaning lady' at the embassy, is also simultaneously the unreliable informant and the unfaithful native; she has a police record as a petty thief and might be a security risk, a potential spy, in the all-important trade deal; even worse, we discover by the end, she is *sexually* unreliable, having worked as 'housegirl' for a number of Western diplomats: she had been steadily 'working her way through the diplomatic corps' when his mate handed her over to Michael. And the worst thing of all: she might even have been lying when she said she was pregnant—or she may have had a secret abortion.

The indecipherability, unknowability, and the sheer *energy* that accumulates around the figure of Katut is in striking contrast to Michael's positioning in relation to her. If, in the *Australian* article cited earlier, Foreign Minister Evans's seeming accommodation of the Malaysian objections to *Embassy* was represented as rolling over for Mahathir, *Embassy* itself represents this scene of Australian diplomatic capitulation as at once an assault and a seduction. The diplomatic body is revealed once more as vulnerable and quiescent, succumbing, first anxiously, then with increasing pleasure, to the knowing and sinuous manipulations of the oriental mistress/servant. I need hardly remark on the significance of casting Katut as the seductress not only of Michael but of the entire diplomatic corps: the body of the oriental woman becomes the means at once of unifying and objectifying, as well as of potentially rupturing or splitting apart, the diplomatic body.

If *Embassy*, as I suggested earlier, replaces the older spies and sailors of Conrad and Kipling with the figure of the diplomat, diplomacy is in many ways a perfect reimagining of colonial contact in the neo- or post-colonial world. It allows questions of cultural conflict, power, and imperialism to be managed and negotiated between West and non-West within a postmodernity characterized by cosmopolitanism and a spurious equality among nations. Like Kipling's Kim, the post-colonial diplomat inhabits two unequal cultures, enacting through work the complicated state of being at home and not at home—though in a world now more uneasy than Kipling's about the need for national belonging. In *Embassy* the demands of national interest often come into conflict with the humane instincts of the diplomats themselves; in one episode Belinda, the young Australian secretary, is threatened with recall to Canberra because in a moment of sympathy she gives her used clothes to her cleaning woman. These are meagre contacts, confined to a benevolent third worldism or to the kind of sexual adventuring indulged in by Michael, but cultural accommodation of any kind also puts the diplomatic body at risk, exposing it to the overflow of national and ethnic excess.

In this episode ethnic excess is represented by Katut's non-English-speaking parents. When the charges against Michael become public and he is in danger of losing his position at the embassy, Belinda persuades the other Australian staff into threatening mass resignations if he is sent home; then she decides to appeal to Katut herself. The redeployment of mateship as a discourse of Australian solidarity here—and the consequent containment of gender as a function of difference within the diplomatic body itself—is accomplished by making Belinda, the youngest and institutionally the least powerful woman at the embassy, the one who puts mateship into action. When 'good old Belinda' later takes matters even more firmly into her own hands and decides to meet Katut face to face, Belinda and Katut become jointly responsible for 'saving' Michael from being sent back to Canberra.

Belinda's confrontation with Katut and her parents is the emotional high point of the episode; I want to discuss briefly my own sense of being positioned and ethnicized by that scene in a very specific way. In watching that scene I was suddenly made intensely conscious of how language is used here both in the words that are spoken by the actors and in the subtitles that begin to appear on the screen. The parallel use of language works here to construct ethnicity as at once an interruption and a hysteria. Throughout the episode Katut's mother, who tries frantically to prevent her daughter leaving the house with Belinda, is represented as the irrational, frantic, and *impenetrable* native, in contrast to her daughter who has learned the skills of manipulation of and collaboration with the West. When Katut's mother speaks in this scene, the subtitles no longer translate what she says; instead they comment or paraphrase. A long passionate outburst, for example, is subtitled 'speaks angrily'. When I played this episode to my students at the University of Technology, Sydney, last year, the entire class broke out in laughter during this scene. The students' assumption was a perfectly legitimate and appropriate one within the codes of production through which they were understanding the scene: for them the woman spoke gibberish which the subtitles tried to reproduce as words.

Any Sinhala speakers in the ABC's viewing audience, however, would have realized that the mother was not, in fact, speaking nonsense; she was speaking a real, living language, a language that I as a Sri Lankan spectator instantly understood. Like the class, I too laughed aloud at the scene, but *my* laugh was one of recognition and pleasure to hear profanities from the back streets of Colombo, a speech I haven't heard in over ten years, transmitted to me over the ABC. This is not to suggest mine was a unique experience; instead I want to point out the shifts by which intelligibility is first procured here—presumably with some effort—by having an actress speak perfectly appropriate lines (though admittedly in one of the least recognizable languages in Asia), then repressed in the subtitles which are supposed to render meaning legible.

There is also a second, more crucial, repressing: the mother is the only one who makes a spoken accusation, in words, of Michael and by extension the other diplomatic masters Katut has worked for. (Katut herself comes to blame her parents rather than any of her lovers.) Yet the mother's protests and resentment are not available, in words, to anyone except the ethnicized spectator who, like myself, is directly interpellated by her speech (but who remains, in the context of *Embassy*'s codes of production, a *misinterpreter* and misreader).[19]

Two complementary constructions of cultural difference, then, are identifiable here: The first is an *accommodation* of difference—it includes not only the alliance between Belinda and Katut but also Katut's manœuvres and manipulations within the compound, hybridized space provided by Western presence. This could perhaps be described as the text of ethnic embarrassment. The second, an unforgiving, hysterical and uncompromising ethnicity is available only in the mother's anger, though it recalls other frantic representations permanently available in Western cultural memory: the scenes recreated and endlessly recycled as the materiality of the Gulf War and the Rushdie Affair, for instance. This is the text of ethnic excess. It is incomplete, violent, untranslatable, represented only metonymically as fragments of gesticulating bodies, upraised arms, veiled heads; or in scraps of chants and indecipherable text: half-slogans, bits of flaming effigies waved frantically in the wind.

Precarious Postures III: The Post-Colonial Subject

'[I]t may well be', Stephen Slemon hopefully concludes his essay in *Past the Last Post*, an Australian–Canadian anthology on postmodernism and post-colonialism, 'that the postmodernist debate can become one of the key sites upon which the Anglo-American West, if it is to unravel its own moment of cognitive and cultural aporia, finds itself *forced* to take the representational claims of the post-colonial world seriously.'[20] Leaving aside the issue of

19 I thank John Frow for making this last point.

20 Stephen Slemon, 'Modernism's Last Post', in Ian Adam and Helen Tiffin (eds.), *Past the Last Post* (Hempstead: Harvester, 1991), 1–11, at p. 9.

whether moments of aporia are, indeed, 'unravellable', and even the some-what questionable division of labour implied by Slemon in his positioning of 'the post-colonial world' as, once again, the potential salvation of the 'Anglo-American West', the last section of this essay examines the orthodoxies of institutionalized 'post-colonial criticism' and its preoccupation with issues of representation.

To return for a moment to Chow's reading of *The Last Emperor*. Chow cites her mother's reaction to Bertolucci's film to suggest how the polarized opposition between 'truth' on the one hand and 'illusion' or 'lies' on the other is sometimes inadequate in understanding the positioning of the eth-nicized spectator in relation to the orientalist text. Chow's mother responded to the many-Oscared *Last Emperor* by saying, 'It is remarkable that a foreign devil should be able to make a film like this about China. I'd say he did a good job!' (p. 24). For Chow, this remark encompasses her mother's experience of the Japanese atrocities committed in China with the collabora-tion of Emperor Pu Yi, and her (the mother's) historically informed suspi-cion of Bertolucci as a westerner and foreigner, *as well* as her intense absorption, as an exile, in the visual pleasure and nostalgia so expertly pro-duced by the film. The unexamined, or as Chow calls it, the academic, orien-talist reading of *The Last Emperor* would write off her mother's response as 'simplistic' or 'manipulated', thus failing to take into account specific histo-ries within the Chinese diaspora. 'The ethnic[ized] spectator', Chow con-cludes, 'occupies an impossible space that almost predetermines its dismissal from a theoretical reading that is intent on exposing the "ideologically sus-pect" technicalities of production alone' (p. 24).

Chow's reading demands that we do not discount or avoid her mother's implication, as a viewer, in the undeniably orientalist structures of Bertolucci's film. Entangled in orientalist discourse, the mother responds by redeploying it ('in spite of being a foreign devil he did a good job') rather than with an outright rejection or unqualified approval.

I will conclude by introducing a piece of text that can be put next to the *Embassy* episode representing Katut 'working her way through the diplo-matic corps'. The quotation is from a brochure designed by the Malaysian government to attract technologically advanced industries into that coun-try's Free Trade Zone. These zones, everyone knows, offer the appeal of cheap labour combined with no taxes and almost non-existent union regu-lation; the brochure promises in addition one other very specialized local product as part of its multiple attractions:

> The manual dexterity of the oriental female is famous the world over. Her hands are small and she works fast with extreme care. Who, there-fore, could be better qualified by nature and inheritance to contribute to the efficiency of a bench assembly production line than the oriental girl?[21]

As Gayatri Spivak has pointed out, 'for reasons of collusion between pre-existing structures of patriarchy and transnational capitalism, it is the urban

---

21 This is quoted in A. Sivanandan, 'Imperialism and Disorganic Development in the Silicon Age', *Race and Class*, 21/2 (1979), 111–26, at p. 122.

sub-proletarian female who is the paradigmatic subject of the current con-figuration of the International Division of Labor'.[22] The structure of that col-lusion is evident here: the celebration of 'manual dexterity' by the FTZ authorities refers not only to the industrial skills publicly advertised in the brochure; it also alludes, carefully and knowingly, to the massage parlours of Bangkok and Manila. The 'oriental girl' invoked here as the handmaiden of hi-tech and heroine of the bench assembly production line has her more familiar counterparts in whole generations of Singapore Girls, and in many similar constructions, as well as in *Embassy*'s Katut.

In citing the brochure here, I want to do more than simply suggest that ori-ental femininity is produced and reproduced as a national commodity in texts as different as *Embassy* and a Malaysian trade publication. I want to show how the circulation of such representations is regulated and managed as part of official Malaysian policy in its exchanges with post-colonizing or imperialist nations. In this instance the brochure, primarily designed to attract foreign investment from industrialized Western Europe and North America, manipulates and repackages orientalist discourses for its own ends. I select this example to demonstrate how, in an instance like this, the repack-aging of colonial constructs confirms in the most damaging way the post-colonized state's official collusion in the orientalizing and mass-marketing of its women. But there is also a different point that it is very important to make here: whereas what Slemon calls 'the representational claims of the post-colonial world' have appeared in recent instances as unintelligible or untranslatable excesses of hysteria and fanaticism, a more careful examina-tion might reveal a programmatic logic at work, a logic that redeploys orien-talist constructs to its own ends. These, I need hardly add, are not always unimpeachable. The official cultural production of the post-colonized state does not spring new-made from the void but is shaped by its own long his-tory of de-formation.[23]

I have already discussed how the postmodernist delegitimation or disper-sal of categories like nation and ethnicity work to disempower the strategic and oppositional functioning of these categories; but the answer, as Chow points out, is not to register the 'representational claims' of the post-colonized in a polarized relation of 'truth and illusion' or referentiality and representation. To recognize and permit the thinking of difference in a way that neither dissipates and disallows it nor distorts, literally, beyond inter-pretation, calls for attention to local stories and local conditions and a care-ful examination of how these intersect and are intersected by global discourses. Then, to cite a recent article by Said, individual 'cultures may . . . be represented as zones of control or of abandonment, of recollection and of forgetting, of force or of dependence, of exclusiveness or of sharing, all tak-ing place in the global history that is our element'.[24]

22 Gayatri Spivak, *In Other Worlds* (New York: Methuen, 1987), 218.

23 Cf. Spivak's suggestion that the Indian government's staging of its early campaign against *The Satanic Verses* was influenced by the need to manage the political damage to the Muslim vote follow-ing the Shahbano trial: in Afsaneh Najmabadi, 'Interview with Gayatri Spivak', *Social Text*, 28: 122–34, at pp. 133–4.

24 Edward Said, 'Representing the Colonized: Anthropology's Interlocutors', *Critical Inquiry*, 15/2 (Winter 1989), 205–25, at p. 225.

This chapter was first delivered at the symposium 'Practising Postmodernism', held at the University of Newcastle in November 1991, at which time I was the recipient of a University of Newcastle post-doctoral research fellowship.

Bibliography

ABERNATHY-LEAR, GLORIA, *African American Viewers and Daytime Serials* (Philadelphia: Univ. of Pennsylvania Press, forthcoming).

ABRAHAMSSON, ULLA B., 'When Women Watch Television', *Nordicom Review*, 2 (1993), 37–52.

ALCOCK, BEVERLEY, and ROBSON, JOCELYN, 'Cagney and Lacey Revisited', *Feminist Review*, 35 (Summer 1990), 42–53; and 37 (Spring 1991), 117–21.

ALEXANDER, KAREN, 'Karen Alexander: Video Worker, Interviewed by Mica Nava', *Feminist Review*, 18 (1984), 29–34.

—— 'Mothers, Lovers, and Others', *Monthly Film Bulletin*, 56/669 (1989), 314–16.

ALLEN, ROBERT C., *Speaking of Soap Operas* (Chapel Hill: University of North Carolina Press, 1985).

—— (ed.), *Channels of Discourse: Television and Contemporary Criticism* (Chapel Hill: University of North Carolina Press, 1987).

—— (ed.), *To Be Continued . . .: Soap Operas Around the World* (New York: Routledge, 1995).

ANG, IEN, 'The Battle Between Television and Its Audiences: The Politics of Watching Television', in Phillip Drummond and Richard Peterson (eds.), *Television in Transition* (London: British Film Institute, 1985), 250–66.

—— *Watching Dallas: Soap Opera and the Melodramatic Imagination* (London and New York: Methuen, 1985).

—— 'Feminist Desire and Female Pleasure', *Camera Obscura*, 16 (1988), 179–91.

—— 'Melodramatic Identifications: Television Fiction and Women's Fantasy', in Mary Ellen Brown (ed.), *Television and Women's Culture* (1990), 75–88 (in this volume).

—— *Desperately Seeking the Audience* (New York: Routledge, 1991).

—— *Living Room Wars: Rethinking Media Audiences for a Postmodern World* (London: Routledge, 1995).

—— and HERMES, JOKE, 'Gender and/in Media Consumption', in James Curran and Michael Gurevitch (eds.), *Mass Media and Society* (Sevenoaks: Edward Arnold, 1991), 307–28.

ARTHURS, JANE, 'Technology and Gender', *Screen*, 30/1–2 (1989), 40–59.

—— 'Spot the Difference: BBC Conference on Women in Television', *Screen*, 32/4 (1991), 447–51.

—— 'Women and Television', in Stuart Hood (ed.), *Behind the Screens: The Structure of British Television in the Nineties* (London: Lawrence and Wishart, 1994), 82–101.

Association of Cinematograph and Television Technicians (ACTT), *Patterns of Discrimination Against Women in the Film and Television Industries* (London: ACTT, 1975).

ATKIN, DAVID J., 'The Evolution of Television Series Addressing Single Women, 1966–1990', *Journal of Broadcasting & Electronic Media*, 35/4 (1991), 517–23.

AUFDERHEIDE, PAT, 'Latin American Grassroots Video: Beyond Television', *Public Culture*, 5/3 (1993), 579–92.

BACON-SMITH, CAMILLE, *Enterprising Women: Television, Fandom and the Creation of Popular Myth* (Philadelphia: University of Pennsylvania Press, 1992).

BAEHR, HELEN, 'The Impact of Feminism on Media Studies—Just Another Commercial Break?', in Dale Spender (ed.), *Men's Studies Modified: The Impact of Feminism on the Academic Disciplines* (Oxford: Pergamon Press, 1980), 141–53.

—— 'The "Liberated Woman" in Television Drama', *Women's Studies International Quarterly*, 3/1 (1980), 29–39.

—— (ed.), *Women and Media* (New York: Pergamon Press, 1980).

BAEHR, HELEN, 'Women's Employment in British Television', *Media, Culture and Society*, 3/2 (1981), 125–34.

—— and DYER, GILLIAN (eds.), *Boxed-In: Women and Television* (London: Pandora, 1987).

—— and GRAY, ANN (eds.), *Turning It On: A Reader in Women and Media* (London: Arnold, 1996).

BARRY, ANGELA, 'Black Mythologies: Representations of Black People on British Television', in John Twitchin (ed.), *The Black and White Media Book* (Stoke-on-Trent, Staffs.: Trentham Books, 1988), 83–102.

BATHRICK, SERAFINA, '*The Mary Tyler Moore Show*: Women at Home and at Work', in Feuer *et al.* (eds.), *MTM: 'Quality Television'* (1984), 99–131.

BAUGHMAN, CYNTHIA (ed.), *Women on Ice: Feminist Responses to the Tonya Harding/Nancy Kerrigan Spectacle* (New York: Routledge, 1995).

BAUSINGER, HERMANN, 'Media, Technology and Daily Life', *Media, Culture and Society*, 6/4 (1984), 343–51.

BERTRAND, INA, 'Australia's *Come In Spinner*: Feminist Ideology as Best Seller (1946) and Television Mini-series (1990)', *Historical Journal of Film, Radio, and Television*, 12/3 (1992), 231–44.

BETTERTON, ROSEMARY (ed.), *Looking On: Images of Femininity in the Visual Arts and Media* (London: Pandora, 1987).

BIRD, LIZ, and ELIOT, JO, 'The Life and Loves of a She-Devil (Fay Weldon–Ted Whitehead)', in George Brandt (ed.), *British Television Drama in the 1980s* (Cambridge: Cambridge University Press, 1993), 214–33.

BLUM, LINDA M., 'Feminism and the Mass Media: A Case Study of *The Women's Room* as Novel and Television Film', *Berkeley Journal of Sociology*, 27 (1982), 1–26.

BOBO, JACQUELINE, 'Black Women in Fiction and Nonfiction: Images of Power and Powerlessness', *Wide Angle*, 13/3–4 (1991), 172–81.

—— *Black Women as Cultural Readers* (New York: Columbia University Press, 1995).

—— and SEITER, ELLEN, 'Black Feminism and Media Criticism: *The Women of Brewster Place*', *Screen*, 32/3 (1991), 286–302 (in this volume).

BODDY, WILLIAM, 'Electronic Vision and the Gendered Spectator', *Screen*, 35/2 (1994), 105–22.

BODROGHKOZY, ANIKÓ, ' "Is This What You Mean By Color TV?": Race, Gender, and Contested Meanings in NBC's *Julia*', in Spigel and Mann (eds.), *Private Screenings* (1992), 143–68.

BONNER, FRANCES, 'Confession Time: Women and Game Shows', in Frances Bonner *et al.* (eds.), *Imagining Women: Cultural Representations and Gender* (Cambridge: Polity with the Open University Press, 1992), 237–46.

—— and DU GAY, PAUL, 'Representing the Enterprising Self: *thirtysomething* and Contemporary Consumer Culture', *Theory, Culture and Society*, 9/2 (1992), 67–92.

BRONSTEIN, CAROLYN, 'Mission Accomplished? Profits and Programming at the Network for Women', *Camera Obscura*, 33–4 (1994–5), 213–40.

BROWER, SUSAN, 'TV "Trash" and "Treasure": Marketing *Dallas* and *Cagney and Lacey*', *Wide Angle*, 11/1 (1989), 18–31.

BROWN, JANE D., and CAMPBELL, KENNETH, 'Race and Gender in Music Videos: The Same Beat but a Different Drummer', *Journal of Communication*, 36/1 (1986), 94–106.

—— and SCHULZE, LAURIE, 'The Effects of Race, Gender, and Fandom on Audience Interpretations of Madonna's Music Videos', *Journal of Communication*, 40/2 (1990), 88–102.

BROWN, MARY ELLEN, 'The Dialectic of the Feminine: Melodrama and Commodity in the Ferraro Pepsi Commercial', *Communication*, 9/3–4 (1987), 335–54.

—— 'The Politics of Soaps: Pleasure and Feminine Empowerment', *Australian Journal of Cultural Studies*, 4/2 (1987), 1–25.

—— (ed.), *Television and Women's Culture: The Politics of the Popular* (London: Sage, 1990).

—— 'Knowledge and Power: An Ethnography of Soap Opera Viewers', in Leah R. Vande

Berg and Lawrence A. Wenner (eds.), *Television Criticism: Approaches and Applications* (New York: Longman, 1991), 178–98.

—— *Soap Opera and Women's Talk: The Pleasure of Resistance* (Thousand Oaks, Calif.: Sage, 1994).

—— and BARWICK, LINDA, 'Fables and Endless Genealogies: Soap Opera and Women's Culture', *Continuum*, 1/2 (1988), 71–82.

BRUNSDON, CHARLOTTE, '*Crossroads*: Notes on Soap Opera', *Screen*, 22/4 (1981), 32–7.

—— 'Writing About Soap Opera', in Len Masterman (ed.), *Television Mythologies: Stars, Shows, and Signs* (London: Comedia, 1984), 82–7.

—— 'Women Watching Television', *MedieKultur*, 4 (Nov. 1986), 100–12.

—— 'Feminism and Soap Opera', in Davies *et al.* (eds.), *Out of Focus* (1987), 147–50.

—— 'Pedagogies of the Feminine: Feminist Teaching and Women's Genres', *Screen*, 32/4 (1991), 364–81.

—— 'Identity in Feminist Television Criticism', *Media, Culture and Society*, 15/2 (1993), 309–20 (in this volume).

—— *Screen Tastes* (London: Routledge, 1996).

BRUNT, ROSALIND, '*What's My Line?*', in Len Masterman (ed.), *Television Mythologies: Stars, Shows, and Signs* (London: Comedia, 1984), 21–8.

—— 'A "Divine Gift to Inspire"? Popular Cultural Representation, Nationhood and the British Monarchy', in Dominic Strinati and Stephen Wagg (eds.), *Come On Down? Popular Culture in Post-War Britain* (London: Routledge, 1992), 285–301.

—— JONES, KAREN, and PERKINS, TESSA, 'A Conversation About Contemporary Television', *Women: A Cultural Review*, 2/1 (1991), 1–10.

BUCKINGHAM, DAVID, *Public Secrets:* EastEnders *and Its Audience* (London: British Film Institute, 1987).

—— *Moving Images* (Manchester: Manchester University Press, 1996).

BUDD, MIKE, CRAIG, STEVE, and STEINMAN, CLAY, '*Fantasy Island*: Marketplace of Desire', *Journal of Communication*, 33/1 (1983), 67–77.

BUDGE, BELINDA, 'Joan Collins and the Wilder Side of Women: Exploring Pleasure and Representation', in Gamman and Marshment (eds.), *The Female Gaze* (1988), 102–11.

BUTCHER, HELEN, COWARD, ROSALIND, EVARISTI, MARCELLA, GARBER, JENNY, HARRISON, RACHEL, and WINSHIP, JANICE, 'Images of Women in the Media', stencilled occasional paper (CCCS, University of Birmingham, 1974).

BUTLER, JEREMY, 'Redesigning Discourse: Feminism, the Sitcom, and *Designing Women*', *Journal of Film and Video*, 45/1 (Spring 1993), 13 ff.

BUTLER, MATILDA, and PAISLEY, WILLIAM, *Women and the Mass Media: A Sourcebook for Research and Action* (New York: Human Sciences Press, 1980).

BUTSCH, RICHARD, 'Class and Gender in Four Decades of Television Situation Comedy: Plus ça change', *Critical Studies in Mass Communication*, 9/4 (1992), 387–99.

BYARS, JACKIE, 'Reading Feminine Discourse: Prime-Time Television in the U.S.', *Communication*, 9/3–4 (1987), 289–303.

—— 'Gazes/Voices/Power: Expanding Psychoanalysis for Feminist Film and Television Theory', in Pribram (ed.), *Female Spectators* (1988), 110–31.

—— and MEEHAN, EILEEN R., 'Once in a Lifetime: Constructing the "Working Woman" through Cable Narrowcasting', *Camera Obscura*, 33–4 (1994–5), 13–41.

CANADIAN RADIO-TELEVISION AND TELECOMMUNICATIONS COMMISSION, *Images of Women: Report of the Task Force on Sex-Role Stereotyping in the Broadcast Media* (Ottawa: Canadian Govt. Publishing Centre, 1982).

CANTOR, MURIEL G., 'Women and Public Broadcasting', *Journal of Communication*, 27/1 (1977), 14–19.

—— 'Daytime Serial Drama: Our Days and Our Nights on TV', *Journal of Communication*, 29/4 (1979), 66–72.

—— *Prime Time Television: Content and Control* (Beverly Hills: Sage, 1980).

—— 'Feminism and the Media', *Society*, 25 (July/Aug. 1988), 76–81.

—— and PINGREE, SUZANNE, *The Soap Opera* (Beverly Hills: Sage, 1983).

CASHMORE, ELLIS, 'In Pursuit of Women', in . . . *And There Was Television* (New York: Routledge, 1994), 115–27.

CASSATA, MARY B., and SKILL, THOMAS D. (eds.), *Life on Daytime Television: Tuning-in American Serial Drama* (Norwood, NJ: Ablex, 1983).

—— —— and BOADU, SAMUEL OSEI, 'Daytime Serial Drama: In Sickness and in Health', *Journal of Communication*, 29/4 (1979), 73–80.

CLARK, DANAE, '*Cagney and Lacey*: Feminist Strategies of Detection', in Mary Ellen Brown (ed.), *Television and Women's Culture* (1990), 116–33.

CONDIT, CELESTE, 'The Rhetorical Limits of Polysemy', *Critical Studies in Mass Communication*, 6/2 (1989), 103–22.

COWARD, ROSALIND, *Female Desire* (London: Paladin, 1984).

—— 'Women's Programmes: Why Not?', in Baehr and Dyer (eds.), *Boxed-In* (1987), 96–106.

CULLEY, JAMES D., and BENNETT, REX, 'Selling Women, Selling Blacks', *Journal of Communication*, 26/4 (1976), 160–74.

D'ACCI, JULIE, 'Defining Women: The Case of *Cagney and Lacey*', in Spigel and Mann (eds.), *Private Screenings* (1992), 169–202.

—— *Defining Women: Television and the Case of Cagney and Lacey* (Chapel Hill: University of North Carolina Press, 1994).

—— (ed.), *Lifetime: A Cable Network 'For Women'* (Special Issue), *Camera Obscura*, 33–4 (1994–5).

—— 'Leading up to *Roe v Wade*: Television Documentaries in the Abortion Debate', in Mary Beth Haralovich and Lauren Rabinovitz (eds.), *Tell a Vision: Feminist Approaches to US TV History* (Durham, NC: Duke University Press, 1997) (in this volume).

—— 'Nobody's Woman? *Honey West* and the New Sexuality', in Spigel and Curtin (eds.), *The Revolution Wasn't Televised* (New York, Routledge).

DANIELS, THÉRÈSE, 'Programmes for Black Audiences', in Stuart Hood (ed.), *Behind the Screens: The Structure of British Television in the Nineties* (London: Lawrence and Wishart, 1994), 65–81.

—— and GERSON, JANE (eds.), *The Colour Black: Black Images in British Television* (London: British Film Institute, 1989).

DATES, JANETTE, 'Gimme a Break: African-American Women on Prime Time Television', in Alan Wells (ed.), *Mass Media and Society* (Lexington, Mass.: D. C. Heath, 1987).

DAVENPORT, RANDI, 'The Knowing Spectator of *Twin Peaks*: Culture, Feminism, and Family Violence', *Literature/Film Quarterly*, 21/4 (1993), 255–9.

DAVIES, J., 'Soap and Other Operas', *Metro*, 65 (1984), 31–3.

—— 'The Television Audience Revisited', *Australian Journal of Screen Theory*, 17–18 (1986), 84–105.

DAVIES, KATH, DICKEY, JULIENNE, and STRATFORD, TERESA (eds.), *Out of Focus: Writings on Women and the Media* (London: The Women's Press, 1987).

DEMING, CAREN J., 'For Television-Centered Television Criticism: Lessons from Feminism', in James A. Anderson (ed.), *Communication Yearbook*, 11 (Newbury Park: Sage, 1988), 148–76.

—— and JENKINS, MERCILEE M., 'Bar Talk: Gender Discourse in *Cheers*', in Leah R. Vande Berg and Lawrence A. Wenner (eds.), *Television Criticism: Approaches and Applications* (New York: Longman, 1991), 47–57.

DEMING, ROBERT, '*Kate and Allie*: "New Women" and the Audience's Television Archive', *Camera Obscura*, 16 (1988), 154–67.

DENSMORE, DANA, *Syllabus Sourcebook on Media and Women* (Women's Institute for Freedom of the Press, 1990).

DESJARDINS, MARY, '*Baby Boom*: The Comedy of Surrogacy in Film and Television', *Velvet Light Trap*, 29 (1992), 21–30.

DESMOND, JANE, 'How I Met Miss Tootie: *The Home Shopping Club*', *Cultural Studies*, 3/3 (1989), 340–7.

DHILLON-KASHYAP, PERMINDER, 'Locating the Asian Experience', *Screen*, 29/4 (1988), 120–6.

DINES, GAIL, and HUMEZ, JEAN M. (eds.), *Gender, Race and Class in the Media* (Thousand Oaks, Calif.: Sage, 1995).

DOANE, MARY ANN, 'Information, Crisis, Catastrophe', in Mellencamp (ed.), *Logics of Television* (1990), 222–39.

DOTY, ALEXANDER, 'The Cabinet of Lucy Ricardo: Lucille Ball's Star Image', *Cinema Journal*, 29/4 (1990), 3–22.

—— *Making Things Perfectly Queer* (Minneapolis: University of Minnesota Press, 1993).

DOUGLAS, SUSAN, *Where the Girls Are: Growing Up Female with the Mass Media* (New York: Random House, 1994).

DOW, BONNIE J., 'Hegemony, Feminist Criticism, and *The Mary Tyler Moore Show*', *Critical Studies in Mass Communication*, 7/3 (1990), 261–74.

—— 'Femininity and Feminism in *Murphy Brown*', *Southern Communication Journal*, 57/2 (1992), 143–55.

DOWELL, PAT, 'Ladies' Night', *American Film*, 10/4 (1985), 44–9.

DROTNER, KIRSTEN, 'Girl Meets Boy: Aesthetic Production, Reception, and Gender Identity', *Cultural Studies*, 3/2 (1989), 208–25.

—— 'Media Ethnography: An Other Story?', in Ulla Carlsson (ed.), *Nordisk Forskning Om Kvinnor Och Medier* (Göteborg: Nordicom, 1993), 25–40.

DYER, RICHARD, GERAGHTY, CHRISTINE, JORDAN, MARION, LOVELL, TERRY, PATERSON, RICHARD, and STEWART, JOHN, *Coronation Street* (London: British Film Institute, 1980).

—— LOVELL, TERRY, and McCRINDLE, JEAN, 'Women and Soap Opera', *Edinburgh Television Festival Magazine* (1978); repr. in Ann Gray and Jim McGuigan (eds.), *Studying Culture* (London: Edward Arnold, 1993), 35–41.

EDWARDS, AUDREY, 'From Aunt Jemima to Anita Hill: Media's Split Image of Black Women', *Media Studies Journal*, 7/1–2 (1993), 215–22.

EHRENREICH, BARBARA, 'Mary Hartman: A World Out of Control', *Socialist Revolution*, 6/4 (1976), 133–8.

ELLIOTT, JODY, 'Television and Female Viewers', *Australian Communication Review*, 14/3 (1993), 53 ff.

FEDER, ELENA, 'In the Shadow of Race: Forging Images of Women in Bolivian Film and Video', *Frontiers*, 15/1 (1994), 123–40.

FERGUSON, MARJORIE, 'Images of Power and the Feminist Fallacy', *Critical Studies in Mass Communication*, 7/3 (1990), 215–30.

FEUER, JANE, 'Melodrama, Serial Form and Television Today', *Screen*, 25/1 (1984), 4–16.

—— 'Genre Study and Television', in Allen (ed.), *Channels of Discourse* (1987), 135–60.

—— 'Reading *Dynasty*: Television and Reception Theory', *South Atlantic Quarterly*, 88/2 (1989), 443–60.

—— 'Feminism on Lifetime: Yuppie TV for the Nineties', *Camera Obscura*, 33–4 (1994–5), 133–45.

—— *Seeing Through the Eighties: Television and Reaganism* (Durham: Duke University Press, 1995).

—— KERR, PAUL, and VAHIMAGI, TISE (eds.), *MTM: 'Quality Television'* (London: British Film Institute, 1984).

FINCH, MARK, 'Sex and Address in *Dynasty*', *Screen*, 27/6 (1986), 24–42.

FINE, MARLENE G., 'Soap Opera Conversations: The Talk that Binds', *Journal of Communication*, 31/3 (1981), 97–107.

FINNEGAN, MARGARET, 'From Spurs to Silk Stockings: Women in Prime-Time Television, 1950–1965', *UCLA Historical Journal*, 11 (1991), 1 ff.

FISKE, JOHN, 'British Cultural Studies', in Allen (ed.), *Channels of Discourse* (1987), 254–89.

—— '*Cagney and Lacey*: Reading Character Structurally and Politically', *Communication*, 9/3–4 (1987), 399–426.

—— 'Gendered Television: Femininity', in *Television Culture* (London: Routledge, 1987), 179–97.

—— *Media Matters: Everyday Culture and Political Change* (Minneapolis: University of Minnesota Press, 1994).

FLITTERMAN, SANDY, 'The *Real* Soap Operas: TV Commercials', in Kaplan (ed.), *Regarding Television* (1983), 84–96.

FLITTERMAN-LEWIS 'Thighs and Whiskers: The Fascination of *Magnum p.i*', *Screen*, 26/2 (1985), 42–58.

—— 'All's Well That Doesn't End: Soap Opera and the Marriage Motif', *Camera Obscura*, 16 (1988), 118–27.

—— 'Psychoanalysis, Film, and Television', in Robert C. Allen (ed.), *Channels of Discourse, Reassembled* (Chapel Hill, NC, 1992), 203–46.

FRANKLIN, SARAH, LURY, CELIA, and STACEY, JACKIE (eds.), *Off Centre: Feminism and Cultural Studies* (London: Harper Collins, 1991).

FRANZWA, HELEN H., 'The Image of Women in Television: An Annotated Bibliography' (US Commission on Civil Rights, 1976).

FRENTZ, SUZANNE (ed.), *Staying Tuned: Contemporary Soap Opera Criticism* (Bowling Green: Bowling Green State University Press, 1992).

FRISSEN, VALERIE, 'Trapped in Electronic Cages? Gender and New Information Technologies in the Public and Private Domain: An Overview of Research', *Media, Culture and Society*, 14/1 (1992), 31–49.

FURNHAM, ADRIAN, and VOLI, VIRGINIA, 'Gender Stereotypes in Italian Television Advertisements', *Journal of Broadcasting & Electronic Media*, 33/2 (1989), 175–85.

GAINES, JANE, and RENOV, MICHAEL, 'Female Representation and Consumer Culture', *Quarterly Review of Film and Video*, 11/1 (1989), vii–viii.

GALLAGHER, MARGARET, *Unequal Opportunities: The Case of Women and the Media* (Paris: Unesco, 1981).

—— *Unequal Opportunities: Update* (Paris: Unesco, 1985).

—— 'Refining the Communications Revolution', in Baehr and Dyer (eds.), *Boxed-In* (1987), 19–37.

—— 'Shifting Focus: Women and Broadcasting in the European Community', *Studies of Broadcasting*, 26 (Tokyo: NHK Research Institute, 1990), 61–82.

—— 'Women and Men in the Media', *Communication Research Trends*, 12/1 (1992), 1–36.

GALPERIN, WILLIAM, 'Sliding Off the Stereotype: Gender Difference in the Future of Television', in E. Ann Kaplan, *Postmodernism and Its Discontents* (London: Verso, 1988), 146–62.

GAMMAN, LORRAINE, 'Response: More *Cagney & Lacey*', *Feminist Review*, 37 (Spring 1991), 117–21.

—— and MARSHMENT, MARGARET (eds.), *The Female Gaze: Women as Viewers of Popular Culture* (London: The Women's Press, 1988).

GEORGE, DIANE HUME, 'Lynching Women: A Feminist Reading of *Twin Peaks*', in David Lavery (ed.), *Full of Secrets: Critical Approaches to* Twin Peaks (Detroit: Wayne State University Press, 1995), 109–19.

GERAGHTY, CHRISTINE, *Women and Soap Opera: A Study of Prime Time Soaps* (Oxford: Polity Press, 1991).

—— 'British Soaps in the 1980s', in Dominic Strinati and Stephen Wagg (eds.), *Come On Down? Popular Culture in Post-War Britain* (London: Routledge, 1992), 133–49.

—— 'Feminism and Media Consumption', in James Curran, David Morley, and Valerie Walkerdine (eds.), *Cultural Studies and Communications* (London: Arnold, 1996), 306–22.

GEVER, MARTHA, 'Seduction Hot and Cold', *Screen*, 28/4 (1987), 58–65.

GILLESPIE, MARIE, 'Technology and Tradition: Audio-visual Culture Among South Asian Families in West London', *Cultural Studies*, 3/2 (1989), 226–39.

—— 'Soap Opera, Gossip and Rumour in a Punjabi Town in West London', in Duncan Petrie (ed.), *National Identity and Europe: The TV Revolution* (London: British Film Institute, 1993), 25–43.

—— *Television, Ethnicity and Cultural Change* (London: Routledge, 1995).

GILLY, MARY C., 'Sex Role in Advertising: A Comparison of Television Advertisements in Australia, Mexico, and the United States', *Journal of Marketing*, 52/2 (1988), 75–85.

GIVANNI, JUNE (ed.), *Remote Control: Dilemmas of Black Intervention in British Film and TV* (London: British Film Institute, 1995).

GLASS, DIANE M., 'Portia in Primetime: Women Lawyers, Television and *L.A. Law*', *Yale Journal of Law and Feminism*, 2/2 (1990), 371 ff.

GLEDHILL, CHRISTINE, 'Pleasurable Negotiations', in Pribram (ed.), *Female Spectators* (1988), 64–89.

—— 'Speculations on the Relationship Between Soap Opera and Melodrama', *Quarterly Review of Film and Video*, 14/1–2 (1992), 103–24.

GOODSTEIN, ETHEL, 'Southern Belles and Southern Buildings: The Built Environment as Text and Context in *Designing Women*', *Critical Studies in Mass Communication*, 9/2 (1992), 170–85.

GOODWIN, ANDREW, 'Music Video in the (Post)Modern World', *Screen*, 28/3 (1987), 36–55.

GRAY, ANN, 'Behind Closed Doors: Video Recorders in the Home', in Baehr and Dyer (eds.), *Boxed-In* (1987), 38–54 (in this volume).

—— 'Reading the Audience', *Screen*, 28/3 (1987), 24–35.

—— *Video Playtime: The Gendering of a Leisure Technology* (London: Routledge, 1992).

—— 'I Want to Tell You a Story: The Narratives of *Video Playtime*', in Skeggs (ed.), *Feminist Cultural Theory* (1995), 153–68.

—— 'Report on 4th Annual Console-ing Passions Conference, Seattle', *Screen*, 36/4 (1995), 418–21.

GRIPSRUD, JOSTEIN, *The Dynasty Years: Hollywood Television and Critical Media Studies* (New York: Routledge, 1995).

GROSS, LARRY, 'What Is Wrong With This Picture? Lesbian Women and Gay Men on Television', in R. Jeffrey Ringer (ed.), *Queer Words, Queer Images: Communication and the Construction of Homosexuality* (New York: New York University Press, 1994), 143–56.

GROSSBERG, LARRY, and TREICHLER, PAULA, 'Intersections of Power—Criticism, Television, Gender', *Communication*, 9/3–4 (1987), 273–87.

GUNTER, BARRIE, *Television and Gender Representation* (London: J. Libbey, 1995).

HALLAM, JULIA, and MARSHMENT, MARGARET, 'Framing Experience: Case Studies in the Reception of *Oranges Are Not the Only Fruit*', *Screen*, 36/1 (1995), 1–15.

—— —— 'Questioning the "Ordinary" Woman: *Oranges Are Not the Only Fruit*, text and viewer', in Skeggs (ed.), *Feminist Cultural Theory* (1995), 169–89.

HAMER, DIANE, and ASHBROOK, PENNY, 'OUT: Reflections on British Television's First Lesbian and Gay Magazine Series', in Hamer and Budge (eds.), *The Good, the Bad, and the Gorgeous* (1994), 166–72.

—— and BUDGE, BELINDA, *The Good, the Bad, and the Gorgeous: Popular Culture's Romance with Lesbianism* (London: Pandora, 1994).

HANSON, CYNTHIA A., 'The Women of *China Beach*', *Journal of Popular Film & Television*, 17/4 (1990), 154–63.

HANTZIS, DARLENE M., and LEHR, VALERIE, 'Whose Desire? Lesbian (Non)Sexuality and Television's Perpetuation of Hetero/Sexism', in R. Jeffrey Ringer (ed.), *Queer Words, Queer Images: Communication and the Construction of Homosexuality* (New York: New York University Press, 1994), 107–21.

HARALOVICH, MARY BETH, 'Suburban Family Sitcoms and Consumer Product Design: Addressing the Social Subjectivity of Homemakers in the 50s', in Phillip Drummond and Richard Paterson (eds.), *Television and its Audience* (London: British Film Institute, 1988), 38–60.

—— 'Sitcoms and Suburbs: Positioning the 1950s Homemaker', *Quarterly Review of Film and Video*, 11/1 (1989), 61–83.

HARRINGTON, C. LEE, and BIELBY, DENISE D., *Soap Fans: Pursuing Pleasure and Making Meaning in Everyday Life* (Philadelphia: Temple University Press, 1995).

HARTLEY, JOHN, 'Invisible Fictions: Television Audiences, Paedocracy and Pleasure', *Textual Practice*, 1/2 (1987), 121–38.

HASKELL, DEBORAH, 'The Depiction of Women in Leading Roles in Prime Time Television', *Journal of Broadcasting*, 23/2 (1979), 191–6.

HAYWARD, JENNIFER, ' "Day After Tomorrow": Audience Interaction and Soap Opera Production', *Cultural Critique*, 23 (Winter 1992–3), 83–109.

HEIDE, MARGARET J., 'Mothering Ambivalence: The Treatment of Women's Gender Role Conflicts over Work and Family on *thirtysomething*', *Women's Studies*, 21/1 (1992), 103–17.

—— *Television Culture and Women's Lives:* thirtysomething *and the Contradictions of Gender* (Philadelphia: University of Pennsylvania Press, 1995).

HENDERSHOT, HEATHER, 'Media Reform in the Age of Toasters: *Strawberry Shortcake*, the Continuum of Gender Construction, and the Deregulation of Children's Television', *Wide Angle*, 16/4 (1994), 58–82.

HERZOG, HERTA, 'What Do We Really Know About Daytime Serial Listeners?', In Paul F. Lazarsfeld and Frank N. Stanton (eds.), *Radio Research, 1942–3* (New York: Duell, Sloan and Pearce, 1944), 3–33.

HIGASHI, SUMIKO, '*Charlie's Angels*: Gumshoe in Drag', *Cinema Papers*, 2/2–3 (1978), 50–7.

—— 'Hold It—Women in Television Adventure Series', *Journal of Popular Film & Television*, 8/3 (1980), 26–37.

HILL, GEORGE, H., RAGLIN, LORRAINE, and JOHNSON, CHAS FLOYD, *Black Women in Television: An Illustrated History and Bibliography* (New York: Garland, 1990).

HINDS, HILARY, 'Fruitful Investigations: The Case of the Successful Lesbian Text', *Women: A Cultural Review*, 2/2 (1991), 128–33 (in this volume).

—— '*Oranges Are Not the Only Fruit*: Reaching Audiences Other Lesbian Texts Cannot Reach', in Sally Munt (ed.), *New Lesbian Criticism* (New York: Columbia University Press, 1992), 153–72.

HOBSON, DOROTHY, Crossroads: *The Drama of a Soap Opera* (London: Methuen, 1982).

—— 'Housewives and the Mass Media', in Stuart Hall *et al.* (eds.), *Culture, Media, Language* (London: Hutchinson, 1984), 105–14.

—— 'Soap Operas at Work', in Seiter *et al.* (eds.), *Remote Control* (1989), 150–67.

HONEYFORD, SUSAN, 'Women and Television', *Screen*, 21/2 (1980), 49–52.

HOOKS, BELL, *Black Looks: Race and Representation* (Boston: South End Press, 1992).

HOUSTON, BEVERLE, 'Viewing Television: The Metapsychology of Endless Consumption', *Quarterly Review of Film Studies*, 9 (1984), 183–95.

How Women are Represented in Television Programmes in the EEC (Luxembourg: Office for Official Publications of the European Communities, 1987).

HOWELL, SHARON, *Reflections of Ourselves: The Mass Media and the Women's Movement, 1963 to the Present* (New York: Peter Lang, 1990).

HUYSSEN, ANDREAS, 'Mass Culture as Woman: Modernism's Other', in *After the Great Divide: Modernism, Mass Culture, Postmodernism* (Bloomington: Indiana University Press, 1986), 44–62.

ISBER, CAROLINE, and CANTOR, MURIEL, *Report of the Task Force on Women in Public Broadcasting* (Washington, DC: Corporation for Public Broadcasting, 1975).

JADDOU, LILIANE, and WILLIAMS, JON, 'A Theoretical Contribution to the Struggle Against the Dominant Representations of Women', *Media, Culture and Society*, 3/2 (1981), 105–24.

JANUS, NOREENE Z., 'Research on Sex-Roles in the Mass Media: Toward a Critical Approach', *Insurgent Sociologist*, 7/3 (1977), 19–32.

JAPP, PHYLLIS M., 'Gender and Work in the 1980s: Television's Working Women as Displaced Persons', *Women's Studies in Communication*, 14/1 (1991), 49–74.

JENIK, ADRIANE, 'Distribution Matters: "What Does She Want?" ', *Screen*, 28/4 (1987), 70–2.

JENKINS, III, HENRY, '*Star Trek*: Rerun, Reread, Rewritten: Fan Writings as Textual Poaching', *Critical Studies in Mass Communication*, 5/2 (1988), 85–107.

—— ' "Going Bonkers!": Children, Play and Pee-Wee', *Camera Obscura*, 17 (1988), 168–93.

—— ' "It's Not a Fairy Tale Anymore": Gender, Genre, Beauty and the Beast', *Journal of Film and Video*, 43/1–2 (1991), 90–110.

JOHNSON, EITHNE, 'Lifetime's Feminine Psychographic Space and the "Mystery Loves Company" Series', *Camera Obscura*, 33–4 (1994–5), 43–74.

JOSEPH, GLORIA I., and LEWIS, JILL, 'Sexual Subjects of Media', in *Common Differences: Conflicts in Black and White Feminist Perspectives* (Garden City, NY; Anchor, 1981), 166–77.

JOSHI, ILA, *Women Dimension on Television: Policy, Personnel and Programme* (New Delhi: Concept, 1991).

JOYRICH, LYNNE, 'All That Television Allows: TV Melodrama, Postmodernism and Consumer Culture', *Camera Obscura*, 16 (1988), 129–54.

—— 'Going Through the E/Motions: Gender, Postmodernism, and Affect in Television Studies', *Discourse*, 14/1 (1991), 23–40.

—— 'Tube Tied: Reproductive Politics in *Moonlighting*', in James Naremore and Patrick Brantlinger (eds.), *Modernity and Mass Culture* (Bloomington: Indiana University Press, 1991), 176–202.

JUHASZ, ALEXANDRA, 'The Contained Threat: Women in Mainstream AIDS Documentary', *Journal of Sex Research*, 27 (Feb. 1990), 25–46.

—— *AIDS TV: Identity, Community, and Alternative Videos* (Durham, NC: Duke University Press, 1995).

KAHN, KIM FRIDKIN, and GOLDENBERG, EDIE N., 'The Media: Obstacle or Ally of Feminists?', *Annals of the American Academy*, 515 (May 1991), 104–13.

KALER, ANNE K., '*Golden Girls*: Feminine Archetypal Patterns of the Complete Woman', *Journal of Popular Culture*, 24/3 (1990), 49–60.

KANE, KATE, 'The Ideology of Freshness in Feminine Hygiene Commercials', *Journal of Communication Inquiry*, 14/1 (1990), 82–92 (in this volume).

KAPLAN, E. ANN (ed.), *Regarding Television: Critical Approaches—An Anthology* (Frederick, Md.: University Publications of America, 1983).

—— 'History, Spectatorship and Gender Address in Music Television', *Journal of Communication Inquiry*, 10/1 (1986), 3–14.

—— 'Sexual Difference, Pleasure and the Construction of the Spectator in Music Television', *Oxford Literary Review*, 8/1–2 (1986), 113–23.

—— 'Feminist Criticism and Television', in Allen (ed.), *Channels of Discourse* (1987), 211–53.

—— *Rocking Around the Clock: Music Television, Postmodernism, and Consumer Culture* (London: Methuen, 1987).

—— 'Whose Imaginary? The Television Apparatus, the Female Body and Textual Strategies in Select Rock Videos on MTV', in Pribram (ed.), *Female Spectators* (1988), 132–56.

—— (ed.), *Girls: The Representation of Femininity in Popular Culture* (Boulder, Colo.: Westview Press, 1995).

KELLEY, PEGGY, 'When Women Try to Work with Television Technology . . .', *Canadian Journal of Communication*, 14/3 (1989), 63–75.

KENNEDY, ROSANNE, 'The Gorgeous Lesbian in *L.A. Law*: The Present Absence?', in Hamer and Budge (eds.), *The Good, the Bad and the Gorgeous* (1994), 132–41 (in this volume).

KERR, PAUL, 'Classic Serials—To Be Continued', *Screen*, 23/1 (1982), 6–19.

KERVIN, DENISE, 'Gender Ideology in Television Commercials', in Leah R. Vande Berg and Lawrence A. Wenner (eds.), *Television Criticism: Approaches and Applications* (New York: Longman, 1991), 235–53.

KINDER, MARSHA, 'Phallic Film and the Boob Tube: The Power of Gender Identification in Cinema, Television, and Music Video', *ONE TWO THREE FOUR*, 5 (Spring 1987), 33–49.

KING, JOSEPHINE, and STOTT, MARY (eds.), *Is This Your Life? Images of Women in the Media* (London: Virago, 1977).

KODAMA, TOMIKO, 'Rhetoric of the Image of Women in a Japanese Television Advertisement: A Semiotic Analysis', *Australian Journal of Communication*, 18/2 (1991), 42 ff.

KRAY, SUSAN, 'Orientalization of an "Almost White" Woman: The Interlocking Effects of Race, Class, Gender, and Ethnicity in American Mass Media', *Critical Studies in Mass Communication*, 10/4 (1993), 349–66.

KREUTZNER, GABRIELE, *Next Time on Dynasty* (Trier: Wissenschaftlicher Verlag Trier, 1990).

—— and SEITER, ELLEN, 'Not All "Soaps" are Created Equal: Towards a Crosscultural Criticism of Television Serials', *Screen*, 32/2 (1991), 154–72.

KRISHNAN, PRABHA, and DIGHE, ANITA (eds.), *Affirmation and Denial: Construction of Femininity on Indian Television* (New Delhi: Sage, 1990) (excerpts in this volume).

KRISTEVA, JULIA, 'Le Temps des Femmes', *Revue du Département de Sciences des Textes* (Université de Paris VII, Paris, 1979), 34/44.

KUHN, ANNETTE, 'Women's Genres', *Screen*, 25/1 (1984), 18–28 (in this volume).

LA FIA, C., ' "Superwoman" in Television Situation Comedies of the 1980s', *Studies in Popular Culture*, 11/2 (1988), 78–90.

LA FOUNTAIN, MARC J., 'Foucault and Dr. Ruth', *Critical Studies in Mass Communication*, 6/2 (1989), 123–37.

LARSON, STEPHANIE GRECO, 'Black Women on *All My Children*', *Journal of Popular Film & Television*, 22/1 (1994), 44–8.

LEAL, ONDINA FACHEL, 'Popular Taste and Erudite Repertoire: The Place and Space of Television in Brazil', *Cultural Studies*, 4/1 (1990), 19–29.

LEE, JANET, 'Subversive Sitcoms: *Roseanne* as Inspiration for Feminist Resistance', *Women's Studies*, 21/1 (1992), 87–101.

LEE, MINU, and CHO, CHONG HEUP, 'Women Watching Together: An Ethnographic Study of Korean Soap Opera Fans in the United States', *Cultural Studies*, 4/1 (1990), 30–44.

LEIBMAN, NINA, 'Leave Mother Out: The Fifties Family in American Film and Television', *Wide Angle*, 10/4 (1988), 24–41.

—— *Living Room Lectures: The Fifties Family in Film and Television* (Austin: University of Texas Press, 1995).

LEMAN, JOY, 'Wise Scientists and Female Androids: Class and Gender in Science Fiction', in John Corner (ed.), *Popular Television in Britain* (London: British Film Institute, 1991), 108–24.

LEMON, JUDITH, 'Women and Blacks on Prime Time Television', *Journal of Communication*, 27/4 (1977), 70–9.

LEO, JOHN R., 'Television and Narrative Structures of Discourse and Difference ("Consenting Adults", Gender Regulation, and Gay Stereotyping)', *Journal of Film and Video*, 43/4 (1991), 45–55.

LEWIS, LISA, A., 'Consumer Girl Culture: How Music Video Appeals to Women', *ONE TWO THREE FOUR*, 5 (Spring 1987), 5–15.

—— 'Female Address in Music Video', *Journal of Communication Inquiry*, 11/1 (1987), 73–84.

—— 'Form and Female Authorship in Music Video', *Communication*, 9/3–4 (1987), 355–78.

—— 'Being Discovered: Female Address on Music Television', *Jump Cut*, 35 (1990), 2–15.

—— *Gender Politics and MTV: Voicing the Difference* (Philadelphia: Temple University Press, 1990).

—— (ed.), *The Adoring Audience: Fan Culture and Popular Media* (New York: Routledge, 1992).

LIEBES, TAMAR, and KATZ, ELIHU, *The Export of Meaning: Cross-Cultural Readings of Dallas* (Oxford: University Press, 1990).

—— and LIVINGSTONE, SONIA, 'Mothers and Lovers: Managing Women's Role Conflicts in American and British Soap Operas', in Jay Blumler *et al.* (eds.), *Comparatively Speaking: Communication and Culture Across Space and Time* (Newbury Park, Calif.: Sage, 1992), 94–120.

LIVINGSTONE, SONIA, 'Viewers' Interpretations of Soap Opera: The Role of Gender, Power and Morality', in Phillip Drummond and Richard Paterson (eds.), *Television and Its Audience* (London: British Film Institute, 1988), 83–107.

—— *Making Sense of Television: The Psychology of Audience Interpretation* (Oxford: Pergamon Press, 1989).

—— 'Watching Talk: Gender and Engagement in the Viewing of Audience Discussion Programmes', *Media, Culture and Society*, 16/3 (1994), 429–47.

LONG, ELIZABETH, 'Women, Reading, and Cultural Authority: Some Implications of the Audience Perspective in Cultural Studies', *American Quarterly*, 38/4 (1986), 591–612.

LOPATE, CAROL, 'Daytime Television: You'll Never Want to Leave Home', *Radical America*, 11/1 (1977), 32–51.

LOPEZ, ANA M., 'Our Welcomed Guests: Telenovelas in Latin America', in Allen (ed.), *To Be Continued . . .* (1995), 256–75.

—— 'I Love Ricky Too: The Oft-Forgotten Cuban in the Text' (forthcoming).

LUBIANO, WAHNEEMA, 'Black Ladies, Welfare Queens, and State Minstrels: Ideological War by Narrative Means', in Toni Morrison (ed.), *Race-ing Justice, En-Gendering Power: Essays on Anita Hill, Clarence Thomas, and the Construction of Social Reality* (New York: Pantheon Books, 1992), 323–63.

LUKE, CARMEN, 'Feminist Pedagogy and Critical Media Literacy', *Journal of Communication Inquiry*, 18/2 (1994), 30–47.

LULL, JAMES, 'Girls' Favorite TV Females', *Journalism Quarterly*, 57/1 (1980), 146–50.

—— (ed.), *World Families Watch Television* (Newbury Park, Calif.: Sage, 1988).

—— *Inside Family Viewing: Ethnographic Research on Television's Audiences* (New York: Routledge, 1990).

—— MULAC, ANTHONY, and ROSEN, SHELLEY LISA, 'Feminism as a Predictor of Mass Media Use', *Sex Roles*, 9/2 (1983), 165–77.

MCCARTHY, ANNA, 'Reach Out and Touch Someone: Technology and Sexuality in Broadcast Ads for Phone Sex', *Velvet Light Trap*, 32 (1993), 50–7.

MCCLARY, SUSAN, 'Living to Tell: Madonna's Resurrection of the Fleshly', *Genders*, 7 (Spring 1990), 1–21.

MACDONALD, MYRA, *Representing Women: Myths of Femininity in the Popular Media* (New York: St. Martin's Press, 1995).

MCLAUGHLIN, LISA, 'Feminism, the Public Sphere, Media and Democracy', *Media, Culture and Society*, 15/4 (1993), 599–620.

MCPHERSON, TARA, 'Disregarding Romance and Refashioning Femininity: Getting Down and Dirty with *Designing Women*', *Camera Obscura*, 32 (1993–4), 103–23.

MAHAJAN, KAMLESH, *Television and Women's Development: Patterns of Televiewing Among College Girls* (New Delhi: Classical, 1990).

MANKEKAR, PURNIMA, 'National Texts and Gendered Lives: An Ethnography of Television Viewers in a North Indian City', *American Ethnologist*, 20/3 (1993), 543–63.

—— 'Television Tales and a Woman's Rage: A Nationalist Recasting of Draupadi's "Disrobing" ', *Public Culture*, 5/3 (1993), 469–92 (in this volume).

MANN, DENISE, 'The Spectacularization of Everyday Life: Recycling Hollywood Stars and Fans in Early Television Variety Shows', in Spigel and Mann (eds.), *Private Screenings* (1992), 41–70.

MANUEL, PREETHI, 'Black Women in British Television Drama—A Case of Marginal Representation', in Kath Davies *et al.* (eds.), *Out of Focus* (1987), 42–4.

MARKS, LAURA U., 'Tie a Yellow Ribbon Around Me: Masochism, Militarism, and the Gulf War on TV', *Camera Obscura*, 27 (1991), 55–75.

MARSHMENT, MARGARET, and HALLAM, JULIA, 'From String of Knots to Orange Box: Lesbianism on Prime Time', in Hamer and Budge (eds.), *The Good, the Bad, and the Gorgeous* (1994), 142–65.

MASCIAROTTE, GLORIA-JEAN, 'C'mon Girl: Oprah Winfrey and the Discourse of Feminine Talk', *Genders*, 11 (Fall 1991), 81–110.

MATTELART, MICHÈLE, 'Women and the Cultural Industries', *Media, Culture and Society*, 4/2 (1982), 133–51.

—— *Women, Media and Crisis: Femininity and Disorder* (London: Comedia, 1986) (excerpt in this volume).

MAYERLE, JUDINE, 'Character Shaping Genre in *Cagney and Lacey*', *Journal of Broadcasting & Electronic Media*, 31/2 (1987), 133–51.

MAYNE, JUDITH, '*L.A. Law* and Prime-Time Feminism', *Discourse*, 10/2 (1988), 30–47 (in this volume).

MEEHAN, DIANE M., *Ladies of the Evening: Women Characters of Prime-Time Television* (Metuchen, NJ: Scarecrow, 1983).

—— and FALUDI, SUSAN, 'Are Media Messages About Women Improving?', in Alison Alexander and Jarice Hanson (eds.), *Taking Sides: Clashing Views on Controversial Issues in Mass Media and Society* (Guilford, Conn.: Dushkin, 1993), 46–64.

MEEHAN, EILEEN R., 'Why We Don't Count: The Commodity Audience', in Mellencamp (ed.), *Logics of Television* (1990), 117–37.

—— 'Heads of Household and Ladies of the House: Gender, Genre, and Broadcast Ratings, 1929–1990', in William S. Solomon and Robert W. McChesney (eds.), *Ruthless Criticism: New Perspectives in U.S. Communication History* (Minneapolis: University of Minnesota Press, 1993), 204–21.

MELLENCAMP, PATRICIA, 'Situation and Simulation: An Introduction to *I Love Lucy*', *Screen*, 26/2 (1985), 30–40.

—— 'Situation Comedy, Feminism, and Freud: Discourses of Gracie and Lucy', in Modleski (ed.), *Studies in Entertainment* (1986), 80–95 (in this volume).

—— (ed.), *Logics of Television: Essays in Television Criticism* (Bloomington: Indiana University Press, 1990).

—— *High Anxiety: Catastrophe, Scandal, Age and Comedy* (Bloomington: Indiana University Press, 1992).

MERCK, MANDY, 'Portrait of a Marriage?', in *Perversions: Deviant Readings* (New York: Routledge, 1993), 101–17.

MODLESKI, TANIA, 'The Search for Tomorrow in Today's Soap Operas: Notes on Feminine Narrative Form', *Film Quarterly*, 33/1 (1979), 12–21 (in this volume).

—— *Loving with a Vengeance: Mass-Produced Fantasies for Women* (Hamden, Ct: Shoestring Press, 1982; London, Methuen 1984).

—— 'The Rhythms of Reception: Daytime Television and Women's Work', in Kaplan (ed.), *Regarding Television* (1983), 67–75.

—— 'Femininity as Mas[s]querade: A Feminist Approach to Mass Culture', in Colin McCabe (ed.), *High Theory/Low Culture: Analyzing Popular Television and Film* (Manchester: Manchester University Press, 1986), 37–52.

—— (ed.), *Studies in Entertainment: Critical Approaches to Mass Culture* (Bloomington: Indiana University Press, 1986).

—— 'Some Functions of Feminist Criticism, Or the Scandal of the Mute Body', *October*, 49 (Summer 1989), 3–24.

MONTGOMERY, KATHRYN C., *Target Prime Time: Advocacy Groups and the Struggle Over Entertainment Television* (New York: Oxford University Press, 1989).

MORITZ, MARGUERITE J., 'American Television Discovers Gay Women: The Changing Context of Programming Decisions at the Networks', *Journal of Communication Inquiry*, 13/2 (1989), 62–79.

—— 'Old Strategies for New Texts: How American Television Is Creating and Treating Lesbian Characters', in R. Jeffrey Ringer (ed.), *Queer Words, Queer Images: Communication and the Construction of Homosexuality* (New York: New York University Press, 1994), 122–42.

MORLEY, DAVID, *The Nationwide Audience* (London: British Film Institute, 1980).

—— *Family Television: Cultural Power and Domestic Leisure* (London: Comedia, 1986).

—— *Television, Audiences and Cultural Studies* (London: Routledge, 1992).

MORRIS, MEAGHAN, *The Pirate's Fiancée: Feminism, Reading, Postmodernism* (London: Verso, 1988).

MORSE, MARGARET, 'Sport on Television: Replay and Display', in Kaplan (ed.), *Regarding Television* (1983), 44–66.

—— 'Talk, Talk, Talk—The Space of Discourse in Television', *Screen*, 26 (1985), 2–15.

—— 'The Television News Personality and Credibility: Reflections on the News in Transition', in Modleski (ed.), *Studies in Entertainment* (1986), 55–79.

—— 'Artemis Aging: Exercise and the Female Body on Video', *Discourse*, 10/1 (Fall–Winter 1987–8), 20–53.

—— 'Video Mom: Reflections on a Cultural Obsession', *East-West Film Journal*, 3/2 (1989), 53–73.

—— 'An Ontology of Everyday Distraction: The Freeway, the Mall, and Television', in Patricia Mellencamp (ed.), *Logics of Television: Essays in Cultural Criticism* (Bloomington: Indiana University Press, 1990), 193–221.

MOSS, GEMMA, 'Children and TV: Exploring Gendered Reading', *Women: A Cultural Review*, 2/1 (1991), 18–28.

MULVEY, LAURA, 'Melodrama In and Out of the Home', in Colin McCabe (ed.), *High Theory/Low Culture: Analyzing Popular Television and Film* (Manchester: Manchester University Press, 1986), 80–100.

MUMFORD, LAURA STEMPEL, 'Stripping on the Girl Channel: Lifetime, *thirtysomething*, and Television Form', *Camera Obscura*, 33–4 (1994–5), 167–90.

—— *Love and Ideology in the Afternoon: Soap Opera, Women, and Television Genre* (Bloomington: Indiana University Press, 1995).

NOCHIMSON, MARTHA, *No End to Her: Soap Opera and the Female Subject* (Berkeley: University of California Press, 1992).

OWEN, A. SUSAN, 'Oppositional Voices in *China Beach*: Narrative Configurations of Gender and War', in Dennis K. Mumby (ed.), *Narrative and Social Control: Critical Perspectives* (Thousand Oaks: Sage, 1993), 207–31.

PARMAR, PRATIBHA, 'Hateful Contraries: Media Images of Asian Women', *Ten. 8*, No. 16 (1984).

PATERSON, RICHARD, 'Planning the Family: The Art of the Television Schedule', *Screen Education*, 35 (Summer 1980), 79–85.

PEDERSEN, VIBEKE, 'Soap, Pin-up and Burlesque: Commercialization and Femininity in Danish Television', *Nordicom Review*, 2 (1993), 25–35.

PENLEY, CONSTANCE, 'Brownian Motion: Women, Tactics, and Technology', in Constance Penley and Andrew Ross (eds.), *Technoculture* (Minneapolis: University of Minnesota Press, 1991), 135–61.

—— 'Feminism, Psychoanalysis, and the Study of Popular Culture', in Lawrence Grossberg, Cary Nelson, and Paula Treichler (eds.), *Cultural Studies* (New York: Routledge, 1992), 479–500.

PENN, RAY, 'What Designing Women Do Ordain: The Women's Ordination Movement Comes to Prime Time', *Studies in Popular Culture*, 13/1 (1990), 89–102.

PERERA, SUVENDRINI, 'Representation Wars: Malaysia, *Embassy*, and Australia's *Corps Diplomatique*', in John Frow and Meaghan Morris (eds.), *Australian Cultural Studies: A Reader* (Sydney: Allen and Unwin, 1993), 15–29 (in this volume).

PETERSON, ERIC E., 'Media Consumption and Girls Who Want to Have Fun', *Critical Studies in Mass Communication*, 4/1 (1987), 37–50.

PETRO, PATRICE, 'Mass Culture and the Feminine: The "Place" of Television in Film Studies', *Cinema Journal*, 25/3 (1986), 5–21.

PINGREE, SUZANNE, 'The Effects of Non-Sexist Television Commercials and Perceptions of Reality on Children's Attitudes About Women', *Psychology of Women Quarterly*, 2/3 (1978), 262–77.

—— et al., 'A Scale for Sexism', *Journal of Communication*, 26/4 (1976), 193–200.

POLLOCK, GRISELDA, 'What's Wrong With Images of Women?', *Screen Education*, 24 (Autumn 1977), 25–33.

PORTER, DENNIS, 'Soap Time: Thoughts on a Commodity Art Form', *College English*, 38/8 (1977), 782–8.

PRESS, ANDREA L., 'New Views on the Mass Production of Women's Culture', *Communication Research*, 13/1 (1986), 139–50.

—— 'Class and Gender in the Hegemonic Process: Class Differences in Women's

Perceptions of Television Realism and Identification with Television Characters', *Media, Culture and Society,* 11/2 (1989), 229–51.

PRESS, ANDREA L., 'The Ongoing Feminist Revolution', *Critical Studies in Mass Communication,* 6/2 (1989), 196–202.

—— 'Class, Gender and the Female Viewer: Women's Responses to *Dynasty*', in Mary Ellen Brown, *Television and Women's Culture* (1990), 158–82.

—— *Women Watching Television: Gender, Class, and Generation in the American Television Experience* (Philadelphia: University of Pennsylvania Press, 1991).

—— 'Working-Class Women in a Middle-Class World: The Impact of Television on Modes of Reasoning About Abortion', *Critical Studies in Mass Communication,* 8/4 (1991), 421–41.

—— and STRATHMAN, TERRY, 'Work, Family, and Social Class in Television Images of Women: Prime-Time Television and the Construction of Postfeminism', *Women and Language,* 16/2 (1993), 7–15.

PRIBRAM, E. DEIDRE (ed.), *Female Spectators: Looking at Film and Television* (London: Verso, 1988).

PROBYN, ELSPETH, 'TV's Local: The Exigency of Gender in Media Research', *Canadian Journal of Communication,* 14/3 (1989), 29–41.

—— 'New Traditionalism and Post-Feminism: TV Does the Home', *Screen,* 31/2 (1990), 147–59 (in this volume).

PUNWANI, JYOTI, 'The Portrayal of Women on Indian Television', in Rehana Ghandially (ed.), *Women in Indian Society: A Reader* (New Delhi: Sage, 1988), 224–32.

RABINOVITZ, LAUREN, 'Sitcoms and Single Moms: Representations of Feminism on American TV', *Cinema Journal,* 29/1 (1989), 3–19.

—— 'Soap Opera Bridal Fantasies', *Screen,* 33/3 (1992), 274–83.

RADNER, HILARY, 'Quality Television and Feminine Narcissism: The Shrew and the Covergirl', *Genders,* 8 (Summer 1990), 110–28.

RADWAY, JANICE, *Reading the Romance: Women, Patriarchy, and Popular Literature* (Chapel Hill: University of North Carolina Press, 1984).

—— 'Reception Study: Ethnography and the Problem of Dispersed Audiences and Nomadic Subjects', *Cultural Studies,* 2/3 (1988), 359–76.

RAKOW, LANA F., 'Feminist Approaches to Popular Culture: Giving Patriarchy its Due', *Communication,* 9/1 (1986), 19–41.

—— 'Rethinking Gender Research in Communication', *Journal of Communication,* 36/4 (1986), 11–26.

—— 'Feminist Studies: The Next Stage', *Critical Studies in Mass Communication,* 6/2 (1989), 209–15.

—— (ed.), *Women Making Meaning: New Feminist Directions in Communication* (New York: Routledge, 1992).

—— and KRANICH, KIMBERLIE, 'Woman as Sign in Television News', *Journal of Communication,* 41/1 (1991), 8–23.

RAPPING, ELAYNE, 'Made for TV Movies: The Domestication of Social Issues', *Cineaste,* 14/2 (1985), 30–3.

—— *The Looking Glass World of Nonfiction TV* (Boston: South End Press, 1986).

—— *The Movie of the Week: Private Stories/Public Events* (Minneapolis: University of Minnesota, 1992).

—— *Media-tions: Forays into the Culture and Gender Wars* (Boston: South End Press, 1994).

REID, EVELYN CAULETA, 'Viewdata: Television Viewing Habits of Young Black Women in London', *Screen,* 30/1–2 (1989), 114–21.

RHODES, JANE, 'Television's Realist Portrayal of African-American Women and the Case of *L.A. Law*', *Women and Language,* 14/1 (1991), 29–34.

RIAÑO, PILAR, *Women in Grassroots Communication: Effecting Global Social Change* (Thousand Oaks, Calif.: Sage, 1994).

ROBERTS, ROBIN, ' "Sex as a Weapon": Feminist Rock Music Videos', *National Women's Studies Association Journal,* 2/1 (1990), 1–15.

—— 'Music Videos, Performance and Resistance: Feminist Rappers', *Journal of Popular Culture*, 25/2 (1991), 141–52.

—— ' "Ladies First": Queen Latifah's Afrocentric Music Video', *African American Review*, 28/2 (1994), 245–57.

ROBINSON, LILLIAN S., 'What's My Line: Telefiction and Women's Work', in *Sex, Class, and Culture* (Bloomington: Indiana University Press, 1978), 310–42.

ROGERS, DEBORAH D., 'Daze of Our Lives: The Soap Opera as Feminist Text', *Journal of American Culture*, 14/4 (1991), 29–41.

ROGERS, EVERETT M., and ANTOLA, LIVIA, 'Telenovelas: A Latin American Success Story', *Journal of Communication*, 35/4 (1985), 24–35.

ROMAN, LINDA, CHRISTIAN-SMITH, LINDA, and ELLSWORTH, LIZ (eds.), *Becoming Feminine: The Politics of Popular Culture* (London: Falmer Press, 1988).

ROOT, JANE, *Pictures of Women: Sexuality* (London: Pandora, 1984).

ROSE, TRICIA, 'Never Trust a Big Butt and a Smile', *Camera Obscura*, 23 (1990), 108–31 (in this volume).

ROSEN, RUTH, 'Search for Yesterday', in Todd Gitlin (ed.), *Watching Television* (New York: Pantheon, 1986), 42–67.

ROWE, KATHLEEN K., 'Roseanne: Unruly Woman as Domestic Goddess', *Screen*, 31/4 (1990), 408–19 (in this volume).

—— *The Unruly Woman: Gender and the Genres of Laughter* (Austin: University of Texas Press, 1995).

RUBEY, DAN, 'Voguing at the Carnival: Desire and Pleasure on MTV', *South Atlantic Quarterly*, 90/4 (1991), 871–906.

SCHLESINGER, PHILIP, DOBASH, R. EMERSON, DOBASH, RUSSELL P., and WEAVER, C. KAY, *Women Viewing Violence* (London: British Film Institute, 1992).

SCHRØDER, KIM, 'The Pleasure of *Dynasty*: The Weekly Reconstruction of Self-Confidence', in Phillip Drummond and Richard Paterson (eds.), *Television and Its Audience* (London: British Film Institute, 1988), 61–82.

SCHULMAN, NORMA MIRIAM, 'Laughing Across the Color Barrier: *In Living Color*', *Journal of Popular Film & Television*, 20/1 (1992), 2–7.

SCHULZE, LAURIE, '*Getting Physical*: Text/Context/Reading and the Made-for-Television Movie', *Cinema Journal*, 25/2 (1986), 35–50.

—— 'The Made-for-TV Movie: Industrial Practice, Cultural Form, Popular Reception', in Tino Balio (ed.), *Hollywood in the Age of Television* (New York: Unwin Hyman, 1990), 351–76.

SCHWICHTENBERG, CATHY, '*Charlie's Angels*: A Patriarchal Voice in Heaven', *Jump Cut*, 24–5 (1981), 13–16.

—— 'Critical Dialogue: Women and Power Relations', *Jump Cut*, 27 (1982), 71.

—— '*Dynasty*: The Dialectic of Feminine Power', *Central States Speech Journal*, 34/3 (1983), 151–61.

—— '*The Love Boat*: The Packaging and Selling of Love, Heterosexual Romance, and the Family', *Media, Culture and Society*, 6/3 (1984), 301–11.

—— 'Madonna's Postmodern Feminism: Bringing the Margins to the Center', *Southern Communication Journal*, 57/2 (1992), 120–31.

—— (ed.), *The Madonna Connection: Representational Politics, Subcultural Identities, and Cultural Theory* (Boulder, Colo.: Westview Press, 1993).

—— 'Reconceptualizing Gender: New Sites for Feminist Audience Research', in John Cruz and Justin Lewis (eds.), *Viewing, Reading, Listening: Audiences and Cultural Reception* (Boulder, Colo.: Westview Press, 1994), 169–80.

SEITER, ELLEN, 'Eco's TV Guide—The Soaps', *Tabloid*, 6 (1982), 35–43.

—— 'Promise and Contradiction: The Daytime Television Serials', *Screen*, 23 (Winter 1982), 150–63.

—— 'Men, Sex and Money in Recent Family Melodramas', *Journal of the University Film and Video Association*, 35/1 (1983), 17–27.

—— 'Stereotypes and the Media: A Re-evaluation', *Journal of Communication*, 36/2 (1986), 14–26.

SEITER, ELLEN, 'Different Children, Different Dreams: Racial Representation in Advertising', *Journal of Communication Inquiry*, 14/1 (1990), 31–47.

—— *Sold Separately: Parents and Children in Consumer Culture* (New Brunswick: Rutgers University Press, 1993).

—— 'Mothers Watching Children Watching Television', in Skeggs (ed.), *Feminist Cultural Theory* (1995), 137–52.

—— BORCHERS, HANS, KREUTZNER, GABRIELE, and WARTH, EVA-MARIA, ' "Don't Treat Us Like We're So Stupid and Naive": Towards an Ethnography of Soap Opera Viewers', in Seiter *et al.* (eds.), *Remote Control* (1989), 223–47.

—— —— —— —— (eds.), *Remote Control: Television, Audiences, and Cultural Power* (New York: Routledge, 1989).

SHATTUC, JANE, *The Talking Cure: Women and TV Talk Shows* (New York: Routledge, 1996).

SHAW, MARION, and VANACKER, SABINE, *Reflecting on Miss Marple* (London: Routledge, 1991).

SIGNORELLI, NANCY, *et al.* (eds.), *Role Portrayal and Stereotyping on Television—An Annotated Bibliography of Studies Relating to Women, Minorities, Aging, Sexual Behavior, Health, and Handicaps* (Westport, Conn.: Greenwood Press, 1985).

—— McLEOD, DOUGLAS, and HEALY, ELAINE, 'Gender Stereotypes in MTV Commercials: The Beat Goes On', *Journal of Broadcasting & Electronic Media*, 38/1 (1994), 91–101.

SIMPSON, AMELIA S., *Xuxa: The Megamarketing of Gender, Race, and Modernity* (Philadelphia: Temple University Press, 1993).

SIU, YVONNE, 'TV Images of Chinese Women', *Asian Messenger*, 5/3 (1981), 39–42.

SKEGGS, BEVERLEY (ed.), *Feminist Cultural Theory* (Manchester: Manchester University Press, 1995).

SKIRROW, GILLIAN, 'Representations of Women in the Association of Cinematograph, Television and Allied Technicians', *Screen*, 22/3 (1981), 94–102.

—— 'Hellivision: An Analysis of Video Games', in Colin McCabe (ed.), *High Theory/Low Culture* (Manchester: Manchester University Press, 1986), 115–42.

SOHN, IRA, 'Critical Dialogue: Sexism and Class Oppression', *Jump Cut*, 27 (1982), 71.

SPANGLER, LYNN C., 'A Historical Overview of Female Friendships on Prime-Time Television', *Journal of Popular Culture*, 22/4 (1989), 13–23.

SPENCE, JO, and WATNEY, SIMON, 'An *Omnibus* Dossier', *Screen*, 24/1 (1983), 40–51.

SPENCE, LOUISE, 'Life's Little Problems . . . and Pleasures: An Investigation into the Narrative Structures of *The Young and the Restless*', *Quarterly Review of Film Studies*, 9/4 (1984), 301–8.

SPIGEL, LYNN, 'Installing the Television Set: Popular Discourses on Television and Domestic Space, 1948–1955', *Camera Obscura*, 16 (1988), 10–47.

—— 'The Domestic Economy of Television Viewing in Postwar America', *Critical Studies in Mass Communication*, 6/4 (1989), 337–54.

—— 'From Domestic Space to Outer Space: The 1960s Fantastic Family Sit-Com', in Constance Penley, Elisabeth Lyon, Lynn Spigel, Janet Bergstrom (eds.), *Close Encounters: Film, Feminism, and Science Fiction* (Minneapolis: University of Minnesota Press, 1991), 205–23.

—— *Make Room for TV: Television and the Family Ideal in Postwar America* (Chicago: University of Chicago Press, 1992).

—— 'The Suburban Home Companion: Television and the Neighborhood Ideal in Postwar America', in Beatriz Colomina (ed.), *Sexuality and Space* (Princeton: Princeton Architectural Press, 1992), 185–217 (in this volume).

—— 'From the Dark Ages to the Golden Age: Women's Memories and Television Reruns', *Screen*, 36/1 (1995), 16–33.

—— and MANN, DENISE (eds.), *Private Screenings: Television and the Female Consumer* (Minneapolis: University of Minnesota Press, 1992).

—— and CURTIN, MICHAEL (eds.), *The Revolution Wasn't Televised* (New York: Routledge, forthcoming).

SQUIRE, CORINNE, 'Empowering Women? The *Oprah Winfrey Show*', *Feminism and Psychology*, 4/1 (1994), 63–79 (in this volume).

STANNARD, KATHERINE, 'Technology and the Female in the *Doctor Who* Series: Companions or Competitors', in Ronald Dotterer and Susan Bowers (eds.), *Politics, Gender and the Arts: Women, the Arts, and Society* (London: Associated University Press, 1988), 64–71.

STEEVES, H. LESLIE, 'Feminist Theories and Media Studies', *Critical Studies in Mass Communication*, 4/2 (1987), 95–135.

—— and SMITH, MARILYN CRAFTON, 'Class and Gender in Prime-time Television Entertainment: Observations from a Socialist Feminist Perspective', *Journal of Communication Inquiry*, 11/1 (1987), 43–63.

STEWART, JULIANNE, 'Micronesian Women and Television', *Australian Journal of Communication*, 18/1 (1991), 80 ff.

STRAAYER, CHRIS, 'The She-Man: Postmodern Bi-Sexed Performance in Film and Video', *Screen*, 31/3 (1990), 262–80.

STRAINCHAMPS, ETHEL (ed.), *Rooms With No View: A Woman's Guide to the Man's World of the Media* (New York: Harper & Row, 1974).

STREETER, THOMAS, and WAHL, WENDY, 'Audience Theory and Feminism: Property, Gender, and the Televisual Audience', *Camera Obscura*, 33–4 (1994–5), 243–61.

SWANSON, GILLIAN, '*Dallas*: Part 1', *Framework*, 14 (Spring 1981).

TAYLOR, ELLA, *Prime-Time Families: Television Culture in Postwar America* (Berkeley: University of California Press, 1989).

TAYLOR, S., 'Days of their Lives?: Popular Culture, Femininity and Education', *Continuum*, 2/2 (1989), 143–62.

THOMAS, LYN, 'In Love with *Inspector Morse*: Feminist Subculture and Quality Television', *Feminist Review*, 51 (Autumn 1995), 1–25 (in this volume).

THORBURN, DAVID, 'Television Melodrama', in Horace Newcomb (ed.), *Television: The Critical View* (New York: Oxford University Press, 1979), 536–53.

THORNTON, EDITH, 'On the Landing: High Art, Low Art, and *Upstairs, Downstairs*', *Camera Obscura*, 31 (1993), 27–46.

THOVERON, GABRIEL, 'European Televised Women', *European Journal of Communication*, 1/3 (1986), 289–300.

THUMIN, JANET, 'A Live Commercial for Icing Sugar; Researching the Historical Audience: Gender and Broadcast Television in the 1950s', *Screen*, 36/1 (1995), 48–55.

TORRES, SASHA, 'War and Remembrance: Televisual Narrative, National Memory, and *China Beach*', *Camera Obscura*, 33–4 (1994–5), 147–64.

TREICHLER, PAULA, 'Beyond *Cosmo*: AIDS, Identity, and Inscriptions of Gender', *Camera Obscura*, 28 (1992), 20–77.

—— and WARTELLA, ELLEN, 'Interventions: Feminist Theory and Communication Studies', *Communication*, 9/1 (1986), 1–18.

TUCHMAN, GAYE, 'The Symbolic Annihilation of Women by the Mass Media', in Tuchman *et al.* (eds.), *Hearth and Home* (1978), 3–38.

—— 'Women's Depiction by the Mass Media', *Signs*, 4/3 (1979), 528–42.

—— DANIELS, ARLENE KAPLAN, and BENET, JAMES (eds.), *Hearth and Home: Images of Women in the Mass Media* (New York: Oxford University Press, 1978).

TULADHAR, SUMON, 'Participatory Video as Post-Literacy Activity for Women in Rural Nepal', *Convergence*, 27/2–3 (1994), 111–17.

TURIM, MAUREEN, 'Viewing/Reading "Born to be Sold: Martha Rosler Reads the Strange Case of Baby S/M" or Motherhood in the Age of Technological Reproduction', *Discourse*, 13/2 (1991), 21–38.

TUROW, JOSEPH, 'Advising and Ordering: Daytime, Prime Time', *Journal of Communication*, 24/2 (1974), 138–41.

TYLER, CAROLE-ANNE, 'The Supreme Sacrifice? TV, "TV", and the Renee Richards Story', *Differences*, 1/3 (1989), 160–86.

UMPHREY, DON, and ALBARRAN, ALAN B., 'Using Remote Control Devices: Ethnic and Gender Differences', *Mass Communications Review*, 20/3–4 (1993), 212–19.

UNITED STATES COMMISSION ON CIVIL RIGHTS, *Window Dressing on the Set: Women and Minorities in Television* (Washington, DC: Commission on Civil Rights, 1977).

VANDE BERG, LEAH R., 'Using Television to Teach Courses in Gender and Communication', *Communication Education*, 40/1 (1991), 105–11.

—— 'China Beach, Prime Time War in the Postfeminist Age: An Example of Patriarchy in a Different Voice', *Western Journal of Communication*, 57/3 (1993), 349–66.

—— and STRECKFUSS, DIANE, 'Prime-time Television's Portrayal of Women and the World of Work: A Demographic Profile', *Journal of Broadcasting & Electronic Media*, 36/2 (1992), 195–208.

VARTANIAN, CAROLYN REED, 'Women Next Door to War: *China Beach*', in Michael Anderegg (ed.), *Inventing Vietnam: The War in Film and Television* (Philadelphia: Temple University Press, 1991), 190–203.

VIDA, GINNY, 'The Lesbian Image in the Media', in *Our Right to Love: A Lesbian Resource Book* (Englewood Cliffs, NJ: Prentice-Hall, 1976), 240–5.

VINCENT, RICHARD C., 'Clio's Consciousness Raised? Portrayal of Women in Rock Videos, Re-examined', *Journalism Quarterly*, 66/1 (1989), 155–60.

WALKERDINE, VALERIE, 'Video Replay: Families, Films and Fantasy', in Victor Burgin, James Donald, and Cora Kaplan (eds.), *Formations of Fantasy* (London: Methuen, 1986); repr. in Valerie Walkerdine, *Schoolgirl Fictions* (London: Verso, 1990).

WALKOWITZ, REBECCA L., 'Reproducing Reality: Murphy Brown and Illegitimate Politics', in Marge Garber, Jann Matlock, and Rebecca L. Walkowitz (eds.), *Media Spectacles* (New York: Routledge, 1993), 40–56 (in this volume).

WALLACE, MICHELE, *Invisibility Blues: From Pop to Theory* (London: Verso, 1990).

WALTERS, SUZANNA DANUTA, *Material Girls: Making Sense of Feminist Cultural Theory* (Berkeley: University of California Press, 1995).

WATSON, MARY ANN, 'From *My Little Margie* to *Murphy Brown*, Images of Women on Television', *Television Quarterly*, 27/2 (1994), 4–24.

WHITE, MIMI, 'Ideological Analysis and Television', in Allen (ed.), *Channels of Discourse* (1987), 134–71.

—— *Tele-Advising: Therapeutic Discourse in American Television* (Chapel Hill: University of North Carolina Press, 1992).

—— 'Women, Memory and Serial Melodrama: Anecdotes in Television Soap Opera', *Screen*, 35/4 (1994), 336–53.

WHITE, SUSAN, '*Veronica Clare* and the New *Film Noir* Heroine', *Camera Obscura*, 33–4 (1994–5), 77–100.

WILCOX, RHONDA V., 'Shifting Roles and Synthetic Women in *Star Trek: The Next Generation*', *Studies in Popular Culture*, 13/2 (1991), 53–65.

WILLIAMS, CAROL T., 'It's Not So Much "You've Come a Long Way, Baby"—as "You're Gonna Make It After All" ', in Horace Newcomb (ed.), *Television: The Critical View* (New York: Oxford University Press, 1976), 43–53.

—— *It's Time for My Story: Soap Opera Sources, Structure, and Response* (Westport, Conn.: Praeger, 1992).

WILLIAMSON, JUDITH, 'How Does Girl Number Twenty Understand Ideology', *Screen Education*, 40 (Autumn–Winter 1981–2), 80–7.

WILSON, PAMELA, 'Upscale Feminine Angst: *Molly Dodd*, the Lifetime Cable Network and Gender Marketing', *Camera Obscura*, 33–4 (1994–5), 103–30.

WLODARZ, JOE, 'Smokin' Tokens: *thirtysomething* and TV's Queer Dilemma', *Camera Obscura*, 33–4 (1994–5), 193–211.

Women in the Wasteland Fight Back: A Report on the Image of Women Portrayed in TV Programming (Washington, DC: National Organization for Women, 1972).

WOMEN'S ADVISORY AND REFERRAL SERVICE ACTION GROUP, 'Opportunity Knocks (But Not Very Hard)', in Simon Blanchard and David Morley (eds.), *What's This Channel Four?* (London: Comedia, 1982), 104–9.

Women's Studies International Quarterly, 3/1 (1980). Special issue on 'Women and Media'.

YOUNG, LOLA, *Fear of the Dark: 'Race', Gender and Sexuality in the Cinema* (London: Routledge, 1996).

ZECK, SHARI, 'Female Bonding in *Cagney and Lacey*', *Journal of Popular Culture*, 23/3 (1989), 143–54.

ZELIZER, BARBIE, 'CNN, the Gulf War, and Journalist Practice', *Journal of Communication*, 42/1 (1992), 66–81.

ZIEGLER, DHYANA, and WHITE, ALISA, 'Women and Minorities on Network Television News: An Examination of Correspondents and Newsmakers', *Journal of Broadcasting & Electronic Media*, 34/2 (1990), 215–23.

ZIMMERMAN, PATRICIA R., 'Good Girls, Bad Women: The Role of Older Women on *Dynasty*', *Journal of Film and Video*, 37 (Spring 1985), 66–74.

—— 'The Female Bodywars: Rethinking Feminist Media Politics', *Socialist Review*, 23/2 (1993), 35–56.

ZOONEN, LIESBET VAN, 'Rethinking Women and the News', *European Journal of Communication*, 3/1 (1988), 35–53.

—— 'Feminist Perspectives on the Media', in James Curran and Michael Gurevitch (eds.), *Mass Media and Society* (Sevenoaks: Edward Arnold, 1991), 33–54.

—— 'A Tyranny of Intimacy? Women, Femininity and Television News', in Peter Dahlgren and Colin Sparks (eds.), *Communication and Citizenship: Journalism and the Public Sphere in the New Media Age* (London: Routledge, 1991), 217–35.

—— 'Feminist Theory and Information Technology', *Media, Culture & Society*, 14/1 (1992), 9–29.

—— 'The Women's Movement and the Media: Constructing a Public Identity', *European Journal of Communication*, 7/4 (1992), 453–76.

—— 'Rethinking Feminist Media Politics', *Socialist Review*, 23/2 (1993), 35–56.

—— *Feminist Media Studies* (London: Sage, 1994).

Index